ADVENTURES IN THE HUMAN SPIRIT

ADVENTURES IN THE HUMAN SPIRIT

SECOND EDITION

PHILIP E. BISHOP

VALENCIA COMMUNITY COLLEGE

PRENTICE HALL, INC., UPPER SADDLE RIVER, N.J. 07458

Publisher: Bud Therien
Editorial Director: Charlyce Jones Owen
Marketing Manager: Sheryl Adams
Manufacturing Buyer: Bob Anderson
Assistant Editor: Marion Gottlieb
Editorial Assistant: Maureen Diana

For Calmann & King Ltd.
Project Manager (second edition): Elisabeth Ingles
Development Editor: Richard Mason
Copy Editor: Matthew Taylor
Designers: Richard Foenander (first edition), Karen Stafford
Picture Research: Susan Bolsom-Morris (first edition), Maureen Cowdroy

This book was designed and produced by Calmann & King Ltd., London
Typeset by Fakenham Photosetting Ltd., U.K.

COVER ART: FRONT
Claude Monet: *Boulevard des Capucines*, 1873 (detail). Oil on canvas, $31^3/_4$ x $23^1/_2$ ins (81 x 58 cm). The
Nelson-Atkins Museum of Art, Kansas City, purchase: the Kenneth A. and Helen F. Spencer Foundation
Acquisition Fund. (See illustration 13.9 for whole painting.)
BACK
Interior, Great Mosque of Córdoba, Spain, c. 736. Photo Sonia Halliday, Weston Turville, U.K.

© 1999, 1994 by Prentice Hall, Inc.
Simon & Schuster/A Viacom Company
Upper Saddle River, N.J. 07458

Printed in China
10 9 8 7 6 5 4 3 2 1
ISBN 0-13-727306-1

Prentice Hall International (UK) Limited, *London*
Prentice-Hall of Australia Pty. Limited, *Sydney*
Prentice-Hall Canada Inc., *Toronto*
Prentice-Hall Hispanoamericana, S.A., *Mexico*
Prentice-Hall of India Private Limited, *New Delhi*
Prentice-Hall of Japan, Inc., *Tokyo*
Simon & Schuster Asia Pte. Ltd., *Singapore*
Editora Prentice-Hall do Brasil, Ltda, *Rio de Janeiro*

CONTENTS

Acknowledgments 12
Photo Credits 13
Preface 15

1 THE HUMANITIES: AN INTRODUCTION TO THE ADVENTURE 16

Finding a Voice 16
Tradition: Nurturing the Creative Spirit 16
Modes of Expression and Reflection 17

The Arts 17
The Pictorial Arts 17
Sculpture: The Art of Shaping 18
Architecture: The Art of Shelter 20
Music: The Art of Sound 21
Dance: The Art of Movement 23
The Art of Theater 24
A Note about Opera 25
The Literary Arts 25

An Invitation to the Adventure 26

Chapter Summary 26

2 THE ANCIENT WORLD 27

The First Humans 27

Mesopotamia 29
The Sumerians 29
Key Concept: Myth 31
Empires of the Near East 32

Ancient Egypt 32
Egypt: Religion and Society 33
The Arts of Egypt 33
Window on Daily Life: Death at an
   Egyptian Banquet 35

Early Asian Civilizations 36
The Indus Valley 36
Bronze-Age China 37

The Aegean World 39

Minoan Civilization 39
Mycenaean Civilization 40

Chapter Summary 41

3 ANCIENT GREECE: THE CLASSICAL SPIRIT 42

Early Greece 42
The Homeric Poems 43
Sappho's Lyric Poetry 45
The Visual Arts in Early Greece 45
Key Concept: Rationalism 48

The Classical Period 48
Window on Daily Life: The Plague of Athens 49
Athens in Its Golden Age 49

The Greek Temple 50
The Parthenon 50
The Parthenon Sculptures 52
Key Concept: Classical Humanism 55

Greek Sculpture 54
The Classical Style 56
The Hellenistic Style 58

Greek Theater 59
Greek Tragedy 59
Greek Comedy 61

Greek Philosophy 61
Early Greek Philosophy 62
Socrates 62
Plato 62
Aristotle 63
Global Perspective: Confucius and
   Philosophy 64

Greek Music 65

The Hellenistic Age 66
The Hellenistic Legacy 67

Chapter Summary 68
Critical Question 44, 55, 63
The Write Idea 45, 54, 59, 61, 64

4   ANCIENT ROME: THE SPIRIT OF EMPIRE   69

The Drama of Roman History   70
The Rise of Republican Rome   71
Imperial Rome   74
Key Concept: Imperialism   72

The Art of an Empire   73
Sculpture as Propaganda   73
The Forum of Trajan   76

The Architecture of Rome   78
The Romans as Builders   79
Roman Buildings   81

Roman Art and Daily Life   83
Roman Daily Life   83
Window on Daily Life: A Marriage
   Contract of the Roman Era   85
Key Concept: The Antiquarian Spirit   86

Roman Theater and Music   89
Roman Theater   89
Music and Dance   91

The Roman Poets   92
Early Roman Poetry   92
Virgil's Roman Epic   93
Roman Satire   94

Roman Philosophy   95
The Epicurean Lucretius   95
The Stoics   95
Global Perspective: The Buddha's
   Teaching   96
Rome's Division and Decline   98

Chapter Summary   99
Critical Question   86, 94
The Write Idea   72, 73, 88

5   THE JUDEO-CHRISTIAN SPIRIT   100

The Judaic Tradition   101
History and the Israelites   101
The Hebrew Bible   102
Key Concept: Monotheism   104
Job and the Trials of Israel   105

Window on Daily Life: The Siege of
   Jerusalem   107

The Rise of Christianity   106
Jesus of Nazareth   106
Early Christianity   107
Christianity in the Late Roman Empire   109

Christian Philosophy   112
From Classical to Christian   112
Augustine of Hippo   112
Key Concept: Original Sin and Human
   Nature   113

**The Christian Empires: Rome and
Byzantium**   114
St. Peter's and the Pope   114
Justinian and the Byzantine World   115
Ravenna: Showcase of the Christian Arts 119

Christianity and the Arts   123
Early Christian Music   123
The Christians and Theater   125
Global Perspective: Teotihuacán:
   Sacred City of Mesoamerica   126

The Rise of Islam   127
The Foundations of Islam   127
Islamic Arts and Science   129
Dawn of The Middle Ages   131

Chapter Summary   132
Critical Question   104, 107, 113, 129
The Write Idea   104, 112

6   THE EARLY MIDDLE AGES: THE FEUDAL SPIRIT   133

The Age of Charlemagne   135
The Carolingian Renaissance   135
The Culture of the Book   137
Window on Daily Life: Work in
   Charlemagne's World   138
Charlemagne's Court   138

Feudal Europe   139
Feudalism   140
The *Song of Roland*   141
Key Concept: Chivalry   142
The Bayeux Tapestry   143

The Flowering of Muslim Spain 145

Monasticism 146
Key Concept: The Monastic Ideal 144
Monastic Life 146
Global Perspective: The Blood of Maya
Kings 147
Hrotsvit and the Classical Tradition 149

The Romanesque Style 149
Imperial Revival and the Romanesque
Style 149
The Abbey of Cluny 150
The Pilgrimage Churches 151
Romanesque Sculpture 153

Early Medieval Music and Drama 154
Musical Notation 154
Hildegard of Bingen: Musical Mystic 156
Drama in the Medieval Church 156

The Medieval Philosopher 159
Early Medieval Philosophy 159
Abelard 160
A New Spirit of the Middle Ages 160

Chapter Summary 161
Critical Question 142, 143, 145
The Write Idea 136, 143

7 THE LATE MIDDLE AGES: THE GOTHIC AWAKENING 162

The Gothic Awakening 163
The Crusades 163
The Decline of Feudalism 164
The Rise of Towns and Cities 164
Key Concept: Pilgrimage 167

The Gothic Style 165
Abbot Suger and the Gothic Style 165
The Cathedral at Chartres 168
Gothic Sculpture 171
Global Perspective: Buddhism in Asia 174

Music and Theater in the Gothic Age 174
The Evolution of Organum 174
Gothic Theater: From Church to Town 176

The New Learning 179
Key Concept: Scholasticism 178

The Universities 179
Thomas Aquinas 181

Courtly Life in the Middle Ages 181
Courtly Love 181
The Medieval Romance Tradition 182
Music in the Late Middle Ages 183

Poets and Pilgrims 183
Dante's *Divine Comedy* 183
Window on Daily Life: The Plague and
Prosperity 186
Chaucer's Canterbury Pilgrims 187

Prelude to the Renaissance 187
Reclaiming the Classical Past 187
Giotto's Pictorial Revolution 188

Chapter Summary 190
Critical Question 177, 178, 182
The Write Idea 167, 169

8 THE RENAISSANCE SPIRIT IN ITALY 191

The Renaissance in Italy 192
The Italian City-states 192
Key Concept: Renaissance Humanism 193
Lorenzo "the Magnificent" 196
Window on Daily Life: The Violence of
Renaissance Youth 197

The Arts in Renaissance Florence 198
Ghiberti's Baptistery Doors 200
Brunelleschi's Domes 201
Florentine Painting: A Refined Classicism 204
Early Renaissance Music 204
Key Concept: The Science of Perspective 206

Early Renaissance Sculpture 205
Donatello 205
Michelangelo in Florence 208
The Decline of Florence 209
Global Perspective: The Sculpture of West
Africa 210

Humanist Realism 211
Machiavelli's *The Prince* 211

The Genius of Leonardo 212
Leonardo as Scientist 212

Leonardo as Painter 214
Key Concept: The Renaissance Man ... and Woman 214

The High Renaissance in Rome 216
Patronage of the Renaissance Arts 217
Josquin des Préz 217
Raphael 218
Michelangelo in Rome 219
The New St. Peter's 223
An Age Of Giants 226

Chapter Summary 226
Critical Question 197, 215, 221
The Write Idea 194, 209, 212, 225

9 THE NORTHERN AND LATE RENAISSANCE 227

The Northern Renaissance 227
Kings, Commerce, and Columbus 229
The Northern Renaissance Courts 229
Window on Daily Life: A Midwife's Advice 231

The Reformation 231
Luther's Challenge 231
The Appeal of the Reformation 233
Calvinism 233
Key Concept: The "Protestant Ethic": God, Work, and Wealth 234

Painting in Northern Europe 235
Van Eyck's Visual Realism 236
Faith and Humanism in the Northern Arts 238
Pieter Bruegel: Painter of Country Life 241

Humanism in the North 242
Erasmus and Satire 243
Humanism and the Reformation 243
Key Concept: Utopia 245

The Elizabethan Age 244
The Reformation in England 244
Theater in the Elizabethan Age 247
The Genius of Shakespeare 248
Elizabethan Music 250

The Late Renaissance in Italy 251
Palestrina: Reaction to the Renaissance 251
Renaissance Theater in Italy 253

The Venetian Renaissance and Mannerism 254
Venetian Music 255
Palladio, Architect of Venice 257
Venetian Painting 259
Mannerism 260

Chapter Summary 261
Critical Question 228, 235, 244, 248
The Write Idea 231, 234, 244

10 THE SPIRIT OF BAROQUE 262

The Baroque in Spain 262
El Greco and Catholic Mysticism 262
Global Perspective: The Taj Mahal 267
Spanish Baroque Architecture 269
Velázquez 269
Cervantes and *Don Quixote* 270

The Baroque in Italy 272
Bernini as Architect 273
Bernini as Sculptor 275
Caravaggio 276
The Birth of Opera 277

The Baroque in France 280
Key Concept: Absolutism 279
The Palace of Versailles 281
The Performing Arts at Versailles 283
Rubens and Poussin: Painters of the Court 285

Music of the Protestant Baroque 287
J. S. Bach 287
The "Well-Tempered Keyboard" 287

The Dutch Baroque 288
Vermeer 289
Rembrandt 291

The New Science 294
Key Concept: The Scientific Revolution 293
Tools of the New Science 294
Descartes and the Philosophy of Science 294

The English Compromise 295
English Baroque Poetry 295
Christopher Wren's London 296
Handel 297

Window on Daily Life: The Fire of London 297
The Politics of England 298

Chapter Summary 299
Critical Question 270, 279, 286
The Write Idea 292

11 THE SPIRIT OF ENLIGHTENMENT 300

The Enlightenment 300
The Philosophes 300
Rousseau 303
Key Concept: The Social Contract 304

The Rococo Style 305
The Salons 306
The Art of Rococo 306
Eighteenth-century Ballet 312
Mozart and Opera 312

The Bourgeois Response 313
The Bourgeois Style in Painting 314
The Rise of the Novel 315
Global Perspective: Kabuki Theater 316
The Bourgeois Theater in Germany 317

The Neoclassical Style 317
Neoclassical Architecture 317
Key Concept: Neoclassicism 318
Neoclassical Painting 319
The Classical Symphony 322

The Age of Satire 324
Swift 324
Window on Daily Life: Women Gladiators 326
Satire and Society in Art 326
Voltaire 327

Chapter Summary 328
Critical Question 304, 317, 326
The Write Idea 303, 306

12 REVOLUTION AND ROMANTICISM 329

Revolutions and Rights 329
The Revolution in America 330
The Revolution in France 331

The Napoleonic Era 331
The Romantic Hero 337
Beethoven 337
Key Concept: Romantic Genius 336
Musical Virtuosos 338
Goethe and Faust 338
Delacroix and the Byronic Hero 340

Elements of Romanticism 342
Romantic Social Protest 342
The Romantics and Nature 344
Romantic Landscapes 346
Key Concept: The Noble Savage 347
The Return to the Past 348
Window on Daily Life: Native Storytellers 350
Romantic Exoticism 351

Romantic Demons 352
Berlioz's *Fantastic Symphony* 352
The Romantic Novel 352

Chapter Summary 354
Critical Question 336
The Write Idea 331, 345, 353

13 THE INDUSTRIAL AGE: THE SPIRIT OF MATERIALISM 355

Realism 356
Realism in Painting 356
The Realist Novel 359
Key Concept: Socialism 360
Karl Marx and Communism 360

The Spirit of Progress 361
Voices of a New Age 361
Monuments of Progress 361
The Modern City 364
Key Concept: Modernity 368

Music and Modernity 366
Verdi's Operas 366
Wagner's Musical Revolution 367
Late Romantic Music 368
Window on Daily Life: A Musical Career 370

The Last Romantics 370
Symbolism and Art for Art's Sake 370
Debussy's Musical Impressions 373

Rodin   374

Impressionism and Beyond   375
Manet: Prelude to Impressionism   375
Monet and the Impressionists   376
Global Perspective: The Japanese Color
    Print   378
Post-Impressionism: Seurat and Cézanne   381
Toward Expressionism: Gauguin and
    Van Gogh   383

The Dark Side of Progress   385
The Realist Theater   386
The Novel and Modern Philosophy   386

Chapter Summary   388
Critical Question   360, 369, 371
The Write Idea   357, 387

**14   THE SPIRIT OF
    MODERNISM**   389

A Turbulent Century   389
The Great War   390
Fascism and the Rise of Mass Society   392
Window on Daily Life: War, Fashion, and
    Feminism   393

Modernism in Art   393
Picasso's Revolution in Art   394
Key Concept: Primitivism   396
Cubism   398
Toward Formal Abstraction   398
Dada and Anti-Art   399
Expressionism   401

The Freudian Revolution   402
Freud and Human Sexuality   402
Surrealism   403
Key Concept: The Unconscious   404

Modernism in Literature   406
The Modernist Style   406
Modern Heroes   406

Modernist Music and Architecture   407
Stravinsky and Ballet   407
Schoenberg and Atonal Music   408

Modernist Building   410

Art and Politics   411
Brecht's Epic Theater   411
Picasso's *Guernica*   412
The Political Art of the Camera   413

In the American Grain   415
Regionalism and Renaissance   415
The American Scene   415
The Age of Jazz   417

Chapter Summary   419
Critical Question   393, 397, 405
The Write Idea   407, 415

**15   THE CONTEMPORARY
    SPIRIT**   420

Holocausts   421
Post-War America   421

Exploring the Absurd   422
Key Concept: Existentialism   422
The Existentialist in Action   423
The Theater of the Absurd   423
The Existential Hero   424

Art in the Post-war Era   425
The New York School   425
Pop, Minimalism, and the Avant-garde   426
Key Concept: The Avant-garde   427
Sculpture in the Post-war Era   429

The Trials of Modern Architecture   432
Triumph of the International Style   432
Building as Sculpture   433

Post-1945 Music   435
The Avant-garde in Music   435
The Pop Rebellion   435

Post-modern Styles   436
Post-modern Architecture   437
Minimalism in Music   439
The Contemporary Visual Arts   441
The New Fiction   442

Revising the Canon 443
African and American Voices 443
Women's Voices 445

Themes for a New Age 447
AIDS and the Arts 447
Toward a World Culture 447
Window on Daily Life: Living and Dying
  with AIDS 447

Chapter Summary 450
Critical Question 426, 443
The Write Idea 422, 432, 446

Notes 451
Glossary 453
Bibliography 458
Index 459

EXTRACTS

This book includes poems or short extracts
from the following authors and works.
Copyright information is given in the Notes on
page 451.

The Great Hymn to Aten 35
Homer, *Iliad*, Book XXIV 44
Sappho 45
Sophocles, *Antigone* 55
Catullus, *To an Unfaithful Lover* 92
Virgil, *Aeneid*, Book I, Book IV 93, 94
Juvenal, *Satires* 94
Lucretius, *On the Nature of the Universe* 95
Marcus Aurelius, *Meditations* Book VII 98
Book of Genesis 103
Book of Job 105
Gospel of Matthew 106
Qur'an (Sura 55) 129
Song of Roland (stanzas 173, 176) 141
Hildegard of Bingen 156
Bernart de Ventadorn 182
Beatriz de Dia 183
Dante, *Inferno* Canto V 186
Geoffrey Chaucer, "The Wife of Bath's Tale" 187
Francis Petrarch, Sonnet 187
Lorenzo de' Medici, *Song of Bacchus* 197
Benvenuto Cellini, *Autobiography* 197
Niccolò Machiavelli, *The Prince* 212
Erasmus, *In Praise of Folly* 243
William Shakespeare, *Hamlet*, Act II sc. ii, Act
  III sc. i 249

Miguel de Cervantes, *Don Quixote* Part I 170
John Donne, *The Canonization* 295
John Milton, *Paradise Lost* 295
The Diary of Samuel Pepys 297
John Locke, *Two Treatises on Government* 298
Jean-Jacques Rousseau, *The Social Contract* 303
Samuel Richardson, *Pamela* 315
Jonathan Swift, *A Modest Proposal* 325
Voltaire, *Candide* 328
Johann Wolfgang von Goethe, *Faust* Part 1, Part
  2 338, 339
William Blake, *London* 342
William Wordsworth, *The Prelude* 344
William Wordsworth, *The World is Too Much
  with Us* 345
Mary Shelley, *Frankenstein* 353
Gustave Flaubert, *A Sentimental Education* 360
Karl Marx, *The Communist Manifesto* 361
Walt Whitman, *Leaves of Grass* 361
Charles Baudelaire, *Les Fleurs du Mal* 371
Henrik Ibsen, *A Doll's House* 386
Fyodor Dostoyevsky, *The Brothers Karamazov*
  387
William Butler Yeats, *The Second Coming* 390
Franz Kafka, *The Metamorphosis* 407
Allen Ginsburg, *Howl* 421
Jean-Paul Sartre, *Existentialism* 423
Jorge Luis Borges, *Tlön, Uqbar, Orbis Tertius* 443
Denise Levertov, *In Mind* 446
Paul Monette, *Borrowed Time: An AIDS Memoir*
  447

TIMECHARTS
Greece and the Ancient World 42
The Roman and Early Christian Worlds 70
The Middle Ages 134
The Renaissances 195
The Baroque and Enlightenment 265
The Nineteenth Century 332
The Twentieth Century 391

MAPS
The Ancient World (Eastern Hemisphere) 29
Ancient Greece 38
The Roman Empire 74
Israel at the Time of Jesus 108
The Spread of Christianity 108
The Byzantine Empire under Justinian 115
The Rise of Islam 128
The Crusades 163
Renaissance Italy 192
Religious Divisions in 16th-century Europe 235

OTHER TABLES AND CHARTS
Prehistoric Cultures 29
Ancient Egypt 33
Notable Roman Emperors 72
History of the Israelites 101
The Hebrew Bible 105
The New Testament 107
Medieval Philosophy 181
Popular Classical Musical Forms 322
Revolutionary Milestones 331
Later 19th-century Music 369
Modernist -isms 403

Difficult and unfamiliar names and terms in the text are followed by their phonetic pronunciation in square brackets. A simple phonetic system is used which includes the symbols:

ah = r*a*w	ow = b*ow*
ay = l*a*te	uh = pl*u*mb
g = *g*et	tch = ri*ght*eous
igh, eye = b*i*te	zh = A*s*ia
oh = b*oa*t	(n), (r), etc. = barely
oo = b*oo*t	voiced or nasal

ACKNOWLEDGMENTS

As with the original edition, this edition owes a great debt to the good counsel and diligent effort of many besides myself. Many improvements here should be credited to those who reviewed the manuscript:

Larry L. Brock, Brevard Community College
Rick Davis, Ricks College
Craig L. Hanson, Muskingum College
Kimberley M. Jones, Seminole Community College
Stanley J. Kajs, Chesapeake College
Leslie Lambert, Santa Fe Community College
James G. Massey, Polk Community College
Jane Pyle, Miami-Dade Community College
Gregory P. Rich, Fayetteville State University
Sharon Rooks, Edison Community College
Donald L. Tuthill, Valencia Community College
Gilbert F. Tierney, Harper College

In addition to Donald Tuthill, many other colleagues at Valencia Community College have been great supporters and good critics: Mary Jo Pecht, Elizabeth Eschbach, Carol Foltz, Kenneth Marshall, David Sutton, Lois McNamara, Andrew Alexander, and Kevin Mulholland. My chairman Richard Rietveld has been constantly encouraging and our departmental staff constantly helpful. Only people as good as they are would tolerate someone as trying as I can be.

At Prentice Hall, my publisher Bud Therien and editorial supervisor Marion Gottlieb have been responsive in the largest and the smallest detail. At Calmann & King, Karen Stafford has created a spacious and appealing design for the new edition. Richard Mason and Elisabeth Ingles have been most patient with an author often busy at other tasks. Their meticulous attention to the particulars of this text has improved it immeasurably. The errors that remain, in spite of their efforts, are entirely mine.

I am grateful that my children, Shaughna and Aaron, on reaching their majority, have absolved me of the neglect caused by this and other projects. They defer gladly to the other constant of my life, Kira, whose lightheartedness is my salvation and to whom I dedicate this humble volume.

PHOTO CREDITS

PREFACE

The original edition of *Adventures in the Human Spirit* may have earned its truest accolade in a chance conversation I had with a student. As we paused in a walkway, the student mentioned – for the first time in our year-long acquaintance – that he suffered from a reading disability. But, he said, he had been able to read *Adventures in the Human Spirit*, on the first try. The definitions, the explanations, the questions, he said, all were laid out in a way that helped him get to the gist of what he wanted to know.

That chance endorsement, seconded by other students and my teachng colleagues, is the inspiration for this new edition of *Adventures in the Human Spirit*. This edition preserves the conciseness and coherence of the original, with its broad history of the arts, philosophy, and religion in Western civilization. It retains the engaging features that were designed to open a conversation about the humanities among the book's readers. And it is expanded and re-organized in ways that should make it an even more inviting introduction to the human adventure.

Most evidently, the material on the ancient world has been re-shaped, now with a new Chapter 2 – The Ancient World, covering the period before classical Greece. This alteration allows the text to begin with stone-age culture and to cover ancient Egypt in greater detail, a request from many teachers and students. The beginnings of civilization are now traced across Eurasia and then back to the Aegean world.

The remaining chapters largely preserve the shape of the original edition, but incorporate significant new material. Chapter 3, Classical Greece, now focuses strictly on ancient Greece from the Archaic to the Hellenistic eras. Chapter 4, Ancient Rome, includes a new section on satire. Each of these chapters contains examples of the text's most dramatic new feature, entitled "Global Perspectives." The teachings of Confucius and Gautama Buddha are linked, respectively, to Socrates and the doctrines of stoicism.

The treatment of Islam's rise in Chapter 5, The Judeo-Christian Spirit, has been expanded, and the sacred Meso-american city of Teotihuacán is compared to the pilgrimage cities of Rome and Mecca. The sacred blood-letting of Maya civilization is treated in the context of European feudalism in Chapter 6, The Feudal Spirit, and a new section on Muslim Spain appears alongside the discussion of medieval courtly love in Chapter 7, The Gothic Awakening. Coverage of the late Middle Ages in Chapter 7 now includes Chaucer, Petrarch, and Guillaume de Machaut.

The discussion of West African portrait sculpture provides a global perspective on the Italian Renaissance (Chapter 8), while Chapter 9, The Northern Renaissance, includes a treatment of Montaigne and the essay. In Chapter 10, The Baroque Spirit, a feature on the Mogul tomb of the Taj Mahal appears alongside discussions of Baroque architecture. Chapter 10 and Chapter 11, The Enlightenment Spirit, both contain a more diverse treatment of music (Vivaldi, Haydn, Mozart's operas) and of literary topics (English Baroque poetry, the novel of manners).

In covering the nineteenth and twentieth centuries, we have likewise broadened and updated coverage of key topics and trends. Chapter 12, Revolution and Romanticism, now covers the colonial revolutions in Latin America and incorporates a re-organized section on "Romantic Demons." A discussion of the Japanese *ukiyo-e* print in Chapter 13, The Industrial Age, links to an earlier feature on Japanese kabuki theater (Chapter 11), as well as impressionist innovations in art. North American topics, from the transcendentalists to Eakins' realism, enjoy fuller coverage, too. Chapter 14, The Modernist Spirit, adds discussion of the painter Dalí and the Harlem Renaissance, while the final chapter on the contemporary scene takes us to the brink of a new century, with new sections on "AIDS and Art," and "The Global Culture."

Generally, we have sought to include more American topics, from the Latin American baroque to the Hudson River School to Charles Ives. The coverage of music has been diversified: Chopin and the romantic virtuosos; Alban Berg's atonal opera *Wozzeck*; and a new section on Giuseppe Verdi. Our growing understanding of women's contributions to Western civilization enriches the new edition: Aspasia and Hypatia in the ancient world, Hildegard of Bingen and the women troubadour poets in the Middle Ages, romantic feminism and the confessional poets, are among the new topics that readers will discover here. There are also more of the popular "Windows on Daily Life."

These and other additions to the text are intended to provide new "handles" for readers to lay hold of, by connecting to their prior knowledge or stimulating a new interest. In most cases, room has been made for new material by condensing the original text, so that the overall length of the reading remains about the same.

The new edition's additional pages are largely devoted to some 47 new illustrations, many enlarged and in color, and handsomely printed. Such high-quality illustrations are still the most effective visual resource for most readers. Many captions have been rewritten to encourage thoughtful study and reader response. We have expanded and refined the book's other stimuli to critical thought, especially the WRITE IDEA and CRITICAL QUESTION prompts. These questions derive from the lesson I have learned as a teacher, critic, and lecturer: people learn the most when the discussion begins with a question they care about or an issue that involves them. I trust that this new edition will help readers to ask those questions and to begin to find answers.

1 The Humanities: An Introduction to the Adventure

In 1800, a boy was discovered in Aveyron, southern France, who evidently had lived in the wilds much of his young life. The child could only growl and grunt, and, as one would expect, had frightful table manners. The so-called "wild boy of Aveyron" provoked a debate among scientists and philosophers over the definition of human nature. Yet the boy himself could not join the debate because he lacked the most basic faculties of human culture: the ability to think and the capacity to explain himself intelligibly to others. The "wild boy of Aveyron" could take no part in the adventure of the human spirit.

FINDING A VOICE

Human beings are distinguished from other creatures by the richness of their inner life, the constant flow of thoughts and feelings that constitutes human experience. Deprived of the means to express this experience, the boy of Aveyron suffered an impoverished inner life as well. By comparison, consider the famous dramatic character Hamlet, in the tragedy by William Shakespeare (Fig. **1.1**). With his university education, Hamlet jokes easily with his companions, stages an impromptu drama, and philosophizes about the human condition. Even as he contemplates suicide, Hamlet's keen mind grasps the complexity of the human soul and the potential for human achievement. In Hamlet's words:

> *What a piece of work is a man! how noble in reason! how infinite in faculties! in form and moving, how express and admirable! in action, how like an angel! in apprehension, how like a god! the beauty of the world! the paragon of animals!*

Most of all, through his capacity for artful speech and action, Hamlet makes his inner life intelligible to Shakespeare's audiences, enriching us through the character's own self-understanding. The boy of Aveyron could never overcome his isolation from human culture, while Hamlet's voice – anguished but eloquent – has spoken to countless generations.

TRADITION: NURTURING THE CREATIVE SPIRIT

Since their beginnings as nomads and cave-dwellers, humans have transformed the wisdom and beauty of human experience into works of art and thought. The process of nurturing and transmitting this creative spirit is called tradition – a process which sustains a civilization's essential values and impresses them on succeeding generations. Some human traditions may be transmitted informally, through family customs and children's play. However, a civilization's core traditions are passed on by organized intention, usually by training or schooling. A religious faith, for example, does not leave it to chance that children learn the faith's essential beliefs

1.1 Laurence Olivier as Shakespeare's Hamlet, in the 1948 filmed version of *Hamlet*, also directed by Olivier.

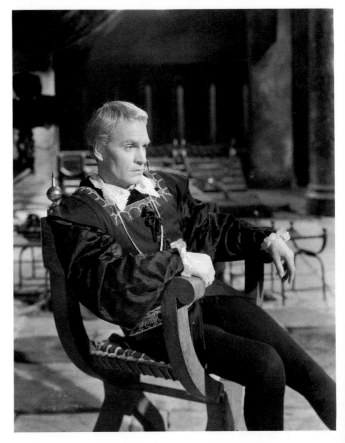

and history: in the ritual of Passover, Jewish children repeat an ancient story of God's blessing; during Ramadan, the Islamic month of fasting, young Muslims observe the annual rituals of purification; and at a first Holy Communion, a Christian child re-enacts the faith's sacred meal and ritually joins the community of believers.

Yet tradition is not a one-way process of transmitting culture to individuals. Tradition shapes the experience of each generation and stimulates new creativity. Every creative spirit depends on the models of tradition, the accumulated expression and reflection of past generations. Through the traditions of the past, humans may discover a unique experience of the present.

MODES OF EXPRESSION AND REFLECTION

The **humanities** are the study of the creative process of tradition as it occurred in the past and continues in the present. Through the humanities, we learn how humans have expressed their most intense experiences and reflected on their most essential truths. The humanities encompass what may be called **modes of expression**, including the visual arts (painting, sculpture, architecture, photography, and film); the performing arts (music, dance, and theater); and the literary arts (poetry and prose). The modes of expression also include such decorative arts as embroidery and metalworking, which are often employed in association with other arts.

Closely allied to these arts are what may be called **modes of reflection**, such as philosophy, religion, and history. In these modes, humans reflect on the most fundamental questions of their experience: "What is truth?", "What is the nature of the divine?", or "What is the meaning of the past?". In pursuing such questions, the modes of reflection may often borrow from artistic expression. The humanities understand these diverse modes – the arts, religion, philosophy – in their fruitful interaction and development.

This textbook is concerned chiefly with the historical development of arts and ideas in Western civilizations – the Mediterranean region, Europe, and the Americas – from about 3000 B.C. to the present day. Within several chapters, the reader will find a unit devoted to other civilizations – Chinese, African, Indian – that provides a global perspective on Western civilization. Also, the features entitled "Windows on Daily Life" provide brief portraits of everyday experience.

The purpose of this book is to introduce the humanities in such a way that the reader may take a more active part in the creative process of tradition. As we learn to command more fully the modes of expression and reflection, our experience is enriched and our powers of thought and creativity are enlarged. Study of the humanities is a part of this individual development. The humanities teach us to understand the languages of tradition, so that we may speak more effectively in the present.

THE ARTS

The following section offers a brief introduction to the arts and suggests critical questions to encourage the reader's active response.

THE PICTORIAL ARTS

In what medium is the picture created?
What are the picture's important lines and shapes?
How does the picture use color and light?
Does the picture contain significant patterns?
How are the parts of the picture combined into a meaningful whole?

One of humankind's most ancient skills is the ability to make **pictures**. The primal impulse to visualize the world is embodied in the pictorial arts of painting, printmaking, and photography. In today's culture, pictorial images surround us in astounding number and intensity, providing endless opportunity for questioning the pictorial arts.

1.2 Hubert and Jan van Eyck, *God the Father*, detail of the *Ghent Altarpiece*, St. Bavo, Ghent, completed 1432. Tempera and oil on wood.
Oil permits the painter to achieve the brilliant colors and gem-like detail of the robes and crown.

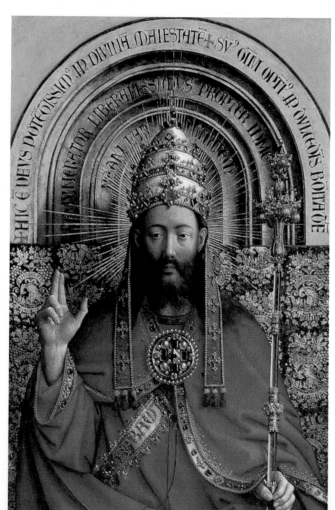

In what medium is the picture created? The **medium** (pl. **media**) is the physical or material means by which a picture is communicated. A painter might choose the medium of oil paint applied to wood (Fig. **1.2**) or canvas, or watercolor applied to paper. Each painting medium has its own technical requirements and pictorial qualities. The transparent wash of a watercolor contrasts sharply with the tangible density of oil paint. Likewise, the pictorial media of printmaking and photography have their own complex technical requirements and unique aesthetic effects.

What are the picture's important lines and shapes? A **line** is an extended point, the most basic element of pictorial communication. Lines help to define the picture as a whole: horizontal and vertical lines tend to define space as stable and orderly, while diagonal lines create tension and motion. Lines can establish a direction for the eye to follow, even when the line is implied. A **shape** is the space bounded by a line, and may be curved or linear, regular or irregular. Shapes also help to create a pictorial structure, and are used to evoke in the viewer a certain feeling. A viewer responds differently, for example, to the organic shape of a shell than to the shapes of machines and buildings.

How does the picture use color and light? Pictures act directly on the viewer by their color (Fig. **1.3**). Aside from their visual and emotional quality, colors also have symbolic importance within a culture. In the Middle Ages, for example, red and blue were traditionally associated with the Virgin Mary. Additionally, **light** creates a sense of depth when it falls across an object. Light also creates dramatic interest by emphasizing important elements or creating a play of light and shadow (Fig. **1.4**).

Does the picture contain significant patterns? A **pattern** is the repetition of a pictorial element according to a particular design. The pattern may consist of line, shape, color, or some other significant pictorial element. Patterns create a visual structure or rhythm that make a picture's meaning more intelligible.

How are the parts of the picture combined into a meaningful whole? **Composition** is the combination of a picture's elements into one whole. Composition may involve the picture's division into major parts, such as foreground and background. Johannes Vermeer's *The Allegory of Painting* (see Fig. 10.33) creates a clear division between the background figure of the model (well-lighted, costumed, and on display), and the foreground figure of the painter (in shadow, self-effacing, anonymous). With composition an artist can orchestrate the picture's elements into a complex pictorial statement.

Many pictorial works communicate a narrative or symbolic message. In such cases, the following questions are also useful in understanding the pictorial arts:

Does the picture tell a story?
Does it contain important symbols?
Is there a dramatic action?

SCULPTURE: THE ART OF SHAPING

Is the sculpture full-round or in relief?
From what materials is the sculpture shaped?
What is the sculpture's texture?
Does the sculpture imply movement?
What is the sculpture's relation to site?

Sculpture is the shaping of material into a three-dimensional work of art. Like painting, it is one of the most ancient arts. Sculpture can take virtually any shape and can be crafted in virtually any material. This art form ranges from the exquisitely proportioned stone of ancient Greek statuary (see Fig. 3.9) to the playfully modern combinations of Alexander Calder (see Fig. 15.8). Of such different sculptural works, the thoughtful student may ask the following questions:

Is the sculpture full-round or in relief? A **full-round** (also called "free-standing") sculpture is shaped so that the work stands freely and can be seen from all sides (see Fig. 8.22). Full-round statues of human figures may be on any scale, from small figurines to colossal statues. **Relief sculpture** is attached to a wall or panel and is commonly used to decorate a building, as in the reliefs on the Parthenon in Athens (Fig. **1.5**) and the sculptural decoration on the Gothic cathedral at Chartres, France (see Fig. 7.15).

From what materials is the sculpture shaped? Sculpture can be made from any material able to be carved, molded, assembled, or cast. As with painting, a sculptor may work in a variety of media or materials. Some materials, such as stone and wood, are shaped by chipping away the excess, a **subtractive** process (Fig. **1.6**). Plaster sculptures, on the other hand, are created by an **additive** process of building up layers of material. Metal can be beaten or bent into the desired shape, or melted and then poured into a mold.

What is the sculpture's texture? **Texture** is the way an object feels to the sense of touch. A painting can only suggest textures, whereas a sculpture's textures may actually be touched and explored. Sculptural materials appeal to the touch in different ways. Marble, for example, can be finished to an extremely smooth texture that resembles glass or human flesh. Michelangelo's late-fifteenth-century sculpture the *Pietà* (see Fig. 8.23), for example, has a remarkably flawless texture that suggests the perfection of Christ's sacrifice.

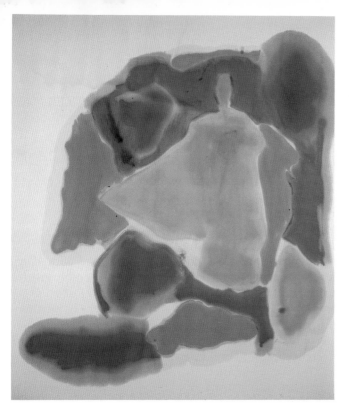

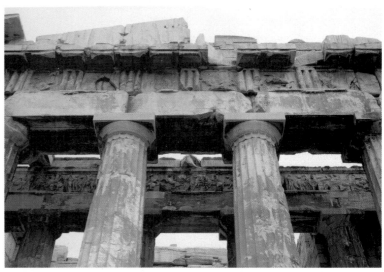

1.5 Above **Relief sculpture decorating the Parthenon, Athens, c. 440 B.C.**
Because relief sculptures can extend hundreds of feet, they are often used to tell stories on a grand scale. On the Parthenon in Athens, a stately procession of Athenian citizens stretches around the entire temple, a length of more than five hundred feet (152 m).

1.3 Above **Helen Frankenthaler, *Formation*, 1963. Acrylic on canvas, 6 ft 4 ins x 5 ft 5 ins (1.93 x 1.65 m). Collection Alexis Gregory, New York.**
Compare the mood created by Frankenthaler's acrylic blues, yellows, and pinks, to the colors of the medieval stained-glass window, *Notre-Dame-de-Belle-Verrière* (Fig. 7.1).

1.4 Below **Caravaggio, *David with the Head of Goliath*, 1609–10. Oil on canvas, 4 ft 1½ ins x 3 ft 3⅜ ins (1.25 x 1 m). Borghese Gallery, Rome.**
The Italian painter Caravaggio achieves a gruesome effect by his lighting of Goliath's severed head, held by the Biblical hero David. Note the direction of the light and the powerful contrast between foreground and background.

1.6 Right **Isamu Noguchi, *Kouros* (in nine parts), 1944–45. Pink Georgia marble, height approx. 9 ft 9 ins (2.97 m). The Metropolitan Museum of Art, New York, Fletcher Fund, 1953.**
Noguchi chooses a traditional material, stone, for this abstractly shaped freestanding sculpture. Compare this with the traditional Greek *kouros* (Fig. 3.6).

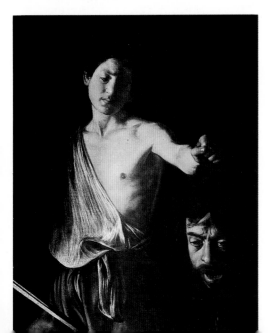

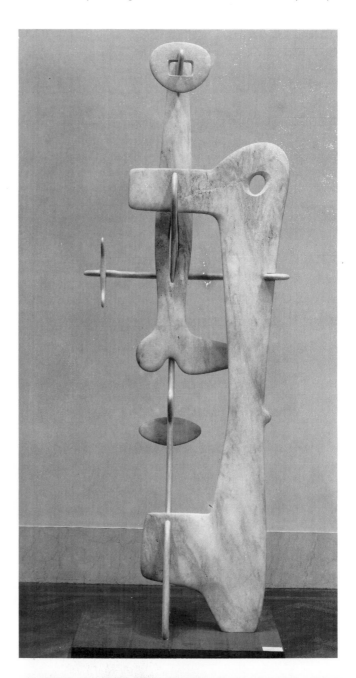

Does the sculpture imply movement? Though most sculptures are immobile, some can appear to move through the space that they occupy. Bernini's fearsome *David* (see Fig. 10.11) has drawn his sling and is about to unleash the missile that will kill Goliath, while in Donatello's more static version (see Fig. 8.22), David rests his foot on Goliath's head. Twentieth-century artists freed sculpture so that some parts could actually move. The first "mobile" was invented in the early twentieth century, when the irreverent modernist Marcel Duchamp (see page 400) placed a bicycle wheel on a stool.

What is the sculpture's relation to site? Sculpture may have a specific relation to its site, that is, its location in a surrounding space. Naturally, a religious sculpture is vitally related to the church or temple in which it is housed.

1.7 Eero Saarinen, Main lobby of the Trans World Flight Center, Kennedy International Airport, New York, 1962. Modern architecture often leaves concrete undecorated, but reinforces it internally with steel rods, allowing the creation of the fluid lines of this Flight Center.

ARCHITECTURE: THE ART OF SHELTER

What is the building's function?
From which materials is the building constructed?
What is the building's design?
What is the relation between the exterior and interior of the building?
How does the building employ the other arts?

The most ambitious of the arts is **architecture**, the art of enclosing a space to provide shelter. Compared with sculpture or painting, architecture requires considerably greater resources of wealth, materials, technical knowledge, and labor. For this reason, significant works of architecture are often associated with wealth and power. Usually only the most powerful members of a society can afford to construct large buildings.

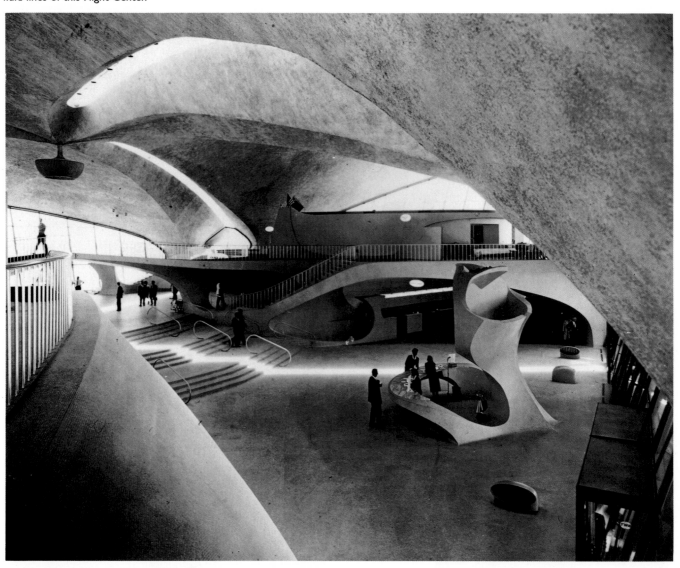

What is the building's function? Nearly all buildings serve a function in the community that constructs them. The earliest great buildings were temples built to honor the gods or palaces that housed the families of kings and pharaohs. Temples had a sacred function, because they were associated with the divine and holy, whereas a royal palace had a secular function, serving everyday needs. Because the temple and the palace involved the community as a whole, their function was public.

Houses and other structures used strictly by individuals are termed private or domestic architecture. Virtually all significant buildings have a function that combines sacred or secular, private or public use.

From which materials is the building constructed? Materials are as essential to architecture as to sculpture. The ancient Greeks (see Chapter 3) built their houses from wood and their temples from stone. Consequently, Greek private architecture has disappeared, while ancient Greek temples still inspire architects today. Often new architectural materials incorporate the old. The Romans developed the use of concrete – a material made of cement, sand, stone, and water – but decorated this unsightly material with an outer layer of stone, in order to make their buildings look like those of the ancient Greeks. Twentieth-century builders improved concrete by adding steel reinforcement.

What is the building's design? The most important and complex aspect of a building is its **design**, the way the building is assembled to create a sheltering space. Architectural design is akin to composition in painting, yet more essential. A poorly composed painting will merely languish in an attic; a poorly designed building may collapse. Architectural design is so closely tied to function and materials that these three elements of architecture – design, function, materials – form an interdependent triad. Eero Saarinen's Trans World Flight Center at the Kennedy International Airport, New York (Fig. **1.7**), can assume such a flowing, bird-like design because it is made of steel-reinforced concrete. The blocks of stone used in ancient Greek and Egyptian buildings (see Fig. 2.9) could not have achieved such flexibility of design. However, their carved columns and sculpture created a monumental presence appropriate to their religious function.

What is the relation between the exterior and interior of the building? A building presents itself to the world through its exterior, yet usually serves its function through the interior. A building's exterior and interior may reflect a common design, as with Frank Lloyd Wright's Guggenheim Museum in New York (see Fig. 15.15). Exterior and interior may exhibit different principles of design, creating a tension between outside and inside.

How does the building employ the other arts? Most commonly, a building employs the other arts, especially painting and sculpture, for decorative purposes. Temples and churches commonly use exterior relief sculpture to attract and educate the faithful. However, buildings can also employ performing arts such as music or theater, often creating a mutual influence among the arts. The sound of choirs singing in St. Mark's in Venice in the fifteenth century was so distinctive that the church's architecture helped shape the development of Renaissance music (see page 255).

MUSIC: THE ART OF SOUND

What are the music's basic melody and rhythm?
What instruments or voices perform the music?
Where is the music performed, and for what purpose?
What is the form of the musical composition?

Music is an art that depends upon performers – players or singers – to bring it to life. It is an abstract and ephemeral art, consisting only of sounds stretched across time. Music differs from ordinary sound – noise – in that it is organized in a way meaningful to the ear. The basic component of music is the **tone**. A musical tone has a certain **pitch** that sounds either high or low. A flute can play tones of a higher pitch than a cello, just as a soprano's voice is pitched higher than a tenor's. A musical tone also has **color**, which means simply how the tone sounds. Because they produce sound in different ways, the flute and violin have different color, even when playing the same tone. Finally, musical tones have **dynamics**, depending on how loudly or softly the tones are played. When these elements of musical tone – pitch, color, dynamics – are combined, composers and musicians create the infinite variety of the world's music.

What are the music's basic melody and rhythm? A **melody** is a series of tones that make some sense to the ear, that create a tune that the ear can follow. Anything the listener can hum is a melody. A **rhythm** is anything one can tap a foot to, a beat created by regularly accented tones. Rhythm is essential to one of music's most important functions, as an accompaniment to dance. In African musical cultures, rhythm dominates other elements of musical expression. The combination of drums and other percussion instruments of different colors creates a rich texture of rhythmic patterns.

The possibilities of melody and rhythm are infinite, yet most music follows particular rules for inventing melodic and rhythmic arrangements. In Western music melodies are expressed in a **key** – a series of seven tones with set intervals between tones. Some twentieth-century musical innovators like Arnold Schoenberg discarded these melodic rules, creating a music that to some people may sound like noise but is, in fact, highly organized. Rhythm is usually determined by a basic **meter**, the set number

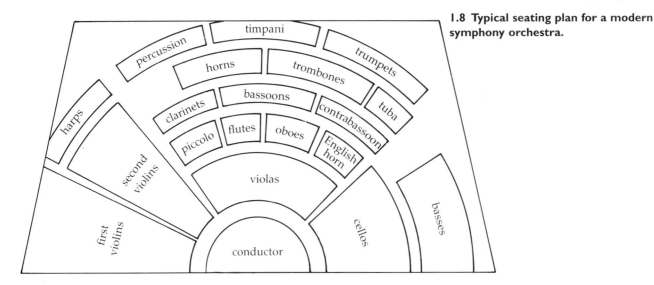

1.8 Typical seating plan for a modern symphony orchestra.

of beats per musical unit. The form of dance music called the waltz is easily recognized by its triple meter, or three beats per measure.

What instruments or voices perform the music? The color of a musical work depends on the combination of musical instruments or voices that perform it. In recent centuries, composers have written music calling for a specific combination of instrumental or choral voices. Mozart (see page 312) composed frequently for a string quartet, while Brahms' symphonic works require the orchestra to have a large brass section (Fig. **1.8**). Vocal music is written for voices in a certain range: an opera role, for example, may require a tenor voice or a baritone. A composition for voice may call for a specified number of soloists (one singer per part) and a chorus (several singers singing the same part).

Where is the music performed, and for what purpose? The setting of a musical performance is usually closely related to its function. As with architecture, music can serve either sacred or secular functions, depending on whether it is performed in a religious service or a concert hall. The setting and function also help determine the choice of instruments – a parade calls for a marching band, while a wedding reception would more likely employ a string ensemble.

What is the form of the musical composition? As in the other arts, musical **form** means the arrangement of a composition's parts into a unified and meaningful whole. A musical form may be very simple and brief, like a nursery rhyme with a single verse, or it may be very large, with the performance lasting several hours and requiring a full orchestra and a large chorus. Popular songs, for example, usually take the form of A–B–A. An initial melody and rhythm (A) are stated and often repeated. Then a verse is sung to a different but closely related

second melody (B). Finally, the opening melody (A) is repeated to create closure. In the Western musical tradition, even larger and more complex forms – such as the movements of a **symphony** – follow this pattern of statement, variation, and restatement. Understanding any musical composition can usually begin by identifying its parts and seeing their relation.

The number of musical forms can be overwhelming. During the last three hundred years, composers have

1.9 Jazz pianist and composer Thelonius Monk.
Though often based on simple melodies, jazz music in performance achieves remarkable melodic and rhythmic complexity.

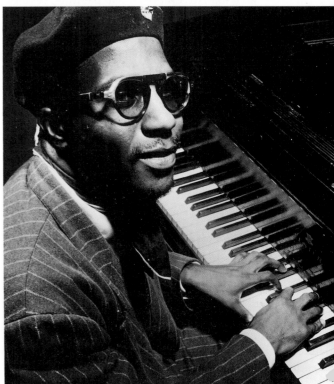

invented and practiced dozens of different musical forms (Fig. **1.9**). The origin of these musical forms is closely related to the setting and function of the composition. For example, the **cantata** was a choral work that set a biblical story to music and was often performed in churches. The **blues** was a mournful song form that originated from the hollers of African-American slaves as they worked in the fields. Both forms are still performed today, the cantata in churches and the blues in night clubs.

DANCE: THE ART OF MOVEMENT

What kind of dance is it?
What is the relation between the dance and the music?
Is the dance mimetic?
How are the dancing movements combined into a meaningful
  whole?

Like music, the performing art of dance is difficult to capture. **Dance** is the rhythmic and patterned movement of the human body, usually to musical accompaniment. It is perhaps the most ancient art, and one that is still practiced in every known human culture. Dance can be as simple and spontaneous as the gyrations of a stadium crowd cheering for their favorite team. Or it can be as formalized and complex as a classical ballet. Our historical knowledge of dance is limited since, like music, its performance leaves few historical traces.

What kind of dance is it? Dance is generally categorized according to three types: popular dance, ballet, and modern dance. **Popular dance** includes forms of dance passed on traditionally, such as folk dances, or dances practiced for social occasions. Popular dances can be highly complex and artistic, and may require considerable training. Popular dances are usually not performed for an audience.

Ballet is a theatrical dance that combines highly formalized steps and poses with athletic leaps and turns. The five "positions" of classical ballet were prescribed in the seventeenth century and are still learned in ballet studios today (Fig. **1.10**). The term ballet also describes the combination of ballet dance, music, and staging in a theatrical work such as *Swan Lake* or *Sleeping Beauty*. In a ballet, the dancers' steps and movements are orchestrated by the **choreographer**, who must coordinate the music, story, and dance to form an intelligible whole. A dance choreographer is part composer, part theatrical director, and part dance master.

The last of the dance types is **modern dance**, which includes the forms of dance created in reaction to classical ballet. Modern dance seeks more freedom and expressiveness than ballet, but still involves choreography and theatrical performance. It is often more abstract and less oriented toward a story than traditional ballet, and it often incorporates modern music and art.

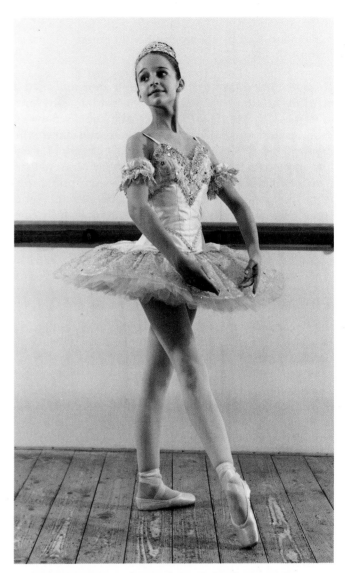

1.10 The formalized poses of classical ballet stem from the 17th century.

What is the relation between the dance and the music? Dance is so closely allied with music that musical styles are often named for the dance they accompany. From the waltz to hip-hop, dance and music have been melded to one another. The dance form of the minuet, originated in France, was preserved in the eighteenth-century symphonies of Mozart (see page 323). In the 1970s, disco music fueled a popular dance revival among young people dissatisfied with rock-and-roll's informal dance styles. In the same way, the improvisational music of jazz (see page 418) has fostered the equally inventive form of jazz dance.

Is the dance mimetic? The term "mimetic" stems from the Greek word for "imitation." Mimetic dance imitates the gestures and actions of real life, and is especially important in ballet and other narrative forms. In a romantic ballet, for example, the dancers' calculated poses and movements may be choreographed to imitate the joy of a couple in love.

How are the dancing movements combined into a meaningful whole? A dance's form, much like the form of music or theater, is the artful combination of dancing gestures and movements. In a dance performance, the dancers' movements create a changing combination of line, motion, pattern, tension, and rhythm. More so than with any other art, the form of dance is perceptible only in performance. The three-dimensional energy and complexity of a dance performance cannot be fully captured by a system of notation or even by film, although filmed dance has been revived by the popularity of music video.

THE ART OF THEATER

How is the play staged through set, lighting, and costume?
How do the director and actors and actresses interpret the dramatic script?

Theater is the art of acting out dramatic literature in a live performance. Since most readers will have studied dramatic works as literature, this introduction considers aspects of theatrical performance.

How is the play staged through set, lighting, and costume? The stage is the physical space in which a dramatic work is performed. Most Western theaters today use a conventional **proscenium** stage. The proscenium stage is enclosed within a rectangular frame, and the audience views the action through an invisible "fourth wall." A theater may instead have a **thrust** stage, in which a stage platform projects into the audience, or a stage **in-the-round**, which has a performance area completely surrounded by the audience.

The most complex elements of staging involve the theatrical **set**, made up of lighting and scenery. The set design creates the imaginary space in which the dramatic action is performed (Fig. **1.11**). Sets may incorporate elaborate scenery and stage machinery. Some medieval dramas known as morality plays managed to represent the Garden of Eden, a fiery hell, and the throne of heaven, all in one elaborate set. Twentieth-century expressionist theater used complicated revolving stages and sets to accommodate huge casts. With the advent of electrical lights, theatrical **lighting** became essential in shaping the theatrical performance. Lighting helps to underscore mood, character, and other elements of the dramatic action.

The **costumes** worn by actors and actresses are also part of the staging and set the tone of a theatrical performance. The choice of costumes is an especially impor-

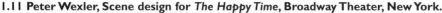

1.11 Peter Wexler, Scene design for *The Happy Time*, Broadway Theater, New York.

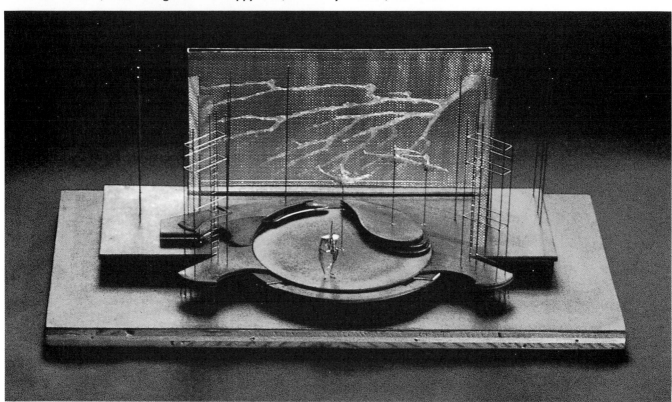

tant decision when performing a play from the past. For example, should a director costume Shakespearean characters in modern dress or period costume? Like theatrical lighting, costume can also emphasize an aspect of the character or imply changes in a character during the performance.

How do the director and actors and actresses interpret the dramatic script? **Acting** is probably the aspect of theatrical performance that audiences are most sensitive to and critical of. Under the director's guidance, actors and actresses are responsible for realizing the dramatic script in their words and actions on stage. An actor's or actress' performing skill and discrimination largely determine the impact a character will have on the audience.

The **director** of a play governs every aspect of the performance, including staging, acting, and changes in the script. Yet the director has no immediately visible role in the performance. The director's decisions can only be inferred from the performance itself. A critical audience should appreciate the director's choices in casting – the choice of particular actors or actresses for certain roles. The director also determines how they move together on stage, and how quickly or slowly the action proceeds. With such decisions, the director controls the essential character of the whole theatrical performance.

A NOTE ABOUT OPERA

Opera can be defined simply as theater set to music. Yet such a simple definition cannot suggest opera's spectacular effects. Opera combines all the performing arts – music, dance, and theater – in an artistic experience that cannot be matched by any of these arts alone.

Unfortunately, opera suffers from an inaccessibility to audiences and an elitist reputation. The need for a precise match between the words of an opera and its music makes it difficult for operas to be translated. An opera written in Italian or French is usually performed in the original language, so an English-speaking audience must be satisfied with a program summary or translated dialogue titles projected over the stage. In addition, opera has historically been an art of the upper classes, and it is still associated with elite audiences.

Still, opera is a stunning art form that can, with a little cultivation, provide pleasure for any humanities student. From a student's point of view, opera is interesting if only because it can stimulate so many of the questions asked already in this brief introduction to the arts:

How is opera staged?
What is the relation between the words and the music?
How has a director interpreted the script?
What instruments and voices are used?
How has a singer interpreted the musical score and the dramatic script?
How is dance incorporated into the operatic narrative?

The variety of questions suggests that opera, perhaps the least-known of the performing arts, is the best-chosen introduction to those arts.

THE LITERARY ARTS

Literature divides generally into two kinds: **fiction**, composed from the author's imagination; and **non-fiction**, recounting the author's actual thoughts or real events. The largest body of literature is fictional and divides further into three main genres: drama, poetry, and narrative fiction.

Drama is literature to be acted out in theatrical performance, an art discussed as the art of theater, above. **Poetry** is a literature of rhythmic sound and concentrated imagery. Poetry usually employs a regular pattern of stresses (called a **meter**) and often contains highly condensed metaphor and symbol. Poetry may actually take the form of drama (Greek tragedy, for example) or narrative (the ancient epics). Poetry of the most personal and concentrated kind is called **lyric**, which can be written in particular forms (for example, the sonnet, elegy, or ode). About poetry, one may ask:

What form does the poem take?
What are its patterns of sound (meter, rhythm)?
How does it employ metaphor or symbol?

Narrative fiction is literature that tells a story. The most common forms of narrative fiction are the novel and the short story, which usually describe events and characters in believable, true-to-life detail. However, narrative can also take the form of fantasy, recounting a dream or vision. The narrator or author often sees the action from a specific point of view, and may comment on the action or characters. In reading narrative fiction, it helps to observe:

What form does the narrative take?
What is the action (plot)?
Who are the chief characters, and what are their significant speeches and actions?
What is the author's point of view?

Fictional works often contain underlying ideas, or **themes**, that develop across the whole work. Identifying a literary work's themes often helps to understand it as a whole and connect it to other works.

Non-fictional literature takes such forms as **biography**, the literary account of a person's life, and the **essay**, a brief exposition of the author's views on a particular subject.

AN INVITATION TO THE ADVENTURE

In considering any work of art, it is always important to concentrate not only on the work itself, but also on one's own responses. We acquire a voice in the human conversation by asking ourselves:

What is my response to the work of art?
How is that response shaped by the work itself and by my own experience?

If, as some say, knowledge is power, knowledge is also pleasure. Knowledge of a human culture gives us power in that culture and pleasure in being a part of it. This is just as true for pop music's latest fad as it is for the classical symphonies of Mozart and Beethoven. A knowledge of both musical cultures broadens a person's potential to have power and find pleasure in his or her world.

The works of culture discussed in this survey offer a rich texture of meaning and experience. Understanding them is often hard work – one must grasp the basic principles of music, for example, while also attending to the subtleties of a symphony or opera. The rewards are substantial. As we learn to command more fully the cultures around us, our own powers of thought and creativity are enlarged. This text aims to prepare readers for the challenges of the humanities and introduce them to their pleasures. It is an invitation to join, actively and intelligently, the adventure of the human spirit.

Chapter Summary

A summary of questions to help the reader discover the pleasures of the humanities:

The Pictorial Arts
In what medium is the picture created?
What are the picture's important lines and shapes?
How does the picture use color and light?
Does the picture contain significant patterns?
How are the parts of the picture combined into a meaningful whole?

Sculpture
Is the sculpture full-round or in relief?
From what materials is the sculpture shaped?
What is the sculpture's texture?
Does the sculpture imply movement?
What is the sculpture's relation to site?

Architecture
What is the building's function?
From which materials is the building constructed?
What is the building's design?
What is the relation between the exterior and interior of the building?
How does the building employ the other arts?

Music
What are the music's basic melody and rhythm?
What instruments or voices perform the music?
Where is the music performed, and for what purpose?
What is the form of the musical composition?

Dance
What kind of dance is it (popular, ballet, modern)?
What is the relation between the dance and the music?
Is the dance mimetic?
How are the dancing movements combined into a meaningful whole?

Theater
How is the play staged through set, lighting, and costume?
How do director and actors interpret the dramatic script?

Opera
How is opera staged?
What is the relation between the words and the music?
How has a director interpreted the script?
What instruments and voices are used?
How has a singer interpreted the musical score and the dramatic script?
How is dance incorporated into the operatic narrative?

Poetry
What form does the poem take?
What are its patterns of sound (meter, rhythm)?
How does it employ metaphor or symbol?

Narrative Fiction
What form does the narrative take?
What is the action (plot)?
Who are the chief characters, and what are their significant speeches and actions?
What is the author's point of view?

Personal Response
What is my response to the work of art?
How is that response shaped by the work itself and by my own experience?

2 The Ancient World

In 1922 a British archaeologist and his Egyptian assistants were the first to look on this face (Fig. 2.1) in nearly 3500 years. In the 1970s, millions more would file through the exhibition of King Tutankhamen's tomb. What was the fascination of this god-king, dead at age nineteen, buried in such glittering splendor in Egypt's fertile valley? Perhaps, King Tutankhamen could reveal the secrets of the **ancient world**: its stories of creation and the gods, its rulers worshiped as gods, its monuments to divine power and the mystery of death. In the eyes of King Tutankhamen, so ancient yet so familiar, perhaps we see the elemental beginnings of human civilization; from his lips, perhaps we hear the tales of the first adventures of the human spirit.

THE FIRST HUMANS

Characterize the likely purpose or function of stone-age art.

The first humans of our kind appeared some 100,000 years ago, spreading from Asia to Europe and Africa, sustaining themselves by hunting and food-gathering. Their primitive culture bore the essential features of later human civilization. They honored the mysterious forces of the cosmos with painted and carved images. They built monumental structures – mystic circles of stone and swelling mounds of soil – to commune with the awesome heavens and the dark earth. They buried their dead with provisions to console their spirits in the next life. Around their fires, they must have chanted stories of cosmic battles and heroic deeds.

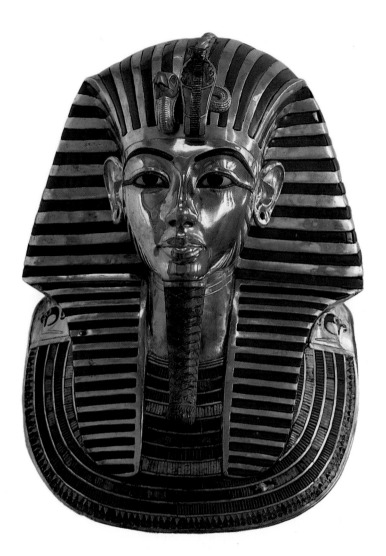

2.1 Funerary mask of King Tutankhamen, c. 1340 B.C. Gold inlaid with enamel and semi-precious stones, height 21 ins (54 cm). Egyptian Museum, Cairo.
The coffin of King Tutankhamen contained his mummified body beneath this splendid gold mask. The belief that the human soul lived on after death was one of the first and most important religious ideas of humans in the ancient world. Ancient tombs in Egypt, China, and the Aegean are essential sources for our knowledge of ancient civilizations.

Living in the Paleolithic period, or Old Stone Age (see chart), these first adventurers of the human spirit left only isolated traces of their achievement. In southwest Europe, **cave artists** painted Paleolithic beasts with uncanny realism, sometimes using humps in the rock to suggest the natural forms of animals. At Lascaux [LAH-skoh] in France, cave artists sketched immense "bulls" that seem to thun-

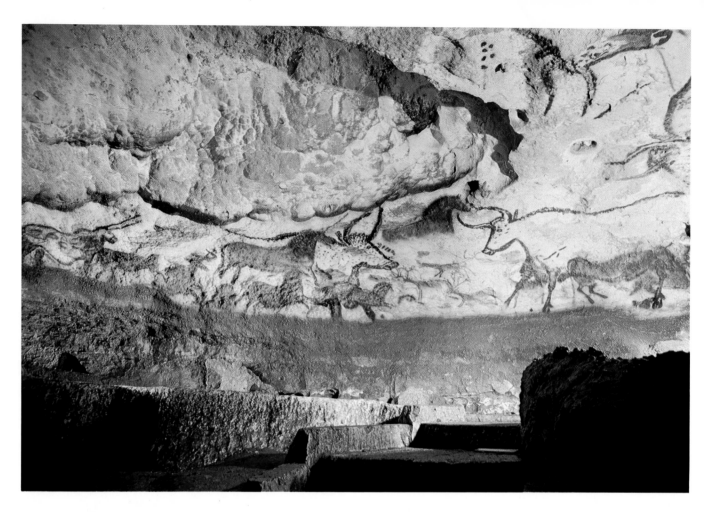

der across the cave wall (Fig. **2.2**). The barely accessible painted chambers must have been the site for ritual ceremonies, illuminated by flickering lamps.

Paleolithic sculptors rendered the human image in a vivid and often naturalistic style. Carved figures were usually female, often pregnant or with exaggerated sexual features. These first sculptures were possibly used for adornment or magical charms to induce fertility and ease childbirth.

By the Neolithic period, or New Stone Age (see chart), humans had begun to shape the physical environment itself, creating **megalithic** (large stone) structures. The most famous megalith stands at Stonehenge in England (Fig. **2.3**), where stone-age architects erected a circle of huge standing stones. Stonehenge's outer ring is a series of post-and-lintel forms, one of the earliest architectural structures. The stones are aligned with astronomical positions and may have served as an observatory as well as a center of religious worship.

The Bronze Age (see chart) emerged in the wake of perhaps the most important shift in human history, from food-gathering to food-growing economies. As human settlement stabilized around intensive agriculture in the **Near East** (present-day Turkey to Iran and Arabia), the first cities – and the first centers of human civilization – appeared on the plains of Mesopotamia [mez-oh-po-TAY-mee-uh].

2.2 Hall of Bulls, c. 15,000–13,000 B.C., Lascaux, France. Paint on limestone.
Paleolithic artists may have applied paint by chewing charcoal and animal fat, and spitting the mixture onto the cave walls. Note how the animal forms at center left are superimposed on one another, perhaps a representation of spatial depth.

2.3 Stonehenge, Salisbury Plain, England, c. 2100–2000 B.C.
Originally, the outer circle was topped by a continuous lintel, or beam, that unified the entire structure. The largest stones, weighing 50 tons, were hauled from a site 150 miles away.

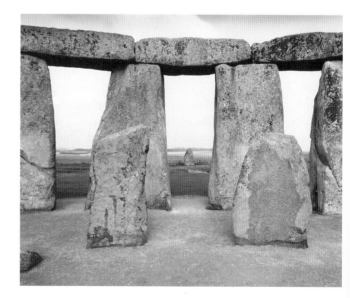

MESOPOTAMIA

Identify similar religious themes and artistic features in ancient Near Eastern civilizations.

The region of **Mesopotamia** (literally "between the rivers," located in present-day Iraq) is justifiably called the cradle of human civilization (Fig. **2.4**). The urban centers that formed along the Tigris and Euphrates [yoo-FRAY-teez] rivers nurtured achievements in the arts, writing, and law. Mesopotamia's rich cities were also the prize for a succession of empires that dominated the Near East and northern Africa during ancient times.

THE SUMERIANS

By 3500 B.C., Mesopotamia's fields and pastures supported a dozen cities inhabited by the **Sumerians** [soo-MER-ee-uns], the first people to use writing and construct monumental buildings. The Sumerians' writing (called **cuneiform**) consisted of pictographs pressed into clay tablets used to record contracts and to track wealth. Sumeria's riches supported a substantial ruling class and the leisure time necessary for fine arts. In a Sumerian

PREHISTORIC CULTURES
Paleolithic (Old Stone Age)
40,000–8000 B.C.
Chipped stone tools; earliest stone sculptures; cave paintings; migration into America
Neolithic (New Stone Age)
8000–2300 B.C.
Polished stone tools; domestication of plants and animals; Stonehenge; potter's wheel (Egypt); rock art (Africa)
Bronze Age
2300–1000 B.C.
Metal tools and weapons; development of writing (China, India)

tomb at Ur, archaeologists have found the soundbox of a spectacular lyre, decorated with a bull's head (Fig. **2.5**). The head itself is gold-covered wood, with a beard of lapis lazuli, a prized blue stone. The lyre was probably

2.4 The Ancient World (Eastern Hemisphere).

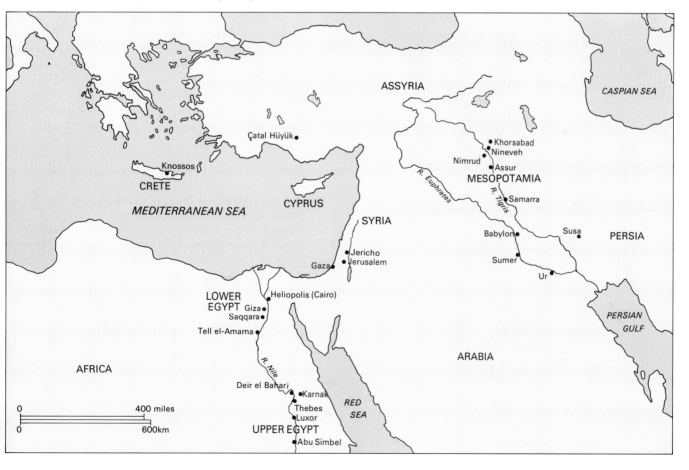

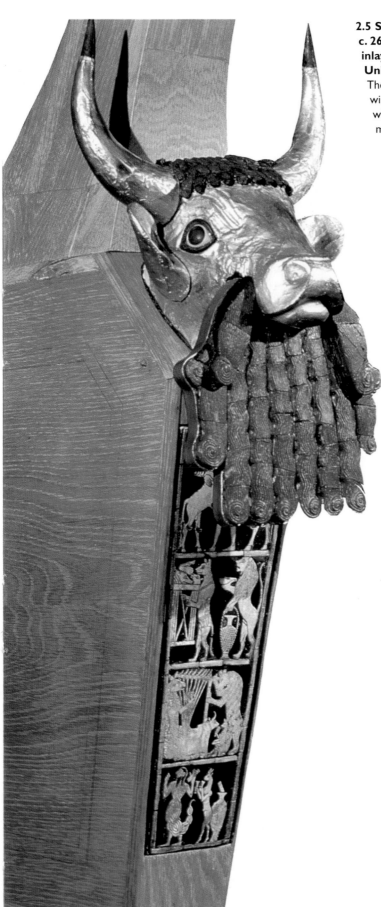

2.5 Soundbox of a lyre from a royal tomb at Ur, Iraq, c. 2685–2550 B.C. Wood with gold, lapis lazuli, and shell inlay, height 17 ins (43 cm). University Museum, University of Pennsylvania, Philadelphia.
The decorative panel shows mythic animals bearing food and wine to a banquet. An ass plays a version of the bull's head lyre, while at bottom a scorpion man gives a dinner oration to musical accompaniment.

used in a funeral rite that included the ritual sacrifice of the musician who played it.

The Sumerian religion, as with most ancient faiths, is known through surviving fragments of myth (see 'Key Concept'). The Sumerian creation myth, called the *Enuma elish* [ay-NOO-mah AY-leesh], reflects the violence of the ancient world. The mother goddess Tiamat does battle with the rowdy seventh generation of gods, led by the fearsome Marduk. After Marduk slays Tiamat, he cleaves her body in half to create the mountains of Mesopotamia. The rivers Tigris and Euphrates arise from the flow of Tiamat's blood. The creation of humanity is equally gruesome. Marduk shapes the first man from the blood of a sacrificed deity, to serve the gods as a slave.

In their sacred buildings, the peoples of ancient Mesopotamia honored the divine forces that controlled the rain and harvests. The first monumental religious structures were Sumerian stepped pyramids called **ziggurats**. Often made of mud brick, the ziggurat was actually a gigantic altar. In mounting its steps, worshipers rose beyond the ordinary human world into the realm of the gods. The great ziggurat at Ur-Nammu (*c.* 2100 B.C.) was dedicated to the moon-god and was probably topped by a temple for sacrifices (Fig. **2.6**).

2.6 Reconstruction drawing of the ziggurat of Ur-Nammu at Ur, Iraq, c. 2100 B.C.
Rising from the Mesopotamian plain, the ziggurat lifted the altars of Sumerian worshipers toward the sacred region of the gods. Comparable "sacred mountains" can be seen in the pyramids of Egyptian and Meso-American civilizations.

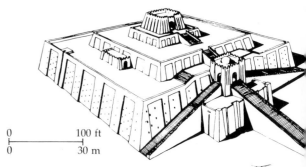

0		100 ft
0		30 m

KEY CONCEPT

MYTH

The unifying ideas of ancient societies were contained in **myths** – stories that explained, in metaphoric or symbolic terms, the nature of the universe and humans' roles and relations in the cosmos. Mythic stories were rooted in the human experience of the divine and the sacred: they often concerned the deeds of the gods, or of god-like heroes who communicated with the divine. Myths were passed on orally in ancient societies, evolving with each generation, until being recorded in the epics and sacred scriptures of the ancient world. The symbolic logic of myth is also elaborated in folk tales, legends, fables, and folk wisdom.

Myths served as the science and philosophy of ancient peoples, explaining cosmic mysteries in the graphic terms of human experience – human sexuality, war, birth and death. In the Sumerian creation myth, for example, the world arises from the sexual union of the gods of fresh water and salt water. In the vivid account of the Hebrew Bible, God shapes the first human from the earth, and then breathes divine life into the man's nostrils. Myths and their related rituals celebrated the cosmic events through which divine forces acted and enabled humans to feel a part of the cosmic dramas.

For mythic cultures, myths also provided compelling explanations for the origins and organization of human society. Anthropologist Bronislav Malinowski saw them as social charters in narrative form, the equivalent of today's political constitutions and social histories. Myths were "not merely a story told but a reality lived," he explained. This lived reality is evident in some of the oldest human artifacts, such as the woman or goddess from Willendorf (Fig. 2.7). These goddess images reflect the earliest humans' reverence for the female body; for them, the mystery of female gestation and birth was bound to the earth's fertility and the renewal of life. When early goddess religions gave way to patriarchal (male-ruled) myths, their memory was preserved in such goddess figures as the Mesopotamian Inanna-Ishtar and the Egyptian Isis, both of whom inspired cultic reverence among women throughout the ancient Near East.

Today, some regard ancient myths as merely fantastic fables, while others perceive in them a profound spiritual or psychological truth. Pioneer psychologist C. G. Jung claimed that myths expressed universal mental images, or **archetypes**, images that

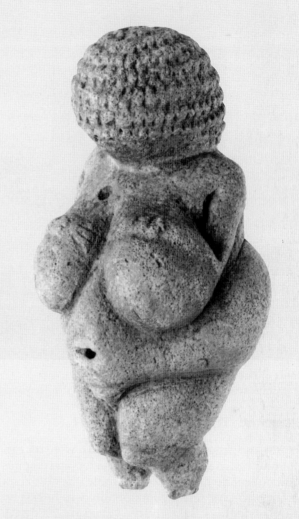

2.7 Woman from Willendorf, Austria, c. 30,000–25,000 B.C. Limestone, height 4¹/₂ ins (11.5 cm). Naturhistorisches Museum, Vienna.
The swelling forms of the figure's breasts, belly, and thighs are symbolic of the female's (and therefore of the earth's) fertility.

also appear in dreams, literature, and art. Religious scholar Mircea Eliade argued that myths revealed a "sacred history," a mysterious and sublime truth that could not be explained by rational or scientific language. Some modern feminists and spiritualists believe that contemporary civilization, with its destructive and exploitative technologies, can only be redeemed by recovering the gentle wholeness of ancient earth and goddess religions.

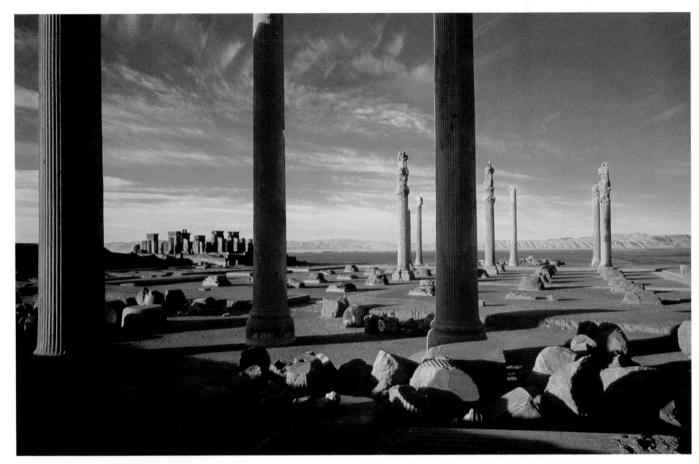

2.8 Ruins of Persepolis, Iran, c. 500 B.C.
Classical Greek sculptors may have seen and imitated the decoration of the Persian palace in the friezes on Athens' Parthenon.

EMPIRES OF THE NEAR EAST

The myths and art of the ancient Near East were repeatedly transformed as a succession of conquerors and empires gained political dominance. For example, the myth of a Sumerian hero-king seeking immortality was re-cast by the **Old Babylonians** as the *Epic of Gilgamesh* (*c.* 2000 B.C.). The myth of Gilgamesh included a version of the Great Flood story also told in the Hebrew Bible. Old Babylon's most significant king was Hammurabi [hah-moo-RAH-bee] (ruled 1792–1750 B.C.), who instituted a legal code dictating the orderly resolution of disputes and uniform punishments for crime. The Code of Hammurabi specified retributions for particular crimes, codifying the ancient legal principle of "an eye for an eye."

The Old Babylonian Empire was followed by that of the Assyrians, skilled and ruthless warriors whose conquests extended to lower Egypt. One Assyrian ruler decorated his palace at Nimrud (in modern-day Iraq) with scenes of lion hunts and luxurious gardens. When Babylonian rule was revived in the seventh century B.C., Nebuchadnezzar II [neh-buh-kahd-NEZZ-er] (ruled 604–562 B.C.) rebuilt the capital. It included the imposing Ishtar Gate, made of turquoise bricks, and a great ziggurat described as having seven levels, each painted a different color.

The last and greatest Near Eastern empire was that of the Persians, established by the conqueror Cyrus II (ruled 559–530 B.C.). His successor Darius built a palace at Persepolis that boasted towering columns and a grand staircase, decorated by a procession bearing taxes and tribute from Mesopotamia's rich cities. It was an unmistakable statement of Persian domination. In the fourth century B.C., however, Persepolis itself fell to the Greek general Alexander the Great, who left its ruin to stand in the desert as a reminder of the vanity of power (Fig. **2.8**).

ANCIENT EGYPT

Explain the religious function of Egyptian art.

In contrast to the upheaval and diversity of the Near East, the people of Egypt created a remarkably stable and homogeneous civilization that endured some three thousand years. Geographically, Egypt was unified by the Nile River and enriched by its annual floods. Politically and religiously, it was united under the rule of the **pharaohs**, god-kings who erected stupendous monuments along the banks

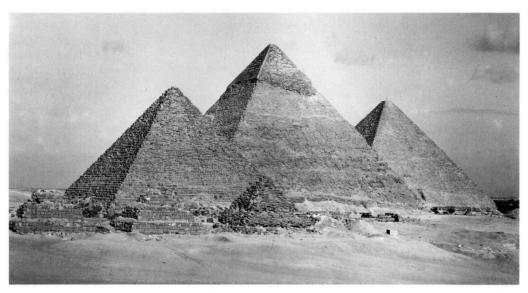

2.9 Pyramids of Mycerinus, Chefren, and Cheops at Giza, Egypt, c. 2525–2460 B.C.
In addition to the religious and political significance, the pyramids were massive state-sponsored employment projects.

of the Nile. The vitality of Egypt's religion fostered an achievement in the arts that still inspires awe today.

EGYPT: RELIGION AND SOCIETY

The Greek historian Herodotus said the Egyptians were the most religious people he knew, and their religious faith inspired much of Egypt's greatest art. Like most ancient peoples, the Egyptians believed in many gods, a form of religion known as **polytheism**. Some gods (often portrayed as animals) had only local powers. Other deities played roles in mythic dramas of national significance. The myth of Isis and Osiris, for example, re-enacts the political struggle between lower and upper Egypt. The god Seth (representing upper Egypt) murders and dismembers his brother Osiris. But Osiris' wife Isis gathers his scattered limbs and resurrects him in the underworld. Henceforth, Osiris rules the realm of life after death. Seth, meanwhile, is defeated by the falcon-god Horus, in whose name Egypt's pharaohs ruled the realm of the living.

The early Egyptians believed that life continued unchanged after death, an expectation that gave rise to the great pyramids of the Old Kingdom (see chart). The **pyramids** were monumental tombs built to contain the bodies of the pharaohs. The great pyramids at Giza (Fig. **2.9**) were gigantic constructions of limestone block. The largest covered thirteen acres at its base, and was built of more than two million huge stone blocks. Shafts and rooms in the interior accommodated the pharaoh's mummified body and the huge treasure of objects required for his happy existence after death. The pyramids were part of a vast funerary complex that included lesser buildings and processional causeways lined with statues.

ANCIENT EGYPT		
Date (app.)	**Period**	**Events**
3150–2700 B.C.	Early Dynastic (Archaic)	Egypt united; first hieroglyphic writing
2700–2190 B.C.	Old Kingdom	Great Pyramids at Giza
2200–c. 2160 B.C.	First Intermediate	Political division; literary flowering
2040–1674 B.C.	Middle Kingdom	Rock-cut tombs
1675–1553 B.C.	Second Intermediate	Hyksos invasion
1552–1069 B.C.	New Kingdom	Amarna period; Temple of Abu Simbel
1069–702 B.C.	Third Intermediate	Political decline; Assyrian conquest

Attention to the spirits of the dead remained a central theme of Egyptian religion and art. Though they never duplicated the pyramids' scale, rock-cut tombs were carved into the rocky cliffs along the Nile in the so-called Valley of the Kings during the Middle Kingdom period (Fig. 2.10). These tombs were hidden to protect them (unsuccessfully) from grave robbers.

THE ARTS OF EGYPT

Even in the wall painting, informal sculpture, and other arts that made their lives colorful and pleasant, the Egyptians were conservative and restrained. The one exception was during the brief reign of **Akhenaten** [ahk-NAH-tun] (ruled 1353–1336 B.C.), who established a cult to the god Aten and fostered a new and distinctive artistic style of great intimacy. Shortly after he came to power,

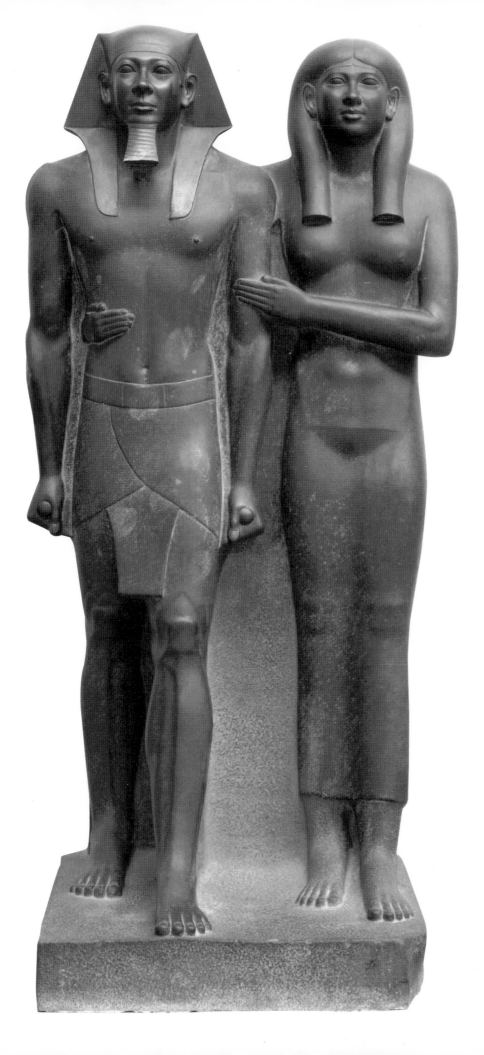

2.10 Mycerinus and Queen Khamerernebty, Giza, c. 2515 B.C. Slate, height 54¹/₂ ins (139 cm). Harvard Museum Expedition. Courtesy, Museum of Fine Arts, Boston.
This sculptural pair stood on the processional causeway leading to Mycerinus' pyramid. The figures' bodily proportions were calculated on a grid determined by a strict rule, or "canon," of proportion, like Greek statues of the Greek classical era.

WINDOW ON DAILY LIFE

DEATH AT AN EGYPTIAN BANQUET

Well-to-do ancient Egyptians often dined on fish and roasted birds and drank a wine made from barley. When they were finished, reports the Greek historian Herodotus, they reminded themselves of their own mortality with this morbid custom:

In social meetings among the rich, when the banquet is ended, a servant carries round to the several guests a coffin, in which there is a wooden image of a corpse, carved and painted to resemble nature as nearly as possible, about a cubit or two cubits in length. As he shows it to each guest in turn, the servant says, "Gaze here, and drink and be merry; for when you die, such will you be." [1]

HERODOTUS
The Persian Wars

Akhenaten broke with the dominant cult of Amon-Re and its powerful priesthood at the temple complex in Thebes. He fostered the worship of the little-known god Aten, the sun-disc, whose life-giving powers he praised in a famous hymn:

> *Earth brightens when you dawn in lightland,*
> *When you shine as Aten of daytime;*
> *As you dispel the dark,*
> *As you cast your rays,*
> *The Two Lands are in festivity.*
> *Awake they stand on their feet,*
> *You have roused them;*
> *Bodies cleansed, clothed,*
> *Their arms adore your appearance.*
> *The entire land sets out to work,*
> *All beasts browse on their herbs;*
> *Trees, herbs are sprouting,*
> *Birds fly from their nests,*
> *Their wings greeting your* ka. [2]

The Great Hymn to Aten was inscribed on a tomb at **Amarna**, the site about 200 miles up the Nile from Thebes where Akhenaten established a new court. Distanced from the temples of Karnak and Luxor, the court at Amarna fostered a style of unprecedented intimacy and innovation. In one famous scene, the royal family – Akhenaten, his queen Nefertiti, and their children – lounge beneath the life-giving rays of the sun-disc. The pharaoh kisses one child, while Nefertiti bounces another on her knee.

Akhenaten's religious and artistic innovations were short-lived. His successor Tutankhamen [too-tahnk-AHH-mun] (1361–1352 B.C.) – whose tomb made such a rich and famous discovery in the twentieth century – restored the cult of Amon-Re and destroyed most of the buildings dedicated to Aten. A late blossoming of Egyptian art under Ramesses II (ruled 1292–1225 B.C.) saw yet more monuments to power and richly decorated tombs.

It was not uncommon for Egyptian queens to attain considerable status and power within the royal court. Early in the New Kingdom, Queen Hatshepsut ruled all of Egypt for two decades (1479–1458 B.C.), and memorialized herself with a huge colonnaded temple near the Valley of the Kings. The famous site of Abu Simbel, carved into the side of a cliff, bears witness to another prominent queen: there, equal in size to the colossal statue of Ramesses II, was the figure of his favored queen **Nefertari**. Tradition holds that Nefertari assisted Ramesses on diplomatic missions that helped expand the Egyptian empire.

Queen Nefertari's tomb in the Valley of the Queens represents Egyptian art at a height of the nation's international power (Fig. **2.11**). The richly carved and painted walls depict the descent of the queen's *ka*, or spirit, into the underworld. Gently led by the figure of Isis, the queen greets the pantheon of Egyptian gods, still celebrated in their ancient animal aspects. From each deity, Nefertari's spirit acquires the powers that prepare her soul for final judgment before the imposing figure of Osiris. The delicate artistry of Nefertari's tomb celebrates the continuity of a religious belief and artistic tradition that had evolved for thousands of years.

The height of Ramesses II's rule was followed by a long decline in Egypt's power, as foreign incursions alternated with periods of independence. The Persian empire imposed a hated regime on Egypt that was ended in 332 B.C. by the conquests of Alexander the Great, whom Egyptians welcomed as a liberating hero.

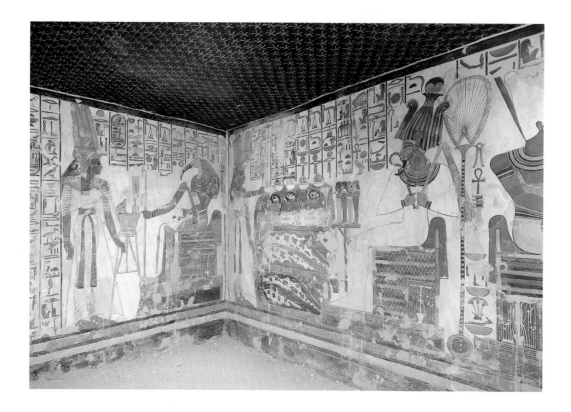

2.11 Painting from the tomb of Queen Nefertari at Thebes, Egypt, 1290–1224 B.C.
At the left, the crowned queen approaches the ibis-headed god Thoth, the divine scribe who records human deeds. To the right, Osiris is seated at the throne where he judges the souls of the dead. Nefertari's figure is carved in a high relief that captures the contours of fingers, legs, and facial detail.

EARLY ASIAN CIVILIZATIONS

Identify the religious and philosophical achievements of early Asian civilizations.

In the third millennium B.C., the wave of urbanization that brought the first human civilization also reached Asia. The most important centers of Asian civilization were in the Indus River Valley (modern Pakistan and India) and cities along the great rivers of China.

THE INDUS VALLEY

The rich valley of the Indus River in southern Asia produced a remarkable civilization that thrived for over 1000 years but was lost to human memory until rediscovered in the 1920s. The **Indus Valley civilization** (2600–1500 B.C.) produced cities of unmatched comfort and design, as archaeologists have discovered at the sites of Mohenjo-Daro and Harappa. Here they have found remains of unfortified cities laid out on an orderly grid plan, with baths, sanitary sewers, and a spacious assembly hall. A system of writing is preserved on seals used to compute agricultural wealth.

Surprisingly, archaeologists have uncovered little evidence of the elaborate temple culture and artistic production that characterize the Near East and Egypt. Indus

Valley sculptural artifacts are nearly all small, personal items. The Indus sculptors demonstrated a distinctive sense of movement and tension, using terracotta (a ceramic) and soft stones. Most remarkable are two male torsos, one a dancing figure, that capture the interacting planes and rounded shapes of the human form (Figs. **2.12, 2.13**). Nothing comparable is found elsewhere in the ancient world.

About 1500 B.C., the commodious Indus Valley cities declined as a foreign people infiltrated southern Asia and transformed its civilization. These newcomers, called **Aryans**, subjugated the native peoples and imposed their own language and religious belief. The Aryans' religious prayers and hymns, called the **Vedas** [VAY-duhz], are among the world's most ancient surviving religious texts. The Vedas contains hymns to the Aryan sky-god and chants to accompany fire-sacrifice. About 800 B.C., Vedic sages composed philosophical commentaries, known as the *Upanishads*, that speculated on the unity of the individual soul and the universe. The Vedic tradition blossomed again about 400 B.C. with the composition of the popular epics

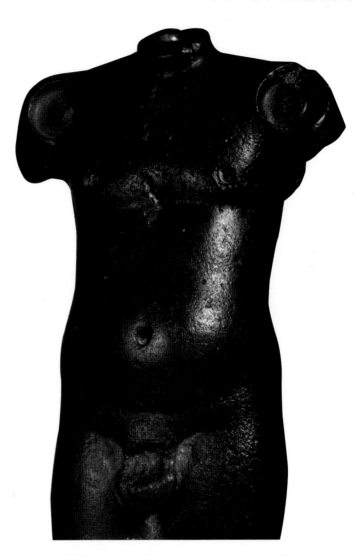

2.13 **Male torso, Harappa, Indus Valley, c. 2300–1750 B.C. Limestone, height 3¹/₂ ins (8.9 cm). National Museum of India, New Delhi.**

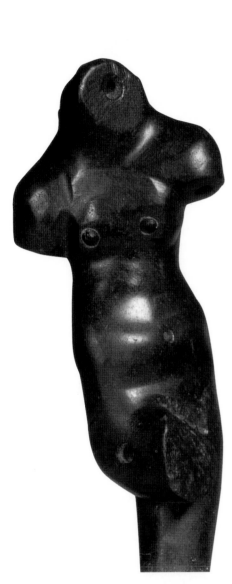

2.12 **Dancing figure, Harappa, Indus Valley, c. 2300–1750 B.C. Limestone, height 3⁷/₈ ins (9.8 cm). National Museum of India, New Delhi.**
Compare the torsion and vitality of these small figures with the rigid formality of the Egyptian royalty in Fig. 2.10.

Mahabharata and *Ramayana*. This rich body of scripture and poetry became the basis for India's dominant faith, Hinduism, which took shape in the sixth century B.C. Hinduism sanctioned a rigid class or caste system, through which virtuous souls might ascend in a cycle of death and re-birth. Hinduism's beliefs were the foundation of other Asian faiths, including Buddhism (see page 96).

BRONZE-AGE CHINA

Of all the ancient civilizations discussed here, only China can trace its unbroken development from the present day to its Bronze-Age beginnings. Agriculture in ancient China dates to around 5000 B.C., town life to around 4000 B.C. Chinese civilization appeared in the valleys of the three great rivers of its central region.

Bronze-Age China divides its history between two great dynasties. The **Shang** [shahng] dynasty (*c.* 1700–1100 B.C.) was a warrior culture whose rulers built walled cities and gigantic tombs in the Yellow River Valley. Their principal artistic media were carved jade (a hard green stone) and cast bronze. Shang bronzes included ritual vessels (Fig. **2.14**) and great bells decorated with fantastic animals,

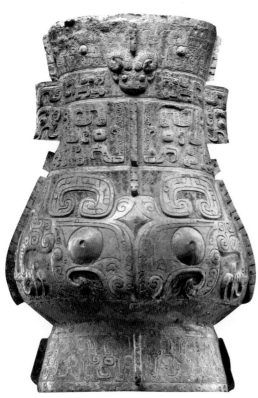

including a complex design called the *taotie*, which may be an animal mask or two dueling dragons.

The Shang fell to the conquering **Zhou** (1100–221 B.C.), a feudal kingdom whose king reigned as the Son of Heaven. Like the Shang, the Zhou [tchoh] practiced a form of ancestor worship and also excelled at the manufacture of ritual bronze objects. As evidence of his exorbitant love of music, one Zhou ruler was buried with a carillon of sixty-five bronze bells, among hundreds of other musical instruments. The later Zhou period was marred by warring factions, until the Warring States period (402–221 B.C.) finally splintered the dynasty.

2.14 Left Ritual wine vessel or *hu*, Shang Dynasty, c. 1300–1100 B.C. Bronze, height 16 ins (40.6 cm). Nelson-Atkins Museum, Kansas City (Purchase: Nelson Trust).
The ambiguous, mask-like design on this vessel, the *taotie*, can be interpreted as a face with the flaring nostrils of an ox, or as two dragons with serpent tails facing each other in profile.

2.15 Ancient Greece.

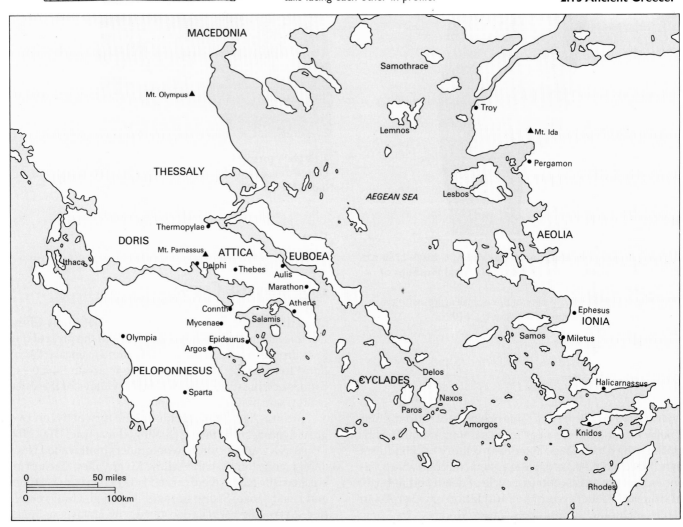

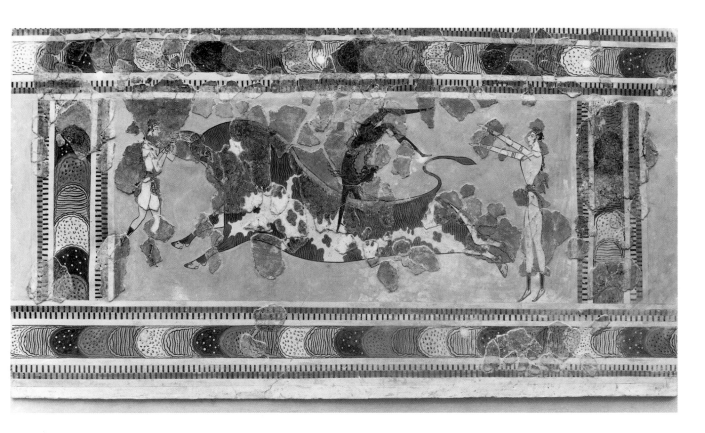

2.16 Bull-leaping in ancient Crete, fresco from the royal palace at Knossos, Crete, c. 1500 B.C.
The painter has portrayed the athletes as if in a multi-exposure photograph: one grasps the horns, a second vaults across the bull's back, and the third finishes her stunt.

THE AEGEAN WORLD

Contrast the character and achievements of the Minoan and Mycenaean civilizations.

In the Mediterranean basin, two smaller Bronze Age civilizations would be of enormous importance for the history of the Western world. These peoples, called **Minoans** [muh-NOH-uns] and **Mycenaeans** [my-suh-NEE-uns], settled the islands and coastal rim of the Aegean Sea (Fig. **2.15**), where their ships had ready access to the wealthy civilizations of Egypt and the Near East. Despite their different characters – one peaceful, the other warlike – together these Aegean peoples were the precursors of the classical civilization that would dominate the West for a thousand years.

MINOAN CIVILIZATION

Minoan civilization (*c.* 2500–1250 B.C.) was located on the island of Crete, home to a pleasure-loving people skilled in small crafts. The Minoans reached a high point of social and artistic development around 1400 B.C. They constructed sprawling palace-cities of brightly colored and undefended buildings. Archaeologists named the island civilization after the legendary King Minos, whose queen bore the feared monster, the Minotaur. The bull was an important part of Minoan religious ceremony, which featured the spectacular sport of bull-leaping (Fig. **2.16**). Male and female athletes grasped the horns of a charging bull and performed a somersault over its back. As this example suggests, the Minoans were a spontaneous and pleasure-loving people who preferred outdoor entertainments.

The Minoans were also skillful artisans of small crafts, producing objects easily traded with their Mediterranean neighbors. Minoans crafted jewelry and figurines in precious metal and ceramics, like the earthenware *Snake Goddess* (Fig. **2.17**). The figure actually depicts a priestess engaged in cultic worship of a Minoan deity. The Minoan religion centered on the worship of female deities, and Minoan society granted women an equality and freedom unusual in the ancient world.

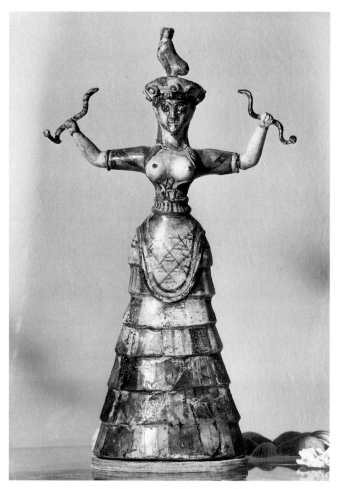

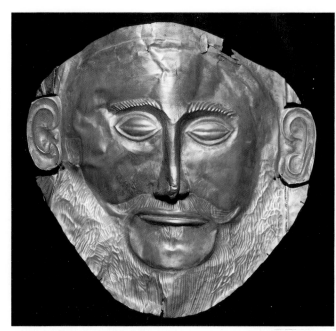

2.18 "Mask of Agamemnon", from a grave in Mycenae, c. 1500 B.C. Beaten gold, height 10¹/₈ ins (26 cm). National Archeological Museum, Athens.
Such portraiture, delicately wrought in the region's most precious metal, was reserved for Mycenaean royalty. In other ancient cultures (Egypt, China), such costly objects were buried with the owner to ease his life in the afterworld.

2.17 *Snake Goddess* from the royal palace at Knossos, Crete, c. 1600 B.C. Faience, height 11 ins (30 cm). Archeological Museum, Heraklion.
The bare bodice and flounced skirt were part of Minoan religious costume. The snakes in the priestess's hands and the owl on top of her head were symbols of sacred power in ancient goddess-centered religions.

MYCENAEAN CIVILIZATION

The Mycenaeans were an aggressive warrior civilization (*c.* 1600–1150 B.C.) that accumulated fabulous wealth. They lived in brooding palace-cities on the Greek mainland, including the city of Mycenae, for which historians name this civilization. From their citadels, Mycenaean warriors mounted pirate expeditions to the rich cities of the Aegean basin. Later Greek stories of the Trojan War dimly recalled Mycenaean expeditions in search of plunder and slaves. Modern archaeology confirms the possibility of a Mycenaean expedition to Troy in Asia Minor, which was burned around 1180 B.C.

Excavations inside the Mycenaean palaces reveal a civilization swollen by plunder and fascinated by death and the afterlife. At Mycenae, archaeologists have unearthed labyrinthine shaft graves where Mycenaean royalty was entombed. The rows of graves inside the fortress' main gate most likely served as a circle of honor for ancestral heroes. The face of one such hero is visible in the famed "Mask of Agamemnon" (Fig. **2.18**), discovered by the archaeologist Heinrich Schliemann in 1876.

The Mycenaeans' predominance in the Aegean was brief. About 1150 B.C., not long after the supposed Trojan expedition, invaders swept into Greece from the north, destroying the Mycenaean palaces and dispersing their civilization. Only a few Mycenaean centers (Athens, for one) remained intact. Following Mycenae's fall, Greece entered the Dark Age (about 1150–900 B.C.), a period when writing, artistic crafts, and other cultural skills were lost. Out of the turmoil of the Dark Age, a people emerged whom we call the Greeks.

Chapter Summary

The First Humans. The first humans appeared about 100,000 years ago and developed a culture that revered the forces of nature and remembered the dead. The first human expression in the arts took the form of elaborate cave paintings, with their dynamic animal figures, and small sculptures of clay and stone, often depicting powerfully symbolic female figures. Megalithic complexes such as Stonehenge in England – the first monumental human buildings – indicate early humans' profound religious connection to the universe.

Mesopotamia. The first great cities appeared in the Bronze Age Near East, on the fertile river plains of Mesopotamia. Here the Sumerians developed the first forms of writing and recorded their mythic thought in the *Enuma elish.* Myths were also celebrated in rituals on huge temple-altars (ziggurats). The succession of great empires that dominated Mesopotamia included the Babylonian, with its law-giving king Hammurabi, and the Persian, remembered for its great palace at the capital Persepolis.

Ancient Egypt. The geography of Egypt – protected by desert and unified by the Nile River – fostered a stable civilization ruled by pharaoh-kings. Egypt's complex myths and rituals centered on the afterlife. To contain the mummified dead, the Egyptians built huge pyramids and elaborately decorated tombs. To honor the gods, they constructed vast temple complexes at Karnak and elsewhere. Egyptian arts reached a high point under the unorthodox pharaoh Akhenaten and in the gracefully decorated tomb of Nefertari.

Early Asian Civilizations. In the Indus Valley of southern Asia (today's Pakistan and India), a highly developed civilization left the ruins of great cities such as Mohenjo-Daro but little in the form of art. This so-called Harappan civilization was supplanted by Aryan settlers, whose great legacy was the Vedic tradition of mystical prayers and hymns. In China, the Bronze Age dynasties of the Shang and Zhou left masterpieces of jade and bronze, the foundation of China's immensely rich artistic tradition.

The Aegean World. The roots of the Western world as we know it can be traced to the Minoan civilization of ancient Crete (an eastern Mediterranean island) and the Mycenaean cities of mainland Greece. The peace-loving Minoans were masters of fine craft and practiced a goddess-centered religion. The Mycenaeans were fierce warriors and pirates who buried their warlords in tombs filled with fantastic riches. From the ruins of Mycenaean palace-cities (sacked by invaders c. 1150 B.C.), the civilization of classical Greece was to arise.

3 | Ancient Greece: The Classical Spirit

*Even in ruins, the Parthenon of Athens stands perfectly balanced and noble in its proportions (Fig. 3.1). The temple stood above Athens as the city reached a pinnacle of cultivation and achievement seldom equaled in history. The Parthenon's harmonious outlines embody the **classical spirit** of ancient Greece: the belief that human intelligence could bring order to the world and that art could capture the essence of human form and feeling. From its height in ancient Athens, this spirit spread across the Mediterranean, becoming a standard by which later civilizations would measure themselves.*

EARLY GREECE

Describe early Greek civilization and its most celebrated artistic achievements.

The early Greek civilization (900–480 B.C.) that emerged from the Dark Age was backward by comparison with its Mediterranean neighbours. Stimulated by contact with Egypt and Persia, however, the early Greeks soon built new cities and established colonies along the northern Mediterranean. They recited the heroic deeds of a single event – the siege of Troy – that was the focus of early Greece's most important literary achievement, the Homeric poems. The early Greeks also excelled at gentler lyric poetry and, in the visual arts, began the rapid stylistic innovation that culminated in the classical style.

GREECE AND THE ANCIENT WORLD

	GENERAL EVENTS	ARCHITECTURE	VISUAL ARTS	LITERATURE AND PHILOSOPHY	THEATER AND MUSIC
4000 B.C. **THE ANCIENT WORLD** **1000 B.C.**	c. 3500 1st Mesopotamian cities c. 2500 Beginning of Minoan civilization, Crete c. 1180 Mycenaeans conquer Troy	c. 2525 Great Pyramids begun at Giza, Egypt (**2.9**) 1379–61 Temple to Aten built in Egypt	c. 2300 Dancing figure, Indus Valley (**2.12**) c. 1550 *Mask of Agamemnon*, Mycenae (**2.18**)	c. 1790–1750 Law code of Hammurabi	c. 2685–2550 Soundbox from royal tomb at Ur, Sumeria (**2.5**)
750 B.C. **ARCHAIC PERIOD** **480 B.C.**	612 New Babylon kingdom rules Mesopotamia 480 Greeks defeat Persians at Salamis	c. 500 Palace of Darius and Xerxes at Persepolis (**2.8**)	c. 615 *Kouros* from Attica (**3.6**)	c. 800–650? Composition of Homeric epics c. 600 Sappho, lyric poet c. 563 Gautama Buddha born in northern India 480 Confucius active in China	c. 550 Pythagoras, numerical basis of music
CLASSICAL PERIOD **323 B.C.**	432–404 Peloponnesian Wars, Athens defeated 336–323 Conquests of Alexander the Great	447–432 Parthenon, Athens (**3.12**) c. 421–409 Erechtheum, Athens (**3.20**) c. 350 Theater at Epidaurus (**3.28**)	c. 450 Myron, *Discus Thrower* (**3.24**) c. 438–432 *Three Goddesses*, Parthenon, Athens (**3.17**) c. 340 Praxiteles, *Hermes and Dionysus* (**3.21**)	399 Socrates' trial and execution 387 Plato founds Academy 342 Aristotle tutors Alexander	429 Sophocles, *Oedipus the King* 411 Aristophanes, *Lysistrata*
HELLENISTIC PERIOD **146 B.C.**	146 Roman conquest of Greece		c. 150 Agesander, Athenodorus, and Polydorus of Rhodes, *Laocoön and his Sons* (**3.27**)	c. 200 Indian verse epic the *Ramayana*	c. 300 Menander, Hellenistic comic playwright

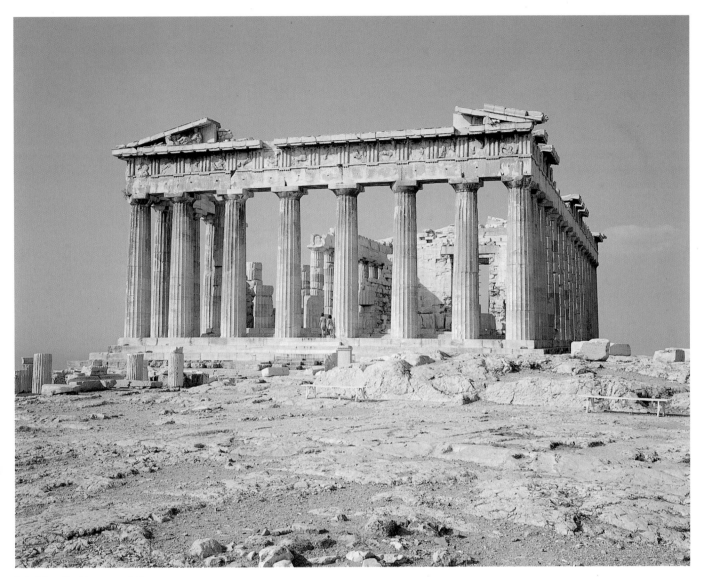

3.1 The Parthenon, Athens.
As the Athenian leader Pericles predicted, the ruins of Athens'
temples still stand as "mighty monuments of our power, which will
make us the wonder of this and of succeeding ages."

THE HOMERIC POEMS

Though the ancient Mycenaean citadels lay in ruins, the
early Greeks preserved the memory of Mycenae's glory
in nostalgic legends of the fall of Troy, an ancient city in
Asia Minor. Greek legend embellished the story of the Trojan War until its Mycenaean heroes became examples of
bravery and folly for all Greeks. The story was told in two
remarkable poems entitled the *Iliad* and the *Odyssey*, both
attributed to the poet Homer and possibly composed in
the eighth century B.C. The ancient Greeks acknowledged
Homer as the greatest poet of the Greek language. Modern scholars, however, cannot agree on whether a poet
named Homer ever existed, or if the two Homeric poems
had the same author. Nonetheless, they recognize the
poems as the first masterpieces of Western literature.

The Homeric poems are both **epics**, long narrative
works that recount deeds on a heroic scale, centered on
a hero who defines a sense of ethnic or national identity. Homer's epics are the well-spring of Greek storytelling, much like the Babylonian *Epic of Gilgamesh* (c. 2000
B.C.), and the Anglo-Saxon epic *Beowulf* (first recorded
c. A.D. 800) in Babylonian and Anglo-Saxon cultures. Later
generations retold their hero's deeds – Gilgamesh's search
for eternal life, Beowulf's battle with the monster Gren-
del – to celebrate their language and national identity, and
also to explore the essential truths of human experience.
Homer's epic heroes were Achilles [ah-KILL-eez], the
greatest warrior of the Greek forces at Troy, and Odysseus
[oh-DIS-ee-us], the great adventurer who voyaged home
from Troy. Homer's heroes served as models of rightful
action and skillful speech, much as biblical heroes did for

3.2 Paris abducting Helen, scene from a red-figure vase, 500–480 B.C. Height 8¹/₂ ins (21.5 cm). Museum of Fine Arts, Boston, Francis Bartlett Fund (1912).
In Homer's *Iliad*, the Greek assault on Troy is justified as an attempt to reclaim Helen, who has been abducted by the Trojan prince Paris.

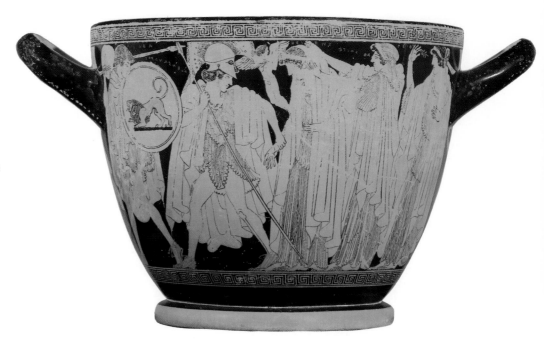

Jews and Christians. Indeed, educated Greek men could still quote the speeches of Homer's warriors seven centuries after the Mycenaean palaces had fallen into ruin.

In the *Iliad*, ethnic warfare between Trojans and Greeks (called Achaeans [ah-KEE-uns]) provides the setting for a deeply human drama of honor, love, and tragic loss (Fig. **3.2**). The proud hero Achilles quarrels with his chieftain Agamemnon and angrily withdraws from battle. When his closest comrade is killed, Achilles rejoins the fray, moved by a grieving rage. He challenges the Trojan prince Hector, kills him, and defiles his body, leaving it unburied for dogs and vultures to feed on. Homer follows this gruesome confrontation with a scene of great tenderness and sympathy. King Priam of Troy steals into the Achaeans' camp to ask for his son's body. Touched by the old man's courage and grief, Achilles weeps with him over their lost kin. The epic concludes with Hector's stately funeral. In spite of its hero's cruelty and violence, Homer's saga of human pride and error ultimately confirms the nobility of human life.

So he [Priam] spoke, and stirred in the other [Achilles] a passion of grieving for his own father. He took the old man's hand and pushed him gently away, and the two remembered, as Priam sat huddled at the feet of Achilleus and wept close for manslaughtering Hektor[a] *and Achilleus wept now for his own father, now again for Patroklos.*[b] *The sound of their mourning moved in the house. Then when great Achilleus had taken full satisfaction in sorrow and the passion for it had gone from his mind and body, thereafter he rose from his chair, and took the old man by the hand, and set him on his feet again, in pity for the grey head and the grey*

beard, and spoke to him and addressed him in winged words: "… Such is the way the gods spun life for unfortunate mortals, that we live in unhappiness, but the gods themselves have no sorrows. There are two urns that stand on the door-sill of Zeus. They are unlike for the gifts they bestow: an urn of evils, an urn of blessings. If Zeus who delights in thunder mingles these and bestows them on man, he shifts, and moves now in evil, again in good fortune. But when Zeus bestows from the urn of sorrows, he makes a failure of man, and evil hunger drives him over the shining earth, and he wanders respected neither of gods nor mortals."[1]

HOMER
Iliad, Book XXIV

a. Hektor (Hector), son of Priam, and the Trojans' greatest fighter, killed by Achilles to avenge the death of Patroclus.

b. Patroklos (Patroclus), Achilles' best-loved companion, killed by Hector while wearing the armor that Achilles had lent him.

CRITICAL QUESTION

The Homeric poems were probably composed orally and remembered for generations without being written down. Imagine the ways that today's civilization would change if all writing and the capacity for literacy disappeared. Are modern societies becoming less literate by relying on visual and "virtual" means of communication?

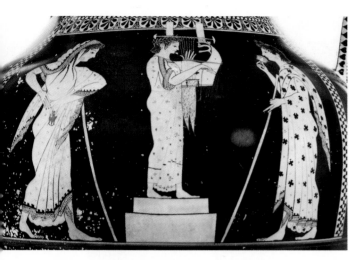

3.3 Citharode and listeners, from a vase painting by the Attic master Andokides, c. 530 B.C. Louvre, Paris.
A lyric singer accompanies herself on the cithara, a larger and more elaborate version of the lyre.

SAPPHO'S LYRIC POETRY

When the Greeks tired of the epic's high drama and elevated style, they could turn to lyric poetry. **Lyric poetry** took its name from the lyre, the stringed instrument used to accompany the recitation of these poems (Fig. **3.3**). Lyric poems were brief, often written for a specific occasion, and expressed the speaker's inner thoughts and feelings more directly than the epic. While an epic bard might sing his poem at a royal court, lyric poetry was probably reserved for less formal occasions, such as a dinner banquet among friends.

The most renowned of Greek lyric poets was Sappho, who lived on the Aegean island of Lesbos around 600 B.C. Sappho was the leader of a circle of female friends devoted to music and poetry. Many of her poems, most preserved as fragments, speak passionately to younger members of this group. Sappho's surviving poetry preserves the immediacy and passion that made her the most admired lyric poet in the ancient Greek world.

In the fragment quoted here, Sappho contrasts a woman's gentle love for friends and family with her subservient love for a man called to war. Yet Sappho's regret does not cloud her tender love for Anaktoria, whose beauty surpasses the military splendor of the battlefield.

> Some say cavalry and some would claim
> infantry or a fleet of long oars
> is the supreme sight on the black earth.
>
> I say it is
>
> the girl you love. And easily proved.
> Did not Helen,[a] who was queen of mortal
> beauty, choose as first among mankind
>
> the very scourge
>
> of Trojan honor? Haunted by Love
> she forgot kinsmen, her own dear child
> and wandered off to a remote country.
>
> O weak and fitful
>
> Woman bending before any man:
> So Anaktoria, although you are
> Far, do not forget your loving friends.
>
> And I for one
>
> Would rather listen to your soft step
> and see your radiant face – than watch
> all the dazzling horsemen and armored
>
> Hoplites[b] of Lydia.[2]

SAPPHO

---

a. Helen, wife of Menelaus, who eloped with the Trojan prince Paris and supposedly caused the Trojan War.

b. Hoplite, an armored foot soldier.

THE VISUAL ARTS IN EARLY GREECE

From 650 to 490 B.C., the Greeks developed a distinctive style in the visual arts, now called **Archaic**. Although the Archaic style in Greece borrowed liberally from more advanced Egyptian and Persian civilizations, the Greek artisans transformed these borrowings into an art concerned with natural beauty and the human form.

Since few early Greek wall paintings survive, we know early Greek painting chiefly through pottery vases. Manufactured at commercial centers like Corinth and Athens, these vases were initially decorated with abstract geometric designs. The **geometric** technique, as it is now called, demonstrated the Greeks' interest in intricate, rationalized patterns. Soon, painters incorporated rudimentary

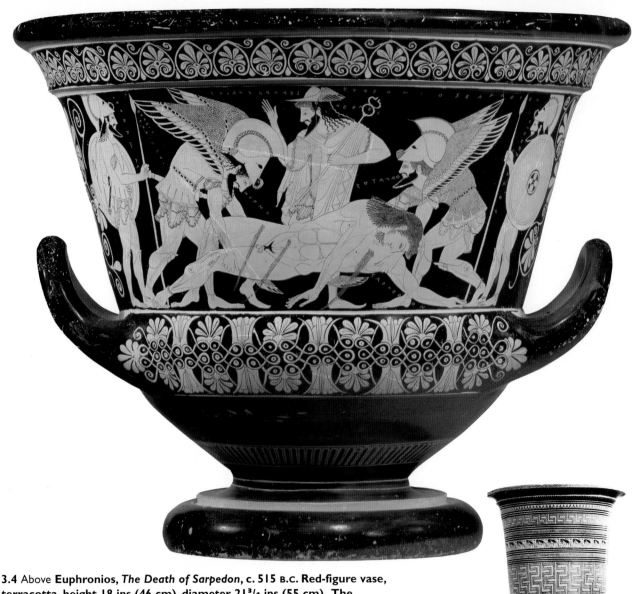

3.4 Above **Euphronios, *The Death of Sarpedon*, c. 515 B.C. Red-figure vase, terracotta, height 18 ins (46 cm), diameter 21³/₄ ins (55 cm). The Metropolitan Museum of Art, New York, Bequest of Joseph H. Durkee, gift of Darius Ogden Mills, and gift of C. Ruxton Love, by exchange, 1972.**
Blood streaming from his fatal wounds, the Homeric warrior Sarpedon is borne to the underworld by the figures of Death and Sleep. The red-figure painting technique permitted greater naturalistic detail than earlier methods.

3.5 Right **Dipylon vase (Attic geometric amphora), c. 750 B.C. Height 5 ft (1.53 m). National Archeological Museum, Athens.**
Amid the abstract geometric designs, a scene shows a funeral bier and mourners drawn in rudimentary style. The vase originally served as a grave marker.

human figures, most likely adapted from Egyptian painting, that showed an increasing **naturalism** – the attempt to represent objects as they appear in nature (Fig. **3.5**).

The most advanced form of vase painting was the **red-figure technique**, in which the background of a scene was entirely painted (appearing as black) and the figures were left unpainted (appearing as red) except for fine details of anatomy. The red-figure technique permitted subtle effects of bodily movement and expressive storytelling. Red-figure vases like the "Euphronios vase" (Fig. **3.4**) illustrate early Greek artists' command of the full range of human feelings and activity.

Archaic sculpture showed a similar development from formalized representation to naturalism. The most common form of Archaic statue was the *kouros*, a free-standing nude male youth that served as a grave-marker or stood outside a temple. The early *kouros* in Fig. **3.6** shows the rigid symmetry and geometric hairdressing that the Greeks had borrowed from Egyptian statuary. The figure stands in a typical pose, with arms held stiffly at the sides, fists clenched, and the left foot in front of the right. The human form here is an exercise in stylized geometry, treated as if the body were an abstract and symmetrical design.

Late in the Archaic period, sculptors began to soften the rigid geometry of the Archaic style, lending their figures more supple curves (Fig. **3.7**). The *koré* [KOH-ray], or female version of the *kouros*, was less stringent in design, in part because the *koré* was always clothed (Fig. **3.8**). The drapery created more varied lines, although the hair is still arranged in stylized geometric patterns. The lips are pulled back in the "Archaic smile," perhaps to lend the face more animation. However, the rationalized design and symmetry of these late Archaic figures remain their most striking stylistic feature. The Greeks' growing interest in anatomical naturalism would eventually give rise to the more humanist approach of the classical period.

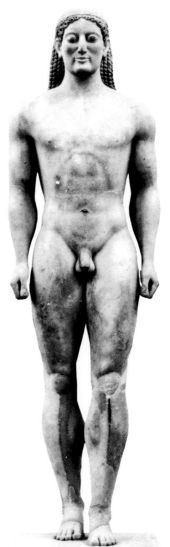

3.8 Below *Koré* **from Chios, c. 520 B.C. Marble, height 22 ins (56 cm). Acropolis Museum, Athens.**
In Archaic and early classical sculpture, the female figure was always clothed. Compare the drapery of this *koré* to the more fluid treatment in the Parthenon goddesses (see Fig. 3.17).

3.6 Right *Kouros* **from Attica, c. 615 B.C. Marble, height 6 ft 4 ins (1.93 cm). The Metropolitan Museum of Art, New York, Fletcher Fund, 1932.**
The Greek *kouros* represented the ideal of youthful male beauty. In what features of this Archaic sculpture can one find evidence of the early Greek interest in symmetry, balance, and geometric order?

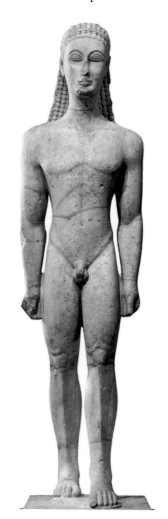

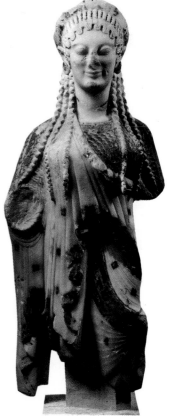

3.7 Above *Kouros* **from Anavyssos, c. 530 B.C. Marble, height 6 ft 4 ins (1.93 m). National Archeological Museum, Athens.**
Note the growing naturalism in anatomical form compared to Fig. 3.6.

KEY CONCEPT

RATIONALISM

The elaborate designs and strict symmetry of Archaic Greek art provide the first hints of classical Greek rationalism. **Rationalism** is the belief that human reason is the primary source of truth and order in the world. To the rationalist, human reason offers better answers to life's questions than mystical faith or knowledge gained through the senses. Rationalism was the classical Greeks' response to a world of conflicting and irrational forces, where gods battled one another, storms threatened, and fate might snatch away happiness in a moment. To protect against uncertainty, the Greeks searched for a knowable and unchanging design in the capricious world of experience. Not surprisingly, ancient Greek rationalists were the philosophical ancestors of modern science, which today predicts the behavior of atomic particles by mathematical calculations, and affirms the Greek belief that human reason can solve the world's enigmas.

The ancient Greeks preferred the idealized creations of human intelligence to the imperfect examples of nature. For example the philosopher Pythagoras (*c.* 530–*c.* 500 B.C.) held that all things could be expressed in number. To Pythagoras, the number four represented as a square :: symbolized justice, a notion that survives in the expression "a square deal." Pythagoras represented love by the number five, a perfect union of the first even (two) and first odd (three) numbers. The same impulse to express reality as an abstract formula can be seen in the rigorous symmetry of the Archaic *kouros*. The classical sculptor Polyclitus [po-lee-KLEYE-tuss] devised a more flexible system for calculating the body's proportions as multiples of a basic unit of measure (Fig. **3.9**). Thus, a sculpture's proportions might be calculated as multiples of a hand's length.

Greek rationalism had an immense impact on later civilizations in science, philosophy, and the arts. The seventeenth-century French painter Nicolas Poussin (see page 286) painted landscapes by breaking them into triangles, circles, and squares. The Italian Renaissance architect Filippo Brunelleschi (see page 201) designed his buildings on the modular principle of Polyclitus. One legacy of the classical spirit is this fascination with the abstract designs of the human mind.

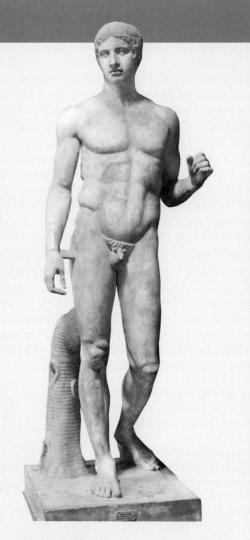

3.9 Polyclitus, *Doryphorus* (*Spear-bearer*), Roman copy of bronze original, c. 440 B.C. Marble, height 6 ft 6 ins (1.98 m). National Museum, Naples.
Polyclitus altered the body's natural proportions to achieve his idealized canon, or "rule," of modular proportion.

THE CLASSICAL PERIOD

Briefly tell the story of Athens' Golden Age.

The **classical period** in Greece opened with the Greeks' victory over the Persian army in 490 B.C. Athenian soldiers prevailed, with brave stands at Thermopylae and Marathon. When the Persian force returned in 480 B.C., the Athenians had to abandon their city and watch it burned by enemy soldiers. But Athens had its revenge a few days later, when Athenian naval commanders slyly lured the Persian navy into a trap and destroyed it at the Battle of Salamis, between the island of Salamis and the Athenian port of Piraeus.

The Athenians interpreted their victories as a sign that Athens was destined to lead all Greece. Indeed, Greece now entered a period of achievement virtually unparalleled in the history of Western civilization. This classical age lasted until the death of Alexander the Great in 323 B.C. It brought remarkable accomplishments in theater, architecture, sculpture, and philosophy, and helped to define the essential character of Western civilization.

ATHENS IN ITS GOLDEN AGE

Athens was the glory of classical Greece, a vibrant center that spawned geniuses of the arts and ideas. Between 480 B.C. and its military defeat in the Peloponnesian Wars in 404 B.C., Athens enjoyed a period of prosperity and accomplishment known as the **Golden Age**. The heart of Athens, as with every Greek city, was its *polis*, a term usually translated as "city-state." To the Greeks, the *polis* meant the citizens themselves, including their civic values and aspirations. The Greek philosopher Plato assumed that a properly organized *polis* would produce perfectly happy citizens. When Aristotle, the late classical philosopher, said that the human was a "political animal" (a *zoon politikon*), he meant that it was human nature to live in a *polis*.

Membership of the Athenian *polis* was limited to adult male citizens of the city, excluding all women, slaves, and non-native residents. In a city like Athens, with a population of perhaps 250,000, the *polis* may have been no larger than ten or twenty thousand men. Within this limited group, however, Athenians of the Golden Age practiced a vigorous democracy, or "rule by the people" – they chose important offices by lot and decided important questions by majority vote of the whole *polis*. Athens' government was thus in some ways more democratic than today's common system of elected representatives. Still, as the civic leader Pericles [PAIR-uh-kleez] proclaimed, in Athens "the claim of excellence is also recognized; and when a citizen is in any way distinguished, he is preferred to the public service, not as a matter of privilege, but as the reward of merit."[4]

Pericles led Athens to a pinnacle of political power and influence. After the Persian Wars, Athens formed an alliance called the Delian League to defend itself against future attack. The Athenians soon began to bully the alliance's members; and by the mid-fifth century B.C., the Delian League had become an Athenian empire. The Athenians eventually appropriated the league's treasury to rebuild the city's burned temples.

The Athenians' arrogant hunger for power led them into a disastrous war with Sparta, Athens' chief rival and a great military power. The Peloponnesian Wars (431–404 B.C.) resulted in the loss of Athens' navy and its surrender to Sparta in 404 B.C. After the war, Athens retained its prominence as a cultural center. The philosopher Plato founded his Academy there and actors performed tragedies beneath the city's grand temples. The city remained the "school of Hellas," as Pericles had called it, but it never regained the power and creative energy of its Golden Age.

Women in Classical Athens   The adult women of Athens – whether they were wives, slaves, or prostitutes – were all excluded from the city's public affairs. Nearly all female citizens were married. Their duties as wives were restricted to organizing the household, supervising slaves, and performing domestic labor (Fig. **3.10**). Pericles said that the happiest wife was one about whom nothing was said, either good or bad. Athenian wives lived in quarters separate from the men and customarily did not even share the evening meal with their husbands. The bawdy jokes of Aristophanes' comedy *Lysistrata* (see page 61), in which Greek women hold a sex strike to end the Peloponnesian Wars, indicate that wives were commonly accused of gossiping and drunkenness.

Foreign women could gain a place in Athenian society as *hetaerae* [he-TAIR-eye], a euphemism for courtesan or prostitute. Some courtesans were highly educated and trained as musicians, and so were favored as companions as well as sexual partners. *Hetaerae* accompanied men to evening banquets and may have been the only women permitted to attend the Greek theater. They had legal recognition and some apparently accumulated property, a right denied to female citizens. The most famous of these women was Aspasia [ah-SPAY-zhuh], companion of

WINDOW ON DAILY LIFE

THE PLAGUE OF ATHENS

In the second year of the Peloponnesian [pell-oh-poh-NEE-zhun] Wars, a plague struck Athens, devastating its population and disrupting social and religious customs. The historian Thucydides [thyoo-SID-uh-deez] reports that bodies filled the temples and sacred precincts.

The sacred places also in which they had quartered themselves were full of corpses of persons that had died there, just as they were; for as the disaster passed all bounds, men, not knowing what was to become of them, became utterly careless of everything, whether sacred or profane. All the burial rites before in use were entirely disregarded, and they buried the bodies as best they could. Many from want of the proper appliances, through so many of their friends having died already, lost all shame in burying the dead; sometimes, when a man had prepared a funeral pile, another came and, throwing his dead on it first, set fire to it; sometimes they tossed the corpse which they were carrying on the top of another that was burning, and went off.[3]

THUCYDIDES
The History of the Peloponnesian War

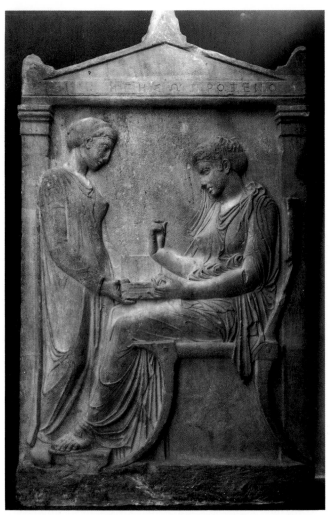

3.10 Grave stele of Hegeso, c. 410–400 B.C. Marble, height 4 ft 11 ins (1.5 m). National Museum, Athens.
This stele, or gravestone relief, depicts a Greek matron adorning herself with jewelry. After marriage, Athenian women customarily led secluded lives of child-rearing and domestic labor.

Pericles from 445 B.C. until his death. Aspasia bore Pericles a son and was suspected of advising him on political affairs. Because of her influence, she attracted the worried criticism of Athens' orators and playwrights.

THE GREEK TEMPLE

Analyze the Parthenon as a symbol of the civic pride and humanist self-confidence of Athens during the classical period.

Athens' most spectacular achievement was the complex of temples on its acropolis, towering over the city as skyscrapers soar above a modern metropolis. An acropolis was a hill in the center of an ancient city (Fig. **3.11**), used originally as a fortress. The acropolis was usually a city-state's most sacred district, containing temples dedicated to the city's patron deities. In classical Greece, such temples were the largest and most expensive buildings constructed, impressive announcements of religious devotion and civic pride.

THE PARTHENON

In 447 B.C., Athens began to rebuild the acropolis temples burned by Persian attackers. The building program began with the **Parthenon**, a temple dedicated to the city's patron deity, Athena. The Parthenon also expressed Athens' prestige and cultivation at the height of the Golden Age (Fig. **3.12**). It was one of the largest temples to be built in Greece during the classical period, supervised by Athens' leading citizen-artists and fashioned by craftsmen from all over Greece.

The temple's construction and sculptural decorations represent a high point of the classical style in the arts. Its basic form, like most Greek temples, was the **post-and-lintel**. The post-and-lintel form consisted of a series of columns (posts) with beams (lintels) laid across the top. Walls and a roof were added to this basic skeleton. The types of Greek temples were distinguished by their decoration of the vertical column and the horizontal beam, called the **entablature**. The decoration of column and entablature was classified according to the classical **orders**, or styles: the Doric order communicated a stolid strength and

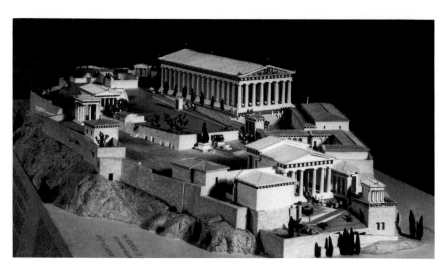

3.11 Model reconstruction of the Athenian acropolis. View from the northwest. Plaster copy of the original model by G. P. Stevens, American School of Classical Studies. Scale 1:200. Royal Ontario Museum, Toronto.
As a sacred precinct, the acropolis was crowded with temples and statues. The Parthenon occupied the acropolis' highest point.

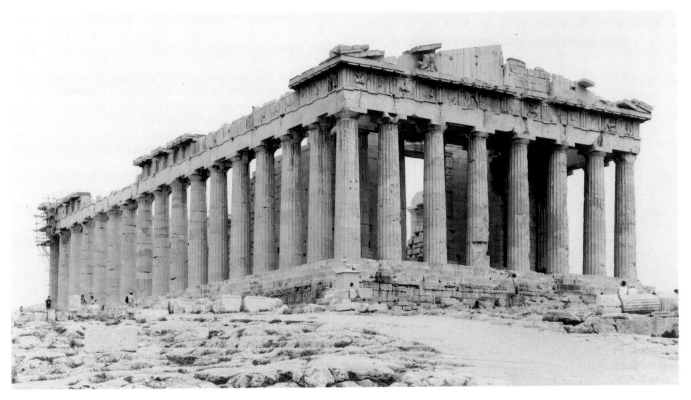

3.12 Ictinus and Callicrates, the Parthenon, Athens, 447–432 B.C. Pentelic marble, length 228 x 104 ft (69.5 x 31.7 m), height of columns 34 ft (10.36 m).
While austerely grand as a ruin today, the Parthenon appeared much gaudier in Classical times, with its sculptures brightly painted in red, gold, and blue.

3.13 Below The Greek orders.
The classical architectural orders varied according to their decoration of the vertical and horizontal elements (column and entablature).

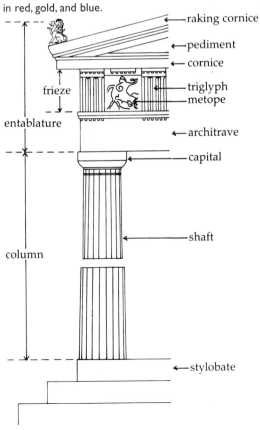

raking cornice
pediment
cornice
triglyph
metope
architrave
capital
shaft
stylobate

frieze
entablature
column

Doric

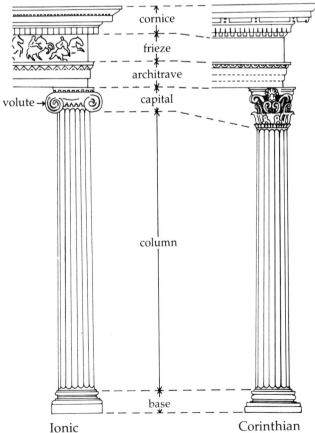

cornice
frieze
architrave
capital

volute

column

base

Ionic   Corinthian

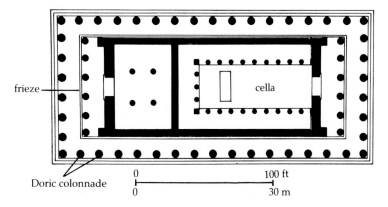

frieze

cella

Doric colonnade

0   100 ft
0   30 m

3.14 Left **Plan of the Parthenon.**
The Parthenon shows evidence of a recurring mathematical ratio of 1:2 + 1, as in the number of columns (8:17).

3.16 Below **Section view of the Parthenon, reconstructed, showing the pediment, Doric frieze, and cella frieze.**
The pediment sculptures stood in the recessed pediment, sheltered by the roof's edges. The cella frieze – nearly 40 feet (12.2 m) above ground and shaded by the ceiling – must have been difficult to view. All the sculptures were probably brightly painted.

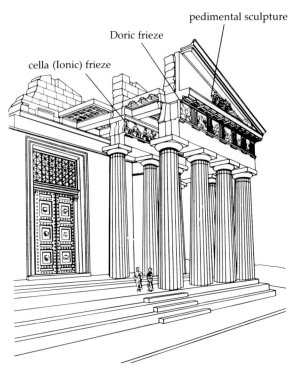

pedimental sculpture

Doric frieze

cella (Ionic) frieze

simplicity; the Ionic order possessed an aura of refinement and sophistication; and the Corinthian order, developed in the later Hellenistic period, projected imperial wealth and grandeur (Fig. 3.13).

The Parthenon was the most advanced example of the Doric order, the climax of two centuries of architectural development. Its Doric columns rested directly on the temple's step and were topped by heavy, square-block capitals. Deep grooves called **flutes** were carved into the column's shaft, creating a shifting play of light and shadow as sunlight struck the column from different angles. The columns surrounded the enclosed inner room, or **cella** (Fig. **3.14**), that held the huge cult statue of Athena by Athens' leading sculptor, Phidias (*c.* 490–432 B.C.).

The Parthenon's construction showed subtle deviations from regularity. Apparently, Greek architects wished to balance their precise rationalism against the need for

3.15 The Parthenon's refinements, exaggerated for effect. The upper diagram is based on N. Balanas, *Les Monuments de l'Acropole*, pl. 2, fig. 2.

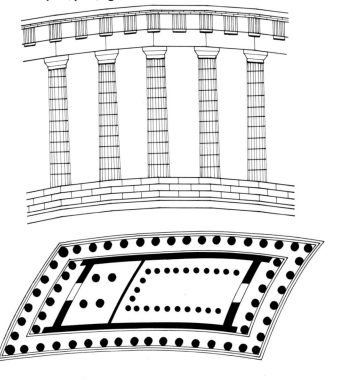

aesthetic appeal to the eye. Throughout the building the numerical ratio of 1 : 2 + 1 recurs, evident in the number of columns across the end (eight) and along the sides (seventeen). The Parthenon's columns bulge slightly, as if they strain under the weight of the roof, and they also lean inward slightly. The corner columns are slightly thicker and closer to their neighbors, as if to compensate for space visible between them. The temple floor rises about 4 inches (10 cm) in the center on all four sides (Fig. **3.15**). These refinements were not unique to the Parthenon, but they were seldom combined with such stunning results.

THE PARTHENON SCULPTURES

While the Athenians dedicated their temple to Athena, they regarded the building as a mirror of their own civic and artistic achievements. The human character of the Parthenon is visible in the temple's decorative sculptures, which occupy three different spaces: the pediment, the outer (Doric) frieze, and the inner (cella) frieze. The sculptural program was supervised and probably designed by Phidias.

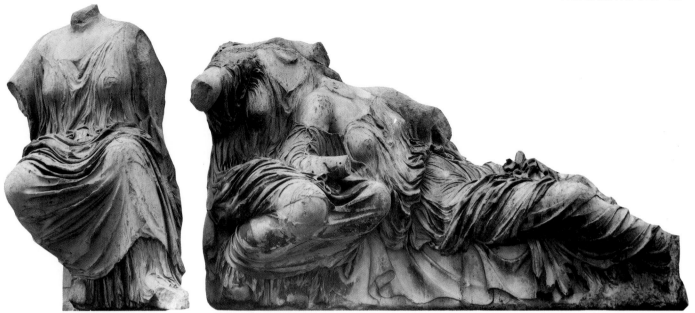

3.17 Three Goddesses, from the Parthenon's east pediment, c. 438–432 B.C. Marble, more than life-size. British Museum, London.
Though missing their heads and arms, these figures still express Greek classicism's balance between naturalism and idealized beauty. Note how the finely carved drapery defines the figures' poses and their dynamic connection to the central event of Athena's birth.

3.18 Lapith and Centaur, metope from the Parthenon's outer frieze (south face), c. 448–442 B.C. Marble, 3 ft 11 ins x 4 ft 2 ins (1.19 x 1.27 m). British Museum, London.
Such scenes of the Doric frieze may have symbolized the Athenians' victory over the Persians, or, more generally, Greek civilization's triumph over barbarism.

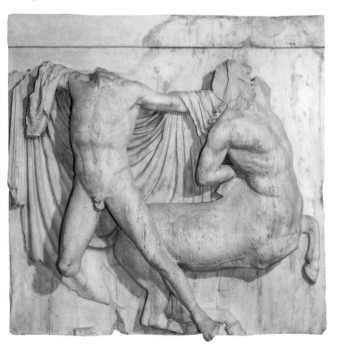

on a broad ledge (Fig. 3.16). The Parthenon's pedimental sculptures depicted important events in the life of Athena: the goddess' birth full-grown from Zeus' head (on the east) and (on the west) Athena's competition with the god Poseidon.

The pediments' graceful and life-like figures contain the essence of classical Greek sculpture. On the east pediment, for instance, the *Three Goddesses* (Fig. 3.17) are divine witnesses to Athena's remarkable birth. Beneath the graceful and fluid lines of their garments, the deities have the solid form of Athenian matrons. The drapery defines each figure individually, unifies the group, and carries the news of Athena's birth outward to the pediment's corner. The original sculptural group must have been a triumph of humanist grace and vitality.

Beneath the cornice on all four sides was a **frieze**, the name given to any continuous band of relief sculpture. In the Doric order, the frieze consisted of three-part geometric panels called **triglyphs** that alternated with pictorial scenes called **metopes**. The metopes were carved in high relief, meaning that the figures project outward from the background. The artistic challenge in the metopes was to create a dramatic action with only two figures, compressed onto a small block (Fig. **3.18**). The figures and background were brightly painted and sometimes adorned with brass detailing, such as horses' reins.

The Parthenon was unique among Doric temples in having a second frieze that ran along the cella wall and across the inner columns. The Parthenon's **cella frieze** was a stroke of genius, a sculpted advertisement of Athenian civic virtue, which ran for more than 500 feet (152 m). The frieze is carved in low relief, with figures projecting only slightly from the background, and depicts a noble procession of Athenian citizens, reminiscent of the city's festival to Athena held every four years. Nude horsemen sit astride their horses with a bearing typical of the classical period (Fig. **3.19**). Athenian maidens lead a parade

The temple's most important sculptures occupied the **pediment**, the triangular space formed by the roof's gable. Pedimental groups were sculpted in the round and rested

3.19 Right *Athenian Horsemen*, from the Parthenon's inner frieze (west face), c. 442–432 B.C. Marble, height of panel 3 ft 7 ins (1.07 m). British Museum, London.
The Parthenon cella frieze celebrated the heroism and nobility of Athens' citizens. The number of horsemen (approx. 192) matches the number of Athenians who died fighting the Persians at Marathon.

3.20 Below Mnesicles, Erechtheum (from south), Athens, c. 421–409 B.C. Marble, length of temple 37 ft (11.3 m), width 66 ft (20.1 m).
Instead of fluting to emphasize their stature, the caryatid columns have the fluid vertical lines of their gowns.

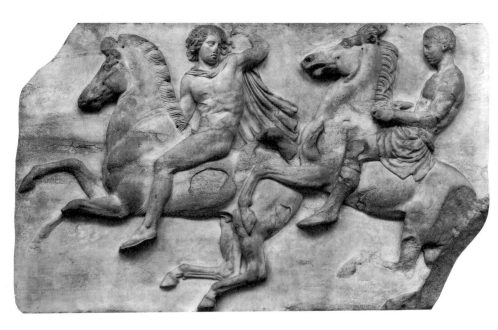

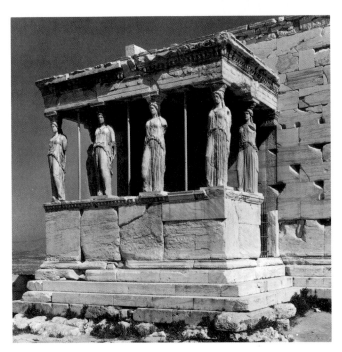

to the thrones of Zeus and Athena, who preside benignly over the celebration. Inspired by their supremacy among Greeks, the Athenians dared to portray themselves among the gods.

Other Acropolis Buildings After the completion of the Parthenon, Athens' leaders turned to other buildings on the acropolis. They built a massive gateway called the **Propylaea** [pro-puh-LEE-uh], with ramps leading through a temple-like building. The Propylaea was notable for its combination of the Doric and Ionic orders. Late in the Peloponnesian Wars, the Athenians began the **Erechtheum** [er-ick-THEE-um], an Ionic temple that encom-

passed several sacred sites. The Erechtheum was built on two levels and had two porches, one in the Ionic style with a continuous frieze, and the other with columns in the shape of maidens, called **caryatids** [kair-ee-AT-ids]. The caryatid columns of the south porch bear the heavy entablature on baskets atop their heads (Fig. **3.20**). The Erechtheum was truly an all-purpose temple: within its grounds were the sacred spring of Poseidon, Athena's sacred olive tree, and the tomb of the city's legendary King Erechtheus.

GREEK SCULPTURE

Describe Greek sculpture of the classical and Hellenistic periods.

To a non-Western observer, ancient Greek sculpture may seem obsessed with the human figure. Few other eras have concentrated so completely on sculpting the human anatomy. This concentration was evident already in the early Archaic *kouroi*, the stylized male youths modeled after Egyptian statuary (see Fig. 3.6). The evolution of Greek sculpture from the Archaic period can be traced in the Greeks' increasingly refined command of the human image.

THE WRITE IDEA
Imagine your home town as a ruin five hundred years from now. What buildings might remain standing and what would they look like? How might a tourist of the year 2500 judge today's civilization based on the architectural monuments left behind?

KEY CONCEPT

CLASSICAL HUMANISM

The peoples of ancient civilization lived in a world where the power of nature and the power of rulers dwarfed ordinary human effort. In the face of these forces, the ancient Greeks proclaimed the nobility of human intelligence and action, believing fiercely in the human ability to understand and control the world, a belief called **classical humanism**. Classical humanism was reflected in every aspect of Greek life. The tragic poet Sophocles, in his play *Antigone*, offers this hymn to the powers of humanity:

Numberless wonders,
terrible wonders walk the world but none the match for
man –
. . . The blithe, lightheaded race of birds he snares
the tribes of savage beasts, the life that swarms
the depths –
with one fling of his nets
woven and coiled tight, he takes them all,
man the skilled, the brilliant! . . .
And speech and thought, quick as the wind
and the mood and mind for law that rules the city –
all these he has taught himself

and shelter from the arrows of the frost
when there's rough lodging under the cold clear sky
and the shafts of lashing rain –
ready, resourceful man![5]

Classical humanism expressed the Greeks' soaring confidence in their civilization, bolstered in fifth-century Athens by wealth and power. Artists and thinkers focused their attention on the human and became more skeptical about traditional belief. When the philosopher Protagoras (see page 62) said, "Man is the measure of all things," he referred to the belief that truth and value were determined by human standards, not by the gods. Such humanist belief helped to create the noble characters of Greek tragedy and the marble beauties that adorn the Greek temples (Fig. **3.21**).

Although the Greeks' humanist confidence eventually faded, the idea of humanism remained a powerful legacy. It was often revived in later ages of great confidence or skepticism. Renaissance thinkers and artists challenged the medieval Church by studying the culture of Greek humanism. Modern existential philosophers maintained that humans were absolutely free to create themselves – a radical humanism. Protagoras' motto is as contemporary and controversial today as it was 2500 years ago.

CRITICAL QUESTION

In what social and scientific debates are humanist beliefs most prevalent today? What ideas or systems of thought are most vigorously opposed to modern humanism?

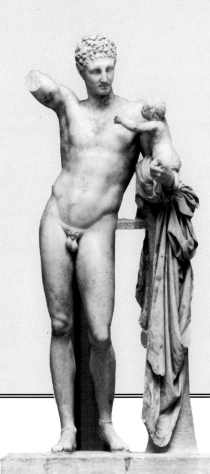

3.21 Praxiteles,
Hermes and the Infant
Dionysus, c. 340 B.C.
Marble copy of
original, height 7 ft 1
in (2.16 m).
Archeological
Museum, Olympia.
Praxiteles mastered the
relaxed stance and fluid,
S-shaped torso that
were typical of late
classical sculpture.

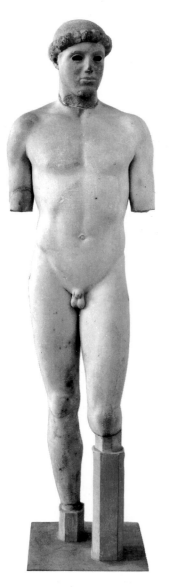

3.22 Left *Kritios Boy*, c. 490 B.C. Marble, height 34 ins (86 cm). Acropolis Museum, Athens.
Here the frontal stance of the *kouros* dissolves and the figure turns ever so slightly in space. The Archaic smile of earlier sculptures has disappeared.

3.23 Right and opposite *Riace Warrior*, mid-5th century B.C. Bronze with glass-plate, bone, silver, and copper inlay. Height 6 ft 6 ins (2 m). Museo Nazionale, Reggio Calabria, Italy.
Note the balance of the warrior's pose, a shield on his left arm as against a spear in his right hand (both now missing). The torso's animated S-curve is created by placing the figure's weight on the right foot, which causes the pelvis and shoulders to tilt in opposite directions. Such figures were Greek ideals of male prowess and nobility.

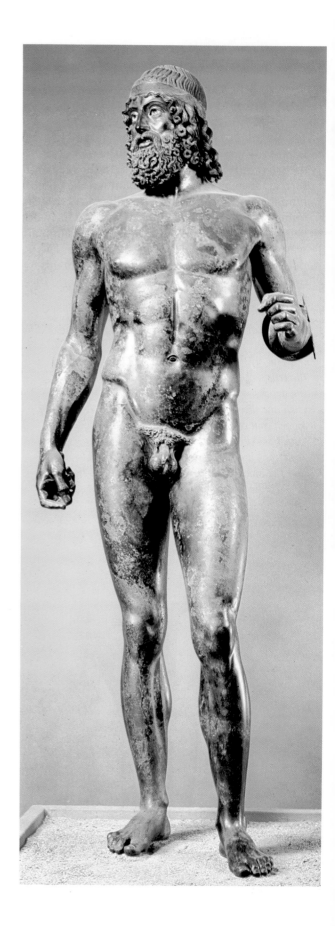

The turning point between Archaic and classical sculpture came when Greek sculptors learned to represent the human figure in motion. The most dramatic example of this lesson was the *Kritios Boy* (Fig. **3.22**), found among the debris of the Persian sack of Athens' acropolis. The differences from the symmetrical Archaic *kouros* are subtle but decisive. The weight is thrown onto the back leg, slightly lowering the opposite hip. The head turns slightly to the left, and the Archaic smile has disappeared. The lines of the torso are softened and filled, as if the statue had taken a breath. Although still highly idealized, the *Kritios Boy* looks forward to the naturalism of the classical style.

THE CLASSICAL STYLE

The classical style in Greek sculpture (*c.* 480–323 B.C.) represented a marriage of idealism and naturalism, much like the compromise between rationalism and the senses in

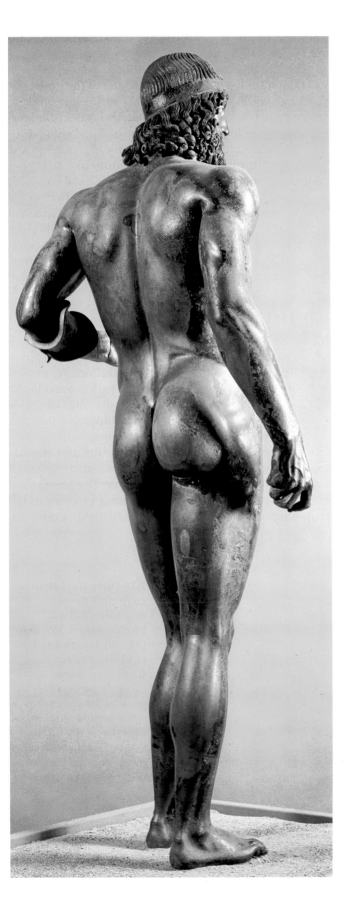

the Parthenon. The greatest statues of this period were nearly always an ideal figure, usually an athlete or a god, yet they were approachably human.

The male ideal of the classical style is evident in the bronze warrior discovered near Riace [ree-AH-chay], Italy. The *Riace Warrior* (Fig. **3.23**) is one of a handful of original bronze statues from the classical period, possibly the work of Phidias himself. Cast in exacting detail, the *Riace Warrior* projects the supreme confidence and powerful athleticism of the hero. One arm is raised to hold a shield and the other one grasped a spear, both now lost. Clearly, classical sculptors could portray a nobility of character and bearing in the male figure that matched the feminine grace of the Parthenon's *Three Goddesses* (see Fig. 3.17).

The most admired classical sculptors set the human figure in complex and expressive motions, while maintaining harmony and balance. Myron's *Discobolus (Discus Thrower)* (Fig. **3.24**), for example, is poised to release his discus and thus filled with potential energy. Yet his stance

3.24 Myron, *Discobolus (Discus Thrower)*. Roman copy after bronze original, c. 450 B.C. Marble, life-size. Museo Nazionale, Rome.
Myron's idealized athlete is poised in the moment just before he unleashes the discus.

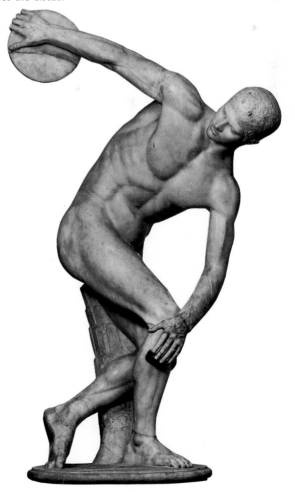

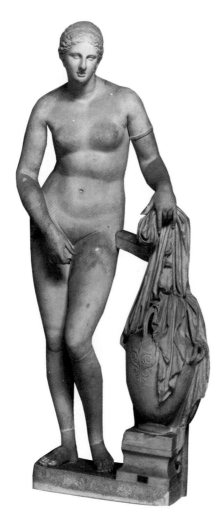

3.25 Above **Praxiteles, *Aphrodite of Cnidos*. Roman copy after original of c. 350–340 B.C. Marble, height 6 ft 8 ins (2.03 m). Vatican Museums, Rome.**
One of several versions of Aphrodite attributed to the late classical sculptor Praxiteles, whose works were among the most-admired and most-copied statues of antiquity. The original statue was probably colorfully decorated with gilded hair and jewelry, and rouged cheeks.

is restrained so that the figure is as calm as the Parthenon horsemen (see Fig. 3.19). The geometric symmetry of Archaic sculpture has given way to a statue of complex angles and arcs.

The late classical sculptor Praxiteles (born *c.* 390 B.C.) was famed for his humanized portraits of the gods. His *Hermes and Dionysus* (see Fig. 3.21) captures the gods in a moment of playful intimacy. Praxiteles [prax-IT-uh-leez] was known for his life-like versions of Aphrodite [af-ro-DYE-tay], the goddess of love, and took advantage of late classical sculptors' new-found freedom in portraying the female nude. The alluring *Aphrodite of Cnidos* (Fig. **3.25**) is captured as she prepares for a bath. Both the *Hermes and Dionysus* and the *Aphrodite* sculptures show the graceful S-curve that was perfected by Praxiteles. This life-like stance, called in Italian *contrapposto*, required that shoulders and hips be slightly angled in opposite directions. The result was the final stage of late classical naturalism.

THE HELLENISTIC STYLE

In its later stages, Greek sculpture developed from classical idealism toward the emotionally charged realism of the Hellenistic style. During the Hellenistic period (323–146 B.C.), Greek civilization spread to Persia and Egypt in the wake of the conquests of Alexander the Great (see page 66). The patrons of Hellenistic sculpture were often private individuals, rather than city-states, as in the classical age. For this reason, Hellenistic sculptures emphasized the individuality of their subjects and strived for a direct emotional impact on the viewer. The *Dying Gaul* (Fig. **3.26**) is one of a statue group commissioned by a Hellenistic ruler to commemorate his battlefield opponents.

3.26 *Dying Gaul*, **Roman copy after bronze original, c. 225 B.C. Marble, height 35¹/₂ ins (91 cm), length 6 ft 3 ins (1.91 m). Museo Capitolino, Rome.**
Compare the pose and mood of this Hellenistic statue with the classical *Riace Warrior* (Fig. 3.23). What different emotional responses might the two works cause in a viewer?

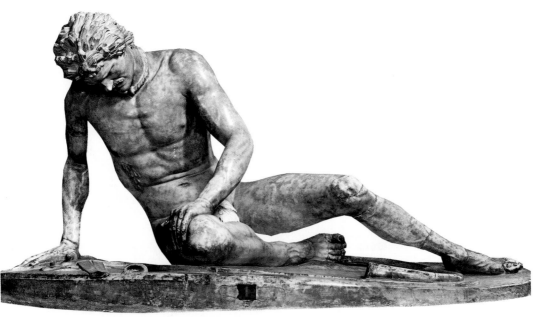

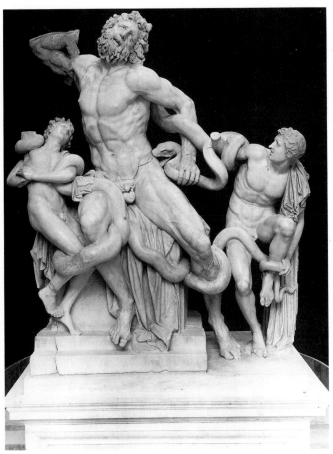

3.27 Agesander, Athenodorus, and Polydorus of Rhodes, *Laocoön and his Two Sons,* **c. 150 B.C. Marble, height 8 ft (2.44 m). Vatican Museums, Rome.**
Trace this dynamic sculpture's crisscrossing diagonal lines overlaid with the contorted serpent's body. Laocoön had tried to warn the Trojans against accepting the Greeks' fateful gift of a wooden horse.

The soldier has just committed suicide with his sword, which lies within his reach. The sculptor has made no effort to idealize the subject. Instead, the figure's heroic resignation is communicated by individualizing detail, such as his coarse hair and his necklace.

The most dramatic of Hellenistic sculpture may be *Laocoön and his Two Sons* (Fig. **3.27**), which portrays a Trojan priest and his sons as they are drowned by serpents. The treatment of the *Laocoön* [lah-OH-koh-on] is more turbulent and impassioned than any classical sculpture. The figures' violent struggle creates a sense of dramatic con-

---

THE WRITE IDEA

Describe the change in Greek attitudes toward the role of art, as it is illustrated in the development of Greek sculpture. What does each phase say about the human aspect of the Greeks who created and patronized it?

---

flict and emotion. The face of Laocoön shows the agony of one terrible moment, rather than the calm balance of a timeless pose, such as in Myron's *Discus Thrower* (see Fig. 3.24).

GREEK THEATER

Describe the most important types of Greek theater.

Many Greek cities joined Athens in creating the architecture and sculpture of the period. However, Athens alone bears the honor of inventing the Greek theater. Seated beneath their acropolis, Athenians witnessed the birth of one of Western literature's first great dramatic forms. Theater was the medium in which Athenians reflected on their culture's most essential questions: the powers of the gods, the course of human destiny, the nature of love and justice. It was at once drama, poetry, religion, and philosophy. Their solemn spectacles of passion and suffering have been acted out countless times in succeeding centuries, yet later imitations of Greek tragedy would never wholly recreate its complex artistic form.

Classical tragedy and comedy both originated in the Greeks' worship of Dionysus [dye-oh-NYE-sus], god of wine, revelry, and intoxication. Worshipers of Dionysus disguised themselves with masks, dressed in animal costumes, carried oversized fertility symbols, and sang hymns of praise to the god. The most solemn hymns were sung and danced by a chorus of performers. These choral recitations became theater when a singer separated from the group and held a dramatic conversation with the **chorus**. From this elemental beginning evolved the Greek **tragedy**, a drama involving mythic characters whose pride leads them into suffering and death. Although scholars disagree about its origins, Athenian tragedy as we know it had evolved by the early fifth century B.C.

GREEK TRAGEDY

The performance of Greek **tragedy** was unlike the performances we experience today. Staged in open-air theaters seating up to fifteen thousand spectators (Fig. **3.28**), the plays were a solemn religious occasion where the priest of Dionysus presided. Wealthy citizens underwrote dramatic productions, and playwrights submitted their plays in a yearly competition. The audience viewed the action from the *theatron*, or "viewing place," originally a bare hillside and later covered by stone seats. Individual actors spoke their lines while standing in front of the *skenē* (the root of our word "proscenium"), a building that housed the props and provided a backdrop for the action. The actors wore heavy wool costumes and large masks that amplified their words (Fig. **3.29**). The chorus of twelve to fifteen actors chanted its songs rhythmi-

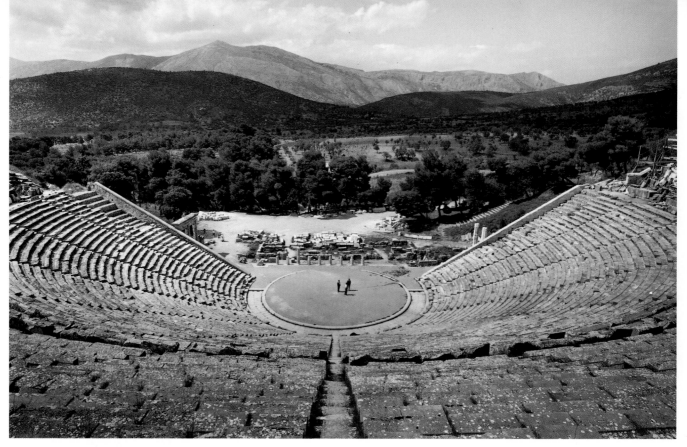

3.28 Theater at Epidaurus, Greece, c. 350 B.C. Diameter 373 ft (114 m), orchestra 66 ft (20 m).
Remains of the *skene* are visible at the rear of the orchestra. The chorus entered and exited through the post-and-lintel gateways at left and right, called *parodoi* (singular, *parados*).

3.29 Fourth-century tragic actor. Vase painting from Tarentum, c. 340 B.C. Würzburg University Museum.
The actor holds a mask suitable for playing a tragic king like Agamemnon or Oedipus.

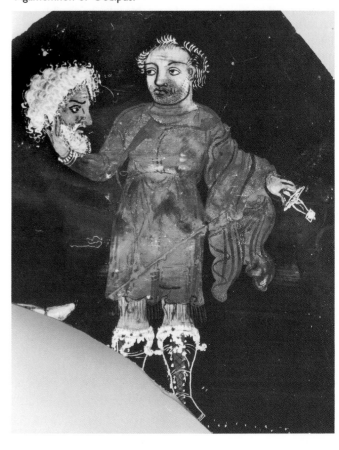

cally to a flute's accompaniment, while engaging in a solemn dance on the **orchestra**, the circular area surrounded by the theatron.

The Greek tragedy was part opera, part ballet, part religious pageant, a mixture that the nineteenth-century German composer Richard Wagner called the *Gesamtkunstwerk*, the "total work of art." Wagner's own operas (see page 366) were an attempt to recreate the Greek tragedy for modern circumstances.

Although many Athenians wrote tragedies, the works of only three great tragedians are known, each responsible for new accents in the tragic idiom. **Aeschylus** [ESS-kuh-lus] (525–456 B.C.) reduced the role of the chorus and added a second actor, making true dialogue possible. The most famous of Aeschylus' seven known works is a three-play cycle called the *Oresteia*. In this gory saga, King Agamemnon returns from the Trojan War to be murdered by his wife Clytemnestra, who then is killed by her son. The murderous cycle finally ends when Athena intervenes and decrees that the rule of law will replace justice by vengeance. As was typical in Aeschylus' dramas, human suffering and guilt eventually led to the recognition of divine wisdom.

The most admired and prolific Athenian playwright was **Sophocles** (*c.* 496–406 B.C.), whose career coincided with the Golden Age of Athens. Sophocles may have written 123 tragedies in all, although only seven are known.

Sophocles added a third actor and created more tightly unified plots than Aeschylus. Sophocles' *Oedipus the King* was the most admired tragedy of the classical period. It told the story of a man prophesied to murder his father and marry his mother, and like most classical tragedies, it retold a legend already familiar to the audience. In this story, Oedipus' [ED-i-pus] royal parents try to evade the divine prophecy by having their child killed. A soft-hearted shepherd saves the infant, who is adopted in neighboring Corinth. As a young man, Oedipus unknowingly murders his true father. His cleverness wins him the throne of Thebes and an unwitting marriage to his own mother, the queen.

Sophocles begins his tragedy of Oedipus after these fateful events are complete, dramatizing Oedipus' agonizing search for his own identity. In the beginning, Oedipus seems to be a paragon of humanism, a man whose intelligence and nobility raise him to the level of a god. Oedipus' self-confidence is later shown to be **hubris**, an arrogant pride that ignores the limits on human understanding. The gods' power over human lives is vindicated in spite of all efforts to evade it. When Oedipus stabs out his own eyes, his action symbolizes the blindness of human intelligence and the folly of defying the gods.

To the philosopher Aristotle (see page 63) *Oedipus* contained the essential elements of tragedy, which Aristotle analyzed in his *Poetics*. When the hero's hubris leads him to commit a tragic error, he suffers a reversal of fortune and recognizes his folly. In witnessing the hero's pathetic fate, the audience experiences a cleansing, called **catharsis**, of their own fear and pity. Aristotle's notion of catharsis demonstrates the serious purpose of Athenian tragedy. Audiences were witnessing acts of primal suffering and religious faith, and few Greeks left the theater unaffected by the spectacle.

Athens' last great tragedian was **Euripides** (*c.* 480–407 B.C.), who saw the city succumb to plague, war, and internal division. Euripides' tragedies were filled with realism and biting social comment, often using unorthodox characters and plots. Sophocles himself acknowledged that his own plays showed people as they should be, while the plays of Euripides showed people as they were. Euripides' characters are often gripped by violent passions. His *Medea* depicts the mythic sorceress who murders her own sons in vengeance against a husband who has abandoned her. Euripides' own death was no less gruesome and bizarre. He was torn to pieces by dogs belonging to the king of Macedon, in whose palace he had taken refuge.

GREEK COMEDY

Although tragedy dominated the Greek theater, ancient Greeks enjoyed comedies of great wit and irreverence. **Comedy** is a dramatic form that humorously portrays everyday themes and characters. Originating in Dionysian fertility rites, Greek comedy featured choruses dressed as animals and actors in obscenely padded costumes. Comic plots were usually fantastic, yet included bawdy dialogue, slapstick shenanigans, and biting comment on the contemporary scene.

The greatest comedian of Athens' Golden Age was Aristophanes [air-i-STOFF-uh-neez] (*c.* 445–*c.* 383 B.C.), who wrote comic satires on philosophy, war, and the relations between the sexes. Aristophanes' *Clouds* depicts the philosopher Socrates sitting in a basket suspended in air. In *Lysistrata* the women of Greece engage in a sex strike to halt the Peloponnesian Wars. Because its subject matter was less high-minded than that of tragedy, comedy did not enjoy the same prestige. In fact, Aristotle hardly mentioned it in the *Poetics*. Comedy was, however, enthusiastically adapted in Hellenistic and Roman times.

In the Hellenistic period (323–146 B.C.), comedy played the role that the social comedies of today's television and film do. The Athenian Menander (342–292? B.C.) was a master of tightly plotted action, full of twists and surprises, where a slave might turn out to be free-born, or where impossible lovers suddenly marry. During the Hellenistic period, theaters were equipped with a raised stage and an elaborate backdrop containing several doors for appearances and disappearances. Because Hellenistic comedy abandoned the religious overtones of earlier Greek theater, it proved a more broadly appealing entertainment.

GREEK PHILOSOPHY

Summarize the aim of philosophy, as understood by Greek philosophers from the materialists to Aristotle.

Sophocles' tragic hero Oedipus possessed the "swiftness of mind" that allowed humans to understand and master their world. The ancient Greeks' fascination with rational inquiry gave rise to **philosophy**, which in Greek meant the "love of wisdom." It encompassed every rational pursuit of knowledge, including mathematics and science. For educated Greeks, philosophy competed with myth in explaining the nature of the universe and the workings of human society. By the fifth century B.C., philosophy's attention had turned to human morality and society. This new concern with human affairs set the stage

---

THE WRITE IDEA

Compare the social and philosophical concerns of Greek tragedy to issues in today's dominant dramatic forms (theater, film, and television). In what ways are today's dramatic artists reflecting the most important social questions of the present?

for Socrates, Plato, and Aristotle, the Greeks who defined the essential questions of Western philosophy.

EARLY GREEK PHILOSOPHY

Early Greek philosophers were primarily concerned with the material substance and ideal structure of the universe. They addressed themselves to the question: "What is the nature and origin of the universe?" Early Greek philosophers were thus also the first Greek scientists. Their scientific theories derived from speculation and contemplation, however, not from closely observing the world or performing experiments, as modern science does.

The earliest Greek philosophers, called **materialists**, searched for the elemental substance of which all other matter was composed. The first great materialists, active in the city of Miletus during the sixth century, speculated that this primal substance was water or air. Later, materialists asserted that all materials were composed of four different elements: earth, air, fire, and water. The last Greek materialists held that the cosmos was made of indivisible particles called atoms (*a-tomos* means "uncuttable"). Thus, early Greek philosophy anticipated the atomic theory of modern science. With the atomists, however, materialist speculation reached a philosophical dead end: the existence of atoms could not be demonstrated or investigated further with the naked eye.

A different vein of early Greek philosophy, called **idealism**, sought evidence of a divine and rational plan in the workings of the cosmos. The founder of Greek idealism was Pythagoras (active 6th century; see page 48), who held that numerical relations were the basis of all existence. Pythagoras made great practical discoveries, including a geometric theorem and the expression of musical tones as mathematical ratios (see page 66). Idealism evolved into a belief that the world was divided into two separate realms: one realm was material and known through the senses; the other was ideal and known only through rational contemplation. The ideas of early idealist philosophers later reappeared in the works of Plato, the greatest of the Greek idealists.

The early Greek philosophers, however, influenced few Greek citizens of the classical age: their speculations were too abstract, their treatises too obscure. The first philosophers to change Greek society were the **sophists**, professional teachers who embodied the humanist spirit of skepticism and self-reliance. The sophists scoffed at the materialists' dry speculations; instead they debated with their students about such practical matters as love, justice, truth, and beauty. The sophists were attracted to Athens, the vibrant "school of Hellas." Here they employed themselves as teachers to the sons of wealthy families, and taught public speaking and debate, the skills of Athenian democracy. The sophists' skepticism reflected the confident sophistication of Athens in the Golden Age. Protagoras (480–411 B.C.), a well-known sophist, pronounced,

"Man is the measure of all things," meaning that truth was always relative to the individual person's knowledge and perceptions. Laws, customs, concepts of right and wrong, were all the creation of humans, not the gods.

While Protagoras gave voice to the new humanist spirit, other sophists fostered cynicism. They taught their pupils to gain advantage through verbal trickery, a technique still called "sophistry." Our knowledge of the sophists is obscure, since few of their writings were preserved. We know them chiefly through the vehement anti-sophist writings of Plato.

SOCRATES

The sophists' abuses rankled their rival **Socrates** (469–399 B.C.), the Athenian who founded classical Greek philosophy without writing a word. Like the sophists, Socrates examined human affairs and taught through questioning. Socrates' philosophical technique, called the Socratic method, was based on question and answer in which the careful definition of terms ("love," "justice," "the good") produced insights into the truth. Unlike his rivals, Socrates believed firmly that absolute truths could be known and taught, although he denied that he himself possessed correct knowledge. He described himself as a "midwife" for knowledge borne from the minds of his students. Socrates' pot-bellied figure was a familiar sight to Athenians, pestering complacent citizens and playing the gadfly that stung Athens into action. "The unexamined life is not worth living," Socrates is quoted as saying.

In 399 B.C., however, the philosopher became bitterly and fatally entangled in affairs of state. In the turmoil following Athens' military defeat, Socrates was tried for religious and moral offenses, and sentenced to die. His trial was apparently motivated by anti-intellectual resentment and enmity toward Socrates' anti-democratic associates.

If his disciple Plato's accounts are to be believed (see below), Socrates' life was a model of principled integrity. He refused to take payment for teaching or to flee from the city whose laws he had respected all his life. In Plato's *Crito*, Socrates resolutely rejects his friends' urging to escape from prison. Such an action would violate the moral principles of a lifetime, principles worth more to Socrates than his own life. Socrates vowed that death would bring his final release from ignorance and desire, the philosopher's ultimate goal.

PLATO

Since Socrates wrote no books, we know his teachings only through the works of his student **Plato** (427–347 B.C.), whose vast writings and influence make him one of history's most important philosophers. Plato's early works are in the form of dialogues which Socrates may actually have held with students. These works include the *Apology*, an account of Socrates' trial, and the *Phaedo*, Socrates' last conversation. Plato maintained the dialogue form in later works, where Socrates becomes the voice of Plato's ideas. The dialogue provided Plato with an accessible and engaging form of philosophical exposition. In these works, he analyzed the most pressing moral and political issues of late classical Greece (404–323 B.C.), when order and harmony seemed to be breaking apart.

In this time of uncertainty, Plato believed in idealist absolutes. He taught that truth, justice, beauty, and virtue could be defined and known with certainty. In Plato's idealist view, these values existed in an ideal realm separate from everyday experience. He believed that what humans knew through the senses, was actually a copy of an unchanging form, known through the mind. For example, a horse cantering across a field was actually an imperfect replica of the ideal horse, which existed as a perfect form. One discovered the true essence of "horse-ness" not by touching or seeing any real horse, but through rational contemplation of the true form. Plato called this form the *eidos*, or "pattern." Mathematical ideas – the circle, triangle, and square – were the simplest versions of these patterns. Plato urged that philosophers be trained in mathematics and dedicate themselves to the contemplation of perfect forms.

Plato applied his doctrine of ideal forms to the questions that perplexed late classical Greeks – questions of justice, law, politics, and aesthetics. His most famous work, *The Republic*, considered all these questions in describing the ideal city-state, a utopia based on enlightened authoritarianism rather than Athenian-style democracy. Plato's ideal society would be ruled by philosopher-kings who had glimpsed absolute truth and therefore cared little about wealth or power. The decrees of Plato's philosopher-kings would be enforced by military guardians, while all labor would be performed by a large under-class of artisans. Plato's ideal society reflects his three-part division of the human soul: reason, the faculty most prominent in philosopher-kings; moral courage, which helps enforce the dictates of reason; and the appetites, which were concerned with material gratification.

In a famous passage from *The Republic* entitled the *Allegory of the Cave* (Fig. **3.30**), Plato described the complacent ignorance of citizens governed by their appetites. The *Allegory* describes the citizens as prisoners chained in a cave, who see shadows flicker across the wall and think the images are real. The cave metaphor illustrates the difficulty of arriving at knowledge, something Plato knew well from his efforts in philosophical education. He once visited the Greek colony of Syracuse to make a philosopher-king of its ruler and establish an ideal state, but he failed to achieve any practical improvement in the colony's government.

ARISTOTLE

In Athens, Plato founded a school called the Academy that attracted scholars from all over Greece. The Academy's most renowned student was **Aristotle** (384–323 B.C.), who challenged Plato's teachings and also became a towering figure in the history of philosophy. Like Plato, Aristotle gained the chance to apply his philosophy. He was appointed tutor for young Alexander, the Macedonian prince who became conqueror of the Mediterranean world. Aristotle's teachings encouraged Alexander's enthusiasm for Greek civilization, which he later imposed on Persia and Egypt.

As a philosopher, Aristotle's aim was to describe and analyze the world as it actually was. Together Ari-

---

CRITICAL QUESTION
How might Plato have criticized the organization of today's democratic governments?

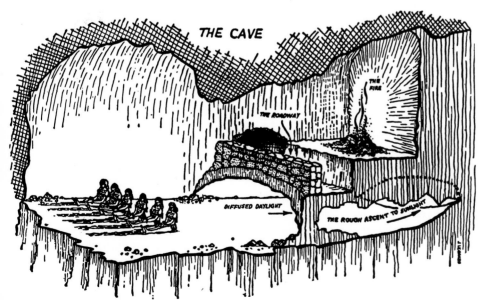

3.30 Allegory of the Cave, from The Great Dialogues of Plato, translated by **W. H. D. Rouse,** translation copyright © 1956, renewed 1984 by J. C. G. Rouse.

GLOBAL PERSPECTIVE

CONFUCIUS AND PHILOSOPHY

To later generations of Western philosophers, Socrates was the model of the wise and virtuous man, leading a life of rigorous self-examination. In Chinese philosophy, this role of the exemplary sage was filled by Kong-Fuzi, better known as **Confucius** (551–479 B.C.), the founder of Chinese philosophy. Like Socrates, Confucius defined a humanistic ideal of character and right action. And like the teachings of classical Greek philosophy, Confucius' ideal of the cultivated person – someone who acts in accord with tradition and propriety – was an abiding influence on Chinese politics and art for centuries.

Born to a poor family of noble origins, Confucius served as a minister of state and overseer of granaries for rulers of China's "Warring States" period. Eventually, however, he left official service to become a teacher and advisor. His teaching emphasized the duty of the gentleman (or "superior man") to fill his assigned role with ethical integrity and respect for tradition.

Like the Greeks of classical Athens, Confucius emphasized the responsibility of the individual to the community. He urged China's rulers to give up their aristocratic concept of exalted birth and inherited privilege. Instead, he advised, they should adopt a personal ethic of wisdom and humanity, and rule by example and moral persuasion rather than by force or punishment.

The Confucian gentleman exhibited an individual virtue that he termed *jen* [run], meaning "human-heartedness." *Jen* required the cultivation of individual benevolence and humanity, as expressed in a life of right action. The cultivation of *jen* led to a respect for custom and propriety (*li* [lee]), another essential Confucian idea. *Li* included obedience to one's parents and to the rulers of the state, and was also demonstrated in the arts, which honored and preserved abiding traditions.

At the heart of Confucian thought was the relation of private virtue and public conduct. Confucius viewed the cultivation of harmony and order in the individual soul as the means to an orderly society. The state could not create justice among citizens who did not seek justice in their own hearts. In *The Great Learning*, a disciple's synopsis of Confucius' moral and social program, the teacher said, "From the emperor down to the common people, all, without exception, must consider cultivation of the individual character as the root. If the root is in disorder, it is impossible for the branches to be in order."[6]

In his respect for the past and down-to-earth practicality, Confucius actually shared more with later Roman philosophy than with the speculative Greeks. The true way (or *tao* [dow]) was to be found in respecting one's elders and social traditions, and filling one's proper role in the family and society.

---

stotle's works form an encyclopedia of Greek knowledge about the world, including treatises in science, ethics, logic, politics, and literature, among other disciplines. His reasoning was clear and logical in a fashion much imitated by later philosophers. In his *Ethics*, Aristotle reasoned that happiness was found in a balance between two extremes. In other words, virtue lay at a "golden mean" between extreme self-denial and utter self-indulgence. Aristotle's "golden mean" expressed in philosophical terms the Greek desire for balance and harmony, the same values visible in the Parthenon's proportions (see page 50).

One of Aristotle's disputes with his teacher Plato concerned the nature of forms. Aristotle claimed that an object's form was contained within the object itself, rather than existing in a separate realm, as Plato believed. For example, a particular horse consisted of both the material individual and the ideal pattern of all horses. The same was true of a table, an olive tree, and a tragic poem. In his *Poetics*, Aristotle described the formal pattern of the tragic drama. Tragedy had, for example, an inherent structure (a beginning, a middle, and an end), and imitated events in the real world. By seeking the formal structures within the material world, Aristotle achieved a reconciliation of Greek philosophy's materialist and idealist traditions. Later generations would admire Aristotle for the clarity of his reasoning and the encyclopedic range of his thought.

THE WRITE IDEA

Reflect on the traditional teachings or ideals that you think are most important, ideals passed on to you by your parents or other elders. Tell a story, addressed to a younger sibling or friend, that illustrates the value of preserving and respecting these traditional teachings.

GREEK MUSIC

Explain the Greeks' beliefs about music and its relation to human character.

It is difficult for modern readers to appreciate the central place of music in classical Greek civilization. In the contemporary world one may be surrounded by music, but music is hardly considered a basic skill, like reading or mathematics. Yet Plato believed that a child's early education should consist only of gymnastics and music, training for the body and for the soul. To the ancient Greeks, music contained the principles of harmony that unified both nature and human society. One philosopher claimed that music was the basis of "the best government in the universe." It is difficult to imagine the response today if leading thinkers were advised to study music as the key to science and government.

The Greeks incorporated all the arts into music. The term **music** meant "of the Muses," the Muses being the goddesses who inspired the creative arts. Music was especially important in poetry, which was usually sung with musical accompaniment. Poems were recited to music from the **lyre**, an instrument with five to seven strings on a U-shaped bow and a sounding board made of tortoise shell. A lyric poet like Sappho (see page 45) probably accompanied herself by plucking the lyre's strings. Dramatic poetry called for the use of a double reed pipe called the **aulos** (Fig. **3.31**), played as the tragic chorus chanted and danced about the orchestra. The aulos continued to be used in drama through the Roman era.

The Greeks were convinced that the human soul attuned itself to music. Music could directly stimulate an emotional state like sadness or courage. The lyre was part of the cult of Apollo, god of rationality and intelligence, and was thought to calm and elevate the soul. The aulos was an instrument of excitement and enthusiasm, sacred to Dionysus, god of intoxication. The theater's intoxicating effect was amplified by the chorus's mimetic dance, which represented in mime the play's important actions. Part of the tragedy's emotional power must have come from this combination of poetry, music, and dance. Plato developed the doctrine of **ethos**, which held that music could be used to train human character and influence behavior. The modern term **ethics**, the study of moral behavior, is derived from ethos. Plato believed that by excluding certain kinds of music from his ideal republic, he could foster moral sternness and courage.

Music appealed to the Greek mind as well as to their passions. In fact, Greek theories of music have influenced Western civilization more than Greek music itself, since its actual sounds and performance cannot be reconstructed. The greatest theoretical discovery is owed to Pythagoras (see page 48), who learned to express musical tones mathematically. Pythagoras established a system of **intervals**, the distance between two musical tones. The Greeks' preferred intervals were the octave, produced when the length of a string was halved and expressed numerically as 1 : 2, and the fourth, which was expressed as

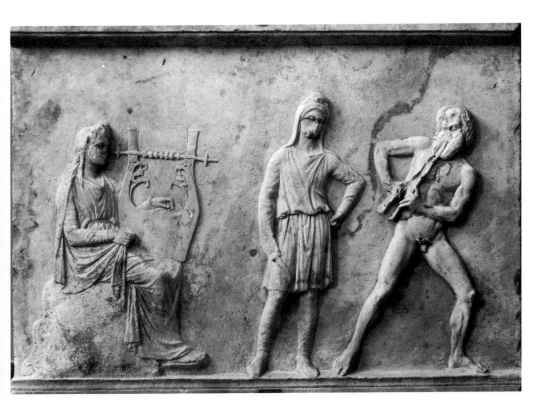

3.31 *Contest of Apollo and Marsyas.* **Relief from Mantineia, Greece, c. 350 B.C. National Museum, Athens.**

The Greeks associated the lyre with Apollo, god of light and knowledge, and the reed pipe (or *aulos*) with Dionysus, god of intoxication and patron of tragedy.

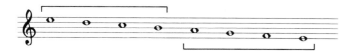

3.32 Greek modes.
Each four-note group was supposed to arouse different feelings in the listener.

4 : 3 and corresponds to the interval between C and the F above it in a modern Western musical scale.

Pythagoras transformed the intervals into a system of four-note groupings called tetrachords. The combination of two tetrachords formed a **mode**. The modes were associated with different emotional states, such as the somber and military Dorian mode preferred by Plato (Fig. **3.32**). Pythagoras enthusiastically applied his musico-mathematical system to the heavenly bodies. He theorized that each body revolved according to a different tone, producing a "music of the spheres." As Aristotle said, Pythagoras supposed "the elements of numbers to be the elements of all things and the whole heaven to be a musical scale and a number." Music, perhaps more than any other Greek art, embodied the harmony of reason and feeling in classical humanism.

3.33 *Alexander at the Battle of Issus*, from the House of the Faun, Pompeii, 2nd century B.C. Copy after original painting of c. 320–311 B.C. Mosaic, 8 ft 10 ins x 16 ft 9 ins (2.69 x 5.11 m). Museo Nazionale, Naples.
In the decisive battle of 333 B.C., the bareheaded Alexander (at left) leads a cavalry charge that causes the Persian king Darius to flee.

THE HELLENISTIC AGE

Compare Hellenistic civilization with the classical Greek civilization that preceded it.

The classical age in Greece ended when the general Philip of Macedon (ruled 359–336 B.C.) managed to subdue and unite the independent Greek city-states. Philip was succeeded in 336 B.C. by his twenty-year-old son Alexander the Great (356–323 B.C.), a pupil of Aristotle, who became one of the world's greatest conquerors. Alexander was a great lover of classical civilization. In the wake of his military conquests, Greek culture was diffused across a vast Mediterranean empire. This **Hellenistic**, or "Greek-like" culture dominated the eastern Mediterranean world for the next thousand years.

Beginning in 333 B.C., Alexander launched a whirlwind campaign against the great empires of Persia and Egypt (Fig. **3.33**). Without losing a battle, he brought their vast territories and resources under his rule. Alexander's armies continued into what is now India until the hero succumbed to a fever in 323 B.C. On his death, Alexander's military empire was divided into three large kingdoms, which adopted the Persian-style government of absolute monarchy and a strong central state. The wealthy Hellenistic rulers proved to be generous sponsors of the arts, libraries, and other intellectual pursuits.

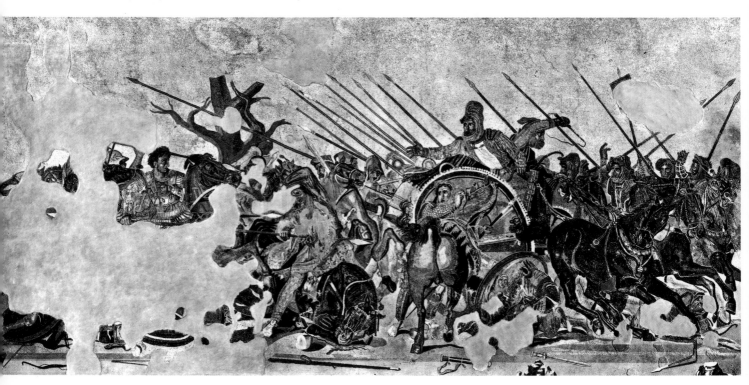

THE HELLENISTIC LEGACY

Hellenistic civilization was a composite of Greek and Oriental elements that differed substantially from its classical predecessor. Politically, the Greek city-states lost the self-sufficiency that had encouraged Athens' burst of classical creativity. Hellenism replaced this freedom with the absolute rule of a king and his royal bureaucracy. At the same time, standards of living rose, and women gained wider respect and legal standing.

In the arts and letters, Hellenistic civilization lacked the audacious originality of classical Greece. Hellenistic kings collected classical manuscripts in great libraries that served as centers of scholarship. The most famous of these libraries was in Egyptian Alexandria, a sprawling cosmopolitan city with perhaps one million inhabitants. Artists were keen to imitate and elaborate the forms and ideas of classical Greece, and in theater, the dramatists proved most inventive in comedy, developing Menander's comedy of manners (see page 61). In philosophy, new schools formed around figures like Zeno (see page 96) and Epicurus (see page 95), who based their teachings on Socrates and the other founders of classical Greek philosophy.

In sculpture, Hellenistic artists achieved a new realism of presentation. Their statuary often portrayed ordinary individuals in fine detail and with sympathy (see Fig. 3.26). Official sculpture, like the frieze of the Altar of Zeus (Fig. **3.34**) in Pergamon in Turkey, also showed the Hellenistic interest in conflict and emotional drama.

The concentration of learning in the cities fueled a burst of scientific discovery in astronomy, medicine, and mathematics. During this period, Euclid (*c.* 300 B.C.) devised his system of geometry and it was asserted for the first time that the planets revolved around the sun. This period was also the first to look back on classical Greece as the standard against which to measure its accomplishments. By emulating and preserving classical Greek culture, Hellenistic scholars and artists revered classical Greece even as they sought to surpass it – an attitude which was to be shared by the ancient world's new rising power, the Romans.

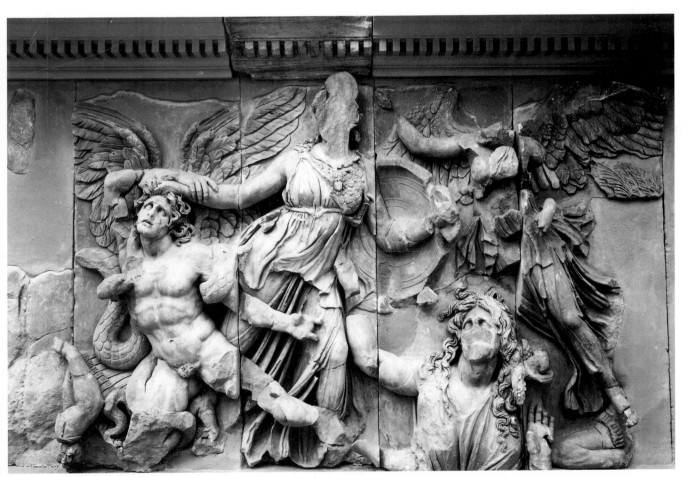

3.34 *Athena Slaying Giant*, **detail of frieze from the Altar of Zeus, Pergamon, c. 180 B.C. Marble, height 7 ft 6 ins (2.29 m). Antikensammlung, Staatliche Museen, Berlin.**
Amid the turmoil of battle, Athena lifts a giant by the hair to slay him. Compare this frieze with the more restrained classical style of the Parthenon's *Lapith and Centaur* (Fig. 3.18).

Chapter Summary

Early Greece. The civilization of early Greece (c. 900–480 B.C.) arose from a Dark Age that followed the ruin of Mycenaean civilization. The first great poetic works of early Greece were Homer's epic poems, the *Iliad* and the *Odyssey*. The Homeric epics – the foundation of Western literature – recount the deeds of heroes from the legendary Trojan War, the formidable warrior Achilles and the wily adventurer Odysseus. The lyric poet Sappho achieved intimacy and tenderness in shorter poems often dedicated to her beloved female friends. The vase painters and sculptors of early Greece showed increasing mastery of human anatomy and naturalism. In the so-called Archaic period especially (650–490 B.C.), sculpture underwent a rapid stylistic evolution, reflecting the early Greeks' fascination with rational order.

The Classical Period. The classical period (480–323 B.C.) of ancient Greece began with Athens' triumph over Persian armies. Under the political leadership of Pericles, Athens entered a Golden Age (480–404 B.C.), developing a vigorous democracy that, despite its achievements, denied most women any rights and eventually brought ruin on itself.

The Greek Temple. The temple was the focus of Greek art in the classical period. The Parthenon's construction and sculptural decoration represented the classical balance between rational design and humanistic vitality. The Parthenon and other Athenian acropolis buildings are the highest expression of Athens' Golden Age.

Greek Sculpture. The concern with human values also characterized the evolution of Greek sculpture from the stylized Archaic style to classical naturalism. Classical Greek sculpture typically portrayed an idealized physical type – a nude god, warrior, or athlete – in a stance suggesting prowess and restrained energy. Late classical sculpture first began to portray the nude female figure. As Greek culture spread to the Mediterranean world, the Hellenistic style in sculpture showed an increasing emotionalism and realism.

Greek Theater. Greek theater was the source of the Western dramatic forms of tragedy and comedy. Arising from the ritual worship of Dionysus, classical tragedy re-enacted ancient legends to teach lessons about human ambition and suffering. Aeschylus was the first tragic playwright, while Sophocles' version of the Oedipus legend was acclaimed as the purest example of Greek tragedy. Classical Greek comedy – a bawdy dramatic form intended to provoke laughter and ridicule – was brought to its highest form by Aristophanes; in the Hellenistic era, comedy lost its religious overtones and, with Menander, developed the twists of plot familiar today.

Greek Philosophy. Early Greek philosophy pursued an inquiry into the nature of the physical universe along both materialist and idealist paths. The sophists turned their attention to human affairs, examining such issues as morality and law. The Athenian Socrates adapted the sophists' methods but rejected their relativism. Socrates' exemplary life and death inspired his student Plato to write the dialogues that elaborated Western philosophy's first great philosophical system. Plato's idealism culminated in his utopian description of the ideal city-state, *The Republic*. The thought of Aristotle, Plato's student, was equally influential, encompassing every realm of human knowledge from ethics and poetics to science and logic.

Greek Music. The Greeks also believed music had a profound effect on human character (*ethos*). The Greek philosopher Pythagoras discovered music's underlying mathematical structure and connected music to the structure of the universe.

The Hellenistic Age. The Hellenistic age (323–145 B.C.) saw the spread of Greek civilization to the eastern Mediterranean world, in the wake of Alexander's conquests. Hellenistic cities in Asia Minor and Egypt were great centers of learning and Hellenistic art achieved a new realism and emotional directness. The Hellenistic elaboration of classical ideas and achievements set the stage for Roman civilization, which would enthusiastically absorb Greek art and ideas.

4 Ancient Rome: The Spirit of Empire

Sprawling imperial Rome – crowded with stupendous buildings, alive with pleasures and entertainment, the hub of a world that stretched from England to Iraq (Fig. *4.1*). Here was where Roman emperors paraded their war captives. Here was where Romans brought their plundered Greek treasures. Here was where future empires would look for an example of greatness. This was the *imperial spirit* of Rome: the power to impose the city's law on subject peoples, the will to civilize them in the Roman way, the sense of destiny that they could bring peace and order to the world.

4.1 Scale model of ancient Rome. Museo della Civiltà, Rome.
Rome at the height of its power, crowded by imperial buildings: at upper right, the Colosseum; center, the Emperor's palace and race course; and upper left, the forum of Trajan.

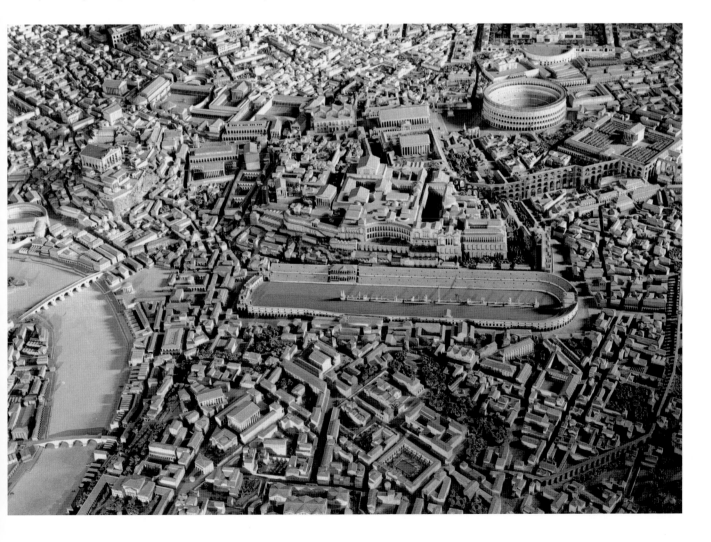

THE ROMAN AND EARLY CHRISTIAN WORLDS

	GENERAL EVENTS	ARCHITECTURE	VISUAL ARTS	LITERATURE AND PHILOSOPHY	RELIGION
1000 B.C.					
	753 Rome founded				c. 960 Temple of King Solomon, Jerusalem
				c. 530 The Buddha's sermon at the Deer Park, Benares, India (**4.32**)	587 Babylonians destroy temple; Israelites in exile
500 B.C.	509 Roman republic established		c. 500 Etruscan *Apollo of Veii* (**4.2**)		
REPUBLICAN ROME	146 B.C. Rome conquers Carthage, Greece			c. 300 Epicurus teaching in Athens	
				c. 65 B.C. Lucretius, *On the Nature of Things*	
30 B.C.					
	27 B.C.–A.D. 14 Octavian rules as Emperor Caesar Augustus	23–13 B.C. Theater of Marcellus, Rome (**4.27**)	13–9 B.C. *Ara Pacis Augustae* (Altar of Peace), Rome (**4.7**)	29–19 B.C. Virgil, *The Aeneid*	c. 4 B.C. Jesus born in Palestine, crucified A.D. 30
ROMAN EMPIRE			A.D. 109–13 Column of Trajan, Rome (**4.10**)		
		c. A.D. 120 Pantheon, Rome (**4.18**)			
A.D. 180				c. 175 Marcus Aurelius, *Meditations*	
DECLINE OF ROMAN EMPIRE	330 Constantinople founded as capital of eastern empire	c. 320–30 St. Peter's, Rome (**5.12**)			313 Emperor Constantine legalizes Christianity
400				397 Augustine, *Confessions*	
BYZANTINE WORLD	527–65 Reign of Justinian	c. 500 Sacred pyramids of Teotihuacán, Valley of Mexico (**5.32**) 532–7 Hagia Sophia, Constantinople (**5.15**)	c. 547 Mosaics at San Vitale, Ravenna (**5.26**, **5.27**)		
					622 Muhammad's flight (*hegira*) from Mecca
700	622–722 Muslim conquests from India to Spain				

THE DRAMA OF ROMAN HISTORY

Trace Rome's historical development from early republic to imperial power.

Few peoples have been as conscious of their history as the ancient Romans, and few histories have been re-enacted as often as ancient Rome's. Shakespeare's Brutus, standing over the murdered Julius Caesar, asks how many times their scene will be enacted on the world's stage. He spoke more prophetically than even Shakespeare could have known. The drama of Roman history has provided the script for revolutions and conquests many times over. Even Rome's fall as an empire has been compared to the decline of the British and Russian empires in recent history.

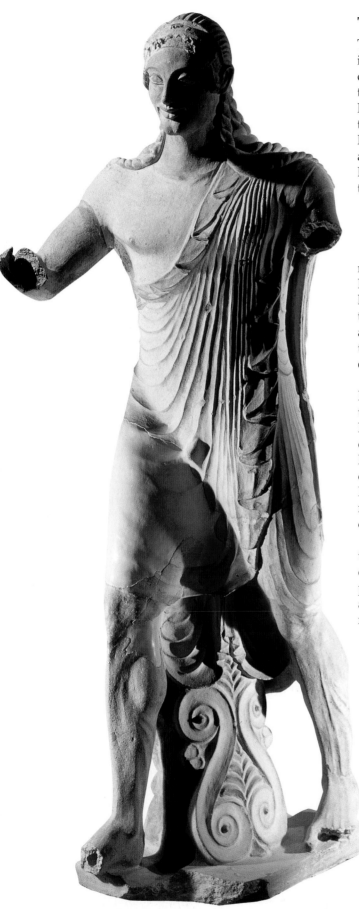

THE RISE OF REPUBLICAN ROME

The Romans' sense of history began with the city's founding, set by legend in 753 B.C. However, Roman cultural development dates from the era of Etruscan domination. The Etruscans were a resourceful people of central Italy, who dominated the Italian peninsula in the sixth century B.C. When the last Etruscan king was expelled from Rome around 510 B.C., the Romans were left with a valuable Etruscan legacy. Although its origins are obscure, Etruscan art (Fig. **4.2**) shows a vigor and confidence that the Romans would not match for some centuries. The Romans had also learned essential skills in engineering and architecture, including the use of the arch for construction.

In 509 B.C., the Romans established a **republic** – a government of representatives chosen to act for the people at large. Etruscan rule had left the early Romans with a distaste for kings, and they intended republican government to protect them from the abuses of monarchy. In modern times and for similar reasons, revolutionaries in eighteenth-century North America and France founded republics modeled after the Roman republic.

From 509 to *c.* 250 B.C., two struggles propelled Roman history: externally, the Romans set out to conquer the Italian peninsula, establishing themselves as a leading Mediterranean power; internally, the Romans struggled over the distribution of political power within the republic. The struggle was won at first by the conservative upper-class **patricians** [pah-TRIH-shuns], who ruled through the Roman Senate. Gradually, the opposing class of poor commoners (called **plebeians** [pleb-EE-uns]) gained political power and constitutional recognition of their rights.

Once the Romans had achieved control of Italy, they turned to subdue their Mediterranean rivals. Rome's chief opponent was the north African commercial and naval power of Carthage. The Romans defeated the Carthaginians in a series of three wars called the Punic [PYOO-nik] Wars (264–146 B.C.), the last of which ended in the vengeful razing of Carthage and Rome's total domination of the western Mediterranean. By this time, Rome's eyes were already turning east, and in 146 B.C., Romans conquered the Greek capital of Corinth. In the next decades, Rome's empire absorbed virtually the entire Hellenistic world, with its wealth, libraries, and art treasures.

4.2 *Apollo*, **from the Portonaccio Temple, Veii, Etruscan, c. 520–500 B.C. Terracotta, height 5 ft 9 ins (1.75 m). Museo Nazionale di Villa Giulia, Rome.**
This Etruscan statue shows the influence of the Archaic Greek *kouros*, especially in its striding stance and formalized smile.

NOTABLE ROMAN EMPERORS

Name	Ruled	Significance
AUGUSTUS	27 B.C.–A.D. 14	Established emperor as dictator of Roman society; promoted peace and traditional Roman values.
NERO	A.D. 54–68	Patronized the arts and built "Golden House"; blamed Christians for devastating fire in Rome (A.D. 64).
HADRIAN	117–38	Most cultivated of the emperors; built the Pantheon and a grand villa at Tivoli.
MARCUS AURELIUS	161–80	Wrote *Meditations*, significant work of stoic philosophy; led military campaigns against foreign invaders.
DIOCLETIAN	284–305	Divided empire into four parts for more efficient administration; retired to palace in Split (present-day Croatia).

By the second century B.C., Rome was no longer an agrarian city peopled by yeoman farmers and small merchants. It had become a vast and wealthy empire with large professional armies. Tantalized by the prospect of ruling this empire, power-hungry leaders convulsed Rome in a series of civil wars (90–31 B.C.). Private armies clashed in distant provinces, while thousands died in political assassinations and reprisals. The leading player in this turbulent era was Julius Caesar (100–44 B.C.), a charismatic figure who reformed Roman law and reorganized its public administration. Playing on his military successes in Gaul (modern France), Caesar had himself named dictator for life in 46 B.C. However, he was assassinated two years later by senators fearful that he would establish a monarchy. Caesar's death set off another bloody civil conflict, from which his adopted nephew Octavian emerged victorious. Octavian (63 B.C.–A.D. 14) defeated his uncle's assassins and then faced his own former ally, Mark Antony. In 31 B.C., Octavian vanquished the forces of Antony and his sponsor Cleopatra, the Egyptian queen, leaving Rome to his own command.

IMPERIAL ROME

During the early republican era, the Romans remained uncivilized, at least compared with their Greek contemporaries. At the time of Athens' Golden Age, the Romans were little more than rude farmers and villagers. In the late republican era, contact with Hellenistic Greece stimulated the first bloom of Roman literature. The Romans' greatest cultural achievements did not begin until the reign of Octavian, who called himself Caesar Augustus (ruled 27 B.C.–A.D. 14). Although the Senate called him Rome's "First Citizen," Augustus was in fact dictator of Rome from 27 B.C. onwards. His reign inaugurated the long succession of Roman emperors who would rule the Western world for five centuries.

Caesar Augustus established a period of relative peace and prosperity commonly called the **Pax Romana**, which lasted until the death of Emperor Marcus Aurelius [oh-REEL-yuss] (in A.D. 180). During his reign, Augustus carefully consolidated his imperial power, even while he preserved the illusion of republican rights and senatorial prerogatives. In the arts, he sponsored a building program that would make Rome the equal of the grand Hellenistic capitals which it now controlled. Augustus proclaimed proudly that he had found Rome a city of bricks and left it a city of marble.

Augustus' protégé, the epic poet Virgil (70–19 B.C.), stated Rome's cultural ambitions with more modesty. In his poem the *Aeneid*, Virgil acknowledged that other races would "hammer forth more delicately a breathing likeness out of bronze, coax living faces from the marble, [and] plead causes with more skill." "Romans," wrote Virgil, "concern yourselves with commanding the nations; your arts shall be to impose the rule of peace, to spare the submissive, and to crush the proud."[1]

Despite Virgil's proclamation, Caesar Augustus and, later, his successors were determined to develop a distinctive Roman civilization, even if much of it had to be borrowed from the Greeks. Two essential observations can be made of the Roman civilization of the late republic and the empire: firstly, the Romans avidly absorbed

---

THE WRITE IDEA

Compare the course of Roman history with that of the United States or of another great modern nation. What do the Romans' ambitions, achievements, and failures have in common with the modern historical experience?

classical Greek and Hellenistic civilization; and secondly, they remained resolutely practical and utilitarian in their attitude toward the arts and philosophy. For the Romans, culture had to serve the useful ends of justifying imperial power and providing comfort and entertainment for Roman citizens.

THE ART OF AN EMPIRE

Analyze the political message in examples of Roman imperial art.

After the leadership of Julius Caesar, virtually every Roman leader strove to leave a memory of himself in stone. The emperors of the Roman Empire built statues and buildings that were both political advertisements and artistic statements, impressing upon their people a message of their power and generosity expressed through the styles of classical and Hellenistic Greece. By adopting the Greek-style arts, the Romans could associate themselves with the prestige of classical Athens and Alexander the Great.

During the reign of Augustus the art of the Roman Empire began to flourish. Artists skillfully adapted classical Greek sculpture to the emperor's propaganda purposes. Augustus and his successors built elaborate new complexes at the center of Rome, the grandest of which was the Forum of Trajan, built at the height of Rome's power in the second century A.D.

SCULPTURE AS PROPAGANDA

Augustus was the first Roman ruler to place statues and busts of his own image in public squares and buildings. The so-called *Augustus of Primaporta* (Fig. **4.6**), discovered in a provincial Roman town, is typical of these official portraits. The figure's stance and proportions are reminiscent of Polyclitus' *Spear-Bearer* (see Fig. 3.9), the classical Greek statue greatly admired by the Romans. Augustus' face is slightly idealized, though still recognizable. The armor breastplate depicts his greatest diplomatic achievement, the return of Roman army standards captured by a foreign rival. The dolphin at his side alludes to the goddess Venus, mother of the Trojan hero Aeneas, from whom

4.3 *Ara Pacis Augustae* **(Altar of Augustan Peace), Rome, 13–9 B.C. Marble, 36 x 33 ft (11 x 10 m).**
This elaborately symbolic work represented Augustus' political program of peace and agrarian values. The right front panel depicts the sacrifice of Aeneas, an episode from Virgil's *Aeneid*.

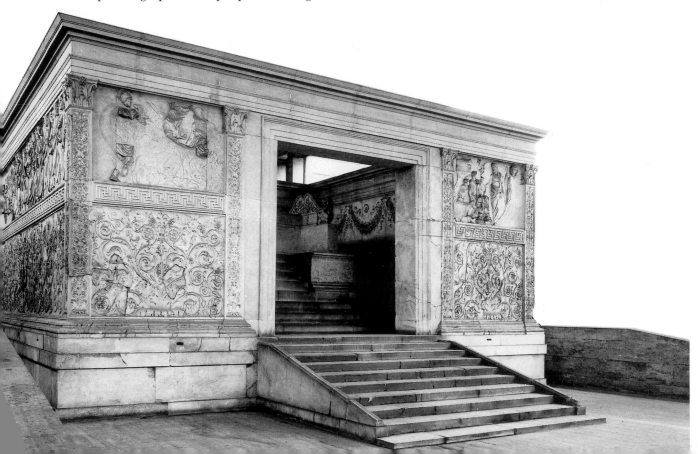

KEY CONCEPT

IMPERIALISM

The concepts of **empire** and **imperialism** suggest both great achievement and hateful oppression. An empire is a large territory or a number of territories dominated by a single political authority. The imperial authority may be a city-state such as Rome, or a nation such as Great Britain, which once controlled a vast empire including the present-day United States and Canada. Now, some call the United States itself an imperial power, dominating the smaller nations of Central and South America and the Caribbean.

Imperial authority often brings cultural progress and political unity to the diverse territories under its rule. For example, the Indian parliament still uses English, the language of its imperial oppressor, as a principal language, and only the English language transcends India's regional and cultural divisions. Ancient

Rome also brought the rule of law and a cosmopolitan culture to its imperial territories. Rome's provinces enjoyed these gifts at the cost of bowing to the Roman eagle and worshiping the Roman emperor.

The ancient Romans built their empire with an aggressive and well-trained army and a talent for efficient administration. By 265 B.C., the Romans controled all of the Italian peninsula. Within a hundred more years, it controlled much of Europe and the entire Mediterranean rim (Fig. **4.4**). Like the westward expansion of the United States during the 1800s, Rome's rise to power seemed to fulfill a divinely sanctioned national destiny. Unlike North American pioneers, however, Rome did not usually displace the residents of conquered territories. Instead, it instituted Roman law and culture alongside native customs and offered citizenship to the social elite of subject nations. Rome's imperial system was so vast and effective that it thrived under good emperors,

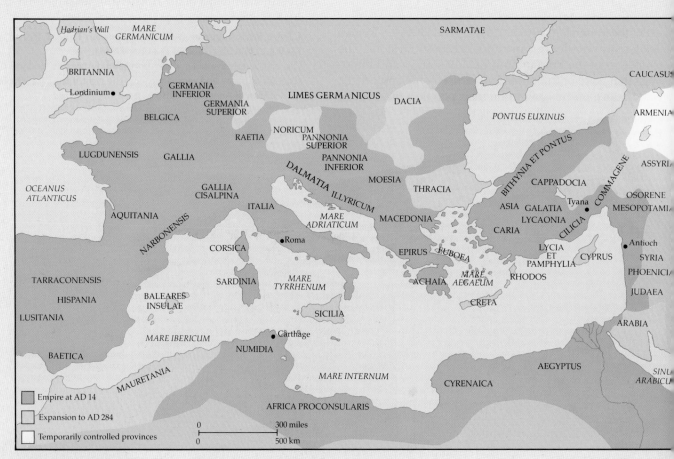

4.4 The Roman Empire.

Augustus claimed descent. By associating the emperor with gods, heroes, and Roman history, this work of art is effective propaganda.

A more elaborate work of sculptural propaganda was the *Ara Pacis Augustae* (Altar of Augustan Peace) (Fig. **4.3**). The *Ara Pacis* [AH-ruh PAH-kiss] shows how effectively the Romans adapted the classical style to convey a social and political message. The altar was built to commemorate Augustus' safe return from a campaign in Gaul. In a larger sense, it celebrated the emperor's twin goals of general peace (after a century of civil war) and a return to Rome's agrarian traditions. The altar itself and the wall

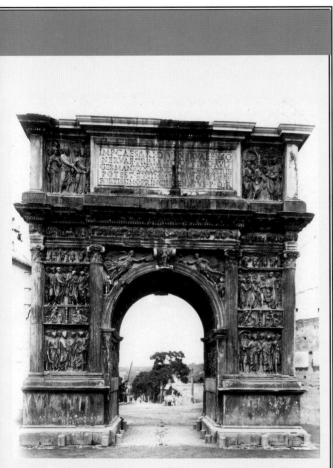

4.5 Arch of Trajan, Benevento, A.D. 114–117. Marble, height 51 ft (15.55 m).
In ancient Rome, the triumphal arch became a symbol of imperial power and achievement. Compare this arch with that built by Napoleon Bonaparte in the early 1800s (Fig. 12.4).

such as Caesar Augustus (see page 72) and Trajan [TRAY-jun] (see page 77), and survived under bad ones, such as Caligula and Nero (see list, page 72).

Later empires and would-be emperors measured themselves against the standard of Roman greatness (Fig. **4.5**). Examples from recent history are the French military genius Napoleon (see page 331), who adopted the symbols and fashions of imperial Rome, styling himself a world conqueror in the Roman mold, and Adolf Hitler (see page 392), who boasted that his Nazi regime would last a thousand years. Napoleon honored his victories with a triumphant arch in Paris that was twice the size of any in Rome, while Hitler ordered his architect to design buildings in Berlin that would surpass those of both Rome and Paris. In fact, an empire as vast and as durable as the empire of ancient Rome has not been achieved since.

4.6 *Augustus of Primaporta*, c. 20 B.C. Marble, height 6 ft 8 ins (2.03 m). Vatican Museums, Rome.
Caesar Augustus propagated such official images throughout his empire, fostering a personal cult of the emperor.

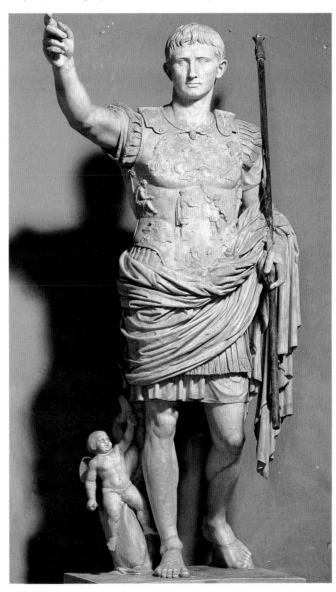

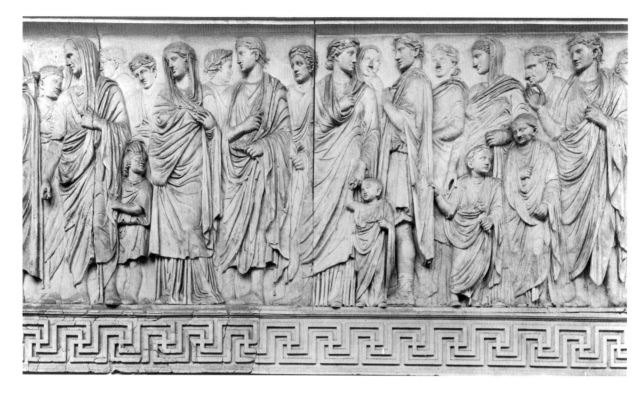

4.7 *Imperial Procession*, detail of the *Ara Pacis Augustae*, Rome, 13–9 B.C. Marble relief, height approx. 5 ft 3 ins (1.6 m).
Compare the Roman classical style of this procession to the Parthenon frieze (Fig. 3.19).

enclosure are decorated with relief sculpture, probably executed by Greek artists. On the screen enclosure, an elaborate two-part frieze consists of floral designs and the procession led by Augustus to consecrate the altar (Fig. **4.7**). The procession resembles the Parthenon frieze, except that the Parthenon glorified the dead heroes of Athens, while this frieze glorifies Augustus himself. Even the altar's site was symbolic of Augustus' program of peace – it

was built in a park that had once been a drill field for the Roman army.

THE FORUM OF TRAJAN

The most impressive monument to Augustus' reign was the forum he built at the center of Rome, of which little now remains. A **forum**, originally a "marketplace," was

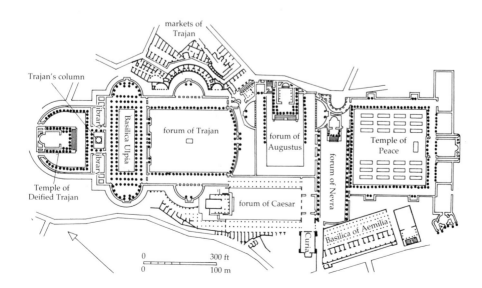

4.8 Plan of the Imperial forums, Rome.
Built to glorify imperial rulers, the forums crowded Rome's center with Greek-inspired temples and buildings. The largest forum was Trajan's, dominated by the imposing Basilica Ulpia.

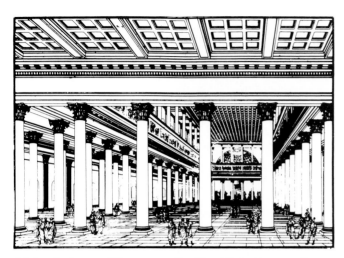

4.9 Apollodorus of Damascus, Basilica Ulpia, Forum of Trajan, Rome, A.D. 113. Reconstruction drawing of the interior. Imperial Romans transacted their legal affairs in such splendid public buildings.

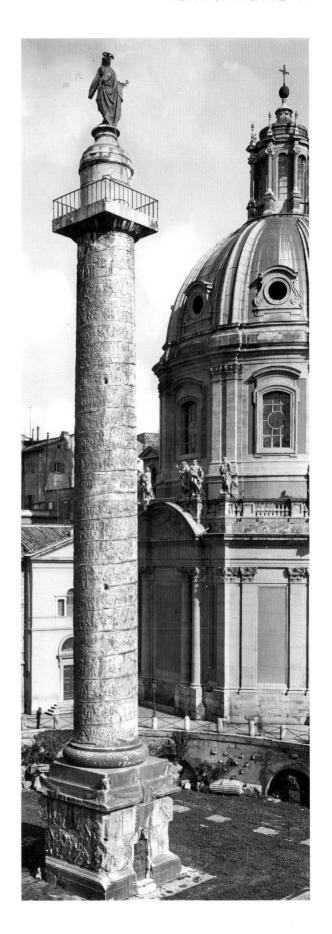

the social and political center of a Roman city. Rome's oldest forum, the republican Forum, was the site of important temples and law courts, as well as shops, banks, and schools. Julius Caesar and Augustus both built new forums, glorifying their own names, adjacent to the old republican Forum.

It was the Emperor Trajan (ruled A.D. 98–117) who built the grandest of the imperial forums (Fig. **4.8**), a suitable monument to the peace and prosperity which characterized his reign. The Forum of Trajan included an expansive marketplace, a hall of justice, and two libraries, one each for Greek and Latin texts. The hall of justice of Trajan's Forum, named the Basilica Ulpia (Fig. **4.9**), was a typical Roman **basilica** – a rectangular public hall, usually with a flat ceiling. The Basilica Ulpia's roof was supported by double rows of handsome Corinthian columns. Traffic circulated outside the columns, and court was held in semicircular niches recessed in the end walls. The basilica was a traditional Roman building, old-fashioned even in Trajan's day but still expressing the imperial grandeur of Rome. Two centuries later, the prestigious basilica form was adapted for the first great Christian churches in Rome (see page 114).

The centerpiece of Trajan's Forum was the Column of Trajan (Fig. **4.10**), a sculpted column depicting scenes of the emperor's victories over the rebellious Dacians (in

4.10 Apollodorus of Damascus, Column of Trajan, Rome, A.D. 106–13. Marble, height of base 18 ft (5.5 m), height of column 97 ft (29.6 m).
In Trajan's time, the column could be viewed from the upper stories of the adjoining libraries and Basilica Ulpia.

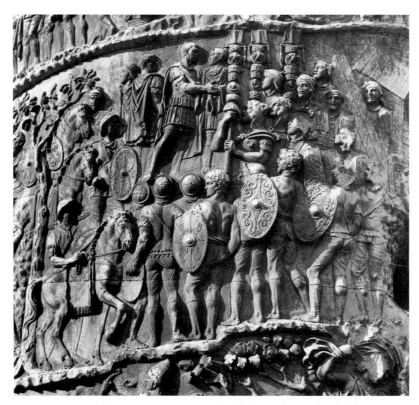

4.11 *Trajan Addressing his Troops* (the *Adlocutio*), detail of Trajan's Column, Rome, A.D. 113. Height of figures approx. 27¹/₂ ins (70 cm). Note the larger scale of the figure of Trajan (center top), which identifies him clearly. What realistic details can you identify in the figures' dress and posture?

present-day Romania). The campaign was a suitable topic for imperial propaganda: the gold from Dacian mines funded public welfare and imperial construction during Trajan's reign. The column is, nonetheless, a remarkable work of art. The narrative sculpture spirals around the column to a length of more than 650 feet (200 m). The story is told in a continuous scene, as if to recount a series of uninterrupted events. The Emperor Trajan appears frequently to indicate distinct episodes – from addressing the troops (Fig. **4.11**) to the display of Dacian commanders' severed heads. While the sculptural style is still governed by Augustan classicism, the concept of a continuous relief narrative was unprecedented in the Greek world.

THE ARCHITECTURE OF ROME

Explain the Romans' important innovations in large-scale public architecture.

For all their splendor, many of ancient Rome's great buildings (Fig. **4.12**) were dedicated to practical ends: the basilicas served as areas where Romans could settle their legal and political affairs; they accommodated religious ceremonies (a matter of civic obligation); the baths were where men exchanged gossip while lounging in the pools; and in the library women might read a Hellenistic romance. Many Roman public buildings were used daily and served multiple purposes, in contrast to classical Greece, where most significant buildings had only a religious function. The Romans constructed their public buildings on a grand scale, decorating the buildings' interiors with colored marble, gilded statues, and wall paintings. The grandeur and comfort of Roman buildings depended on the Romans' revolutionary innovations in construction, particularly the use of concrete and the arch.

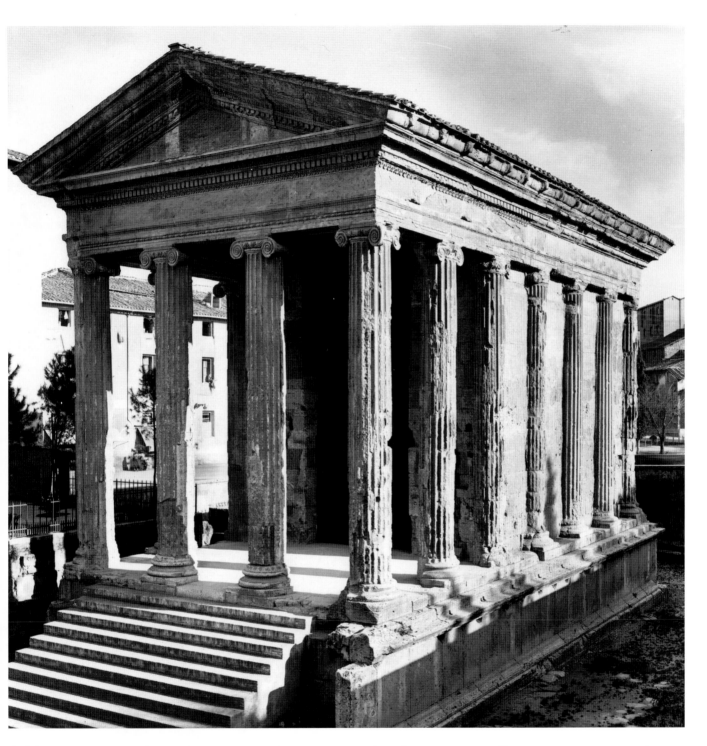

4.12 Temple of Portunus (also known as Temple of Fortuna Virilis), Rome, late 2nd century B.C.
The Roman variation of the classical Greek temple had a clear orientation to the front. They were commonly placed on forums, overlooking the Roman city's civic center.

THE ROMANS AS BUILDERS

The Romans developed the **arch** into a highly flexible architectural form, which could be used in many types of constructions. The arch was superior to the post-and-lintel design of Greek temples (see Fig. 3.12) for a simple technical reason – too much weight on the stone lintel would cause it to snap. Because in an arch the stones are compressed and not bent, it can bear more weight than the post-and-lintel. The arch's simplest use was in bridges, such as the Pont du Gard in France (Fig. **4.13**), in which

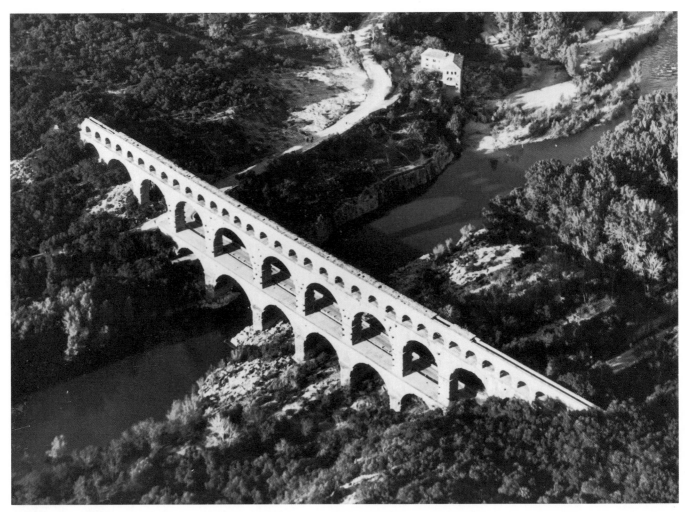

4.13 Pont du Gard, near Nîmes, France, late 1st century B.C. Stone, height 162 ft (49.4 m).

4.14 The arch and its applications.

In the basic **arch** (*a*), wedge-shaped stones called *voussoirs* transferred the weight to load-bearing vertical piers. A connected series of arches created a **barrel** or **tunnel** (*b*) vault. The intersection of two barrel vaults formed a **cross vault** (*c*), open on four sides and supported by piers at the four corners. In a **dome**, a series of arches intersected around a central axis.

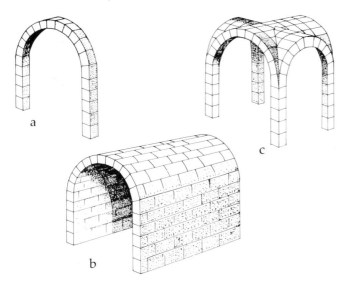

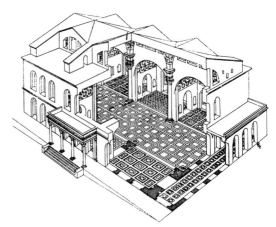

4.15 Reconstruction drawing of the Basilica of Constantine (after Huelsen).

three series of arches are stacked on top of each other. Running across the top of the Pont du Gard was an aqueduct that carried water to a provincial Roman city. While arched bridges and aqueducts were essential to commerce and everyday living, Roman architects learned to use the arch for more daring constructions. The **barrel vault** (Fig. **4.14**) could bear tremendous weight and was often used as a structural support in buildings' foundations. The **cross vault** was often connected in a series to form an open rectangular hall, with ceilings as high as 180 feet (55 m). The **dome** created a spacious and majestic interior space, of which the grandest was in the Pantheon (see Fig. 4.20).

Equal in importance to the arch was the use of concrete in Roman building. Concrete was a mixture of rubble and a mortar that hardened when mixed with water. Concrete was customarily used with brick to construct a building's core; the exterior was then decorated with a marble veneer. This enabled the Romans to construct buildings with the grand appearance of Greek classicism but without the expense of a quarried stone core.

ROMAN BUILDINGS

The flexibility and economy of Roman construction and the cramped conditions of building in Rome produced buildings of a different nature from those of classical and Hellenistic Greece. Instead of creating spectacular exterior settings, like the Parthenon's in Athens, the Romans created spacious interiors with lavish marbles, mosaics, and gilding, and emphasized the usefulness of their buildings, in keeping with the practical spirit of Roman civilization.

The most spectacular interiors are those in buildings devoted to recreation. The Roman baths were the ancients' combination of health spa, beauty salon, public library, and shopping mall. The baths' central hall consisted of connected cross vaults soaring high above the floor. These vaults were supported on either side by barrel-vaulted chambers, like the ones that remain from the Basilica of Constantine (Figs. **4.15** and **4.16**). Under this spectacular vaulting, decorated with colored marble

4.16 Basilica of Constantine (or Maxentius), Rome, c. 306–13. Brick and concrete.
The high vaulted ceilings and large windows allowed light to flood the spacious interior, illuminating the colorful mosaic decoration. This basilica, the only law court built in the grand style of the Roman baths, was the last great pagan building of ancient Rome.

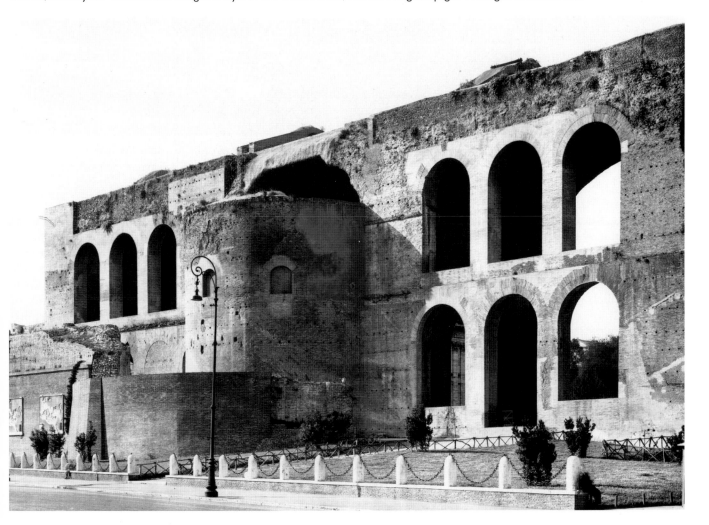

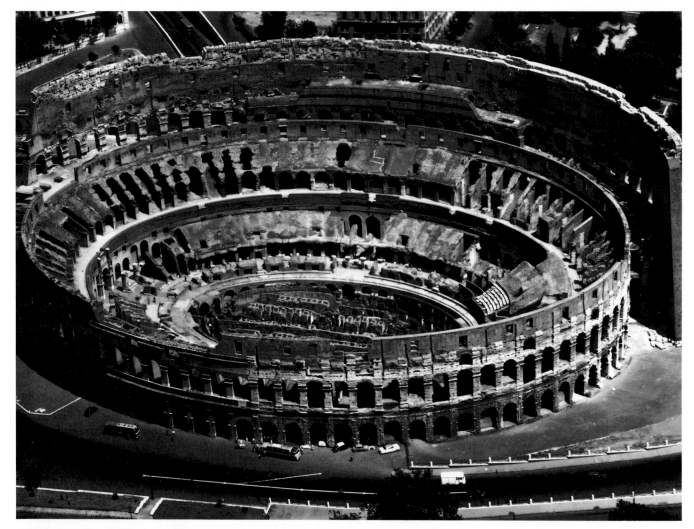

4.17 Colosseum, Rome, c. A.D. 72–80. Long axis 620 ft (189 m), short axis 513 ft (156 m), height 160 ft (49 m).
Site of bloody spectacles, the Colosseum's exterior was nevertheless austerely classical, decorated by relief columns in three different classical orders.

and painting, Romans languished in pools of hot, warm, and cold water. The Baths of Caracalla also housed a separate swimming pool, gymnasium, massage and steam rooms, restaurants, and a library. It is no wonder that Romans flocked to the baths, and that an elaborate system of aqueducts was required to supply these baths with water.

The Romans loved entertainment as much as they loved pleasure, and theaters, amphitheaters, and race-tracks were spread throughout the city. Romans crowded their stadiums for entertainments that were every bit the match of today's stadium events. The most famous Roman amphitheater was the Colosseum (Fig. 4.17), which dominated the skyline of imperial Rome from its location near the republican Forum. The Colosseum's outer walls rose nearly 160 feet (49 m) high. Inside, a complex arrangement of arches and barrel vaulting supported seating for fifty thousand spectators. The arena floor could be landscaped for wild animal combats or flooded for mock naval battles. The Romans preferred their entertainment to be spiced with violence and gore. According to the historian Suetonius, five thousand wild beasts were slaughtered in a single day at the Colosseum's inauguration. Thousands of gladiators and some Christian martyrs also met their deaths on the Colosseum's sand floor. Such scenes of Roman cruelty make the padded combat of today's sporting events seem rather tame by comparison.

The Pantheon The beauty and grandeur of one Roman building far outweighed its usefulness. The Pantheon (Fig. 4.18) was famed for its magnificent dome, rising above the interior in a perfect hemisphere, resting on a cylinder of exactly the same diameter (144 feet; 44 m; Fig. 4.19). The Pantheon's perfect geometry and lavish interior decoration made it one of antiquity's most admired buildings. For a Roman, to stand under this magnificent dome was like standing under the heavens themselves.

The Pantheon was built around 120 by the Emperor

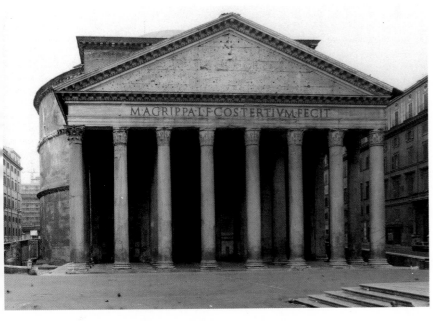

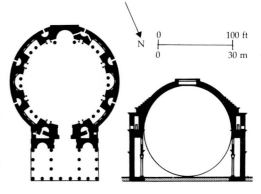

4.19 Pantheon, Rome, c. A.D. 120. Plan and cross-section.

4.18 Pantheon, Rome, c. A.D. 120. Height of portico 59 ft (18 m).
To Romans, the Pantheon symbolized the unity of the cosmos and of the Roman imperial world.

Hadrian at the height of Rome's power. The temple was dedicated to the seven planetary gods, although Hadrian also used it for Senate meetings and other ceremonial occasions. Seen from the outside, the Pantheon now appears rather dull, especially as it has been stripped of its marble covering and bronze pedimental relief sculpture. Inside, however, the observer can still sense the building's original beauty (Fig. **4.20**). The dome was punctuated by a 30-foot (9 m) opening called an **oculus**. The oculus was the principal source of interior light and also repeated the interior's geometric motif. Around the walls were niches, containing divine statues and recesses behind Corinthian columns of colored marble. With its geometric rhythms and soaring interior, the Pantheon seemed to merge all of creation in a perfectly harmonious whole.

ROMAN ART AND DAILY LIFE

Analyze what the arts of painting and sculpture reveal about the lives of ordinary Romans.

The imperial buildings of Rome tell us much about the Romans as engineers, conquerors, and administrators, but little about them as ordinary people. Christian historians later condemned the licentious style of Roman living, blaming Rome's fall on sinful ways. In fact the daily life of a Roman was modest and centered on the family. The Romans' character and customs are best revealed in the arts of painting and portrait sculpture, preserved in the excavated sites of Pompeii and Herculaneum in Italy.

ROMAN DAILY LIFE

In ancient Rome, family ties were the basis of social identity. The male head of the family, known as the paterfamilias [PAH-ter fah-MEE-lee-us], controled the family's membership and its fortunes. A newborn infant was not legally a family member until the paterfamilias had recognized the infant and given it his name. Unrecognized children were sometimes given for adoption to other families. More commonly, newborns (especially girls) were "exposed," that is, left in the forum to die or be adopted as foundlings. Bearing a family name through adoption was no disadvantage: the young Octavian became Rome's first emperor after he had been adopted by Julius Caesar.

Married women enjoyed relative freedom, but still suffered confined social roles. Roman women accompanied their husbands in public, often to banquets and other

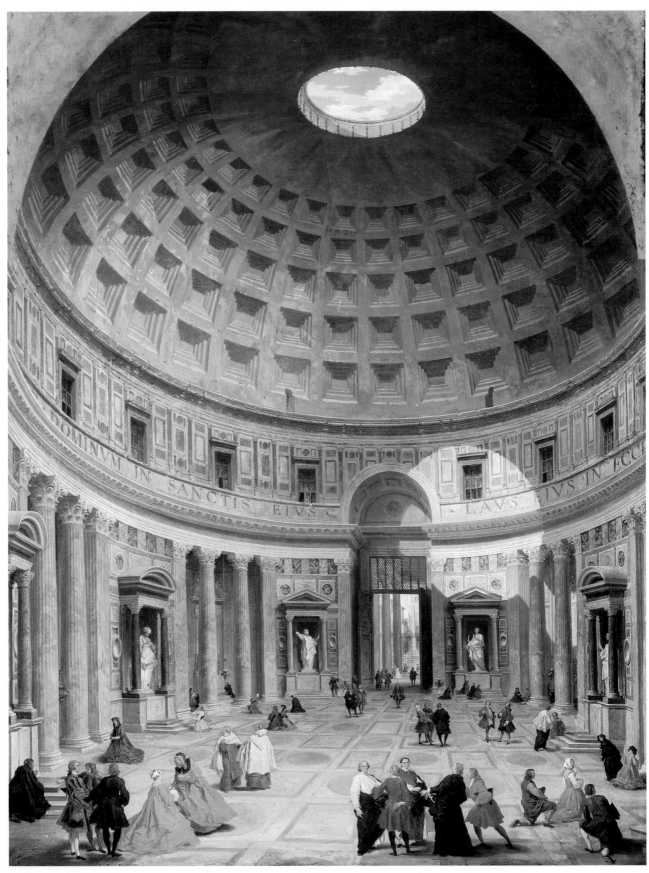

4.20 Giovanni Paolo Pannini, *Interior of the Pantheon,* **c. 1740. Oil on canvas, 50¹/₂ x 39 ins (128 x 99 cm). National Gallery of Art, Washington, D.C., Samuel H. Kress Collection, 1939.**
This eighteenth-century painting provides the best view of the Pantheon's grand interior. Disregard the visitors in modern dress, and imagine the building as it appeared in Roman times: the coffered ceiling covered with gilded bronze, statues disputing a point of Stoic philosophy.

WINDOW ON DAILY LIFE

A MARRIAGE CONTRACT OF THE ROMAN ERA

In the Roman era, marriage among the upper classes customarily required only a simple contract between husband and wife (Fig. **4.21**). A Roman wife maintained control of her own property, including the right to her dowry should the husband seek divorce. The marriage contract below bound a couple living in Alexandria, the cosmopolitan Hellenistic capital, in the first century B.C.

Let Apollonia be the wife of Philiscus, having been persuaded by him that it is fitting for her to be his wife, and let her have mastery in common with him over all their possessions. And let Philiscus provide for Apollonia all the things that she needs and her clothing and all the rest that is suitable for a married woman to have provided for her – and let him do this wherever they live,

according as their means allow. And let him take no other wife but Apollonia, and no concubine, and let him have no boyfriends or beget children from any other woman so long as Apollonia is living nor inhabit any other household than the one over which Apollonia rules; nor let him repudiate her or do violence to her or treat her badly or alienate any of their property in a manner which is unfair to Apollonia. If he is caught doing any of these things ... then let him pay back immediately to Apollonia her dowry of two talents and four thousand drachmas of bronze. By the same token, let Apollonia not be permitted to spend the day or the night away from the house of Philiscus without his knowledge, nor may she sleep with another man, nor may she squander their common household property, nor may she disgrace Philiscus in the ways in which men get disgraced. But if Apollonia willingly does any of these things, let her be sent away from Philiscus, and let him repay to her the dowry simply within ten days of her departure.[2]

4.21 *Portrait of a Magistrate and His Wife*, **Pompeii, Italy, mid-1st century** A.D. **Mural painting, 22⅞ x 20½ ins (58 x 52 cm). National Archeological Museum, Naples.**
This Pompeiian couple was well-educated, as seen in the scroll, stylus, and wax tablet that they hold. Roman married couples frequently portrayed themselves together.

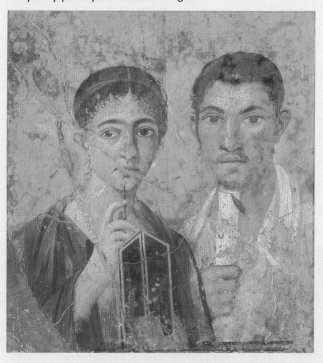

KEY CONCEPT

THE ANTIQUARIAN SPIRIT

The antique store beside a country road is selling more than old dressers and pictures: it nurtures the antiquarian spirit – the desire to study, collect, and imitate things of the past. Antiquarians often believe that antique arts represent a higher standard of beauty and craftsmanship than those of the present. By collecting fine objects of the past, however, antiquarians help to sustain cultural traditions. Surrounded by their relics, they revive the past.

Both the Hellenistic Greeks and the Romans were avid antiquarians. Hellenistic kings founded the ancient world's first great libraries and museums in Alexandria, Egypt, and Pergamon in Asia Minor. In these centers, scholars meticulously edited classical manuscripts and undertook the first textual criticism. The first scholarly editions of Homer were compiled in Hellenistic libraries. When the Romans conquered the Hellenistic world in the second century B.C., they stepped into a vast museum of Greek antiquities. The Roman conquerors shipped these treasures home to Italy, where fine Greek originals were used by the wealthy to decorate their villas and gardens (Fig. **4.22**). When this supply was exhausted, Roman sculptors learned to make precise mechanical copies of Greek statuary and painting.

The Romans' plunder of Greek civilization should not obscure their antiquarian achievement. Much of what we know about classical Greece is owed to Roman collectors, scholars, and artists, who preserved Greek art by imitating it. The antique legacy of Rome proved an enormous stimulus to later artists, especially in the Renaissance (see Chapter 8). The antiquarian labors of the scholar, connoisseur, and collector often light the fuse for a new burst of artistic creativity.

Antiquarianism is often a creative pursuit in its own right. By studying a fragment of sculpture or an ancient manuscript, the antiquarian imaginatively recreates the human spirit contained in that antique object. The twentieth-century originator of psychoanalysis, Sigmund Freud (see page 402), was an avid collector of classical and Egyptian antiquities. To him these ancient objects represented a riddle of the past – a mystery much like the dreams and musings of his patients.

CRITICAL QUESTION

How valuable to you and your community are relics of the past like historic buildings and neighborhoods? How should the value of preservation be weighed against the rights of those living in the present?

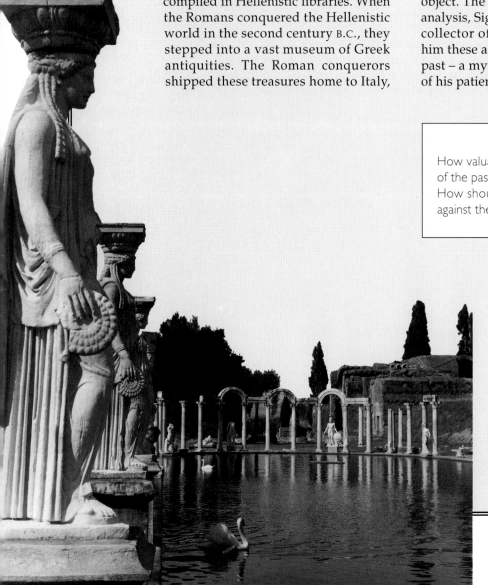

4.22 Hadrian's Villa, Tivoli, Italy, A.D. 124–33.
The emperor Hadrian, like many wealthy Romans, collected original Greek statuary or commissioned Roman copies to decorate his estate.

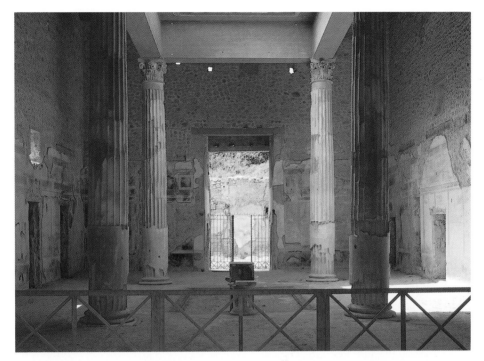

4.23 Atrium, House of the Silver Wedding, Pompeii, Italy, early 1st century A.D. This house belonging to a wealthy Pompeiian family is much grander than the norm. The Corinthian columns surround a pool in the room's center.

public occasions. As in Greece, they supervised the household, but in Rome women might also hold and inherit property. Women could divorce their husbands and be divorced, often through a simple public declaration. If her husband died or was sent into exile, a wife would inherit her husband's household and wealth. She could entertain suitors, take a lover, or cloister herself in mourning, sheltered from the world's hypocrisy.

Pompeii The houses, forums, theaters, and amphitheaters of one entire Roman city were preserved by a great accident of history, the destruction of Pompeii [pom-PAY-ee] in A.D. 79. Pompeii was buried under a 15-foot (4.6 m) layer of ash when the nearby volcano Mount Vesuvius erupted and spewed its ash over the city. The town's inhabitants were smothered by toxic gas, and their bodies left hardened volcanic casts where they fell. The Pompeiians' houses and domestic possessions were preserved virtually intact and were first excavated in the eighteenth century, offering a glimpse of the Roman household and its artistic decoration.

Even the finest Pompeiian city houses were relatively dark and crowded. The largest houses were centered on an **atrium**, a reception room with an open roof and a pool beneath. The atrium in the House of the Silver Wedding (Fig. **4.23**) is exceptional in its size and grandeur. The other rooms were windowless, and usually several people slept in the same room. The most pleasant aspect of the finer

houses was an adjacent garden, surrounded by a colonnade, where Pompeiians dined.

In fine Roman households, the walls themselves were decorated with lavish paintings in a variety of styles. A famous example is contained in the so-called Villa of the Mysteries (Fig. **4.24**) in Pompeii, named for the wall painting in its spacious dining room. The paintings apparently depict the re-enactment of scenes from the life of the god Dionysus. One section shows a group of women miming the birth of the god; one woman is in the throes of labor and sits in the lap of a companion, while a nude figure on the right celebrates the birth with cymbals and a dance. Other wall paintings from the same period create elaborate architectural perspectives, probably to lend rooms a sense of spaciousness. Such pictures show that Roman artists could master large subjects, including the human figure. In general, however, wall paintings of this period were not pictorial masterpieces and were derived from superior Hellenistic examples. The Romans were more interested in pleasant domestic surroundings than in high standards of artistic beauty.

A minor Roman art related to painting was **mosaic**, pictures made from tiny bits of colored marble or ceramic cemented to a floor or wall. Like so many Roman arts, mosaic developed in ancient Greece and was avidly imported to Roman cities. Hellenistic designs often consisted of geometric patterns or mythological scenes. One of the most imitated pavement mosaics was the *Unswept*

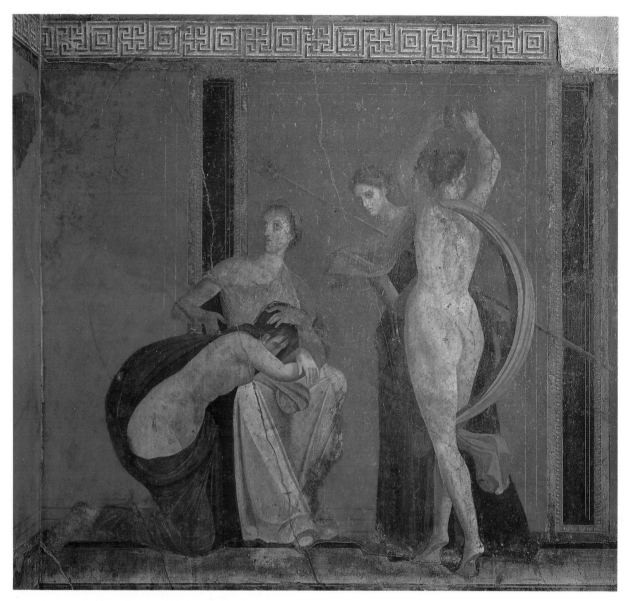

4.24 *The Dionysian Mysteries* (detail), Villa of the Mysteries, Pompeii, Italy, c. 60 B.C.
The scenes depict the rites of initiation into the cult of Dionysus. At right a nude worshiper of Dionysus dances ecstatically, while the initiate (left) prepares for a ritual flagellation.

Floor (Fig. **4.25**), attributed to the Hellenistic artist Sosus. With his delicate bits of mosaic tile, Sosus created realistic effects such as the chicken's leg, the fish's skeleton, and the snail's shell. In later Rome, mosaic was used for the more exalted purpose of religious art.

Portrait Sculpture The Romans' veneration of the family and interest in realism can be seen in the most original of Roman arts, portrait sculpture. To honor and remember their loved ones, the Romans commissioned portrait busts. Portrait sculpture of the Roman era showed attention to individual detail and in some cases a psychological insight into character. Early Roman portraits captured the rugged naturalism of republican Rome, when Romans

---

THE WRITE IDEA

Imagine the city or town in which you live were buried, just as it is today, and uncovered a thousand years from now. Write the account of archaeologists excavating a local site. What physical evidence might be the most puzzling to future scholars and scientists? What arts of daily life might interest students a thousand years from now?

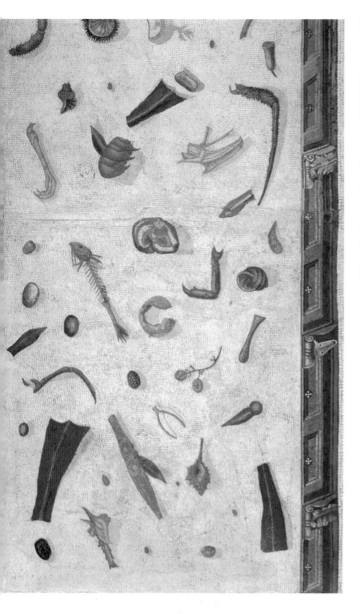

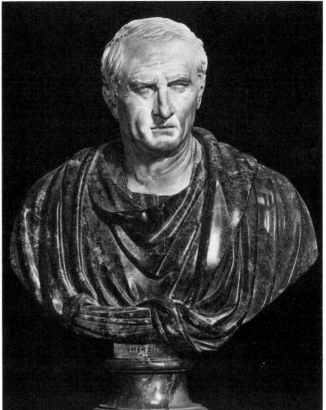

4.25 Left **Sosus, *Unswept Floor* (detail). Roman copy of Hellenistic original, 2nd century B.C. Mosaic. Vatican Museums, Rome.**
Like much Roman decorative art, this realistic floor mosaic was copied from an original by Sosus at Pergamon, the Hellenistic capital.

4.26 Above **Bust of Cicero, 1st century B.C. Marble, life-size. Uffizi, Florence.**
Inspired by the Romans' veneration of their ancestors, Roman sculptors excelled in portraiture. Here the late Republican orator and philosopher Cicero is portrayed as a man of principle and deep conviction.

proudly extolled the virtues of courage, patriotism, and hard work. The bust of Cicero (Fig. **4.26**) suggests the hard-headed realism and self-reliance of this leader of the republican era.

ROMAN THEATER AND MUSIC

Characterize the ancient Romans' tastes in popular entertainment.

The ancient Romans considered public entertainment to be a birthright of the Roman citizen. In Rome itself, lavish public shows helped occupy the sometimes threatening masses of poor and unemployed. In the provinces, theater and sporting spectacles were a measure of the good life. In theater, the Romans produced sophisticated comedies that were imitated by later dramatic geniuses, such as Shakespeare (see page 248) and the French playwright Molière. Roman music was largely an accompaniment to theater, sport, and banqueting.

ROMAN THEATER

The origins of Roman drama lie probably in ancient religious dances. The development of a genuine theater, however, began with the influx of Greek culture. The first Roman play with a plot was attributed to a Greek slave of the third century B.C., and nearly all known Roman plays, both comedy and tragedy, are derived from Greek originals. Comedy and tragedy coexisted in the Roman theater, although comedy was more popular, and both became important influences on later drama.

Romans borrowed their comedy directly from the comic theater of Hellenistic times, with its stock characters and slapstick comic devices. Audiences were well acquainted with Hellenistic comedy's misers, braggart soldiers, and good-hearted prostitutes. The first well-known Roman comic playwright was Plautus (c. 254–184 B.C.), whose plays apparently all followed Greek plots. Plautus [PLAH-tus] relied heavily on the comedy of exaggerated and absurd situations known as **farce**, a style which satisfied the Romans' taste for coarse humor. Roman audiences were known to ask for a performing bear show between acts of a play. Despite his audiences' low demands, Plautus' plays are still admired for their wit and literacy.

A more important innovator in Roman drama was Terence (193–159 B.C.), who developed character more fully than was usual in Hellenistic comedy. Terence instituted more complicated double plots, often revolving around mistaken identities. A favorite device was a boy and girl who think they are twins but still fall in love. In the final scene they are revealed as adopted orphans who are free to marry. Like his predecessors, Terence set his plays in Greece and used Greek characters – it was easier to mock the folly of the Greeks than that of his Roman audience. Terence's plays were widely read throughout the Middle Ages and frequently adapted: the medieval canoness Hrotsvit (see page 149) wrote Christianized versions of Terence's plays, and Shakespeare rather frankly borrowed one of Terence's plots in his *Comedy of Errors*.

The most important Roman tragedian was Seneca (c. 4 B.C.–A.D. 65), who adapted Greek stories by making them more sensational and moralistic. In Seneca's version of *Oedipus*, a pregnant Jocasta rips her incestuous offspring from the womb. Roman tragedy's gruesome plots appealed to the same coarse Roman tastes as comic farce. Its melodramatic exaggeration was, again, much imitated in the English theater of Shakespeare's era.

Under the Roman Empire, the popularity of relatively literate playwrights such as Plautus and Terence faded, to be replaced by bawdier theatrical entertainments. There was rugged competition for audiences in imperial Rome. Spectators were known to leave the theater in midperformance to see a gladiator contest nearby. To keep the public's interest, playwrights and theaters turned to simpler dramatic forms such as pantomime, in which actors used no words. A pantomime might be performed entirely by one actor, accompanied by a chorus. Theaters also mounted elaborate and often obscene spectacles, including mock sea battles that required the theater or amphitheater to be flooded. Farcical comedies mocked social and religious practices, and eventually led the early Christian Church to threaten to expel believers who attended the theater. Roman theater continued to decline and in the fifth century A.D. barbarian emperors halted dramatic performances altogether.

Roman theaters (Fig. **4.27**) were gigantic physical structures with multi-storied stages. Their auditoriums could accommodate as many as sixty thousand spectators. Unlike the classical Greek theaters, the Roman auditorium joined stage and seating into one architectural unit. The stage was narrow and was raised several feet (1–2 m). Behind the stage, a façade called the *scaenae frons* [SAY-nay fronz] rose two or three stories high (Fig. **4.28**). The *scaenae frons* was ornately decorated with pedimented niches, statues, and gilded columns and doors. By the first century B.C., some theaters were equipped with a curtain that was raised from a slot in the stage floor.

As with the Greeks, Roman tragic and comic actors wore masks and wigs. Masks were necessary in part because men played all the roles. Actors had little social standing and were often slaves, kept by their masters for entertainment.

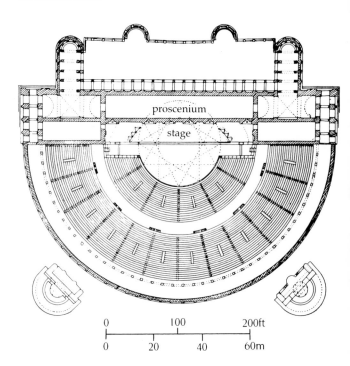

4.27 Plan of the Theater of Marcellus, Rome, 23–13 B.C.
Stage and seating are joined to form a single, freestanding architectural unit.

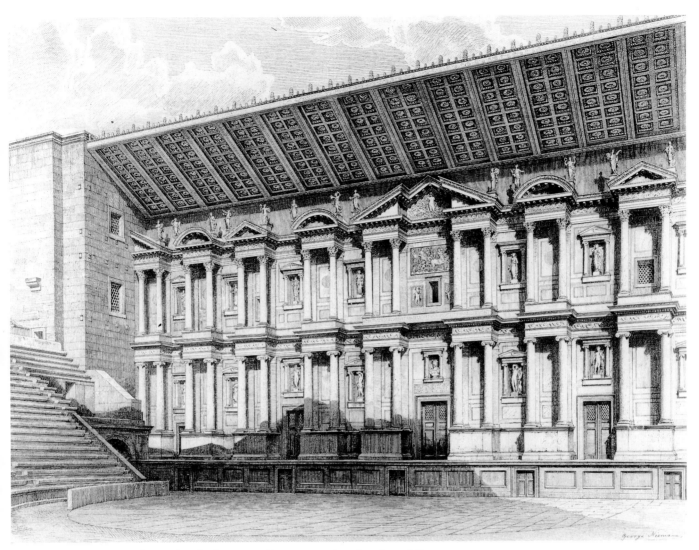

4.28 Roman Theater at Aspendos, 2nd century. Reconstruction drawing of the *scaenae*.
The elaborate, two-storied *scaenae frons* was equipped with several doors, allowing the stage to serve easily as a street scene. What modern plays might be easily accommodated to this stage?

MUSIC AND DANCE

Roman music and dance were strongly associated with bawdy entertainments and orgiastic banquets. The Romans almost certainly imitated the musical forms and instruments of Greek civilization. However, there is little evidence that they shared the Greeks' interest in musical theory. Like the Greeks, the Romans believed that music could have a great emotional effect on the listener. In fact, Roman orators were known to have musicians stand behind them and strike the desired tone at a particular moment in their speech. In their military processions Romans played a **tuba**, a long, straight trumpet, probably invented by the Etruscans. The Romans later also used a horn (Latin *cornu*) with circular tubing, something like today's French horn.

The most spectacular musical instrument used by the Romans was an organ called the *hydraulis* [high-DRAW-liss]. The *hydraulis* had a wide harmonic range and produced piercing tones, easily heard across the expanses of a Roman amphitheater (Fig. **4.29**). Christians later associated the *hydraulis* with religious persecution, which the Romans carried out as public entertainment and accompanied by music. Because of this stigma, the organ was banned from Christian churches for several centuries.

The Romans also adapted versions of the Greek *aulos* (pipes) (see page 65) and the *cithara* [SITH-uh-ruh], a large twelve-stringed lyre. Such instruments were used to accompany poetry in the Greek fashion. On being told that Rome was afire, the Emperor Nero supposedly took up his lyre (not a fiddle, as the saying goes) and sang of ancient Troy in flames. Nero was an exception – an emperor who desired to be an actor and a musician. In most cases, musicians were professionals and treated as menial servants.

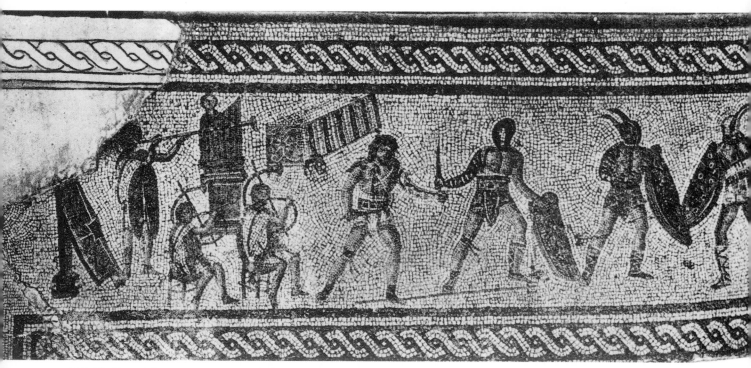

4.29 Gladiatorial contest, accompanied by orchestra. Mosaic from villa near Zilten, North Africa, c. A.D. 70. Museum of Antiquities, Tripoli.
The musicians play a *hydraulis* or organ, a long trumpet, and two curved *corni*, or horns.

THE ROMAN POETS

Identify the achievements of Roman lyric, satire, and epic poetry that most influenced later authors.

Like most other Roman arts, Latin poetry grew up under the powerful influence of Greek civilization. Still, the lyric poet Catullus and the epic poet Virgil created their own significant variations on Greek poetic forms. In poetic satire, Roman poets made their most unique contribution to the Western literary tradition.

EARLY ROMAN POETRY

Poets in late republican Rome imitated the polished forms and meters of Hellenistic verse. Their poetic works circulated among an educated elite that was well versed in Hellenistic literature. The lyric poet Catullus (c. 84–c. 54 B.C.) was part of that elite, an urbane, versatile poet, writing a variety of wedding songs, elegies, and gossipy personal lyrics. He had studied the Greeks well – among his works is a translation of a fragment by Sappho (see page 45).

Catullus is best remembered as a love poet. He wrote about twenty-five poems concerning his love affair with "Lesbia." Lesbia was actually an aristocratic woman named Clodia, sister to a prominent Roman politician and wife to a consul. Catullus' poems frankly disclosed his feelings, from the foolish enthusiasm of new love to the final bitter recrimination.

> *Enough, Catullus, of this silly whining;*
> *What you can see is lost, write off as lost.*
> *Not long ago the sun was always shining,*
> *And, loved as no girl ever will be loved,*
> *She led the way and you went dancing after.*
> *Those were the days of lovers' games and laughter*
> *When anything you wanted she approved;*
> *That was a time when the sun truly shone.*
> *But now she's cold, you must learn to cool;*
> *Weak though you are, stop groping for what's gone,*
> *Stop whimpering, and be stoically resigned.*
> *Goodbye, my girl. Catullus from now on*
> *Is adamant; he has made up his mind:*
> *He won't beg for your favor like a bone.*
> *You'll feel the cold, though, you damned bitch, when men*
> *Leave you alone. What life will you have then?*
> *Who'll visit you? Who'll think you beautiful? Who'll*
> *Be loved by you? Parade you as his own?*
> *Whom will you kiss and nibble then?*
> *   Oh fool,*
> *Catullus, stop this, stand firm, become stone.*[3]

CATULLUS
"To an Unfaithful Lover"

In its easy mixture of colloquial language and learned allusions, Catullus' poetry was unique in its time and widely admired by his successors.

The poet Ovid [AHH-vid] (43 B.C.–A.D. 17) was banished from Rome in late life. His crime may have been to witness a sexual impropriety by the emperor's granddaughter. Ovid's poetic masterpiece was the *Metamorphoses*, a sprawling collection of stories from classical and Near Eastern sources. The *Metamorphoses* was a source for some of the best-known works of later European writers, including Geoffrey Chaucer's *Canterbury Tales* and William Shakespeare's *A Midsummer Night's Dream*.

VIRGIL'S ROMAN EPIC

Under Caesar Augustus, Latin literature enjoyed its "golden age," in some forms equaling its Greek predecessors. Of course, the greatest Greek poems were Homer's epics, and the golden age produced Rome's answer to the *Iliad* and *Odyssey*. The great Roman epic was the *Aeneid* [ee-NEE-id], composed by the poet known as Virgil (70–19 B.C.). Virgil was already an established poet when he began the *Aeneid*, and had written poems celebrating traditional Roman values. With the *Aeneid*, he not only wrote a sprawling tale of passion and heroism: he also served Augustus' propagandistic aim of justifying imperial power and predicting a future of peace and order.

The *Aeneid* (composed 29–19 B.C.) tells of Aeneas, a Trojan warrior who leaves his burning city to travel to Italy. Aeneas is destined to subdue Italy's hostile residents and blaze a glorious path for the Roman race. In his story, Virgil combines the themes of the *Iliad* (the story of a great war) and the *Odyssey* (the story of a hero's adventurous journey):

> *This is a tale of arms and of a man. Fated to be an exile, he was the first to sail from the land of Troy and reach Italy, at its Lavinian shore. He met many tribulations on his way both by land and on the ocean … [And] he had also to endure great suffering in warfare.*[4]

4.30 *Dido Sacrificing*. **Illustration to Virgil's** *Aeneid*, **early 13th century. Vatican Library, Rome.**
Virgil's epic poem has been read and illustrated many times in Western civilization from the poet's day right up to the modern era.

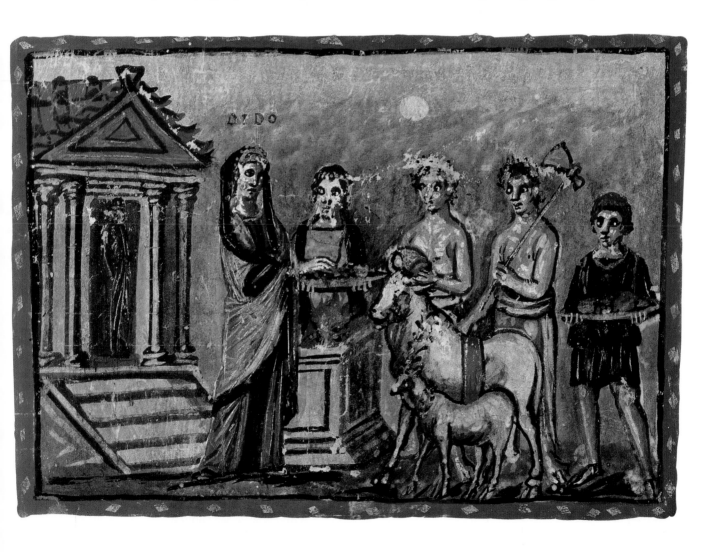

CRITICAL QUESTION

Do you believe that destiny controls some part of your life's course? The life of your family? Or nation? Discuss the ways that destiny might affect the course of a career, love, war, politics, and history.

The *Aeneid*'s unifying theme is destiny, and the poem bestowed upon Aeneas a destiny that anticipated Augustus' own. Roman tradition held that Aeneas was chosen by the gods to found the Latin race. In a similar way, Virgil's epic suggested that Augustus was destined to establish a great and peaceful world empire. Virgil skillfully weaves the history of Rome into the legendary account of Aeneas. In his journey, Aeneas continually glimpses the spirits of Rome's future heroes and the scenes of future Roman victories. His destiny is to inaugurate a history that Augustus will bring to completion.

The epic's most famous and touching episode is Aeneas' encounter with the passionate Queen Dido [DYE-doh], which stirs a conflict between Aeneas' destiny and his personal desires. Dido is the widowed queen of Carthage, in northern Africa, where Aeneas has been shipwrecked (Fig. **4.30**). Aeneas succumbs to his desire for the queen, but after a year, is reminded by the gods of his destiny to reach Italy. As Aeneas' ships sail from Carthage, Dido curses him from atop a funeral pyre. Her wretched death would inspire artists and composers for a thousand years.

Terrible Spirits of Avenging Curse! Angels of Death awaiting Elissa! All of you, hear me now. Direct the force of your divine will, as you must, on the evil here, and listen to my prayer. If that wicked being [Aeneas] must sail surely to land and come to harbor, because it is the fixed and destined ending required by Jupiter's own ordinances, yet let him afterwards suffer affliction in war through the arms of a daring foe, let him be banished from his own territory, and torn from the embraces of Iulus [Aeneas' son], imploring aid as he sees his innocent friends die, and then, after surrendering to a humiliating peace, may he not live to enjoy his kingdom in days of happiness; but may he lie fallen before his time unburied on a lonely strand. That is my prayer and my last cry, and it comes from me with my life-blood streaming.[5]

VIRGIL
Aeneid, Book IV

ROMAN SATIRE

In one literary form, the Romans claimed superiority over the Greeks. They excelled in verse **satire**, the artistic form that wittily ridicules human folly or vice, often with the aim to improve individuals or society. One of Rome's greatest satirists was Horace (65 B.C.–8 B.C.), a contemporary of Virgil's. He wrote two books of satires in the mid-30s B.C., adopting a casual style and avoiding the mockery of individuals. One satire recounts a journey with friends (including Virgil), while another tells humorously of his attempts to escape a boorish friend. Horace's most famous satire compared the virtues of city and country life, ending with the well-known fable "The Town Mouse and the Country Mouse." Horace himself preferred country living and retired to an estate given him by a patron. His satires and other writings (including a famous essay on the art of poetry) would become perhaps the most widely read literature of ancient Rome.

In contrast to Horace's gentle manner, the satires of Juvenal [JOO-vuh-null] (c. A.D. 55–c. 127) are savagely ironic in their criticism of Roman life. Juvenal attacks the corruption and hypocrisy of Roman society at the height of its wealth and self-indulgence. Few aspects of Roman society escaped Juvenal's satirical whip: sexual depravity; the extravagant banquets of the rich; the influence of Greek immigrants; the folly of tyrannical emperors. In this passage, he asks what employment he might find in a city perverted by patronage and deceit:

What should I do in Rome? I am no good at lying.
If a book's bad, I can't praise it, or go around ordering
*   copies.*
I don't know the stars; I can't hire out as assassin
When some young man wants his father knocked off for a
*   price; I have never*
Studied the guts of frogs, and plenty of others know better
How to convey to a bride the gifts of the first man she
*   cheats with.*
I am no lookout for thieves, so I cannot expect a
*   commission*
On some governor's staff. I'm a useless corpse, or a cripple.
Who has a pull these days, except your yes men and
*   stooges*
With blackmail in their hearts, yet smart enough to keep
*   silent?*
. . . Never let the gold of the Tagus,[a]
Rolling under its shade, become so important, so precious
You have to lie awake, take bribes that you'll have to
*   surrender,*
Tossing in gloom, a threat to your mighty patron
*   forever.*[6]

JUVENAL
From the *Satires*

a. A river in Spain and Portugal.

Juvenal's mockery reaches a climax in the famous tenth satire, where he exposes the vanity of human desire for wealth and fame. His call for a life of patient humility would be echoed by the Renaissance satirist Erasmus and the satirical geniuses of eighteenth-century Europe.

ROMAN PHILOSOPHY

Compare Roman epicureanism and stoicism in the rules they prescribe for living a good life.

Roman philosophy was governed by the Romans' sense of the practical and the necessary. From the diverse strands of Hellenistic philosophy, the Romans took what best suited their national character. The poet Lucretius elaborated a Hellenistic philosophy that defined the good as moderate and lasting pleasure. The more widely practiced Roman philosophy, called **stoicism**, was based on duty and world order. Stoicism's most eloquent statement came from the pen of the Emperor Marcus Aurelius, reflecting on life's meaning in the midst of a military campaign.

THE EPICUREAN LUCRETIUS

Late republican Rome was stimulated by Greek ideas, imported by the Greek scholars who tutored Roman youths. A handful of educated Romans was attracted to the hard-headed philosophy of **epicureanism** [epp-uh-KYOO-ree-un-ism], named for its founder Epicurus (341–271 B.C.), who taught in Athens. Epicureanism claimed that humans could live happily by understanding nature and pursuing moderate pleasure. "Pleasure is the beginning and end of living happily," wrote Epicurus. However, he did not teach the hedonistic pursuit of sensation at all cost: unbridled pleasure was certain to end in pain, he warned, and so the wise person learned to moderate desire. The aim of an epicurean's moral conduct was *ataraxia*, "un-troubledness" or "tranquility." Epicurus' theory of nature was heavily influenced by the early Greek materialists (see page 62). He taught that nature resulted from the chance collision of atoms; therefore, divine destiny did not control events. Rather, nature obeyed purely mechanistic laws.

While Greek in its origins, epicureanism found its most gifted spokesman among the Romans. The poet Lucretius [loo-KREE-shus] (98–*c.* 55 B.C.) explained epicureanism in his didactic poem *De rerum natura* (*On the Nature of the Universe*), the most systematic work of philosophical materialism in classical philosophy. *De rerum natura* elaborated epicurean natural philosophy, detailing the movement and collision of atoms. Lucretius' science had a moral purpose: to relieve human guilt and the fear of death. He explained that the gods had no power over human lives

and so could not punish humans for their impiety. As for death, Lucretius wrote:

> *Suppose that Nature herself were suddenly to find a voice and round upon one of us in these terms: "What is your grievance, mortal, that you give yourself up to this whining and repining? Why do you weep and wail over death? If the life you have lived till now has been a pleasant thing – if all its blessings have not leaked away like water poured into a cracked pot and run to waste unrelished – why then, you silly creature, do you not retire as a guest who has had his fill of life and take your care-free rest with a quiet mind? Or, if all your gains have been poured profitless away and life has grown distasteful, why do you seek to swell the total? The new can but turn out as badly as the old and perish as unprofitably. Why not rather make an end of life and labor? Do you expect me to invent some new contrivance for your pleasure? I tell you, there is none. All things are always the same. If your body is not yet withered with age, nor your limbs decrepit and flagging, even so there is nothing new to look forward to – not though you should outlive all living creatures, or even though you should never die at all." What are we to answer, except that Nature's rebuttal is justified and the plea she puts forward is a true one?*[7]

LUCRETIUS
From *On the Nature of the Universe*

Though he wrote, "Death is nothing to us and no concern of ours," Lucretius was not entirely consoled. He admitted that his resolute materialism was not able to still this "deplorable lust of life that holds us trembling in bondage to such uncertainties and dangers."[8]

For all its intellectual clarity, epicureanism did not spread far in the Roman world. Epicurus himself was attacked as a dissolute hedonist by those who misunderstood his philosophy. Roman epicureans found themselves condemned by the stoics (for withdrawing from public life) and by early Christians (for denying divine power). Epicureanism survived mainly through the eloquence and rigor of *De rerum natura*.

THE STOICS

The epic poet Virgil described his hero Aeneas as *pius*, Latin for "virtuous" or "dutiful," a title that Aeneas earned by his loyalty to the gods, his family, and his people. Aeneas represented perfectly the sense of social and familial obligation contained in *pietas* [PEE-ah-toss], the Romans' term for social duty. To justify a life of *pietas*, educated Romans were drawn to the philosophy of **stoicism**, which taught that one must do one's duty, practice virtue, and submit to a divinely ordered destiny.

Stoicism developed through several stages, from its origins in Hellenistic philosophy to its final stage in the writings of Emperor Marcus Aurelius (ruled A.D. 161–80).

It originated in Athens around 300 B.C. in the teachings of the Greek Zeno (*c.* 335–262 B.C.), a student of the Platonic Academy and an admirer of Socrates' ethical teaching. In the late Republic and early Roman Empire, patrician statesmen and soldiers enthusiastically adopted stoicism as a philosophy of life.

Stoicism held that divine reason controlled the universe and that humans should strive to live in harmony with divinely imposed laws of nature. Happiness was to be found in performing public duties while nurturing moral strength and self-restraint. Thus stoics strived to accept all circumstances beyond their immediate control, trusting that fate was ordered by divine reason. The orator Cicero (see Fig. 4.26) declared that all men were united in a universal brotherhood, because all were endowed with divine reason. Cicero's belief did not prevent him from holding slaves, and he did not apply the doctrine to women. Still, stoicism articulated an idea that all humanity was fundamentally endowed with the same divine spirit, a step toward belief in the equality of all humans.

The stoic Roman character was revealed most frankly in the writings of Marcus Aurelius (Fig. **4.31**). During

4.31 Equestrian statue of Marcus Aurelius (ruled A.D. 161–80). Gilded bronze, height 16 ft 8 ins (5.1 m). Capitoline Museums, Rome.
Even in this official statue, the emperor's thoughtful expression confirms the Romans' interest in realistic portraiture.

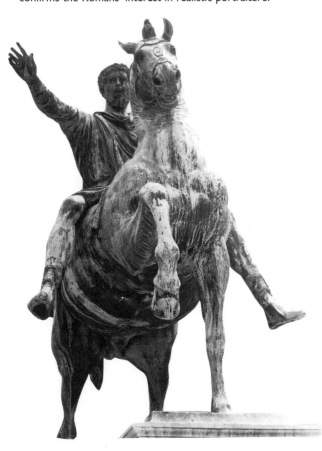

GLOBAL PERSPECTIVE

THE BUDDHA'S TEACHING

As Rome was consolidating its military and political domination of the Western world, Asia was being transformed by a very different force: the teachings of Buddhism, still one of the world's great religions. Where Roman stoicism taught obedience to social obligation, Buddhism preached the withdrawal from family and public life, in the effort to achieve a detached enlightenment.

Buddhism originated in the life of Siddhartha Gautama [sid-DAR-tuh GOW-tuh-muh] (*c.* 560–480 B.C.; the dates are disputed), known as the **Buddha** [BOO-duh], meaning "the enlightened one." According to Buddhist tradition, Gautama was born to a royal family in Nepal but tired of his luxurious existence. He was puzzled by the problem of human suffering (in Pali, *dukkha*). Leaving his family, he sought the advice of Hindu sages, fasted, and performed other ascetic exercises. Finally, while sitting under a tree (the *bo* tree), Gautama attained enlightenment (*bodhi*) – a perfect understanding of the nature of things. He entered upon a life of preaching, showing by example and teaching how others might achieve enlightenment (Fig. **4.32**).

Buddhism appealed to the poor and low-caste, because it taught that salvation did not depend on wealth or high birth. The Buddha's forceful and confident teaching (called the *dharma*) is summarized in the "Four Noble Truths," his fundamental assertions about the nature of existence:

- life is permeated by suffering (*dukkha*)
- suffering originates in craving or grasping
- suffering can be ended by the cessation of craving or desire
- the way to cessation of craving lies in the Noble Eightfold Path.

The Buddha's *dharma* absorbed from Hinduism the belief that life is suffering, and the idea that spiritual peace comes only in the release from a bodily existence. But whereas in Hinduism, the believer's soul rose to salvation through a long cycle of death and rebirth, the Buddha charted a more direct path to spiritual release – the "Noble Eightfold Path." Through clarity of mind, righteous action, and a regimen of meditation, the dedicated believer could cease all striving and attain a mindful detachment from existence. Cultivating this state of being would lead to *nirvana*, a perfect oblivion that released the believer from the cycle of birth, death, and re-birth.

Just as Christianity would prosper by its alliance with Constantine and later Roman emperors, so Buddhism was spread by the Indian conqueror Ashoka (ruled *c.* 270 B.C., the time of the Hellenistic Empire and Rome's first Punic War). Ashoka renounced his brutal military expansionism in favor of a universal religious tolerance. He encouraged Buddhist missionaries to carry the faith into southeast Asia (especially present-day Thailand and Cambodia), where devotees built Buddhist temples and monasteries on a grand scale (see page 174).

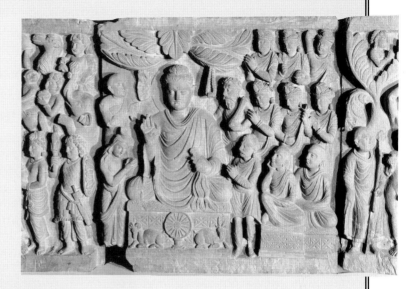

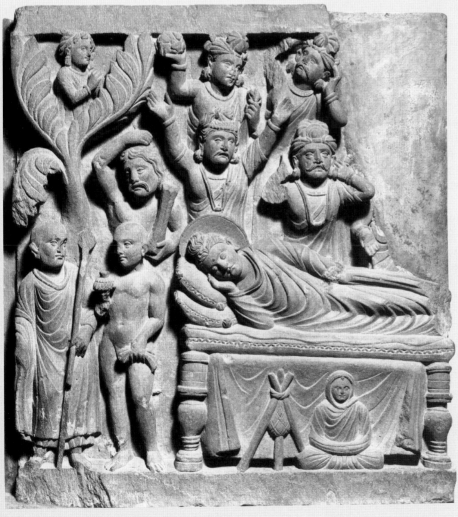

4.32 Above and left **Details of relief from Gandhara showing the First Sermon in the Deer Park and the Death of the Buddha, Kushan, late 2nd century to early 3rd century. Dark gray-blue slate, height 26³/₈ ins (67 cm). Freer Gallery of Art, Smithsonian Institution, Washington, D.C.**

the military campaigns that occupied the last ten years of his reign, Marcus Aurelius wrote twelve books of *Meditations* in the form of diary entries, possibly written in a military tent while his soldiers slept and tapers flickered in the breeze. In these surroundings, Marcus exhorted himself to act always with reason and restraint, to recognize the limit of his power over others, and to accept the necessity of death. His honesty and critical self-examination are all the more notable when one remembers his status: he was honored as a god by the inhabitants of the empire, and his power was virtually unlimited.

In the *Meditations*, Marcus described a universe that was unified by a single natural law, the law of reason that governed all creatures. A human's most important task was to understand and obey this law of reason:

> *All things are interwoven with one another, and the bond which unites them is sacred; practically nothing is alien to anything else, for all things are combined with one another and contribute to the order of the same universe. The universe embraces all things and is one, and the god who pervades all things is one, the substance is one, the law is one, the Reason common to all thinking beings is one, the truth is one, if indeed there is one perfection for the kindred beings who share in this selfsame Reason.*[9]

MARCUS AURELIUS
From *The Meditations*, Book VII

Even an emperor had to practice a disregard for the wrongs of others who harm only themselves. "I do my duty," he wrote; "other things do not disturb me." He assured his happiness by limiting personal desires, relying only on himself, although such happiness was gained at the cost of indifference to others' suffering.

The *Meditations'* tone of self-admonishment sometimes resembles the self-help manuals so popular today, as Marcus reminds himself to concentrate his energies on the present moment. True to the stoic belief, his emphasis was always on duty, surely an admirable moral guide for any ruler: "Firmly, as a Roman and a man should, think at all times how you can perform the task at hand with precise and genuine dignity, sympathy, independence, and justice, making yourself free from all other preoccupations."[10]

ROME'S DIVISION AND DECLINE

The last centuries of the Roman Empire were marked by increasing division and a decline of the empire's cohesion. Diocletian [deye-oh-KLEE-shun] (ruled 284–305) recognized that the empire had grown unwieldy, and for administrative purposes divided it into eastern and western sections. Diocletian himself abdicated the imperial throne, and withdrew in retirement to a palace-fortress he had built at Spalatum on the Adriatic Sea (now Split, in present-day Croatia). The vigorous classicism still visible in Marcus Aurelius' portraits also was transformed. Sculptors reverted to a more formulaic representation of the human figure.

Rome itself, though sapped by corruption, remained the center of Mediterranean civilization. The first Christian emperor, Constantine, was to build a new capital in the east, but even in the Christian era, the city of Rome would remain the psychic center of Western civilization and eventually become the new capital of Western Christianity. All roads still led to Rome, and for centuries pilgrims of all religious and intellectual stripes would feel compelled to journey to Rome and taste of its spiritual riches.

Chapter Summary

The Drama of Roman History. Rome began its rise as a world power with the overthrow of Etruscan domination and the founding of the Roman republic. In the republican era (509–90 B.C.), Romans devoted themselves to military conquest and the resolution of internal conflicts. Following conquests of Carthage and Greece, Rome was convulsed in a period of civil war (90–30 B.C.), marked by the rise of Julius Caesar. Caesar's nephew Octavian finally established himself as absolute ruler and inaugurated the Roman Empire, which reached its height during the *Pax Romana* (27 B.C.–A.D. 180).

The Art of an Empire. Augustus' reign gave rise to an art dedicated to the glorification of empire. Borrowing from the styles of classical and Hellenistic Greece, imperial art celebrated the power and achievements of Rome's emperors. Augustan sculpture served as effective artistic propaganda, while the forum of Trajan and its famous Column of Trajan were the ultimate imperial monuments.

The Architecture of Rome. The splendor of ancient Rome depended on Roman architects' skill in the use of concrete and the arch. By combining the arch in vaulting, Roman builders created spacious and luxuriously decorated interiors. The most common types of buildings — baths, basilicas, amphitheaters — illustrated the Romans' interest in architecture's utilitarian value. Rome's most perfect building, however, was the domed Pantheon.

Roman Art and Daily Life. Roman daily life encouraged the arts of wall painting, mosaic, and portrait sculpture. Roman life can be reconstructed from the remains of Pompeii, a city entombed by volcanic eruption in A.D. 79 that was uncovered centuries later by enthusiastic antiquarians. Pompeii's wall paintings and mosaics demonstrate the influence of Greek artists and the Roman preference for pleasant surroundings. Their portrait sculpture served the veneration of elders and showed a realistic insight into individual character.

Roman Theater and Music. In theater, Romans preferred the entertainment of comedy to tragedy's serious tone. Roman comedies were adapted from Hellenistic theater, as was the Roman theater, with its raised stage and tall architectural backdrop. The comic playwrights Plautus and Terence perfected the complicated plots and stock characters that would be borrowed by later writers. Roman music and dance were a professional affair, used to accompany military parades, theater, and banquets.

The Roman Poets. Roman poets borrowed liberally from Greek authors, especially in the republican period, when the lyric poet Catullus wrote his famous and candid cycle of love poems. The greatest Latin poet was Virgil, author of the *Aeneid*, an epic that rivaled Homer's in its nobility of theme. Virgil's story of the Trojan hero Aeneas depicted Rome's future triumphs as Aeneas' divine destiny, which he must obey at the cost of personal happiness. In satirical verse, the Romans surpassed their Greek predecessors: Horace's satirical tone was gentle, while Juvenal's *Satires* bitterly exposed the corruption and excesses of imperial Rome.

Roman Philosophy. Roman philosophy reflected the qualities of clear-headed resolve and patriotic duty that Romans prized. The epicurean Lucretius composed an eloquent statement of philosophical materialism, reassuring Romans that the gods did not control human destiny and that life ended in nothingness. The Roman character was reflected more directly in the teachings of stoicism, which taught the acceptance of fate and the quiet practice of virtue. The emperor Marcus Aurelius applied these teachings in his *Meditations*, which voiced a determination to perform his civic duties and to disregard anything beyond his immediate control.

By the third century, Rome was suffering increasing division and decline. Even so, the cohesion and grandeur of the Roman Empire would be the envy of every conqueror in subsequent Western history.

5 The Judeo-Christian Spirit

Here Emperor Justinian, master of the Roman Empire in the sixth century, is flanked by soldiers who remind us of the Romans' awesome military power. But he holds the emblems of Christianity, a faith that counseled meekness and promised heavenly kingdoms, not imperial power (Fig. 5.1). How had Christianity conquered mighty Rome?

*Christianity had arisen out of Judaism, the faith of the Israelites, a Near Eastern people that was often conquered and finally crushed by Rome itself. The astounding merger of these two traditions – the classical and the Judeo-Christian – is one of the remarkable moments in Western history. The **Judeo-Christian spirit** brought to the ancient world a belief in a single all-powerful God, who demanded righteousness and promised redemption. For Christians, this redemption came through the teaching and sacrifice of Jesus, God's anointed. By the mid sixth-century, it was at the altar of Jesus that the Roman emperor worshiped, piously bearing the symbols of a new faith.*

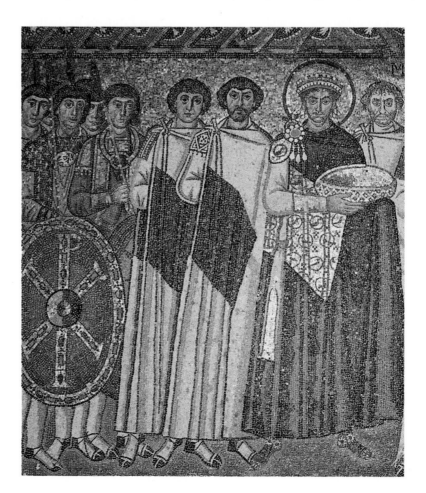

5.1 *Justinian and His Courtiers*, c. 547. Mosaic, San Vitale, Ravenna, Italy.
The Emperor Justinian (527–65) here presents himself as Commander of the Roman world (the last to rule a unified empire) and highest priest of the Christian Church that would become the new unifying force of the Western world.

HISTORY OF THE ISRAELITES

12th century B.C. Settlement in Canaan
Biblical battle of Jericho

1020–922 B.C. United monarchy
Kings David, Solomon; first Temple at Jerusalem

922–722 B.C. Divided monarchy
Division into northern and southern kingdom;
much of Torah written and compiled

722–587 B.C. Assyrian conquest
Assyrians conquer northern kingdom; prophets
active

587–539 B.C. Babylonian exile
Destruction of Solomon's Temple; forced exile

539–332 B.C. Restoration
Persians permit return to Jerusalem; Second
Temple built 538–516 B.C.

332–63 B.C. Hellenistic
Hellenizing of Jews throughout Near East

65 B.C.–A.D. 135 Roman
Roman army sacks Jerusalem and destroys
temple (A.D. 70)

THE JUDAIC TRADITION

Summarize the essential religious ideas of the Jewish people and their sacred scripture, the Hebrew Bible.

Beginning in the fourth century, the Roman Empire was transformed by its conversion to the new Christian religion. To understand the causes of this transformation, we retrace our steps to the ancient Near East, to the time of ancient Egypt, Babylon, and Persia. The Christian faith that would conquer Rome was rooted in the religious ideas of the ancient Israelites (also known as Hebrew or Jews). Few nations or peoples with so small a population as ancient Israel have so greatly influenced Western civilization. The Israelites' belief in one all-powerful God is the cornerstone of modern Judaism, Christianity, and Islam, the faiths that would dominate the Western world.

Politically and culturally, the Israelites were a minor nation of the ancient Near East. They shared the fates of other small nations in the region, suffering domination by the great powers of Egypt and Mesopotamia. Religiously, however, the Israelites were unique: they rejected their neighbors' polytheism and embraced monotheism, devoting themselves to one God (see page 104), who acknowledged them as his chosen people. The special relationship between the Israelite nation and its God was chronicled in the Hebrew Bible, a masterpiece of religious literature that infused Western civilization with its values and wisdom.

HISTORY AND THE ISRAELITES

The first Israelites were a nomadic tribe of shepherds, led by **patriarchs**, or chieftains. Tradition holds that Abraham was the first patriarch and the founder of the Israelite nation. According to the same tradition, the patriarch Moses led the Israelites in a dramatic exodus from Egypt (dated about 1250 B.C.), an event that the Israelites interpreted as God's deliverance of their nation from its captors and tormentors. The exodus was part of a pattern of collective deliverance and punishment at the hands of God that continued throughout the Israelites' tribal history. As told in Hebrew scripture, the Israelites wandered for years in the desert and eventually settled in Canaan (also called Palestine), the homeland that God had promised to Moses. In Palestine, the Israelites lived as farmers and traders.

By the eleventh century B.C., the Israelites' tribal egalitarianism had evolved into a monarchy. The uniting of Israel's tribes under a king marked the high point of the Israelites' national history. Their first great king was David (ruled *c.* 1000–961 B.C.), who centralized Hebrew worship at his court in Jerusalem. David was himself a talented musician and developed a liturgy of psalms of praise to God. King Solomon (ruled 961–922 B.C.) consolidated and expanded the Israelites' power in a splendid reign, remembered by many Jews as a golden age. Solomon built an elaborate temple at Jerusalem, employing artisans and religious symbols from neighboring cultures. The temple and its replacement, destroyed in Roman times, are still the focus of Jewish devotion and nationalism today (Figs. **5.2, 5.3**).

In the centuries after Solomon's reign, the Israelite kingdom declined and in 587 B.C. suffered an invasion by a Babylonian army that razed the temple and forced many Israelites into exile. The years of exile (587–*c.* 450 B.C.) had an immense cultural effect on the Israelites. They adopted a new calendar and a new language, known as Aramaic (the language that Jesus spoke). Their religion absorbed elements from Babylonian and Persian belief, such as the notion of a Satan, an evil force opposing God. The Israelites interpreted the Babylonian exile in the same way as they did other national calamities, as God's punishment for their unfaithfulness.

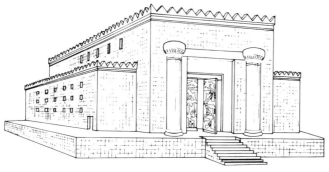

5.2 Solomon's Temple (reconstruction).
The temple's innermost chamber, called the Holy of Holies, contained the Ark of the Covenant, vessel for the laws of God given to Moses.

Some Jews eventually returned to Palestine after the Persian conquest of Babylonia, but suffered successive domination by the Hellenistic and Roman empires (Fig. 5.4). The rebuilt temple at Jerusalem was refurbished grandly under the reign of King Herod the Great (died 4 B.C.). However, repeated Jewish insurrections incited the Romans to storm Jerusalem in A.D. 70. Herod's temple was destroyed and once again many Jews were forced into the **Diaspora** [dye-ASS-por-uh], the "dispersion" of Jews into exile from their homeland and religious cen-

5.3 Jews praying at the Western Wall, the only remains of the Second Temple built by Herod the Great and destroyed by the Romans in A.D. 70.

ter. Wherever they settled, most Diaspora Jews lived as a religious and cultural minority. They resolutely preserved their language and faith in spite of frequent persecution.

THE HEBREW BIBLE

Identify the essential teachings of the Hebrew Bible.

The Israelites' God, named Yahweh [YAH-way], was present to them through his holy scripture, the compilation of history, poetry, and wisdom that is called the Hebrew Bible. The Hebrew Bible (from the Greek *biblos*, or "book") served much the same function for the Israelites as the Homeric epics did for the Greeks. The Bible was a stock of story and wisdom that was transmitted orally for centuries before being written down sometime after 1000 B.C.

The Israelites divided their scriptures into three major parts. The first five books constituted the Torah, or "instruction," a history of the early Israelite nation. The Prophets comprised writings of charismatic leaders such as Isaiah and Jeremiah, who reminded Israelites of their duty to God. Finally, the Writings included psalms and other wisdom literature.

The Hebrew Creation The Hebrew Bible's power and complexity are evident in the first chapters of Genesis, the two accounts of the creation (Genesis 1–3:24). The creation stories illustrate an important difference between the Hebrew God and his pagan counterparts – the Hebrew God was no longer associated with particular locales and aspects of nature, he was the original author of the world, the source of all creation, whose power was universal.

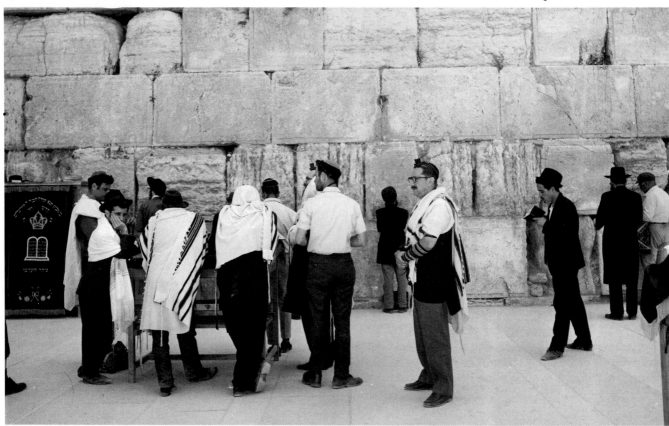

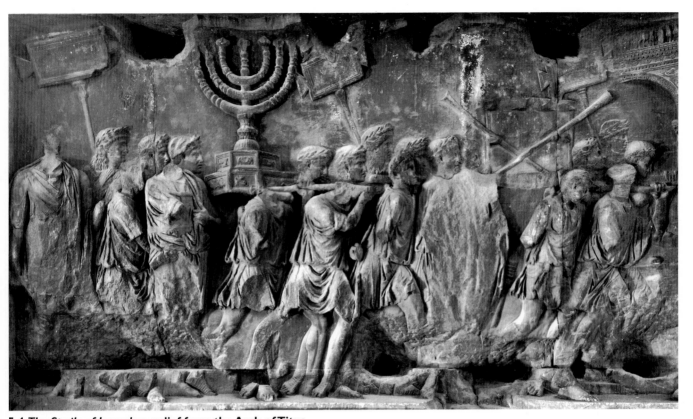

5.4 *The Spoils of Jerusalem*, relief from the Arch of Titus, Rome, c. A.D. 81. Marble relief, height 6 ft 7 ins (2 m).
Roman soldiers sacking Jerusalem carry off the *menorah*, the seven-branched candelabra that is now a national symbol of Israel.

The first Genesis story (1–2:3) tells of a majestic creation that spans six days. Biblical scholars believe this story was written by Israelite priests during the Babylonian exile, after they had heard other creation myths on the same grand scale. In this account, God's creation progresses from a primal world of nothingness to an orderly hierarchy of all creatures. Here, the creation of humanity is a generic, universal act in harmony with the story's tone. Human beings form the capstone of God's universe, the pinnacle of a divinely fashioned order:

Then God said, "Let us make man in our image, after our likeness; and let them have dominion over the fish of the sea, and over the birds of the air, and over the cattle, and over all the earth, and over every creeping thing that creeps upon the earth." So God created man in his own image, in the image of God he created him; male and female he created them. And God blessed them, and God said to them, "Be fruitful and multiply, and fill the earth and subdue it; and have dominion over the fish of the sea and over the birds of the air and over every living thing that moves upon the earth."[1]

GENESIS 1:26–28

The second Genesis story (2:4–3:24) is attributed to a biblical author called the Jahwist, who typically wrote with drama and economy. The Jahwist recounted the memorable episode that proved so influential in Judeo-Christian civilization – the story of Adam and Eve. God forbids Adam and Eve, without explanation, to eat of the tree of the knowledge of good and evil. A serpent appears to tempt Eve to taste of the forbidden fruit and its powers.

He [the serpent] said to the woman, "Did God say, 'You shall not eat of any tree of the garden'?" And the woman said to the serpent "We may eat of the fruit of the trees of the garden; but God said, 'You shall not eat of the fruit of the tree which is in the midst of the garden, neither shall you touch it, lest you die.' " But the serpent said to the woman, "You will not die. For God knows that when you eat of it your eyes will be opened, and you will be like God, knowing good and evil."[2]

GENESIS 3:1–5

Adam and Eve succumb to temptation and suffer expulsion from the Garden of Eden. God declares that as punishment Eve will suffer the pain of childbirth and Adam the toil of labor.

KEY CONCEPT

MONOTHEISM

The Israelites gave the Western religious tradition the unique concept of **monotheism**, the belief in one all-powerful and beneficent god. The Hebrew Bible describes the Israelite God as an all-powerful enigma, the author of all creation, yet himself un-created. Through Moses, God prohibited his followers from representing him in statues and even declined to be named directly. The Israelites called him originally by the sacred consonants YHWH, pronounced as "Yahweh." Despite these mysteries, the faithful believed God revealed himself again and again, commanding their obedience and rewarding their righteousness.

God's most important revelation was the Ten Commandments, which Moses received on Mount Sinai and which became the basis for all Hebrew law. The Commandments established the leading principles of Israelite tribal life. The first was a principle of universal justice, that all humans were governed by one divinely sanctioned law. From this followed a second principle, that all humans (or at least all Israelites) were equal before God's law and worthy in God's sight. Compared to the strict class societies of the ancient world, the Israelites were notably egalitarian, and believed that the principles of their society obliged them to treat the poor and unfortunate with kindness and generosity.

Hebrew moral teachings may be summarized as ethical monotheism, the belief that obedience to God's law implies righteous action in all aspects of moral life. Any sin is disobedience to God and deserves divine punishment. These ethical ideas were developed in later Christianity and Islam. The Hebrew ethical tradition differed significantly from the ethics of Aristotle and other classical philosophers, who believed moral conduct lay in a balance between extreme actions. For the Hebrew tradition, moral conduct lay in rigorous obedience to God's command.

In the ancient world, Hebrew monotheism offered a powerful religious alternative to the dominant polytheism. But monotheism also generated some perplexing theological questions. For example, if God was the source of all things, was he therefore the origin of evil? If God could intervene in history, then why did he not halt war and catastrophes? How did one judge among the religions that each claimed to obey the God of Abraham? Such questions are still confronted by the heirs of Hebrew monotheism: modern-day Jews, Christians, and Muslims. Like the ancient Israelites, modern believers still struggle to understand God's mysterious power and obey his stringent law.

CRITICAL QUESTION

What, in your opinion, is the ultimate cause of evil in the world? How might this cause be reconciled with the belief in a benevolent and all-powerful God?

The Jahwist's story illustrates what the Israelites believed was humanity's most fundamental failing: the disobedience of God's command. Yet the story also contains essential themes found in the myth and legend of the ancient world. In Adam and Eve, we see the human interest in moral knowledge, the desire to escape death, and the violation of a divine taboo, all common themes of ancient myth. These Hebrew creation stories are not only models of concise storytelling – they also echo the most potent ideas of ancient literature, from the Greeks' Oedipus legend to the Egyptian tales of the afterlife.

The God of the Covenant   Most of the Hebrew scriptures recount God's relationship with his chosen people, the Israelite nation. The Israelites viewed this special bond as a covenant, or agreement, between God and themselves, whereby the Israelites were bound to obey God's law, while God promised to favor and defend his chosen nation. Much of the Torah was devoted to a historical account of this troubled but indissoluble bond between God and Israel. Thus, in the Hebrew Bible, religious faith and national history overlap.

THE WRITE IDEA

Explain how the story of Adam and Eve confirms or conflicts with your notions of male-female relations, sin, and sexuality.

The Israelites' covenant with God was confirmed by decisive moments in their history. One such moment was Abraham's sacrifice of Isaac (Genesis 22), in which God commands the aged patriarch Abraham to sacrifice his favored son. Proving his complete obedience to God, Abraham holds the knife to Isaac's throat before God's angel intervenes and halts the killing. Throughout their history, the Israelites celebrated and affirmed their covenant with God in religious ritual. Even today at Passover, for example, modern Jews commemorate an incident from the Egyptian captivity, in which God's angel of death slew the Egyptians' first-born children but spared those of the Israelites.

God's command to moral righteousness was enforced by **prophets** (in Hebrew *navi*), who were fervent mouthpieces of divine judgment. Israelite prophets often opposed the official cult of priests and the temple, criticizing ritualized observance of the law. Prophets such as Isaiah and Jeremiah stressed inner obedience to God and the creation of a just society. The prophets frequently predicted a future of redemption, as in Isaiah's famous saying, "And they shall beat their swords into plowshares, and their spears into pruning hooks; nation shall not lift up sword against nation, neither shall they learn war any more" (Isaiah 2:4).

JOB AND THE TRIALS OF ISRAEL

The trials of the Israelite nation were symbolically represented in the story of Job – a righteous man, once favored by God, who loses his family and fortune through a series of calamities. The Book of Job, dated somewhere between 600 and 400 B.C., is one of the Hebrew Bible's most richly poetic books and compares the humans' narrow moral viewpoint with the immense majesty of God's power. Three friends come to console Job, plying him with the conventional wisdom of Hebrew morality. One says Job must have sinned greatly to deserve so terrible a punishment from God; another proposes that Job's suffering is a test of his faith and that he will be rewarded in the end. Convinced of his own righteousness, however, Job demands that the Almighty show him the nature of his sin. God answers Job but refuses to justify himself in human terms. Instead, he reminds his servant Job of God's incomprehensible power and majesty. Confronted by the vastness and eternity of God's universe, Job acknowledges that his own sufferings are as nothing.

> *Then the Lord answered Job out of the whirlwind:*
> *"Who is this that darkens counsel by words without*
> *knowledge?*
> *Gird up your loins like a man,*
> *I will question you, and you shall declare to me.*
>
> *"Where were you when I laid the foundation of the*
> *earth?*
> *Tell me if you have understanding.*
> *Who determined its measurements – surely you know!*
> *Or who stretched the line upon it?*
> *On what were its bases sunk,*
> *or who laid its cornerstone,*
> *when the morning stars sang together,*
> *and all the sons of God shouted for joy?*
>
> *"Or who shut in the sea with doors,*
> *when it burst forth from the womb;*
> *when I made clouds its garment,*
> *and thick darkness its swaddling band,*
> *and prescribed bounds for it,*
> *and set bars and doors,*
> *and said, 'Thus far shall you come, and no farther,*
> *and here shall your proud waves be stayed'?"* [3]
>
> JOB 38:1–11

The Book of Job echoed the lament of an Israelite nation that, in the centuries after the Babylonian exile, suffered the yoke of conquest and persecution. During the period 200 B.C. to A.D. 50, many Jews expected an **apocalypse** [uh-POCK-uh-lips], a cataclysmic revelation of God's will that would liberate and redeem Israel. At the apocalypse, they believed God would judge all humanity and restore the Jewish temple at Jerusalem as the center of the world. The Jews associated the apocalypse with the appearance of a **messiah**, a leader "anointed" by God, who would overthrow Israel's foreign rulers and restore the glories of David's kingdom. To these potent expectations, founded on Hebrew nationalism, Jesus and his followers would appeal with great success.

THE HEBREW BIBLE

The Torah	The Prophets	The Writings
Genesis	Joshua	Psalms
Exodus	Judges	Proverbs
Leviticus	1st & 2nd Samuel	Job
Numbers	1st & 2nd Kings	Song of Songs
Deuteronomy	Isaiah	Ruth
	Jeremiah	Lamentations
	Ezekiel	Ecclesiastes
	Twelve Minor Prophets	Esther
		Daniel
		Ezra
		Nehemiah
		1st & 2nd Chronicles

THE RISE OF CHRISTIANITY

Explain the appeal of Christian teachings and practices in the late Roman world.

It seems unlikely that belief in an obscure Jewish prophet would supplant the diverse paganism of the late Roman world. In its first two centuries, the new religion of Christianity was just one of many religious cults practiced in the vast Roman Empire. By the early fourth century, however, the Christian faith counted a Roman emperor among its converts, and by 400, Christianity was the Roman Empire's official religion.

Historians cannot fully reconstruct the history of early Christianity. Nevertheless, we know that by the second century early Christians believed that Jesus of Nazareth was the divine Son of God, who had been resurrected from the dead to save all humanity. Believers in Jesus were promised forgiveness of sins and everlasting life after death. Christians eagerly expected the imminent end of time, when Jesus would come again to reward the faithful and judge the wicked. From these fundamentals of faith, Christianity successfully broadened its appeal as it spread through the Roman Empire. The rise of Christianity can be divided into three phases:

- the life of Jesus of Nazareth, the Jewish prophet whom Christians claimed to be both man and god;
- early Christianity as it spread from Palestine to the Greco-Roman cities of late antiquity;
- Christianity as the dominant religion of the Roman Empire.

JESUS OF NAZARETH

Jesus of Nazareth was a Jewish teacher and healer whose life and person became the center of the Christian faith. His teaching attracted a few devoted followers before he was executed for political crimes by Palestine's Roman authority. Jesus' public life preaching to the poor folk of rural Palestine was so brief that no contemporary source refers directly to his ministry. Virtually all that we know of Jesus must be gleaned from the Gospels, the four accounts of his life and teachings composed a generation after his death. These accounts are more professions of Christian faith than historical records of Jesus' life.

Jesus was born at a time (*c.* 4 B.C.) when the Jewish nation was deeply troubled by Roman oppression and ripe with messianic expectations. Thus his preachings that a "kingdom of God" would soon be established appealed to his followers' apocalyptic hopes. The kingdom of God would radically alter human relations and bring a divine

judgment of humanity. To prepare for the coming apocalypse, Jesus urged his followers to abandon their property and families, love one another without reservation, and meet evil with passive resistance.

The Gospels portray Jesus as a skillful teacher. His graphic language and simple stories appealed to his poor, uneducated followers, and he frequently used illustrative stories called **parables** to dramatize his vision of God. In the parable of the "prodigal son" (Luke 5:11–32), for example, a foolish son wastes his inheritance on riotous living. On returning home repentantly, the son is forgiven by his loving father, who had feared he was lost. Jesus' parables illustrated by analogy the nature of God and his kingdom. He stressed that God loved and forgave his faithful servants, as the father did his profligate son.

The teachings of Jesus are summarized in the Sermon on the Mount (Matthew 5–7), a compilation of sayings that reinforced his relation to the Hebrew tradition and scripture. The Sermon on the Mount called for an intensification of ethical monotheism, the ancient Hebrew obligation to respect and care for everyone in the community. Jesus said he had come "not to abolish the law and the prophets, but to fulfill them." By intensifying their love for others, said Jesus, his followers prepared themselves for entry into the impending kingdom of God. Like earlier prophets, Jesus also demanded a righteousness of the heart. Conspicuous acts of faith and formal obedience to the law were not sufficient. A sinful thought was as evil as a sinful action.

"You have heard that it was said, 'You shall not commit adultery.' But I say to you that every one who looks at a woman lustfully has already committed adultery with her in his heart. If your right eye causes you to sin, pluck it out and throw it away; it is better that you lose one of your members than that your whole body be thrown into hell."

"You have heard that it was said, 'An eye for an eye and a tooth for a tooth.' But I say to you, Do not resist one who is evil. But if any one strikes you on the right cheek, turn to him the other also; and if any one would sue you and take your coat, let him have your cloak as well; and if any one forces you to go one mile, go with him two miles. Give to him who begs from you, and do not refuse him who would borrow from you."[4]

GOSPEL OF MATTHEW 5:27–29, 38–42

It is not clear how enthusiastically Jesus' fellow Jews responded to his preaching. The Gospels agree that, in the last weeks or months of his life, Jesus entered Jerusalem to the acclaim of its citizens. Even though he declined the mantle of a political messiah, a new David come to restore Israel's independence, Jesus' apocalyptic teachings had alarmed the Roman authorities. The Roman government seized Jesus and crucified him, a method of execution reserved for political criminals. This humiliating public death was, paradoxically, the starting point of a powerful new religious faith.

The days following the death of Jesus were to become the pivotal moment of the Christian faith. All of the Gospels claim that Jesus rose bodily from the dead and appeared to his disciples in the flesh. His followers believed his resurrection was proof that Jesus was indeed the messiah (in Greek *Christos*), and that soon he would return in a "second coming," to usher in the kingdom of God. Christian belief holds that Jesus predicted his imminent death at the Last Supper (Matthew 26:17–29), a Passover meal shared with his disciples, which later became the core of Christian ritual, celebrating Jesus' bodily resurrection from the dead.

EARLY CHRISTIANITY

The first Christians were Palestinian Jews whose new faith was largely consistent with Jewish nationalism and apocalyptic hope. The spread of Christianity beyond Palestine (Figs. 5.5, 5.6) required that the new faith broaden its appeal. Early Christianity's most effective advocate was the apostle Paul (died A.D. 64?), whose tireless travels and passionate letters to new churches spread Christianity through the Greco-Roman world.

As a Hellenistic Jew and Roman citizen, Paul could move easily through the empire, preaching the gospel of Christ among Jews and non-Jews in Greco-Roman cities. To Jews, Paul proclaimed Jesus as the messiah who would

---

THE NEW TESTAMENT

Gospels
Matthew, Mark, Luke, John
The Acts
Letters of Paul
Romans, 1st & 2nd Corinthians, Galatians, Ephesians, Philippians, Colossians, 1st & 2nd Thessalonians, 1st & 2nd Timothy, Titus, Philemon
Other Letters
Hebrews, Epistle of James, 1st & 2nd Peter, 1st, 2nd, & 3rd John, Jude
Revelation

---

bring imminent redemption to the faithful. Non-Jews could embrace Paul's teaching without submitting to the male circumcision and dietary restrictions required by orthodox Judaism. Paul's letters exhorted new Christians and advised them on marriage, charity, and ritual.

Christian ritual centered on communal celebrations of the **Eucharist** [YOO-kuh-rist], a re-enactment of the Last Supper (Fig. 5.7). The Eucharist meals associated Christians with other mystery cults in the late Roman world. The Dionysians, for example, celebrated their god with wine-drinking and orgiastic banquets. The cult of Isis, the Egyptian goddess, told of a murdered god who was res-

---

WINDOW ON DAILY LIFE

THE SIEGE OF JERUSALEM

When a Roman army besieged Jerusalem in A.D. 70, starvation drove its citizens to madness. This account is from Josephus, a Jewish historian:

Throughout the city people were dying of hunger in large numbers and enduring indescribable sufferings. In every house the merest hint of food sparked violence, and close relatives fell to blows, snatching from one another the pitiful supports of life. No respect was paid even to the dying; the ruffians searched them, in case they were concealing food somewhere in their clothes, or just pretending to be near to death. Gaping with hunger, like mad dogs, lawless gangs went staggering and reeling through the streets, battering upon doors like drunkards, and so bewildered that they broke into the same house

two or three times in an hour. Need drove the starving to gnaw at anything. Refuse which even animals would reject was collected and turned into food. In the end they were eating belts and shoes, and the leather stripped off their shields. Tufts of withered grass were devoured, and sold in little bundles for four drachmas.[5]

JOSEPHUS
The Jewish Wars

CRITICAL QUESTION

In what ways do people still claim divine sanction or approval for their actions? How are calamities and misfortune often still taken as a sign of divine judgment?

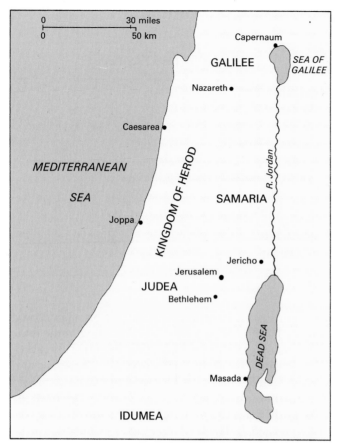

5.5 Israel at the time of Jesus.

5.6 The spread of Christianity.

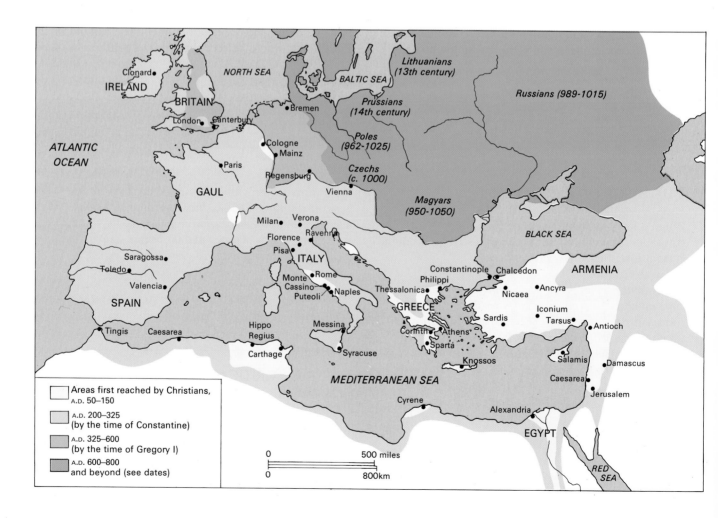

Areas first reached by Christians,
A.D. 50–150

A.D. 200–325
(by the time of Constantine)

A.D. 325–600
(by the time of Gregory I)

A.D. 600–800
and beyond (see dates)

urrected in the afterlife. Converts to Christianity also underwent the rite of baptism, which erased the sins of the old life and prepared the believer to enter the kingdom of God. The Emperor Constantine postponed his baptism until he was near death, hoping to erase all but a few days of sin.

Early Christian ritual was accompanied by readings from a growing body of scripture written in Greek. The Christian New Testament consisted of diverse materials. The letters (or **epistles**) of Paul and other apostles were the earliest Christian writings, while the four Gospels and Luke's Acts of the Apostles (written *c.* A.D. 60–95) were professions of Christian faith written as histories. The Christian New Testament ended with the apocalyptic Book of Revelation, a powerfully symbolic vision of Christ's second coming. The New Testament, like the Hebrew Bible, recorded God's active intervention in the lives of the faithful and promised them redemption.

CHRISTIANITY IN THE LATE ROMAN EMPIRE

By the third century, Christianity had established itself firmly as a leading cult in the Greco-Roman world. Christian churches successfully established tight-knit, supportive communities in the disorderly world of late antiquity. New believers embraced Christianity's benevolent monotheism and welcomed its promise of resurrection after death. To the empire's slaves and lower classes, Christianity granted an equal membership in the community of faith; to the wealthy – especially women – it offered freedom from oppressive family and social obligations. Widows seem to have occupied esteemed positions and women apparently served as church officers.

The religious diversity of the late Roman Empire is illustrated by Dura-Europos, a town in Roman Syria (modern Iraq) that was partially buried in 256. Excavations at Dura-Europos [dyoor-a yoo-ROPE-us] uncovered temples to more than a dozen Greek and Roman gods, as well as smaller sanctuaries of Judaism, Christianity, and other cults. Despite God's ban on images, the Jewish synagogue was decorated with wall paintings of biblical scenes.

5.7 *Last Supper*, **Sant' Apollinare Nuovo, Ravenna, Italy, c. 520. Mosaic.**
Roman mosaicists adopted a new iconography based on Bible stories and Christian symbols. Here a typical Roman banquet scene is recast as the Last Supper, with the purple-robed figure of Christ opposite the traitor Judas. Christ has just announced, "One of you will betray me," and the disciples look expectantly at Judas.

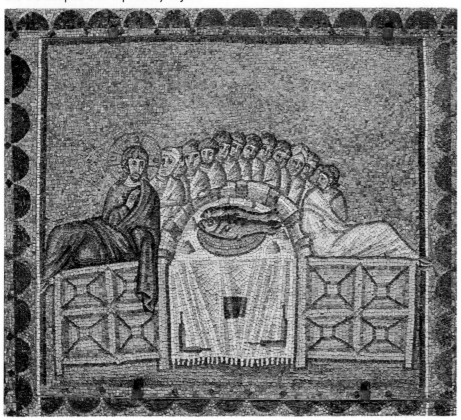

The Christian church, actually a converted house, contained painted scenes of the women who discovered Jesus' empty tomb and of Christ performing miracles.

Early Christian art (Fig. **5.8**) indicated a willingness to synthesize the new faith with dominant styles and imagery of late Roman art. Christian wall paintings depicted Jesus in the guise of Orpheus, the musician of Greek mythology who descends into hell and charms the god of the underworld. Christians also depicted events from the Hebrew Bible that emphasized deliverance and salvation, such as Jonah in the belly of the whale. Early Christians developed an arcane set of symbols that became sacred images, known as **icons**. The fish, for example, represented the initial letters of "Jesus Christ, God's Son, Savior" in Greek: I-CH-TH-Y-S, "fish." Fish imagery also echoed Jesus' promise to his apostles that "I will make you fishers of men" (Matthew 4:19). The merger of Judeo-Christian symbolism and the classical style is evident in the sarcophagus [sar-KOFF-ah-gus] (coffin) of Junius Bassus, a fourth-century Roman official (Fig. **5.9**). In the center top scene, for example, Christ's throne in heaven is supported by the Roman god of the sky. Daniel, the late Hebrew prophet, stands like an Athenian philosopher among the lions.

Constantine and Christianity A turning point in Christianity's rise came under the reign of Constantine [KON-stan-teen] (ruled 312–37), the first emperor to embrace the Christian faith (Fig. **5.10**). The night before a crucial battle, Constantine was said to have seen a fiery cross against the sun, with the words below "In this sign you will conquer." Following his victory, Constantine issued the Edict of Milan (313), which legalized Christianity and ended official persecution. While paying homage to the official pagan gods, Constantine had his sons brought up as Christians and made his new capital, Constantinople [kon-STAN-ti-noh-pull] (the ancient city of Byzantium; now the Turkish city of Istanbul), the first Christian city.

With one exception, every Roman emperor after Constantine favored Christianity, and by the end of the fourth century, the religion had entered a new phase in its devel-

5.8 Painted ceiling from the catacomb of SS. Pietro e Marcellino, Rome, 4th century A.D.
The first Christian art appeared in catacombs, underground chambers where early Christians worshiped and buried their dead.

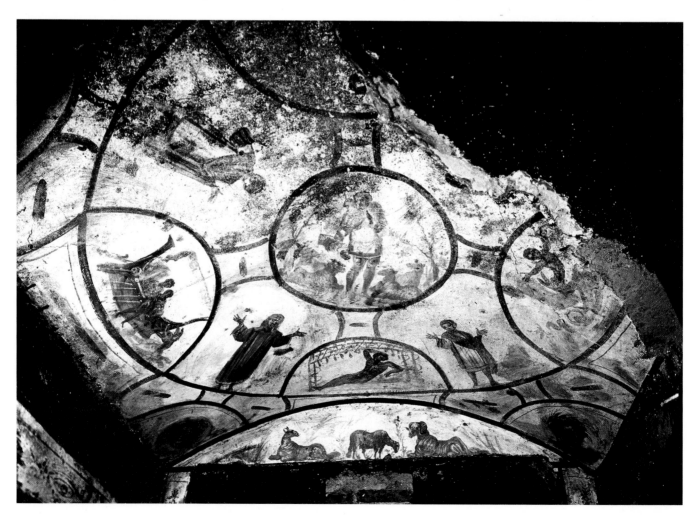

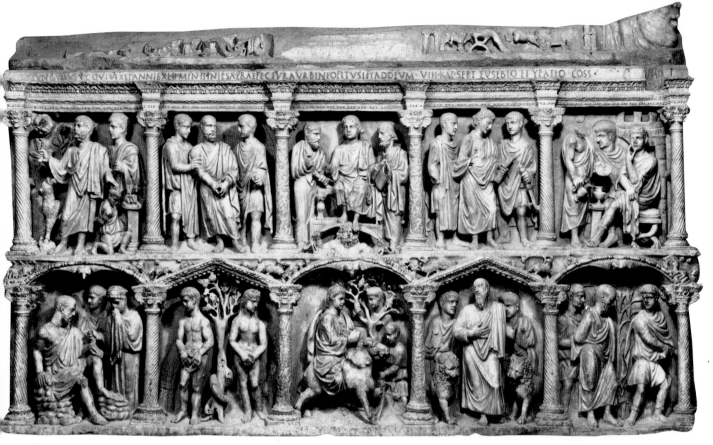

5.9 Above **Sarcophagus of Junius Bassus, 359. Grottoes of St. Peter, Vatican.**
Each relief scene is presented on its own stage, depicting biblical figures in a finely carved classical style. In the lower register, scenes of affliction and sin (Job with the counselors, Adam and Eve in Eden) are counterposed to the theme of redemption and deliverance (Christ entering Jerusalem, the prophet Daniel among the lions).

5.10 Right **Head of Constantine, from a colossal statue that stood in the Basilica of Constantine, Rome (see Fig. 4.16), 313. Marble, height of head 8 ft 6 ins (2.59 m). Palazzo dei Conservatori, Rome.**
Inclined to visionary mysticism, the emperor Constantine founded dozens of Christian churches in Rome and Constantinople, the new capital of his empire.

opment. The emperors built lavish new churches, advancing the synthesis of Christianity and the pagan tradition. With Christianity's new status came an impulse to compromise. Christian leaders now represented the power of the Roman state that had once persecuted them. In the first century A.D., the Christian faith had begun as a radical teaching to impoverished Palestinian Jews. By the fifth century, it had become the wealthiest and most powerful social institution of the Western world.

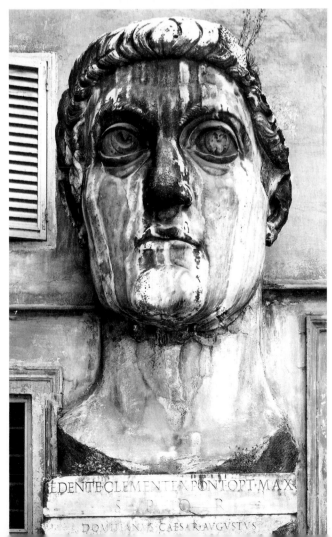

CHRISTIAN PHILOSOPHY

Explain Augustine's views on human nature and human history.

Christianity's first leaders had been martyrs and saints. By 400, the Christian clergy had become politicians and civic leaders in a declining Roman Empire. Once Christianity had become the Empire's official religion, a new relation needed to be forged between the Christian Church and imperial power. Theologians needed to define orthodox belief and enforce Christian doctrine on believers scattered throughout the Empire, while Christian philosophers considered the nature of human character and human society in a Christian age.

FROM CLASSICAL TO CHRISTIAN

The first centuries of Christianity saw an intense intellectual struggle between the pagan traditions of Greek and Roman learning and the new ideas of Christianity. The predominant pagan philosophies were **Manicheism** [man-i-KAY-ism], which saw the world as a conflict between good and evil, and **Neoplatonism**, which characterized all good as flowing from a single, divine force. The Neoplatonists in particular fostered the classical tradition of reason and unity of thought. For example, Hypatia [hyuh-PAY-shuh] (*c.* 370–415), late antiquity's most significant woman philosopher, led a lively Neoplatonist school at Alexandria in Egypt. She made significant contributions to mathematics and astronomy, but suffered a hideous murder at the hands of Christian zealots. Hypatia's death and the burning of Alexandria's famous libraries ended the city's preeminence as a center of classical learning.

Through the fourth century, Christian intellectuals gradually did harmonize their beliefs with classical traditions, affirming Plato's division of body and soul (see page 63) and the stoics' restraint of passion and acceptance of divine will. The agents of this philosophical compromise were the so-called Fathers of the Church, whose writings formed the **patristic** tradition (from Latin *pater*, "father"). One legacy of patristic scholarship was the Latin translation of the Bible by St. Jerome, whose version became the standard Bible of Western Christianity.

AUGUSTINE OF HIPPO

By far the most important patristic philosopher was Augustine of Hippo (354–430). Augustine's best-known writing is the *Confessions* (397–401), a remarkable work of spiritual introspection unparalleled in the classical literature of Augustine's day. It details Augustine's attraction to both Manichean and Neoplatonist doctrines. More important, the *Confessions* describe Augustine's inner struggle against his own sinful will. In repentance, he remembers the youthful theft of some pears with the same bitterness as his years with the anonymous mistress who bore him a son. Of the theft, Augustine writes:

> *Some lewd young fellows of us went and took huge loads, not for our eating, but to fling to the very hogs. And this, but to do what we like only because it was misliked.*[6]

Of the mistress, whom he renounced at his family's insistence, he says, "The heart, to which she stuck fast, was cut and wounded in me, and oozed blood."

In probing "the depths of his soul," Augustine found that only God's immense grace could save him from sin. His own will was too weak. Human freedom, Augustine argued, was only the freedom of the will to commit sin. The *Confessions* portray Augustine's soul in a constant struggle against its desires, in constant conflict with its own sinful nature. Thus, Augustine's Christian view of the human soul differed sharply from the classical tradition in which it was rooted. For classical philosophers such as Socrates and the stoics, the wise soul could successfully live at peace with itself and the cosmos; the Christian's soul, said Augustine, was always at war with itself.

Augustine's **City of God** The barbarian sacking of Rome in 410 shocked Augustine and most citizens of the Empire. Pagan traditionalists blamed Rome's fall on the Christians, who refused to do public service or honor Roman deities. Augustine responded to pagan critics with the *City of God* (413–26), the most comprehensive work of history in the ancient world. He argued that God had a historical design for all humanity's salvation, and Rome's fall was part of that design.

Augustine presented human history as a battle between two symbolic cities. The "city of the world" (*civitas terrena*) was peopled by pagans and Christian heretics. The "city of God" (*civitas dei*) was founded in heaven but encompassed the Christian faithful living on earth. According to God's plan of history, the earthly city would eventually be destroyed altogether and its inhabitants cast into damnation. Righteous Christians would live in a state of blessedness and universal peace at the end of history. Until this time, Augustine advised good Christians to "obey the laws of the earthly city whereby the things necessary for the maintenance of this mortal life are administered." With such words, Augustine commanded Christians to obey

---

THE WRITE IDEA

Given the trends you see now, describe where human history will lead in the next century. What is causing history to move in one direction or another?

KEY CONCEPT

ORIGINAL SIN AND HUMAN NATURE

Augustine believed that sinfulness and the need for repentance were the unrelenting truths of human experience. His beliefs engaged him in fierce debate over sin and human nature. Christian thinkers disagreed on whether baptism erased sinfulness or whether sin remained forever rooted in the human soul. Augustine answered this question with his doctrine of "original sin." A fundamental concept of Western views of human nature, **original sin** refers to Adam and Eve's first violation of divine command in the Garden of Eden (Fig. **5.11**). According to Augustine, when Adam and Eve ate the forbidden fruit, they condemned all humanity to a state of sinfulness. Because all humans descended from Eve, every human soul, including that of a newborn infant, was inevitably wicked.

The Greek scholars of the Eastern Church (which later became the Greek Orthodox Church) disputed Augustine's concept of original sin. As they read the Bible, sin resulted from individual acts of will, and humans were justly punished according to the degree of their sin. However, according to Augustine, sin resulted from human nature, not from human action. The stain of sinfulness existed from conception and could not be erased by acts of repentance. Augustine's more radical interpretation won the day and his view of original sin became official doctrine. It remains a cornerstone of Western Christian belief today.

The concept of original sin had enormous importance in the Western view of human nature. It meant that humans could not naturally govern themselves or achieve a state of goodness by their own effort. As children, humans required the rigorous discipline of parental guidance; as adults, they required the limits imposed by law and a paternal government. Later philosophers would challenge Augustine's doctrine of human depravity, or corruption. Some eighteenth-century philosophers claimed that humans were naturally good and corrupted only by the influence of a depraved society. Augustine's definition of human nature still affects the way that parents rear children, schools instruct students, and governments rule their citizens.

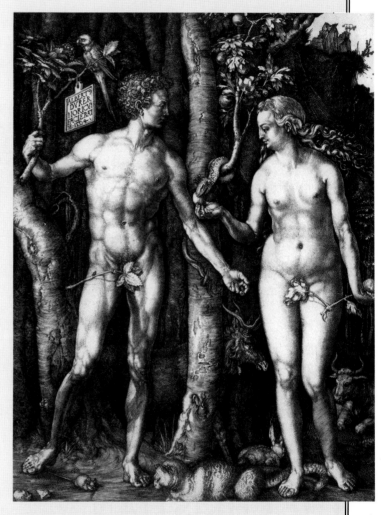

5.11 Albrecht Dürer, *Adam and Eve*, 1504. Engraving, 10 x 7⁵/₈ ins (25.2 x 19.4 cm).
A rendering of the fall of Adam and Eve, when, according to Augustine, both sin and knowledge of good and evil entered the world.

CRITICAL QUESTION

In your opinion, are humans naturally inclined to greed, rebellion, and evil? What forces, both inner and outer, cause humans to do good or evil?

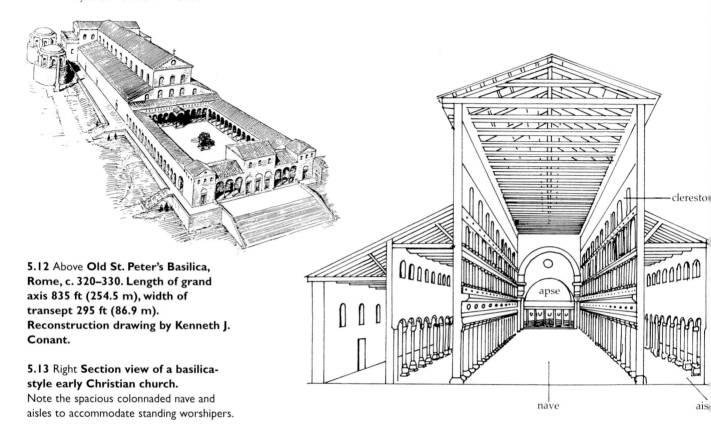

5.12 Above **Old St. Peter's Basilica, Rome, c. 320–330. Length of grand axis 835 ft (254.5 m), width of transept 295 ft (86.9 m). Reconstruction drawing by Kenneth J. Conant.**

5.13 Right **Section view of a basilica-style early Christian church.** Note the spacious colonnaded nave and aisles to accommodate standing worshipers.

the very Roman state that barely a century earlier had bitterly persecuted them.

Historical thinking in Western philosophy continued to be influenced by Augustine's work. Modern versions of his final stage of history can be seen in the "classless society" of Karl Marx's *Communist Manifesto* (1848) and the dark vision of George Orwell's *1984* (1949). The *City of God* established a longstanding tradition of histories that led into the future.

THE CHRISTIAN EMPIRES: ROME AND BYZANTIUM

Summarize the artistic differences between the churches of Latin Christianity and the Byzantine world.

In 330, the Emperor Constantine dedicated a grand new capital of the Roman Empire. Constantine had built his capital at the ancient Greek city of Byzantium and renamed it Constantinople, after himself. The consecration of a "new Rome" at Constantinople indicated a pivotal change in the late Empire. From that moment, the Roman Empire divided into two parts that would suffer different historical fates. The Latin-speaking Western Empire, centered in Rome, suffered barbarian invasions and political turmoil. A Greek-speaking Byzantine Empire, centered in Constantinople, grew more prosperous and powerful. By the sixth century, the Byzantine emperor would rule the entire Empire from his palace in Constantinople.

The Empire's division also affected the newly influential Christian churches. A disaffection grew between the Latin Church, with its centers of power in Rome and northern Africa, and the Greek Church, which was strongly allied with the powerful Byzantine emperors. The division expressed itself in growing theological and artistic differences that would eventually split the Roman Catholic (or "universal") Church and the Byzantine Orthodox Church.

ST. PETER'S AND THE POPE

Roman emperors had always favored their subjects with lavish public buildings, a policy that now benefited the newly legalized Christian Church. In Rome, Constantine endowed about fifteen new churches that rivaled the pagan temples in their size and splendor. The largest and most important was St. Peter's (Fig. **5.12**), built on the Vatican hill outside Rome over the tomb of the apostle Simon Peter. The St. Peter's of Constantine (built *c.* 320–30) was to be Latin Christianity's most famous shrine for a thousand years, until it was demolished and replaced during the Renaissance.

St. Peter's was typical of basilica-style Christian churches, which were modeled after the Roman basilica (see page 77), with its coffered ceilings and rows of columns

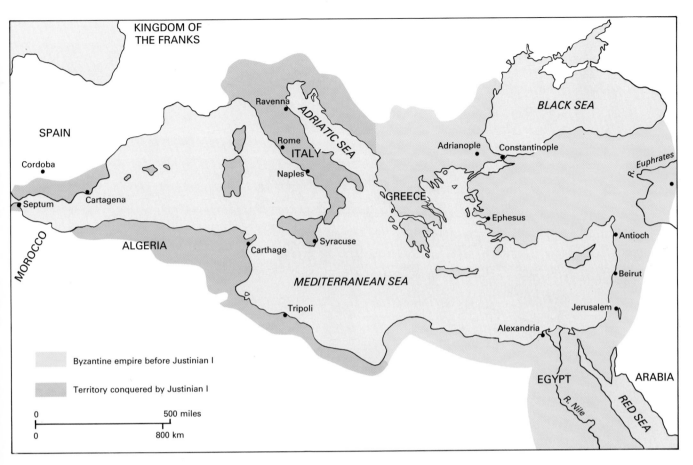

5.14 The Byzantine Empire under Justinian, 527–65.

(Fig. **5.13**). Worshipers entered the church through a wide, shallow **narthex**, or vestibule, and then traveled along the columned aisles. The church's central hall, called the **nave**, had an elevated roof and could accommodate several thousand standing worshipers. The architect of St. Peter's added a crossing **transept** at the altar to provide additional space for worshipers. This created a cross-shaped floor plan. Behind the altar was the **apse**, another holdover from the Roman basilica. The apse's half-dome was typically decorated with sacred images in paint or mosaic. St. Peter's basilica design was to become the basic pattern of Latin Christianity's greatest churches.

Constantine's generosity to the Church did not reverse the decline of Rome or protect it against the barbarians, nomadic peoples of northern Europe who swept over the Rhine River and threatened Roman farms and cities. Barbarian leaders, some already converted to Christianity, pressed in on the Western Empire, demanding tribute and territory. In 402 the Roman government was moved to the more easily defended town of Ravenna, on the Italian Adriatic coast. In 410 Rome itself was sacked by the Goths, shocking the entire Empire, and in 476 the last Roman emperor was forced to abdicate in Ravenna, ending a line of rulers that had originated five centuries earlier with Caesar Augustus. By the sixth century, the old

Roman Empire had become a patchwork of barbarian settlements, its central government and cities in ruin.

In Rome the vacuum of power was quickly filled by the pope, the Christian bishop of Rome. By the fourth century, the pope was acknowledged by Western Christians as the Church's supreme spiritual authority. As imperial order declined in the West, the pope and other bishops played a powerful civic role and were able to encourage lawfulness and censure abuses. In the eastern Byzantine Empire, on the other hand, the emperor's power remained unshakable and the Eastern Church was closely wedded to imperial authority.

JUSTINIAN AND THE BYZANTINE WORLD

Compared with the upheavals in the West, the Byzantine Empire was a paragon of stability and conservatism. Its founder had equiped Constantinople with an imperial palace, a hippodrome, numerous churches, and the other trappings of Roman urban life. Constantinople quickly absorbed the Greek climate of cultivation, spirituality, symbolism, and intrigue, and grew into a vibrant cultural and intellectual center.

The Byzantine world (Fig. **5.14**) reached its height under the rule of the Emperor Justinian (527–65), who

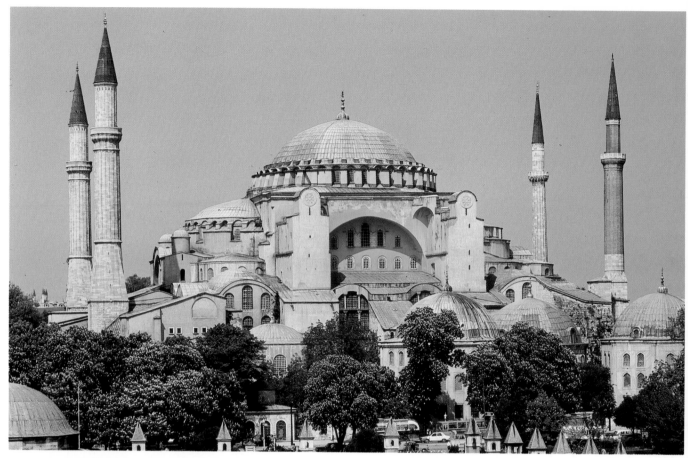

5.15 Anthemius of Tralles and Isidorus of Miletus, Hagia Sophia ("Holy Wisdom"), Istanbul (Constantinople), 532–7.
Though somewhat obscured by additional buttressing, Hagia Sophia's dome rises on a mountain of masonry. The minarets date from after the Turkish conquest of Constantinople in 1453.

achieved significant legal reforms and artistic renewal. Justinian [juss-TIN-ee-un] was a skillful negotiator, more inclined to compromise than conquer. His armies overthrew barbarian rule in the West and briefly reunited the two empires. Justinian is best remembered for his vast reform of Roman law, the so-called Code of Justinian, which was the first thorough revision of Roman law since Julius Caesar.

Justinian was notable also for sharing power with his wife, Theodora, a confident and capable woman who ruled as co-empress. Theodora [thee-oh-DOH-ruh] rose to power from humble beginnings as an actress and courtesan. The empress is credited with saving the emperor when he faced a civil insurrection. Reportedly, Theodora stopped her husband from fleeing the capital, saying of her royal gown, "The empire is a fine winding sheet." Inspired by her example, Justinian ordered his army commander to slaughter thirty thousand protesters in the hippodrome. The emperor's rule was never again seriously threatened.

During this revolt a fire destroyed the center of Constantinople, including the great church of Hagia Sophia [hah-JEE-ah soh-FEE-ah] ("Holy Wisdom"). At Justinian's direction and enormous expense, Hagia Sophia (Fig. 5.15) was quickly rebuilt on a gigantic scale. The church was so large that it seemed a divine miracle to observers in later centuries. The new church's designers, Anthemius of Tralles and Isidorus of Miletus, were both mathematicians and scientists, not professional architects. Their daring plan for a gigantic domed interior astonished even Justinian, who took a personal interest in the construction. Two giant work crews built simultaneously from the north and south. By Christmas 537, less than six years after it was begun, the awesome new Hagia Sophia was dedicated. It would remain the largest church in the Christian world for nine hundred years.

The architects of Hagia Sophia stretched the techniques of domed building to the very limit of possibility (Fig. 5.17). Older domes such as the Pantheon in Rome (see Fig.

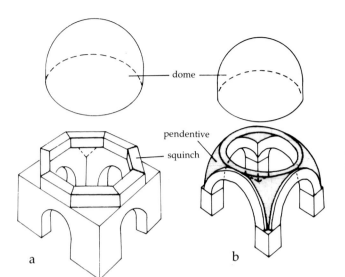

5.16 Supporting a dome.
In (*a*) beams called squinches are placed diagonally across the opening and support the dome. In pendentive construction (*b*) – the method used for supporting the dome in Hagia Sophia – triangular pendentives curve up and in from supporting piers, forming a circular base for the dome. Compare with the Pantheon (Fig. 4.19) in which the dome rests on cylindrical walls.

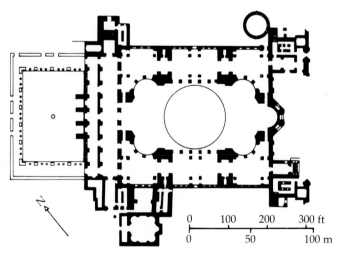

5.17 Plan and section of Hagia Sophia, Istanbul, 532–7. Exterior dimensions 308 x 236 ft (93.9 x 71.9 m).
The central dome was supported by half-domes on the east and west sides, and filled arches on the north and south sides.

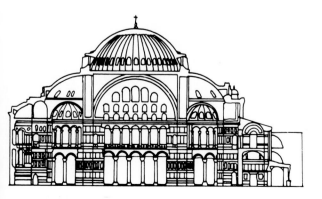

4.18) rested on cylindrical walls. Byzantine architects frequently supported their domes on **squinches** (Fig. **5.16**). In Hagia Sophia, the dome rested on concave, triangular vaults called **pendentives**, which curved gracefully down to four massive corner piers. Pendentive construction allowed the dome to cover a square or rectangular space below, creating a so-called "domed basilica."

The current dome of Hagia Sophia rises to a height of more than 180 feet (55 m), nearly 40 feet (12 m) higher than the Pantheon of Rome. The original dome, which was higher, collapsed twenty years after it was built. From the outside, the dome appears to rest upon a mountain of masonry. On the inside (Fig. **5.18**), the dome floats above the cavernous nave, rising on a combination of columns, arches, pendentives, and half-domes. The interior pays little regard to classical rules of proportion and measure. Instead, Hagia Sophia's combinations of mass and space create an aura of mystery and subtle cultivation well suited to the Byzantine spirit.

Hagia Sophia's interior decoration expressed the Byzantine love of intricate decoration and sumptuous materials. The foundation columns were topped by capitals with the undercut carving of the Byzantine order. The interior walls and domes were decorated with lavish mosaics that covered a total area of 4 acres (1.62 ha). Illuminated by rows of windows, including forty windows in the central dome, these mosaics reflected the brilliance of the Byzantine Church and court. A contemporary observer wrote, "The golden stream of glittering rays pours down and strikes the eyes of men, so that they can scarcely bear to look. It is as if one were to gaze upon the mid-day sun in spring, when it gilds every mountain height."[7]

Standing in his great church for the first time, Justinian compared his achievement to the temple in Jerusalem. The emperor is said to have murmured, "Solomon, I have surpassed thee." In the sheer ambition of its design, Hagia Sophia surpassed every building of classical times.

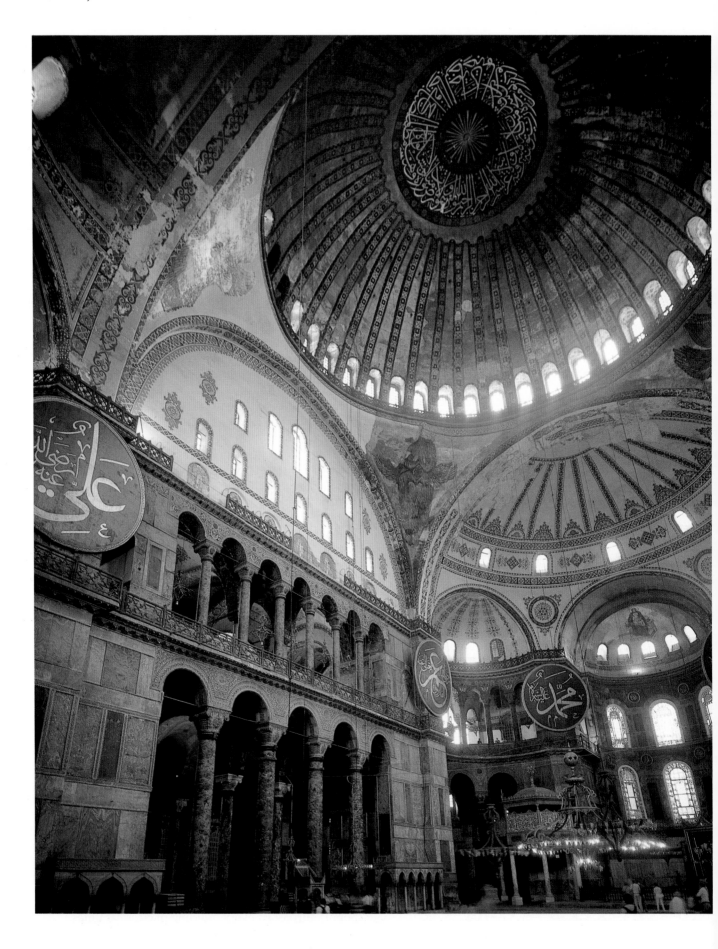

5.18 Opposite **Interior, Hagia Sophia, Istanbul, 532–7. Height of dome 183 ft (55.8 m).**
Weakened by earthquakes, the original dome collapsed in 558 and was replaced with the current, slightly lower version. The shields bearing Arabic script were added when the church was converted by Muslims to a mosque after 1453.

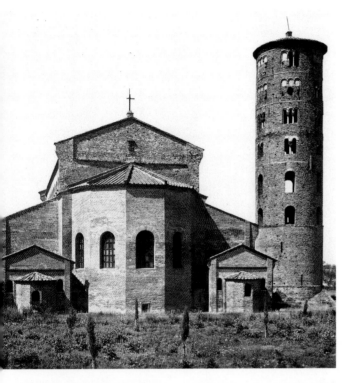

RAVENNA: SHOWCASE OF THE CHRISTIAN ARTS

By historical accident, the best-preserved early Christian art is found not in Rome or Constantinople, but in the small town of Ravenna on Italy's northeast coast. In the fifth and sixth centuries, Ravenna became a refuge for Roman emperors and barbarian rulers. After its capture in 540 by Justinian's army, Ravenna was briefly drawn into the Byzantine orbit and benefited from Justinian's generous patronage. For a century and a half, patrons from both Latin and Greek Christianity built their churches, mausoleums, and baptisteries in Ravenna. They left a record of Christian art that was untouched by later conquest or artistic renewal.

The earliest churches of Ravenna retained the Roman architectural vocabulary: columns, arches, mosaic decoration, and the rectangular basilica plan (Fig. **5.19**). These

5.19 Left **Sant'Apollinare in Classe, Ravenna, Italy, c. 549.**
In this view, the polygonal apse juts out from the nave, with the slanting aisle roofs visible on either side. The bell tower at right dates from a later period.

5.20 Below *Christ as the Good Shepherd*. **Mosaic from the Mausoleum of Galla Placidia, Ravenna, Italy, 5th century.**
In this brilliant mosaic, a scene of Christ as the good shepherd is composed to fit the half-oval shape of a lunette. The youthful Christ tenderly rubs a sheep's chin in this pastoral scene.

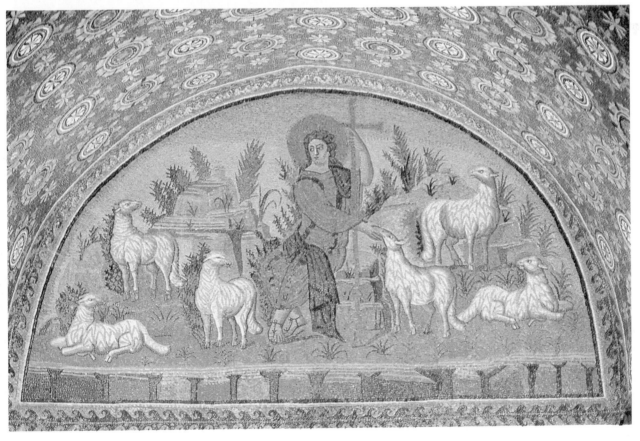

churches were usually plain brick on the exterior. On the inside, their apses and walls were richly decorated with scenes of the Christian faith.

The mosaics of Ravenna reveal the evolution of visual imagery and storytelling in early Christian art. Compared with pagan mythology, early Christianity offered mosaic artists a rather slim stock of stories and images. Artists depicted scenes and stories from the life of Christ, the lives of saints and martyrs, and Hebrew tales. The most familiar images represent Jesus in scenes from the Gospels: Christ as the Good Shepherd (Fig. **5.20**), Christ feeding the multitudes, and Christ calling his disciples.

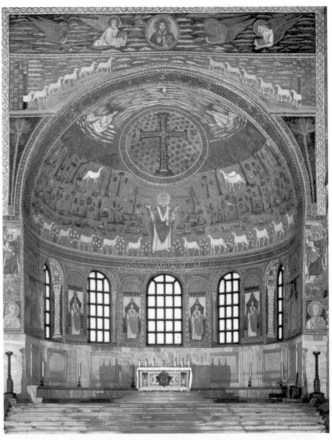

5.21 Right **Interior, Sant'Apollinare Nuovo, Ravenna, Italy, c. 493–526.**
Observe how the apse's half-dome creates a grand theatrical setting for the raised altar, where the Christian mass was celebrated. The apse's mosaic presents Christ with outstretched arms, reigning over the delights of paradise and welcoming the faithful (symbolized as sheep).

5.22 Below *Procession of Virgin Martyrs*, **c. 560. Mosaic. Sant'Apollinare Nuovo, Ravenna, Italy.**
These martyrs represent early female converts to Christianity, who resisted social pressures to marry in favor of pursuing their Christian faith. The Virgin Martyrs bear crowns to the Christ Child, against a background of palm trees.

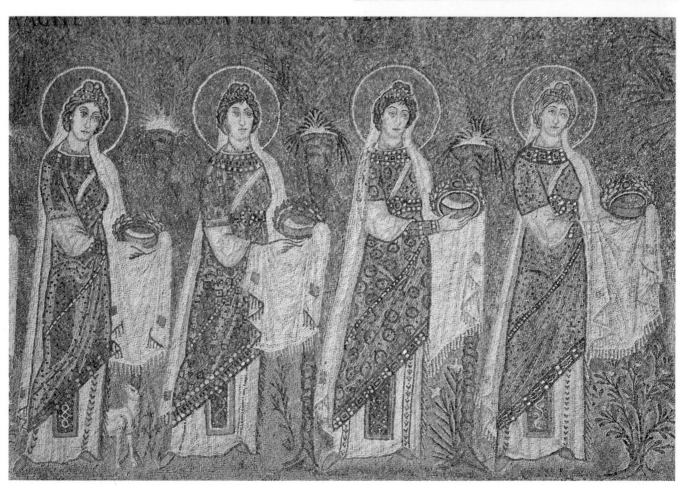

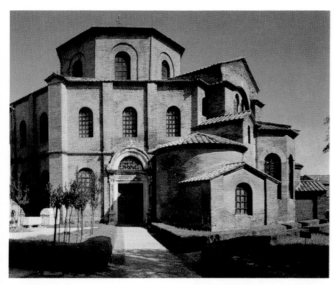

5.23 San Vitale, Ravenna, Italy, c. 527-47. Diameter 112 ft (34.2 m).
The church's plain brick exterior gives little hint of the sumptuous decoration inside.

The noblest work of interior decoration at Ravenna is Sant' Apollinare Nuovo (Fig. **5.21**), built under the reign of the barbarian ruler Theodoric (445–526). Above the nave columns, stately processions of the saints and virgin martyrs (Fig. **5.22**) bear gifts toward Christ and the Virgin Mary.

5.24 Plan of San Vitale, Ravenna, Italy, c. 527–47.
The octagonal plan's symmetry was compromised to create a nave, apse, and atrium.

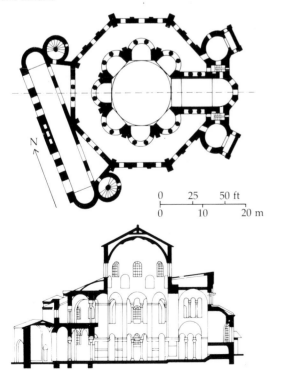

The parade of virgins is led by the Three Wise Men, passing before palm trees that recall Christ's triumphant entry into Jerusalem, when he was supposedly hailed as a king (Mark 11:1–10). To please their imperial patrons, artists stressed such images of Christ's royalty and majesty. The Ravenna mosaics' visual style indicates the weakening hold of Roman naturalism on early Christian artists. The virgins of Sant' Apollinare Nuovo [sant-ah-poll-ee-NAR-ay noo-WO-voh] are abstracted from the background in a way that emphasized their spirituality. This trend toward spirituality and symbolic representation intensified in later Byzantine art.

5.25 Interior looking toward apse, San Vitale, Ravenna, Italy, c. 527–47.
Justinian's generous patronage financed San Vitale's spectacular mosaic decoration.

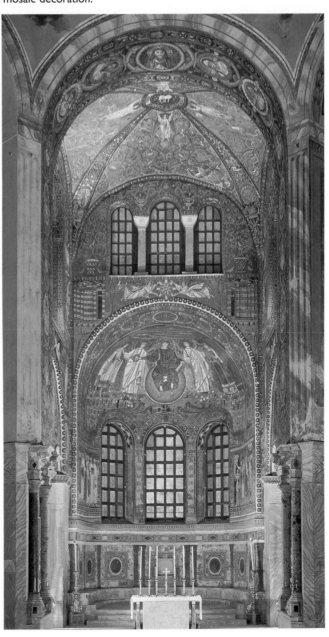

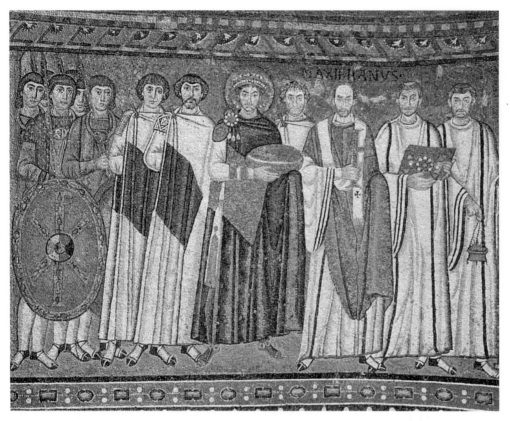

5.26 *Justinian and His Courtiers,* **c. 547. Mosaic. San Vitale, Ravenna, Italy.**
Emperor Justinian holds a bread basket symbolizing an element of the Eucharist (Last Supper). On the soldier's shield are the Greek initials *chi* and *rho,* the first letters of "Christ."

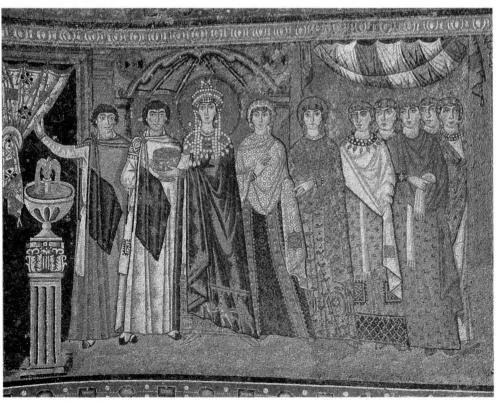

5.27 *Theodora and Retinue,* **c. 547. Mosaic. San Vitale, Ravenna, Italy.**
This scene of a regal Theodora faces *Justinian and his Courtiers* (see Fig. 5.26) on the opposing wall. The shape of the jeweled chalice is echoed in the baptismal font at left; on the hem of Theodora's gown are the Three Wise Men bearing gifts to Christ, a favorite theme of imperial Christian art. What conclusions can be drawn from the mosaic artists' even-handed treatment of emperor and empress in these matching portraits?

San Vitale of Ravenna The only truly Byzantine church in Ravenna is San Vitale (Fig. **5.23**), built during Justinian's reign and emphatically un-classical in its design and decoration. San Vitale [sahn vi-TAHL-ay] is an example of a **central-plan** church, so-called because its dome and walls are organized around a central axis (Fig. **5.24**). The church is a double octagon: the domed inner octagon is supported by arches, while the outer octagon encloses a vaulted walkway. The second-story gallery accommodated female worshipers, who were strictly segregated in the Byzantine liturgy. The walkway is interrupted on one side by a shortened nave and apse, a concession to the classical basilica form. In all, San Vitale's design was compact yet complex, a modest but charming counterpart to the domed grandeur of Hagia Sophia.

San Vitale's interior (Fig. **5.25**) is perhaps the most complete and authentic example of Byzantine decoration from Justinian's era. Most striking are the facing mosaic portraits of Justinian and Theodora with their courtly retinues. Justinian is flanked by clergymen (including the Archbishop Maximian) and by imperial soldiers (Fig. **5.26**); the portrait represents the union of state power and Church power that distinguished the Byzantine from the Roman Church. The portrait of Theodora presents her as a regal figure, holding a jeweled chalice of the Eucharist, while a priest reveals at her right the baptismal font (Fig. **5.27**). The figures' exaggerated eyes and strictly frontal poses are features of Byzantine art, which moved toward greater spirituality and abstraction, away from naturalism.

The church of San Vitale was the ultimate fusion of imperial splendor and Christian piety. The later medieval emperor Charlemagne may have modeled his own royal chapel after San Vitale at Ravenna (see page 138).

CHRISTIANITY AND THE ARTS

Identify the religious and social reasons for early Christians' hostility to the arts.

Early Christians rather easily adopted Roman architecture and decoration in their churches. However, the other arts of pagan Rome – especially music and theater – inspired deep suspicion among the Church fathers. The Roman theater fostered a mocking irreverence that threatened Christian religiosity. In addition, the performing arts competed directly with the Church for the attention of the faithful. A bishop of Carthage even threatened to excommunicate any Christian who went to the theater instead of church on a feast day. Early Christianity's struggle with Roman music and theater was the first of Christianity's many battles with the spirit of artistic creation.

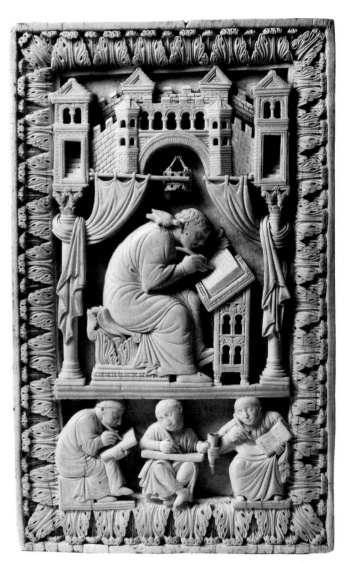

5.28 Tenth-century ivory book cover depicting Gregory recording chants.
Gregory's authorship of the so-called Gregorian chant was more legendary than historical. Tenth-century artists portrayed the early Christian pope as inspired by the Holy Spirit, represented by a dove.

EARLY CHRISTIAN MUSIC

The ancient Roman world possessed a wealth of musical styles and instruments. Music accompanied virtually every public entertainment, from a bawdy farce to the slaughter of wild animals and Christians in the circuses. The Church associated instrumental music with such non-religious pastimes, and therefore banned musical instruments from church services. Thus early Christian music was almost entirely vocal music, and would remain so for centuries.

Early Christian music consisted of chanted hymns and psalms that accompanied worship services and communal meals. The earliest Christian singing may have par-

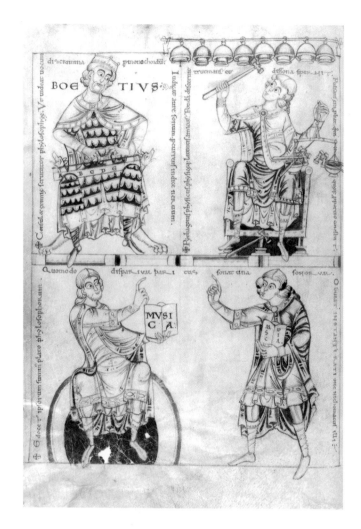

5.29 Illustration from Boethius' *De institutione musica* **(***The Fundamentals of Music***), Cambridge University Library, England.** The illustration honors the revered classical authorities on music: Boethius himself in upper left; Pythagoras striking the bells in upper right; and below, Plato and another philosopher disputing musical theory.

alleled the psalms and hymns sung in Jewish temples. However, local Christian churches were so independent that their sacred music varied widely in form and language. Chants and hymns were sung mainly in two ways – in **responsorial singing**, with the choir responding to a soloist, or in **antiphonal singing**, in which two choirs sang alternating verses. Both responsorial and antiphonal forms of chant and song became ingrained in the Christian musical tradition.

As authority in the Latin Church became more centralized, Christian song was gradually unified into distinct repertories of sacred melody. One style of chant, known as **Ambrosian chant**, was associated with the prestigious bishop of Milan, St. Ambrose, and was practiced in northern Italy. The most influential early Church music was the **Gregorian chant** (also known as plainchant or plainsong), a body of song consolidated in Rome during the seventh century, although tradition grants authorship to Pope Gregory I (590–604; Fig. **5.28**). By the eighth century a Roman school existed for training young men and boy singers of chant. In the ninth century, Gregorian chant was systematically compiled at the court of the Frankish Emperor Charlemagne (see page 154). Charlemagne's priests and monks tried to impose the Gregorian style on all of the Western Church, stamping out Ambrosian and other chant styles.

The Christian liturgy, or Mass, required different music according to the religious season. The Mass accommodated the yearly cycle of Christian holidays, while maintaining its basic conservative form. The chants were largely **monophonic** ("one-voiced"), consisting of a single melodic line, sung in unison, that rose and fell in a mystic undulation. Christian music, always tradition-bound, remained largely monophonic until the twelfth century.

Music was largely responsible for creating an attitude of devotion in Christian worshipers. The classical doctrine of ethos was still echoed in early Christian music. The main influence on the theory of music was the early Christian philosopher Boethius [boh-EETH-ee-us] (*c.* 480–*c.* 524). He theorized that music underlay the harmony of the universe and the soul, and that this harmony rested on the numerical orderliness of musical tones and chords. Music was a demonstration of the order in God's creation. Thus, Boethius transmitted in Christianized form the musical doctrines of Pythagoras and other ancient Greek thinkers. Boethius' treatise *De institutione musica* (*The Fundamentals of Music*, early sixth century; Fig. **5.29**) was the most widely read book of musical theory in the Christian Middle Ages.

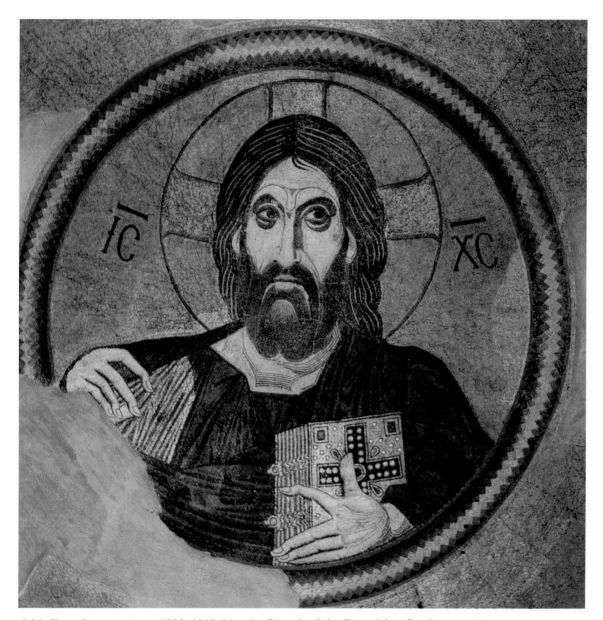

5.30 *Christ Pantocrator*, c. 1080–1100. Mosaic, Church of the Dormition, Daphne.
This image of a stern Pantocrator ("world ruler") was typical of the images that inspired great devotion among Byzantine worshipers, and were eagerly restored after iconoclasm had subsided.

THE CHRISTIANS AND THEATER

In the late Empire, Roman theater had become increasingly lurid and spectacular. Sex acts were permitted on stage, and the Emperor Diocletian decreed that a crucifixion be part of a theatrical performance. Even Augustine confessed, "I had a violent passion for these spectacles, which were full of the images of my miseries and of the amorous flames which devoured me." Besides this sensual wickedness, Roman mimes and comic actors frequently aimed their mockery and sacrilegious outrages at the pious Christians.

Not surprisingly, early Christian authorities condemned the Roman theater more fiercely than any other art. Baptism was forbidden for actors (an exception was made for Justinian's empress, Theodora). Professional actors – never highly esteemed in the Roman world –

virtually disappeared from Western society. The public theaters declined until, in the seventh century, state support was withdrawn and official theater expired in the western Roman Empire. It would not appear again until the beginnings of Christian religious drama some three hundred years later. Theater in the Western world survived in two forms: in the classical texts stored in libraries and read only by monks, and in the pagan folk festivals that gradually infiltrated the Christian calendar.

Early Christianity's hostility to the arts peaked in Byzantine iconoclasm [eye-KON-o-klaz-um], which reached its height from 730 to 843. **Iconoclasm**, which meant "smashing icons," was a violent response to the popular taste for sacred images. The Byzantine faithful attributed healing powers to icons, usually mosaics or painted wooden screens (Fig. **5.30**). Byzantine theologians defended icons

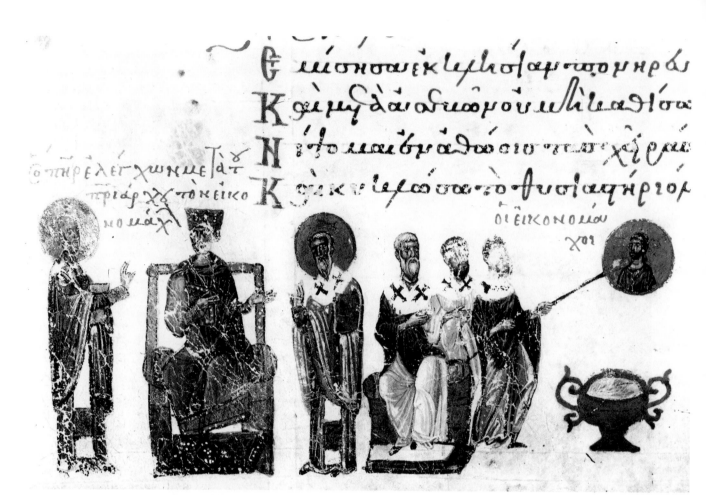

5.31 Iconoclast whitewashing an image. Manuscript illumination. British Library, London (ms. fl 9352 fol. 27v).
An iconoclast whitewashes an image of Christ. The iconoclastic controversy split the Byzantine Church until bans on images were repealed in the ninth century A.D.

GLOBAL PERSPECTIVE

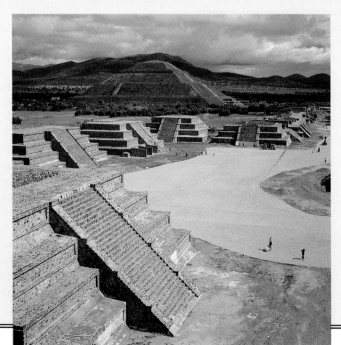

TEOTIHUACÁN: SACRED CITY OF MESOAMERICA

The sacred cities of the Christian and Muslim worlds – Jerusalem, Rome, Mecca – attracted a constant stream of devout visitors, eager to contact the holy sites of their faith. In **Mesoamerica** (present-day southern Mexico and Centra America), a pilgrim's destination would likely have been the great city of Teotihuacán [TAY-oh-TEE-hwah-

5.32 The Way of the Dead, Teotihuacán, Mexico, 1st–6th century A.D.
A view from the Temple of the Moon, with the Temple of the Sun rising in the background. The altars in the foreground radiate around the northern end of the Way of the Dead. The altar terraces show the sloping walls and vertical panels, originally decorated with relief sculpture.

as a way to know spiritual truth through a material form. However, the Byzantine Emperor Leo III blamed icon-worship for the Empire's military losses to the Arabs. In 730 he decreed that icons be removed from churches and palaces. With the emperor's sanction, the iconoclasts splintered iconic panels and painted over mosaics (Fig. **5.31**), often replacing gorgeous images with a rudely painted cross.

Although iconoclasm was official policy, it never enjoyed great popular support. When the controversy subsided in 843, icons soon reappeared in Byzantine churches. The episode echoed the Judeo-Christian tradition's old hostility toward the visual arts – "You shall have no graven images," commanded God – and anticipated future struggles between Christian faith and the creative arts.

THE RISE OF ISLAM

Identify the beliefs of Islam that supported the faith's militant expansion.

The internal dissension of the Christian empires at Rome and Byzantium proved to be mild compared to the onslaught of a new religious force in the Western world. Arising out of Arabia, the faith of Islam inspired a militant expansion that swept across the Near East to southwest Europe.

Founded by the prophet Muhammad [moo-HAM-ad] (570–632), Islamic belief superseded ancient ethnic loyalties and forged a powerful unity among the Arab people. By the time of Muhammad's death, virtually the entire Arabian peninsula was converted to Islam and unified Arabs were poised to expand northward and westward (Fig. **5.33**). Muhammad's successors authorized campaigns of religious conquest against armies of the Byzantine and Persian empires. The Arabs were skilled horsemen and fierce fighters, but they also believed that death in defense of Islam would bring them immediately to the rewards of paradise.

Within two centuries, Islam had expanded its borders east to the Indus River, encompassing much of what is now Pakistan. It stretched in the west to Spain, where its advance was halted by the Frankish army of Charles Martel, Charlemagne's grandfather, in 732. Synthesizing the cultures of its many peoples, Islam entered a "golden age" during which Islamic scholars and artisans surpassed their Christian and Eastern rivals.

THE FOUNDATIONS OF ISLAM

La ilaha illa Allah; Muhammad rasul Allah – "There is no god but Allah, and Muhammad is his prophet." In Arabic, these words are the simple but powerful profession of faith in Islam, the world's youngest great religion. The word *islam* means simply "surrender to God." For Muslims, the believers of Islam, "surrender" requires obedience to a strict reli-

KAHN], located in the Valley of Mexico (about 33 miles northeast of modern Mexico City). With some 200,000 residents at its height (350–650), Teotihuacán was one of the ancient world's largest cities and one of the most sacred. Its residents believed it to be the birthplace of the world, the site at which the gods sacrificed themselves to create the sun and moon. Nearly a thousand years after its ruin, the Aztec rulers of Mexico still made pilgrimages to Teotihuacán's holy temples.

Teotihuacán's most important temples and palaces were arranged along a processional causeway, called the Way of the Dead (Fig. **5.32**), which served as stage for ceremonial processions. The largest temples were the Pyramid of the Sun and Pyramid of the Moon, whose swelling forms mimicked the shape of the surrounding mountains. Beneath the Pyramid of the Sun was a natural lava cavern thought to be the womb from which the gods themselves were born.

The temples' terraced walls sloped up to rectangular panels that were carved with the ferocious heads of feathered or fiery serpents. Inside the city's palaces, painted murals depicted the Spider Woman, a figure still known in American Indian legend, and a Water Goddess whose headdress blossoms into a fertile profusion of butterflies and flowers. The mythical beings that decorated the temples and palaces of Teotihuacán were worshiped throughout Mesoamerica.

Teotihuacán suffered an unexplained decline about 650 when the city was burned, perhaps by invaders or perhaps by its own citizens in an act of ritual self-sacrifice. It continued as a shrine for later peoples until the Spanish conquered Mesoamerica in the sixteenth century.

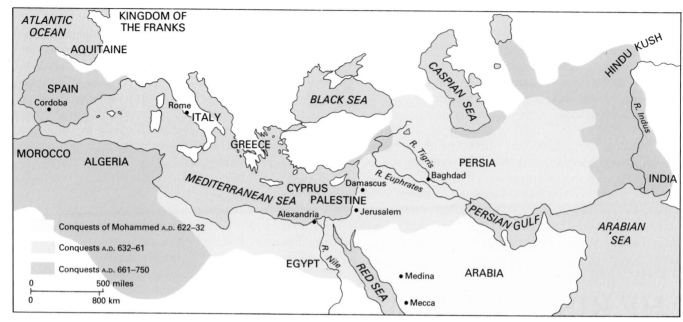

5.33 The rise of Islam.

gious and moral code and unfailing belief in the teachings of the prophet Muhammad.

The life of Islam's founder, the prophet Muhammad, is well known. He was born about 570 in the Arabian trader city of Mecca. In mid-life Muhammad received an angelic command to "rise and warn" the Arabian people in the name of their chief deity, **Allah**. About 613 Muhammad began preaching in Mecca and then had to flee his opponents in 622, settling in Medina, north of Mecca. This flight, called the **hegira** [HEEJ-ruh], is the event from which Muslims date their calendar. Eventually, Muhammad led a force against Mecca and successfully established the worship of Allah at Arabia's holiest shrine, the Qa'aba [KAHH-buh].

Muhammad's message, like that of Moses and Jesus, was radically simple: Allah was the sole god and creator of the universe. All men (though not women, according to Muhammad) were equal before God, and should treat each other as brothers. A day of judgment was coming that would reward the faithful with infinite pleasures and punish the evil with eternal misery. Muhammad acknowledged the prophets of Judaism and Christianity – Abraham, Moses, Jesus – as his predecessors (Fig. **5.34**).

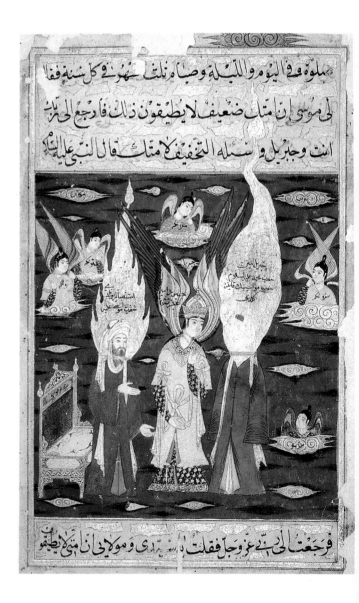

5.34 *The Prophet Muhammad with the Archangel Gabriel Meeting Moses in Heaven.* Persian miniature painting from Mustafa Zarir's *The Book of the Life of the Prophet*, c. 1594. 12¹/₂ x 8 ins (8.31 x 20.3 cm). Museum für Islamische Kunst, Berlin-Dahlem.
Islam saw Muhammad as the successor to the great Jewish prophets Abraham, Moses, and Jesus, but carefully emphasized the status of Muhammad as the last and truest of God's spokesmen.

From Muhammad's teachings evolved the essential tenets of Muslim faith, called the Five Pillars of Islam:

- bearing witness to Allah as the one true God
- prayer, normally five times daily while facing Mecca
- giving alms, both to the poor and to the Islamic state
- fasting during the holy month of Ramadan
- pilgrimage (the *hajj*) to the Qa'aba in Mecca.

The poor and infirm are excused from the obligations of almsgiving and pilgrimage. These pillars of faith remain the precepts of Islam throughout the world today.

The Qur'an Muhammad's most important act was to receive the revelations of God, recited to him by the archangel Gabriel over a period of twenty years. These revelations are inscribed in the Qur'an (Koran), Islam's scriptures (Fig. **5.35**). Written in Arabic, the Qur'an [KOR-ahn] is divided into 114 *suras* [SUH-ruhs], or chapters. It blends ecstatic praise of Allah with wisdom derived in part from Jewish and Christian sources. In most *suras*, Allah speaks directly to the faithful, as in Sura 55, when he describes the judgment of souls:

Mankind and jinn.[a] We shall surely find the time to judge you! Which of your Lord's blessings would you deny?

Mankind and jinn, if you have power to penetrate the confines of heaven and earth, then penetrate them! But this you shall not do except with Our own authority. Which of your Lord's blessings would you deny?

Flames of fire shall be lashed at you, and molten brass. There shall be none to help you. Which of your Lord's blessings would you deny?

When the sky splits asunder, and reddens like a rose or stained leather (which of your Lord's blessings would you deny?), on that day neither man nor jinnee will be asked about his sins. Which of your Lord's blessings would you deny?

The wrongdoers will be known by their looks; they shall be seized by their forelocks and their feet. Which of your Lord's blessings would you deny?

That is the Hell which the sinners deny. They shall wander between fire and water fiercely seething. Which of your Lord's blessings would you deny?

CRITICAL QUESTION

Compare Islam's fundamental beliefs with those of Judaism and Christianity. In what ways would you expect these religions to be compatible or incompatible with one another?

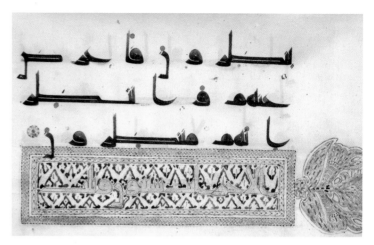

5.35 Qur'an page written in Kufi script, Iraq or Syria, 8th or 9th century. Parchment, 8¹/₂ x 13 ins (21.6 x 32.5 cm). Museum für Islamische Kunst, Berlin-Dahlem.
The Arabic text of the Qur'an, here presented in decorative calligraphy, was also incorporated into Islamic art as a constant reminder of the commanding will of Allah.

But for those that fear the majesty of their Lord there are two gardens (which of your Lord's blessings would you deny?) planted with shady trees. Which of your Lord's blessings would you deny?[8]

THE QUR'AN
Sura 55 The Merciful

---

a. *jinn,* supernatural spirits who, like humans, would face divine judgment.

For Muslims, only the Arabic version of the Qur'an is God's true revelation. Because of its influence, Arabic became the universal language of Islamic faith and learning, much as Latin was the tongue of Western Christianity.

ISLAMIC ARTS AND SCIENCE

In the eighth and ninth centuries, Islamic civilization achieved a remarkable synthesis of the many cultures within its bounds. By the early 800s, Islam's rulers (called **caliphs**) were Persian, not Arab. The caliphs occupied a splendid green-domed palace in their capital, Baghdad (founded 762), which grew to a city of more than a million. In Baghdad, Islam's artists and intellectuals drew from the rich traditions of Byzantine, Persian, Egyptian, and Indian peoples, as well as the Chinese, with whom Arab traders had regular contact.

Muslim art and architecture evolved directly from the tenets of the faith. The Muslims' place of worship, the **mosque**, was usually constructed on a simple plan: a large inner courtyard was surrounded by arcaded aisles to contain the faithful at prayer. The mosque at Córdoba in Spain (begun about 736) shows that Muslim architects willingly

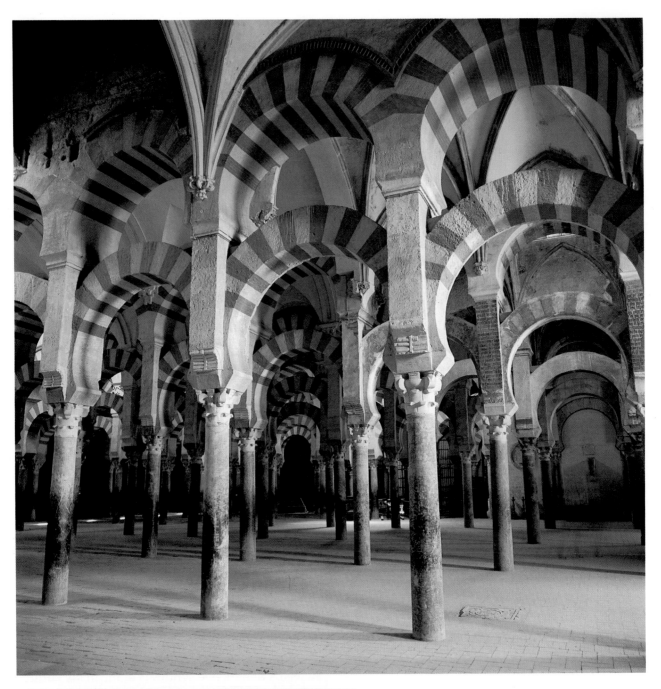

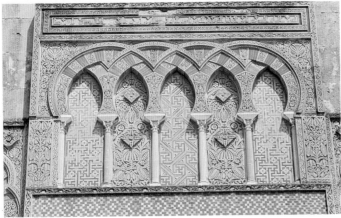

5.36 Above **Interior, Great Mosque of Córdoba, Spain, c. 736.**
Note the doubled horseshoe arches, the upper arches rising on stone or brick impost blocks. This ingenious system was originally devised to compensate for the relatively short columns (less than ten feet high) and was carried out as the mosque expanded to serve Córdoba's faithful.

5.37 Left **Arabesque, Great Mosque of Córdoba, Spain, 785–7.**

adapted the columns and arches of the Roman style (Fig. 5.36). The mosque's aisles oriented the believer in the direction of Mecca, toward which the faithful must turn in prayer. Mosques – as well as Islamic pottery and fine art – were commonly decorated in abstract design, in obedience to the Qur'an's prohibition against images of living things. The typical decoration was the **arabesque**, a design that repeated a basic line or pattern in seemingly infinite variations (Fig. 5.37).

Islamic civilization's greatest achievements were not in the arts, but in science, mathematics, and philosophy. Arabic physicians were licensed by the state and routinely performed surgeries for cancer and other diseases. The physician Razi (865–925) was the first to describe the clinical symptoms of smallpox. Arabic mathematicians shared the Islamic artists' fascination for abstraction and devised a numeral system based on the zero (Arabic *sifr*) and the mathematics of algebra (Arabic *al-jabr*). Arabic centers of learning preserved the heritage of classical philosophy, at a time when many works of Aristotle and Plato were unknown to the Christian world. A ninth-century caliph established an academy at Baghdad after being assured by the ghost of Aristotle that classical philosophy did not conflict with the Muslim faith. Baghdad was also long a center of Hebrew scholarship, thanks to Islam's tolerance for its Jewish minority. The later revival of science and philosophy in Christian Europe owed much to the efforts of Arabic civilization.

The rise of Islam initiated a long history of religious rivalry and uneasy coexistence in the Mediterranean world. Muslims often placed new Islamic shrines on the sacred sites of conquered religions. The Dome of the Rock in Jerusalem, for example (Fig. **5.38**), was erected on the Temple Mount where Herod's temple had stood (see page 102). The rock where Jews believed Abraham had prepared to sacrifice Isaac was where Muslims held that Muhammad ascended to visit heaven. At the same time, Muslim conquerors were comparatively tolerant. In Muslim Córdoba (see page 146), the regional caliph recognized both Muslim and Christian feast days. War erupted frequently, however, and in coming centuries Christian and Muslim often took bloody vengeance on each other. A common religious heritage was insufficient to resolve the political and cultural tensions among Jews, Christians, and Muslims.

DAWN OF THE MIDDLE AGES

Islam's victories completed a transformation of the ancient world that began with the barbarian invasions and the rise of Christianity. In the years from Constantine's conversion to Christianity to the Muslim conquest of Africa and Spain, the Greco-Roman world fell apart. Some of the pieces (Syria, Persia, north Africa) were swallowed up by Islam's advance, others (chiefly northern Europe) fell under the rule of vigorous barbarian tribes. The Mediterranean core of the

5.38 The Dome of the Rock, Jerusalem, late 7th century.
Compare the exterior splendor and symmetry of this domed mosque to the Church of San Vitale in Ravenna (Fig. 5.23). In Jerusalem, Muslim rulers and architects intended this grand mosque to rival the great churches of Jerusalem, built by Constantine and his successors.

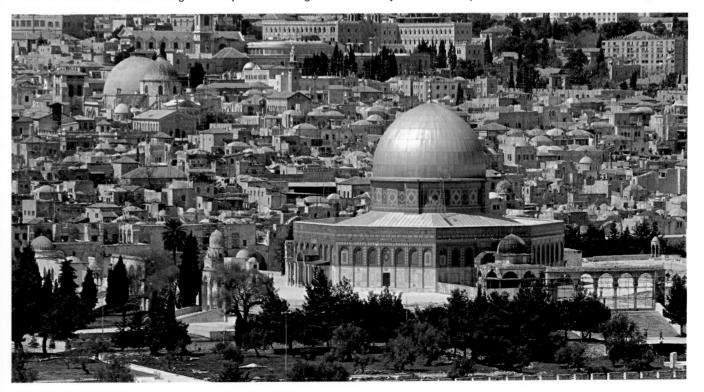

Greco-Roman world (Rome and Byzantium) remained intact, although now thoroughly Christianized.

The classical world had come to an end, and was replaced by what we now call the Middle Ages – the "middle" time between the classical era and the Renaissance (see Chapter 8), which inaugurated our modern age. Some scholars date the medieval period from Constantine, the first Christian Roman emperor; others see its beginning in the barbarian sack of Rome in 410, or in the last Roman emperor's abdication in 476. Yet, these dates focus on the decay of Roman forces, not on the vigorous new forces – of Islam and the European barbarian kings – that would dominate the medieval period. Whatever the date of the dawning of the Middle Ages, the light revealed a Western Europe dominated by two powerful forces – the Roman Catholic Church and the war-lords of northern Europe. The new "middle" age would be shaped by these two ambitious and often incompatible forces.

Chapter Summary

The Judaic Tradition. The Roman Empire's transformation by Christianity is rooted in the ideas of the ancient Jews, or Israelites, a Near Eastern people. In their history, the Israelites saw a pattern of deliverance or punishment at the hands of their God, Yahweh. Israelite national life centered on the temple at Jerusalem, founded by the kings David and Solomon. The Israelites' contribution to Western religion was their concept of monotheism, which held that all were equal before an almighty God. This "ethical" monotheism bequeathed important notions of obedience, righteousness, and sin to Western civilization. The Hebrew Bible revealed the nature of God and illustrated his covenant with the Israelites, who had to obey God's law and, like Job, submit to God's might. Often subjugated and exiled by imperial powers, the Israelites developed the apocalyptic hope that God would restore their nation's glory.

The Rise of Christianity. Out of the Hebrew faith arose Christianity, which originated in Jesus of Nazareth's call for a radically loving and humble communal life. Jesus' followers, especially the apostle Paul, emphasized their belief that Jesus had risen from the dead and offered eternal life to Christians. The Christian scriptures included Paul's letters and the Gospel accounts of Jesus' life, which testified to Jesus' promise of redemption. The Roman Emperor Constantine converted to Christianity and, by the end of the fourth century, Christianity had become the Empire's official religion.

A Christian Philosophy. The early Christian thinkers engaged in an intense struggle with the pagan traditions of Greek and Roman philosophy. The most important synthesis of classical and Christian ideas was achieved by St. Augustine, author of a compelling spiritual autobiography and a Christian philosophy of history. Augustine's concept of original sin had a powerful influence on Christian attitudes toward human nature and politics. His *City of God* envisioned a history that moved according to the majestic plan of God to final salvation and damnation.

The Christian Empires: Rome and Byzantium. The first Christian emperor, Constantine, completed Rome's division into Eastern and Western Empires. The Eastern, or Byzantine, Empire grew increasingly prosperous and powerful, while the Western Empire suffered the onslaught of barbarian armies. Churches built at Rome established a characteristic form of new Christian architecture, while the pope in Rome became the most effective official authority. In the East, Byzantium reached its height in the sixth-century reign of Justinian. During Justinian's rule, great churches built at Constantinople and Ravenna exhibited a fusion of Roman arts and Christian values. San Vitale at Ravenna was a consummate statement of Byzantine architecture, with its mosaic images of imperial faith and power.

Christianity and the Arts. The Christian Church was deeply hostile to the pagan arts of music and theater. Early Christian music consisted of elaborate chants in differing regional styles that served to enhance celebrations of the Christian Mass, or liturgy. Christian leaders condemned and suppressed the theater. This hostility toward art climaxed in the iconoclastic controversy, when officials in the Byzantine Empire systematically destroyed religious mosaics and painted icons.

The Rise of Islam. The Byzantine world was shaken by the rise of Islam, a new religious and political force. Founded by the Arabian prophet Muhammad, Islam worshiped the one god Allah with a regimen of daily prayer and devotion as prescribed by the Islamic scripture, the Qur'an. By 750, Islam had conquered a vast empire and was fostering a rich Islamic civilization. Islamic medicine and science saw important advances, while Muslim and Jewish scholars preserved classical learning. The European Middle Ages opened with the great empires of Byzantium and Islam coexisting on Europe's southern frontier.

6 The Early Middle Ages: The Feudal Spirit

I alone give order to all and crown the righteous;
Those who follow crime, I judge and punish.
Here, let those bound to earthly error be struck
    by terror.
The horror of those you see here will be
    their fate.

With these fearsome words, the image of Christ greets the medieval believers who passed beneath. From his throne, he judges the souls of the dead at the Last Judgment (Fig. 6.1). Some are lifted through the gates of heaven. More – many more – are cast into the torments of hell.

*The hierarchical order of this heaven and hell reflects the **feudal spirit** of the early Middle Ages. God and believer, lord and peasant, ruler and the ruled – all were bound in a system to defend against a violent and demon-infested world. The rise of a new empire in Europe and the Church's efforts to preserve the arts and learning were not always enough to protect the Middle Ages from the fiends of war, ignorance, and folly.*

6.1 Gislebertus, *Last Judgment*, tympanum sculpture, west portal, Cathedral of St-Lazare, Autun, France, c. 1120–35.
At the Last Judgment, Christ calls all souls to rise from the dead (across the lintel); while some are admitted to heaven (left), many more are weighed on the scales of righteousness (right) and damned to punishment.

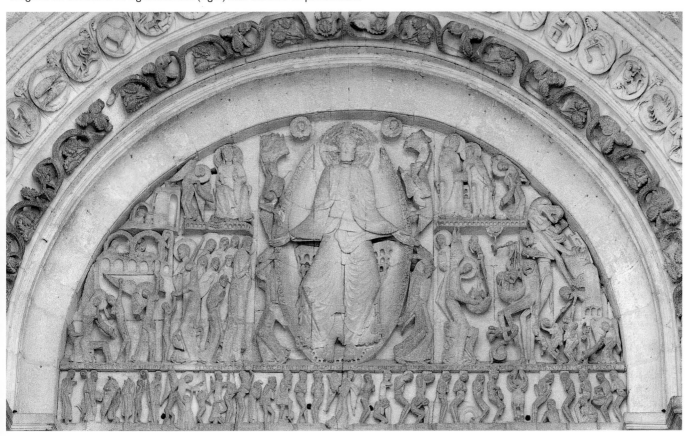

THE MIDDLE AGES

	GENERAL EVENTS	ARCHITECTURE	VISUAL ARTS	MUSIC	LITERATURE AND PHILOSOPHY
800	800 Charlemagne crowned emperor by pope	792–805 Charlemagne's palace chapel at Aachen, Germany (**6.9**)	820–40 *Utrecht Psalter* (**6.5**)	c. 800 Codification of Gregorian chant under Charlemagne	
THE FEUDAL AGE					930–1037 Ibn-Sina, Arabic-language commentator on Aristotle
	c. 960 Ottonian emperors rule in Germany			991–1033 Guido of Arezzo, invention of musical notation	970 Hrotsvit active as medieval dramatist
1000					
	1066 Normans conquer England at Battle of Hastings		c. 1073–88 Bayeux Tapestry (**6.14**)		
	1096–99 First Crusade, sack of Jerusalem	1095–1100 Third abbey church at Cluny, France (**6.22**)	c. 1120–32 Sculpture of La Madeleine, Vézelay, France (**6.27**)	1150–80 Bernart de Ventadorn, troubadour	1121 Abelard, *For and Against*
		1144 Dedication of choir at St. Denis, Paris			
1150	c. 1170 Court of Eleanor at Aquitaine			c. 1170 Léonin compiles book of organum, Paris	
THE GOTHIC AGE		1194–1240 Chartres Cathedral, France, rebuilt in Gothic style (**7.9**)	1200s Ife portrait sculpture, West Africa (**8.26**)		
					1266 Aquinas begins *Summa Theologica*
			1280–90 Cimabue, *Madonna Enthroned* (**7.25**)		
1300			1305–6 Giotto, Arena Chapel frescoes (**7.26**)		1303–21 Dante, *Divine Comedy*
		1354–91 Court of Lions, Alhambra, Granada, Spain (**6.17**)			

THE AGE OF CHARLEMAGNE

Explain the interest of Charlemagne in books, churches, and the arts.

The Emperor Charlemagne came from a line of barbarian chieftains whose war-like values helped shape the early Middle Ages. Charlemagne was a Frank, one of the Germanic peoples who settled in Rome's northern territories in the fourth century. The Franks installed their own social organization, based on personal loyalty and ethnic warfare. Gradually, however, their war-like nature and pagan beliefs merged with the Romanized Christian Church. Early medieval Europe showed many signs of this blend between militant, mystic Germanic cultures and the classical, rationalist Mediterranean civilization.

The compromise between barbarian and classical cultures reached a height in the rule of Charlemagne (768–814). From his Frankish predecessors, Charlemagne [SHARL-main] inherited a kingdom that stretched from the River Rhine, where he built his palace and chapel, to northern Spain. Crowned sole Frankish ruler in 771, Charlemagne quickly expanded his kingdom, thanks to an imposing force of mounted Frankish knights. His warrior nature was ruthless: he once beheaded four thousand Saxon warriors to punish a rebellion and forced the survivors to convert to Christianity. By his death in 814, Charlemagne's realm extended from the River Elbe to the Mediterranean, the largest European territory ever united under one ruler. The period known as the Carolingian renaissance (from *Carolus*, Latin for "Charles") was marked by this creation of a great Frankish empire and a renewed interest in learning and the arts.

THE CAROLINGIAN RENAISSANCE

The Carolingian [kair-o-LIN-jee-un] renaissance briefly centralized a lively feudal culture at Charlemagne's court. Charlemagne's interest in ideas, language, and the arts attracted the brightest scholars of his realm, and using their skills, he administered a vast kingdom. Scholars of Charlemagne's palace school supervised reforms in church music, oversaw the copying and lavish decoration of important manuscripts, and chronicled the life of Charlemagne. After Charlemagne's death, the talent dispersed and within a generation the Carolingian renaissance was extinguished.

The achievements of the Carolingian renaissance were remarkably unified in concept and practice. In concept, Carolingian art and ideas reflected an imperial ideal borrowed from ancient Rome and the still-reigning Byzantine emperors. In practice, Carolingian art works were nearly all produced at Charlemagne's palace school and at monasteries sponsored by the king. Manuscript paint-ing, religious chant, biblical interpretation – all the essential cultural activities – were supervised by scholarly monks and courtiers.

The most influential intellectual in Charlemagne's circle was Alcuin of York (735–804), an Anglo-Saxon monk, librarian, and teacher. Alcuin [AL-kwin] is credited with reforming the Catholic orders of worship and supervising a new translation of the Bible. Perhaps most important, he fostered a general revival of learning under Charlemagne's reign. At the imperial court (which he called a "new Athens"), Alcuin tried to create an aura of biblical royalty and classical achievement, dubbing courtiers with nicknames such as "David" (Charlemagne) or "Homer" (Alcuin himself). Alcuin's greatest talent was as a teacher. He taught the king grammar and read to him from Augustine's *City of God*, Charlemagne's favorite book. Alcuin's quick mind is evident in the following exchange with the eldest prince, Pippin. Alcuin's responses indicate the nature of early medieval philosophy. Philosophy in this age relied on metaphorical associations and leaps of intuitive thought, rather than on systematically logical thinking.

P: What is a letter?
A: The guardian of history.
P: What is a word?
A: The mind's betrayer.
P: What creates the world?
A: The tongue.
P: What is the tongue?
A: Something which whips the air.
P: What is the air?
A: The protection of life.
P: What is life?
A: The joy of the blessed, the sorrow of sinners, the expectation of death.
P: What is death?
A: An unavoidable occurrence, an uncertain journey, the tears of the living, the confirmation of the testament, the thief of man.
P: What is man?
A: The slave of death, a passing wayfarer, the guest of a palace.[1]

Alcuin's influence also indicates the importance of education and literacy in Charlemagne's empire. Charlemagne needed officials who could read his administrative orders, and since he recruited most of his officials from the clergy, Charlemagne advocated clerical education. He urged bishops and abbots to foster literacy in their domains and to promote clergymen based on learning and ability. In one district, priests were ordered to establish free schools for all boys – an early and short-lived attempt at universal education.

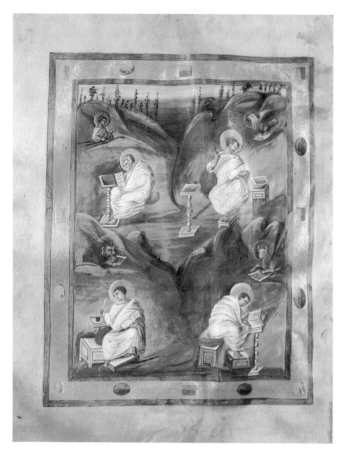

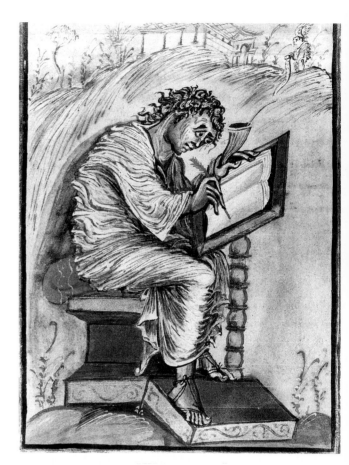

6.2 Above **The four evangelists, from the *Gospel Book of Charlemagne*, early 9th century. Manuscript illustration. Palace School of Charlemagne, Aachen, Germany. Cathedral Treasury, Aachen.**
An illustration produced in the palace workshops of Charlemagne depicts the four gospel-writers with their symbols. They are shown in the pose of the medieval copyist, bent over a stand with quill in hand.

6.3 Above right **St. Matthew, from the *Gospel Book of Archbishop Ebbo of Reims*, c. 816–35. Manuscript illustration, approx. 10 x 8 ins (25 x 20 cm). Bibliothèque Nationale, Paris.**
The evangelist's toga and backgound buildings show the influence of Hellenistic painting, enlivened by the nervous lines and expressive face.

6.4 Right **Crucifixion, from the front cover of the *Lindau Gospels*, c. 870. Gold and jewels, 13³/₄ x 10¹/₂ ins (35 x 27 cm). Pierpont Morgan Library, New York.**
Carolingian artists were devoted to the lavish decoration of books, as in this crucifixion scene with a gem-encrusted border. The beardless Christ is attended by angels above and figures of the Virgin Mary, St. John, and Mary Magdalene (?) in mirror-image below.

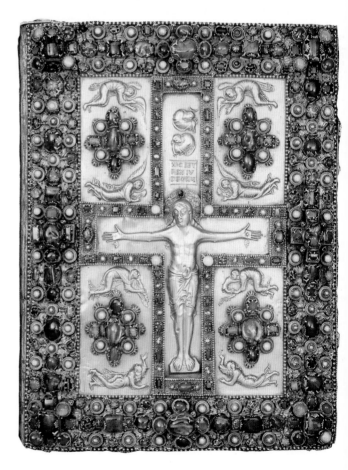

THE WRITE IDEA
Describe the role that today's political leaders should take in supporting the growth of arts and ideas. Should we choose leaders who, like Charlemagne, show an interest and ability in cultural affairs?

THE CULTURE OF THE BOOK

In the early Middle Ages, books were exceedingly rare and costly. Monasteries possessed the largest libraries, where monks studied books as the key to scriptural truth and the classical past. Alcuin energetically supported a thriving "culture of the book," and Carolingian monasteries fervently dedicated themselves to the study and production of books (Fig. **6.2**).

The decoration, or **illumination** (Fig. **6.3**), of books was a primary concern of the visual arts, providing rich opportunities for Carolingian painters and illustrators. The artists at Charlemagne's court consciously imitated the late Hellenistic and Byzantine styles imported from the Mediterranean world. However, the Carolingian artists, some of them immigrants from Byzantium, could not resist Anglo-Saxon art's intricate fantasy and grotesque energy – a style that developed in the remote monasteries of England and Ireland. Much Carolingian art displays a tension between these Mediterranean and Anglo-Saxon influences (Fig. **6.4**).

One notable synthesis of these illumination styles was the *Utrecht Psalter* [OO-trekt SALT-er] (Fig. **6.5**), a collection of the Psalms produced in the workshops of Ebbo, archbishop of Reims in France. The artist depicted each significant phrase as a separate vignette, connecting the vignettes with swirling clouds or landscape. In Psalm 44, the psalmist's words, "Through thee we push down our foes," are illustrated in the quailing army at lower left. Above, a sleeping God is implored by angels, "Rouse thyself! Why sleepest thou, O Lord? Awake! Do not cast us off for ever!" While imitating Roman-style fresco, the workshop artist at Reims animated his figures with a bizarre energy, suffusing the classical Mediterranean style with a mystic aura that emanated from the North.

In the age of Charlemagne, the art of life-size sculpture virtually disappeared, in part because of the iconoclastic controversy (see page 125). Sculpture did find an outlet in the demand for **reliquaries** (Fig. **6.6**), richly decorated containers of holy objects. Possession of an important relic gave a church or monastery considerable prestige, and therefore a reliquary was crafted at huge

6.5 Psalm 44, from the *Utrecht Psalter*, c. 820–40. Pen and ink on vellum, 12⁷/₈ x 10 ins (33 x 25 cm). University Library, Utrecht.
Each page contains several vignettes illustrating different verses of the psalm.

6.6 Burse-reliquary of the tooth of St John the Baptist (front), c. 850–900. Gold and precious jewels, height 13³/₈ ins (34 cm). Cathedral Treasury, Monza, Italy.
Such richly decorated reliquaries demonstrated both religious piety and imperial wealth.

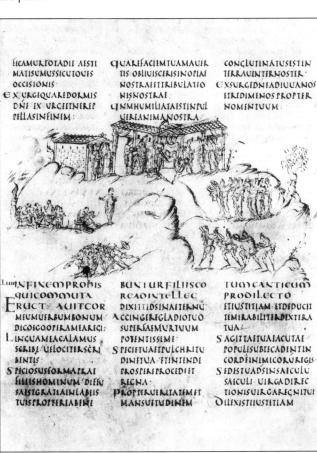

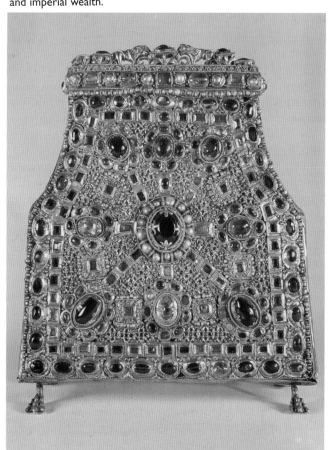

WINDOW ON DAILY LIFE

WORK IN CHARLEMAGNE'S WORLD

From this prohibition against work on Sunday, we gain an idea of the labors that occupied Charlemagne's subjects during the rest of the week:

Let no servile work be done on Sunday and no one be required to work in the fields on that day: none should cultivate the vine nor plow the fields, nor harvest, nor make hay, nor prune the hedges, nor clear forests, nor cut trees, nor dress stones, nor build houses, nor work in their gardens, nor attend law courts, nor hunt. Only three sorts of cartage will be authorized on Sunday: deliveries to the army, deliveries of provisions, and, if the need should arise, the burial of the lord. Women should not work at cloth: none should cut out clothing, nor do needle work, nor card wool, nor pound flax, nor wash clothes in public. For all must be obligated to rest on the Lord's Day.[2]

CHARLEMAGNE
Admonitio, 789

expense, often decorated with precious stones and gold. This form of decoration was also incorporated into the Carolingian culture of the book, since sculptors could decorate book covers without risking the sin of idolatry. The *Crucifixion* shown in Fig. **6.7** compresses the biblical scene into several levels of action, all connected by the cross on which Jesus hangs. Above the arms, angels wait to receive Christ's spirit; below, Mary and other followers mourn Christ's suffering; Roman soldiers with a spear and wine-soaked sponge are flanked by rounded tombs from which figures rise in praise of Christ's sacrifice; and at bottom, the angel points to the empty tomb from which Christ has arisen. The style of drapery cloth and architecture is clearly influenced by Byzantine models, much like the

6.7 *Crucifixion*, **c. 900. Ivory cover of French Evangelistary, from Metz. Church of St-Croix, Gannat, France.**
Compressed within the dimensions of sacred book covers, sculptors in the Carolingian era achieved considerable expressiveness and narrative detail. The snake curled around the foot of the cross refers to the original sin of Adam and Eve, which is erased by Christ's death and resurrection.

Utrecht Psalter drawings. Compared to Greco-Roman sculpture, however, the Carolingian carvers showed little interest in anatomy or realistic space. Instead, they emphasized the spiritual pathos of the biblical scenes.

CHARLEMAGNE'S COURT

In 800, Charlemagne made a pilgrimage to Rome, where on Christmas Day, the pope crowned him "emperor" of the Western Christian world. This made Charlemagne the first acknowledged ruler of all Europe since Roman times. At his palace complex at Aachen [AHKH-un] on the Rhine River, Charlemagne was already building a residence to reflect his imperial office. The palace at Aachen (in French, Aix-la-Chapelle [AYKS-lah-shah-PELL]) included a great hall for imperial business and a chapel modeled after Byzantine churches. As if anticipating his title as emperor, the king imported a statue of Theodoric, the Roman king deposed by Justinian, to stand before his palace. The chapel at Aachen was supposedly inspired by the church of San Vitale in Ravenna (see Fig. 5.23). By the standards of Hagia Sophia or St. Peter's, the chapel was rather modest. However, its sensible eclecticism reveals the tastes of Charlemagne's court. The chapel is a double octagon (Fig. **6.8**), plain brick on the outside in the Byzantine style. Inside (Fig. **6.9**), the chapel has none of the airiness and

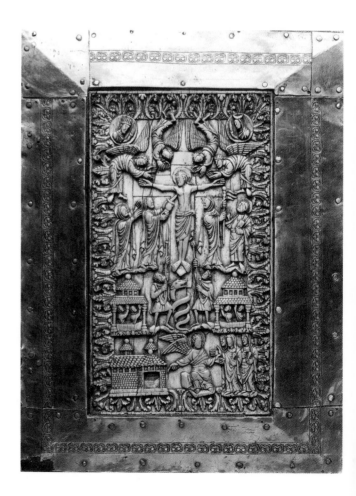

grace of its Byzantine model – instead, the two-story inner octagon is supported by heavy stone piers. The king's marble throne stood in the gallery, from where Charlemagne could overlook the chapel's altars and the throng of courtiers who gathered below.

The palace at Aachen was an appropriate setting for the informal Carolingian court. Here the king and his teacher Alcuin traded riddles, and the king's daughters carried on love affairs with favored courtiers. In formal grandeur, Aachen fell short of the courts at Rome and Constantinople. However, in the power and ambition of its ruler, the palace of Aachen was unrivaled.

Decline of Charlemagne's Empire Unlike Alexander's Hellenistic Empire, Charlemagne's kingdom was split by political dissension and war only a generation after his death. The Frankish kingdom splintered into regional territories, governed by powerful dukes and barons. The disintegration was propelled by a savage new wave of invasions that struck Europe in the ninth and tenth centuries. The Muslims from the south, the Hungarians from the east, above all the Vikings from Scandinavia, all terrorized European settlements and disrupted European society. The Vikings' fierce attacks began in the last years of Charlemagne's reign and continued intermittently for two centuries. Vikings plundered the undefended monasteries of England, robbing their fine reliquaries and treasuries, and then turned to towns and farms all over Europe, devastating agriculture and trade. The Vikings were gradually Christianized, but their aggressive nature was not tamed by Christianity. In 1066 French-speaking descendants of the Vikings invaded England and forever altered Europe's history.

6.9 Interior, Palace Chapel of Charlemagne, Aachen, Germany, 782–805.
Charlemagne's chapel on the Rhine river was a more modest version of the Byzantine imperial style. Compare the arches with those of San Vitale in Ravenna, Italy (Fig. 5.25) and the Córdoba Mosque, Spain (Fig. 5.36).

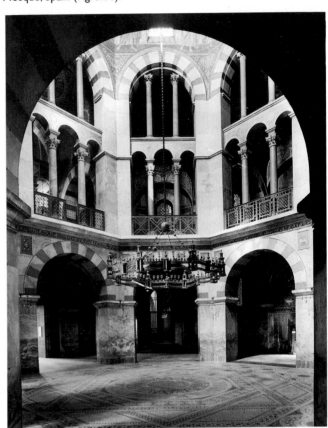

6.8 Restored plan, Palace Chapel of Charlemagne, Aachen, Germany, 782–805.

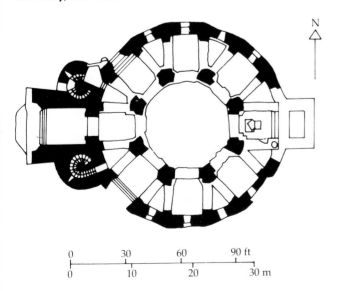

FEUDAL EUROPE

Characterize the achievements of feudal culture in medieval Europe.

Under the pressure of Viking raids and territorial disputes, medieval society labored to preserve its communal life and sustain its fragile agrarian economy. Especially in France and England, which bore the brunt of the Viking onslaught, a decentralized patchwork of small estates evolved from Carolingian society. These rural estates were governed by a system in which land-owning nobles cooperated to defend their property. Largely self-sufficient, these medieval communities functioned effectively without the cities and centralized government that seem so indispensable to modern life. In this era, a European culture arose to reflect the military values of the land-owning class – a culture of epic battles and military conduct that may be called the feudal spirit. Meanwhile, a unique blend of Muslim, Jewish, and Christian cultures was achieved under the relatively tolerant rule of Muslims in medieval Spain.

FEUDALISM

Feudalism is the medieval social system based on the link between vows of military service and the ownership of land. Under feudalism, an aristocratic warrior elite ruled Europe chiefly by military force. The link between war and land was the feudal oath (Fig. **6.10**), which bound a lesser lord, or vassal, to serve a higher lord in battle. In return for his service, the vassal received title to a grant of lands (in Latin, *foedum*). The vassal assumed the right to rule and tax the peasants on his estate, which enabled him to maintain his expensive horses and weaponry, while enjoying the produce of its farms, vineyards, and villages. Virtually the entire life of the feudal nobility – war, marriage, political alliance – concerned the getting and keeping of land.

Life on a medieval estate centered on the castle – the residence of the lord's family and refuge for the estate's population in time of war. In the early Middle Ages, a castle was hardly more than a crude timber house encircled by a stockade. Later, after Christian crusaders (see

6.10 The girding-on of swords, one part of a solemn ritual undertaken in the investiture of a knight. Ms. D XI fol. 134 vi. British Library, London.
Personal oaths of loyalty and service were of vital importance in holding together the feudal political system.

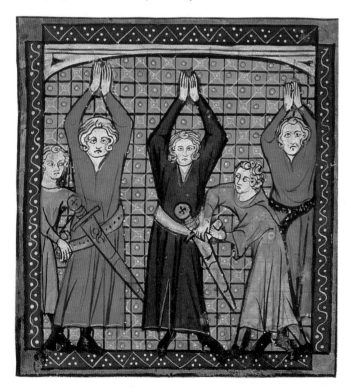

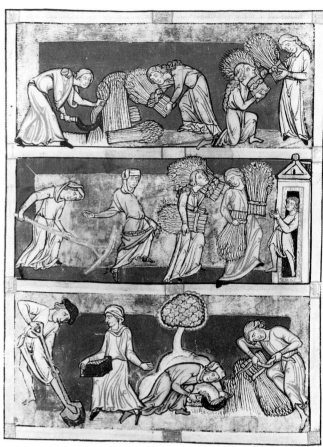

6.11 A 12th-century medieval calendar showing peasants at their labors. Rheinisches Landmuseum, Bonn, Germany.
Peasant life was governed by agrarian labor and cultural traditions rooted in pre-Christian times.

page 163) had studied Byzantine and Turkish castles, noble residences became more imposing. Stone fortresses were carefully designed to defend against military siege. Still, no castle was impregnable. Attackers often tunneled underneath the castle walls, battered them with siege weapons, or simply waited for the defenders' water or food supplies to give out.

Compared with the lavish houses of Pompeii or Byzantium, European castles were rather sparsely furnished and decorated. The walls were typically painted with designs or flowers, or covered by embroidered wall hangings such as the Bayeux Tapestry, which helped subdue wintry drafts. More elaborate tapestries, imported from Islamic regions, did not appear until the fourteenth century.

Outside the castle, the peasants of a feudal estate endured the backbreaking labor of plowing, planting, and harvesting food crops (Fig. **6.11**). Peasants owed their lord a specified amount of rent and labor in kind. To assure a captive labor force, feudal law prohibited serfs from marrying a daughter outside the village or giving a son to a monastery. In return, the lord was obliged to provide a feast for his peasants on harvest days and religious holidays, which occupied as much as one-third of the calendar.

Christian feast days were celebrated with song, dance, and other traditions rooted in ancient pagan ritual. One tradition was **mumming**, in which villagers disguised themselves as animal or human characters. The masked mummers marched silently into the household of a lord or other social superior, danced and celebrated, and then offered gifts to the host and took their leave in silence. Itself obscurely rooted in pagan celebrations, mumming was the origin of masquerades and other masked dances. Like much early medieval peasant dance and music, it thrived on the edge of Christian orthodoxy.

THE *SONG OF ROLAND*

The feudal nobility of early medieval Europe encouraged an oral literature of military exploits and feudal values, similar to the Greek epics which had praised the heroes of the Trojan War. Feudalism's greatest war story was the *Song of Roland* (Fig. **6.12**), an epic that recounts a battle from Charlemagne's campaigns in Islamic Spain. The epic's hero is Roland, a lieutenant of Charlemagne, who fights bravely against an overwhelming force of Muslim knights (called Saracens). The poem embellishes Roland's death with the elements of chivalrous heroism: feudal treachery, combat with evil pagans, a loyal companion, and a sacred sword.

The *Song of Roland* was written in Old French, composed as early as the ninth century and first recorded in the eleventh century. It was the most famous of many *chansons de geste* [shah(n)-SOH(n) duh ZHEST], tales of chivalric deeds sung by minstrels in Europe's feudal courts. The *chansons de geste* celebrated a knight's valor in battle and loyalty to his lord, ideas certain to please a minstrel's host. Unlike the later medieval romances, the *chansons de geste* gave virtually no place to women: the only female in the *Song of Roland* is Aude, the hero's betrothed, who appears at the end and dies on hearing of Roland's death.

The *Song of Roland* is a considerably romanticized account of an episode from Charlemagne's Spanish campaign in 778. As the king's forces withdrew from Spain, his rearguard was ambushed by Christian Basque fighters at the pass of Roncevalles [roh(n)ss-VAHL] in the Pyrenees. According to Charlemagne's biographer, a certain "Hruodlandus, prefect of the forces of Brittany" was included among the Frankish dead. Medieval minstrels transformed this disastrous encounter into a tale of feudal courage, violence, and treachery, told in a manner to gain the admiration of medieval audiences. Instead of Basque peasants, the attackers are devilish Saracen knights, whom the courageous knight Roland impetuously engages. Overwhelmed by the Muslims, Roland finally recalls Charlemagne's main army, blowing his great horn (named Olifant) and bursting his temples with the effort. Delayed by treachery, Charlemagne rushes to Roland's side, to learn the hero has died in battle with his companion Olivier [oh-LIV-ee-ay]. The king vents his anger in vengeful slaughter of the Saracens.

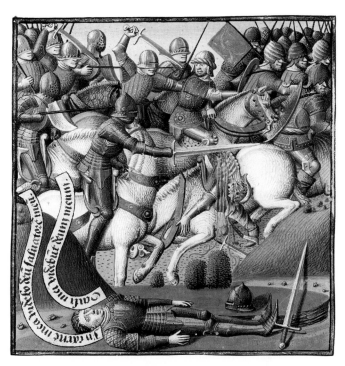

6.12 Illustration from a 15th-century manuscript of the *Song of Roland*. **Musée Condé, Chantilly, France.**
The hero lies dying with his sword Durendal nearby.

Despite its violence, the *Song of Roland* constantly invokes Christian values. Christianity provides the rationale for war against the Saracens, who are a mirror-image of the French in dress, manner, and values. Because they are pagans, however, the Muslims deserve to perish. At the moment of death, Roland tries to break his sword, Durendal, lest it become a trophy for a Saracen knight. He swears by the sacred Christian relics held within the sword's hilt and, in a knight's dying gesture, Roland offers his glove to God in submission, a sign of the poem's union of feudal and Christian values:

Roland the Count strikes down on a dark rock,
and the rock breaks, breaks more than I can tell,
and the blade grates, but Durendal will not break;
the sword leaped up, rebounded toward the sky.
The Count, when he sees that the sword will not be
*   broken,*
softly, in his own presence, speaks the lament:
"Ah Durendal, beautiful, and most sacred,
the holy relics in this golden pommel!
Saint Peter's tooth and blood of Saint Basile,[a]
a lock of hair of my lord Saint Denis,[b]
and a fragment of blessed Mary's robe:
your power must not fall to the pagans,
you must be served by Christian warriors.
May no coward ever come to hold you!
It was with you I conquered those great lands

KEY CONCEPT

CHIVALRY

Medieval romances painted a fanciful picture of chivalrous knights who dueled for the favor of their lady. In fact, chivalry (from the French *chevalier*, or "horseman") was a code of conduct that governed medieval warfare, dictating rules of mercy and fair play. Under the rules of chivalry, medieval knights pledged to serve God and their lord faithfully, and to treat others with courtesy and generosity.

Chivalry most likely sprang from the need to enforce vows of feudal loyalty. By accepting knighthood, a warrior promised not to kill his lord, sleep with the lord's wife, or surrender his lord's castle. Violations of

6.13 Medieval tournament scene from the Manasseh Codex. Universitätsbibliothek, Heidelberg, Germany. Medieval tournaments involved combat nearly as deadly as warfare itself. Here a lady arms her champion for the contest, while courtly spectators applaud.

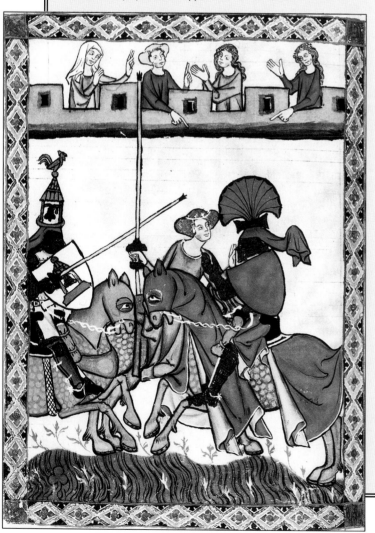

this trust were punished swiftly and brutally. Ganelon, who betrays Roland in the medieval epic *Song of Roland*, is executed by having his limbs torn apart by horses. In the later Middle Ages, chivalry expanded to include religious devotion and service to ladies. Thus, chivalry evolved as a means of civilizing the rough fighting men of feudal Europe, who were otherwise little inclined to acts of kindness and courtesy. In philosophical terms, chivalry established a compromise between medieval warfare and the principles of Christian love.

The cult of chivalry involved an elaborate program of activity to occupy knights during peace-time. The Spaniard Ramon Llull's *Book of the Order of Chivalry* (late thirteenth century) described the chivalric ideal:

> *A knight should ride warhorses, joust, go to tournaments, hold Round Tables, hunt stags and rabbits, bears, lions, and similar creatures: these things are a knight's duty because to do them exercises a knight in the practice of arms and accustoms him to maintain the order of knighthood.*[3]

Chivalric tournaments (Fig. **6.13**) were spectacular competitions that also involved feasting, pageantry, and dance. The competitions resembled military combat, often resulting in serious injury or death. A skilled combatant could enrich himself by capturing horses and armor, or by claiming ransoms from his vanquished opponents. Thus, chivalry opened a narrow path of social advancement in medieval society.

Chivalry led to the creation of a well-trained and ambitious class of professional warriors in medieval Europe, who responded to calls for a military campaign or a crusade to the Holy Land. As part of this military culture, great epic poems such as the *Song of Roland* told of valor and loyalty in battle. Possibly not since the Greece of Homer's epics had warfare and military values so dominated Western civilization as in the medieval "age of chivalry."

CRITICAL QUESTION
Discuss the idea that training a military elite such as the medieval knighthood increases the likelihood of war. Does military training today provide opportunities for social advancement, as it did in the Middle Ages?

that Charles has in his keeping, whose beard is white,
the Emperor's lands, that make him rich and strong."
... He turned his head toward the Saracen hosts,
and this is why: with all his heart he wants
King Charles the Great and all his men to say,
he died, that noble Count, a conqueror;
makes confession, beats his breast often, so feebly,
offers his glove, for all his sins, to God. AOI.[c] [4]

SONG OF ROLAND

a. Saint Basile, the founder of an important monastery.

b. Saint Denis, patron saint of France.

c. AOI, a refrain uttered at the end of stanzas; scholars cannot explain its meaning.

THE WRITE IDEA

To what extent do you believe that religious belief should justify war? What parallels do you see between today's militant religions and the conflict recounted in the *Song of Roland?*

THE BAYEUX TAPESTRY

Chroniclers say that a minstrel sang the *Song of Roland* in 1066 while riding into battle on the field of Hastings. If so, then Roland's epic inspired soldiers whose own valor was commemorated in feudalism's most brilliant pictorial work, the Bayeux Tapestry (Fig. **6.14**). The Bayeux [beye-(y)UH] Tapestry is an embroidered wall hanging that celebrates one of medieval Europe's most decisive conflicts. The tapestry depicts William the Conqueror's victory over the English at Hastings, a battle that deeply affected English history, language, and religion.

William the Conqueror (*c.* 1028–87) was a Norman, descended from Viking invaders who settled in northwest France. In a campaign of territorial expansion, William laid claim to the throne of England, then held by Edward the Confessor (ruled 1046–66). William's rival was Harold, son of England's most powerful family. When Edward died, the disputed succession was decided by war, in typical feudal fashion. William's Norman army invaded England in 1066 and defeated the English at Hastings, killing Harold.

The Bayeux Tapestry recounts this chain of events in a complex pictorial narrative. It is actually not a woven tapestry, but a 231-foot-long (70.4 m) stretch of linen cloth embroidered with figures and captions. This kind of wall hanging commonly decorated feudal halls and depicted scenes from legend or history. The Bayeux Tapestry was probably designed by an English cleric who had studied illuminated manuscripts such as the *Utrecht Psalter*

CRITICAL QUESTION

How does one judge the documentary truth in a visual work like the Bayeux Tapestry? Can the same rules of truth be applied to other documentary works of art?

6.14 Detail from the Bayeux Tapestry, c. 1073–88. Wool embroidery on linen, height 20 ins (51 cm), length of tapestry 231 ft (70.4 m). Town Hall, Bayeux, France.
The Tapestry's embroidery renders the mêlée of battle in gruesome detail, including a severed head and an English foot soldier's assault on a horse. Note the treatment of the horse's rear legs in a contrasting color, a device suggesting spatial depth.

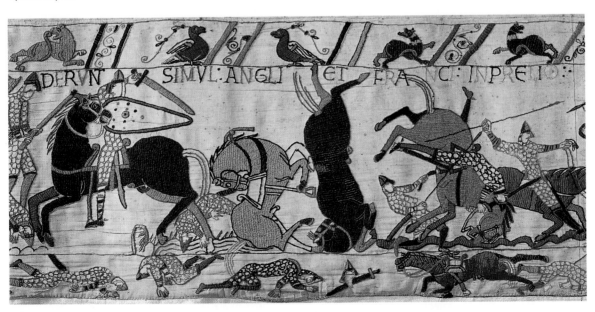

KEY CONCEPT

THE MONASTIC IDEAL

From the beginning of Christianity, believers were called to renounce the world and pursue a solitary existence of prayer and devotion. The first Christians to adopt this austere spiritual ideal were Egyptian hermits who retreated alone to the desert. With time, these solitary believers became known as monks (from the Greek *monos*, or "one"), and by the fourth century, Christian monks had organized themselves in monasteries throughout the Christian world.

On entering a monastery, a Christian monk believed he was adopting the *vita apostolica*, the life of Christ's apostles. Three vows were the essence of the monastic order – poverty, chastity, and obedience. Just as the original apostles had left their homes to follow Christ, so a person entering a monastic order forfeited all property and vowed to live in poverty. A vow of celibacy protected a monk from carnal temptations and concentrated his attention on matters of the spirit. A monk also vowed to obey religious authority. In pursuing the monastic ideal, a Christian renounced the natural community of family and friends and embraced a spiritual communion with God and like-minded companions (Fig. **6.15**).

In the history of monasticism, this rigorous ideal was often compromised. During the Middle Ages, monasteries grew wealthy with feudal lands. Abbots were said to collect jewels and sometimes mistresses, while monks succumbed to the sins of gluttony and drunkenness. Convents for women became refuges for the nobility's unmarried daughters, and often expected a handsome donation for admitting a noble lady. Reform movements arose periodically to root out corruption and restore the monastic ideal. The most well-known reformer was St. Francis of Assisi (1182–1226), a friar who directed his followers to preach in villages and fields, and live from alms in Christ-like poverty. Even the Franciscans, however, were not immune to the attractions of material things – within a generation of their founder's death, the Franciscans had built St. Francis, a spectacular church decorated with scenes of the life of the saint (Fig. **6.16**), in the town of Assisi, Italy.

Today the monastic ideal may seem to pale before the materialism of modern civilization. However, the ideal survives. Christian monasteries still attract initiates, and monks devoted to Eastern religions continue to pursue spiritual purity amid the relentless acquisitiveness of Western societies.

6.15 St. Benedict, founder of the Benedictine Order, blessing Abbot Desiderius. Biblioteca Apostolica Vaticana, Rome.
Desiderius rebuilt Benedict's abbey at Monte Cassino (shown in the background).

6.16 Giotto (?), *St. Francis Renouncing His Father*, c. 1296–1300. Fresco. Upper Church of St. Francis, Assisi, Italy.
The order of mendicant (begging) friars founded by St. Francis stressed humility and poverty. Here, the saint dramatically renounces his father's wealth by disrobing in the square at Assisi.

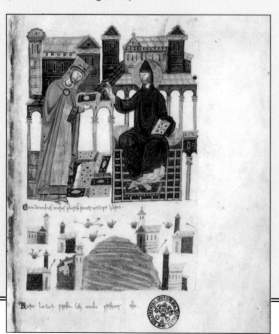

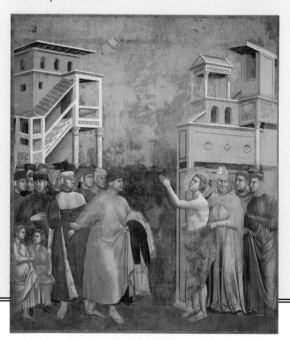

CRITICAL QUESTION

For what reasons might someone your age decide to enter the monastic life? What might be the rewards of poverty and spiritual devotion to a person who has grown up in contemporary society?

(then held at Canterbury Cathedral in England; see Fig. 6.5). The designer was clearly not a propagandist for one side or the other. For example, the tapestry depicts Harold's oath of loyalty to William, an event supporting William's claim to the English throne; yet, it also shows King Edward's death-bed designation of Harold as his rightful successor. The tapestry's stitching was probably performed by female English embroiderers, an art famed throughout Europe as *opus Anglia*, or "English work." In both physical size and the span of its narrative, the tapestry rivals the great continuous friezes left by classical civilization, and is particularly reminiscent of Trajan's triumphal column (see Fig. 4.10), which could still be admired by medieval pilgrims to Rome.

THE FLOWERING OF MUSLIM SPAIN

No court or city of northern Europe could rival the scale and splendor of the medieval Muslim civilization to the south. On the Iberian peninsula, Muslim Spain – known by its Arab name, *al-Andalus* [ahl-AHN-dah-loos] – was an immensely cultivated world, remarkable because its Muslims, Jews, and Christians often coexisted peacefully. This multicultural society's achievements in architecture, poetry, and philosophy would deeply influence Western civilization.

Muslim armies from North Africa first conquered the Iberian peninsula in 711, and Muslim control was most extensive under Abd-ar-Rahman (912–61). Abd-ar-Rahman declared his independence of the Muslim authority in Baghdad and established al-Andalus as an autonomous

6.17 The Court of Lions, the Alhambra, Granada, Spain, 1354–91.
Originally planted with gardens, this courtyard is an architectural rendition of the pleasures of the Islamic paradise. The columned pavilions jut into the yard, creating an interplay of light and shadow. The lions were said to represent the "lions of the Holy War," meaning Muslim Spain's ongoing defense against the *Reconquista*.

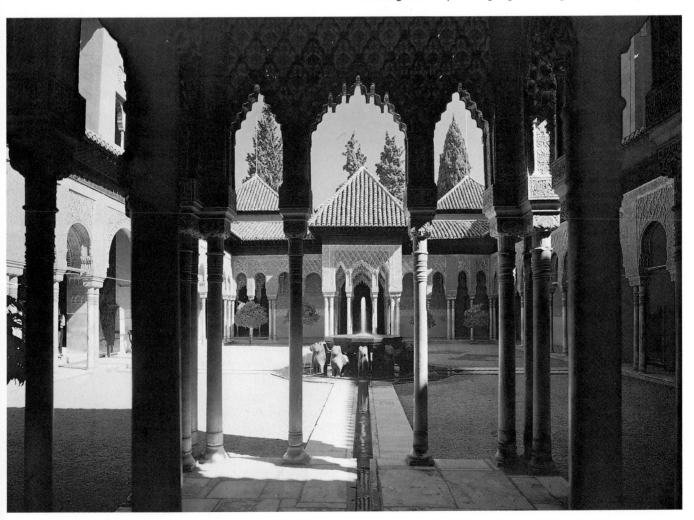

realm. Its capital was Córdoba, a glittering city of half-a-million that rivaled Baghdad and Damascus. Court poets sang the praises of al-Mansur (ruled 979–1002), who sponsored an anthology of Hispano-Arabic poetry called the *Kitab al-Hadàig* (*Book of Orchards*). After 1000, Muslim political power in Spain declined, but its art and science continued to thrive. The poet Ibn Hazm (died 1064) composed idealized love poetry that influenced the troubadour poets of southern France. Grammatical treatises and religious commentaries of Andalusian scholars attained wide currency in the Muslim world.

The Spanish Muslims' tolerance of the Jewish minority fostered a "golden age" of Jewish civilization. As Jewish academies declined in the Near East, Spanish Jews (called **Sephardic** Jews) fostered centers of learning and built lavish synagogues in Córdoba and Granada. Jews attained posts of power and influence. The Jewish physician and diplomat Rabbi Hisdai ibn Shaprut (*c.* 915–*c.* 970) negotiated for Muslim rulers with delegations from Byzantium and the Saxon ruler Otto I. When a Christian ruler reconquered Toledo in 1085, Jewish scholars joined with Christian sages to establish the School of Toledo, a center for translating Arabic and Hebrew works into Latin. The School of Toledo was a conduit for the philosophical and scientific texts that inspired scholasticism, the intellectual renaissance of the later Middle Ages (see page 178).

Christian nobles pursued a campaign of reconquest (in Spanish, *Reconquista*) that gradually pushed back the borders of Muslim rule. Islam's last Spanish capital was at Granada, where the Muslim rulers built the Alhambra palace on a hill outside the city. The palace complex included government buildings, quarters for a large court, and, most notably of all, luxurious gardens. Its centerpiece was the Court of the Lions (Fig. **6.17**), whose graceful colonnaded pavilions were used for musical performances and poetry readings. Muslim Spain's remarkable coexistence of cultures ended emphatically in 1492 with the final reconquest of Granada. Muslims and Jews were forced to convert to Christianity or be expelled; many Sephardic Jews migrated to north Africa, the Americas, and Poland.

MONASTICISM

Describe a typical day of a medieval monk.

By the sixth century, Christian monasticism had spread from its beginnings in Egypt and Syria to Italy, England, and Ireland. The monasteries of Italy and northern Europe became oases of learning in a barbarian world, and also served as outposts of religious fervor in the campaign to convert pagans to the Christian faith. Evangelizing monks managed to instill Christian belief among virtually all the Germanic peoples of Western Europe.

Monks who had no missionary passion remained behind their abbey walls, living by the strict monastic rule of St. Benedict and laboring over their books. Architecturally, monasteries reflected the self-sufficiency of the feudal estate. Separate buildings for dormitories and kitchens were clustered around the abbey church, where monks prayed almost constantly. For centuries in the early Middle Ages, these monks were guardians of the arts and artifacts of Western civilization.

MONASTIC LIFE

The rule of St. Benedict was a set of guidelines for monastic life which nearly all medieval monasteries followed in some form. The rule was authored by Benedict of Nursia (480–*c.* 547), the founder of the first monastic order, in the early sixth century. St. Benedict's rule laid down concise, straightforward instructions that maintained monastic discipline and assured communal harmony. For example, Benedict admonished the abbot, the elected leader of the monastery, to recognize the differences among his brother monks. The advice he gave might well apply to today's business managers.

> *Let him realize also what a hard and difficult task he has undertaken, to rule souls and to adapt himself to many different characters. This one he must praise, that one rebuke, another persuade, and according to each one's character and understanding he must adapt himself in sympathy so that he may not only suffer loss in the flock entrusted to him, but may rejoice in their increase. . . . Let him study to be loved rather than feared. Let him not be impetuous or anxious, autocratic or obstinate, jealous or suspicious, for so he will never be at rest . . . and let him so temper all things that the strong may wish to follow, and the weak may not draw back.*[5]

Benedict recommended a humble diet of bread and vegetables. Meat was permitted only in the infirmary, reason enough for a monk to suffer occasional illness. Monks were not supposed to drink wine. However, "since nowadays monks cannot be persuaded of this," Benedict advised that no more than half a pint a day should be allowed. Abbots were warned to see "that neither surfeit nor drunkenness result."

A monk spent many of his waking hours in prayer. The monastic day was punctuated by the offices, hours of prayer that were sounded by bell. Prayer began with the night office at 2 a.m., followed by Lauds at dawn, and four more offices throughout the day. Twilight brought Vespers. The day's last office, called Compline, was spoken after the evening meal. Monks would also chant psalms and listen to readings from sacred books and the lives of the saints. When followed rigorously, this routine of devotion assured a monk's focus on the life of the spirit. (See Key Concept, page 144.)

GLOBAL PERSPECTIVE

THE BLOOD OF MAYA KINGS

The feudal nobility of Europe engaged in war to acquire lands and wealth. The royal dynasties of Central America engaged in war to capture enemy soldiers for ritual sacrifice. Among these people – the Maya of the Classic Period – humans were duty-bound to shed their own blood as sustenance for the gods, in symbolic return for the gods' gift of a fertile earth and womb. Maya blood sacrifice was not only a reason for war, but also the occasion for religious spectacle, monumental building, and sumptuous art.

The principal Maya centers were independent city-states, ruled by royal dynasties, that spread across the Yucatán peninsula (present-day Mexico, Belize, Guatemala, and Honduras). At the height of the Classic period (300–900), there were a dozen Maya cities with populations as large as 40,000. Architecturally, the Maya centers featured stepped pyramid-temples (probably modeled on Teotihuacán's), as well as vaulted palaces and ball courts that were part of sacrificial rites. The remains of their civilization indicate a remarkable achievement in astronomy, mathematics, and calendar-making.

Carved and painted murals on Maya buildings record the blood sacrifice that was a primary focus of their religious ceremony. At the city of Yaxchilán [yax-chi-LAN], a master sculptor depicted a king and queen in elaborate costume, engaging in a blood-letting ritual that was a royal duty to the gods (Fig. 6.18). The royal blood was usually shed by piercing the tongue, ear-lobe, or penis. Numbed by intoxicants and loss of blood, the participants often experienced intense religious visions. Painted murals at other sites record the torture and heart sacrifice of captive warriors.

Like Teotihuacán, the Classic Maya centers suffered a mysterious decline, perhaps attributable to environmental devastation. By 900, the time of the Viking invasions in Europe, nearly all the Maya cities lay in ruins.

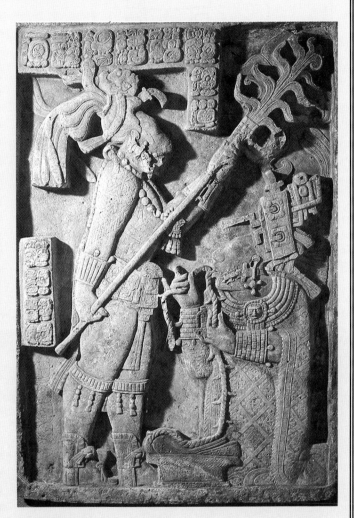

6.18 Maya blood-letting rite, lintel from Yaxchilán, Mexico, c. 725. Limestone, 110 x 81 cm. British Museum, London. A Maya king holds a torch over his kneeling queen, who draws a rope strung with thorns through her tongue in a ritual blood-letting. The blood-soaked paper in the basket below will be burned to sustain the gods. Note the intricate textures of the royal garments and the compositional effect of the ceremonial torch.

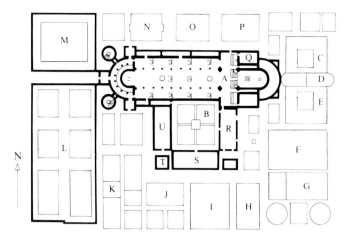

A church	H barn	O school
B cloister	I workshops	P Abbot's house
C infirmary	J brewery and bakery	Q scriptorium and library
D chapel	K stables	R dormitory
E novitiate	L animal pens	S refectory
F orchard/cemetery	M hostel	T kitchens
G garden	N guest house	U cellars

6.19 Plan of the monastery of St. Gall, Switzerland, c. 820.
The idealized plan was based on Roman-style modules, a basic unit of measure multiplied to produce the overall dimensions. The plan of St. Gall provided for an orderly and self-sufficient monastic life and influenced the actual construction of monasteries for centuries.

The Plan of St. Gall Monastic life was sealed off from the world of temptation outside its walls. A monastery's inwardness and self-containment were reflected in its architectural organization. Early medieval monastic architecture is best seen in the plan of St. Gall (Fig. **6.19**), an ideal plan for building a great abbey of the Carolingian age. Although St. Gall in Switzerland was not built exactly to this design, the plan served as a model for other abbeys built in the prosperous regions of Carolingian Europe.

The plan centered on a great church, which had an apse at each end and a pair of towers on the west. The nave was 300 feet long (91 m) and divided into chapels, since there was no need for space for a large congregation. To perform their offices, monks often entered the church from their dormitory, attached directly to the transept. The nearby **cloister** (Fig. **6.20**), the enclosed arched walkway, was a trademark of monastic complexes, and served as a classroom for instruction in music or theology.

By the ninth century, the large monasteries had become feudal estates in their own right, holding lands that extended far beyond their walls. The monastic standard of living rose accordingly. The plan of St. Gall included a large infir-

6.20 The cloister of St. Domingo de Silos, Spain, c. 1085–1100.
The cloister was a center of monastic social life, often sheltering classes in reading and music.

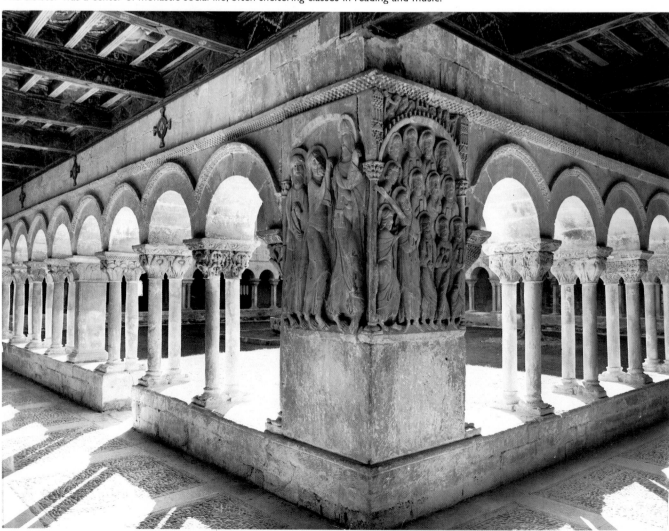

mary, ample lodging for guests, and, despite Benedict's injunctions against meat-eating, a piggery. Quarters were provided for the servants and artisans who performed menial tasks or labored in workshops. Monks themselves worked as cellarers, cantors, and above all, copyists in the **scriptorium**, where manuscripts were copied and preserved. Monastic scriptoria were the sole producers of books in the early Middle Ages.

HROTSVIT AND THE CLASSICAL TRADITION

The monastic scribes and scholars who copied the sacred writings of Christianity also helped to preserve the writings of classical authors. Although monastic life did not encourage artistic creativity, the classical tradition sometimes inspired literary imitators. Perhaps the most remarkable was Hrotsvit [(h)rots-VEET] of Gandersheim (active c. 970), a Saxon noblewoman who wrote witty adaptations of Roman comedies. Most likely, Hrotsvit's dramas were never performed, and instead, were read in the small circle of educated women of the community at Gandersheim in Germany. Hrotsvit's abbey at Gandersheim was supported by wealthy Saxon rulers and accepted only daughters of aristocratic families. In the early Middle Ages, such female communities governed themselves and provided virtually the only avenue for women to pursue a scholarly life. Hrotsvit was a canoness rather than a nun, and so was not bound by a vow of poverty.

Hrotsvit probably entered the abbey of Gandersheim as a young girl and studied in its library of Greek and Roman authors. A gifted scholar, she began writing Latin verse "in the hope that my little talent given by God should not lie in the dark recesses of the mind and be destroyed by the rust of neglect; hoping, rather, that through the mallet of devotion, my little talent may sound the little tinkling chord of divine praise."[6]

Hrotsvit wrote a book of Christian legends in addition to Christianized adaptations of Roman drama. The plots often involved chaste Christian women threatened by lascivious pagans, or harlots whose souls were saved by Christian love. In one play, a chaste wife prays for death rather than submit to a pagan's adulterous advances. The lustful Roman who intends to violate her dead body is converted at her tomb.

Hrotsvit consciously imitated the style and plots of the Roman comedian Terence (see page 90), whose Latin works were widely read in medieval cloisters. Yet, the Saxon scholar was also sensitive to the dangers of Terence's harlots and temptresses to Christian readers. Hrotsvit's women were models of Christian virtue, to counteract the influence of Terence's style:

Therefore I, the Strong Voice of Gandersheim, have not found it objectionable to imitate him in composition,
whom others study in reading, so that in that very same form of composition through which the shameless acts of lascivious women were depicted, the laudable chastity of sacred virgins may be praised within the limits of my little talent.[7]

Not only was Hrotsvit the earliest significant medieval dramatist; in addition, her works provide a compelling alternative to the generally negative view of women in medieval Christianity.

THE ROMANESQUE STYLE

Explain how the Romanesque style served the different needs of German emperors, powerful abbots, and Christian pilgrims.

Beginning about 900, a new line of emperors took power in Germany, reviving imperial traditions and founding impressive new churches. In the same period, an influential monastic order, centered at Cluny in France, sponsored reforms in Western monasticism. Stimulated by these ambitious forces, a building style called the Romanesque developed to meet the demand for splendid new sacred buildings.

IMPERIAL REVIVAL AND THE ROMANESQUE STYLE

In Germany, the title of Holy Roman Emperor was revived by a succession of powerful Saxon rulers, the Ottonians. Beginning with Otto the Great (912–73), the Ottonian emperors actively promoted their claim to the imperial legacy of Charlemagne. Otto the Great held his election as Saxon king in Charlemagne's chapel at Aachen. Later, like Charlemagne, he journeyed to Rome to protect the pope and was crowned emperor in 962. Otto's grandson, Otto III, made a pilgrimage to Aachen in 1000, where he opened Charlemagne's tomb and bowed before the great ruler's seated corpse.

Although its empire never rivaled Charlemagne's, the Ottonian dynasty did earn considerable respect in Europe. The Saxon rulers restored political order to the German provinces, fought back Slavic invaders, and exerted their authority over the Church. In fact, Otto the Great deposed the pope who had crowned him and forced the election of a pontiff friendly to his political aims. Thus the Ottonians became the first of many German rulers to interfere in papal affairs.

The Ottonian ambitions also fostered a new style in sacred architecture. Historians now call this style

Romanesque because it used distinctive elements of Roman architecture, such as the rounded arch and barrel vault. Romanesque churches were the first medieval European buildings to rival the buildings of imperial Rome in their size and beauty. The Romanesque style was characterized by massive walls and piers, and used rich sculptural decoration. It was a style which appealed to the Ottonian emperors because of its associations with Roman imperial tradition. Otto the Great and his successors bolstered their political ambitions with splendid cathedrals and abbey churches on a grand scale. While there were considerable regional differences in the Romanesque style, it stimulated a renewed interest in the arts everywhere.

THE ABBEY OF CLUNY

The Ottonians' secular empire was nearly matched in wealth and expanse by the Abbey of Cluny, a Benedictine abbey founded in 910 in Burgundy, France. It was the most powerful and influential monastic order of its time. The Cluniacs were exempted from control by local bishops and nobles; thus, the order was well situated to reform Europe's monastic houses and bring them under a centralized administration. Eventually Cluny controlled an empire of nearly one thousand five hundred monasteries, both large and small, while reformist Cluniac popes were responsible for the restoration of the papacy's authority and prestige.

Cluniac houses enthusiastically adopted the Romanesque style. The vaulted Romanesque interiors served as an arena for the Cluniacs' processions, and as an auditorium for their great choirs. Not to be outdone by pretentious Saxon kings, the Cluniac abbots even modeled church façades after Roman theaters.

The greatest Cluniac projects were at Cluny itself. The abbey church of Cluny was rebuilt three times in less than two centuries, expanding to accommodate the monastery's growing numbers. The final church, now known as Cluny III, was the centerpiece of a spiritual city, a "new Jerusalem" that must have seemed like an earthly version of Augustine's city of God (Fig. 6.21). A seventeenth-century admirer wrote of Cluny III that "if you see its majesty a hundred times, you are overwhelmed on each occasion."

Like most churches in the Romanesque style, Cluny III was characterized by great masses of stone and the austere rhythm of rounded arches. The church was built (in Roman fashion) according to precise modules. The east end, with its cluster of chapels, was devoted to prayer, while the towering nave (Fig. 6.22) was the setting for litur-

6.21 Elevation and plan of the third Abbey Church of Cluny, France, 1095–1100. From an 18th-century engraving. Cluny was the center of medieval Europe's most powerful monastic order, which built a succession of three great abbey churches.

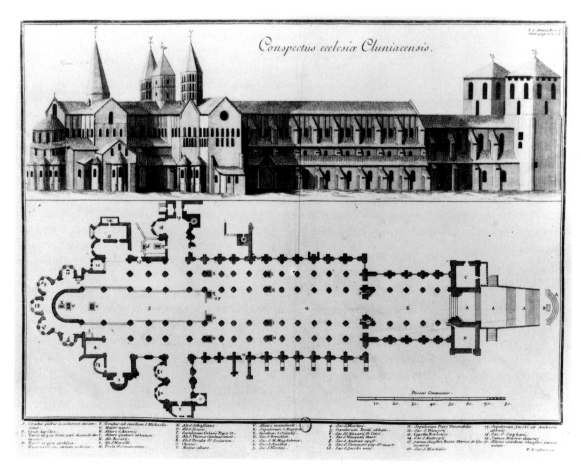

Conspectus ecclesiæ Cluniacensis.

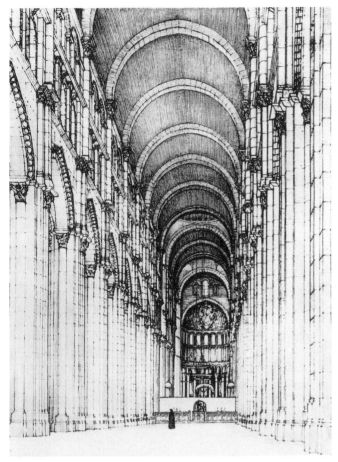

6.22 Nave, third Abbey Church of Cluny, France, 1095–1100. Reconstruction drawing by Kenneth J. Conant.
The cavernous nave, with its Roman-style barrel vaulting, provided a dramatic setting for the Cluniacs' chants and processions.

gical processions. The rounded arches reached 100 feet (30.5 m) above the floor, rivaling the later Gothic cathedrals in height (see page 165). The barrel vaulting provided inspired acoustic effects for the Cluniacs' beloved music.

THE PILGRIMAGE CHURCHES

Like ancient Greek temples and Roman baths, the design of Romanesque churches was determined by their function: the German emperors wanted a symbolic display of imperial grandeur, and the Cluniac abbots wanted a grand setting for their processions and music. The largest Romanesque buildings of all, however, served as medieval tourist centers. These were the great pilgrimage churches, which accommodated believers journeying to Europe's Christian shrines. The grandest pilgrimage churches stood on the routes to the most popular shrine of the Middle Ages, Santiago de Compostela, in Spain.

The church of St. Sernin [san(h) ser-NAN(h)] at Toulouse (Fig. **6.25**) typifies the pilgrimage churches' design and decoration. Its floor plan (Fig. **6.23**) indicates the special needs of a pilgrimage church. A spacious nave (Fig. **6.24**)

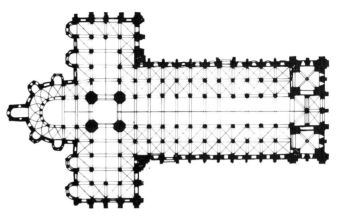

6.23 Plan of the church of St. Sernin, Toulouse, France, c. 1080–1120.
The basic cross-shaped Christian church was expanded to serve medieval pilgrims. An ambulatory carried pilgrims around the choir, where priests could say Mass even during the busiest hours. Large portals, or doors, were added to the transept, creating grand entrances to the north, south, and west. Chapels placed along the apse and transept each contained an altar.

6.24 Nave of the church of St. Sernin, Toulouse, France, c. 1080–1120.

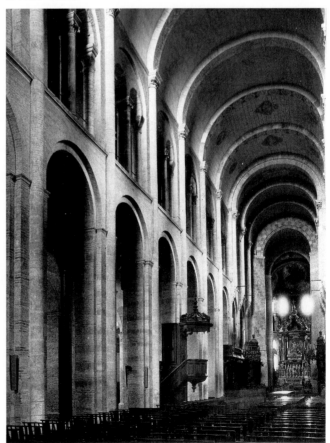

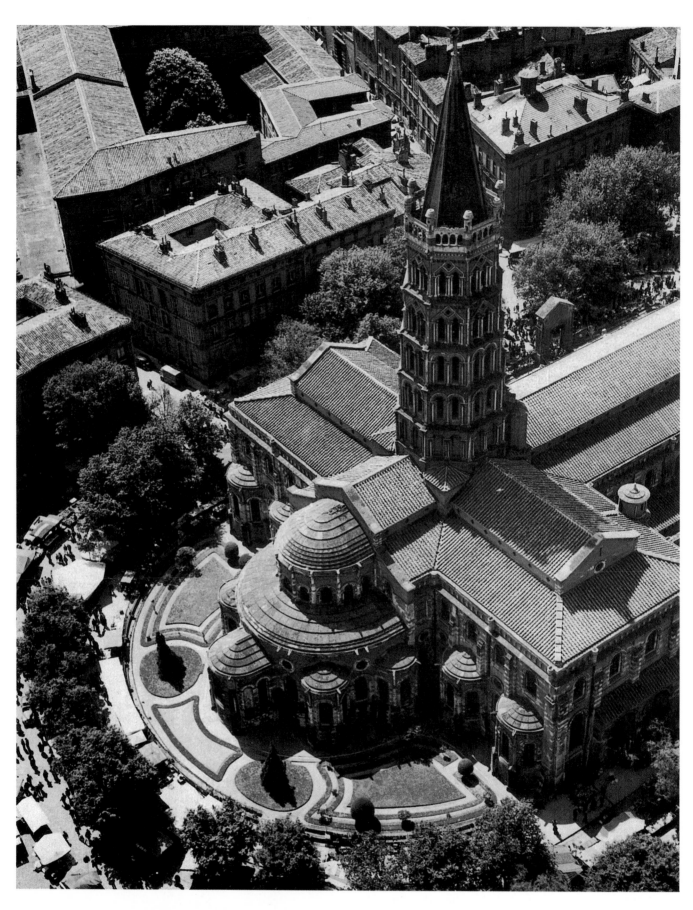

6.25 Crossing and apse, St. Sernin, Toulouse, France, c. 1080–1120. Height of tower 215 ft (65.5 m).
The great Romanesque church at Toulouse was an important way-station on the most traveled pilgrimage routes.

THE ROMANESQUE STYLE • 153

was required to accommodate the masses of pilgrims who gathered during the pilgrimage season. Chapels lined the apse and transept, where the faithful could file by and view the relics displayed there. Three **portals** and wide **ambulatories**, or walkways around the choir, allowed easy circulation of the pilgrim traffic, without disrupting services being held in the choir. Even with these accommodations, a pilgrimage church was likely to have been a noisy and crowded place during the travel season.

Both St. Sernin and the abbey church at Cluny, despite their stunning heights, achieved an overall solidity that was typical of the Romanesque style. This effect came from massive stone columns rising without interruption to the ceiling arches. To pilgrims and monks who filled these churches, their walls were ramparts against the world of sin and temptation outside. The Romanesque's monumental weight of masonry surpassed even the great buildings of ancient Rome.

ROMANESQUE SCULPTURE

While the churches of Charlemagne's era were usually decorated with painting, the Romanesque style increasingly resorted to relief sculpture, in the fashion of ancient Rome. The Romanesque visual style was inspired more by the fantastic shapes of Anglo-Saxon art (see Fig. 6.4) than by Roman classicism. Romanesque sculptors appealed to the believer's imagination with vivid storytelling and an inventive visual style. Mystical events and grotesque beasts adorned the doors beneath which pilgrims walked, no doubt craning their necks at these wonders.

It was the great portal of a Romanesque church that bore its principal exterior sculpture. A portal's sculptural theme was established by the **tympanum**, the large semicircular space above the door. At Autun [OH-tan(h)], in central France, one tympanum bore a great scene of the Last Judgment, carved by a master sculptor named Gislebertus [GEEZ-luh-BAIR-tus] (see Fig. 6.1). As Gislebertus' Christ judges the blessed and the damned, horrible demons try to tip the scale that weighs a soul (Fig. 6.26). On the beam underneath the tympanum, called the **lintel**, Gislebertus shows the hands of God grasping a screaming sinner, while serpents gnaw the breasts of a naked woman. The sculptor intended such vivid images to instruct illiterate churchgoers in the horrors that awaited the sinful.

While Gislebertus worked at Autun, anonymous artisans were decorating the sumptuous pilgrimage church of La Madeleine at nearby Vézelay [vay-zuh-LAY], which reputedly held the bones of St. Mary Magdalene. The tympanum at Vézelay (Fig. 6.27) shows Christ transmitting

6.26 Gislebertus, *Last Judgment*, detail of tympanum sculpture, west portal, Cathedral of St. Lazare, Autun, France, c. 1120–35.
Gislebertus was a master of engaging narrative detail, as shown in the frightened soul who cowers in the hem of the angel's robe at left. What other vivid instructive detail can be discerned in this view?

6.27 Narthex door, tympanum, Church of La Madeleine, Vézelay, France, c. 1120–32.
Note how the Romanesque style entirely surrounded the church's entrance with sculpted images. The coordinated scenes of tympanum, lintel, and archivolts here depict aspects of a single Christian theme or story.

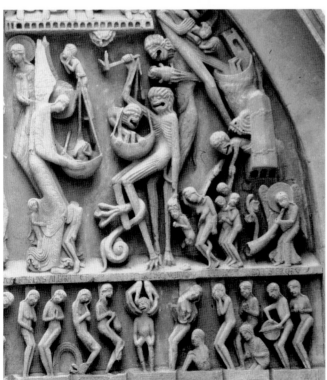

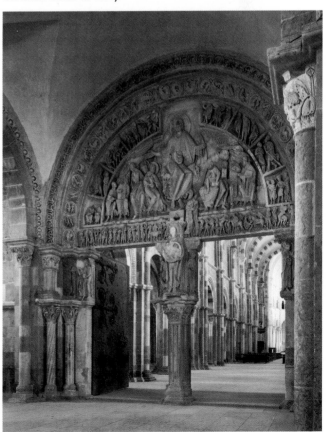

his saving power to the apostles, the eventual founders of the Christian Church. Christ's otherworldliness is emphasized by the sculpture's low relief and by the almond-shaped symbol of eternity which encloses him. The apostles are ranged on either side of Christ in the order of their significance. Across the lintel below, citizens and creatures of the world's different regions are sculpted in high relief. In the **archivolts**, the decorative moldings that frame the arch, there are symbols of the seasons and the astrological zodiac, representing the universe of time and space over which Christ has dominion. Space for lifesize sculpture was provided by the post between the doors, called a **trumeau** [troo-MOH], and by pedestals on the door jambs.

On the interior at Vézelay, sculptural decoration is limited to the capitals of columns, as was typical of the Romanesque style. Sculptors molded their scenes to fit the available space, without regard for naturalism or classical proportion. In the *Mystic Mill* (Fig. **6.28**), Moses pours grain (symbolizing the old law of the Hebrews) into a grinder, while below him, Paul bags the ground meal (representing the new law of the Gospels). Paul's contorted body follows the curvature of the capital, and the back-

6.28 Mystic Mill: Moses and St. Paul Grinding Corn, nave capital sculpture, c. 1130. Church of La Madeleine, Vézelay, France.
In this column capital, the Romanesque sculptors showed a plastic, sometimes grotesque sense of the human form. Observe how the curling lines of St. Paul's hair and beard (right) merge with the abstract lines of his garment.

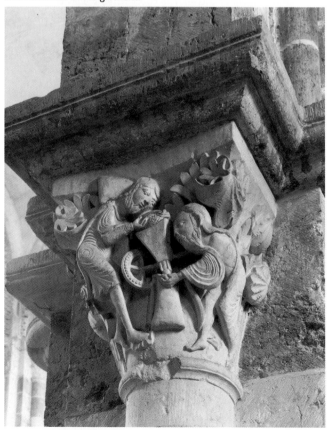

ground foliage contributes to the fantastic effect. The scene is evidence that, in Romanesque sculpture, symbolic meaning prevailed over naturalistic appearance.

Against the soaring stone masses of a church's nave, Romanesque sculpture displayed a rich texture of symbols and stories, a style that seemed alarmingly sensuous to some observers. St. Bernard of Clairvaux [clair-VOH] complained especially of lavishly decorated monastic churches:

> *O vanity of vanities, yet no more vain than insane. The church is resplendent in her walls, beggarly in her poor; she clothes her stones in gold, and leaves her sons naked; the rich man's eye is fed at the expense of the indigent. . . .*[8]

EARLY MEDIEVAL MUSIC AND DRAMA

Show how the invention of musical notation altered the way that music was taught and sung.

The great Romanesque churches provided an awe-inspiring setting for the Catholic Mass, a spectacular ritual of music and ceremony. The singing of monastic brothers and sisters celebrated a novice's first initiation and followed his or her body to the grave. For illiterate peasants and pilgrims, sacred music was an accompaniment to the spectacles of the Christian liturgy. The evolution of medieval music was determined by slow innovation and the need for a system of musical notation. At the same time, medieval drama evolved from the seasonal rituals of Mass. Music and dramatic spectacle both became an adornment to the great stone walls of the Romanesque church.

MUSICAL NOTATION

The most widespread medieval church music was based on the flowing lines of Gregorian plainchant which had been codified under Charlemagne (see page 135). The traditional Gregorian chants changed slowly in the early Middle Ages. The music was taught and performed in monasteries, themselves conservative institutions, and the chants were taught through oral instruction. The range of early medieval music was limited by the memories of medieval choristers. The first cautious innovations came as singers added short chains of notes, called **melismas**, to syllables of key words in the text. Thus, a six-note melisma might be sung on the last syllable of "Alleluia." Melismatic chant, as it was called, gave a modest flourish to the basic Gregorian chant.

By the ninth century, the body of sacred music was outgrowing the limits of oral instruction. As one monk wrote from St. Gall, "When I was still young, and very long melodies – repeatedly entrusted to memory – escaped from my poor little head, I began to reason with myself how I could bind them fast." The solution was to add words to the melisma as an aid to memory. These devices were called **tropes**, musical additions to the traditional Gregorian chant. The most important tropes were set to words, usually a biblical phrase. Tropes either introduced a chant or were sung between phrases of the Gregorian text. A soloist might sing an introductory trope, then be answered by the choir singing the traditional chant. As we shall see, tropes helped to introduce dramatic dialogue into the Mass.

The proliferation of musical tropes eventually complicated the problems of musical instruction. Monastic cantors and choristers had to learn chants for all the Church seasons, plus melismatic variations and tropes, plus a body of psalms and occasional music. It was no wonder, then, that monastic schools devoted so much time to musical education (Figs. **6.29** and **6.30**).

Medieval musical theorists responded to the challenge with new systems of musical notation. Since most monks were trained to read, it was no difficult task for them to learn a system for reading music. The most important steps in musical notation are credited to a Benedictine monk named Guido of Arezzo [GWEE-doh of ah-RETZ-oh] (c. 991–c. 1033), who devised a six-note scale and an ingenious memory device called **solmization**. Solmization associated each tone with the first syllable of a familiar hymn. The musical scale was sung on the syllables *ut*, *re*, *mi*, *fa*, *sol*, and *la*, which could be written above the words of the musical text. (By substituting *do* for *ut* and adding a seventh tone, *si* or *ti*, one has the solmization formula sometimes used to teach scales today.) Guido also invented the "Guidonian hand," which enabled the choirmaster to call for notes by indicating the appropriate knuckle.

Guido's most important invention was the musical **staff**, in which each line and space represented a tone in

6.29 *Monks in choir*. **Illustration from Cotton Domitian A XVII, fol. 122v. British Library, London.**
Several hours in a monk's day were devoted to singing Mass.

6.30 *Nuns in choir*. **Illustration from Cotton Domitian A XVII, fol. 177v. British Library, London.**
Likewise, nuns received a thorough musical education so that they could perform the offices of the Church.

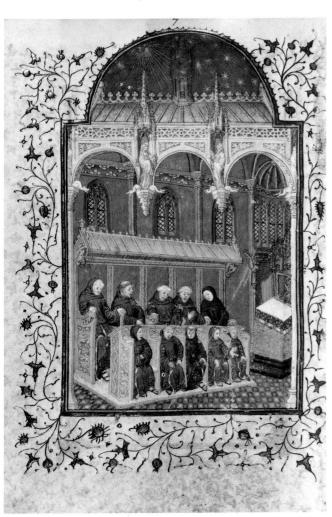

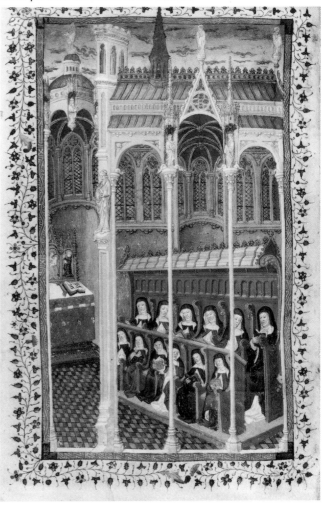

Medieval Notation

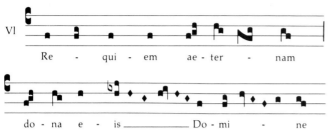

6.31 The Guidonian staff.
The four-line staff attributed to Guido allowed composers to represent precisely musical tones and intervals.

Modern Notation

6.32 The modern staff.
Adapted from medieval notation, the modern staff accommodates a wider range of tones. The sign for treble (upper) clef is adapted from "G" in medieval script, the bass (lower) clef from "F."

the scale. A key letter, or **clef**, set the tone for one line and hence for all the staff's lines and spaces. In the Middle Ages, the customary clefs were F or C, often drawn in red. Since most chants in medieval times required a range of only eight or nine notes, Guido's single four-line staff (Fig. **6.31**) was sufficient. (The modern staff, Fig. **6.32**, adds a fifth line.) Guido's book of musical theory was the most widely read musical treatise written in the Middle Ages. His fame was such that the pope invited Guido in 1028 to instruct the Vatican choir in his methods.

Despite Guido's renown, the early centers of musical innovation were located outside Italy, especially at the abbeys of St. Gall in Switzerland and Cluny in France. The monasteries which had long guarded Christian civilization through writing were now able to preserve Christianity's glorious music through musical notation. Thus, we know far more about medieval sacred music than the secular musical tradition, which was still largely unwritten.

HILDEGARD OF BINGEN: MUSICAL MYSTIC

European monasticism produced its share of geniuses – musicians, scholars, spiritual leaders – but few are more intriguing than Hildegard of Bingen (1098–1179), an influential German abbess who composed a considerable body of mystical poetry and music. In 1151, Hildegard, a bold and confident spiritual leader, organized a secession of her abbey's nuns (with their dowries) from their male-governed abbey. The sisters founded a new independent monastery at Bingen, where Hildegard's achievements and fame drew talented women from all over Germany. The abbess's correspondents included the Holy Roman Emperor and fellow mystics Bernard of Clairvaux and Elizabeth of Schöngau [SHE(R)N-gow].

Hildegard's imaginative works included a morality play set to music (in effect, a medieval opera), and a grand mystical vision entitled *De operatione Dei* (*The Book of Divine Works*). The *Book* laid out an elaborate cosmology that was revealed to Hildegard in painful, ecstatic visions that seized

her for seven years, beginning in 1163 (Fig. **6.33**). Unlike the rationalist arguments of the philosophers, Hildegard's insights were expressed in powerful images – for example, the world conceived as an egg surrounded by luminous fire.

Hildegard's musical works were no less vivid. Her compositions employed the standard church modes, eight scales of notes that were loosely associated with classical Greek sources. Poetically, Hildegard's songs were rich in mythic associations. In one hymn to the Virgin Mary, she describes the mother of Jesus in imagery suggesting the Greek deity Demeter, goddess of the earth's fertility:

Hail to you, O greenest, most fertile branch!
You budded forth amidst breezes and winds
In search of the knowledge of all that is holy.
When the time was ripe
Your own branch brought forth blossoms. . . .
Because of you, the heavens give dew to the grass,
The whole Earth rejoices;
Abundance of grain comes from Earth's womb
And on its stalks and branches the birds nest.[9]

HILDEGARD OF BINGEN

Hildegard's vivid praise of Mary's life-giving female powers made an emphatic theological point. By courageously accepting God's charge to bear his son, Mary had miraculously reversed the first sin of Adam and Eve. For Hildegard, women who modeled themselves after Mary – humble, pure in spirit, receptive to God's divine mystery – could likewise become the vehicle of universal peace and salvation. This idea of their crucial role in God's plan helped fuel women's devotion to the Virgin Mary in the eleventh and twelfth centuries.

DRAMA IN THE MEDIEVAL CHURCH

Like many medieval Europeans, Hildegard thought music was the highest expression of human devotion to God. Little wonder that medieval music was also the vehicle for the re-birth of European theater, largely dormant since late Roman times. In fact, the first known medieval dramas

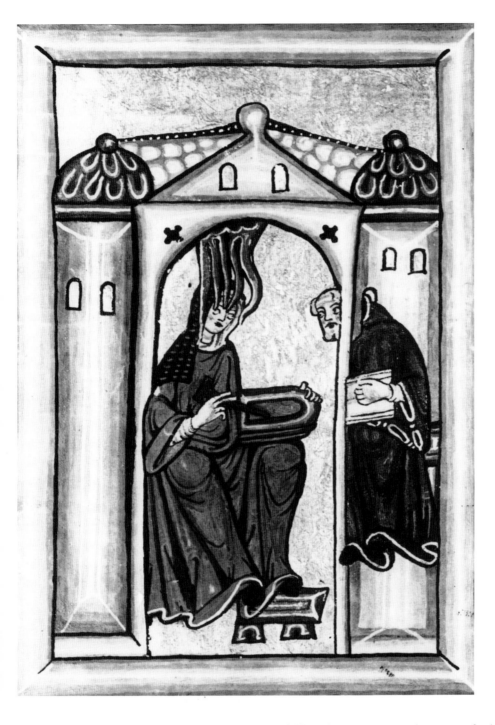

6.33 Hildegard of Bingen. Hessische Landesbibliothek, Wiesbaden.
The Abbess is shown receiving her first vision, while a monastic scribe records her testimony.

were scenarios dramatizing the Mass – scenes of Christ's birth, death, and resurrection.

Monastic records show that sometime during the tenth century, the monks of St. Gall acted out the dialogue of an Easter text. The text, entitled in Latin *Quem queritis* ("Whom do you seek?"), dramatized the scene in which three women came to dress Christ's crucified body (see Mark 16). The angel who guards Christ's empty tomb speaks to them:

1st Voice: Whom do you seek in the sepulcher?
2nd Voice: Jesus of Nazareth.
1st Voice: He is not here; he is risen as foretold when
it was prophesied that he would rise from the dead.
2nd Voice: Alleluia! The Lord is risen!
All Voices: Come and see the place.

According to the St. Gall script, monks were costumed to represent the three women and the angel, and the church altar symbolized the empty sepulcher (Fig. **6.34**). With this rudimentary mime, theater first appeared in the medieval church as part of the ritual drama of the Catholic Mass. Like melismas and tropes, the early music-dramas served to embellish the conservative core of medieval liturgy.

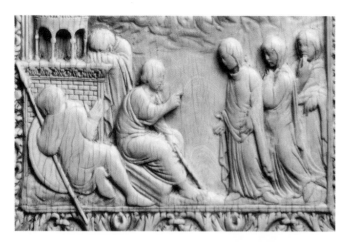

6.34 *The Marys Visiting the Tomb*, detail of ivory panel, c. 820. National Museums and Galleries on Merseyside.
The discovery of Christ's empty tomb was acted out in the earliest known medieval drama, the *Quem queritis* ("Whom do you seek?").

In the next three centuries, such music-dramas evolved and expanded into longer plays. By the twelfth century, medieval playwrights had created a repertory of about fifteen standard sacred plays. These included renditions of the *Three Wise Men*, *Herod's Slaughter of the Innocents*, and the *Raising of Lazarus*. Written by choir-masters and per-

formed in musical Latin, the plays were usually brief. Still, clerical playwrights developed stock characters and spectacular action that appealed to church audiences. For example, the shepherds visited by an angel at Christ's birth were portrayed as clownish bumpkins (Fig. **6.35**). The popular *Play of Herod* featured rowdy swordplay and the histrionic ranting of King Herod the Great, frustrated in his search for the Christ child. Centuries later, Shakespeare's Hamlet would warn his actors not to "out-Herod Herod" in overplaying their scene.

The venue for these playlets was the church itself. Scenes were either staged on elevated platforms in the choir, with players moving from one scene to another, or sets were placed around the church in doorways, arches, or bays, with the audience following from one scene to the next. Costumes were at first just the regular vestments appropriate to the Church season. In time, however, the plays required more elaborate costumes: the *Play of Daniel* called for lion costumes and the *Raising of Lazarus* dictated that Mary Magdalene don the "habit of a whore." While the actor wearing this costume might well have been a man, music-dramas were performed in both convents and abbeys.

Church drama eventually developed a theatrical vigor that overshadowed the solemn rites it was intended to represent. Church officials were unhappy with the "world-

6.35 *Nativity*, c. 1130–40. Ivory panel, 15³/₄ x 4⁵/₈ ins (40 x 12 cm). Schnütgen Museum, Cologne.
The shepherds' ignorant astonishment at Christ's birth was often the pretext for comic dialogue in medieval dramas.

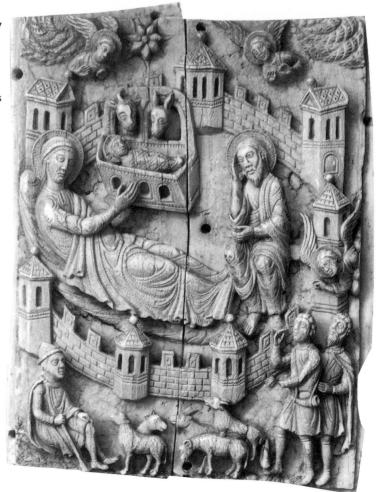

liness" brought into the sanctuary by the plays. By the early thirteenth century, for reasons not entirely known, theater productions were moved outside of churches into the town, although the Church remained an important sponsor of theater into the late Middle Ages.

THE MEDIEVAL PHILOSOPHER

Analyze the role of Abelard in altering the conventions of medieval theology.

Like theater and music, early medieval philosophy was cultivated in the monasteries, the centers of medieval learning. Here, philosophy was governed by a conservative tradition that subordinated reason to Christian faith. Following the example of Augustine (see page 112) and other Church fathers, medieval philosophy was a creature of theology. However, when schools sprang up at cathedrals in Europe's towns, philosophy became more skeptical and contentious. A pivotal figure in this change was Peter Abelard [AB-eh-lard], famous for his passion as well as his philosophy.

EARLY MEDIEVAL PHILOSOPHY

Early medieval philosophers largely restricted themselves to philosophical questions defined by the early Church fathers, who stressed such Christian problems as the nature and existence of God, the freedom of will, and the relationship between faith and reason. The monastic philosophers' commentaries and interpretations nearly always confirmed Catholic orthodoxy. For example, St. Anselm

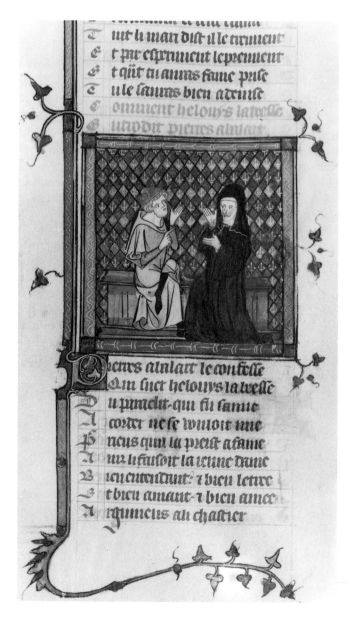

6.36 *Abelard Teaching Heloïse.* **Manuscript illumination from the** *Roman de la Rose* **by Jean de Meun, 13th century. Musée Condé, Chantilly.**
The love affair of this medieval teacher and his pupil inspired the medieval literary imagination. An account of their affair is included in the *Roman de la Rose*, a hugely popular erotic allegory.

of Canterbury (1033–1109) developed a famous proof of the existence of God that claimed God is that "which confers upon and effects goodness in all other things." Anselm's famous motto was *credo ut intelligam* – "I believe in order to understand."

The conservative boundaries of medieval philosophy were stretched by the rise of urban schools, which were usually attached to the cathedrals. Beginning in the late eleventh century, the cathedral schools provided a powerful stimulus to medieval learning. Newly translated classical works, especially the work of Aristotle, provoked an interest in dialectic and disputation. Schoolmasters adopted a method called the *questio* which subjected a traditional commentary to spirited debate. The *questio* produced more comprehensive summations of medieval philosophy, but disturbed the traditionalists, who complained about the schoolmasters that, "as if the works of the holy Fathers are not enough, they dispute publicly against the sacred canons concerning the incomprehensible Deity; they divide and rend the indivisible Trinity; and there are as many errors as there are masters."

ABELARD

The most famous schoolmaster was Peter Abelard (1079–1142), a pivotal figure in medieval philosophy. Abelard was trained at the cathedral schools of several French cities and taught at several others, always quarreling with intellectual authorities. He established himself by writing commentaries on Aristotle's logic and dialectic.

Part of Abelard's fame rests on an incident that had little to do with philosophy. While teaching in Paris in 1119, he began a love affair with Heloïse [ay-loh-EEZ], a young pupil of exceptional intelligence and education (Fig. **6.36**). Abelard's autobiography, *A History of My Calamities*, recounts their ill-fated love. "Under the pretext of study," Abelard wrote of his lessons with Heloïse, "we spent our hours in the happiness of love, and learning held out to us the secret opportunities that our passion craved." Soon pregnant, Heloïse at first refused and then agreed to Abelard's offer of marriage. Their union ended when Abelard was assaulted and castrated by friends of Heloïse's powerful uncle. The lovers both withdrew to a monastic life, and later exchanged passionate, sometimes bitter love letters. Their correspondence reveals that Heloïse was the philosopher's match in strength of will and intellectual honesty.

Aside from this famous romance, Abelard was a thinker of originality and courage. Above all, Abelard used his dialectical method to examine important points of Church doctrine. His best-known work was *Sic et Non (For and Against)*, which posed theological questions and then quoted conflicting Church authorities. The effect was to expose inconsistencies in Church teachings. In the manner of schoolmasters, Abelard examined the articles of Christian faith as one might a scholar's disputation. Condemned for relying on human reason instead of faith, Abelard was nonetheless immensely popular as a teacher. His students followed him whenever he wandered. No other medieval master succeeded so brilliantly, strictly by the power of his teaching and writing.

A NEW SPIRIT OF THE MIDDLE AGES

Peter Abelard's career illustrates a new spirit in medieval life in the twelfth and thirteenth centuries. This new spirit arose most strongly in the growing towns and cities of medieval Europe. Unlike his own teachers, Abelard did not restrict his teaching to the cathedral schools, where the Church's influence was still overpowering. Instead, he spent much of his career at the university in Paris, and his theological teachings shared in the skepticism and practicality of this adventurous urban atmosphere.

Of course, feudalism and monasticism remained powerful institutions in Europe during the later Middle Ages. Indeed, Abelard spent the last years of his life under the protection of the abbot of Cluny. But the conservative traditionalism that governed early medieval life gradually gave way to a spirit of intellectual daring and broad vision. This spirit would be expressed in the great projects of the Gothic builders and in the works of the Italian poet Dante. Peter Abelard may be seen as a pioneer of this new spirit of the late Middle Ages.

Chapter Summary

The Age of Charlemagne. The early Middle Ages in Europe took shape under the reign of Charlemagne, the Frankish king who unified Western Europe into one Christian empire. To recreate the Roman imperial ideal, Charlemagne fostered a renaissance of learning and the arts, drawing talent from monasteries in England and Italy. At Carolingian courts and abbeys, the arts of manuscript illustration, ivory carving, and metalwork produced a rich "culture of the book." Charlemagne built a fine palace at Aachen, including a chapel modeled consciously after Byzantine imperial churches. After his death, Charlemagne's European empire disintegrated under the force of Muslim and Norse invasions.

Feudal Europe. A feudal system emerged to govern medieval Europe, which was ruled by a land-holding class of warrior knights. The feudal estate, encompassing both nobles and peasants, was the center of communal life. The estate's agrarian calendar of feast days gave rise to early forms of popular music and dance. Feudalism also fostered the medieval code of chivalry, which required that knights be loyal to their lord and courteous to ladies. The fusion of medieval Christianity and feudalism is illustrated in the epic poem *The Song of Roland* and the Bayeux Tapestry, a pictorial account of William the Conqueror's conquest of England. In medieval Spain, Muslim rule brought a remarkable coexistence of Muslims, Jews, and Christians. Muslim Spain fostered a lively intellectual culture and artistic achievements such as the Alhambra palace.

Monasticism. One of the strongest forces in medieval life was Christian monasticism, the practice of living in spiritual solitude. Followers of the monastic ideal took vows of poverty, celibacy, and obedience, withdrawing to the sheltered community of the cloister. Most medieval monasteries followed the rule of St. Benedict, a set of guidelines for monastic daily life. Monastic orders also built elaborate complexes to house hundreds of monks and nuns. Monasteries were centers of intellectual activity, where ancient manuscripts were copied and studied. The cloistered scholar Hrotsvit of Gandersheim drew on Roman models to create the first Christian literary drama.

The Romanesque Style. A medieval artistic style, called the Romanesque, developed under the tenth-century reign of the Ottonian emperors in Germany and the powerful abbots of Cluny. The Romanesque style appealed to the Ottonians' desire for churches of imperial grandeur, while also accommodating the Cluniacs' monastic ceremonies. Other Romanesque churches were primarily shrines for pilgrims. As seen in Gislebertus' decoration at Autun and at the sumptuous church at Vézelay, the Romanesque style encouraged a lively and accomplished art of sculpture.

Early Medieval Music and Drama. Both medieval music and drama evolved from the Catholic Mass. The increasing complexity of Gregorian chant required a system for teaching and writing music. The most important innovations of musical notation, including the first musical staff, are attributed to Guido of Arezzo. In Germany, the charismatic Hildegard of Bingen translated her mystic religious vision into compelling songs in praise of the Virgin Mary. The impulse to dramatize liturgical music and Bible stories eventually led to a vigorous sacred drama. As music-dramas grew more theatrical, Church authorities finally excluded them from the churches.

The Medieval Philosopher. The conservatism of medieval Christianity did not suppress the rise of urban schools, where philosophers taught new methods of theological argument and analysis. The most popular teacher from these schools was Peter Abelard, famous for his love affair with Heloïse as well as his daring challenges to the established wisdom. By the twelfth century, the authority of feudalism and monasticism was being challenged by new forces in European life.

7 The Late Middle Ages: The Gothic Awakening

Queen of the skies and regent of the
  earth
And sovereign empress of the realms
  of hell,
Receive me, Mary, though of little
  worth,
Yet heavenward bent, a child of
  Christian birth.[1]

*With these humble words, a
medieval Christian addressed the
Virgin Mary, mother of Christ and
Queen of Heaven. Like the earth
goddesses of old, the Virgin showered
her blessings upon all who appealed
to her mercy: prosperity to the
merchant, wisdom to the scholar,
healing to the sick, forgiveness to the
sinner. From the walls and windows
of medieval Europe's churches, she
gazed upon the faithful with a
mother's kindness (Fig. 7.1).*

*Under the Virgin's benevolent
reign, it seemed that medieval
Europe had awakened from a
nightmare of feudal war and
ignorance. In this Gothic awakening –
the age of the later Middle Ages in
Europe (1150–1400) – towns and
kingdoms thrived, grand churches
were built across Europe, and a new
spirit of learning and beauty suffused
the Western world. It was an age to
match the regal beauty of the Virgin
herself.*

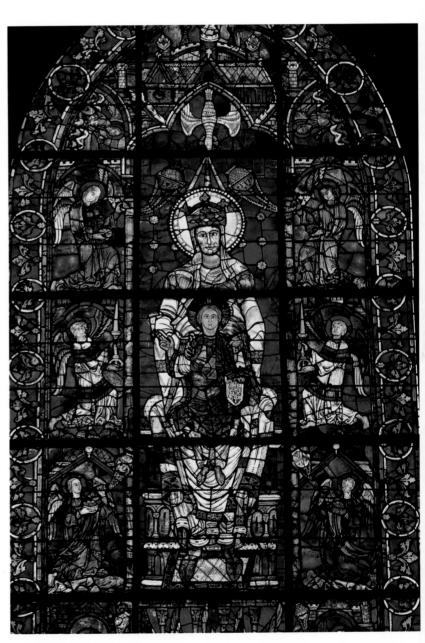

**7.1 Notre-Dame-de-Belle-Verrière (*Our Lady of the Beautiful Glass*), Chartres
Cathedral, France, 12th century. Stained-glass window.**
The Virgin Mary sits on the throne of heaven, the Christ Child in her lap, adored and
praised by heaven's angels. At Chartres, a garment supposedly worn by the Virgin at
Christ's birth attracted pilgrims to Chartres' splendid Gothic church.

THE GOTHIC AWAKENING

Describe the primary factors in the cultural awakening of the late Middle Ages.

In the later Middle Ages, Europe roused itself from a traditional life governed by a conservative Church and the feudal estate. Crusading expeditions (Fig. **7.2**) to the Holy Land brought Christian Europe in contact with the Islamic world. At the same time, the stable hierarchy of feudalism was loosened by the long absences of crusading lords. European society began to move to the quicker rhythms of its growing towns and cities. Enterprising townspeople exploited trading and financial opportunities, increasing Europe's economic interdependence. This new current in European life is called the "Gothic awakening," after the artistic style that it stimulated and supported. The Gothic awakening was shaped above all by the great Crusades, the decline of feudalism, and the growth of the towns and cities.

THE CRUSADES

In 1095 Pope Urban II impulsively called on Christian knights to capture Jerusalem from its Muslim rulers. The pope feared that a new Turkish regime endangered the Holy Land's Christian inhabitants. Although the threat was exaggerated, Europe's response to Urban's appeal was astounding. The call inaugurated the first of the Crusades, wars fought to defend Christians against non-believers or to recover Christian lands. During the following three centuries the Crusades enlisted feudal knights in search of adventure, pilgrims expecting salvation, and

7.2 The Crusades.

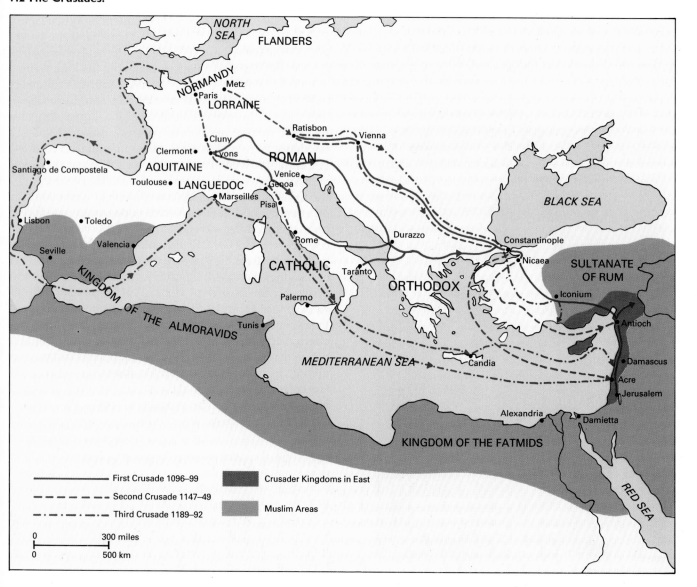

even an army of children, believing their innocence might recover Jerusalem.

In 1099, the first Crusade ended in an orgy of brutality when Christian knights slaughtered Jerusalem's Arabs and Jews. Abandoning their lofty ideals, the Crusade's commanders promptly divided their conquered territory into feudal estates. Within a century, however, Muslims had regained Jerusalem and subsequent Christian crusaders were unable to match the bloody victory of 1099.

Despite failures on the battlefield, the Crusades achieved unintended success in Europe. Crusaders returned to their homelands with Arab foods and cloths, creating a new demand for goods and enlarging Europe's money economy (Fig. **7.5**). Italian ports such as Venice and Genoa profited as departure points for crusading expeditions and as crossroads for Mediterranean commerce. Contact with Arabic civilization also brought to Europe the wisdom of Arabic philosophers, scientists, and mathematicians,

7.3 Murder of St. Thomas. 13th-century miniature. Carrow Psalter Ms W.34f15v. Walters Art Gallery, Baltimore.
Thomas à Becket, Archbishop of Canterbury, was gruesomely decapitated by King Henry II's agents as he prayed at the altar. To atone for the murder, Henry II is said to have worn a hair shirt for the rest of his life.

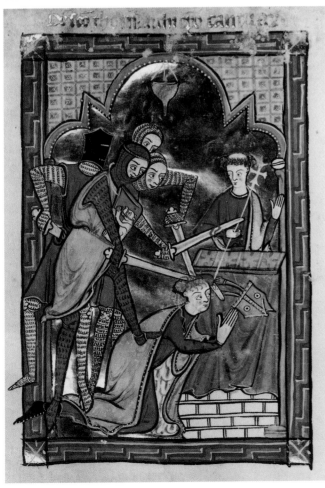

whose translations of, and commentaries on, the classical philosophers fueled an intellectual revival in Europe's schools and universities. While failing in their military aims, the Crusades reinforced social changes already underway in Christian Europe.

THE DECLINE OF FEUDALISM

The militant piety of the Crusaders did not always imply ready obedience to the pope's commands. The later Middle Ages witnessed frequent and bitter conflict between the Church and secular leaders. Their fiercest disputes concerned Church offices and the Church's vast wealth. Feudal nobles wanted to appoint their bishops and tax Church property within their own territory. Pontiffs sought in turn to regain those powers for Rome. The pope's greatest weapon against troublesome rulers and their subjects was excommunication, the power to bar Christians from receiving the Church sacraments, such as marriage, confession, and the Eucharist.

This clash between Church and crown had sometimes dramatic, sometimes bloody consequences. When Henry II of England (ruled 1154–89) tried to expand the power of his royal courts, he quarrelled with the Archbishop of Canterbury, Thomas à Becket. Believing the king wished to be rid of this "troublesome priest," Henry's followers hacked Becket to death at the altar of Canterbury Cathedral (Fig. 7.3). In another episode, the Holy Roman Emperor Henry IV stood three days in the snow outside the pope's residence begging his forgiveness in a quarrel over the emperor's powers. During the period called the Great Schism (1378–1417), there were actually two popes at the head of the Christian Church, one at Rome and the other at Avignon, in France. Each pope had the support of opposing factions and righteously excommunicated his counterpart. The Great Schism represented a low point of papal prestige. As the power of the popes waned, the power of the kings increased, especially in England, France, and Spain. Monarchs such as Henry II of England and Louis XI of France enlarged their royal power and domains at the expense of feudal lords. These same monarchs granted charters to cities, offering the cities autonomy from feudal obligations in exchange for the right to tax urban commerce. Such policies stimulated the cities' prosperity and enhanced royal might at the nobility's expense. Europe's most powerful monarchs were able to oppose the Church's authority and increasingly centralize the royal state.

THE RISE OF TOWNS AND CITIES

The Gothic awakening was most dramatic in Europe's towns and cities. Although small by today's standards (Paris had a population of about fifty thousand), the cities of medieval Europe recovered the vitality lost in the Roman Empire's decline. In contrast to the great cities of antiquity, medieval towns were crude, filthy places. Rats and pigs

ran the narrow streets, and residents enjoyed no facilities comparable to a Roman bath. Yet for the price of this walled squalor, city-dwellers gained important freedoms: urban residents were free from feudal bonds and protected from the rapacious armies of kings and dukes.

The town's citizens, called **burghers** (from *burg*, meaning "town" or "fortress"), jealously guarded their liberties. Burghers sought guarantees from their sponsors in the form of a charter or constitution, forerunners of today's national constitutions. In France, the number of chartered cities increased tenfold in a hundred-year span. Such cities were a significant factor in the generation and development of ideas and provided a haven for schools and universities that vied for the age's most famous scholars. Towns such as Champagne and Chartres held great fairs, where local products could be exchanged for costly goods from Italy or the East. Medieval town-dwellers formed a growing social group known as the middle class, who thrived on a traffic in goods and ideas that neither pope nor king could control.

THE GOTHIC STYLE

Explain how, to a medieval Christian, the beauty of a Gothic-style church symbolized God's presence in the world.

Stimulated by the Gothic awakening, the towns around Paris launched a public building program which, relative to their size and wealth, has few historical parallels. In present-day terms, it would be like a Midwestern farming town building a skyscraper on its town square, financing it with donations from local tradespeople and prominent citizens. In the pious Middle Ages, only one kind of building could command such enthusiasm and sacrifice – a cathedral, the church of the local bishop.

Within a span of a hundred years beginning about 1150, a dozen new cathedrals were begun in such prosperous French towns as Chartres, Amiens, Beauvais, and Sens. These new cathedrals were all dedicated to *Notre Dame*, or "Our Lady the Blessed Virgin." All were built in a daring new style that we now call **Gothic**, characterized by soaring vertical lines and jewel-like stained-glass windows, a synthesis of stone and glass inspired by the most profound religious feeling. The Gothic churches achieved such daring design and rich decoration that they rivaled the ancient temples of Greece.

Abbot Suger and the Gothic Style

The Gothic style in architecture was first realized by Abbot Suger (*c.* 1085–1151), who rebuilt his church's choir to emphasize light and luminosity. Abbot Suger [SOO-zhay] subscribed to a medieval belief that God revealed himself through the material world, allowing God's spiritual truth to be understood through the study of material things.

Light – brilliant but immaterial – offered the abbot the perfect analogy to God's spiritual being. Like the spirit of God, the beauty of light was reflected in precious gems and golden reliquaries. Light could even symbolize the mystic incarnation of Christ: God's holy spirit had passed through Mary's womb without altering her virgin purity, much as light filtered through a stained-glass window. For Suger, the mysticism of light symbolized the deepest mysteries of medieval Christianity, a belief that is inscribed at his church at St. Denis [san(h) duh-NEE], Paris:

The dull mind rises to truth through that which is
*   material*
And, in seeing this light, is resurrected from its former
*   submersion.*[2]

Abbot Suger undertook the reconstruction of the abbey church at St. Denis in the 1130s. By ingenious technical innovation, he was able to surround his new church choir with walls of colored glass, which seemed like a shim-

7.4 Gothic-style construction.
The technical basis of the Gothic style was the pointed arch and cross-ribbed vaulting. The rounded arches of the Romanesque style, (*a*) and (*b*), were limited in width and height. Vaults of pointed arches (*c*) could span a wider, rectangular bay, while rising to a uniform height (*d*).

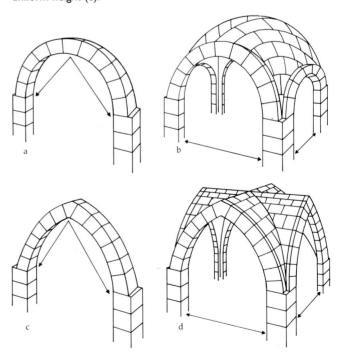

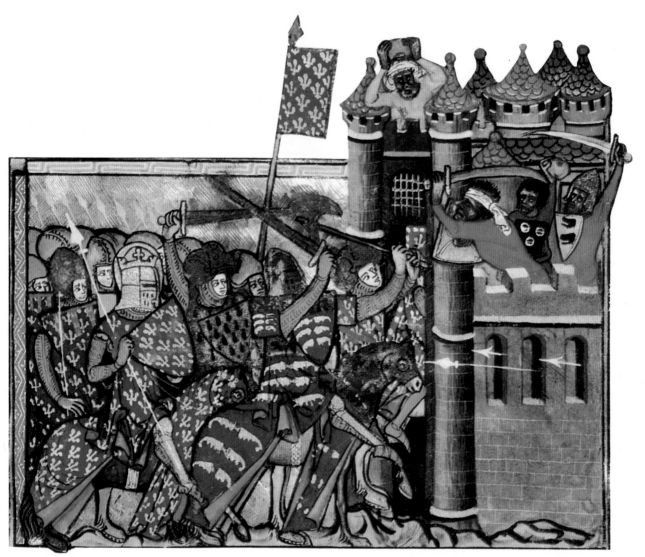

7.5 French knights under Louis XI besieging Damietta, Egypt, 7th Crusade, 1249. Ms. Fr. 13568 fol. 83. Bibliothèque Nationale, Paris.

mering miracle of color and light. The abbot connected his architectural invention with the *lux nova*, the "new light" of Christ's coming. He wrote:

> *For bright is that which is brightly coupled with the*
> *bright,*
> *And bright is the noble edifice which is pervaded by the*
> *new light.*[3]

St. Denis' walls of translucent glass depended on a subtle combination of three architectural elements: the pointed arch, the ribbed vault, and the flying buttress. Abbot Suger and his architect (who is unknown) merged these elements in a daring innovation that defined the Gothic style in architecture. The Gothic **pointed arch** replaced the Romanesque style of rounded arches, which were limited by width and height (Fig. **7.4**). The vaults of the pointed arch could span a wider, rectangular bay,

while rising to a uniform height, and thus permitted enlarged openings for windows. The ceilings were supported by **ribbed vaulting**, thin skeletons of stone that were erected first and then filled with a layer of ceiling masonry. In the Romanesque style, the ceiling's weight was supported by massive piers along the nave. The Gothic architects moved these heavy piers to the exterior, creating buttresses that braced the nave wall through stone arms called **flying buttresses** (Fig. **7.7**). The system of buttresses and flying buttresses supported the ceiling's weight and counteracted its outward thrust, permitting the nave walls to be filled with glass instead of masonry and creating the luminous effects of St. Denis' choir.

The Gothic style's structural elements – the pointed arch, ribbed vaulting, and external buttresses – created a framework of soaring lines which lift the eyes and the spirit. The Gothic ribs and arches were both decorative and functional: they made possible the churches' daring

KEY CONCEPT

PILGRIMAGE

The dynamism of the later Middle Ages was fueled by the popularity of **pilgrimage** – the journey to a saint's shrine or other sacred place. Christian pilgrimage was rooted in Christianity's deep sense of human sinfulness: as one poet explained, "We who live the worldly life are drawn so deeply into sin that it will be a miracle indeed if God has mercy upon us." A public and arduous act of faith such as a pilgrimage was a way of doing penance for a lifetime of sin. A pilgrim might also call on the miraculous powers of the saint whose **relics** – bones or personal possessions – were kept at the shrine. The tunic of the Virgin Mary at Chartres, for example, was believed to ease the pains of childbirth.

In Europe, a great age of pilgrimage dawned about 1000, as the region recovered from war and invasion. The principal destinations for European Christians were Jerusalem, Rome, and Santiago de Compostela, the shrine of St. James located near the northwest coast of Spain. Pilgrimage guide books instructed the believer in the proper dress and equipment – a tunic, staff, and leather purse – and warned of dangers to the traveler. Pilgrims returned with a badge, such as the palm of Jericho or the cockle shell of St. James (Fig. **7.6**).

Christian pilgrimage originated in the so-called "cult of the saints," the pious veneration of the Christian saints and their relics. The collection of saintly relics dated from the earliest days of Christianity, and the Middle Ages saw a lively commerce in saints' bones, slivers of the cross, vials of Christ's blood, and other sacred objects. When European Crusaders on their way to the Holy Land sacked and occupied Constantinople in 1204, they plundered the Byzantine emperor's substantial collection of relics. One prize was a crown of thorns supposedly worn by Jesus at the crucifixion. The possession of an important relic brought prestige and income to a church or town.

The most important medieval cult was devoted to the Virgin Mary, to whom nearly all the great Gothic cathedrals – "palaces of the Virgin" – were dedicated. It was not relics that drew believers to Mary, but rather the passionate belief in her powers of mercy and salvation. Such belief still draws Christian pilgrims to sites such as Lourdes (in France) and Guadalupe (in Mexico).

The journey to a sacred shrine is a motive in many world religions. Muslim pilgrims on the *hajj* flood to

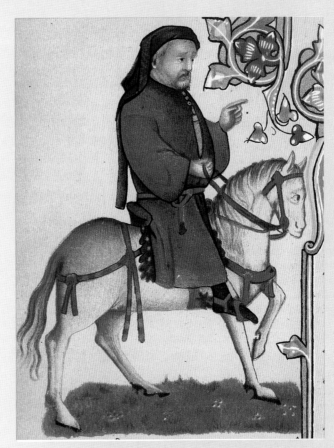

7.6 Geoffrey Chaucer (c. 1340–1400) as pilgrim.

Mecca by the millions. Hindus traditionally journey to the banks of the Ganges or other sacred waters of the faith. The site of the Buddha's enlightenment at Bodh Gaya in India is the first among Buddhism's chief pilgrimage destinations. In all these religions, a pilgrimage brings believers in contact with the sacred.

THE WRITE IDEA

Tell the story of a journey that changed your life or gave you important insight into yourself. Was it necessary to leave your everyday surroundings to have this experience?

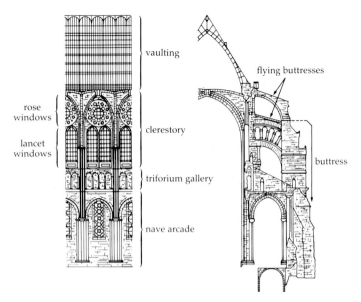

7.7 Section of Gothic nave and diagram of buttresses.
The slender ribs of the cross-ribbed vaulting helped reduce the roof's weight and expense, while giving visual emphasis to the vault's soaring lines. The exterior stone piers, or buttresses, were connected to the exterior walls by stone arms called flying buttresses. The buttressing counteracted the roof's weight and thrust (outward push).

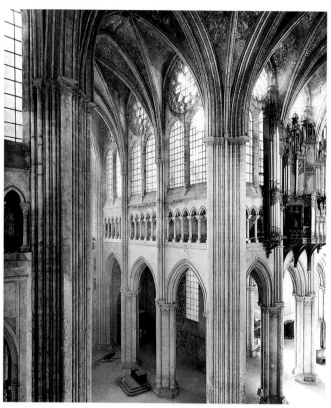

7.8 Interior of Chartres Cathedral, France, c. 1194–1240, showing nave arcade, triforium, and clerestory windows.

heights, and also made the churches a visual metaphor for the orderliness of God's world (Fig. **7.8**).

THE CATHEDRAL AT CHARTRES

In the century after Suger rebuilt St. Denis, Gothic cathedrals arose in the towns around the Ile-de-France, the royal domain surrounding Paris. The towns of the Ile-de-France competed in building higher and more splendid cathedrals. The contest ended in a construction disaster at Beauvais, where the choir collapsed in 1284. While the new style was soon imitated throughout Europe, its origins were unmistakably French, and it was then called simply the "French style."

The cathedral at Chartres [SHART-(r)] (Fig. **7.9**) surpassed all others in the perfection of its architectural design, stained glass, and sculpture. Located in a rich farming town southwest of Paris, Chartres Cathedral was one of Christian Europe's holiest shrines, housing the tunic that believers claimed was worn by the Virgin Mary at Christ's birth. When the town's Romanesque cathedral was burned down in 1194, the Virgin's tunic was rescued from the ruins of the building unharmed. Chartres' citizens interpreted this miracle as a sign that the Virgin desired a new shrine in her honor. Funds were solicited throughout Europe to rebuild Chartres' church. The faithful responded so generously that the church's new Gothic nave was completed in 1220, barely twenty-five years after reconstruction began.

Chartres' new floor plan (Fig. **7.10**) maintained the basic form and dimensions of the earlier Romanesque church, which had partly survived the 1194 fire. The relatively narrow nave and its flanking aisles were reflected on the exterior by the three doors of the west portal. Gothic architects added broader and more elaborate portals on the north and south porches of the transept. The choir, located behind the altar, was screened off from the nave, which was noisily occupied by merchants and townspeople. The coexistence of secular and sacred activity was typical of medieval cathedrals, and for a while, Chartres' wine merchants sold their goods within sight of the altar.

The differences between Gothic and Romanesque styles are more dramatic when one stands inside the Gothic cathedral. Looking down the nave, one sees – instead of massive Romanesque stone walls – a harmony of soaring lines and gem-like luminosity (Fig. **7.8**). Like the floor plan, the Gothic church's vertical design has a three-part division. The **nave arcade** is formed by weight-bearing piers, whose mass is disguised by vertical shafts. Above the arcade are the **triforium**, an arcade of pointed arches sometimes opening onto a gallery, and the tall **clerestory** windows. The upward view along the ribbed piers, past the colored clerestory windows to the delicate web of ribbed vaulting in the ceiling, represented the beauty and pro-

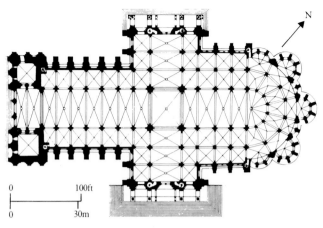

7.10 Plan of Chartres Cathedral, France, 1194–1240.

portion of God's ordered cosmos, a visible manifestation of divine truth. Chartres Cathedral was not the highest or most daring example of the Gothic style. However, its pious beauty made the splendor and meaning of God's revelation manifest to the human senses.

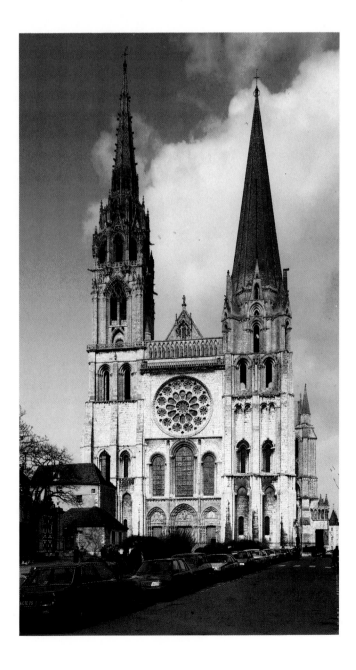

7.9 Chartres Cathedral, France, west façade, 1194–1240. South spire, c. 1180, height 344 ft (105 m); north spire, 1507–13, height 377 ft (115 m).
The original north spire was destroyed by fire and replaced in the late-Gothic "flamboyant" style.

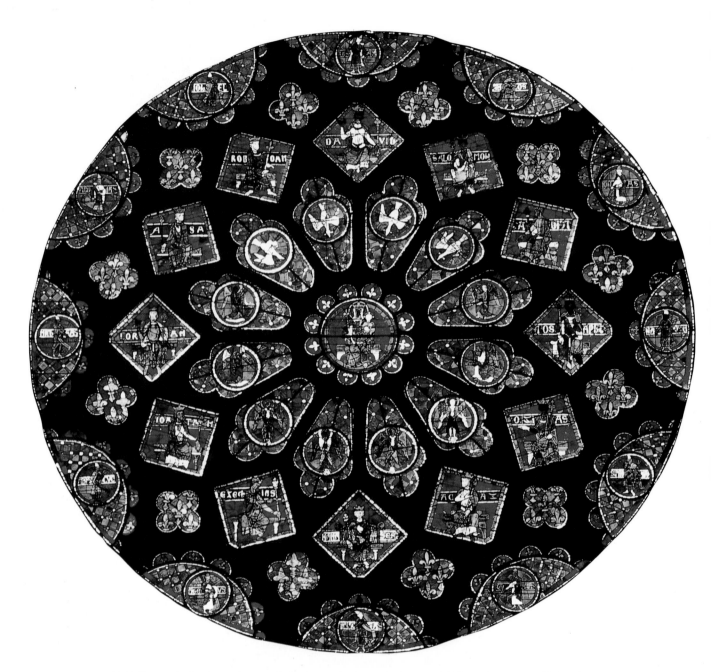

7.11 Rose window, north portal, Chartres Cathedral, France, 1223–6. Diameter 44 ft (13.4 m).
At the center of the rose are Mary and the Christ Child, surrounded by angels and Old Testament kings.

Chartres' Stained-glass Windows In earlier Byzantine and Romanesque churches, paintings and mosaic had decorated the masonry walls. The stone walls of the Gothic church were filled instead with stained glass, an art in which Chartres surpassed all its Gothic rivals. Chartres' windows contained 22,000 square feet (2050 m²) of colored glass, filling the interior with a subdued light that symbolized God's mysteries. The windows represented quite literally the word of God. Each one depicted a biblical story, the life of a saint, or a principle of Church doctrine. A Gothic cathedral's windows therefore created a visual "Bible of the poor," instructing the illiterate citizens and pilgrims who worshiped there.

A rose window (Fig. **7.11**) stood over each portal, representing both the sun, source of light, and the Virgin Mary, the perfect "rose without thorns." The rose windows were outlined by finely carved stone **tracery**, a rose-shaped frame that was assembled in place and then filled with glass. **Lancet windows**, shaped like pointed arches, filled much of the remaining wall space. In all the windows, the pieces of colored glass were held by thin lead strips and reinforced by iron bars. The citizens of Chartres' trade and

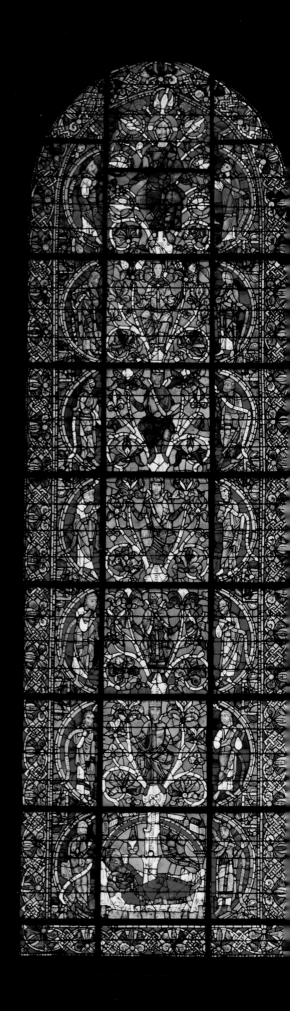

7.12 *Tree of Jesse*, lancet window, west portal. Chartres Cathedral, France, c. 1150.
In a conventional medieval image of Christ's royal ancestry, a tree sprouts from the loins of Jesse, father of the Hebrew king David, and emanates at top in the Virgin Mary and Christ himself. Observe the elaborate floral imagery.

craft guilds underwrote the cost of many windows. Some forty-three different trades are represented in "signature" scenes of Chartres' windows.

The most admired window at Chartres is the *Notre-Dame-de-Belle-Verrière* [NOHT(r) DAHM duh BELL vair-ee-AY(r)], or "Our Lady of the Beautiful Glass" (see Fig. 7.1). The predominant colors of blue and red were the favorites of Gothic glass-makers – they symbolized the Virgin and altered the external light to the shade of ruby and sapphire gems. The *Notre-Dame-de-Belle-Verrière* captured the tenderness and mercy that medieval worshipers attributed to the Virgin.

In another window, the *Tree of Jesse* (Fig. **7.12**) over the west portal, religious devotion was blended with the practical truths of politics. Read in the medieval fashion (left-to-right, bottom-to-top), the window shows the Old Testament lineage of Christ. The figures are framed by lily flowers, symbols of the French king who subsidized the window – no doubt a king's wish to remember his own royal lineage in that of Christ's. Thus, the *Tree of Jesse* offered the viewer a lesson in both medieval faith and medieval politics.

GOTHIC SCULPTURE

On the outside of Chartres Cathedral, the sculpted figures on the massive three-door portals were as detailed and systematic as the writings of the theologians who taught at Chartres' cathedral school. Most likely, the school's teachers supervised the design of Chartres' exterior sculpture. The carved symbols and stories were carefully coordinated to attract and instruct the pilgrims who entered the shrine.

The famed west or "royal" portal of Chartres (Fig. **7.13**), for example, depicts the glory and power of Christ in three aspects. The tympanum over each door states its theme. On the right, Madonna and Child represent the Incarnation of Christ, that is, Christ's descent into the flesh through the womb of Mary. On the left door is Christ's

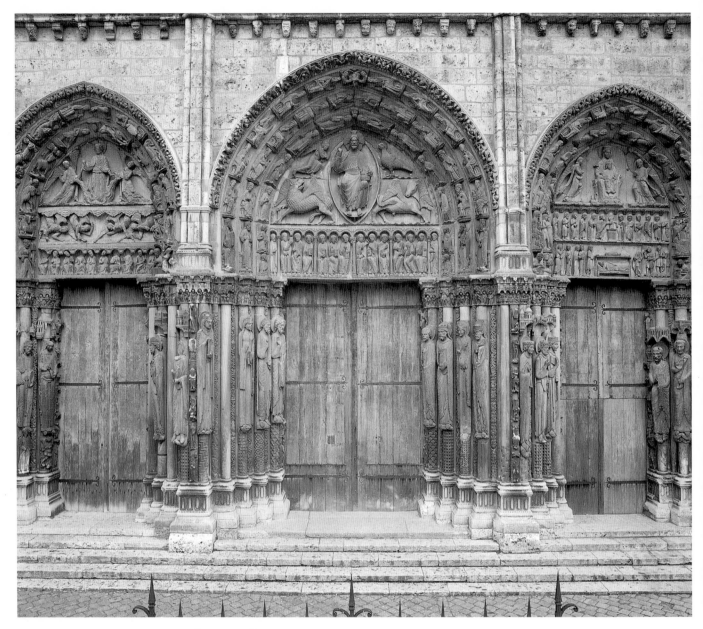

7.13 The three portals of the west façade, Chartres Cathedral, France, c. 1145–70.
The three tympanum scenes depict Christ's birth (right); his ascension into heaven (left); and his reign in heaven (center), where symbols of the four Evangelists surround him and the twelve apostles fill the lintel below.

Ascension into Heaven, his return to the realm of spirit. Over the center door, Christ in His Majesty reigns as king over heaven, ringed by symbols of the four Evangelists (authors of the Gospels). The themes of royal birth and majesty are repeated from the *Tree of Jesse*, one of the lancet windows set above these doors. In some cases, the exterior sculpted figures mirror scenes from the windows.

A closer examination of these doors reveals a complex symbolic meaning. On the right door (Fig. **7.14**), for example, the incarnation is told as the *Life of the Virgin Mary*, a theme of special significance at Chartres. The tympanum scene of the Madonna and Child mirrors

the famed window *Notre-Dame-de-Belle-Verrière*. On the lintel below are scenes from Mary's life, including the Annunciation, the visitation of St. Elizabeth, the birth of Christ, and the presentation of the Christ child at the temple. On this door, the archivolts contain symbols of the seven liberal arts, the curriculum of medieval learning (see page 180). The liberal arts refer both to the cathedral school and to Mary herself, who was considered patron of all learning.

The Gothic spirit effected changes in sculpture that resembled the evolution of ancient Greek sculpture (see Chapter 3), from stylized austerity to a more life-like

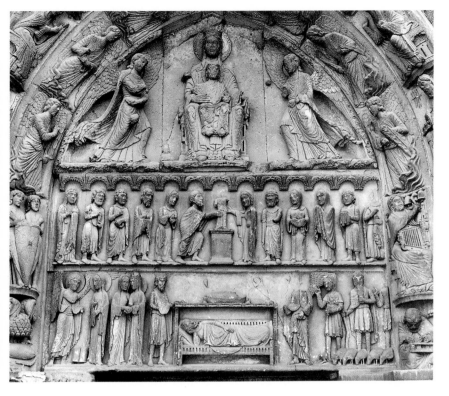

7.14 Left *Life of the Virgin Mary*, tympanum of right door, **Royal Portal, Chartres Cathedral, France, c. 1145–70.**
The different groups of figures narrate the early life of Christ. Across the bottom panel, for example, are: the Annunciation; the visitation of St. Elizabeth, mother of John the Baptist; Mary and the Christ Child in a two-tiered bed; and the shepherds hearing the news of Christ's birth.

7.15 Below *Abraham and Isaac*, **Chartres Cathedral, France.**
Compared to the stiffly elongated figures of the Royal Portal (Fig. 7.14), this jamb sculpture creates an animated drama. Preparing to sacrifice his son, Abraham turns toward the angel who instructs him instead to slay the ram (below).

humanism. This evolution is best illustrated in the **jamb** sculptures of Chartres Cathedral. On the west doors, still in Romanesque style, the sculpted ancestors of Christ are rigid, austere, and clearly bound to the columns behind them. The later Gothic sculptures of the north and south doors are more animated and natural-looking. The most dramatic of these is *Abraham and Isaac* (Fig. **7.15**), showing young Isaac bound for sacrifice and Abraham raising the knife to slay him. Both look up, as if toward the angel who stays Abraham's hand. The angel directs him to sacrifice the ram caught in a thicket at their feet.

Like all the arts of the cathedral, the sculptures are subordinate to the cathedral's main purpose – to represent, in the material forms of stone, the spiritual truth of God's word.

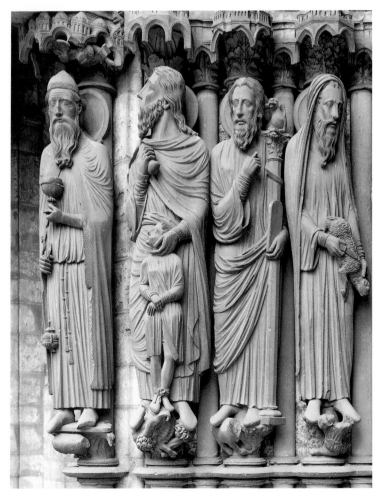

GLOBAL PERSPECTIVE

BUDDHISM IN ASIA

Under the rule of Frankish kings, Christianity was established in medieval Europe as a religion of monastic discipline and a popular faith that mixed easily with pagan belief. In a similar fashion, Buddhism spread eastward through Asia in two guises: a monastic asceticism and a teaching of compassion and salvation.

The first of these paths, based on the Theravada ("Doctrine of the Elders"), adhered to the original teaching of the Buddha. The follower of Theravada [thair-uh-VAH-dah] sought the liberation of self through meditation and moral discipline, a path that required withdrawal into a monastic order (the Sangha). Lay people were obliged to support the Sangha, while postponing their own pursuit of a saintly life. Adherence to the Theravada spread to Sri Lanka (Ceylon) in the third century B.C. and from there to southeast Asia (Burma, Thailand, Vietnam).

A more popular Buddhist faith took shape in the Mahayana, or "Greater Vehicle," which fostered the deification of the Buddha and emphasized personal salvation rather than ascetic denial. In the Mahayana [mah-hah-YAH-nah], some believed that the Buddha continually visited the world in new incarnations. Others appealed to the powers of **Bodhisattvas** [boh-dee-SAHT-vah], pious and generous saints who

postponed their own entry into nirvana in order to save others. Cults of various Bodhisattvas encouraged mythic embellishment of Buddha's teachings, including the belief in a paradise (the Pure Land of the West) waiting after death. A later Chinese version of this belief promised that the Maitreya Buddha (Buddha of the Future) would return to earth and establish paradise in this life. With less emphasis on Hindu ideas of karma and reincarnation, the Mahayana faith was easily embraced in China and Japan, where it was blended with Taoist teachings to create Ch'an (Japanese, Zen) Buddhism.

The enthusiasm of the Buddhist faith in Asia encouraged elaborate artistic expressions. The great temple of Borobudur in Java (present-day Indonesia), for example, was constructed as a vast holy mountain, rising in nine terraces to a sealed chamber containing an image of the Buddha. The central chamber and the surrounding peaks all take the form of a bell-shaped **stupa** (literally, "hair knot"), a rounded sacred enclosure used in Hindu and Buddhist architecture. The temple plan's concentric square and circles, symbolizing the wheel of life, were adopted in other great temple complexes of southeast Asia, such as Angkor Wat (Cambodia) and Ananda (Burma).

MUSIC AND THEATER IN THE GOTHIC AGE

Identify the most important changes in Gothic sacred music and theater.

The Gothic church achieved a rich texture of artistic elements – architecture, stained glass, and sculpture – that were drawn from older medieval traditions. A similar process of evolving traditions brought changes in theater and music during the Gothic age. Musicians devised complex new accents in sacred music, without abandoning traditional chants. Their sophisticated musical techniques affected the course of Western music for centuries. Sacred drama moved outside the church, even though its popular spectacles maintained their religious

emphasis. Thus, the Gothic forms of music and drama grew from deep roots in Christian faith and symbolism, even as they became more worldly.

THE EVOLUTION OF ORGANUM

The most striking development in medieval music was the evolution of **polyphony** ("many voices") from traditional, monophonic plainchant. Polyphony involves two or more melodic lines playing simultaneously. It may have arisen in secular music, as singers "doubled" the melody with a second voice. While polyphony probably began in musical improvisation, it was gradually incorporated into the composed music of sacred chant. This medieval invention of polyphony sets Western music apart from virtually all the world's other musical traditions.

The earliest references to medieval polyphony are in a ninth-century musical handbook, which describes church singing in two voices. This early polyphony was designated **organum**, perhaps because it resembled the sound of an organ. In organum's most basic form, the two voices moved in parallel direction, creating **parallel organum** (Fig. **7.16**). Parallel organum consisted of a principal melody (usually a traditional chant) and a second, "organal" voice

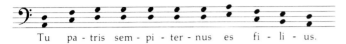

7.16 Parallel organum.

7.17 Organum duplum.

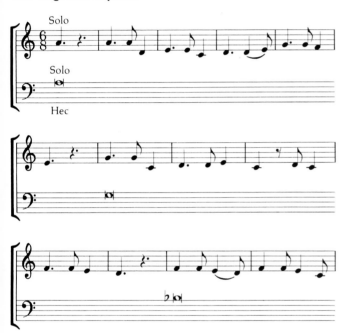

phrases that also derived from earlier church music. However, these developments made possible the great syntheses of medieval music that composers achieved at the cathedral schools during the twelfth and thirteenth centuries.

The Notre Dame School The Gothic era's leading musical inventors gathered at the cathedral of Notre Dame in Paris, where they were called the "Notre Dame School of Music." Here a master composer named Léonin

7.18 Organum triplum.

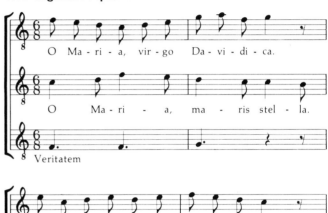

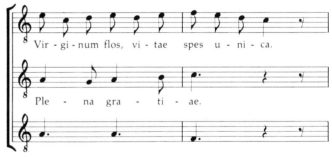

sung below the principal melody. The second voice moved at set intervals (usually an octave, fourth, or fifth) below the basic chant.

Gothic composers began to elaborate on this simple but revolutionary musical invention. They cautiously experimented with different intervals (such as the third), made the two voices move in contrary motion, and added rhythmic variety. By the late eleventh century, a new version of organum had been developed, called **organum duplum** (Fig. **7.17**). In duplum, the traditional plainchant melody was shifted to the lower voice and sung in long, held notes. This lower voice was called the "tenor" (from Latin *tenere*, "to hold"). Above the tenor, the "duplum" voice sang freer, more complex musical phrases. Duplum organum was Western civilization's first truly polyphonic music, since the two distinct melodic lines moved independently of one another.

Despite its novelty, duplum organum was firmly rooted in tradition. The tenor voice intoned a traditional plainchant, a spiritual reminder of Christianity's musical roots. The duplum melody was often composed of melismatic

[LAY-oh-nan(h)] (c. 1163–1201) worked in the years of Notre Dame Cathedral's construction. Léonin compiled an influential book of sacred music in duplum organum called the *Magnus Liber Organi* (*Great Book of Organum*), important above all for recording the improvisational singing techniques of this period. It is most likely that Léonin did not actually compose the *Magnus Liber*'s contents but organized and notated what he had learned as a master singer.

Léonin's successors at Notre Dame and other schools continued to enrich the growing body of organum music. Pérotin [PAIR-oh-tan(h)] (active early thirteenth century) is credited with adding a third (Fig. **7.18**) and sometimes fourth voice above the tenor. In Pérotin's complex works, the organal passages were often balanced against sections of the plainchant melody sung in unison. The rich and sometimes dissonant harmonies of the upper voices were punctuated with forms of **cadence**, the musical resolution at the end of a phrase.

Pérotin's innovations in musical structure and tonality accelerated the development of late medieval music, a complex music which came to be called *cantus firmus* ("fixed song") because of the tenor's melodic fixity. The *cantus firmus* posed new problems of musical composition and training. Coordinating several voices required greater rhythmic precision and stimulated the rise of rhythmic modes. The different organal voices had to be governed by a stricter rhythmic measure, or else the music would come crashing down on their ears. The intricate texture of *cantus firmus* also demanded a more advanced musical notation and training, techniques that were developed and propagated by the Notre Dame Cathedral school. Pérotin's three- and four-voice organum was not always appreciated by Church authorities, who feared that the congregation would go insane from the "riot of the wantoning voice" and the "affectations in the mincing of notes and sentences."

GOTHIC THEATER: FROM CHURCH TO TOWN

By the eleventh century Church authorities were complaining about drama in the church, which was spiced by raging Herods and violent massacre scenes. One German abbess objected to "the clang of weapons, the presence of shameless wenches and all sorts of disorder" that liturgical plays brought to her church's nave. As its scripts and staging became more elaborate, sacred drama outgrew the Catholic Mass that it was supposed to illustrate. The simple scenarios depicting three women at Christ's tomb had become elaborate recreations of the Journey of the Wise Men and the Slaughter of the Innocents. Consequently, sacred drama was shifted outside the church to the town squares, where it was acted by ordinary citizens instead of priests and nuns, and often written in the spoken vernacular instead of Latin.

Like the building of a cathedral, staging a play in the Gothic era was a cooperative effort between the Church and the people of the town. Theatrical productions were based on religious stories and nearly always coincided with religious holidays. The most common occasion for civic drama was the Feast of Corpus Christi, celebrated in late spring. At Chartres, trade guilds and civic leaders had helped to pay for building the town's cathedral. In other towns, these same groups helped to produce the local Cor-

7.19 Scenery for the Valenciennes Mystery Play, 1547. Contemporary drawing. Bibliothèque Nationale, Paris.
The stage provided for elaborate stage effects, including fire spouting from the mouth of hell (right).

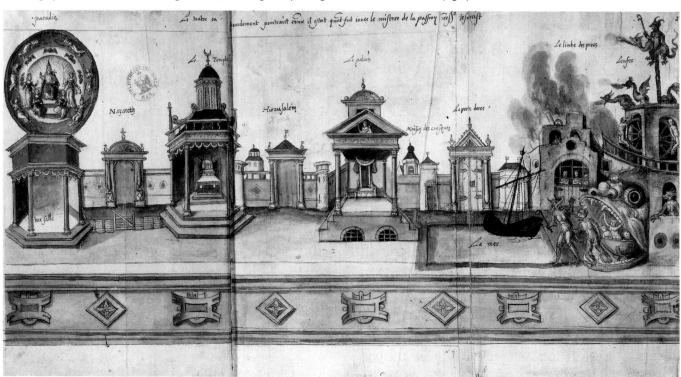

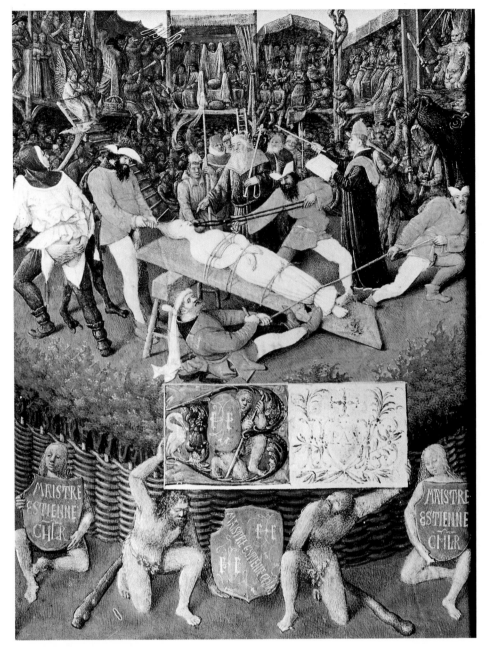

7.20 Scene of the Martyrdom of St. Apollonia, from a 15th-century miniature by Jean Fouquet. Musée Condé, Chantilly, France.
A scene from a miracle play depicting the life and martyrdom of St. Apollonia. The play's director (in miter hat, center right) holds a prompt book and directs the music with his baton. Elaborate scenic scaffolds enclose the stage at the rear.

pus Christi drama cycle. A play involving Noah's Ark would be assigned to the local carpenters, and goldsmiths and money-changers would costume and portray the Three Wise Men. As these examples show, drama festivals were sanctioned and supervised by Church authorities, but depended on hundreds of townspeople to plan, finance, and stage their productions. The scale of participation commanded by the medieval Church might well be the envy of directors of civic theater today.

CRITICAL QUESTION
What projects in your community involve the kind of civic cooperation demonstrated by a medieval dramatic production? What do such projects reveal about the values of your community?

KEY CONCEPT

SCHOLASTICISM

Like many of the Gothic arts, philosophy in the later Middle Ages developed by crossing the boundary between the sacred and secular. The rise of the cathedral schools and disputatious scholars such as Peter Abelard (see page 000) stimulated a philosophical movement called scholasticism. **Scholasticism** encompassed the philosophical debates and methods of learning practiced by theologians during the later Middle Ages. Scholasticism's skepticism and vitality thrived outside the monastic cloister, in the cities' schools and universities.

Although scholasticism was not a unified system of thought, the scholastics did share some fundamental principles for understanding God's truth and his universe. They wanted to incorporate philosophy (the study of truth in general) into theology (the study of God's word). In effect, this made theology a comprehensive system of all human knowledge. Also, scholastics relied on the Greek philosopher Aristotle (see page 63) as a model of logical method, and considered the pagan Aristotle to be an authority equal to the Bible itself. Finally, the scholastics practiced a method of formal argument by which issues could be debated logically and systematically – a method which gave consistency and rigor to medieval philosophical disputes.

Scholastic teachers were famed for the audacity of their reasoning and the size of their student following. These teachers often wandered from school to school, comparing themselves to the sophists of ancient Greece (see page 62). Peter Abelard, who reckoned himself "as the only true philosopher left in the world," attracted students whether he taught at the cathedral school in Paris or a monastery in the wilds of western France.

Nowadays, because of its emphasis on logic and argument, medieval scholasticism suffers from a reputation for arid debates about obscure topics, perhaps in the same way that today's university researchers sometimes suffer ridicule for their obscure and seemingly irrelevant projects. Scholastic philosophers wrote in a specialized and artificial language that non-experts could barely understand, and their argumentation lacked the personal and engaging tone of early Christian writings such as Augustine's *Confessions*. However, the scholastics' disputations addressed issues that still concern today's thinkers: the nature of law, the authority of the state, the definition of life. The scholastics themselves were the precursors of today's university intellectuals, who in their academic enclaves often debate the same vital issues.

CRITICAL QUESTION

Should the academic pursuit of knowledge and truth always have practical consequences? How would you rank the college courses you have taken according to their practical value? According to their genuine devotion to truth?

The actual plays demonstrated a medieval blend of sacred and secular concerns. **Mystery plays** were cycles of plays depicting biblical stories (Fig. **7.19**). A cycle usually centered on the Passion of Christ, but might also re-enact the fall of Adam and Eve, the sacrifice of Isaac, or the Flood. The dramatic climax came when Christ descended through the gaping mouth of hell and defeated a buffoonish devil. Christ then sat in judgment upon the wicked and the pure. A mystery cycle was typically an elaborate affair, lasting several days, with spectacular stage effects such as flying angels and hellish flames.

Another type of play, called the **miracle play**, recounted the lives of saints from childhood to death and often included vivid scenes of battle and torture (Fig. **7.20**). The **morality play**, which appeared in the fifteenth century, depicted the struggle between the vices and virtues over a sinner's soul. The best-known morality play, *Everyman*, represents an ordinary man's struggle to escape the summons of death. *Everyman* required little scenery and scarcely more than an hour to perform. The play was well suited to the fledgling bands of professional actors who were beginning to entertain in Europe's palaces and town squares.

Despite their diversity, the plays of the Gothic era shared some essential traits. First, theater in this age was thoroughly popular. It was written and performed in the **vernacular**, the language spoken by common people, and the plays involved hundreds of citizens in the production itself. The audience may well have been the town's entire population. Second, the mystery and miracle plays emphasized spectacular staging rather than subtleties

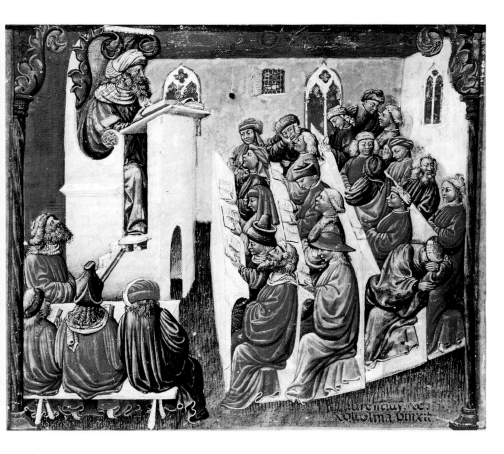

7.21 A master lecturing university students, from a medieval edition of Aristotle's *Nicomachean Ethics*. Manuscript illumination, German, 14th century. Staatliche Museen, Berlin.
Note that some students follow the lecture in their own books, while others converse or doze. How does this image of medieval higher education compare with instruction and learning in today's universities?

of dramatic text. Like the citizens of ancient Rome, medieval townspeople preferred a grand show to literary niceties. Finally, all the plays had a religious message, whether taken from the Bible, the life of a saint, or the struggle of ordinary people against sin. Thus, although performed outside the church walls, Gothic theater stood very much in the Church's shadow.

THE NEW LEARNING

Describe the social atmosphere and course of study at a typical medieval university.

The cities of the Gothic age gave birth to a new learning, based on scholasticism and centered in the cathedral schools and urban universities. In its love of complexity, the new Gothic learning resembled the layered voices of organal song. In its rough-and-tumble vitality, medieval scholarly life shared the spirit of the town dramas. The Gothic intellectual awakening spawned a new kind of social institution called the university. Within the university's lecture halls, scholastic philosophers achieved a grand synthesis of Christian doctrine and the Western philosophical tradition.

THE UNIVERSITIES

The medieval university was quite unlike anything in the ancient world: a self-governing organization of scholars formed to teach and certify a professional class of lawyers and clerks. Medieval universities were governed either by their faculties or by their students, who together formed the *universitas*, or "whole body." Most universities offered the basic baccalaureate (bachelor's degree), while specializing in one of three advanced studies – theology, law, or medicine. University education, however, almost entirely excluded women. The late medieval decline of independent convents and abbeys for women further reduced women's opportunity for advanced learning.

Though they were all men, medieval university faculties and students were a remarkably international group. All teaching and writing were done in Latin, so an English-born scholar could study as easily in Bologna as in Oxford. The preeminent medieval university was at Paris, recognized by the French king in 1200. Paris was famed for its theological faculty and was dubbed "mother of the sciences" by one pope. Universities at England's Oxford and Cambridge modeled themselves after Paris, while the university at Bologna specialized first in law, then in medicine.

Although relaxed and wholly voluntary, life at a medieval university was rather strenuous by today's standards. Students suffered from shortages in lodging, con-

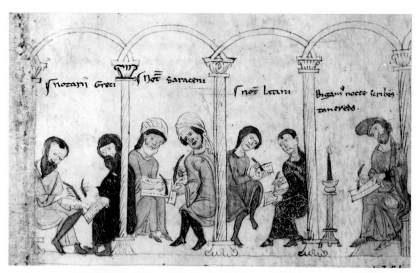

7.22 Medieval scholars studying in Latin, Hebrew, and Arabic at a school in Sicily. Italian, c. 1200. Bürgerbibliothek Bern, Codex 120 II, f. 101r.
Schools in Spain, Sicily, and Italy were vital in the transmission of Arabic and Hebrew scholarship to Christian Europe.

flicts with townspeople, and slow responses to appeals for money from home. A typical day began at 5 a.m. with prayers and study, followed by lectures, a group debate, and further study before bed. Because few students had textbooks, their courses consisted mainly of the master's lectures. Lectures (from the Latin *lectio*, or "reading") in theology consisted of a master reading from the Bible or a standard commentary, followed by his own interpretation (Fig. **7.21**). At Bologna in northern Italy a master could be fined for extending his lecture even a minute past the allotted time.

A course of study usually began in the liberal arts, primarily the *trivium* of grammar, logic, and dialectic. Ideally, the *trivium* comprised the introductory course of study, to be followed by instruction in the *quadrivium* of arithmetic, geometry, music, and astronomy. The medieval curriculum of *trivium* and *quadrivium* could be traced to the writings of the late Roman philosopher Boethius. In practice, teachers had considerable freedom in defining the topics of university education. Advanced students earned a bachelor's degree. At least six years were required to obtain a master's, or teaching degree in the arts, and longer in the more demanding areas of theology, law, or medicine (Fig. **7.22**).

A young scholastic demonstrated his learning in the disputation, a form of philosophical debate modeled on Plato's dialogues. In a disputation, the master announced an issue for discussion, and then his advanced students answered objections from the audience. Finally, the master himself closed the discussion with a definitive and authoritative answer. Student examinations were entirely oral, and usually held during Lent, the season of fasting and self-denial.

The Rediscovery of Aristotle Between 1150 and 1250, scholastic learning in medieval Europe was energized by the "rediscovery" of Aristotle's works on nature and human affairs. European philosophers had long known the "old" Aristotle – his works on logic and rhetoric. In the "new" Aristotle, scholastic thinkers found a comprehensive philosophy that examined problems of ethics, law, and nature. By 1250, a century after the universities were founded at Paris and Oxford, Aristotle's dominance was so complete that he was known simply as "the Philosopher."

Christian Europe owed its rediscovery of Aristotle to the rich intellectual culture of the Islamic world, where Arabic scholars had translated and interpreted Aristotle's works for centuries. At the School of Toledo (see page 146) and other scholarly centers, the Arabic texts and commentaries were translated into Latin and spread into Europe. In fact, many of the new Aristotelian works were known only by Latin versions of Arabic translations, not in the original Greek.

Of the Arabic-language philosophers, Ibn-Sina [EE-bunn SEE-nuh] (980–1037), known in Latin as Avicenna [ah-vuh-CHENN-uh], was perhaps the most original. Ibn-Sina claimed to have read Aristotle's *Metaphysics* forty times before he finally understood it. He also compiled an immense encyclopedia of medical knowledge that was widely used by European physicians. The greatest philosopher of Muslim Spain was Ibn-Rushd (1126–98), known in Latin as Averroës [ah-VER-roh-us], whose commentary was considered by Thomas Aquinas to be the definitive interpretation of Aristotle's philosophy. Ibn-Rushd's attempts to reconcile Muslim faith with Aristotle's natural philosophy were not always welcome. Theologians once

MEDIEVAL PHILOSOPHY

Anselm of Canterbury	1033–1109	Preached faith as the basis for all understanding
Peter Abelard	1079–1142	Defended freedom to doubt and question as a means to truth
Ibn-Rushd	1126–98	Reconciled Aristotle's scientific thought with Muslim scriptures
Thomas Aquinas	1125–74	Taught that revelations of faith were not contrary to truths of reason

incited a mob to attack him, and his philosophical writings were burned by an intolerant caliph. The conflict of reason and faith also engaged the Jewish scholar Moses Maimonides (1135–1204), who wrote (in Arabic) his *Guide for the Perplexed.* Maimonides' [may-MAHN-i-deez] manual gave advice for regaining one's lost faith in God through the use of reason.

Thomas Aquinas

The most influential scholastic thinker was Thomas Aquinas (1125–74), who achieved a vast synthesis of medieval theology and Aristotelian philosophy. Aquinas [uh-KWEYE-nuss] said he wanted to make "a science of faith." His greatest work was the *Summa Theologica* (begun 1266), a summation of medieval knowledge about God's plan for the natural and human world. The *Summa* showed Aquinas' genius for creating harmony and order among diverse philosophical elements. The result was a thoroughly Christian philosophy that still influences thinkers in politics, education, and law.

For Aquinas, the spheres of divine revelation and human reason were distinct but not contradictory. "Reason does not destroy faith but perfects it," he wrote. According to Aquinas, humans came to know God's world both through the Bible's revealed truth and the logical workings of human understanding. God, the highest reality, would always remain a mystery to human reason, hidden even in the words of Christian scripture. Still, Aquinas argued, God revealed himself in other ways, through the works of nature and the workings of human reason. He held that God and nature were one, forming a harmonious order that was intelligible to the human

powers of reason. Thus the study of nature led ultimately to an understanding of God.

Aquinas' synthesis may be illustrated by a common example. Observing a wren from his window, Aquinas could study the bird for itself as a creature of nature, as Aristotle might have. However, Aquinas would also know (as Aristotle would not) that the wren was a part of God's hierarchical order of creation. Aquinas' knowledge of the bird was itself part of God's purpose, which intends for humans to employ their powers of reason.

For Aquinas, the hierarchy of human knowledge reflected the order of creation. His understanding of God's mystery was supported and confirmed by his knowledge of the natural world. Thus, Aristotle's natural philosophy was complemented by Aquinas' rich and flexible understanding of divine purpose.

Like God's world, Aquinas' *Summa Theologica* was encyclopedic in its scope and hierarchical in its organization. His master work examined a universe in which everything had its proper and logical place. The *Summa*'s logical order resembles the great natural system of evolution envisioned by the biologist Charles Darwin, in which the position of every creature was determined by evolutionary law. In its own time, Aquinas' system resembled the detailed symmetry of the Gothic style, the medieval synthesis of intellect and the arts. At his death, Aquinas' *Summa* was left unfinished, appropriately enough, since one's praise of God could never be complete.

COURTLY LIFE IN THE MIDDLE AGES

Give examples of the rules of courtly love professed in medieval courts.

Life at the medieval court achieved a new sophistication in the later Middle Ages. With feudalism's decline, new powers and wealth were accrued at the royal courts of England and France. These courts and their major satellites stimulated a revived interest in poetry and storytelling. Rather than epics of bloody combats, the late medieval minstrels and writers were more likely to tell a story of romantic adventure. Medieval romances, as these stories were called, gave rise to a culture of love, courtesy, and graciousness in some medieval courts. Today's romantic courtesies – those that are left – are rooted in the courtly life of the later Middle Ages.

Courtly Love

The term **courtly love** describes an elaborate code of behavior governing relations between the sexes at medieval

---

CRITICAL QUESTION

What rules might be agreed on to govern love in the modern era? How would these rules differ from the medieval rules of courtly love? Might men impose different rules on love from women?

---

courts. According to the rules of courtly love, the young man pledged spiritual devotion and servitude to his love, usually a noblewoman. The lady, who was usually already married, felt flattered by the lover's attentions, but had to reject him. Knowing that his desire must remain unsatisfied, the lover's mood shifted between joy and despair, devotion and betrayal. The male troubadour's songs and poems alternated between praise for his lady's beauty and complaints about her cruelty. The female troubadour often praised her suitor's character and warned him against betrayal.

The culture of courtly love reached its zenith at the courts of the gracious and powerful Eleanor of Aquitaine (c. 1122–1204). Eleanor was a powerful duchess who became the queen of two kings and was the mother of two sons who became kings. In 1170, the fiery and independent Eleanor was estranged from her royal husband, Henry II of England. She withdrew to her feudal lands in France and revived her court at Poitiers [PWAH-tee-ay]. Here Eleanor established elaborate rules of courtly dress, manners, and conversation.

Scholars are not sure whether Eleanor's prescriptions had any real influence on behavior at Poitiers or elsewhere. The rules of love are recorded in *The Art of Courtly Love* (*Tractatus de Amore*), written about 1180 by Andreas Cappellanus. Andreas defined love as "a certain inborn suffering derived from the sight of and excessive meditation upon the beauty of the opposite sex, which causes each one to wish above all things the embraces of the other and by common desire to carry out all of love's precepts in the other's embrace." Andreas ends his treatise with a faintly mocking list of love's "precepts":

- *Marriage is no real excuse for not loving.*
- *He who is not jealous cannot love.*
- *The easy attainment of love makes it of little value; difficulty of attainment makes it prized.*
- *Every lover regularly turns pale in the presence of his beloved.*
- *Love can deny nothing to love.*[4]

Even if the rules of courtly love were never seriously practiced, they reveal significant paradoxes of medieval society. Since marriage was a social obligation for medieval nobles, it was seldom an occasion for romantic fantasy and tenderness. Instead, romance was expressed through the quasi-adulterous games of courtly love. The rules of courtly love made the lady a powerful lord and the male lover her servant. In this way, courtly love inverted the normal medieval arrangement of male-female power. The lover praised his lady's beauty in the most sensuous language, while knowing that his love could never be physically consummated. The lady's rejection was cruel, but necessary. A lady's indifference to her lover's advances confirmed her purity and chastity, the very qualities that made her worthy of loving.

THE MEDIEVAL ROMANCE TRADITION

The paradoxes of courtly love found poignant expression in the songs of troubadours, the lyric poet-singers of the region of Provence in southern France. The troubadours' love songs celebrated medieval courtly life and idealized the troubadours' aristocratic patrons. Their style was quickly imitated in Germany by the *Minnesänger*, and in northern France by the *trouvères*. Through the bitter-sweet love songs of these poet-composers, the conventions and popular stories of courtly love spread throughout late medieval Europe.

The origins of troubadour song lie probably in the Arabic love poetry of the Muslim culture in Spain. Troubadours mixed the sensual images of Arabic poetry with the Neoplatonist idealism of popular philosophy. The most famous troubadour was Bernart de Ventadorn [vahn-ta-DORN] (c. 1150–c. 1180), who serenaded Eleanor of Aquitaine at the court of Poitiers. In his poems, Bernart's unquenchable hope for love was often mixed with despondency and rejection:

> *My dearest hopes grow grand and bold*
> *When fate presents the lovely face*
> *That I most love and must behold,*
> *Noble, gentle, true, without a trace*
> *Unlovely, and a body sweet with grace.*
> *She could bring salvation to the king;*
> *She has made me rich from nothing.*
>
> *As deeply as I love I fear,*
> *And nothing causes more dismay*
> *Than keeping all her wishes dear.*
> *It seems Christmas every day*
> *Her soul-filled eyes turn my way,*
> *But this they are so slow to do,*
> *It's months till every day is through.*[5]

BERNART DE VENTADORN

Women troubadours (called *trobairitz* [TROH-bair-itz] in their native Provençal language) were frequently noblewomen themselves, like Beatriz de Dia [BAY-uh-treez duh DEE-ah] (born c. 1140), wife of the Count of Poitiers. Women troubadours often spurned the poetic euphemism of male singers, instead demanding a forthright profession of their lover's feelings. These lines from Beatriz assert her own worth and fidelity while questioning her lover's fidelity:

My worth and noble birth should have some weight,
My beauty and especially my noble thoughts;
So I send you, there on your estate,
This song as messenger and delegate.
I want to know, my handsome noble friend,
Why I deserve so savage and so cruel a fate.
I can't tell whether it's pride or malice you intend.[6]

The troubadours and *trobairitz* nurtured a blossoming romance literature in late medieval Europe. The medieval **romance** was a long narrative in verse that told of chivalric adventures and courtly lovers. The same romance stories were revised and elaborated by different medieval authors. The most popular French romance was the *Roman de la Rose* (*Romance of the Rose*), begun by one poet around 1240 and extended by another about 1275. The *Roman de la Rose* was an allegorical tale of ideal love, adventure, and social satire, widely read and imitated throughout Europe.

An equally famous romantic elaboration was the tale of the legendary King Arthur and his court. Eleanor of Aquitaine's daughter encouraged her court poet Chrétien de Troyes [KRAY-tee-an(h) duh TWAH] (active 1160–90) to embellish the Arthurian legend along the lines of courtly love. Chrétien responded, somewhat reluctantly, with his *Lancelot, or the Knight of the Cart*. Chrétien's *Lancelot* introduced the famous love affair between Lancelot, King Arthur's lieutenant, and Guinevere, his queen. These Arthurian lovers became a kind of romantic trope, reappearing in different romantic contexts (see Dante, page 186).

The greatest female writer of medieval romance was also connected to Eleanor's court. Marie de France (active 1160–1215) may have been the half-sister of Henry II and probably lived at English courts. Among other forms, Marie de France composed verse narratives called *lais*, written in medieval French. Of the dozen *lais* that survive, several show a concern for women's experiences that was unique in the romance tradition. Some of Marie de France's heroines escape from their possessive husbands by creating a fantasy of spiritual and fulfilling love. The Frenchwoman's poems circulated widely among European storytellers, perhaps helping to achieve a measure of civility and equality between sexes.

MUSIC IN THE LATE MIDDLE AGES

By the fourteenth century, the monophonic songs of troubadour and *trouvère* were being supplanted by a more refined secular music. Increasingly, secular songs were given polyphonic settings and were enriched by rhythmic complexities. Developed in northern France, this new style was called the ***Ars nova***, or "new art."

The master of the *Ars nova* style was Guillaume de Machaut [gee-YOHM duh mah-SHOH] (*c.* 1300–1377), whose works achieved an unprecedented unity and refinement. Machaut composed in all the principal forms of his day, including monophonic *lais* and a great Mass titled *Messe de Nostre Dame*. He also applied the principles of *Ars nova* to the **motet**, a polyphonic song form in which the higher voices sang different poetic texts. The name is based on the French *mot* [moh], or "word," probably because words were so essential to the motet's beauty. Machaut's sacred motets were typical: an instrument played the lower part (the slow *cantus firmus*), while voices sang the freer upper parts, often with texts in Latin and French.

Though he retired as a cathedral administrator, the bulk of Machaut's music was secular. He composed mostly for the dukes and kings whom he served as poet, musician, and secretary. Like today's popular song, Machaut's poems were sung in stanzas, accompanied by a lute. His innovation came in the songs' subtle rhythm, which often shifted from the traditional triple time to the new duple (two-beat) meter. Harmonically, Machaut also colored his songs with sharp and flat tones. Though they were barely perceptible to the ear, such *Ars nova* refinements appealed to the educated sensibilities of Machaut's courtly audiences.

Guillaume de Machaut died just as the Catholic Church was rent by the Great Schism (see page 164). Machaut's career shows that, in place of a corrupt and discredited Church, Europe's courts and cities had become leading centers of power and patrons of the arts.

POETS AND PILGRIMS

Compare the use of pilgrimage as a metaphor in the major works of Dante and Chaucer.

By 1300, city life and the medieval courts had unleashed a new freedom to interpret medieval traditions. In literature, this blend of freedom and tradition engendered two late medieval masterpieces: the *Divine Comedy* of Dante Alighieri [DAHN-tay al-ig-YAIR-ee] (1265–1321) and the *Canterbury Tales* of Geoffrey Chaucer (*c.* 1340–*c.* 1400). Both works synthesize the medieval literary tradition, using the concept of pilgrimage as a literary and philosophical metaphor.

DANTE'S DIVINE COMEDY

Dante was an active citizen and poet of Florence when he was exiled for political reasons in 1300. In exile, he composed the *Divine Comedy*, a three-part epic that recounts the poet's vision of the afterlife. The *Comedy* is not only a kind of poetic *summa* of medieval values; it is also a syn-

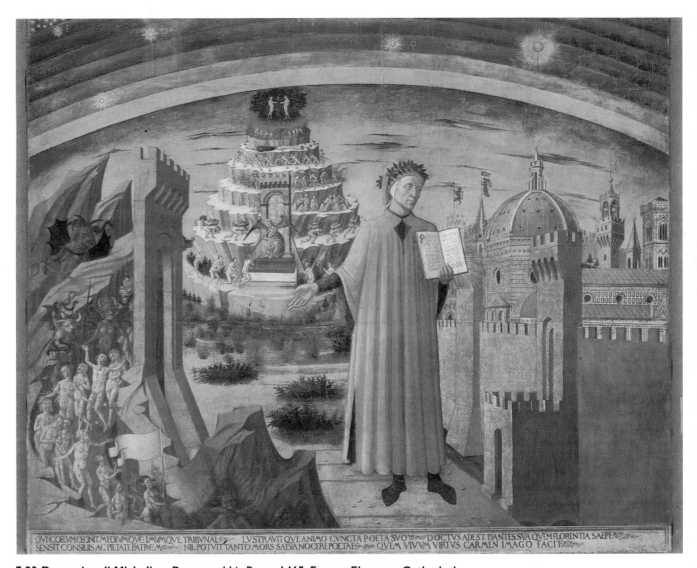

7.23 Domenico di Michelino, *Dante and his Poem*, 1465. Fresco, Florence Cathedral.
Dante stands holding a copy of the *Divine Comedy*. On the left, the damned descend wailing into hell. Behind rises the mountain of purgatory, and on the right is the city of Florence, emblematic of paradise.

thesis of medieval poetic techniques, including courtly love poetry and the classical poetic tradition.

In Dante's epic poem, the poet's own journey through the afterlife is an elaborate metaphor for the pilgrimage through life (Fig. **7.23**). The *Comedy*'s three-part structure mirrors Dante's passage through hell, purgatory, and heaven. In the *Inferno*, Dante is guided through the pit of hell by the classical poet Virgil (see page 93), a symbol of human reason and the classical poet whom Dante most admired. In the *Purgatorio*, the travelers climb the mountain of purgatory, encountering souls whose sins are not yet forgiven. In the *Paradiso*, Dante takes the hand of his idealized lady, Beatrice [bay-uh-TREE-chay]. At the center of heaven, Dante is permitted to look briefly at the blazing glory of God himself. As the pilgrim in his own epic, Dante faces

the trials of the ordinary Christian believer. To reach his destination, he must master his own sinful nature, submitting to the commands of human reason (Virgil) and sacred truth (Beatrice).

The *Divine Comedy* synthesized religious symbolism with Dante's views on politics and language. The entire poem was written in a three-line stanza form called *terza rima* [TAIR-zuh REE-muh]. The holy number three reappears in the 33 cantos of each main section, which (when added to an introductory canto) equal another "perfect" number, 100. The pilgrim's conversations with the souls allow Dante to espouse his political belief that Europe should be governed by a secular emperor, not the pope. Significantly, Dante composed the *Divine Comedy* in the Italian vernacular (spoken language), rather than in Latin.

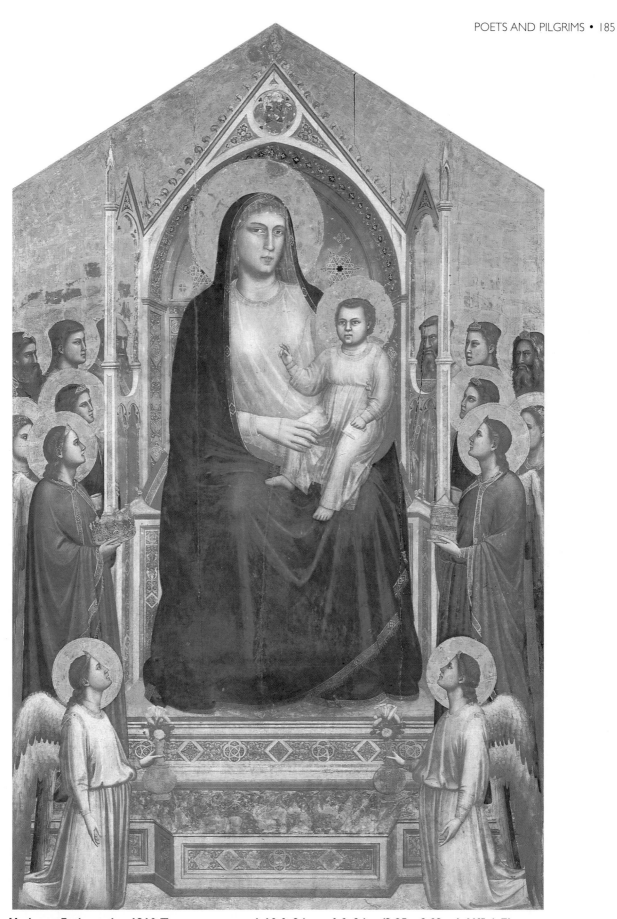

7.24 Giotto, *Madonna Enthroned*, c. 1310. Tempera on wood, 10 ft 8 ins x 6 ft 8 ins (3.25 x 2.03 m). Uffizi, Florence.
Observe Giotto's use of light and dark shading to create a feeling of volume and depth. What other visual clues – angels holding flowers and gifts, the receding lines of the throne, background figures obscured by foreground – contribute to the sense of spatial realism?

WINDOW ON DAILY LIFE

THE PLAGUE AND PROSPERITY

For those in Europe who survived the plague known as the Black Death of 1348, standards of living actually improved. Food was more plentiful and labor more scarce, forcing up wages. The king of England resorted to drastic (and futile) measures to hold wages at their customary levels:

Meanwhile the King sent word into all the separate companies of the kingdom that reapers and other workers should not take more than they were accustomed to take under penalty of the fixed statute. . . . The artisans [laborers], however, so puffed up and contrary, would not heed the mandate of the King, but if anyone wished to have them it was necessary to pay them according to their wish and either to lose his produce and his crops or satisfy the proud and greedy desire of the workers. Wherefore, when it was known to the King that employers would not obey his mandate and that they granted greater payment to the laborers, he imposed heavy fines upon the abbots and the priors, and upon the greater and lesser knights. . . . Then the King set about to arrest many of the laborers and send them to prison; many such withdrew and hid in the forests and woods for the time, and those who were captured were heavily fined. The greater part of them were bound under oath that they would not take daily payments [wages] beyond the old custom, and thus they were freed from prison. In a similar way it happened to the other artisans in the towns and villages.[7]

HENRY KNIGHTON
(1348)

Dante's Lovers Dante's poetic style was shaped by Florentine love poetry and he borrowed characters and stories from the European romance tradition. In the *Inferno's* most famous episode, Dante meets Paolo and Francesca [POW-loh, fran-CHAY-skah], lovers murdered in their bed by Francesca's husband (Paolo's brother). At Dante's request, Francesca describes the moment of their first love, when they sat reading the medieval romance of Lancelot and Guinevere. In his sweet poetic style, Dante celebrates these sinners' romantic passion, while remaining firmly on the path to his heavenly destination.

*"Love, which in gentlest hearts will soonest bloom
Seized my lover with passion for that sweet body
From which I was torn unshriven to my doom.*

*Love, which permits no loved one not to love,
Took me so strongly with delight in him
That we are one in Hell, as we were above.[a]*

*Love led us to one death. In the depths of Hell
Caïna waits for him who took our lives."[b]*

*". . . One day we read, to pass the time away,
Of Lancelot, how he had fallen in love;
We were alone, innocent of suspicion.*

*Time and again our eyes were brought together
By the book we read; our faces flushed and*

To the moment of one line alone we yielded:

*It was when we read about those longed-for lips
Now being kissed by such a famous lover,
That this one (who shall never leave my side)*

*Then kissed my mouth, and trembled as he did.
Our Galehot[c] was that book and he who wrote it.
That day we read no further."[8]*

DANTE ALIGHIERI
From *Inferno*, Canto V

---

a. The pair's bodiless souls are bound together and blown about hell by hot winds, symbolic of the passion that destroyed them in life.

b. Caïna, a region of Dante's hell reserved for murderers of their own kin. Giovanni Malatesta, Francesca's husband and Paolo's brother, will dwell here because his violent sin is more serious than the lovers' lustful passion.

c. Galehot, the go-between who urged on Lancelot and Guinevere; also, in Italian, the word for "pander."

The *Paradiso* is suffused with a more exalted and spiritual love. Guided by Beatrice, a symbol of human beauty, love, and grace, Dante discourses with Thomas Aquinas and heaven's other saintly inhabitants. The great poem ends with a lyrical prayer to the Virgin Mary, who permits Dante to gaze for a moment upon God. Because of that vision, Dante says, he is turned, with "feeling and intellect balanced equally," inevitably toward divine love.

CHAUCER'S CANTERBURY PILGRIMS

Like Dante, Geoffrey Chaucer was a versatile poet, wise in the ways of the world, a diplomat and courtier in London, who wrote his poetic works to entertain a circle of courtly friends. His masterpiece was the *Canterbury Tales* (begun c. 1387), a set of stories told by a group of imaginary pilgrims journeying to Canterbury in southeast England. Chaucer sketches his pilgrims with knowing irony and wit. Each is journeying to Canterbury for a different reason, revealing the spectrum of human motivation, from religious piety to vain self-delusion. The pilgrims also reveal a cross-section of English society, including the dissolute and hypocritical as well as the pious and noble. Chaucer describes them and recounts their tales with a marvelous sense of irony and insight into human psychology.

In its literary form, Chaucer's great work borrows from the *Decameron* of the Italian poet Giovanni Boccaccio [jyoh-VAH-nee boh-KAH-chee-oh] (1313–75), in which the occupants of a country villa, gathered to escape the plague, entertain themselves by telling stories. Originally, Chaucer intended that each of the thirty pilgrims should tell four stories, but only twenty-four tales and a prologue were actually completed.

One of Chaucer's most memorable characters is the Wife of Bath, who has outlived five husbands and seeks a sixth on her journey. Her frank sensualism is a direct challenge to the medieval Church's teachings about women. To those who condemn women who do not seek the chastity of the convent, she says:

> As in a noble household, we are told,
> Not every dish and vessel's made of gold,
> Some are of wood, yet earn their master's praise,
> God calls His folk to Him in many ways.[9]

Chaucer's insight into such ordinary folk makes the *Canterbury Tales* a kind of "human comedy" as profound as Dante's magisterial work. The two poets' appreciation of human diversity and their worldly understanding of human nature engendered the two literary masterworks of late medieval culture.

PRELUDE TO THE RENAISSANCE

Identify the figures who anticipated the Renaissance in Italy.

The fourteenth century was a turbulent age in Europe, marked by war and the pestilence of the Black Death, an epidemic of the bubonic plague that wiped out one-third of Europe's population at mid-century. For the survivors, ironically, living standards improved as wages rose and food was more plentiful.

As Europe recovered from the Black Death, poets and artists pushed forward a new style in the arts. In letters, the poet Petrarch recovered the classics and defined a new poetic style, while the philosopher Christine de Pisan eloquently defended the heritage of women. In painting, Giotto's revolutionary innovations would earn him praise as the one "through whose merit the lost art of painting was revived."

RECLAIMING THE CLASSICAL PAST

Increasingly in the fourteenth century, intellectual life centered in Europe's towns and courts, where it was less restricted by Church doctrines. The Italian poet and scholar Francis Petrarch (1304–74) used this freedom to emphasize the continuity between the Christian faith and the teachings of classical Greece and Rome. This attitude of compromise between classicism and Christianity was called **humanism**, and it would dominate the thinking and art of the next century in Italy. Aside from his studies of classical languages and writings, Petrarch [PET-rark] also defined a lyrical new style of poetry. He perfected a form of the **sonnet** (a fourteen-line poem), dedicating many to his mysterious beloved named Laura. Laura succumbed to the plague in 1348, and in this sonnet, Petrarch praises her beauty while mourning her loss.

> *The eyes that drew from me such fervent praise,*
> *The arms and hands and feet and countenance*
> *Which made me a stranger in my own romance*
> *And set me apart from the well-trodden ways;*
>
> *The gleaming golden curly hair, the rays*
> *Flashing from a smiling angel's glance*
> *Which moved the world in paradisal dance,*
> *Are grains of dust, insensibilities.*
>
> *And I live on, but in grief and self-contempt,*
> *Left here without the light I loved so much,*
> *In a great tempest and with shrouds unkempt.*
>
> *No more love songs, then, I have done with such;*
> *My old skill now runs thin at each attempt,*
> *And tears are within the harp I touch.*[10]

FRANCIS PETRARCH

One of the fourteenth century's most remarkable careers was that of Christine de Pisan (1364–c. 1430), who grew up in the French royal court and eventually supported her family by writing poetry, moral philosophy, and a king's biography. Her most important work was *The Book of the City of Ladies* (1405), which retold the lives of goddesses and heroic women. The "city of ladies" was a heavenly

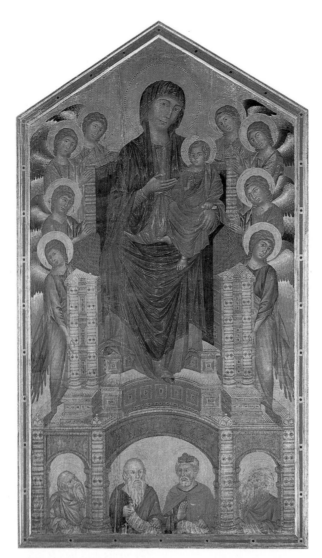

7.25 Cimabue, _Madonna Enthroned_, 1280–90. Tempera on wood, 12 ft 6 ins x 7 ft 4 ins (3.81 x 2.24 m). Uffizi, Florence. Compare the poses and expressions of the figures here to Giotto's version of the same theme (Fig. 7.24). Note also the construction of the throne.

bastion against the contempt for women that Christine found in such medieval works as the _Romance of the Rose._

GIOTTO'S PICTORIAL REVOLUTION

Fourteenth-century Italy was an economic and artistic crossroads. Geographically, Italy's merchants and traders were well positioned to profit from commerce with the rich Byzantine and Eastern empires. The influence of the nearby Byzantine civilization grew in 1204, when Christian crusaders sacked Constantinople. The crusaders returned through Italy, depositing the pirated glories of Byzantine art. Wealth also flowed to Italy from northern Europe, as Italian cities became centers of manufacture and finance.

These diverse influences culminated in a rich diversity of late medieval styles in painting. The Byzantine influ-

ence is evident in the gilded surfaces and other-worldly atmosphere of the _Madonna Enthroned_ (Fig. **7.25**) by Cimabue (_c._ 1240–1302?). Cimabue's [chim-uh-BOO-ay] gigantic panel blends the gilded Byzantine style with an emerging interest in space and human emotion. The picture contains hints of a natural space, such as the throne's receding lines and the Madonna's feet placed obliquely on different steps. In general, however, the central figures, the throne, and the angels all inhabit a spiritual world set apart from the observer.

It was a student of Cimabue's, Giotto di Bondone (_c._ 1266–1337), who was to revolutionize painting in Italy. Giotto [JYAH-toh] was a contemporary of Dante and probably trained in a Florentine workshop. His break with the medieval pictorial style can be seen in his own version of the _Madonna Enthroned_ (Fig. **7.24**). Compared with Cimabue, Giotto gives his figures a new volume and vital-

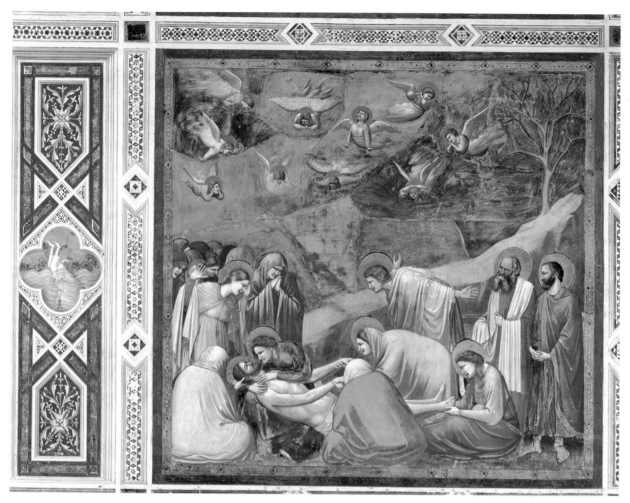

7.26 Giotto, *Pietà* (*Lamentation*), 1305–6. Fresco, 7 ft 7 ins x 7 ft 9 ins (2.31 x 2.36 m). Arena Chapel, Padua.
The unifying diagonal line begins with the tree at upper right and terminates in the head of Christ, toward which the mourners gaze.

ity. The drapery now falls more naturally over the Madonna's knees and breasts. The throne is set in a more believable space, with angels and saints positioned emphatically beside and behind. Some elements of medieval spiritualism remain, in the gold haloes and inconsistent scale of the figures. Still, the picture exhibits a new coherence and realism of visual space.

The Arena Chapel Giotto's masterpiece was a three-part cycle of paintings in the Arena Chapel in Padua, Italy. Italian Gothic churches provided large expanses of wall, which painters decorated in the ancient art of fresco (paint applied to wet plaster). For the frescoes of the Arena Chapel, Giotto chose three great narrative themes: the Life of the Virgin, the Life of Christ, and the Passion of Christ. Each series contained scenes of tenderness and drama, which appealed to Giotto's interest in showing human emotion. The result of his efforts was a pictorial narrative that rivaled Dante's *Divine Comedy* in its emotional force and spare eloquence.

Even to Giotto's contemporaries, the pictures of the Arena Chapel were stunningly new. Giotto radically simplified his compositions, eliminating detail in order to amplify a scene's visual and emotional effect. In the *Pietà* [pee-uh-TAH] (*Lamentation*; Fig. **7.26**), the mourners' eyes converge on the poignant figures of the dead Christ and his grieving mother. This emotional focal point is reinforced by the mountain ridge's bold diagonal slash, drawing the eye toward Jesus. Giotto's realism pioneered a new visual style that would be followed by later Renaissance artists. Most importantly, his interest in human emotion and individuality anticipated the values that would arise in the newly prosperous and sophisticated cities of Renaissance Italy.

Chapter Summary

The Gothic Awakening. The Gothic awakening was stirred by events that transformed medieval European society. The Crusades opened contacts to the Islamic world and loosened the ties of feudal society. Feudalism itself weakened as medieval monarchs in France and England consolidated their power and struggled for influence with popes and bishops. Medieval towns and cities thrived on the new commerce, gaining important freedoms from feudal obligation.

The Gothic Style. The towns and cities around Paris were the site of a splendid new style of building, the "French" or Gothic style. At the royal abbey of St. Denis, Abbot Suger combined architectural elements in a style that gave new prominence to light, the symbol of divine beauty. At Chartres and other cities of the Ile-de-France, soaring Gothic churches symbolized the order of God's universe and celebrated the beauty of the Virgin Mary. Pilgrims were drawn to these splendid new buildings, hoping to find healing or salvation. The Gothic churches' stained-glass windows vividly depicted the stories and teachings of the medieval Church, serving as a "Bible of the poor." Exterior sculpture evolved from Romanesque austerity to increasing naturalism and vitality.

Music and Theater in the Gothic Age. In the cathedral schools, musicians devised more complex forms of sacred music, especially the organum, which introduced polyphony in Western music. Composers of the Notre Dame School of Music compiled a great collection of organum that traced its development. Meanwhile, medieval theater moved from church to town, while keeping its Christian themes and subjects. The Gothic era's spectacular drama cycles and mystery plays were civic pageants, involving the whole town in dramatic production.

The New Learning. Medieval towns also fostered the rise of the university, where medieval scholars achieved a new synthesis of Christian teaching and classical philosophy called scholasticism. Scholasticism was stimulated by Europe's rediscovery of Aristotle through the translations and commentaries of Arabic scholars. Ibn-Rushd and Moses Maimonides explored the conflicts of faith and reason that also concerned Christian scholars. The scholastic theologian Thomas Aquinas reconciled the doctrines of revealed truth with the natural and social philosophy of Aristotle.

Courtly Life in the Middle Ages. Late medieval court life helped foster a culture of courtly love, romantic tales, and refined music. At Eleanor of Aquitaine's court in France, a code of love stressed the beauty and purity of noble women and men's duty to honor and serve them. Troubadours of Provence's courts celebrated the joys and agonies of courtly love in song. The medieval romance encouraged elaboration of stock romantic stories such as the Arthurian legends and stimulated the genius of Marie de France. Guillaume de Machaut applied the musical techniques of *Ars nova* in composing refined songs for his courtly audience.

Poets and Pilgrims. Two poetic masterworks of the later Middle Ages, Dante Alighieri's *Divine Comedy* and Geoffrey Chaucer's *Canterbury Tales*, employed pilgrimage as a literary and philosophical metaphor. Dante's *Comedy* told of his journey through the afterlife, guided by symbols of pagan reason and Christian truth, synthesizing dramatically the philosophical and religious concerns of the Gothic age. Chaucer portrays his Canterbury pilgrims with humor and worldly understanding.

Prelude to the Renaissance. Europe's turbulent fourteenth century was marked by rampant plague, but also by a new prosperity and intellectual dynamism. In this atmosphere, poets and scholars such as Petrarch and Christine de Pisan managed to ally Christian belief with the values of the classical past. In painting, Giotto introduced a new pictorial and emotional realism into Western painting. His frescoes in the Arena Chapel have been hailed as forerunners of the Renaissance, which would begin in the prosperous cities of central Italy.

8 | The Renaissance Spirit in Italy

*With its towering cathedral dome and gracious palaces, the grand city of Florence (Fig. **8.1**) was a center of the **Renaissance spirit in Italy**: a desire to recover the classical beauty and wisdom of old, combined with an innovative spirit and an unfailing belief in human reason and achievement. In Florence and in Rome, this spirit inspired some of history's greatest artists and thinkers. Yet outside Florence's walls, the legions of war and division were camped, ready to destroy what the Renaissance had created. At its height, Renaissance Florence rivaled classical Athens in its* artistic and intellectual genius. *Its workshops trained the greatest artists of the early and High Renaissance. But even this great flowering of the human spirit could not escape the looming shadow of conflict and destruction.*

8.1 Renaissance Florence, from a contemporary painting. During the 14th and 15th centuries, the city's wealthy merchants built dozens of new residences, chapels, and churches. The cathedral dome and the nearby Palazzo Vecchio (City Hall) dominate Florence's profile.

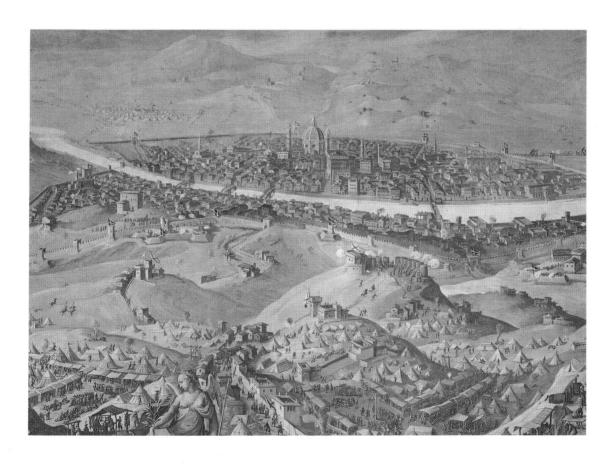

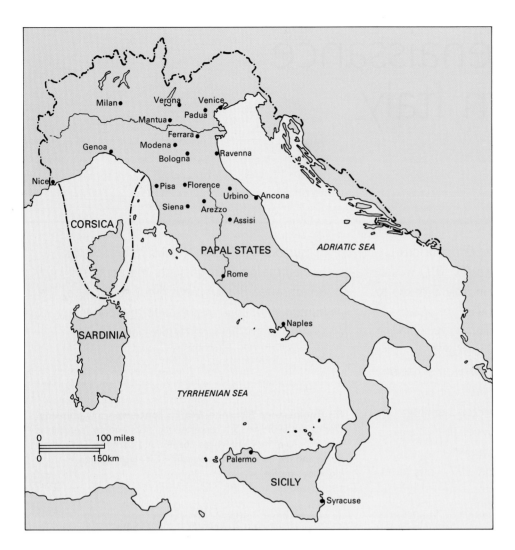

8.2 Renaissance Italy.

THE RENAISSANCE IN ITALY

Describe the conditions in Italian cities that nurtured the creative spirit of the Renaissance.

The **Renaissance** in Italy (*c.* 1400–1550) sprang from a vigorous interest in the culture of the ancient Greeks and Romans and a conviction that the achievements of classical antiquity were being restored in this new age. Hence the name Renaissance, which means "rebirth," a term not applied to the period until the early nineteenth century. The Italian Renaissance was a period of spectacular advances in learning and the arts, led by artists such as Ghiberti, Brunelleschi, Botticelli, Leonardo, Michelangelo and Raphael, whose genius impressed kings and popes and who left works of unmatched excellence. One contemporary Italian described the Renaissance as a "new age, so full of hope and promise, which already rejoices in a greater array of nobly-gifted souls than the

world has seen in the thousand years that have preceded it."

The cultural revolution of the Italian Renaissance was made possible by the wealth of Italy's city-states in this period (Fig. **8.2**). Powerful merchants and bankers, such as the Medici family of Florence, patronized a glittering array of artists, musicians, and scholars. Yet Italy was troubled by political intrigue and wars that often affected artists and thinkers. Still, aside from classical Athens, probably no other age was so confident of its powers and so rich in artistic excellence.

THE ITALIAN CITY-STATES

Italy had long been the conduit for commerce and travel between Europe and the Eastern world, and its cities profited from contact with the wealth Byzantine Empire and the intellectual centers of Islamic civilization. The Renaissance was born in Italy's prosperous and independent city of Florence and spread throughout the other cities of Italy. By the 1400s these cities had established their independence from popes and kings and were counting the

KEY CONCEPT

RENAISSANCE HUMANISM

In contrast to the medieval Christian view of humans as sinful and depraved, Italian Renaissance thinkers praised the human character as God's highest creation. The Renaissance humanists combined respect for classical learning with supreme confidence in human ability. This humanism played a role in the age's greatest achievements, and is evident in the statues modeled after ancient nudes and in the translations of classical authors.

In Renaissance times, a **humanist** was simply a student of Greek and Roman literature, history, rhetoric, and ethics. These subjects comprised the *studia humanitatis*, or the "course that made one human." In the *studia humanitatis*, scholars reconciled Christian belief with the moral teachings of the ancients. Renaissance humanists also challenged the medieval notion that the material world contained only temptation and evil and, instead, glorified the beauty and order in nature – as can be seen in Leonardo's drawing of the geometric proportions of the human body (Fig. **8.3**).

The definition of Renaissance humanism has now broadened to mean the age's glorification of human powers. The human capacity for knowledge and creativity made humans almost the equals of God. The Florentine humanist Pico della Mirandola [PEE-koh dell-ah meer-AHN-doh-lah] (1463–94) exalted human freedom in his *Oration on the Dignity of Man*, in which God says to humanity:

> *We have made you neither of heaven nor of earth, neither mortal nor immortal, so that with freedom of choice and with honor, as though the maker and molder of yourself, you may fashion yourself in whatever shape you shall prefer. You shall have the power to degenerate into the lower forms of life, which are brutish. You shall have the power, out of thy soul's judgement, to be reborn into the higher forms, which are divine.*[1]

Of course, such a divinely sanctioned human freedom presented both opportunity and risk. According to Pico's God, humans could develop and apply their powers until they became like the angels. Yet, humans could also fall into cruelty and corruption, if they ignored the moral teachings of ancient philosophy and the Church. Several prominent figures of the Renaissance agonized in fear that they had gone too far in glorifying the human spirit.

While Renaissance humanism did not immediately affect the lives of common people, its belief in human reason and scholarship soon stimulated monumental changes: the sixteenth-century scientist Galileo pursued experiments that flew in the face of Church doctrine; and the sixteenth-century reformer Martin Luther's Bible translations (see page 232) depended on his humanist training in ancient languages. Humanist printers, such as Aldus Manutius of Venice, who published translations of Plato and Roman dramatists, used their printing presses (Fig. **8.5**) to spread Renaissance ideas throughout Europe. Although its flame was lit by a handful of Italian artists and thinkers, Renaissance humanism inspired human achievement for centuries after its high point.

8.3 Leonardo da Vinci, *Proportions of the Human Figure* ("Vitruvian Man"). Galleria dell' Accademia, Venice.
In this famous image, Leonardo plotted the human figure within a circle and square, recalling the principles of classical rationalism.

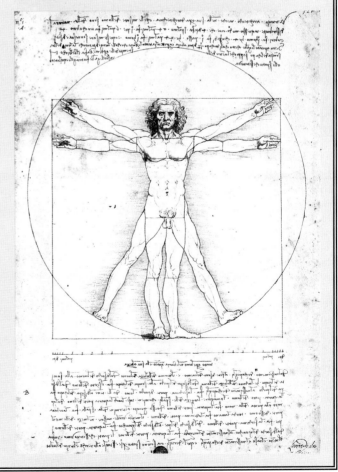

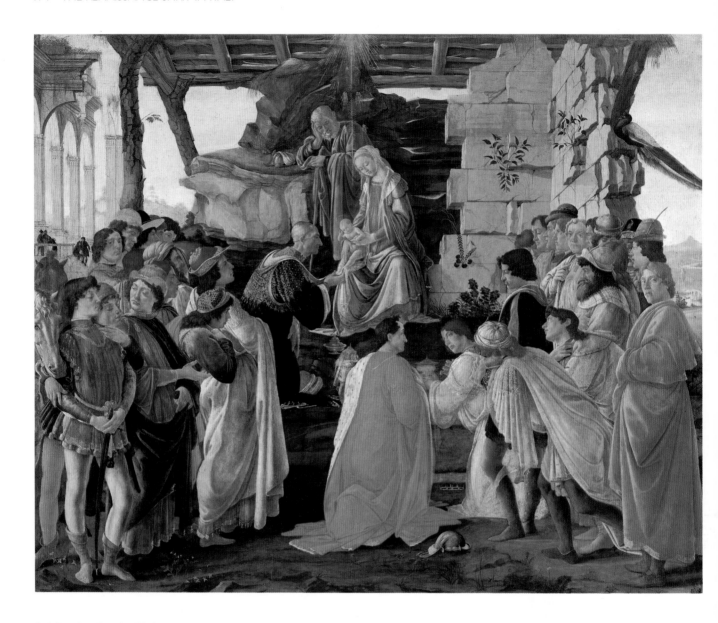

8.4 Sandro Botticelli, *Adoration of the Magi,* **c. 1475. Tempera on wood, 3 ft 7¹/₂ ins x 4 ft 4³/₄ ins (1.1 x 1.34 m). Uffizi, Florence.**
Botticelli honored his Medici patrons by portraying them as Wise Men worshiping the new-born Christ. Note how the classical-style ruins, the rustic shed, and the pyramid-shaped rock formation give the scene spatial depth and a classical flavor.

revenues from their lucrative shipping, manufacturing, and banking enterprises. Like Rome in the age of Augustus, the Italian city-states were keen to claim prestige and status by underwriting the beauties of art, music, and architecture.

Italian merchants ruled their cities as **merchant princes**, wealthy citizens who sometimes held public office but more often wielded power from behind the scenes. The most famous and prominent merchant princes were members of the Medici [MAY-dee-chee] family, who were famed as shrewd businessmen, cunning politicians, and refined patrons of culture. The Medici dynasty in Florence was established by Cosimo de' Medici (1389–1464). Cosimo used the family's financial power – acquired through being the pope's banker – to build a vast commercial empire. Out of gratitude for God's (and the pope's) generosity, the Medici spent staggering sums of money on charity and the arts. Their generosity to the arts compares to that of today's wealthy families, such as the Rockefellers or MacArthurs, who have supported artists and intellectuals through charitable foundations.

THE WRITE IDEA

Write a definition of human nature as you understand it, including the most significant differences between humans and animals. Compare your definition with Pico's description of human nature in his *Oration on the Dignity of Man.*

THE RENAISSANCES

	GENERAL EVENTS	ARCHITECTURE	VISUAL ARTS	MUSIC	LITERATURE AND PHILOSOPHY
1400			1401 Ghiberti wins Baptistery competition, Florence (**8.9**)		
THE EARLY RENAISSANCE	1434 Cosimo de' Medici controls Florence	1420 Brunelleschi begins Cathedral dome, Florence (**8.8**)	1434 Jan van Eyck, *Marriage of Arnolfini* (**9.12**)	1436 Guillaume Dufay motet dedicates Florence Cathedral	1453 Greek scholars flee Constantinople, settling in Florence
	1469–92 Lorenzo de' Medici, patron of learning and the arts, governs Florence		c. 1485 Leonardo, *Madonna of the Rocks* (**8.29**)	1486 Josquin des Préz active in papal choir, Rome	1486 Pico, *Oration on the Dignity of Man*
	1480s Portuguese explorers' contact with Benin, West Africa				
1500	1503–13 Reign of Pope Julius II	1506 Bramante begins new St. Peter's, Rome (**8.46**)	1500 Dürer, *Self-portrait* (**9.15**)		
			1508–12 Michelangelo, *Sistine Ceiling*, Vatican Palace, Rome (**8.41**)		1509 Erasmus, *In Praise of Folly*
	1517 Luther's 95 Theses, marks beginning of Reformation				1517 Machiavelli, *The Prince*
		1529 Francis I builds château at Chambord, France (**9.4**)		1529 Luther's hymn "Ein' feste Burg" published	
THE HIGH RENAISSANCE	1545–64 Council of Trent directs Counter-Reformation	1547 Michelangelo named architect of St. Peter's, Rome (**8.48**)			
		1550 Palladio, Villa Rotonda, Vicenza (**9.33**)		1571–94 Palestrina director of papal choir, Rome	
THE LATE RENAISSANCE	1588 English navy defeats Spanish armada			1585 G. Gabrieli organist of St. Mark's, Venice	
			1592–4 Tintoretto, *Last Supper* (**9.39**)		
1600				1601 Weelkes publishes madrigals dedicated to English queen	1601 Shakespeare, *Hamlet*

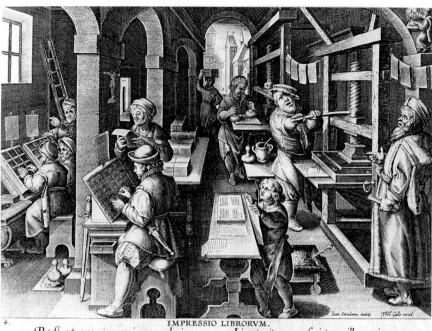

4.
IMPRESSIO LIBRORVM.
Poteſt vt vna vox capi aure plurima :   Linunt ita vna ſcripta mille paginas.

Ioan. Stradanus inuent.   Phls Galle excud.

8.5 A German print shop. Copperplate from Jan van der Straet's *Nova Reperta* by Theodor Galle.
The new printing press fed the Renaissance humanists' hunger for classical writings. The most famous Italian printer was Aldus Manutius of Venice, who published translations of Plato and the Roman playwrights.

8.6 Michelangelo Buonarroti, Laurentian Library, San Lorenzo, Florence, begun 1524, staircase completed 1559.
The Medici were avid antiquarians, commissioning this severely classical library by Michelangelo to house their collection of ancient manuscripts.

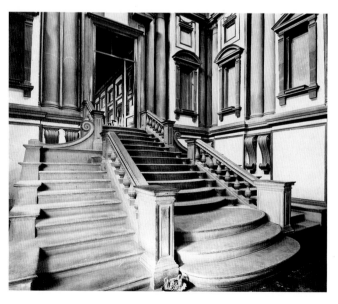

The combination of respect for human achievement and commitment to the public good is called **civic humanism**. Derived from classical writers, civic humanism thrived under the republican government of Florence, in which wealthy and influential families shared power. Merchant princes proudly demonstrated their commitment to the city's welfare, and the Medici family, for example, rebuilt churches, sponsored hospitals and other civic projects, and commissioned public art works (Fig. **8.4**). Cosimo de' Medici subsidized an academy of Renaissance learning that attracted to Florence scholars from all of Europe. Besides pushing the levers of power, the Medici patriarch was himself a Renaissance scholar, who collected a famous treasury of ancient books and manuscripts for which Michelangelo later designed a library (Fig. **8.6**).

LORENZO "THE MAGNIFICENT"

The Medici era in Florence culminated in the reign of Lorenzo de' Medici (ruled 1469–92) (Fig. **8.7**), called "the Magnificent," who not only patronized the arts but was himself an accomplished poet. Lorenzo was the favored son of Florence's lively Renaissance culture. He was tutored by the classical scholar Marsilio Ficino [fi-CHEE-noh] (1433–99), the age's leading translator of Plato. Lorenzo later said that, without knowing Plato, one could not be a good citizen or a good Christian. When, at age twenty-one, Lorenzo was asked to assume political leadership of the city, he responded to his duty with the commitment of a good civic humanist.

Lorenzo's civic obligations did not distract him from the arts. He loved music and wrote bawdy lyrics to be sung in the street or the saddle. Following Dante's lead, Lorenzo

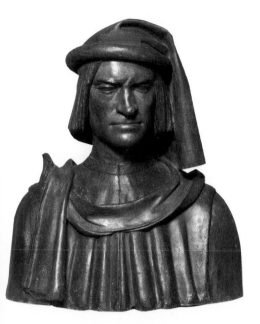

8.7 Andrea del Verrocchio, *Lorenzo de' Medici*, c. 1480. Terracotta, life-size. National Gallery of Art, Washington, D.C., Samuel H. Kress Collection.
Lorenzo de' Medici, grandson of Cosimo, presided over the late bloom of Renaissance culture in Florence. Verrocchio, a favorite of the Medici, was the teacher of Leonardo da Vinci.

composed in his native Tuscan language, not in the stuffy Latin of scholars. His hedonistic carnival songs were sung at Florence's raucous carnival celebrations, and capture the pagan spirit of Florentine life, caught up with the sensual pleasures of love and festivity.

> *Ladies and gay lovers young!*
> *Long live Bacchus, live Desire!*
> *Dance and play; let songs be sung;*
> *Let sweet love your bosoms fire;*
> *In the future come what may!*
> *Youths and maids, enjoy today!*
> *Nought ye know about tomorrow.*
> *Fair is youth and void of sorrow;*
> *But it hourly flies away.*[2]

LORENZO
Song of Bacchus

CRITICAL QUESTION

Do wealthy citizens of today's cities have an obligation to support civic projects and public works of art? What arguments would you make to support or oppose such an obligation?

Lorenzo became the patron and protector of the most prominent artists and intellectuals of the early Renaissance. As youths, Leonardo da Vinci and Michelangelo, who was discovered by Lorenzo copying a Roman statue in his gardens, may have dined at the family table. Lorenzo also saw that the painter Botticelli and the sculptor Verrocchio received generous commissions for their work. When the scholar Pico della Mirandola was tried for heresy in Rome, Lorenzo invited him to Florence and protected him from the pope. The golden age of the Florentine Renaissance came to an end, however, with the decline of the Medici fortune and the death of Lorenzo in 1492.

WINDOW ON DAILY LIFE

THE VIOLENCE OF RENAISSANCE YOUTH

Swordplay and other violence were common in the rough-and-tumble urban life of Renaissance Italy. In his autobiography, the Florentine goldsmith and sculptor Benvenuto Cellini [tcheh-LEE-nee] (1500–71) describes this duel between his fourteen-year-old brother and an older rival in the streets of Florence.

> *They both had swords; and my brother dealt so valiantly that, after having badly wounded him, he was upon the point of following up his advantage. There was a great crowd of people present, among whom were many of the adversary's kinsfolk. Seeing that the thing was going ill for their own man, they put hand to their slings, a stone from one of which hit my poor brother in the head. He fell to the ground at once in a dead faint ... I ran up at once, seized his sword, and stood in front of him, bearing the brunt of several rapiers and a shower of stones. I never left his side until some brave soldiers came from the gate San Gallo and rescued me from the raging crowd....*[3]

BENVENUTO CELLINI
The Life of Benvenuto Cellini (1558–62)

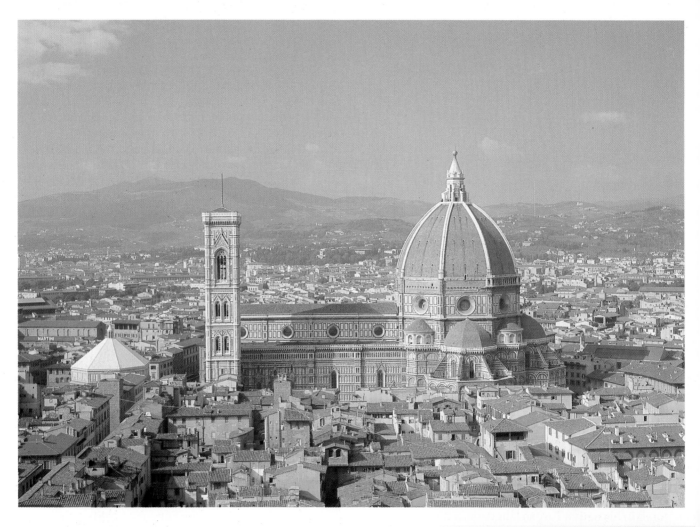

8.8 Florence Cathedral (Santa Maria del Fiore), begun 1296. Dome by Filippo Brunelleschi, 1420–36; façade remodeled late 19th century. Overall length 508 ft (154.9 m), height of dome 367 ft (111.9 m).
The soaring cathedral dome by Brunelleschi, completed in 1436, became the city's trademark. The bell tower (or *campanile*) was designed by Giotto in the previous century. The octagonal roof of the Baptistery is visible at left.

8.9 Right **Lorenzo Ghiberti, *Sacrifice of Isaac*, 1401. Gilt bronze, 21 x 17¹/₂ ins (53 x 44 cm). Museo Nazionale, Florence.**
Judges of the Baptistery contest admired the energetic nudity of Isaac's form, which stretches back to receive the knife's blow. Compare this composition to Giotto's scene of the *Pietà* (Fig. 7.26).

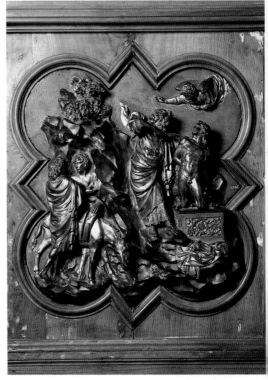

THE ARTS IN RENAISSANCE FLORENCE

Describe the technical innovations in the arts and music that helped define the Florentine Renaissance style.

Towering above Florence was a symbol of Renaissance humanism, the marble-ribbed dome of the Cathedral, designed by the young architect Filippo Brunelleschi (Fig. 8.8). The dome acted as a beacon to artists and scholars:

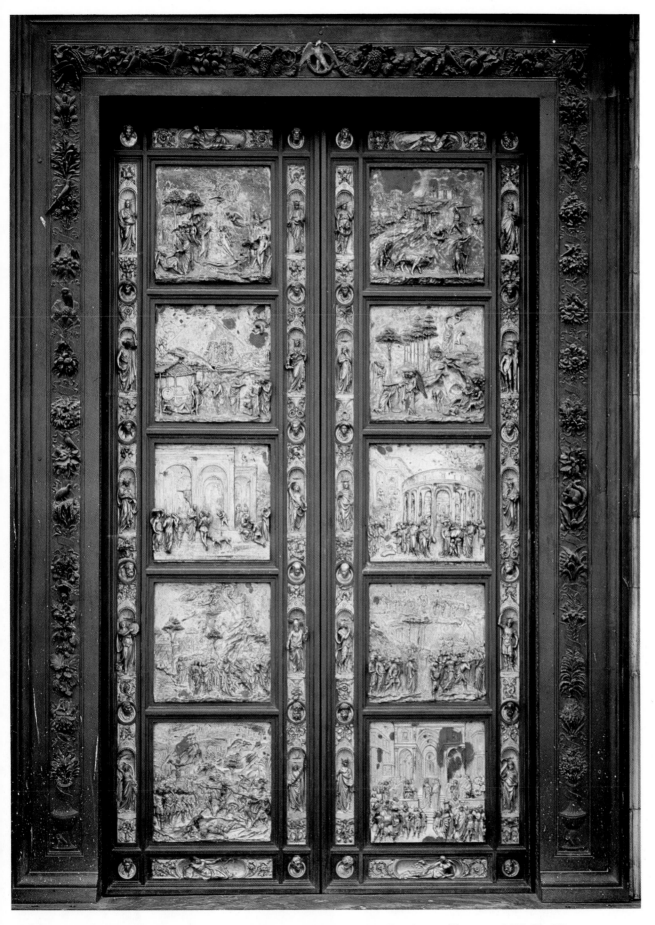

8.10 Lorenzo Ghiberti, *Gates of Paradise*, east doors of the Cathedral Baptistery, Florence, 1425–52. Gilt bronze, height 17 ft (5.2 m).
Ghiberti devoted virtually his entire career to designing and casting the east and north doors of the Baptistery.

when, in 1453, Greek scholars fled the Turkish conquerors of Constantinople, many re-settled in Florence, where they aided Florentine humanists in studying ancient texts. Young artist prodigies such as Leonardo da Vinci and Michelangelo Buonarroti came to apprentice in Florence's workshops and academies, while some of Europe's leading composers served in its courts.

GHIBERTI'S BAPTISTERY DOORS

One might well say the Renaissance began in Florence in 1401. In that year, city officials challenged artists to compete for the honor of decorating the doors of the city's Baptistery. The Baptistery was an eight-sided medieval building that stood before Florence's cathedral. Its massive east doors were to be adorned by gilded bronze panels. In the contest to design a panel depicting Abraham's sacrifice of his son Isaac (Genesis 22), the chosen design was that of Lorenzo Ghiberti [gee-BAIR-tee] (1378–1455; see Fig. 8.12), a young Florentine metalworker who spent much of his creative life working on the Baptistery doors. The judges praised the dramatic unity of Ghiberti's composition and his masterful handling of Isaac's nude body (Fig. **8.9**). To the Florentine humanists, it seemed that Ghiberti had lifted this nude figure directly from a Roman fresco. Its classical qualities were reason enough to praise Ghiberti's panel above all its competitors.

8.11 Lorenzo Ghiberti, *The Story of Jacob and Esau*, left center panel from the *Gates of Paradise*, Cathedral Baptistery, Florence, c. 1435. Gilt bronze, 31¹/₄ ins (79 cm) square.
Ghiberti framed the Biblical story of Jacob and Esau within an arcade that demonstrated the new science of perspective.

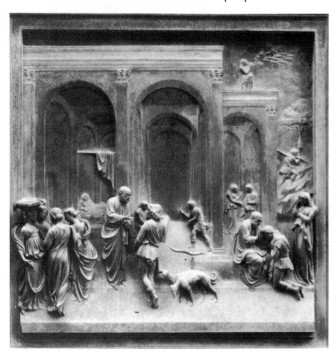

Over the next fifty years, all of Florence watched Ghiberti's progress as he cast panels for both the north and east doors. The Baptistery doors proved to be a fitting challenge to the Renaissance master, since the creative process involved so many different arts: skill in drawing and architectural design to compose the scenes; sculptural technique to shape the wax models for the figures; and finally, expertise in metalworking to supervise the meticulous casting, finishing, and gilding of the panels themselves. Thus, Ghiberti's doors became a catalogue of the evolving Renaissance style in the arts. As he erected each panel,

8.12 Lorenzo Ghiberti, Self-portrait, detail from the *Gates of Paradise*, 1424–52. Cathedral Baptistery, Florence.
In the Italian Renaissance, artists like Ghiberti were no longer anonymous artisans, but famous and prominent individuals.

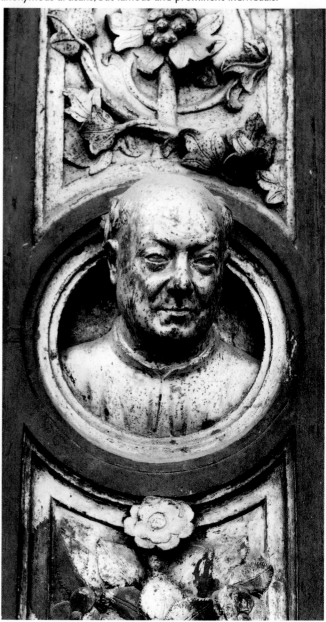

Ghiberti's Florentine colleagues appraised his work. Later, the young Michelangelo so admired the master's accomplishment that he dubbed the east doors the "Gates of Paradise," a name they still bear (Fig. **8.10**).

The panel *The Story of Jacob and Esau* (Fig. **8.11**) from the *Gates of Paradise* indicates Ghiberti's mastery of the arts. The panel depicts the biblical story of Jacob (Genesis 25–27), who purchased his brother Esau's birthright and deceitfully obtained the blessing intended for Esau. In the upper right, the pregnant Rebekah learns of the future conflict between her twin sons. At the lower right, Jacob deceives his blind father and receives the blessing that rightfully belongs to Esau. The figures of the *Gates of Paradise* seem to move beneath their garments, reminiscent of classical Greek statues (see Fig. 3.17). Following the new rules of optical **perspective**, Ghiberti (Fig. **8.12**) unified the story's different episodes in a single architectural space, for example, in the tiled courtyard and receding arches in the panel of *Jacob and Esau*. Only the painter Raphael, in his *School of Athens* (see Fig. 8.36), matched Ghiberti's use of architecture as a setting for dramatic action.

BRUNELLESCHI'S DOMES

The losing finalist in the Baptistery competition was the aspiring young Filippo Brunelleschi (1377–1446), who would become Florence's greatest Renaissance architect. Rather than mourn his defeat, Brunelleschi [BROO-neh-LESK-ee] went to Rome to sketch and measure ancient buildings. He returned to Florence and received the commission to build a domed roof over Florence's cathedral altar (see Fig. 8.8). For years, the cathedral's massive drum had been uncovered because no architect knew how to span such a wide space. Brunelleschi's dome had to stretch as wide as the Pantheon in Rome (see Fig. 4.20) and reach higher than any Gothic cathedral.

Brunelleschi's solution produced a building that truly appealed to Florence's civic vanity. The design was a double roof, with inner and outer shells connected by a hidden system of buttresses and reinforcement (Fig. **8.13**). The double shell was unlike anything built in antiquity, and with its crowning lantern, the finished dome rose 367 feet (112 m) above the floor, inspiring one observer to say that it seemed to rival the hills surrounding Florence. The soaring red-tiled roof was outlined by swelling marble ribs, with each section underscored by a round clerestory window (Fig. **8.18**). The visual effect was a triumph of simplicity and reason. Brunelleschi's dome embodied the humanism of the Florentine Renaissance – a respect for classical models mixed with a celebration of human ingenuity.

The cathedral commission established Brunelleschi's reputation as an architect, and he soon set to work serving the wealthy families of Florence. For the powerful Pazzi [POT-zee] family, rival of the Medici family, Brunelleschi built the Pazzi Chapel (Fig. **8.14**) in the courtyard of a Flor-

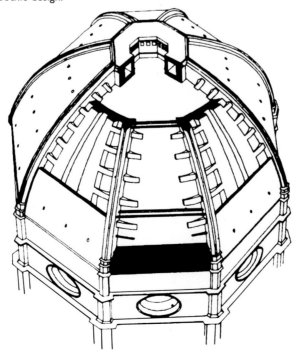

8.13 Brunelleschi's double-shell design for the dome of Florence Cathedral.
A system of internal braces connected the outer roof and interior ceiling, supporting the dome without the elaborate buttressing of Gothic design.

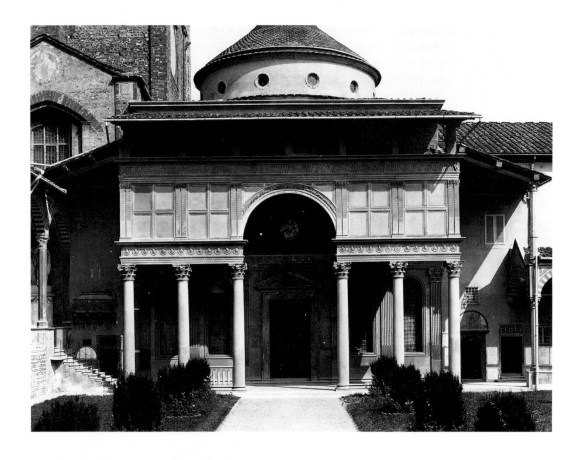

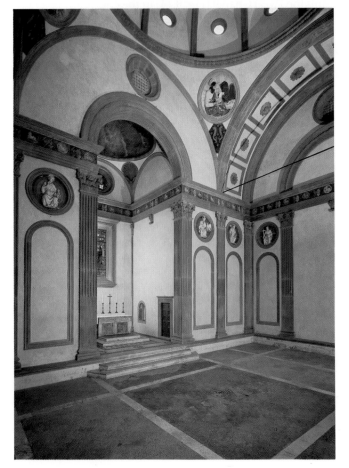

8.14 Filippo Brunelleschi, façade of the Pazzi Chapel, Santa Croce, Florence, c. 1429–33.
A work of serene classicism, the Pazzi Chapel shows Brunelleschi's careful study of ancient Roman buildings. The Corinthian columns, pilasters, and frieze designs were all copied from classical models.

8.15 Filippo Brunelleschi, interior of the Pazzi Chapel, Santa Croce, Florence, c. 1429–33.
The use of gray *pietra serena* emphasizes the geometric shapes and proportions of the chapel's interior.

entine monastery. The Pazzi Chapel's arcaded porch and domed roof were clearly inspired by Roman architecture. Both inside and out, the building's dimensions were multiples of a basic module, creating a mathematical regularity reinforced by the recurring geometric shapes (especially the circle and square). Inside the Pazzi Chapel the dramatic use of gray stone (called *pietra serena*) lends a peaceful simplicity to the pilasters and arches (Fig. **8.15**).

The grace and piety of their chapel did not extend to the Pazzi family themselves. In 1478, the Pazzi tried to assassinate Lorenzo de' Medici in the cathedral on Easter Sunday. Lorenzo survived, and twelve Pazzi conspirators were hanged.

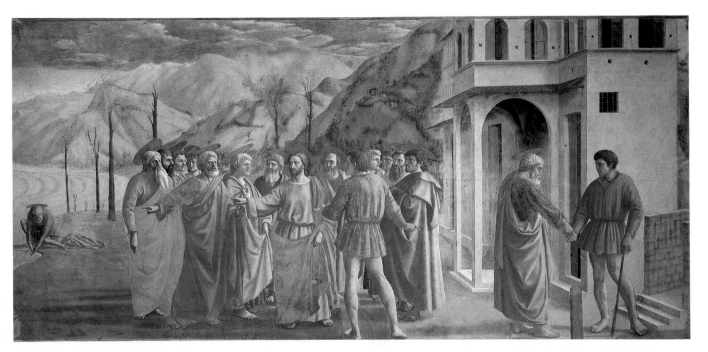

8.16 Masaccio, *The Tribute Money*, c. 1427. Fresco (after restoration, 1989), 8 ft 4 ins x 19 ft 8 ins (2.54 x 5.9 m). Brancacci Chapel, Santa Maria del Carmine, Florence.
Note the painter's emphatic use of light and dark shading (called *chiaroscuro*) to create volume in the cloaks. Is there inconsistency in the linear perspective of the building and the atmospheric landscape?

8.17 Sandro Botticelli, *La Primavera (Birth of Spring)*, c. 1478. Tempera on panel, 6 ft 8 ins x 10 ft 4 ins (2.03 x 3.14 m). Uffizi, Florence.
The painting's symbolic references include the orange fruits (an allusion to the Medici family crest), the bed of flowers (for the city of Florence), and Venus' red and blue garments, which associate her with the Virgin Mary.

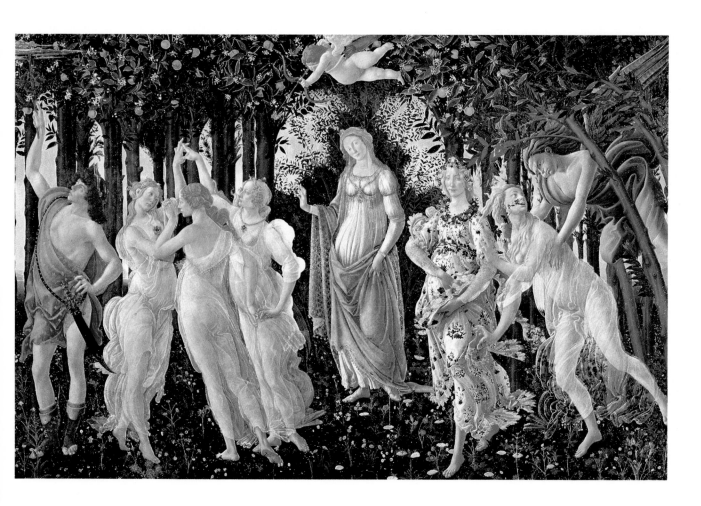

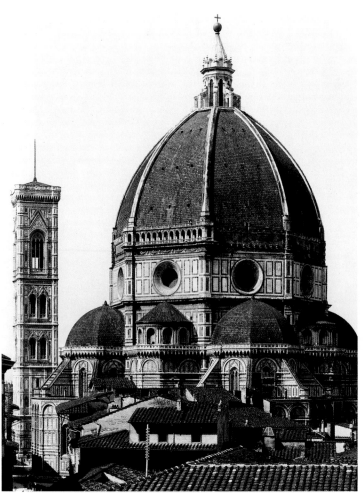

8.18 Filippo Brunelleschi, dome of Florence Cathedral, 1420–36. Height 367 ft (112 m).
The red-tiled roof and swelling marble ribs project a classical simplicity.

FLORENTINE PAINTING: A REFINED CLASSICISM

Early Renaissance Florence was justifiably famous for its painters, whose techniques established a striking new visual style in the arts. To satisfy their patrons' demands, Florentine artists were trained in anatomy (to create life-like figures), modeling (to suggest volume in round objects), and perspective (to organize and unify the pictorial space). The Florentine painters were especially known for their technique in fresco, suited to decorating the walls of Florence's new churches and chapels.

One of the most influential Florentine innovators was Tommaso di Giovanni, known as Masaccio [mah-ZAHH-chee-oh] (1407–28), who learned to create the illusion of three-dimensional space through modeling and atmospheric effects. Masaccio's masterpiece was a series of frescoes painted in the Brancacci [brahn-KAH-chee] Chapel in the church of Santa Maria del Carmine; the frescoes served as a "school of art" for the most celebrated artists and sculptors of the time.

Masaccio's painting technique can be studied in *The Tribute Money* (Fig. **8.16**), a three-part scene based on the gospel story (1 Matthew 17:24–7). In the center, a tax collector demands a tax from Christ and his apostles. At Christ's direction, Peter finds the money in the mouth of a fish (left) and "renders unto Caesar what is Caesar's" by paying the tax (right). Though his theme was biblical, Masaccio's picture had its relevance to the politics of his day, since Florence's clergymen were being asked to "render unto Caesar" by paying a new tax for the city's military defense. The figures in *The Tribute Money* leave an impression of solidity and depth created by the light and dark shading in the figures' robes, a technique called *chiaroscuro* [KYAH-ruh-SKOO-roh]. *Chiaroscuro* enabled Florentine painters to create the illusion of volume – the solid forms of living, breathing men and women – that classical Greek sculptors had achieved in their clothed figures. The illusion of depth is enhanced by blurring the hills and trees, a technique called **atmospheric perspective**, which Masaccio invented. Finally, the impression of space is reinforced by the lines of the building on the right. Here the use of **linear perspective** (see page 206) in the building's receding lines creates a sense of space behind the crowd of figures.

Florentine painting took on a more learned and refined aspect in the works of Sandro Botticelli [BAH-ti-CHELL-ee] (1444–1510), a member of the Medici circle. In his *La Primavera* (*Birth of Spring*) (Fig. **8.17**), the theme is taken from classical mythology and is blended with Christian symbols – a prime example of the Renaissance humanist spirit.

Scholars still dispute the precise meaning of Botticelli's picture. It is agreed that the central figure is Venus, the classical goddess of love and fertility, who raises her hand in benediction over the scene. Venus' gesture and the color of her robe associate her with the Virgin Mary, the Christian embodiment of maternal love. On the right, the wind god Zephyr pursues a nymph who is miraculously transformed into Flora, goddess of the flowers. In the foreground, Botticelli recreated the classical nude female in the figures of the Three Graces, whose forms are idealized by the translucent gauze of their garments. To the far left stands the god Mercury, while above Cupid prepares to shoot his arrow into the scene. One of the Renaissance's best-loved paintings, the *Birth of Spring* portrayed the Renaissance's intellectual synthesis of Christian and classical ideas.

EARLY RENAISSANCE MUSIC

European music in the early Renaissance continued to take the forms preferred in the Middle Ages:

- the Mass and other liturgical music
- sacred motets, with texts in Latin
- secular song.

An important figure in the transition from medieval to Renaissance music was Guillaume Dufay (c. 1398–1474), a French native who served many patrons in Italy. Dufay [doo-FAY-ee] served in the glittering court of Burgundy in France, where his music was prized for its lyricism and charm. Dufay also spent several years in Italy, composing a famous motet, entitled *Nuper rosarum flores*, that was sung at the dedication of Florence's cathedral in 1436.

In Florence, humanist intellectuals such as Marsilio Ficino, Lorenzo de' Medici's tutor, attempted to reproduce ancient Greek music. These scholars were familiar with classical musical theory, but had no idea what Greek music actually sounded like. They performed chanted translations of classical poetry, accompanied by a lyre. This half-sung recitation of poetry, called **monody**, was dry and academic, and did not faintly resemble the music of the ancient Greeks. Monody did serve to inspire the more colorful musical form of opera, which was invented in Florence later in the Renaissance.

Meanwhile, in Florence's festive streets and courts, citizens wooed each other with secular ballads and songs. Florentine music was sweetly lyrical, well suited to the affairs of courting a lover or mourning love's loss. Popular song forms were usually polyphonic, such as the *frottola* (pl. *frottole*) – a ballad-like song with refrain. The *frottola* [FROTT-oh-lah] arose under the patronage of Isabella d'Este of Mantua, and spread to other Italian courts and cities. Although *frottole* were often composed for four voices, the parts were usually based on a few musical chords. This chordal structure permitted *frottole* to be sung by a single voice, accompanied by a lute. The popularity of Renaissance songs was exploited by the new commercial printers. Books of *frottole* advertised themselves as "suitable compositions for all occasions and situations of amorous and courtly life." Every Renaissance courtier was expected to be an amateur musician, ready to woo a lover or charm the court with a beautiful song.

The opportunities for patronage in prosperous Italian courts drew musicians trained in the schools of northern Europe, including professional musicians from Burgundy (in northern France) or Flanders (present-day Belgium). Lorenzo de' Medici favored the well-traveled Flemish composer Heinrich Isaac (c. 1450–1517), who also served at courts in Vienna, Austria and Konstanz, Germany. Isaac's musical talents were eclectic, exploiting many musical forms and influences. While in Florence, he set to music more than a hundred Italian songs and composed about forty masses. Isaac's most famous work is a lyrically polyphonic song entitled *In Innsbruck muss ich dich lassen* (*In Innsbruck I must leave you*). Isaac probably served as tutor to Lorenzo's children, including the son who would become Pope Leo X, the most musical of Renaissance popes.

In Italy, the Flemish composers blended their technical brilliance with the Italian humanist love for poetry. The result was a new importance for language in both sacred and secular music. In Flemish music, poetic verses were often a pretext for abstract exercises in musical polyphony. In Italy, Renaissance composers learned to express the words' sense in musical tones, a technique called **word-painting**. In word-painting, the words "and glad joy" would be sung in ascending tones. The musical expressiveness of word-painting was perfected by another composer of Flemish origin in Italy, Josquin des Préz (see page 217), who served the popes in Rome.

EARLY RENAISSANCE SCULPTURE

Identify the themes and techniques of Michelangelo's early sculptures.

By the 1490s, the century-long ascendancy of Renaissance Florence was threatened by decline. Lorenzo de' Medici's neglect of family finances threatened the Medici's hold on political power, and the incompetence of Lorenzo's successor exposed Florence to its political enemies and to popular challenge within. The political turmoil of these years actually served as a stimulus to the city's sculptors. Renaissance sculpture achieved a new heroic power portrayed in the works of Donatello and the young Michelangelo. Eventually, however, the decline of the Medici family and civic turmoil in Florence shifted the center of Renaissance culture to Rome.

DONATELLO

The dominant figure in early Renaissance sculpture was Donatello (1386–1466), who virtually reinvented the free-standing nude in classical style. Donatello assisted Ghiberti on the Baptistery doors and accompanied Brunelleschi on his trips to Rome, to study antique sculpture and building. Donatello left an imposing legacy of stone and bronze statuary – works which decorate Florence's cathedral and palaces.

Donatello's revival of antique sculpture is most striking in his *David* (Fig. **8.22**). This statue was the first life-size, free-standing bronze nude since classical times. *David* stands with one foot on Goliath's head, clad in boots and a Tuscan hat. Although the theme is biblical, Donatello's treatment is entirely pagan. He adopted the S-shaped pose of classical Greek statuary, but not its treatment of anatomy. The adolescent lines of David's torso could be described as lyrical, almost sweet. The contrast between the extravagant hat and Goliath's burly head emphasize David's boyishness rather than his heroic strength.

KEY CONCEPT

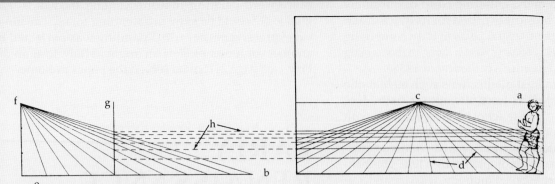

8.19 Design of Alberti's perspective construction, according to recent discoveries.
Alberti's perfected system involved a single vanishing point for lines perpendicular to the canvas, and additional points on either side at which oblique lines seemed to converge (*a* height of person, *b* base line, *c* vanishing point, *d* orthogonals, *e* "little space," *f* distance point, *g* vertical intersection, *h* transversals).

THE SCIENCE OF PERSPECTIVE

The Renaissance's greatest advance in the pictorial arts was the invention of **perspective** – a pictorial technique for representing a two-dimensional scene so that it appears to be three-dimensional. As Masaccio showed in his *Tribute Money*, painted objects could be shaded to create the illusion of volume, or slightly blurred to create the illusion of distance. Painters achieved the most dramatic illusion of depth with **linear perspective**, in which a picture's straight lines all converge toward a vanishing point.

Although Brunelleschi probably invented linear perspective, it was his colleague Leon Battista Alberti (1404–72) who codified linear perspective's elaborate rules. In the treatise *On Painting* (1435), Alberti detailed a system for projecting a pictorial scene on to a grid of perspective lines. Perspective (Fig. **8.19**) involved one or two vanishing points for lines perpendicular to the canvas, and additional points on either side at which

8.20 Leonardo da Vinci, *Last Supper*, 1495–8. Oil and tempera on plaster, 14 ft 5 ins x 28 ft ¹/₄ in (4.39 x 8.54 m). Refectory, Santa Maria delle Grazie, Milan.

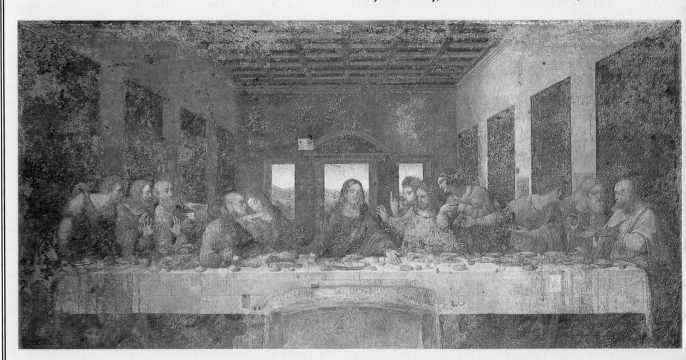

oblique lines seemed to converge. Ghiberti, the artist who created the panels of the *Gates of Paradise*, faithfully adopted Alberti's rules in the representation of the tiled courtyard and the receding arches of *Jacob and Esau* (see Fig. 8.11).

Perspective also served to unify and harmonize a picture's dramatic moment. In Leonardo da Vinci's famous *Last Supper* (Fig. **8.20**), lines created by the coffered ceiling and side windows converge to a vanishing point just above Christ's head (Fig. **8.21**). Thus,

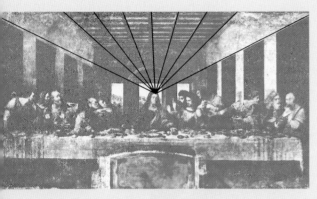

8.21 Perspective lines of Leonardo's *Last Supper*, with the vanishing point at Christ's head.

the animated action of the moment of Jesus' betrayal centers upon the peaceful form of Christ himself. The result is not only the illusion of a three-dimensional space behind the table, but also a feeling of mathematical balance and design.

In an age when artists were also engineers and mathematicians, perspective offered a scientific way of mapping and mastering the world. Its principles echoed the ancient Greeks' belief that mathematical values were the foundation of the universe. It established the individual's mind and eye as the origin of knowledge and perception. Renaissance perspective was, in sum, the visual equivalent of Renaissance humanism, confirming both the wisdom of the ancients and the glory of human intelligence.

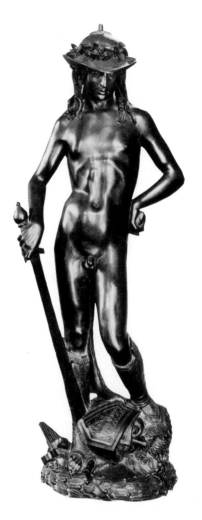

8.22 Donatello, *David*, c. 1430–32. Bronze, height 5 ft 2¹/₄ ins (1.58 m). Museo Nazionale, Florence.
With this graceful youth, Donatello revived the classical tradition of nude statuary in bronze. The young hero's Tuscan hat gives a Florentine accent to the biblical theme.

MICHELANGELO IN FLORENCE

By the age of twenty-two, Michelangelo Buonarroti [BWAH-na-RAH-tee] (1475–1564) had already established himself as a rival to Donatello. In the late 1490s, Michelangelo was called to Rome, where he executed a work every bit as lyrical as Donatello's *David*. Michelangelo's *Pietà* (Fig. **8.23**) was a graceful interpretation of the Virgin mourning the dead Christ. The Madonna's face is like that of a maiden's, its purified beauty unmarked by age or grief. Yet, from this delicate apex, the Madonna's form broadens into a massive pedestal for the body of Christ. Posed against the cascading drapery of his mother's garment, Christ's nudity becomes an emblem of suffering and grief. In the *Pietà* Michelangelo makes artistic technique serve the pathos of his subject, as Giotto had done in his earlier fresco version (see Fig. 7.26). With this statue, the young Michelangelo announced his own heroic talent and ambition, and a new heroic scale in Renaissance art.

Michelangelo's heroic aspirations were first realized in his statue of *David* (Fig. **8.24**), a statement of the sculptor's – and his city's – audacious confidence. Florence's city fathers had lured Michelangelo back from Rome with the opportunity to carve, from a giant block of marble, a male statue for Florence Cathedral. Michelangelo chose to create a David that combined classical values with a biblical theme. The slayer of Goliath is portrayed as a Greek god, who looks defiantly over the countryside in search of his enemy. The muscled torso of the naked figure suggests monumental energy, while the right hand is calm as it loosely grasps a stone. The combination of energy and control recalls the classical balance of Polyclitus (see Fig. 3.9), yet what distinguishes Michelangelo's statue is the heroic force that exceeds the classical rules of measure and moderation. The statue, completed in 1504, surpassed even the ancients in its self-assurance and power. It also expressed Michelangelo's confidence in the Florentine republic, restored after the Medici's fall in

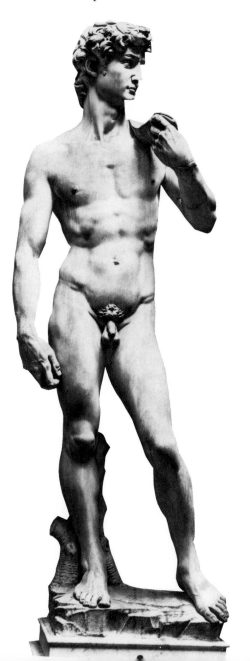

8.23 Michelangelo Buonarroti, *Pietà*, 1498–9. Marble, height 5 ft 9 ins (1.75 m). St. Peter's, Rome.
Consider the emotional impact achieved by Michelangelo's distortion of the figures' relative scale: the adult body of Jesus cradled in Mary's gigantic lap. How might a more realistic scale be less affecting to the viewer?

8.24 Right **Michelangelo Buonarroti, David, 1501–4. Marble, height 18 ft (5.49 m). Accademia, Florence.**
Compare Michelangelo's heroic Renaissance nude to the bronze Riace Warrior of ancient Greece (Fig. 3.23). Note the similarities and differences – subject, style, material, treatment of the figure etc. – in these two representations of the male heroic ideal.

1494. When the stupendous figure was unveiled, the Florentines chose to place it in the city square, next to Donatello's statue of the Hebrew heroine Judith. Donatello's work bore the inscription, "Kingdoms fall through luxury, cities rise through virtues; behold the neck of pride severed by humility." Donatello's and Michelangelo's defiant works of art were intended as talismans against tyranny.

THE DECLINE OF FLORENCE

The end of the fifteenth century saw a decline in Florence's status as a center of innovation in the Renaissance. The voice of this decline belonged to the fiery monk Savonarola (1452–98), whose fierce sermons made him virtual dictator of the city for four years (1494–8). Savonarola [sah-VAH-nah-ROLL-ah] condemned the pleasure-seeking paganism of Florentine Renaissance culture. As evidence of Florentine sinfulness, he cited a popular melody in praise of the Virgin Mary, entitled "Queen of Heaven." The same tune, Savonarola complained, served as a love song to the "Queen of my heart." With his puritanical message, so much like the ancient Hebrew prophets, Savonarola rose to power in the vacuum created by Lorenzo de' Medici's death in 1492.

Appealing to Florence's poor and working people, Savonarola condemned the Church's corruption and the excessive displays of wealth and fashion among Florence's

privileged families. In 1497, his supporters created a great "bonfire of the vanities" in Florence's town square, and piled the fire high with dice, playing cards, cosmetics, indecent books and pictures, and other evidence of Florence's sinful luxury. However, just one year later, Savonarola was defeated by his rivals and was burned at the stake as a heretic near the site of his "bonfire" (Fig. **8.25**).

While wealthy Florentines reverted quickly to their lavish gaiety, Savonarola's message was not entirely forgotten. This message affected the age's greatest figures,

---

THE WRITE IDEA

Michelangelo sculpted the biblical figure of David to represent Florence's courage and independence. What person (real or fictional) would you choose to represent the heroism of the nation or group to which you belong? What heroic qualities does this figure symbolize?

8.25 *The Execution of Savonarola*, **from a contemporary painting. Museo San Marco, Florence.**
Savonarola's charismatic moralism affected the age's greatest figures, including Botticelli, Michelangelo, and Lorenzo de' Medici himself.

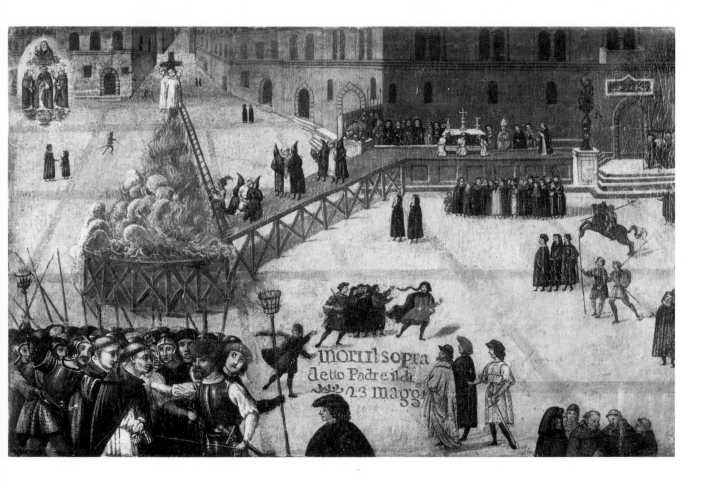

GLOBAL PERSPECTIVE

THE SCULPTURE OF WEST AFRICA

The art of sculpture thrived in Renaissance Italy because of several powerful factors: the genius of Donatello and Michelangelo; the presence of classical models; and the enthusiasm of wealthy patrons such as the Medici family. Sculpture enjoyed a comparable heyday in the city-states of West Africa during the period 1100–1500, when a royal class commissioned sculpted images of itself in bronze and brass.

West Africa in this period (equivalent to the Middle Ages and early Renaissance) was governed by regional kingdoms centered in principal cities such as Ife [EE-fay] and Benin [buh-NEEN] (in present-day Nigeria). These nations maintained a lively commerce with the Muslim world (via trans-Saharan caravans) and Asia (via sea routes across the Indian Ocean).

Despite the lack of a unifying language or religious faith, west African sculptors demonstrated a remarkably consistent style, working in ceramic and bronze. They excelled in the "lost-wax" method of bronze-casting, probably learned from African Muslims, who also supplied the requisite metals. Lost-wax casting had been used in ancient Greece and Rome and was revived by Donatello and others in Renaissance Europe.

The innovators of the west African style resided in Ife, a Yoruba-speaking city-state. Ife is especially noted for the serene naturalism of its portrait sculpture, which glorified royalty and preserved the memory of royal ancestors (Fig. 8.26). The statues may have been used as a substitute for the deceased monarch during elaborate funeral rituals. They depict their subjects as somewhat idealized youths, with elongated brows, decorative headdresses, and facial decoration that may represent scarification patterns. Like the *kouroi* of archaic Greece (see Fig. 3.6), these heads may memorialize their subject at a youthful peak of handsome vitality. In glorifying rulers both living and dead, Ife sculpture is equivalent to the Italian Renaissance's portraits of merchant princes and popes.

The sculptural style of Ife migrated in the late 1300s to the Edo-speaking kingdom of Benin, where it con-

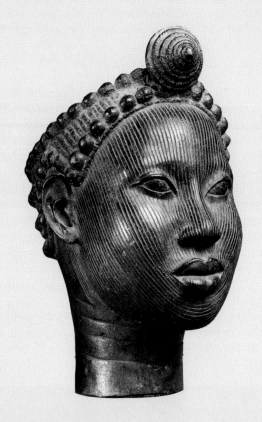

8.26 Ife portrait head. Bronze, height 9 ins (22.9 cm). Detroit Institute of Art.
Ife artisans compromised their portraits' realism with certain stylized features, such as the overlapping eyelids and the slight ridge surrounding the lips. The sinuous grooving may represent ritual scars or be yet another stylization.

tinued to develop until European forces sacked the city in 1897. The realism of Ife and Benin portraiture is found nowhere else in African sculpture.

---

including Botticelli, who destroyed the nude paintings in his workshop and afterward painted only religious themes, and Michelangelo, who forty years later, while working on a scene of the *Last Judgment*, said he could still hear Savonarola's condemnations ringing in his ears. Savonarola's regime emphatically ended the glittering age of Lorenzo the Magnificent, and the artists who had prospered in Florence were now drawn to other Italian cities.

HUMANIST REALISM

Summarize the rules of government prescribed in Machiavelli's The Prince.

During the cultural Renaissance, Italy was plagued by violent political conflicts among its five independent states: Florence, Milan, Venice, the papal states, and the Kingdom of Naples. Besides these divisions, Italians suffered the interference of foreign rulers who sought to dominate the Italian peninsula. These political factions were quick to form alliances for their own advantage and just as quick to betray their allies. As a result, Renaissance Italy was a viper's nest of political intrigue and cynicism, without rules or principles to guide it.

MACHIAVELLI'S *THE PRINCE*

During this period, there was one person who gave order to the chaos in Italy. Niccolò Machiavelli [MAH-kee-ah-VELL-ee] (1469–1527), a Florentine diplomat, described the harsh realities of power in Italy in his masterpiece of political philosophy entitled *The Prince* (1532). *The Prince* was the first attempt in the Christian era to analyze politics from an entirely secular viewpoint. Like the classical Greek philosopher Plato in *The Republic*, Machiavelli reflected on his age's politics in the hope of saving a declining form of government. Where Plato was an idealist of political philosophy, however, Machiavelli was the clear-headed realist (Fig. **8.27**).

Machiavelli was an active Florentine diplomat for fourteen years, until he was dismissed from his diplomatic post in 1512, when the Medici returned to power. Writing (as Dante had) in exile from his native Florence, Machiavelli coldly analyzed the motives and methods of political power. In *The Prince* he describes the ideal "prince," or ruler, of an Italian city-state, modeled on the cruel Cesare Borgia, illegitimate son of Pope Alexander VI, who plotted with his father to unify Italy under his control. Though Borgia's plans were foiled, Machiavelli urged Italian rulers to be equally ruthless in seizing and preserving power. He believed that only strong rulers could keep Italy's city-states free from foreign domination. Such ruthless politics earned Machiavelli a reputation for cold-heartedness, and he was condemned for counseling ambition, cruelty, and deceit in the pursuit of political aims. This trait has carried over in the term "Machiavellian," which describes a person believed to be unscrupulously pursuing political gain at any cost. Yet, Machiavelli demonstrated a humanist conception of political behavior. Politics embodied rational action in a world where humans were responsible for their behavior – a concept in keeping with the time, and guided by the classical authors.

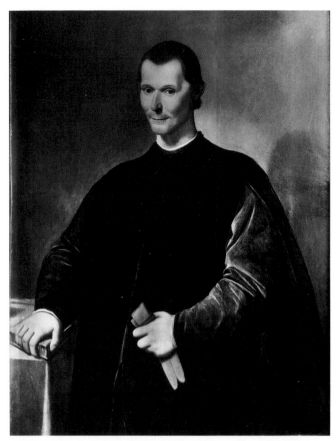

8.27 Tito, *Niccolò Machiavelli.* **Palazzo Vecchio, Florence.** Though his name is now a synonym for devious and ruthless politics, Machiavelli in fact remained loyal to his native Florence in spite of torture and exile. Machiavelli's *The Prince* (1532) offered advice to Florence's new Medici ruler.

Machiavelli's analysis of politics can still throw light on the actions of people in power today. His writing is remembered and quoted in aphoristic sayings that have become well-known.

It is better for a prince to be feared than loved.

In the actions of all men, and especially princes, where there is no court of appeal, the end is all that counts.

As I have said, so far as he is able, a prince should stick to the path of good but, if the necessity arises, he should know how to follow evil.

Now since the prince must make use of the characteristics of beasts he should choose those of the fox and the lion, though the lion cannot defend himself against snares and the fox is helpless against wolves. One must be a fox in avoiding traps and a lion in frightening wolves.

It [cruelty] *may be said to be well used (if we may speak of using well a thing in itself bad) when all cruel deeds are committed at once in order to make sure of the state and thereafter discontinued to make way for the consideration of the welfare of the subjects.*

But a prince who consults with more than one advisor, unless he be a wise man, will never know how to coordinate the advice given him. For each of his advisors will see the matter from his own point of view, and a stupid prince will be unable to make allowances and distinctions. Advisors are of necessity of such a nature because unless men are compelled to be good they will invariably turn out bad.

My conclusion is, then, that, as fortune is variable and men are fixed in their ways, men will prosper so long as they are in tune with the times and will fail when they are not.

MACHIAVELLI
From *The Prince* (1517)

Judged by his own standard, Machiavelli was certainly not in tune with his times. When Florence's republic fell in 1512, he was tortured briefly and exiled. He could not please either of Florence's rival factions. His service to the republic made him suspicious to the Medici family, while his overtures to the Medicis tainted him in the republicans' eyes. Machiavelli died in 1527, a few months before the Holy Roman Emperor Charles V's troops sacked Rome, when Machiavelli's worst fears about foreign domination of Italian politics were realized.

THE GENIUS OF LEONARDO

The most diverse and enigmatic talent of the Renaissance was Leonardo da Vinci [da VEEN-chee] (1452–1519), a genius of the arts, science, engineering, and mathematics. Leonardo was universally admired in his day as a paragon of artistic skill, grace, and wit. Yet he remained a remote and mysterious character, even to his contemporaries. As a painter, Leonardo was capable of exquisite perfection, yet hardly more than a dozen of his completed pictures

---

THE WRITE IDEA

How would you apply Machiavelli's maxim "the end is all that counts" to your own education and career? At what times might you expect to concentrate only on your aim, regardless of the costs?

---

survive. His scientific explorations reached to the mysteries of birth and life, yet he was equally fascinated by the machinery of destruction and envisioned the world's end in a catastrophic deluge.

Trained as a painter and sculptor in Florence, Leonardo abandoned that vibrant city to seek new interests. He served the Duke of Milan as a designer of fortifications and water projects. When the duke was deposed by a French invasion, Leonardo left behind in Milan some of his greatest works. Never loyal to one city or patron, Leonardo was consumed by an insatiable appetite for knowledge about the world. In his notebooks, projects, and paintings, he demonstrated an understanding of the world that still amazes. Western civilization has probably never known a greater or more restless intelligence.

LEONARDO AS SCIENTIST

Leonardo filled the pages of his *Notebooks* (Fig. **8.28**) with thousands of sketches and designs that attest to his keen insight. Leonardo was fascinated with the

8.28 Below Page from Leonardo's *Notebooks*, 1510. Pen and ink. Royal Collection, Windsor Castle, © Her Majesty Queen Elizabeth II.
Leonardo's interests in anatomy, mechanics, engineering, and botany were not uncommon for a Renaissance artist, who was expected to be able to design a hoist as readily as to paint a portrait.

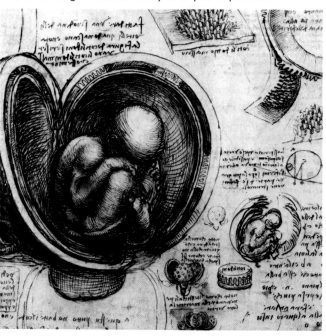

8.29 Opposite Leonardo da Vinci, *Madonna of the Rocks*, c. 1485. Oil on panel, 6 ft 3 ins x 3 ft 7 ins (1.91 x 1.09 m). Louvre, Paris.
Compare the mood created by Leonardo's mystical landscape – the grotto and the distant river – to Raphael's architectural background in *The School of Athens* (Fig. 8.36). How is each setting well-matched to the painting's theme?

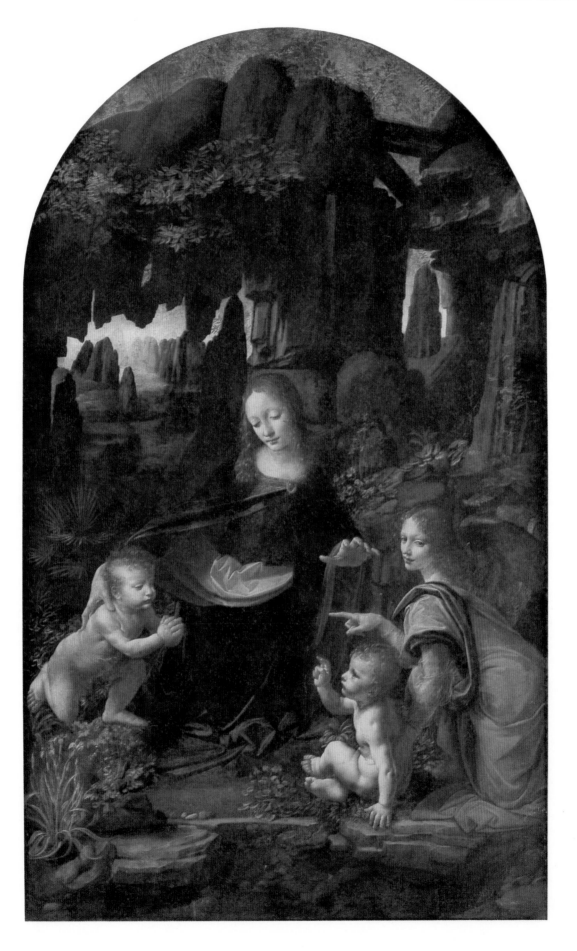

natural world in all its aspects. His notebooks contain sketches and written descriptions of such things as the movements of water, and of the foetus in the womb, the motion of birds in flight, and the circulation of blood. His fascination with the human body and his interest in the mathematics of nature are represented in a famous (and inaccurate) drawing of a human figure graphed within a circle and square (see Fig. 8.3). "Let no one read this book who does not know mathematics," he wrote in his *Treatise on Painting.*

Believing that machines were more reliable than men, Leonardo designed countless devices that were ahead of his time. His notebooks outline versions of such modern technology as the tank, submarine, and airplane. Mechanically, Leonardo's machines were perfectly designed, though they lacked a means of propulsion. Yet, in his lifetime, most of Leonardo's designs remained unrealized – Leonardo was himself more interested in the theoretical solution of a problem than the ful-fledged execution of an idea. His scientific insights, which might have revolutionized the field of anatomy and many other fields, remained locked in his unpublished notebooks.

8.30 Leonardo da Vinci, *Mona Lisa*, c. 1503–5. Oil on panel, 30 x 20 ins (76 x 53 cm). Louvre, Paris.
The sitter's bemused calm contrasts to the spectacular landscape, with its craggy peaks and misty rivers. Leonardo's skill in portraiture made him the most sought-after painter of his age, even though he completed only a handful of pictures in his long career.

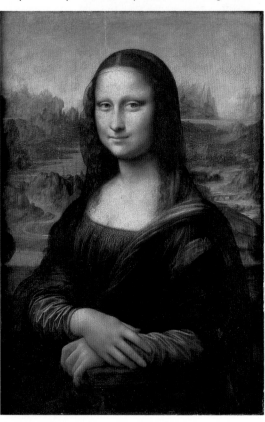

LEONARDO AS PAINTER

Leonardo's mastery of drawing and pictorial mood ranks him as one of the greatest painters ever to live. The *Last Supper* (see Fig. 8.20), a crumbling fresco in Milan, has become an icon of Western art. Leonardo's technical skills may be best appreciated in lesser-known works. In his *Madonna of the Rocks* (Fig. **8.29**), for example, Leonardo captured a graceful beauty reminiscent of Botticelli's *Birth of Spring* (see Fig. 8.17). Leonardo surpassed his predecessor in the complexity of foreground and background and the deeply symbolic effects of light and dark. The foreground group of the *Madonna* includes the infant John the Baptist, the Virgin Mary, an angel, and the Christ child. The group forms a solidly classical triangle, a favorite compositional technique of the Renaissance. The gestures of praying, pointing, and benediction unify the group psychologically. The same motions also create implied lines

KEY CONCEPT

THE RENAISSANCE MAN... AND WOMAN

To many of his contemporaries, Leonardo embodied the ideal of the Renaissance courtier: witty, handsome, learned, and skillful in many arts. Leonardo could have been the model for the ideal gentleman described in *The Book of the Courtier* (1528) by Baldassare Castiglione (1478–1529) (Fig. **8.31**). Castiglione [kass-TEE-lee-OH-nay] defined the Renaissance ideal of the *uomo universale* ("universal man") skilled in the arts and sciences valued by the Renaissance. The *uomo universale* [WO-mo oon-ee-ver-SALL-ay] had to be adept at soldiering and riding, well-bred and handsome. He should be able to dance, read music, quote ancient authors, and woo a lover. And the Renaissance man had to do all this with a carefree disdain that Castiglione called *sprezzatura* [sprets-a-TOOR-a].

While Castiglione's courtiers agreed about the Renaissance man, they loudly disputed the qualities of a Renaissance woman. One speaker passionately claimed that women could match the perfection of the Renaissance man, that women "do not wish to become men in order to make themselves more perfect but to gain their freedom and shake off the tyranny that men have imposed on them by their one-sided authority."[5] The woman who best realized this Renaissance ideal of courtliness and independence was Isabella d'Este [DESS-tay] (1474–1539). Isabella had the education, family connections, and refined tastes of a Renaissance aristocrat. By the age of fourteen she was an

that further connect the figures. Behind the central group, through an arch of rocks, a mysterious landscape opens into an infinity of time and distance. Across the whole picture is a hazy aura created by the use of **sfumato** [sfoo-MAH-toh], a shading technique in which outlines are slightly blurred. *Sfumato*, also used to supreme effect in the *Mona Lisa* (Fig. **8.30**), imitated the effects of human vision, and was Leonardo's own variation on the *chiaroscuro* technique developed by Masaccio and other early Renaissance masters.

Leonardo defended painting as the highest art, and claimed that painting permitted unlimited range to the artist's imagination. "If the painter wishes to see enchanting beauties," he wrote in his *Treatise on Painting*, "he has the power to produce them." If the painter wants to create "towns or deserts," if "from high mountain tops he wants to survey vast stretches of country . . . he has the power to create all this." Leonardo concluded, "Indeed, whatever exists in the universe, whether in essence, in act, or in the imagination, the painter has first in his mind and then in his hands."[6] Leonardo was so fascinated with the material world, so imaginative in seeing its beauty and logic, that his tantalizing legacy in the arts still fascinates.

CRITICAL QUESTION

Should college and university curricula be redesigned to provide a more all-rounded education in the arts, history, science, and mathematics? Should students be educated in the social graces?

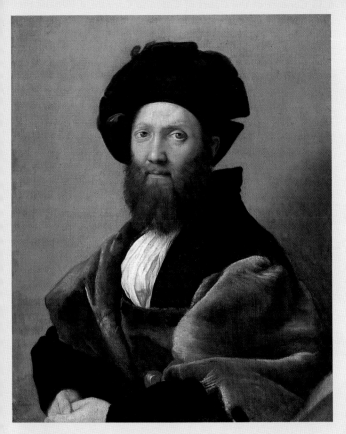

accomplished dancer, could quote Virgil, and played the lute. She had seen the dramatic works of the classical authors Plautus and Terence performed in her father's court. As a Renaissance woman, Isabella energetically patronized the arts and charmed her companions. She toured Rome's classical ruins with Castiglione and repeatedly implored Leonardo to paint her portrait. Isabella also proved herself an able political manager, much to her husband's discomfort – after six years as a political prisoner, the duke returned to find his city running a bit too well under the rule of a woman.

The ideal man of the Renaissance could, like Isabella, master the practical problems of government or, like Leonardo, produce elegant works of imagination. The ideal of excellence lay in the versatility of the person, in contrast to the modern ideal, which values specialized abilities and single-minded determination. Rather than nonchalance, modern artists and executives display their fierce competitiveness and power of concentration. Renaissance and modern societies seem to demand different – one might say opposing – qualities from their model citizens.

8.31 Raphael, *Baldassare Castiglione*, 1510–16. Oil on panel, 29¹/₂ ins x 25¹/₂ ins (75 x 65 cm). Louvre, Paris.
Castiglione's *The Book of the Courtier* (1528) defined the qualities of the Renaissance individual, which included skills in combat, music, riding, and conversation.

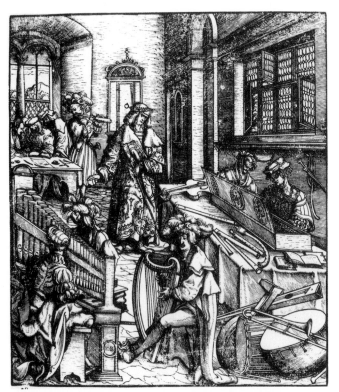

THE HIGH RENAISSANCE IN ROME

Compare the heroic style of the Renaissance in Rome with the early Renaissance style in Florence.

While the Italian Renaissance blossomed in Florence, the age bore its greatest fruit in the city of Rome. Rome had long been famed for its dedication to high living and fine art. About 1500, it witnessed an outburst of artistic creation and imitation that transformed the city. The period known as the High Renaissance saw the masterful application of techniques and ideas developed in Florence. The achievements of Raphael and Michelangelo in painting, Josquin des Préz in music, and Leonardo da Vinci in several arts, make this an unsurpassed age of heroic genius. The High Renaissance was centered in Rome but also spread to other cultural centers of southern Europe.

8.32 Hans Burgmair, *Maximilian with His Musicians*, illustration from *Der Weisskönig*, 16th century. Woodcut.
Renaissance musicians migrated to the courts of patrons such as Maximilian, the Holy Roman Emperor. Among the instruments shown here are early versions of the harp, organ, trombone, flute, and viola.

8.33 *Concert at the Court of Caterina Cornaro*, a Renaissance music party. Attingham, Shrewsbury, England.
An amateur's skill in music, aided by printed music from the new presses, was expected of any Renaissance courtier.

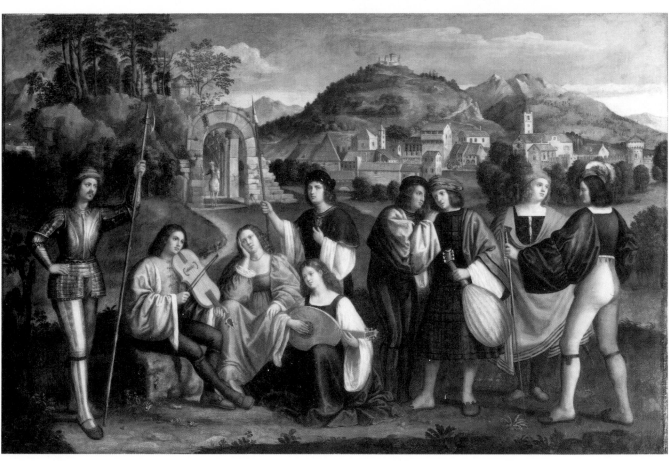

PATRONAGE OF THE RENAISSANCE ARTS

Rome's prominence in Renaissance art rested on a system of patronage, by which wealthy families and individuals employed artists. A Renaissance **patron** normally engaged an artist through a written contract that outlined the work's specifications and a schedule of payments. The wealthiest patrons might maintain an artist at their court, expecting the performance of certain duties, such as supervising building projects or directing a choir (Figs. **8.32**, **8.33**). The most prominent patrons were often popes, including the imperious Pope Julius II and the extravagant Medici pope, Leo X. The system of patronage sometimes brought troubled relations between artists and their patrons. In his *Lives of the Painters* (1550), the biographer Giorgio Vasari told of a painter who was locked in a room to finish a commission. The recalcitrant artist escaped through the window to spend three days in Florence's taverns and brothels. In another example, Pope Julius II, impatient with Michelangelo's progress on the Sistine Chapel ceiling (see page 220), once threatened to throw the artist off his scaffolding. Michelangelo replied quietly but forcefully, "I think not, my lord."

In a lifetime, an artist might serve many patrons – the composer Josquin des Préz, for example, served several kings, emperors, and popes – and could offer many services, as the skills of Leonardo da Vinci clearly testify.

JOSQUIN DES PRÉZ

Pope Leo X, the successor to Julius II, liked to meditate while his choir filled the papal chapel with music whose nobility matched Michelangelo's paintings. The rich blend of northern polyphony and Italian lyricism was called the *ars perfecta*, or "perfect art," the highest development of Renaissance sacred music.

The great master of *ars perfecta* was the northern French composer of Flemish origin Josquin des Préz [zhoss-KAN(h)-day-PRAY] (c. 1440–1521). Although he served many masters, for almost a decade (c. 1486–94) Josquin (Fig. **8.34**) sang and composed for the pope's Sistine Choir in Rome,

the finest choral group in Europe. The Sistine Choir sang without musical accompaniment, a technique still called *a cappella* because it was practiced almost exclusively in the Sistine Chapel.

Josquin's compositions were admired for their harmonious architecture and for their match between words and music. By 1500, composers such as Josquin had freed themselves from the traditional texts and melodies of the medieval tradition. They could compose all the voices of a composition at once, blending them harmonically and matching the music's melody to the words. Josquin blended the north European style of complex polyphony (several melodies played simultaneously) and the Italian preference for chordal harmonies (based on three-tone chords). Josquin's mastery of the *ars perfecta* style made him the best-known and best-paid composer of the High Renaissance. The reformer Martin Luther (see page 231) said Josquin was "master of the notes," making them do as he willed.

Josquin's preferred form was the motet (see page 183), of which he composed more than a hundred examples. The motet form permitted Josquin freedom in creating sweet harmonies and exploring the musical qualities of words. Josquin excelled at word-painting – matching a descending melody to words of grief, or a quickened rhythm to an expression of joy.

Like his Flemish predecessors, Josquin made frequent use of polyphony, especially a technique known as **imitation**, in which one voice states a melody that is duplicated in turn by succeeding voices (Fig. **8.35**). Such imitation marks the opening of the motet *Ave Maria . . . virgo serena* (*Hail, Mary . . . serene virgin*) (1520), where the voices

8.35 Example of imitation, from a motet by Josquin des Préz.

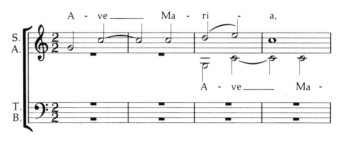

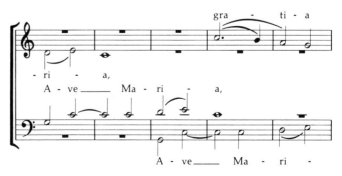

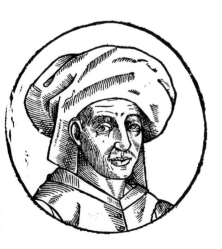

8.34 Portrait of Josquin des Préz, published in 1511. Josquin des Préz, of whom Martin Luther wrote: "He is the master of the notes. They must do as he wills; as for the other composers, they must do as the notes will."

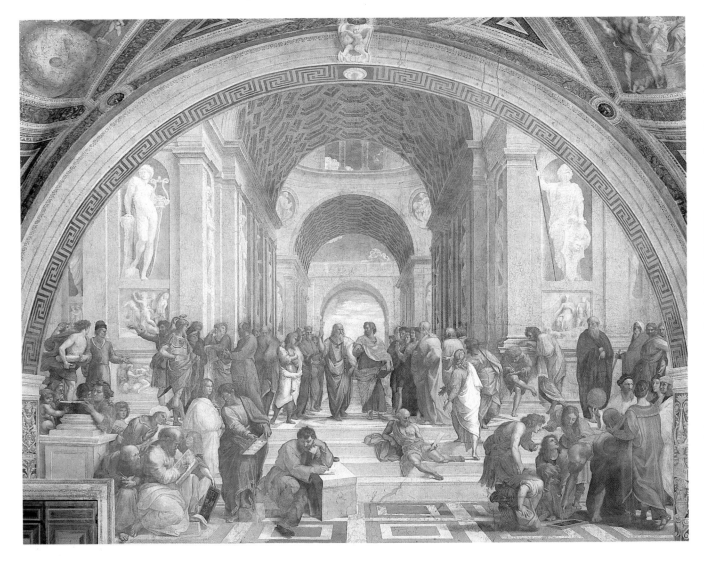

8.36 Raphael, *School of Athens*, 1509–11. Fresco, 26 ft x 18 ft (7.92 x 5.48 m). Stanza della Segnatura, Vatican Palaces, Rome.
Bisecting the painting horizontally allows a comparison of its human action and its architectural setting; bisecting it vertically underlines the philosophical theme of abstract thought (left) and practical knowledge (right).

build and overlap in an architecture of melody. Josquin frequently balances counterpoint against simpler choral passages, and voices are paired to emphasize the clarity of the text.

Josquin's musical complexities demanded an attentive and educated audience, which he found at the pope's court in Rome. He inspired an unbounded admiration among his humanist patrons and musical contemporaries, who compared his stature in music to that of Michelangelo's in painting and sculpture.

RAPHAEL

In 1509, Pope Julius II followed his architect's advice and commissioned a young painter to decorate his apartment chambers. The artist, known as Raphael, was already famed for a series of graceful Madonnas painted in Florence. Working under the pope's patronage, Raffaello Sanzio (1483–1520) became Renaissance Rome's busiest and most beloved artist. Besides painting, Raphael used his talents on projects for the pope, such as the excavation of Roman ruins and the construction of the new St. Peter's basilica. In a city of intrigues and jealousies, Raphael was loved for his good humor and modesty. When he died at thirty-seven ("of too many women," grumbled one rival), he was the most popular artist of the Renaissance.

As a painter, Raphael was known for the clarity and spiritual harmony of his works, which eloquently embodied the High Renaissance style. His most famous work, the *School of Athens* (Fig. **8.36**), is a virtual textbook of Renaissance painting, a synthesis of humanism and Renaissance technique. The *School of Athens* depicts a gathering of the great pagan philosophers. The two central figures

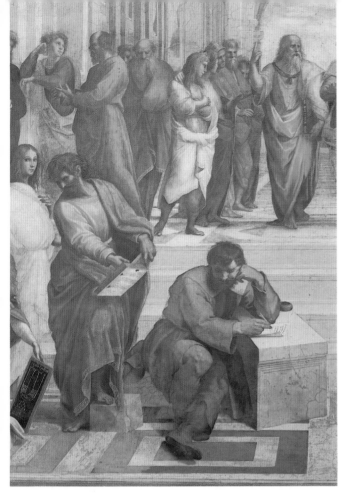

8.37 Above **Raphael, *The School of Athens*, 1509–11, detail showing Michelangelo (seated, bottom right).**
What clues do you find here that the figure of Michelangelo and the stone block on which he writes were added at the last moment?

8.38 Right **Michelangelo Buonarroti, *Captive*, 1527–8. Marble, height 7 ft 6¹/₂ ins (2.3 m). Accademia, Florence.**
One of the unfinished figures for Pope Julius' tomb, this "captive" symbolizes the soul's struggle against confining flesh.

are Plato, who points to the world of ideal forms above, and Aristotle, reaching for the natural world below. On either side, figures representing ancient philosophy are arranged in lively symmetry, balanced between the abstract and the practical. To Plato's right, for example, a brown-cloaked Socrates ticks off arguments on his fingers and Pythagoras checks proportions on a slate. On Aristotle's side, practitioners of the applied sciences include the astronomer Ptolemy holding a globe in the right foreground. The diverse group is unified by the great arch that encloses the whole scene. The barrel vaults recede to a vanishing point between the heads of Plato and Aristotle. The painting's overall effect is of learning, tolerance, perfect harmony, and balance.

The philosophers portrayed in the *School of Athens* may have been ancient but some of their faces were based on contemporary figures. Plato may be a portrait of the aged master Leonardo; the bearded sage beneath the statue of Minerva resembled Raphael's patron, Pope Julius II; the bending figure of Euclid paid homage to Raphael's spon-

sor, the architect Bramante [brah-MAHN-tay]; and next to Ptolemy, the face of Raphael himself peers out at the viewer. The most striking figure, however, was the brooding man leaning on a stone block and dressed in the smock and boots of a sixteenth-century stonecutter. Here, portrayed as the philosopher Heraclitus, Raphael created a portrait of Michelangelo (Fig. **8.37**). Michelangelo was then at work on the Sistine Chapel ceiling, only a stone's throw away from the wall of the Vatican that Raphael painted. In this portrait, drawn in the bold and muscular style of Michelangelo's athletes, Raphael recognized the colossal achievement of his colleague.

MICHELANGELO IN ROME

Show how Michelangelo's artistic works balance the pagan classical tradition with Christian values.

In 1505, Michelangelo was ordered to Rome by Pope Julius II, who wished the brilliant young sculptor to build his tomb. Michelangelo's designs demonstrate the heroic scale

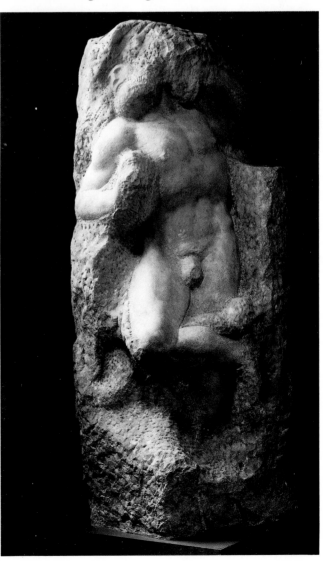

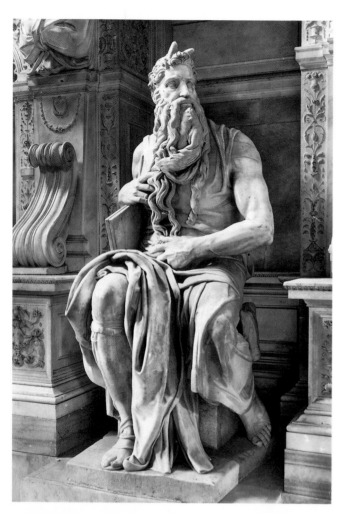

8.39 Michelangelo Buonarroti, *Moses*, 1513–15. Marble, height 8 ft 4 ins (2.54 m). San Pietro in Vincoli, Rome.
Moses prepares to rise in anger against his faithless people. Note the statue's poised energy, evident in the tensed legs and the left arm's bulging muscles and sinews.

anticipated by his Florentine *David.* For the tomb the sculptor envisioned a gigantic facade rising in three stages, decorated with forty life-size statues. The designs for the tomb represent the Neoplatonist passage from material to spiritual existence, recalling Plato's three-part division of the soul. The unfinished sculptures intended for the tomb reinforce this Neoplatonist motif. The so-called *Captives* (Fig. **8.38**) appear to struggle against the stone that binds them, just as the soul strives against the restraints of the flesh. Michelangelo's grandiose tomb remained unfinished, although the project occupied him for thirty years. Michelangelo himself referred to this project as his "tragedy."

One sculpted figure from Julius' tomb ranks among Michelangelo's greatest works. The *Moses* (Fig. **8.39**) embodies the fierce power called *terribilità* that Michelangelo himself possessed in abundance. Moses holds the tablets of commandments received from the hand of God. Looking over his shoulder, Moses sees the Israelites worshiping a pagan idol. Possessed by righteous anger, he rises to dash the tablets of God's law and condemn his tribe. The muscular pose of *Moses* embodies the fierce power of God's judgment, and even his beard is like a living thing, animated by anger. Next to this work of mature vigor, Michelangelo's *David* (see Fig. 8.24) seems like a lyrical poem of youth.

The Sistine Chapel Ceiling

In 1508, Julius directed Michelangelo to interrupt the tomb project and paint the ceiling of the Sistine Chapel. Michelangelo protested that he was a sculptor, not a painter. Nevertheless, here, in the same chapel where Josquin had sung, Michelangelo created a visual poem on the powers of creation and the frailty of human flesh that was to become his most famous work.

For the Sistine Chapel ceiling (Figs. **8.40**, **8.41**), Michelangelo employed a complex philosophical and religious scheme based on Platonic and Christian ideas. The central panels depict scenes from Genesis – the Creation, the Fall, and the story of Noah. Arranged around the narrative scenes are figures that symbolize the reconciliation of Christian and classical ideas – Hebrew prophets to represent divine revelation, and Roman sibyls (pagan prophetesses; Fig. **8.42**) to symbolize human wisdom. In the corners are four narrative scenes that foretell the coming of Christ. The various parts are delineated by an architectural border and nude "athletes."

Despite its obscurity, the Sistine Chapel ceiling is clearly a work of Renaissance humanism. It combines classical and Christian ideas, recognizing in humanity the tension between a divine spirit and sinful flesh. When read from the Creation to the story of Noah, the central panels tell how the divine beauty and order of creation were corrupted by human weakness. The frailty of human will is visible in the shamed and shriveled Adam and Eve as they are driven from paradise (Fig. **8.43**).

However, Michelangelo actually painted the panels in reverse order. Read from Noah to the Creation, the

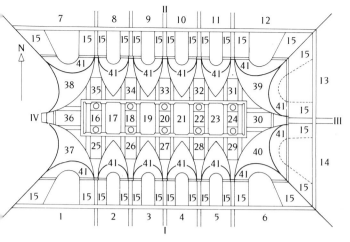

8.40 Plan of the Sistine Chapel ceiling.
Michelangelo probably devised his grand iconographic scheme with advice from papal scholars. Among its guiding ideas were a neo-Platonic symbolism of light and dark, and the Old Testament's prefiguring of Christ's coming. The walls and niches (1-15) were painted by early Renaissance masters.

CRITICAL QUESTION

Does the Sistine Chapel ceiling express optimism or pessimism about the future of humanity? How might Michelangelo have judged the centuries of human history that have followed his great work on the creation?

8.41 Michelangelo Buonarroti, Sistine Chapel ceiling, 1508–12. Fresco, 44 ft x 128 ft (13.41 x 39.01 m). Vatican Palaces, Rome.
Michelangelo painted the gigantic ceiling while standing (not lying on his back) on scaffolding of his own design.

I, II South and north walls: scenes painted by early Renaissance masters

Michelangelo's ceiling frescoes (1508–12)
16 God Separates Light and Darkness
17 God Creates the Sun and the Moon and the Plants on Earth
18 God Separates the Water and Earth and Blesses his Work
19 Creation of Adam
20 Creation of Eve
21 Fall of Man and Expulsion from Paradise
22 Sacrifice of Noah
23 The Flood
24 The Intoxication of Noah
25 Libyan Sibyl
26 Daniel
27 Cumaean Sibyl
28 Isaiah
29 Delphic Sibyl
30 Zechariah
31 Joel
32 Eritrean Sibyl
33 Ezekiel
34 Persian Sibyl
35 Jeremiah
36 Jonah
37 The Brazen Serpent
38 The Punishment of Haman
39 David Slaying Goliath
40 Judith with the Head of Holofernes
41 Lunettes above windows: portraits of ancestors of Christ and scenes from the Old Testament

IV West wall: Michelangelo, *The Last Judgment* (1534–41)

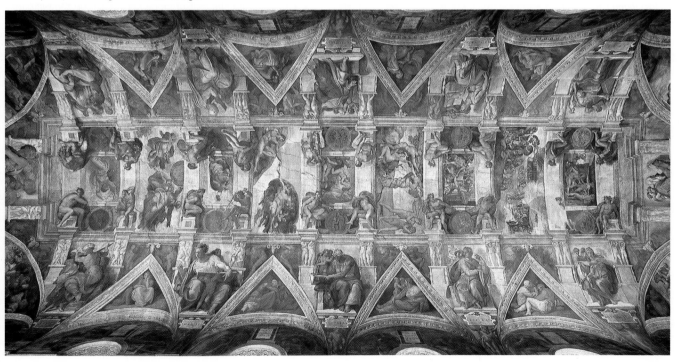

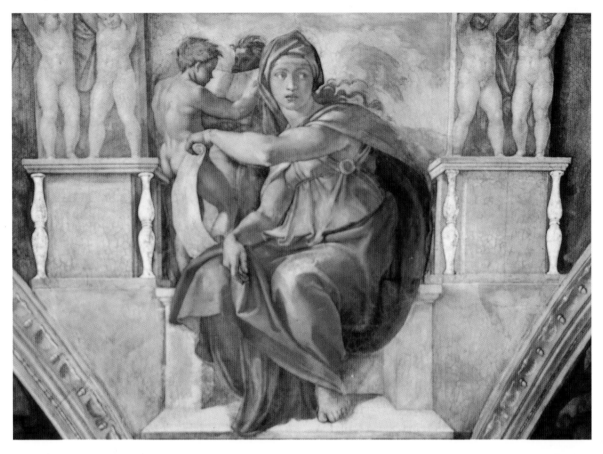

8.42 Michelangelo Buonarroti, *Delphic Sibyl*, detail of the Sistine Chapel ceiling, 1509. Fresco. Vatican Palaces, Rome.
The sibyls, symbols of classical wisdom, alternated with figures of Old Testament prophets. The swirl of this sibyl's garment and the curving scroll define an oval shape, in contrast to the painted architectural setting.

8.43 Michelangelo Buonarroti, *Temptation and Expulsion from the Garden*, detail of the Sistine Chapel ceiling, 1509–10. Fresco. Vatican Palaces, Rome.
The forbidden tree divides these two fateful scenes: on the left Adam and Eve reach eagerly for the fruit of moral knowledge; on the right, they cower in fear as God's angel drives them from the garden.

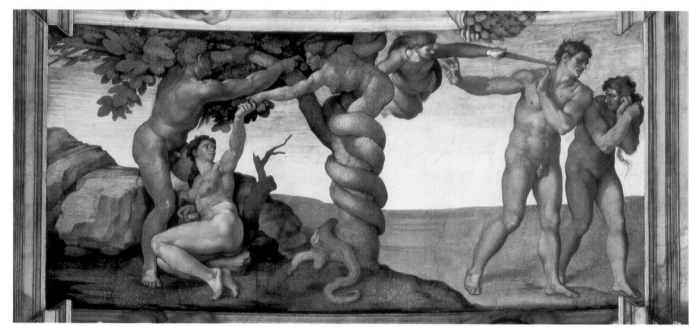

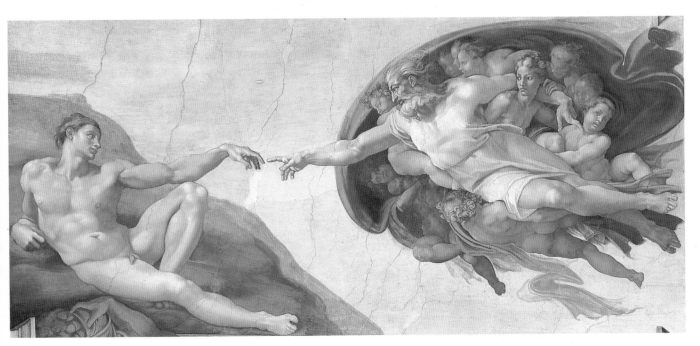

8.44 Michelangelo Buonarroti, *Creation of Adam*, detail of the Sistine Chapel ceiling, 1508–12. Fresco. Vatican Palaces, Rome.
The cloak of God teems with life (Eve awaits her creation in the crook of God's arm), while Adam lies passively against a lifeless hillside.

8.45 Donato Bramante, Tempietto, San Pietro in Montorio, Rome, 1502. Height 46 ft (14 m), diameter of colonnade 29 ft (8.84 m).
Here, on a small scale, we see the domed symmetry and overt classicism that Bramante employed in his designs for St. Peter's in Rome.

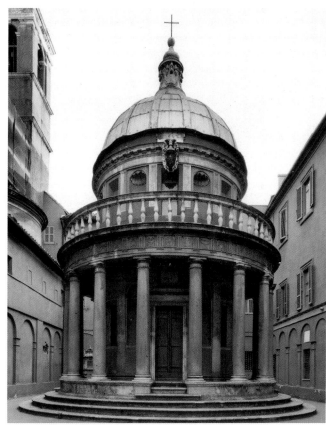

central panels show the triumph of the creative spirit, as Michelangelo becomes more confident of his vision and overcomes the cramped composition of earlier scenes. In the *Creation of Adam* (Fig. **8.44**), God moves toward a languid Adam with a commanding divinity. He holds Eve in the crook of his arm and trails a cloak that contains all of future humanity. The final paintings show God creating the cosmos from a void, scenes that remind us of Michelangelo's own heroic creativity.

Michelangelo's Sistine figures have long been admired for their muscular energy. During the 1980s, the cleaning and restoration of the Sistine Chapel ceiling revealed that Michelangelo was also an inventive and confident colorist. Scholars have re-evaluated a work that, perhaps more than any other, embodied the heroic will of the High Renaissance.

THE NEW ST. PETER'S

Michelangelo spent his last years devoted to architecture. In 1547, he was appointed chief architect of St. Peter's, a project which had already suffered delays and complications. The rebuilding of St. Peter's had begun under Pope Julius II. The old basilica, first built by the Emperor Constantine, had become a crumbling hodgepodge of old-fashioned designs. In a bold act of Renaissance confidence, Pope Julius II ordered that the great church be demolished and replaced with a modern design. When the cornerstone of the new St. Peter's was laid in 1506, it began the High Renaissance's largest and most expensive undertaking. The mammoth project would take more than 150 years to build and would occupy the epoch's leading architects.

As chief architect for the new church, Pope Julius II first engaged Donato Bramante (c. 1444–1514). Bramante produced a symmetrical design shaped like a Greek cross and centered around a flattened dome. His inspiration had come from Brunelleschi's dome in Florence, and from the sketches of Leonardo, which included a central-plan church much like Bramante's. Bramante's plan was never built. The classical symmetry of its exterior is suggested, however, by the architect's Tempietto (Fig. **8.45**), a chapel he completed in another part of Rome in 1502. The Tempietto's delicately classical proportions would have been enlarged to a gigantic scale in the new St. Peter's.

8.46 Plans for the new St. Peter's, Rome, 1506–1606.
The Greek-cross plans of Bramante and Michelangelo were compromised in Maderno's completed version, which added the traditional long nave.

8.47 St. Peter's, Rome, interior of dome.
The dome's symbolism as the dome of the heavens and the perfect circle is stressed by the repetition of circular shapes (arches, medallions, oculus). Compare this gilded brilliance to the church's austere classical exterior (Fig. 8.48).

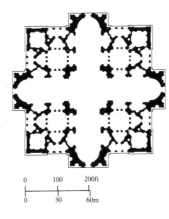

Bramante, 1506.

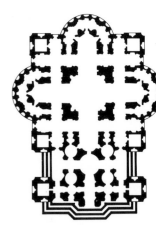

Sangallo, 1539.

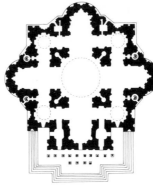

Michelangelo, 1547.

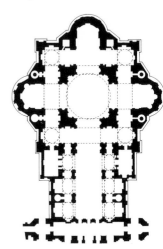

Carlo Maderno, 1606.

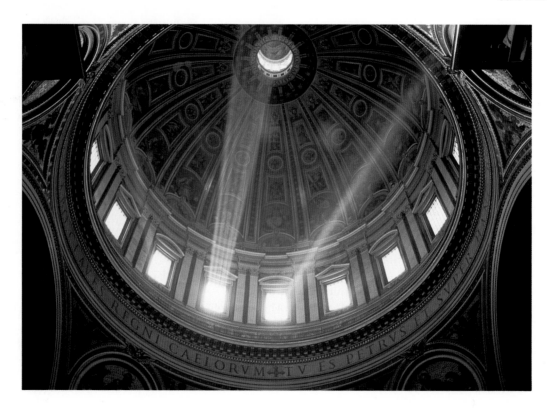

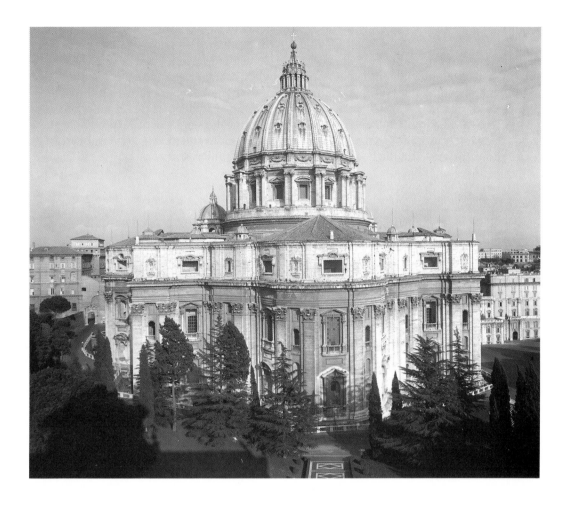

8.48 Michelangelo Buonarroti, St. Peter's, Rome, view from west, begun 1547. Dome completed by Giacomo della Porta, 1590. Height of dome 452 ft (137.8 m).
Michelangelo intended the church to be dominated on all sides by the massive dome, as it is in this view, which shows only the three short arms of the Greek-cross plan. Note the restrained classical decoration: gigantic Corinthian pilasters on the ground story and double engaged columns around the dome, separating pedimented windows.

Bramante's plan of monumental simplicity was expanded and revised by his successors (including Raphael) (Fig. **8.46**). When Michelangelo assumed the project in 1547, he returned to the idea of a symmetrical, Greek-cross plan – a central dome surrounded by four arms of equal length. The dome itself was actually built much as Michelangelo envisioned. On the exterior, it is ribbed in the style of Brunelleschi and unified by repeating pairs of Corinthian columns circling the base and giant pilasters on the outer wall. On the interior, the dome rises in gilded splendor over the altar of St. Peter (Fig. **8.47**). However, where Michelangelo's Greek-cross plan would have been dominated by the dome, later architects lengthened the nave

and added a giant façade, obscuring the dome in the front view (see Fig. 8.46). On the exterior, Michelangelo's intentions are visible today only when St. Peter's is viewed from the rear (Fig. 8.48).

The construction of a new St. Peter's revealed the Renaissance spirit at its best and worst. The grand church was a monumental project, influenced by classical models but conceived on a heroic Renaissance scale. However, the ambitions of patrons and designers (a total of twelve architects and twenty-two popes) far exceeded their ability to execute. Actual construction was hampered by the Church's limited treasury and by a conflict of architectural purposes. In the end, like the sketches in Leonardo's *Notebooks*, St. Peter's was more perfect in conception than in reality.

THE WRITE IDEA
How might a Church leader of the Renaissance have responded to the criticism that the Church should devote its resources to helping the poor and not to constructing grand buildings?

AN AGE OF GIANTS

We cannot fully explain the concentration of artistic talent in Italian cities of the fifteenth and sixteenth centuries. Wealth, classical influences, and cultural ferment cannot account for the birth – within a few miles and a few years – of talents like Leonardo and Michelangelo. Consequently there has been a tendency to lionize the Italian Renaissance. Many historians date the beginning of modern civilization from this one time and locale but much in Renaissance Italy was an extension of the Middle Ages that preceded this fertile era. This was, however, a place and time of great achievement. Fifteen centuries earlier, the ancient Romans had imported the beauty and genius of ancient Greece. In the Renaissance, Italy itself became the source of beauty and learning – a fount of cultural achievement in its own right and a glorious triumph of the human spirit.

Chapter Summary

The Renaissance in Italy. What is called the Renaissance ("rebirth") began in the prosperous Italian city-states of the fifteenth century. Renaissance humanism arose from an interest in classical antiquity and a desire to match the intellectual and artistic achievements of ancient Greece and Rome. Italy's merchant princes supported this effort by extravagant patronage of the arts and learning. In Florence, the Medici family's influence culminated in the reign of Lorenzo the Magnificent, first patron of Michelangelo and a poet in his own right. In applying his classical learning to government, Lorenzo applied the ideal of Renaissance civic humanism.

The Arts in Renaissance Florence. Renaissance Florence's civic pride sustained a remarkable blossoming of the arts. Ghiberti's gilded Baptistery doors became a catalogue of the evolving Renaissance style, including the technique of perspective. Florence's landmark cathedral dome was the ingenious creation of Brunelleschi, its leading Renaissance architect. Florentine painters made revolutionary strides, led by Masaccio's use of *chiaroscuro* and atmospheric perspective. Botticelli's reconciliation of Christian and pagan ideas exemplified the refined classicism of Renaissance learning.

Music in Italy combined the polyphonic textures of northern European composers (Dufay, Heinrich Isaac) with the Italians' love of sweet melody and vivid poetry. Music, in forms such as the *frottola*, adorned Italian courts and filled its streets.

Early Renaissance Sculpture. Early Renaissance sculptors were the artists most directly affected by the classical tradition. Donatello revived the ancient tradition of the free-standing nude in his bronze version of *David* (at a time when west African sculptors had long created realistic portraits in cast bronze). Michelangelo's *Pietà* and *David* combined biblical themes with a classicism of heroic scale.

In the same years as these works, however, Renaissance Florence was chastened by the reformer Savonarola, who zealously condemned the Florentines' luxury and corruption.

Humanist Realism. By applying Renaissance humanism to treacherous Italian politics, the Florentine Machiavelli produced a masterpiece of political philosophy. *The Prince* counseled Italian rulers to pursue their aims with clear-eyed realism, combining a knowledge of the historical past with a ruthless sense of purpose.

The Genius of Leonardo. The Renaissance ideal of the "universal man" was represented by the enigmatic genius Leonardo, whose *Notebooks* reveal a restless and diverse intelligence. Leonardo's meticulous observation of the natural world produced insights in anatomy and mechanics. His mastery of painting technique produced a handful of masterpieces that are icons of world art.

The High Renaissance in Rome. In the High Renaissance, European artists were drawn to Rome, where papal patrons offered immense opportunities for achievement. The composer Josquin des Préz, called "master of the notes," blended northern polyphony and Italian lyricism in his sacred motets and secular songs. The painter Raphael decorated the pope's dwellings at the Vatican with works of perfect balance and harmony. Michelangelo created the awesome figure of *Moses* for the tomb of Pope Julius II, and painted the Sistine Chapel ceiling. Both works symbolized Michelangelo's titanic will and creative achievement.

The High Renaissance's greatest undertaking was the building of a new St. Peter's in Rome. The new basilica was topped by Michelangelo's great dome, a synthesis of Renaissance classicism and heroic ambition, the crowning achievement of an age of giants.

9 The Northern and Late Renaissance

*Tradition holds that, in October 1517, a plump young professor tacked a notice to the wooden door of the Castle church in Wittenberg. With that hammer, Martin Luther (Fig. **9.1**) drove a wedge between the Mother Church and her German followers. He was challenging the practices of the Roman pope, whose agents were selling salvation to German peasants. The slogan from Rome was, "As the coin into the coffer springs, then the soul from purgatory springs." But (Luther asked indignantly), if the pope could so easily grant entry into heaven, why did he not freely release all the souls from purgatory, regardless of whose relatives could pay? And (German princes added), why should German money flow back to Rome to fund its extravagant artistic projects?*

*Luther's reformation of the Church was the pivotal event of the **Northern Renaissance**: a combination of religious zeal and love of learning that divided Europe into Roman Catholic and Protestant faiths. The northern reformers' fervor was soon matched by a counter-movement in Italy, where the Catholic religious reaction coexisted uneasily with the pagan spirit of late Renaissance classicism.*

THE NORTHERN RENAISSANCE

Identify the political and economic causes of the Northern Renaissance.

As the 1500s began in northern Europe, a new political stability was forming in the wake of plague, famine, and dynastic wars. Strong monarchs in England, France, and

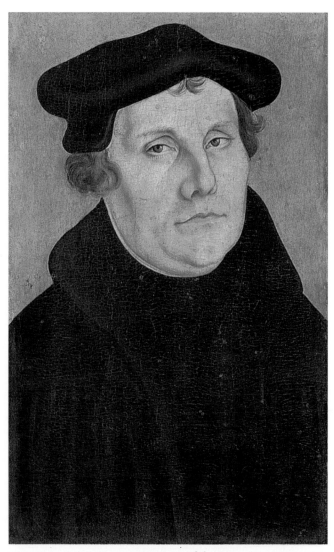

9.1 Lucas Cranach the Elder, *Portrait of Martin Luther,* **c. 1526. Oil on wood, 15 x 19 ins (38 x 24 cm). Uffizi, Florence.**
The pious Augustinian monk, Martin Luther, set off a religious revolution when he questioned the Church's teachings on confession and forgiveness.

Spain, had centralized their power and subdued feudal rivalries between the crown and lesser nobles. The pace of commerce and manufacture in Europe quickened,

CRITICAL QUESTION

Discuss the paradoxes of Holbein's portrait *The Ambassadors* (Fig. **9.2**). What does it say about the spirit of science and exploration and the inevitability of death? In what ways are we reminded of death in the midst of technological and scientific confidence?

9.2 Hans Holbein the Younger, *Allegorical Portrait of Jean de Dinteville and Georges de Selve* **("The Ambassadors"), 1533. Oil and tempera on wood, 6 ft 9¹/₈ ins x 6 ft 10¹/₄ ins (2.06 x 2.09 m). National Gallery, London.**

These Renaissance courtiers stand next to the navigational instruments that guided Europe's merchant fleets. The hymn book and the lute (with a broken string) refer to the discord of northern Europe's religious disputes, while the distorted skull is a reminder of death.

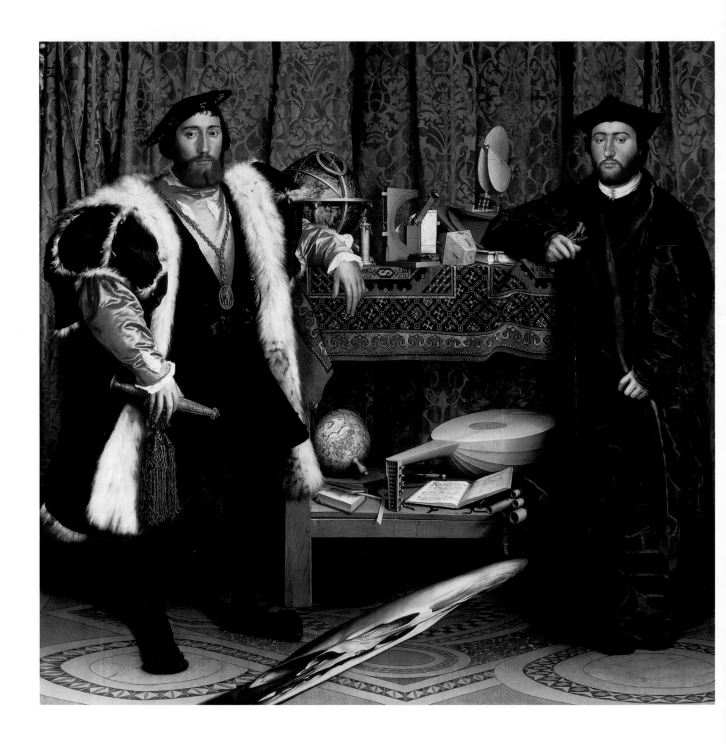

especially with the discovery of the New World and the East. This prosperity and stability fostered a "renaissance" in northern Europe quite different from the Renaissance in Italy. The Northern Renaissance did not cast off medieval attitudes and embrace the glories of antiquity, as Italian humanism had. Some achievements of the Northern Renaissance did show the influence of classicism – Luther's German Bible was translated from the Greek, and the German painter Dürer (see page 239) revived classical proportion. However, many northern artists – for example, Shakespeare and Bruegel – relied little on Italian models and evolved a Northern Renaissance humanism, which was deeply affected by the religious fracture in sixteenth-century European life. The first and greatest "rebirth" in northern Europe was religious, not artistic or political. More than classical learning, it was religious reform that gave rise to the spirit of the Northern Renaissance.

KINGS, COMMERCE, AND COLUMBUS

The nation-states of England, France, and Spain dominated the European continent during the sixteenth century. The monarchs of these strong nations had each consolidated power in their own way. In France, Louis XI (ruled 1461–83) regained territories from England and strengthened his power to levy taxes. In Spain, Ferdinand and Isabella combined their regional thrones in 1479 and ended the Muslim rule in southern Spain. They were succeeded by a line of Spanish monarchs called the Hapsburg dynasty, who eventually controlled territories through much of Europe. Henry VII of England (ruled 1485–1509) ended a period of civil war and established the Tudor dynasty which later included the famous monarchs Henry VIII and Elizabeth I.

Europe's strong monarchs encouraged a commercial revolution that brought wider prosperity to towns and cities. An economic revival in the fourteenth century had been concentrated in a few dominant trading cities, such as Venice in Italy and Bruges in present-day Belgium. The 1500s offered broader opportunities for commercial success, both for individuals and cities. As the commercial revolution spread, traditional restraints against enterprise weakened. The Church relaxed its rules against charging interest on loans, allowing banking houses such as the Fuggers of Augsburg in Germany to accumulate enormous profits. Traditional communal farms were divided up and planted for cash crops. Many peasants either became landowners or sought their fortunes as laborers in the growing towns. Martin Luther's father was a displaced German peasant, who left his family's farm and worked as a miner. He eventually acquired his own mines and foundries, and thus could well afford a university education for his son Martin – who, to his father's chagrin, became a monk instead of a lawyer.

An entirely new factor in the sixteenth-century commercial revolution was Europe's exploration and colonization of the Americas. Financed by Ferdinand and Isabella of Spain and guided by new inventions in navigation, the explorer Christopher Columbus (1451–1506) opened the "New World" to European exploration in 1492. Exploitation followed, and Spanish colonies were established to mine South American silver and gold. The influx of precious metals temporarily made Spain the wealthiest nation in Europe, and inspired adventurers and explorers with hopes of fantastic wealth. The new sea routes to India and the East Indies (via the African coast) shifted Europe's trade to the Atlantic ports of London in England and Amsterdam in the Netherlands. As a result, Europe's balance of economic power shifted toward the north.

THE NORTHERN RENAISSANCE COURTS

Economic prosperity and royal power created an extravagant court life in northern Europe's royal palaces. For all their gaiety and cultivation, however, the English and French courts produced few original works and usually imported their artistic talent. The French King Francis I (Fig. 9.3) sheltered Leonardo da Vinci at his château in Amboise in the Loire Valley in France and invited the

9.3 Jean Clouet (?), *Francis I,* **c. 1525–30. Tempera and oil on wood, 37³/₄ x 29¹/₈ ins (96 x 74 cm). Louvre, Paris.**
A humanist and a generous patron of the arts, Francis I negotiated with Erasmus to establish the Collège de France, a French academy. Despite his humanist principles, he ordered the slaughter of French Protestants after a Lutheran indiscreetly posted a religious bulletin on his bedroom door.

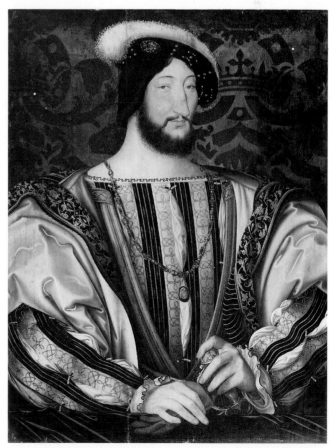

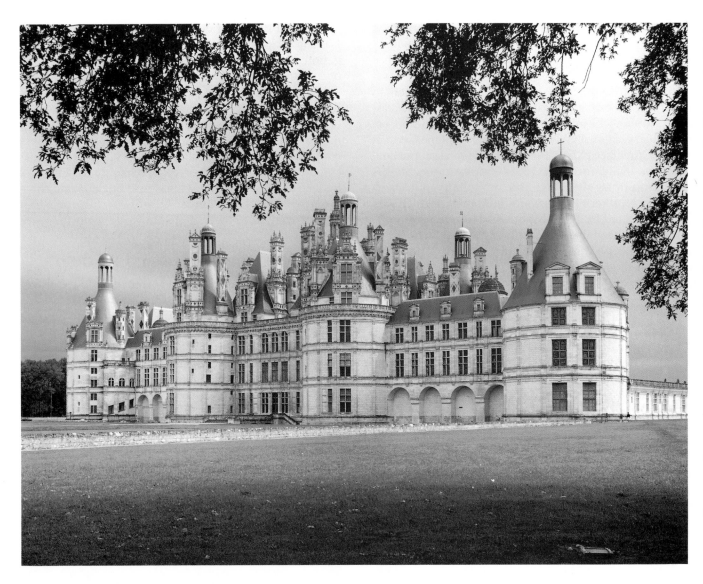

9.4 Château de Chambord, France, begun 1529 to the designs of Domenico da Cortona and Trinqueau: façade (above) and plan (right).
The simplicity of the residence's round turrets with their cupolas is compromised by the irregular eruptions of dormers and chimneys. Note the continuous moldings and balustrades that unify the building's central portion. The plan is symmetrical and unified.

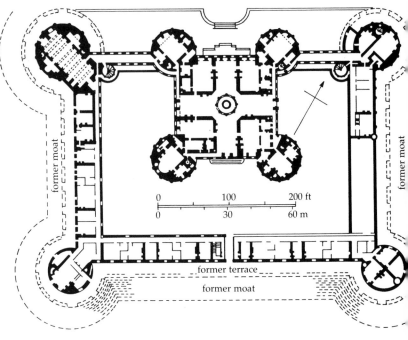

former moat

former moat

former terrace

former moat

0   100   200 ft

0   30   60 m

WINDOW ON DAILY LIFE

A MIDWIFE'S ADVICE

Diane de Poitiers [dee-AHN duh PWAT-ee-ay] was famed for her beauty and influence, as cherished companion of King Henry II of France (ruled 1547–59), but also for her skills in medicine and midwifery. Here she gives advice about a wet nurse to the infant prince of France, the Duke of Orleans.

Madame my ally, I am well pleased about what has happened at Blois, and that you are in good health; as to that which I am overseeing, you would do well to do what is necessary there. The King and Queen are writing to you concerning the health of monsieur d'Orléans, and also to see whether the wet nurse has milk as good as required. For here they say that it is not good and that it upsets him, on account of which it seems to me that you would do well to investigate the situation, and if she is not good, to hire another for him. And I believe that if her milk has worsened since I saw her, it is because she has not conducted herself as she should have. It seems to me that if you make her drink cider or beer, that should refresh her thoroughly. I think that the doctors would agree with me on this. I trust you to put all this in good order....[1]

DIANE DE POITIERS
May 20, 1551

Italian mannerist painters to his court. Henry VIII favored the German portraitist Hans Holbein [HOHL-bine], native of the vibrant Renaissance city of Augsburg.

While Northern Renaissance kings engaged in substantial building programs, their architecture generally retained its medieval character. The most truly Renaissance building of this period was Francis I's château at Chambord [shan(h)-BOH(r)] (Fig. **9.4**), also in the Loire valley. Chambord's busy mass of roof dormers, chimneys, and turrets suggests medieval haphazardness. The decorative details, however, are borrowed from Italian Renaissance models and the floor plan reveals an Italian Renaissance heart. Framed in the shape of a Greek cross, like Michelangelo's plan for St. Peter's (see Fig. 8.46), the château had large stairwells at each corner and a modular plan for interior rooms. Chambord was rare because an Italian

architect had planned it from the beginning. More typical was the château at Fontainebleau, to which Francis simply attached an Italian-style façade.

THE REFORMATION

Summarize the beliefs which led Protestantism to separate from the Roman Catholic faith.

The people of sixteenth-century Germany had survived war and plague, but one burden seemed inescapable: the unending pursuit of salvation through confession and penance. For many, repentance became an empty ritual: prosperous citizens could simply purchase papal documents that guaranteed the forgiveness of sins. In need of revenue for its building projects, the Roman Church was all too eager to offer salvation for sale.

In 1517, few Germans – least of all the monkish scholar Martin Luther (1483–1546) – wanted to cure this hypocrisy of confession by killing the patient. Yet, Luther's challenge to the Roman Church exploded into a religious revolt. Inspired by Luther's broadsheets and pamphlets, the common people of Germany rallied to the religious barricades. They fervently echoed his call for freedom from Rome's tyranny and a return to the true faith of the Bible.

Luther's challenge inspired the sixteenth-century religious movement called the **Reformation**, which split Western Christianity into the Roman Catholic and the new Protestant faiths. For a thousand years, the Roman Catholic Church had been the supreme unifying force in Western civilization. The Reformation shattered that unity, by breaking with the Catholic Church and spawning many "reformed" creeds, whose followers were called **Protestants** because of their protest against Catholic doctrine. The Reformation's effects were broader than the Church itself. Theologically, the Reformation revived the Christian debate over free will and human nature. Intellectually, it elaborated the ideas of Christian humanist scholars, although reformers and humanists sharply disagreed on some issues. Socially, the Reformation appealed to a German people who resented the Catholic Church's heavy taxation. Martin Luther's revolt touched every aspect of European life.

THE WRITE IDEA

State, as clearly as you can, your five most fundamental beliefs about the nature of the divine, the nature of human beings, and their relationship with each other. Do your beliefs have anything in common with Lutheran ideas?

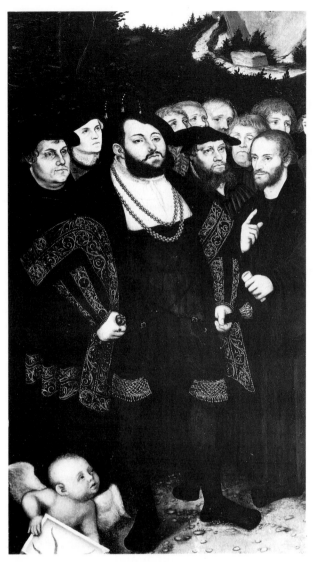

9.5 Lucas Cranach the Younger, *Martin Luther and the Wittenberg Reformers*, c. 1543. Oil on wood, 27⁵/₈ x 15⁵/₈ ins (70 x 40 cm). Toledo Museum of Art, Toledo, Ohio, purchased with funds from the Libbey Endowment, gift of Edward Drummond Libbey.
Martin Luther (left) stands behind his political protector, Frederick the Wise, Elector of Saxony. The German princes and cities who harbored reform resented the heavy taxes paid to the Church in Rome.

LUTHER'S CHALLENGE

In 1517 Luther published his ninety-five theses (see page 227) questioning the theological basis for the sale of indulgences – written guarantees of forgiveness stamped by the pope's own seal. Within months, German printers made Luther's dry theological argument a bestseller.

The theological challenge to the Roman Church was stated in the motto *"Scriptura sola, fide sola, gratia sola"* ("Only scripture, only faith, only grace"). Luther insisted

that Christian faith be based on the words of the Bible. He rejected every aspect of the Catholic faith that had no biblical authority, including the holy sacraments, the celibacy of priests, and the authority of the pope. Luther also rejected the notion of earning salvation. He quoted the apostle Paul: "For by grace are you saved by faith; and that not of yourselves; it is the gift of God: not of works, lest any man should boast" (Galatians 2:16). If salvation was a gift of divine grace, then Christian believers did not need the Catholic Church and its burden of offerings, confession, and penance.

Luther's message of religious freedom and nationalism was published in three pamphlets in 1520. In the first pamphlet, Luther pleaded with Germany's princes to reform the Church and asserted the individual believer's right to appeal directly to God, without a priest as intermediary. In another tract, titled *Treatise on Christian Liberty* (1520), he declared that Christian believers were bound only to the word of God, not to the doctrines and institutions of the Church. By the end of 1520, Luther's writ-

First Phrase of Chorale

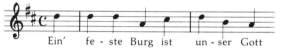

Opening Tenor Phrase of Cantata

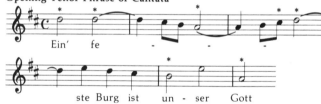

9.6 Martin Luther, opening measures of *Ein' feste Burg ist unser Gott (A Mighty Fortress Is Our God)*, a popular Lutheran hymn.
Hymns based on simple melodies and written in German helped involve Protestant congregations more directly in worship.

ings had sold more than three hundred thousand copies, a figure that attests to Luther's popularity and to the literacy of his German followers.

A generation earlier, such a brash reformer would quickly have been burned at the stake. Luther, however, was saved by circumstance. In Rome, Pope Leo X was too busy with his artistic projects to bother with this "monkish squabble." Also, Church authorities hesitated to anger Luther's political sponsor, a powerful German noble (Fig. **9.5**). When finally, in 1521, Luther was threatened with excommunication, he burned the papal edict in Wittenberg's town square. Summoned to a trial before the Holy Roman Emperor, Luther entered the city of Worms [vorms] like a conquering hero – walls were plastered with his portrait and pamphlets. To the demands that he recant, Luther replied with the simple words: "I neither can nor will recant anything, since it is neither right nor safe to act against conscience. God help me. Amen." Luther had defied the powers of the Church and was outlawed by the Emperor Charles V. Leaving Worms, Luther was seized by agents of his political protector and taken into hiding, where he translated the New Testament into German.

THE APPEAL OF THE REFORMATION

Luther's challenge was theological in its substance, but political and social in its appeal. His writings contained an underlying message of freedom and equality: that God offered divine grace equally to rich and poor, clergy and lay, and that believers could speak directly to God and interpret the Bible themselves. Such radical ideas had unforeseen consequences in Germany. Luther's ideas helped to inspire peasant revolts that German rulers bloodily suppressed, with Luther's tacit approval.

Protestantism also succeeded in making the Christian faith accessible to the common believer. Luther translated the New Testament into ordinary German, enabling a pious Lutheran family to read the Bible in their own language. For Protestant worship, Luther wrote simple hymns such as *Ein' feste Burg ist unser Gott* (*A Mighty Fortress is Our God*) (Fig. **9.6**), based on familiar popular melodies. Thus, instead of listening to a remote choir singing Latin polyphony, Lutheran congregations could sing their own hymns of piety and nationalism.

The Reformation also appealed to Europe's humanist intellectuals, who recognized their own ideas in Luther's doctrines. Protestantism echoed the humanist criticism of religious corruption and ignorance, and it shared humanists' interest in studying and translating ancient texts. Humanists also approved of Luther's preference for simple piety over the Church's quibbling scholasticism and elaborate ritual. At the same time, reformers and humanists differed on crucial philosophical points. Where the humanists asserted the nobility of the human spirit, Luther insisted (in the tradition of Augustine) that humans could not achieve goodness by their own effort. For Luther, human freedom led straight to moral damnation.

CALVINISM

A second wave of Protestant successes originated in Geneva, the Swiss city where John Calvin (Fig. **9.7**) emerged as a new leader of the Reformation. John Calvin (1509–64) was a Reformation thinker of precision and subtlety, and a reformer whose influence was felt in France, Scotland, England, and America. The French-born Calvin received a humanist training in the works of classical and early Christian authors. Because of his radically Protestant views, he was forced to leave predominantly Catholic France, and

settled in Geneva, which welcomed his strict moral teachings. Calvin's *Institutes of the Christian Religion* (1536) defined Protestant doctrine and became the Reformation's most widely read theological work. It elaborated the principle of **predestination**, the belief that God determines before their birth which Christians will gain salvation. If believers could not affect their destiny by good works ("by faith alone," cried Luther), then God must designate the saved before birth. Calvin's idea had political consequences. He asserted that God's righteous elect were justified in opposing civil authority, whenever a king's decree contradicted God's higher law. This radical belief contributed to a wave of European political rebellions over the next two centuries.

In Geneva, Calvin instituted a moral regime that prohibited dancing, drinking, and dissent. His government established "Blue Laws" that regulated the city's taverns and employed a cadre of civic informers and spies.

9.7 The reformer John Calvin, here shown in his study holding a copy of his *Institutes of the Christian Religion*.

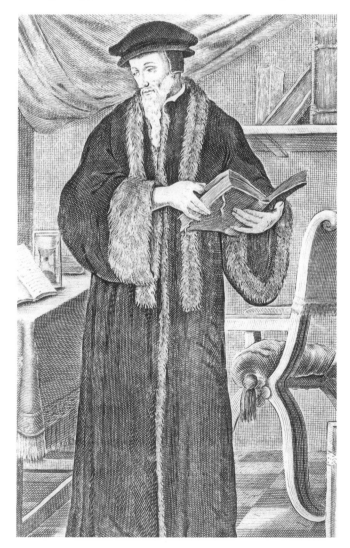

KEY CONCEPT

THE "PROTESTANT ETHIC": GOD, WORK, AND WEALTH

The Reformation's success among the prospering town-dwellers of northern Europe created an apparent paradox. Enterprising Protestant merchants and artisans busily enriched themselves, while they condemned the greed of priests and popes. In modern times, the sociologist Max Weber coined the term **Protestant ethic** to describe the ascetic industriousness encouraged by Calvinist theology. In his controversial study *The Protestant Ethic and the Spirit of Capitalism* (1904), Weber argued that the Calvinists' single-minded effort and self-denial helped nurture northern Europe's budding capitalist economy.

The Protestant ethic was rooted in the anxieties brought on by Calvinist religious ideas. If believers could not earn salvation, Weber asked, how could they know if they belonged to God's "elect" – those destined for salvation and everlasting life? The Calvinists' answer, said Weber, was to define hard work and wealth as the visible signs of election. Thus, wealth was a sign of God's blessing, so long as it was not misused in idleness, leisure, or the spontaneous enjoyment of material possessions. This Protestant ethic, with its mixture of acquisitiveness and asceticism (Fig. 9.8), encouraged small-scale capitalism and may have contributed to Protestants' material success.

The English Puritans who migrated to North America brought this Calvinist attitude with them. Today many people will recognize it in some North Americans' approval of a strong work ethic and disapproval of a life of contemplation or pleasure-seeking.

Weber's thesis has been discounted by modern sociologists, however, because it proved no causal relation between Calvinist doctrine and economic behavior. It is true that capitalist economies have succeeded mightily in such places as Hong Kong and Japan, where acquisitiveness and asceticism stem from Eastern religions, not Calvinism. Yet the essential features of Weber's Protestant work ethic – work, self-denial, the moral virtue of wealth – are still visible in attitudes and behavior today, and maintain a form of religious significance.

THE WRITE IDEA

Describe your own attitudes toward work and material success. What influences have instilled those attitudes in you? What religious associations or overtones can you detect in your own work ethic?

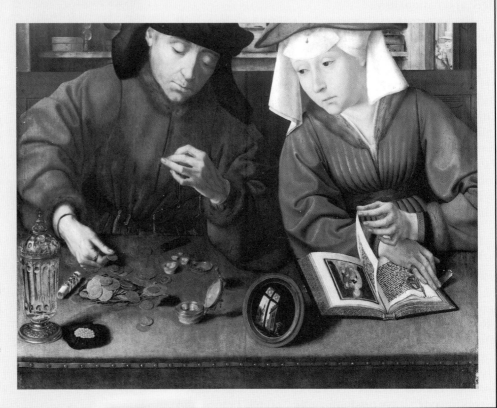

9.8 Quentin Massys, *Moneychanger and His Wife*, 1514. Oil on wood, 28 x 26³/₄ ins (71 x 68 cm). Louvre, Paris.
In this Renaissance portrait, the husband counts his gold and the wife turns pages of her devotional.

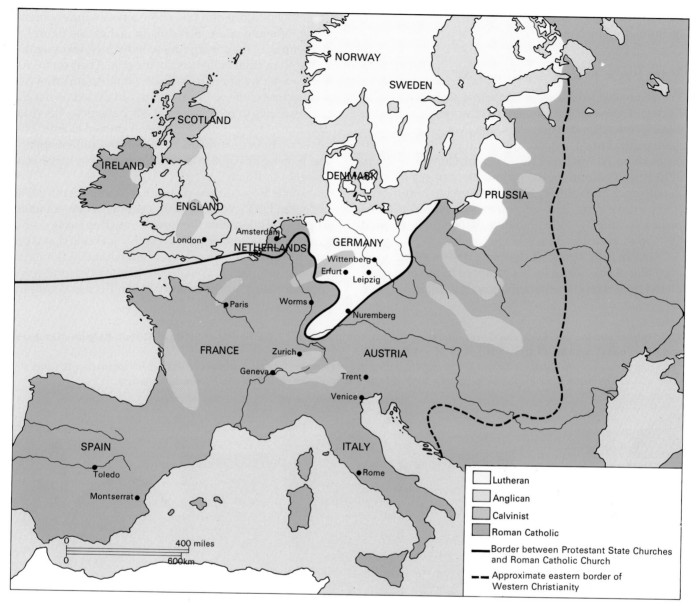

9.9 Religious divisions in 16th-century Europe.

Confident of their predestined place in paradise and busy with God's work on earth, most Genevans submitted willingly to an exceptionally rigid and intolerant social discipline. Ironically, Calvinist sects suffered persecution elsewhere in Europe. By the second half of the sixteenth century, bloody religious wars had spread to most of northern Europe (Fig. **9.9**).

CRITICAL QUESTION

In today's society, who ought to be responsible for the moral regulation of community life? From what sources and principles should we derive laws that govern moral behavior?

PAINTING IN NORTHERN EUROPE

Compare the Renaissance painters of northern Europe, in style and subject, with the masters of the Italian Renaissance.

Northern European painters of the fifteenth century at first paid little attention to the revolutionary innovations of the Italian Renaissance. Northern painters were more interested in an intense visual realism than in the Italian tendency toward intellectual unity and depth of idea. Although some northern artists did adopt aspects of classical humanism, by the late sixteenth century it was Italy's turn to be influenced by Northern Renaissance painting.

Van Eyck's Visual Realism

The acknowledged master of northern realism was Jan van Eyck (*c.* 1390–1441), a Flemish painter who excelled in jewel-like detail and vivid colors. Van Eyck's masterpieces were painted in oil, usually applied to wood. As a painting medium, oil was better suited to achieving subtle effects of light and color than the technique of fresco used by Renaissance Florentines. Also, the churches of northern Europe were more often decorated with elaborate altarpieces – painted wooden cabinets that could be opened for display and closed for storage.

Jan van Eyck's greatest altarpiece was the *Ghent Altarpiece* (Fig. **9.10**), begun by his brother Hubert and completed by himself. The panels depicting Adam and Eve

(Fig. **9.11**), credited to Jan, show a new subtlety in handling light and space. Standing in niches, the figures are presented as they would be seen by a viewer standing at the altar, from below and to the side. Their torsos turn to recede backward into the space, while Adam's foot steps forward out of the niche. Although van Eyck does not glorify his nudes in the manner of Michelangelo, his Adam and Eve bear no trace of medieval sin and shame. Their naturalism of gesture and subtle three-dimensionality make them the equal of any nudes painted in Renaissance Florence or Rome.

While Masaccio was pioneering pictorial depth in Florence, van Eyck's portraits demonstrated a new command of pictorial detail in the Low Countries (today's Belgium and the Netherlands). Van Eyck excelled as a portraitist for wealthy nobles and merchants. Like Italian painters, he often incorporated his patrons' faces into scenes of religious significance. In 1434 van Eyck was commis-

9.10 Hubert and Jan van Eyck, the *Ghent Altarpiece* (open), completed 1432. Cathedral of St. Bavo, Ghent, Belgium. Tempera and oil on panel, approx. 11 ft x 15 ft 1 in (3.35 x 4.6 m).
The upper portion of this altarpiece depicts Christ reigning among the heavenly host; below, a pageant of worshipers approaches to adore the Lamb of God. The subtle detail of Flemish oil painting inspired hasty and avid imitation among Italian Renaissance artists.

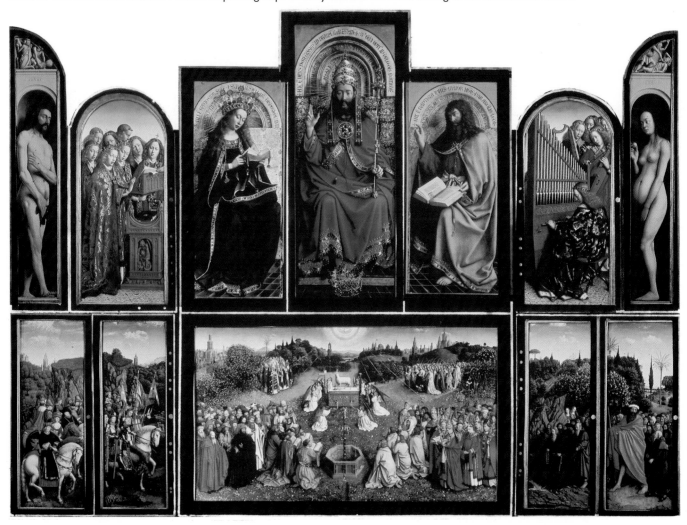

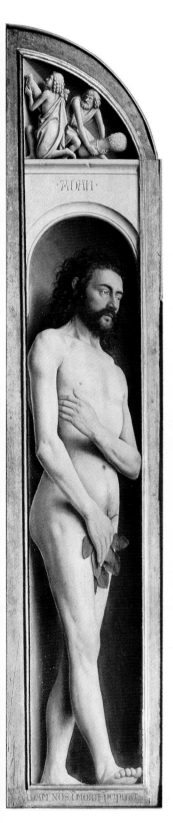
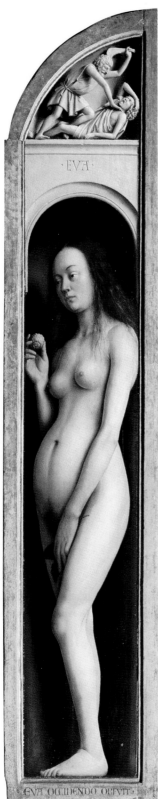

9.11 Left **Jan van Eyck, *Adam and Eve*, detail of the *Ghent Altarpiece*, completed 1432. Cathedral of St. Bavo, Ghent, Belgium. Tempera and oil on panel, each panel 6 ft 8 ins x 18 ins (2.04 x 32 cm).**
The figures are contained within cleverly lighted architectural niches. How do the scenes of Cain and Abel (above; see Genesis 4) relate symbolically to Adam and Eve?

9.12 Below **Jan van Eyck, *Marriage of Giovanni Arnolfini and Giovanna Cenami*, 1434. Oil on panel, 33 x 22¹/₂ ins (84 x 57 cm). National Gallery, London.**
The portrait, which served as a pictorial wedding certificate, shows the couple surrounded by symbols of fidelity and fertility.

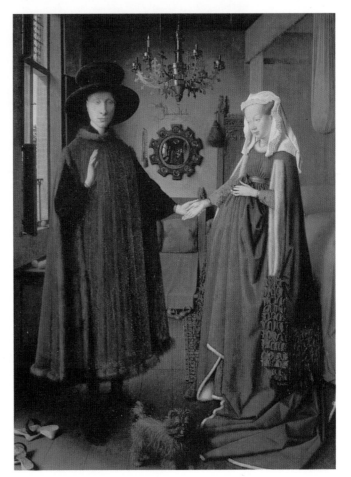

sioned to paint the *Marriage of Giovanni Arnolfini and Giovanna Cenami* (Fig. **9.12**). Van Eyck surrounded the shrewd merchant Arnolfini and his demure young wife with symbols of their matrimony, each painted with a jeweler's precision. The dog represents marital fidelity.

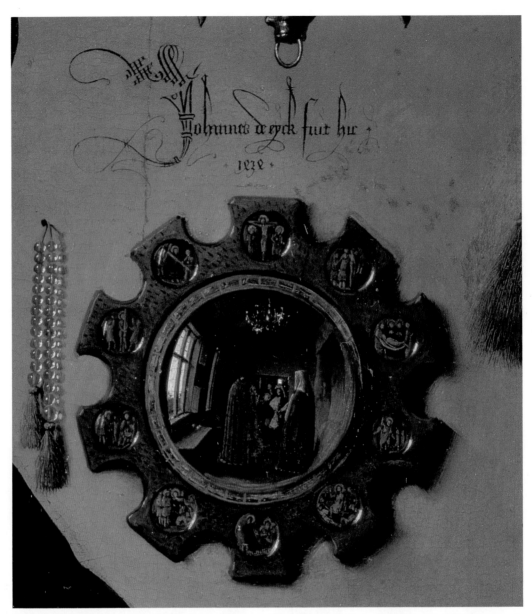

9.13 Jan van Eyck, detail of *Marriage of Giovanni Arnolfini and Giovanna Cenami*, 1434. National Gallery, London.
The painter van Eyck serves as witness to the rite of marriage, depicting himself in the mirror and signing the picture "Jan van Eyck was here, 1434." The mirror frame underscores the painting's theme of sacred devotion (it depicts scenes of Christ's last hours). The mirror also enhances the sense of perspective in the compact room, providing a vanishing point for the sharply angled lines of the window frame and bed.

The single candle may stand for the one true light of Christ, who blesses their union. The fruit symbolizes the fertility that the newly-weds hope will grace their wedding bed, which is hung in a vibrant red. A convex mirror on the back wall reflects the entire room (Fig. **9.13**), including the artist and an assistant standing in the doorway. No painter of his day could rival van Eyck's mastery of light, color, and pictorial space.

FAITH AND HUMANISM IN THE NORTHERN ARTS

As northern painters absorbed the lessons of the Italian revolution in painting, some maintained a religious mood of medieval intensity. This combination of Renaissance technique and Gothic mood is visible in such works as Matthias Grünewald's *Crucifixion* (Fig. **9.14**), a panel of the *Isenheim Altarpiece*. Grünewald [GRYOO-nuh-vahlt] (1475?–1528) portrays the agonized figure of Christ as pocked by the effects of the bubonic plague (the altarpiece was commissioned by a monastery that cared for plague victims). His tortured figure communicates an intense piety and almost grotesque emotionalism that belong to the Northern Renaissance sensibility.

The first genuinely humanist artist of the Northern Renaissance was the German Albrecht Dürer (1471–1528), a master painter and graphic artist who also wrote treatises on pictorial technique. Dürer [DYOO-ruh(r)] was trained as an engraver in the imperial city of Nuremberg, a center of Germany's thriving printing trade. However, the young artist was not satisfied as an artisan who dutifully executed his patrons' orders. Like Leonardo da Vinci and the other Italian masters, he wanted to exalt the artist's standing as a thinker and creator. Dürer traveled twice to Italy, where he embraced Italian theories of proportion and perspective. He envied the prestige of his Italian counterparts – from Venice he wrote a German colleague, "Here I am a gentleman; there I am a parasite."[2] More than the Italian Renaissance masters, Dürer praised the artist as genius and justified the artist's vocation. In the drafts

for his book on proportion, Dürer echoed the humanist enthusiasm of Pico (see page 193):

Through instruction we would like to be competent in many things, and would not tire thereof, for nature has implanted in us the desire of knowing all *things . . . If we want to sharpen our reason by learning and to practice ourselves therein, having once found the right path we may, step by step, seek, learn, comprehend, and finally reach and attain unto some of the truth.*[3]

9.14 Matthias Grünewald, *Crucifixion,* **exterior panel from the** *Isenheim Altarpiece,* **completed 1515. Oil on panel, 8 ft x 10 ft 1 ins (2.44 x 3.07 m). Musée d'Unterlinden, Colmar, Germany.**
John the Baptist (right) points to the sacrifice of Christ while Mary Magdalene (kneeling) and the Virgin Mary, supported by the apostle John, mourn the tortured Christ. The *Agnus Dei* (Lamb of God) stands over the chalice which will hold the sacrificial blood of Christ.

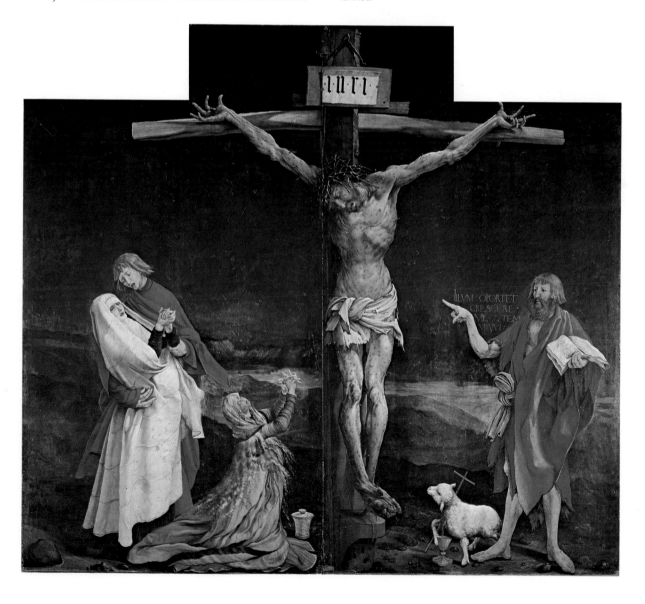

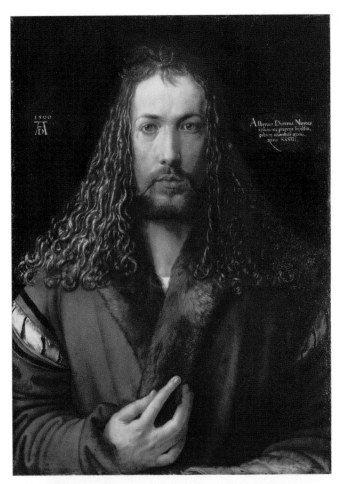

9.15 Albrecht Dürer, *Self-Portrait in a Fur-collared Robe*, 1500. Oil on panel, 26¹/₄ x 19¹/₄ ins (67 x 49 cm). Alte Pinakothek, Munich.
The long fingers of the right hand draw attention not only to the collar's delicate texture but also to the hand itself, the repository of Dürer's painting skill. The inscription says "I, Albrecht Dürer, painted myself with everlasting colors in my twenty-eighth year."

Dürer portrayed himself with a self-absorption bordering on vanity. In *Self-portrait in a Fur-collared Robe* (Fig. **9.15**), the artist's flowing hair and thoughtful face suggest an image of Christ, an idea reinforced by the subdued colors and pyramid-like composition, which lend the image a religious solemnity. Yet Dürer painted the beard and fur collar with a precision characteristic of Jan van Eyck.

Dürer achieved widest success in his woodcuts and engravings – graphic arts associated with the rise of the printing press. In sixteenth-century Europe, woodcuts and engravings had the immediacy of today's photography and video, and were frequently used as weapons in the age's political and religious controversies. For example, Dürer's engraving *Knight, Death, and the Devil* (Fig. **9.16**), may be an illustration of the works of Luther or Erasmus, a Dutch contemporary of Luther and the leading Christian humanist of northern Europe. The resolute Christ-

ian knight sits astride a well-proportioned horse. He shows no fear of Death at his side – holding an hourglass – or of the grotesque devil at his rear – disguised as a wild boar. The celestial city of God rises atop a mountain landscape behind him. The city may symbolize the inner moral virtue that is protected by the knight's armor. Dürer's scene of militant piety recalls the words of Erasmus in his *Handbook of the Christian Knight*, written ten years earlier:

> *We must forge a handy weapon, an* enchiridon, *a dagger, that you can always carry with you. You must be on guard when you eat or sleep, even when you travel in the course of worldly concerns and perhaps become weary of bearing this righteous armor. Never allow yourself to be totally disarmed, even for a moment, lest your wily foe oppress you.*[4]

As this engraving suggests, Dürer actively involved himself in the intellectual controversies of his day, supporting the humanist Erasmus and sympathizing with Luther. When his native city of Nuremberg converted to

9.16 Albrecht Dürer, *Knight, Death, and the Devil*, 1513. Engraving, 9³/₄ x 7¹/₂ ins (25 x 19 cm).
The symbolism of this engraving is obscure. The dog may represent loyalty or vigilance, while the salamander customarily symbolized a creature invulnerable to fire. Some have speculated that the salamander and the "S" in the monogram allude to Savonarola, burned at the stake in Florence in 1498 (Fig. 8.25).

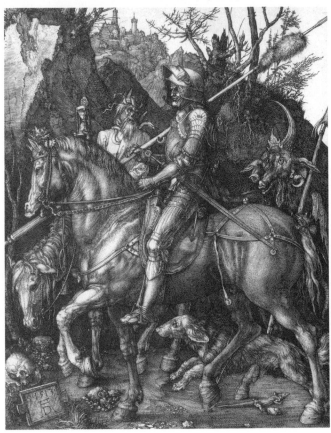

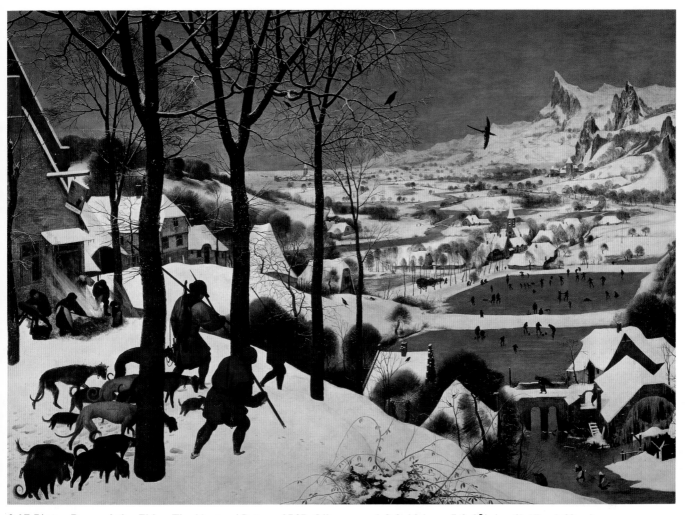

9.17 Pieter Bruegel the Elder, *The Hunters' Return*, 1565. Oil on panel, 3 ft 10 ins x 5 ft 3³/₄ ins (1.17 x 1.62 m). Kunsthistorisches Museum, Vienna.
This painting was one of a series of calendar paintings, a medieval pictorial tradition. Analyze the relations among the returning hunters, their village, and the natural world, as depicted in the painting's complex composition.

Lutheranism, Dürer presented to it a large portrait called the *Four Apostles* that was inscribed with quotations from Luther's German Bible. Few other artists of the Renaissance showed such sensitivity to the intellectual and artistic currents that swirled around them.

PIETER BRUEGEL: PAINTER OF COUNTRY LIFE

In contrast to Dürer, Pieter Bruegel (*c.* 1525–69) showed little interest in Italian technique and humanist debate. Bruegel [BROY-gull] expressed a profound affection for natural beauty and the simple life of Flemish peasants. At the same time, he chose to paint landscapes and scenes of daily life in part because of Protestant hostility to religious art. His worldly subjects and attitude make Pieter Bruegel the North's first important post-Reformation painter.

Bruegel was fascinated by the lives of common folk and their relationship to the land. An early biographer told how the painter disguised himself as a peasant to join in village festivals. He depicted common people in many **genre** pictures, or scenes of daily life. However, besides their rustic charm, Bruegel's genre scenes often achieved a breathtaking perspective and philosophical sophistication. In *The Hunters' Return* (Fig. **9.17**), the failure of the hunt is evident in the dogs' drooping tails. In emotional contrast, a group on the left prepares to slaughter a hog, a promise of feasting and gaiety. From this foreground action, the eye follows the trees down the hill to the skaters below. The distant skaters are oblivious to the returning hunters and seem insignificant against the vast winter landscape. A single bird floats across the sky, unifying the human drama with the timeless Alpine peaks in the upper right. Compared to much Renaissance painting, *The Hunters' Return* is notable for the absence of religious themes. Bruegel

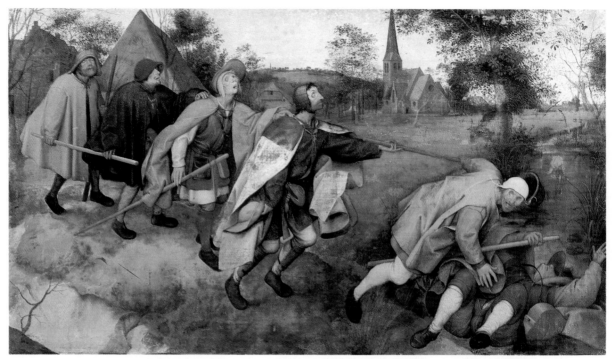

9.18 Pieter Bruegel the Elder, *The Parable of the Blind*, 1568. Tempera on canvas, approx. 34 x 68 ins (86 x 173 cm). Museo Nazionale, Naples.
Note the falling diagonal line of action in this picture, in contrast to the rising diagonal in *The Hunters' Return.* The parable concerns a dispute between Christ and the Pharisees over the interpretation of religious rules, a comment perhaps on the religious controversies of the Reformation.

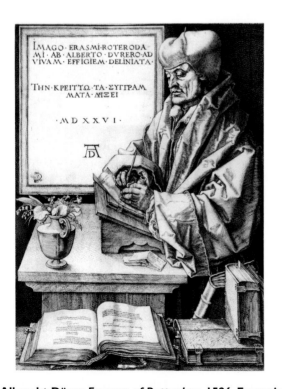

9.19 Albrecht Dürer, *Erasmus of Rotterdam*, 1526. Engraving, 9³/₄ x 7¹/₂ ins (25 x 19 cm). British Museum, London.
Dürer shows Erasmus surrounded by his books, in an attitude of scholarly concentration.

is more interested in the unity of humans and nature than in Christian moral lessons. With his mastery of space and perspective, Bruegel binds his ordinary peasants to the eternal rhythms of the seasons.

Bruegel's insight into the ways of humans often had a sardonic twist. *The Parable of the Blind* (Fig. **9.18**), for example, illustrated Christ's saying to the Pharisees, "And if the blind lead the blind, both shall fall into the ditch" (Matthew 15:14). From the leader who falls pell-mell into the ditch, an abrupt diagonal line of arms and canes leads back to the blissful oblivion of the last blind man to follow. Surely, Bruegel was commenting on spiritual as well as physical blindness. The men's folly contrasts with the peaceful and stable church in the background. The blind men might even represent the religious zealots of Bruegel's century, both Catholic and Protestant, blindly leading each other into folly and destruction.

HUMANISM IN THE NORTH

List the major points of agreement and disagreement between Erasmus and the Reformation.

The most important voice of Northern Renaissance humanism was Desiderius Erasmus (1466–1536; Fig. **9.19**), famed for his learning and satirical wit. Born in the Netherlands, Erasmus was trained early in a simple life of piety and humility based on the Gospels. Ordained as a priest in 1492, he began a campaign to free the Church from corruption and scholastic pretension, while himself pursuing a life of quiet devotion and moral virtue.

Erasmus' translations of classical and biblical texts, along with his satire *In Praise of Folly*, established him as northern Europe's leading intellectual. His fame as a scholar earned him the patronage of Pope Leo X, who praised Erasmus' works even while Church scholars were attacking them. Erasmus refused to take up the Reformation banner, despite his criticism of the Church.

ERASMUS AND SATIRE

Erasmus' best-known work was *In Praise of Folly* (1509), an exposé of the vanity and corruption in Renaissance society. *In Praise of Folly* was the Renaissance's greatest example of **satire**, a work that criticizes society through humorous exaggeration and parody. The book's Latin title, *Encomium Moriae*, is a pun meaning both "praise of Folly" and "praise of More," in tribute to Erasmus' friend and fellow humanist Thomas More (see page 245). Though its author considered the book a trifle, *In Praise of Folly* became immensely popular – in Erasmus' lifetime, it appeared in forty-two Latin editions and in English and German translations.

In Praise of Folly takes aim at the hypocrisy and vanity of Renaissance society, and contrasts its vices with the inner piety and moral striving that lead to Christian salvation. Speaking in the satirical voice of Folly, Erasmus rails against the folly of war, especially as practiced by warrior popes such as Julius II. Folly reserves her most biting criticism for Erasmus' constant adversaries, the scholastic theologians. In the author's view, the pretensions of the scholastics kept them from true piety. Folly suggests that study of the Bible itself should replace scholastic commentaries and Church dogmas. While readers were delighted with Erasmus' mockery of lawyers, merchants, monks, and theologians, his satire earned him intellectual enemies throughout Europe, reason enough for the scholar to seek protection from the pope.

Erasmus' opinion on lawyers: . . . *the most self-satisfied class of people, as they roll their rock of Sisyphus[a] and string together six hundred laws in the same breath, no matter whether relevant or not, piling up opinion on opinion and gloss on gloss to make their profession seem the most difficult of all. Anything which causes trouble has special merit in their eyes.*

On the pope's court: *Countless scribes, clerks, lawyers, advocates, secretaries, muleteers, grooms, bankers and pimps (and I nearly added something rather more suggestive, but I didn't want to offend your ears) – in*

short, an enormous crowd of people now a burden on the Roman See (I'm sorry, I meant "now an honor to") . . .

On scholastic theologians: . . . *so happy in their self-satisfaction and self-congratulation, and so busy night and day with these enjoyable tomfooleries, that they haven't even a spare moment in which to read even once through the gospel or the letters of Paul. And while they're wasting their time in the schools with this nonsense, they believe that just as in the poets Atlas[b] holds up the sky on his shoulders, they support the entire Church on the props of their syllogisms and without them it would collapse.[5]*

ERASMUS
From *In Praise of Folly* (1509)

---

a. Sisyphus [SIZ-i-fuss], the Greek condemned to roll a stone perpetually up a hill.

b. Atlas, the Greek god who supports the sky.

HUMANISM AND THE REFORMATION

Erasmus was a leader of the Christian, or evangelical, humanists, as distinct from the classical humanists of

9.20 Albrecht Dürer, *St. Jerome in His Study*, 1514. Engraving, 9³/₄ x 7³/₈ ins (24.7 x 18.8 cm).
The fourth-century scholar and translator St. Jerome was considered the patron saint of Christian humanism, a model of scholarship and humility. Dürer had never seen a real lion.

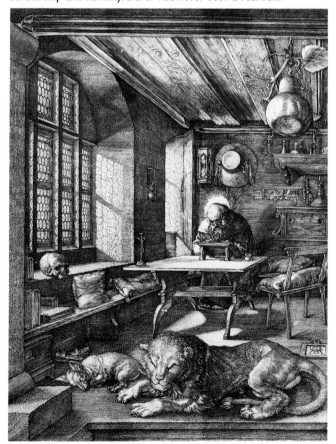

the Italian Renaissance. Christian humanists were chiefly concerned with the translation of biblical manuscripts and the writings of the early Church fathers, such as St. Jerome (Fig. **9.20**). In 1516, Erasmus made a revolutionary advance by publishing a version of the New Testament in the original Greek, accompanied by his own commentary. Erasmus' Greek Bible exposed substantial errors in the Church's official Latin translation, and Church scholars vigorously attacked it as a threat to the Church's religious authority.

Despite his differences with the Church, Erasmus remained distant from Martin Luther's reforms, for reasons of both philosophy and self-preservation – Erasmus' patrons all opposed Luther. Philosophically, Erasmus held the humanist view that people were, by free acts of will, able to improve themselves morally. Luther, on the other hand, saw humans as absolutely dependent on God's grace for salvation. Erasmus finally voiced his disagreement with Luther in a critical treatise entitled *De libero arbitrio* (*On the Freedom of the Will*, 1524), which challenged Luther's fundamental belief in human sinfulness. Luther replied with his own pamphlet, pointedly titled *De servo arbitrio* (*On the Slavery of the Will*), which argued that nothing good came through human freedom. Erasmus agreed with the reformers that God's word was supreme and that piety was more important than good works. But he never abandoned his Catholic faith or his belief in human freedom and self-determination.

Montaigne Where Erasmus prized piety and humility, the Renaissance humanist Michel de Montaigne (1533–92) practiced skepticism and an unflinching self-examination. Montaigne [mohn(h)-TEN(y)] was born to a noble family in Bordeaux (in southwest France), received an exemplary humanist education, and served as a courtier and advisor. In 1571, however, he retired to his family home and began to write his *Essais* (*Essays*; 1580, 1588), conversational and introspective prose works that defined a new literary type: the **essay**.

Montaigne's essays were uniquely personal, full of anecdote and self-observation and ranging over every topic of concern to him – friendship, religious toleration, death, nature. Montaigne's most famous essay, *Apology for Raymond Sebond*, questioned the superiority of humans to other creatures, a commonplace of humanist thought. "When I play with my cat, who knows if I am not a pastime to her more than she is to me?" he asks in a

---

THE WRITE IDEA

In outline form, describe the perfect society as you envision it. How does your utopia reflect your beliefs and values as a person?

CRITICAL QUESTION

Are you inclined, like Erasmus, to remain loyal to groups or institutions that you recognize are sometimes flawed? Or are you, like Montaigne, basically skeptical about commitment and belief?

---

famous illustration. Montaigne's skepticism toward the Renaissance's intellectual pretensions led him to rely chiefly on his own experience and observation – a starting point for the scientific attitude that would revolutionize European thought in the coming centuries.

THE ELIZABETHAN AGE

Describe the social and religious circumstances in England that contributed to the success of Elizabethan theater.

England was able to match the Renaissance achievements of Italy and Germany only in the late sixteenth century. By this time, navigational inventions such as the telescope had helped to expand England's maritime economy, while agricultural production had also increased. The new prosperity and political stability maintained by the English monarchy created the conditions for a renaissance in England. Although influenced by European fashions, it achieved its own artistic and philosophical expression in music and theater.

THE REFORMATION IN ENGLAND

The English Reformation began as a political dispute that resulted in religious schism. King Henry VIII (ruled 1509–47) appealed to the pope to dissolve his marriage with Catherine of Aragon, which had produced no male heir. When the pope refused, Henry split with the Roman Church, and established himself as head of the Anglican (English) Church, enabling him to divorce his wife by his own decree. He also confiscated monastic lands, and sold them at a large profit. While rejecting papal authority, the Anglican Church maintained its Catholic religious beliefs and vigorously opposed Lutheranism. The English king even-handedly burned Protestants for religious heresy and Catholics for political treason. Under Henry VIII's successors, first Edward VI and then Mary I, Protestant and Catholic factions alternately gained the upper hand, each persecuting their religious opponents.

Finally under Elizabeth I (ruled 1558–1603; Fig. **9.22**), the Anglican faith was reinstated and religious toleration prevailed. Elizabeth demanded outward obedience

KEY CONCEPT

UTOPIA

The evangelical humanists aimed to create a better world, where piety triumphed over corruption. This better world was sketched vividly by Erasmus' humanist friend, the English scholar Thomas More (1477–1535), in his book *Utopia* (1516) – a title which meant literally "no place." More's book describes a fictional island where industrious citizens have solved the problems of war, poverty, and crime. We now apply the term "utopia" to any such fictional description or philosophical theory of a perfect society. Most utopias envision a community of social harmony and justice where human needs are satisfied (Fig. **9.21**).

The island paradise of *Utopia* is a republic of industrious austerity, whose citizens all wear the same plain woolen clothing and go to bed at eight o'clock. Evening lectures offer education and self-improvement. First-time criminals are sentenced to a period of slavery instead of prison, and illicit sexual activity is severely punished, because otherwise, More suggested, no one would have reason to get married. More's Utopia has no money, unlike existing European society, which, according to More, was a "conspiracy of the rich to advance their own interests under the pretext of organizing society."

More's *Utopia* belongs to a tradition of utopian writing that began in classical philosophy. His island society is modeled on *The Republic*, Plato's elaborate description of a perfect Greek city-state. Later utopias stemmed from economic, technological, and psychological theories. The nineteenth-century social theorist Karl Marx envisioned a "classless society" that had abolished private wealth. In *Walden II* (1948), a utopian novel by the twentieth-century psychologist B. F. Skinner, happiness is achieved by behavioral engineering.

The modern era has more often seen anti-utopias, called dystopias, where evil and wretchedness prevail instead of orderly happiness. Fictional works such as George Orwell's novel *1984* (1949) or Anthony Burgess's *A Clockwork Orange* (1962, also a Stanley Kubrick film, 1973) describe a fearsome world of bureaucratic control and sadistic violence.

9.21 Pieter Bruegel the Elder, *Tower of Babel*, c. 1563. Oil on panel, 3 ft 11⁷/₈ ins x 5 ft 1 ins (1.22 x 1.55 m). Kunsthistorisches Museum, Vienna.
This painting shows a vast image of the Tower of Babel, biblical symbol of human vanity. Evaluate the painting as a comment on the Renaissance rulers' construction of grand new palaces and churches.

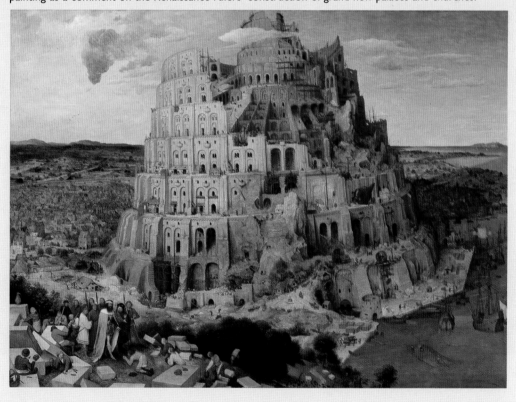

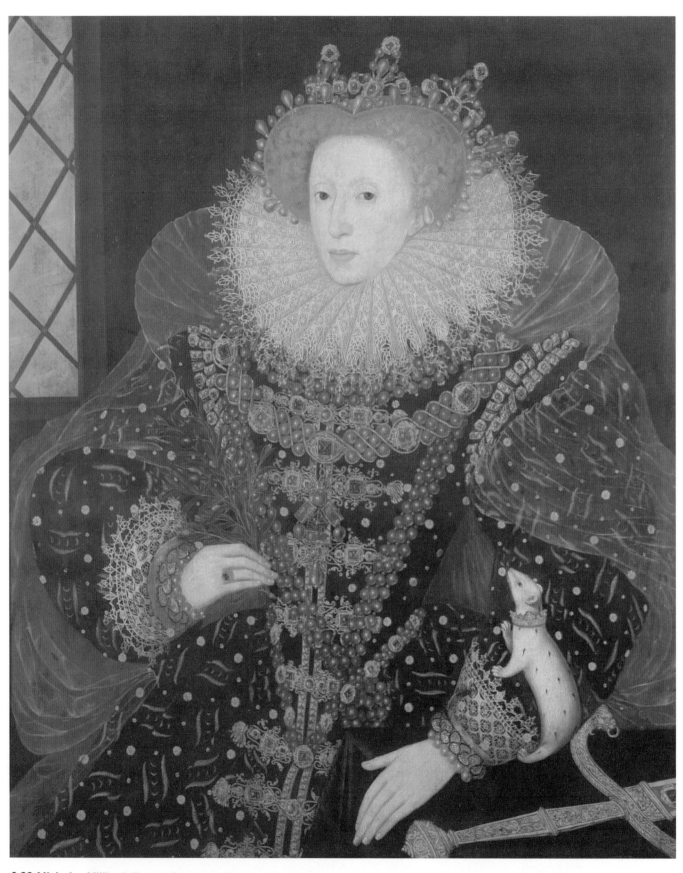

9.22 Nicholas Hilliard, *Ermine Portrait of Queen Elizabeth I*, 1585. Oil on canvas, 41³/₄ x 35 ins (106 x 89 cm). Hatfield House, England. Collection of the Marquess of Salisbury.

As evident from her costume here, the queen loved sumptuous displays of wealth. The ermine on her sleeve is a symbol of Elizabeth's virginity.

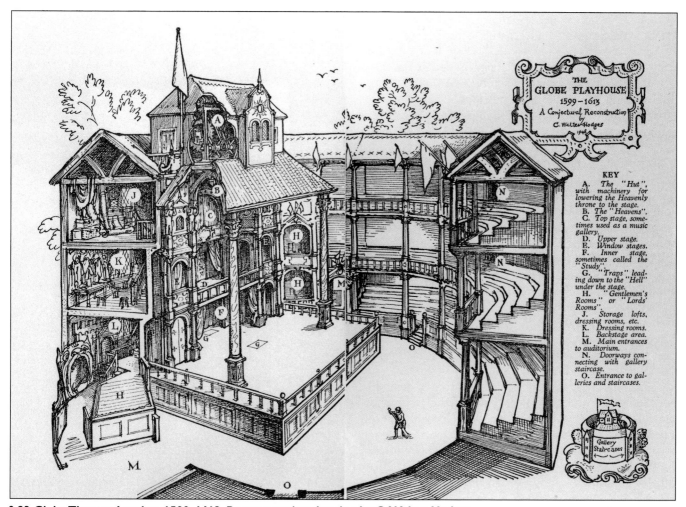

9.23 Globe Theater, London, 1599–1613. Reconstruction drawing by C. Walter Hodges.
Shakespeare's theater was amply provided with stage machinery beneath the roof and a trap door (used in the ghost scene in *Hamlet*). Privileged spectators often sat on the upper stage, where they preened themselves and commented on the play.

to the official Anglican faith, while allowing Catholics to practice their faith secretly. As for the Protestants, Elizabeth frequently suppressed the Puritans, whose Calvinist doctrine threatened royal power. Thus, while the European continent was ravaged by bloody religious wars, England enjoyed relative religious peace, prosperity, and cultural revival – a period known as the Elizabethan Age.

This revival commenced in 1588 with the English naval victory over Spain, which boosted England's national spirit and maritime economy. At the same time, refugees from Europe's religious wars fled to English cities, joining the flood of peasants displaced from the countryside. London, the site of Elizabeth's lavish and pleasure-loving court, swelled with new inhabitants and became the capital of Elizabethan civilization.

THEATER IN THE ELIZABETHAN AGE

One art thrived above all others in Elizabethan times: the theater. Religious divisions in England's towns had virtually ended the production of medieval drama cycles by the mid-sixteenth century (see page 178). In their place, touring companies of professional actors presented plays in inn courtyards and other makeshift theaters. Actors' companies were often censored by town authorities, who feared for their citizens' morals. To thwart this censorship, acting troupes gained the sponsorship of prominent nobles, who also employed the company to perform at their courts. With a virtual monopoly on theatrical entertainment, the professional companies enjoyed commercial success and produced plays of high literary quality.

The era of prosperity of the Elizabethan theater began in 1576, when the Theatre in London was built. This was the first of London's public theaters, permanent houses whose popular plays attracted a diverse audience. The Theatre was later renamed the Globe (Fig. **9.23**), the famous "wooden O" where many of William Shakespeare's plays were first performed. London's public theaters were built on the Thames River's south bank, where they were free of the city's censorship. Here, theaters were also handy to such alternative entertainments as bear-baiting and prostitution. London's glittering Elizabethan society streamed across the Thames' bridges to see plays there – for a penny admission, even a humble apprentice might see a dramatic spectacle that rivaled those of ancient Rome.

The public theaters reflected the needs of their diverse clientele and the demands of public performance. They were polygonal or circular structures, and could accommodate as many as two thousand spectators. The wealthiest patrons sat comfortably in the galleries, while common playgoers (including a cadre of pickpockets and prostitutes) stood crowded together in the "pit," the area around the stage. Because the stage jutted into the central yard, an actor standing downstage was surrounded on three sides by a noisy audience. Thus, Elizabethan actors favored a declamatory acting style, with broad gestures to demonstrate the character's emotional state. Also, the open-air arrangement of the theaters meant that actors had to be quick enough to finish a long play by dusk.

Elizabethan plays were a lively mixture of dramatic types that drew on both classical and medieval forerunners. Elizabethan comedies were modeled loosely on those of the Roman playwrights Plautus and Terence (see page 90), whose plays were read in Latin by schoolboys such as Shakespeare. Whatever its literary pedigree, Elizabethan comedy contained enough broad humor and slapstick to please the illiterate commoners in the pit. History plays, or chronicles, were also immensely popular in the patriotic aftermath of England's naval victory over the Spanish. The chronicles incorporated elements of the medieval mystery plays, with their panoramic biographies of saints and gory on-stage torture. Elizabethan tragedy borrowed from the Roman Seneca's sensational plots (see page 90), often mixing themes of revenge with a severe Calvinist morality. Late Elizabethan tragedies were often set in Italy, which seemed the perfect setting for political intrigue, murder, and depraved sexuality. With its variety and inventiveness, the theater captured the essence of Elizabethan society, much as Hollywood films' gangsters and love stories captured America in the 1930s and 1940s.

CRITICAL QUESTION

What popular art best captures the essence of North American civilization today? What aspects of this civilization are most clearly mirrored in the art form?

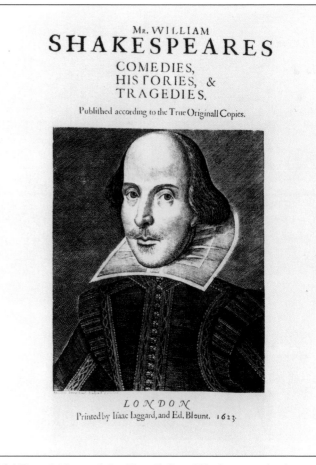

9.24 Frontispiece of the First Folio of Shakespeare's plays, 1623.

Shakespeare cared so little about the literary value of his plays that he retired to Stratford-upon-Avon without publishing them. The first complete edition, with a dedication by Ben Jonson, appeared seven years after Shakespeare's death.

THE GENIUS OF SHAKESPEARE

The most acclaimed dramatist of the English language is William Shakespeare (1564–1616), the genius of Elizabethan theater. Shakespeare was a provincial who, like many Elizabethans, came to London to seek his fortune. He found rich opportunities awaiting him in the theater. By the 1580s, several professional acting companies were well established and the public theaters were a commercial success. Christopher Marlowe (1564–93), Shakespeare's most talented contemporary, had pioneered the verse forms of Elizabethan drama. Marlowe's play *The Historical Tragedy of Doctor Faustus* (first performed 1588) anticipated Shakespeare's great tragedies – such as *Hamlet*, *Macbeth*, *Othello*, and *King Lear* – in its psychological depth and epic sweep. Marlowe's Faustus is motivated by a boundless thirst for knowledge and power, which leads him into a bargain with the devil. The popularity of such

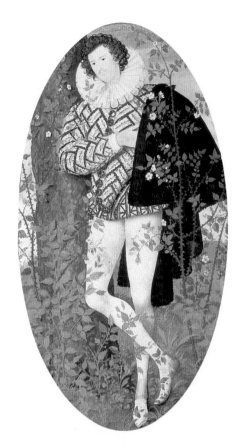

9.25 Nicholas Hilliard, *A Youth Leaning Against a Tree with Roses*, c. 1590. Parchment, 5³/₈ x 2³/₄ ins (14 x 7 cm). Victoria & Albert Museum, London.

works helped create the conditions for Shakespeare's success.

As a dramatist, Shakespeare disdained the classical rules of form favored by his university-trained rivals, who included his younger friend and protégé Ben Jonson (1572–1637). Shakespeare's plays were loosely plotted, with action that sprawled across weeks or even years. Instead of imitating Latin poetry, Shakespeare shaped Elizabethan speech into **blank verse**, using the five-stressed poetic line (pentameter) that in English had both naturalness and dignity. Shakespeare (Fig. **9.24**) may not have been a humanist, but to his contemporaries he was a poet of great humanity.

Shakespeare's Hamlet The play that best reveals Shakespeare's bond to the Renaissance is the tragedy *Hamlet*, the tale of the brooding prince. Called home to Denmark from his university studies, Hamlet is commanded by his father's ghost to avenge his murder at the hands of Hamlet's uncle. The uncle, Claudius, has been elected king and has married Hamlet's mother, the widowed queen. Hamlet is tortured by doubt and disgust, and he delays action by feigning madness. Finally, he orchestrates a duel in which the innocent die along with the guilty.

In *Hamlet*, Shakespeare engages in his own dialogue with leading ideas of the Renaissance. To begin with, young Hamlet is a Renaissance gentleman fashioned after Castiglione's *Book of the Courtier* or Hilliard's *Youth Leaning Against a Tree* (Fig. **9.25**). Hamlet has an abundance of what Castiglione called *sprezzatura*, or accomplished style: he banters wittily with companions, improvises a court drama, and handles a sword with deadly effect. But Hamlet is also touched by the darker Renaissance skepticism of Montaigne, who questions whether humanity is much superior to the animals. Hamlet's famous praise of human nobility turns suddenly to pessimism and disgust:

> *What a piece of work is a man! how noble in reason!*
> *how infinite in faculties! in form and moving, how*
> *express and admirable! in action, how like an angel! in*
> *apprehension, how like a god! the beauty of the world!*
> *the paragon of animals! And yet, to me, what is this*
> *quintessence of dust? man delights not me . . .*[6]

Called to action by his father's ghost, Hamlet is torn between Machiavellian expedience and moral ambiguity. He mocks a rival who, in the spirit of the Machiavellian warrior ideal, is willing to risk fortune and death "even for an egg-shell." Yet, once decided on vengeance, Hamlet readily sacrifices the lives of friends and family to his vendetta.

Hamlet's feigned madness is a metaphor for the conflicting ideals that enliven his character: Renaissance courtliness, rationalist skepticism, and bold action. His beloved, Ophelia (who has been bitterly rejected by Hamlet), describes his conflicted soul in eloquent words.

> *O, what a noble mind is here o'erthrown!*
> *The courtier's, soldier's, scholar's, eye, tongue, sword;*
> *The expectancy and rose of the fair state,*
> *The glass of fashion, and the mould of form,*
> *The observed of all observers, quite, quite down!*
> *And I, of ladies most deject and wretched,*
> *That sucked the honey of his music-vows,*
> *Now see that noble and most sovereign reason,*
> *Like sweet bells jangled, out of time and harsh;*
> *That unmatched form and stature of blown youth,*
> *Blasted with ecstasy:*[a] *O, woe is me!*
> *To have seen what I have seen, see what I see!*[7]

WILLIAM SHAKESPEARE
Hamlet, Act III, Scene i

---

a. ecstasy, madness.

For all its rich philosophical overtones, Shakespeare's *Hamlet* was filled with engaging dramatic action. Educated theater-goers might savor themes of moral corruption and philosophical speculation, whilst the unlettered customer enjoyed a good show of verbal wit, pageantry, and swordplay. *Hamlet* was in every way a paragon of Elizabethan theater.

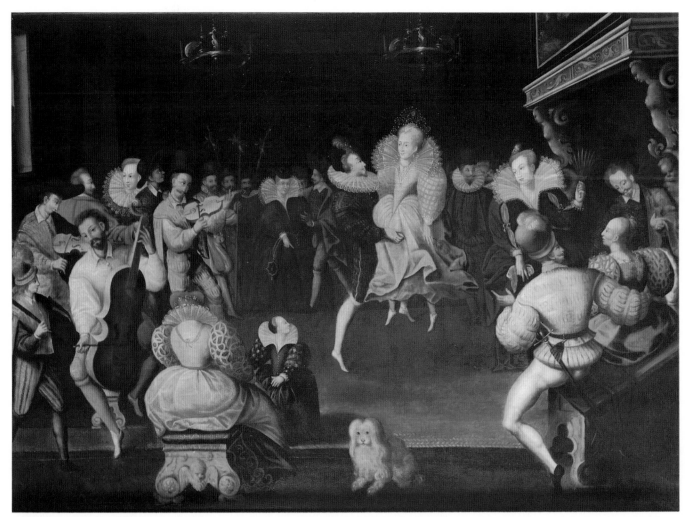

9.26 Anon., *Dancers at the Court of Elizabeth I,* **16th century. Oil on panel, 30 x 40 ins (76.2 x 101.6 cm). Collection Viscount de L'Isle, Penshurst Place, Kent, England. Reproduced by permission of Viscount de L'Isle, from his private collection.**
This courtly couple may be dancing a galliard, a dance with many leaps and kicks. Elizabeth I was an avid dancer and as a child had learned such stylish Italian dances as the lavolta.

ELIZABETHAN MUSIC

Queen Elizabeth admired pageant and festivity, and her royal court was alive with music, dance, mime, and other spectacles (Fig. **9.26**). The Elizabethan court followed the fashion set by Castiglione's *Book of the Courtier* (see page 214). A courtier was expected to play a musical instrument, most likely the lute or virginal (a type of harpsichord favored by the queen), and to join in a vocal ensemble. The most popular songs and dances were imported from Italy but were usually imbued with English vitality.

The Elizabethan court's most gifted and versatile composer was William Byrd (1543?–1623), whose diverse productivity matched Shakespeare's output in drama. As a composer, Byrd was forced to contend with his country's religious divisions; he fended off the Puritans, who considered all sacred music mere "popish" ornament, and wrote music for both the Anglican Church and his own

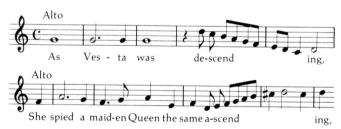

9.27 Thomas Weelkes, "As Vesta Was Descending," from *The Triumphes of Oriana,* **1601.**

Catholic faith. Though he wrote three Catholic masses, these works could not be performed publicly in Protestant England. Byrd also labored in service to royal and noble patrons, for whom he composed music for all occasions. Emulating Shakespeare's versatility in the theater, Byrd excelled in all the musical types, including the motet and the popular madrigal.

The **madrigal** was a secular (i.e. non-religious) form, originally sung in four parts but eventually in five or six. Voices were commonly "doubled" by instruments. In this period, the Italian madrigal was originally inspired by the musical poetry of the Italian humanists and so expressed the Renaissance love of word-painting. Imported to England, the madrigal showed itself equally suited to English songs of love and lament. Elizabethan poets produced witty lyrics for madrigals and other popular songs. Musicians, like the other artists in Elizabethan times, successfully adapted forms borrowed from Italy to the tastes of their English public.

In England, the madrigal fashion arose in the late 1580s, led by composer and publisher Thomas Morley (1557–1602). He lived in the same London district as Shakespeare and set some of the playwright's verse to music. At the height of the madrigal's popularity, Morley published nine volumes of madrigals in seven years. His most famous work was a volume of songs from twenty different composers called *The Triumphes of Oriana* (published 1601). Oriana was a fanciful name for Elizabeth, the "maiden queen." Each of the madrigals ended with the homage "Then sang the shepherds and nymphs of Diana: 'Long live fair Oriana' " (Fig. **9.27**). Music, as any other art, served the cult of royal adulation that surrounded Elizabeth I during her reign.

THE LATE RENAISSANCE IN ITALY

Explain the reasons for the late Renaissance's conservatism in music and theater.

By the middle of the sixteenth century, Renaissance Italy was in political decline. The papacy was jolted by Luther's German revolt and in 1527 suffered the humiliating sack of Rome by Emperor Charles V. Charles' mercenaries plundered the city and stabled their horses in the Sistine Chapel. Renaissance art suffered losses as well. By the end of 1520,

Leonardo and Raphael were dead. Of the High Renaissance masters, only Michelangelo lived on, stifling others by his greatness while suffering his own profound religious doubts.

In late Renaissance Italy, a conservative reaction arose against Renaissance humanism, weakening the High Renaissance impulse toward harmony, reason, and intellectual order. In Rome, the reaction was audible in the marbled smoothness of Palestrina's sacred music. A conservative classicism also governed Italian theater, influencing theater construction and stagecraft.

PALESTRINA: REACTION TO THE RENAISSANCE

The Catholic reaction against the Reformation was slow. When Catholic bishops finally met in the Council of Trent (1545–63), they scrutinized Church doctrine and practice. The result was called the **Counter-Reformation**, the Catholic Church's effort to reform itself and mount a religious offensive against Protestantism. The Counter-Reformation drafted the arts into its reform program, often censoring artistic subjects and prescribing technique. Regarding music, the Council of Trent declared:

> *. . . in the case of those Masses which are celebrated with singing and with organ, let nothing profane be intermingled, but only hymns and divine praises. The whole plan of singing in musical modes should be constituted not to give empty pleasure to the ear, but in such a way that the words be clearly understood by all . . .*[8]

This pronouncement by the Council challenged two basic principles of Renaissance music: first, it criticized

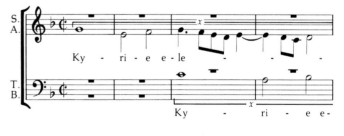

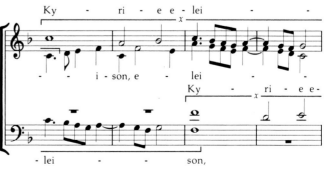

9.28 Palestrina, opening measures from *Missa Brevis*, "Kyrie," 1570.
Note the step-like progress of the melodic line and the simplified polyphony, using only three voices.

x = imitation

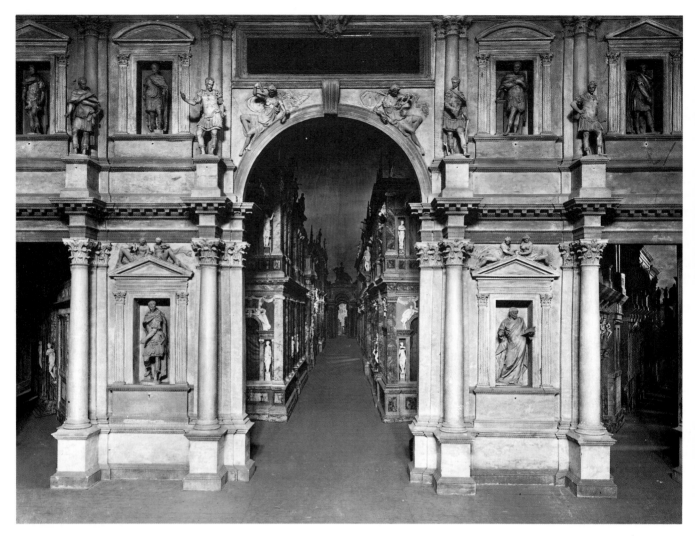

9.29 Andrea Palladio and Vincenzo Scamozzi, Teatro Olimpico, interior, Vicenza, Italy, 1580–4.
The decoration of the stage's façade is a Renaissance conglomeration of classical elements, including the alternating rounded and triangular pediments also visible in the Roman Pantheon (Fig. 4.18).

9.30 Right **Sebastiano Serlio, stage setting from D'Architettura, 1540–51.**
Such illusionistic stage settings applied the rules of perspective to stage design.

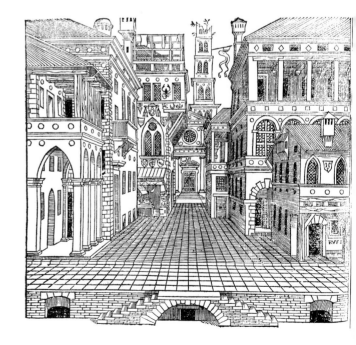

complex polyphony in the style of Josquin des Préz and other northern French and Flemish-born composers; second, it condemned the "intermingling" of religious and non-religious elements common in Renaissance sacred music.

The condemnation gave rise to a new conservatism among Italian composers. The composer best attuned to the changes was the Italian Giovanni da Palestrina (c. 1525–94). He abandoned secular composition, saying of the composers of such works, "I blush and grieve to

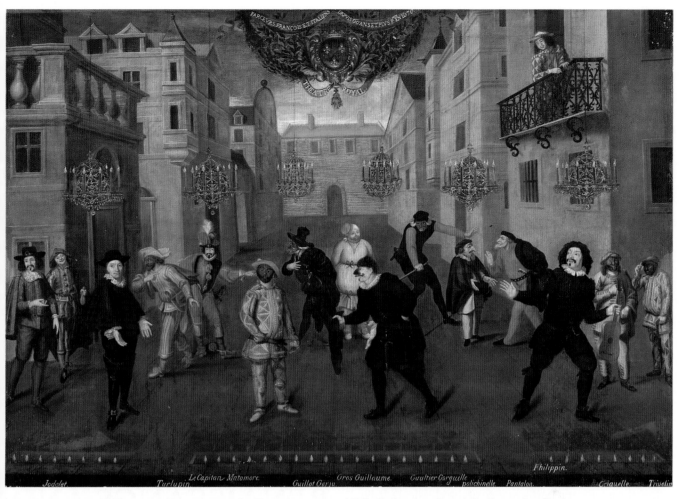

9.31 A *commedia dell'arte* performance at the French court, c. 1670. Collection Comédie Française, Paris.
A *commedia* troupe included stock figures such as the Harlequin (left of center, in his identifying brightly colored costume) and the slapstick pair of Pantalone and Pulchinella (far right). Notice the illusionist perspective scenery of buildings on either side.

think that once I was of their number." Palestrina's recantation was opportune, for he later occupied several prestigious musical posts in Rome, and finally became director of the pope's Sistine Choir. Palestrina's stately and flawless compositions were the high point of sacred music in late Renaissance Italy.

Musically, Palestrina returned to sacred compositions based on traditional plainchant, while using more restrained dissonances than Josquin's. He composed the *Mass of Pope Marcellus* (1567) in six voices to demonstrate that complex polyphony need not violate the dictates of piety. His elegiac motet *Super flumina Babylonis* (*By the Rivers of Babylon*, 1581) matched the musical rhythms perfectly to the mournful words of the Biblical text (from Psalm 137). Palestrina's polyphonic imitation is always controlled, and imitative passages are balanced against chordal phrases. In Palestrina's sacred music, the voices blend into a whole of exceptional clarity and grace (Fig. **9.28**). It was as if he had purified the Church's music of the sinfulness which infected it in the early Renaissance.

RENAISSANCE THEATER IN ITALY

Renaissance theater in Italy was governed by a different sort of conservatism from that of music. In their enthusiasm for ancient Greek and Latin drama, Renaissance Italian dramatists rejected popular theater and instead imposed classical formulas – entirely the opposite of what was taking place in Shakespearean England. The result in Italy was an intellectualized theater that was performed in beautiful classical settings but had little popular appeal.

Italian dramatists were preoccupied with translated classical plays, chiefly ancient Roman comedies and tragedies. This theatrical classicism was nurtured by a learned Florentine society called the Camerata, devoted to the revival of Greek tragedy. The Florentine Camerata mounted a landmark performance of *Oedipus the King* that incorporated dance and music into the performance. The production bore no resemblance to Sophocles' ancient Athenian tragedy, but it was immensely influential in creating a new theatrical art, the opera.

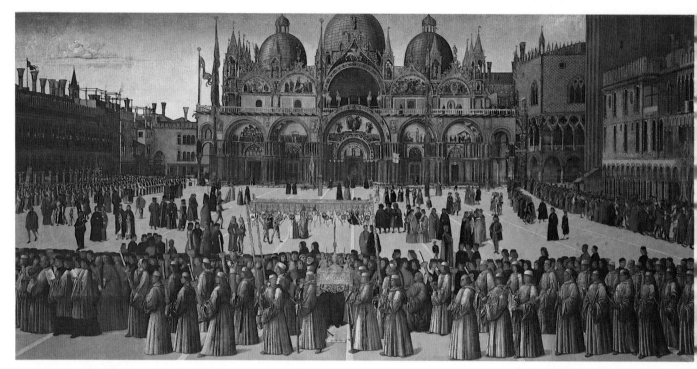

9.32 Gentile Bellini, *Procession in St. Mark's Square,* **1496. Oil on canvas, 12 ft x 24 ft (3.66 x 7.32 m). Galleria dell'Accademia, Venice.**
The square of St. Mark, shown here before it was renovated by Palladio, was the focus of Venetian pomp and festivity. In the background are the great cathedral's gilded domes and, visible to the right, the Doge's Palace, residence of the city's elected governor.

Italian theater's great innovation came in solving the problems of building a theater what would accommodate the needs of a performance of the classical plays. Andrea Palladio's Teatro Olimpico (Fig. **9.29**), for example, was designed in the spirit of the Camerata. The Teatro Olimpico was a small-scale replica of an ancient Roman theater, with a multi-storied facade and decorative statues and columns. The theater's arched opening was enlarged in later theaters to accommodate the new techniques of stagecraft, especially scenery. Using the techniques of perspective in Renaissance painting, designers created the illusion of a deep, three-dimensional space on stage (Fig. **9.30**). Painted wing scenery was angled inward to create the appearance of a long city street or a forest vista. From the center seats, at least, spectators could view a dramatic space that obeyed the same perspective rules as a Renaissance painting.

In contrast to the tedious classicism of Renaissance theater, a robust new form of theater appeared in Italy, the *commedia dell'arte* (Fig. **9.31**) – improvisational comedy in which actors invented dialogue to fit the bare outline of a plot. Performances drew freely on popular novels, gossip, and current events. The scenario involved a cast of stock characters, including the innocent young lady, the spendthrift lover, and the stuffy doctor. The improvisational skill of *commedia dell'arte* actors delighted the Italian audiences, and the form was later exported to northern Europe.

THE VENETIAN RENAISSANCE AND MANNERISM

Analyze the differences between artists and composers of the Venetian Renaissance and their High Renaissance precursors.

Late Renaissance Venice was a liberal and cosmopolitan city, largely untouched by the age's religious conflicts. The wealthy aristocracy supported a rich artistic culture, and commissioned portraits and built country villas in neoclassical style. The city's grand St. Mark's Square (Fig. **9.32**) was not only a splendid architectural landmark, but also the center of a rich musical culture. Based on a friendly accommodation between state and Church, Venetian civic life glittered with lavish processions, sumptuous festivity, and artistic brilliance.

The late Renaissance reached a bloom in Venice, especially in the works of Palladio and Titian. Meanwhile, other Italian artists began to stretch and distort the Renaissance style, inventing a new style which was called mannerism. Thus, in the twilight of the Italian Renaissance, some artists returned to old truths while others struck out in bold new directions.

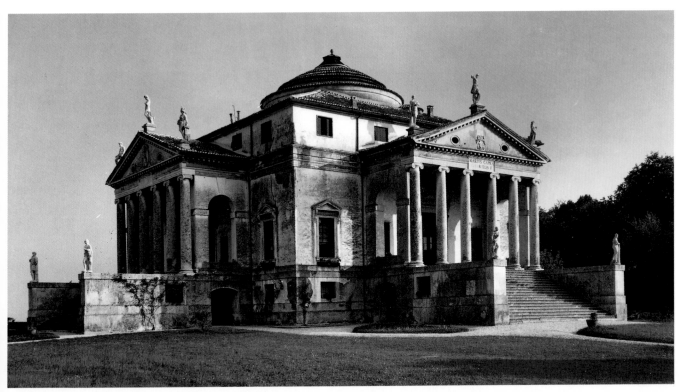

9.33 Above **Andrea Palladio, Villa Rotonda (Villa Capra), Vicenza, Italy, begun 1550. 80 ft (24.38 m) square, height of dome 70 ft (21.34 m).**
The classical porticoes on all four sides took advantage of the surrounding vistas. The hilltop site inspired, among others, Thomas Jefferson's Monticello in Virginia (Fig. 11.25).

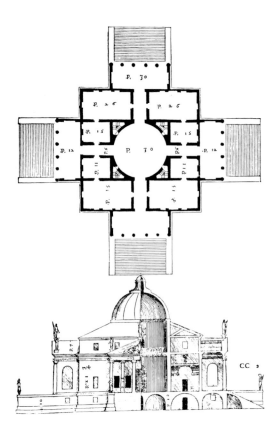

9.34 Left **Plan of the Villa Rotonda, Vicenza, Italy, begun 1550. From Palladio's** *Quattro libri dell'architettura* **(***Four Books of Architecture***), 1570.**

VENETIAN MUSIC

The grand style of Venetian music provided a suitable accompaniment to the city's habitual pomp and celebration. Renaissance Venice was a city of festivity, whose taste in music was lively and adventurous – unlike the conservative music of Palestrina. The city was served by a line of distinguished composers, first Flemish musicians and later native-born composers. The last of the Venetian Renaissance composers was Giovanni Gabrieli (1558–1612), whose uncle had composed the music for the Florentine Camerata's version of *Oedipus the King*. Like that of his predecessors, Gabrieli's sacred music was strongly affected by the unique architecture of the city cathedral. Instead of just one choir space, St. Mark's Cathedral had two opposing choirs, each with its own organ. Venetian composers exploited this setting by devising a **polychoral style**, which used two or more groups of singers spaced some distance apart. Backed by the cathedral's two organs, Venetian choirs engaged in great stereophonic musical duels, their voices crashing against each other across St. Mark's gilded vastness.

Giovanni Gabrieli and his uncle Andrea were among the first to specify the instruments that doubled the choral voices. The soprano part might be played by recorder or violin, for example, and the tenor part by a tenor recorder or viola. Increasingly in Gabrieli's late Renaissance style,

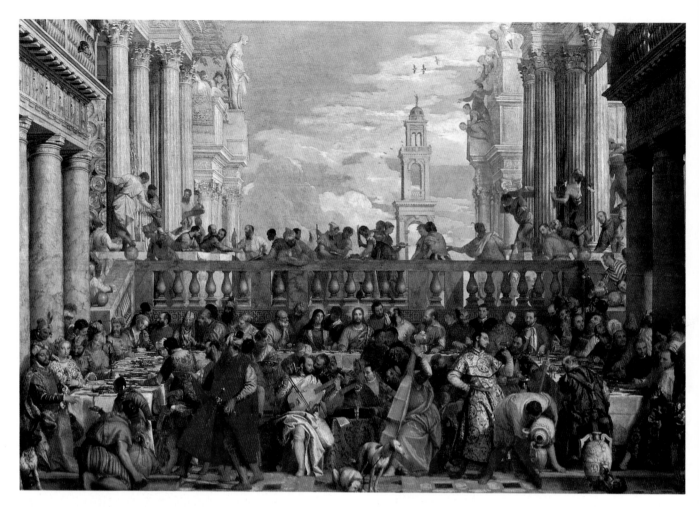

9.35 Above **Paolo Veronese,** *Marriage at Cana,* **c. 1560. Oil on canvas, 21 ft 10 ins x 32 ft 6 ins (6.65 x 9.88 m). Louvre, Paris.**
Christ and the Virgin Mary, seated at center, are distinguishable only by their haloes; among the musicians (foreground) is a self-portrait of the artist. The architectural setting resembles a perspective theater set (Fig. 9.30). What are the possible explanations for the butcher above the head of Christ?

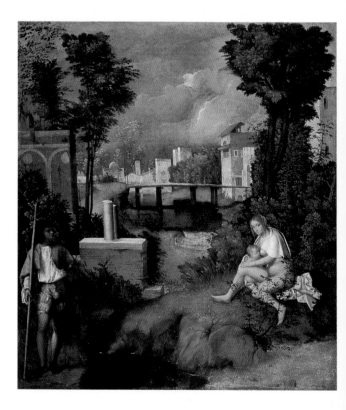

9.36 Giorgione, *Tempest,* **c. 1505. Oil on canvas, 32¹/₄ x 28³/₄ ins (82 x 73 cm). Galleria dell'Accademia, Venice.**
The painting's allegorical meaning is obscure. The stork on the rooftop and the mother's white cloak are traditional symbols of purity; the sentinel's staff and the broken columns both allegorically suggest fortitude. Note the contrast in mood between the stormy background and the foreground figures.

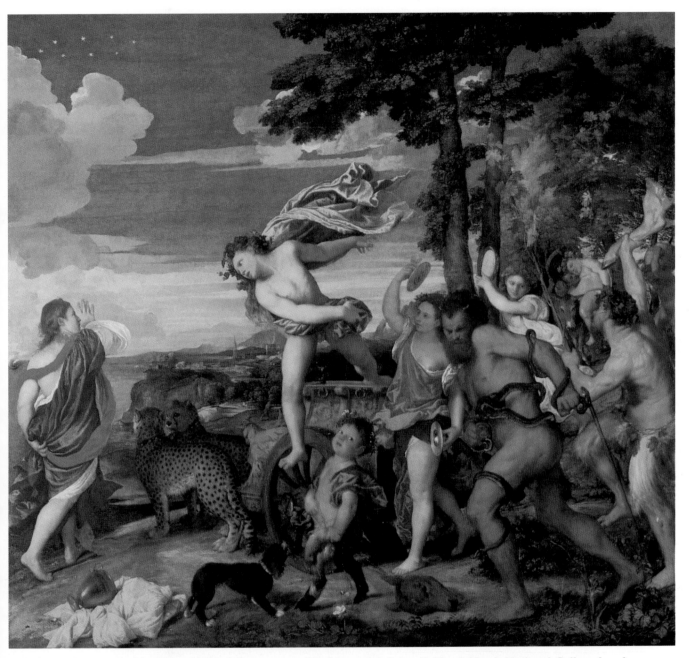

9.37 Titian, *Bacchus and Ariadne*, c. 1520. Oil on canvas, 5 ft 8 ins x 6 ft ⁷/₈ ins (1.73 x 1.85 m). National Gallery, London.
Divide the picture diagonally into four triangles and note that Bacchus' revelers fill one triangle at right, while Ariadne stands alone in the triangle on the left. Connecting both triangles at the center is the leaping Bacchus. Compare this dynamic composition with Leonardo's *Madonna of the Rocks* (Fig. 8.29).

the different vocal parts united in a final chord (two or more tones played at the same time). These chordal endings were called **cadences**, musical resting points that provided a sense of resolution and completion. The pronounced cadences in Gabrieli's music produced a more harmonic effect, especially at the end of a musical piece – a trend which later intensified in baroque music (see page 287). This harmony of chords moved away from the polyphony of the Renaissance and signified an end to the Renaissance style.

PALLADIO, ARCHITECT OF VENICE

The Venetians' grand style of living proved fortunate for its most prominent Renaissance architect, Andrea Palladio (1508–80). Although he designed numerous churches, usually with a central plan and a classical temple façade, Palladio is best-known for his country estates. Venetian economic troubles had forced many of its wealthy merchants to take up farming, and Palladio showed skill in adapting his classical style to building country villas for

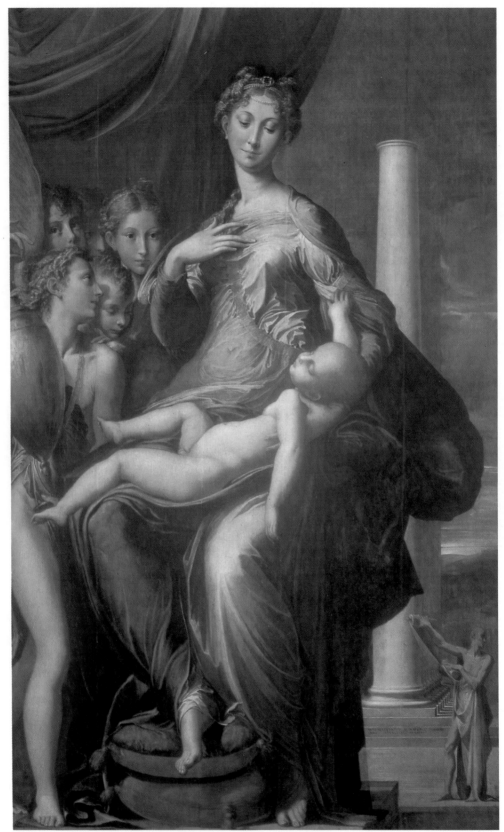

9.38 Parmigianino, *Madonna with the Long Neck*, 1534–40. Oil on panel, 7 ft 1 ins x 4 ft 4 ins (2.16 x 1.32 m). Uffizi, Florence.

Compare the space at left, with its crowded band of angels, to the space at right, where the prophet Isaiah stands before the columns of an unfinished classical building. What is "mannerist" about the picture's differing scales and definition of space?

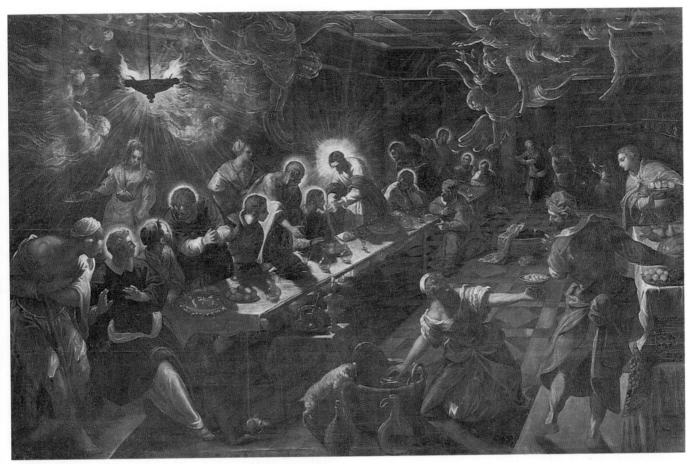

9.39 Jacopo Tintoretto, *Last Supper*, 1592–4. Oil on canvas, 12 ft x 18 ft 8 ins (3.65 x 5.7 m). San Giorgio Maggiore, Venice. The apostles are arranged behind a table that stretches diagonally back into the pictorial space. Contrast the effect of the smoking lantern and ghostly angels to the action in the right foreground.

such patrons. Palladio's designs of classical symmetry and simplicity influenced architects into the nineteenth century.

A typical design of the country villa was the Villa Rotonda (Fig. **9.33**), with its rigorously symmetrical floor plan (Fig. **9.34**) and domed central hall. Partly through Palladio's influence, such pedimented temple facades became a common feature of secular buildings in later periods. Palladio was an enthusiastic antiquarian (see page 86). His *Four Books of Architecture* (1570), a copy-book of classical designs and decoration, became a textbook for architects of the next two centuries. As late as 1800, the American President Thomas Jefferson copied Palladio's drawings directly into designs for his residence at Monticello.

VENETIAN PAINTING

Painters appealed to the Venetians' taste for pageantry and beauty with works of rich color and a festive mood. Venetian painters preferred oil paint, which was more durable than fresco in Venice's damp climate and permitted rich hues of color to dominate the Venetian style. Even religious subjects, such as Paolo Veronese's [vair-oh-NAY-zay] *Marriage at Cana* (Fig. **9.35**), reflected the Venetians' love of scenes crowded by festive revelers.

The most mysterious painter of the Venetian Renaissance was Giorgione [jyor-jee-OH-nee] (1478–1511), who in a brief career became a master of pictorial mood. In the *Tempest* (Fig. **9.36**), for example, the city landscape manages to suggest both profound peacefulness and the foreboding threat of a storm. The figures in the foreground – the sentinel and the nude mother with infant – remain largely unexplained. They suggest the complementary qualities of strength and tenderness. Apart from the hint of Madonna and Christ Child, Giorgione's pastoral scene is entirely non-religious.

Giorgione's brief career contrasts with the life of Titian (*c.* 1488–1576), a master of color who became the wealthiest and most successful artist of his day. While Michelangelo's energies were absorbed by the new St. Peter's, Titian [TEE-shun] fulfilled commissions for the Italian aristocracy. Titian excelled at every type of Renaissance painting, including portraiture and sacred themes. One of his most striking works, *Bacchus and Ariadne* (Fig. **9.37**), is a celebration of the pagan spirit, painted to decorate a duke's country home at Ferrara in northern Italy. The wine god Bacchus impetuously leaps from his chariot to wed Ariadne. The torsion and movement in the figures provide a sharp contrast to the restful harmonies of works by Leonardo and Raphael. The entire picture is dominated by exuberant blues, golds, and pinks, reflecting the mood of the revelers who crowd in from the right.

MANNERISM

The tension and dynamism in Titian's later work suggest the direction of many artists in the aftermath of the Renaissance. The term **mannerist** was given to Italian artists who used exaggeration, distortion, and expressiveness to free themselves from the late Renaissance style. Scholars originally applied the term derisively, implying a derivative or decadent style. More recently, mannerism has been seen as a search for new expressive methods outside the formal standards of Renaissance harmony and order.

The carefully refined distortions of the mannerist style are visible in the *Madonna with the Long Neck* (Fig. **9.38**) by Parmigianino [PAR-mee-juh-NEE-noh] (1503–40). The central figures violate the rules of proportion that had been elaborated by Renaissance studies of anatomy. The Christ child lolls in his mother's arms like a corpse. The row of unfinished columns echoes the Madonna's vertical form, but the use of perspective is unorthodox, abandoning the carefully calculated pictorial space that we saw in Ghiberti's *Gates of Paradise* (see Fig. 8.10).

The same self-conscious exaggeration and distortion were evident in the works of the Venetian mannerist Jacopo Tintoretto (1518–94). Tintoretto's dramatic *Last Supper* (Fig. **9.39**) is a masterpiece of the mannerist style and a striking contrast to Leonardo's version (see Fig. 8.20). Where Leonardo placed Christ at the geometric focal point of his painting, Tintoretto's Christ is distinguished mainly by his mysterious halo. The lantern's smoke is transmuted into angels, while in the foreground servants and everyday objects glow in a mystical light. The picture communicates the profound mystery of the Last Supper, suggesting the transformation of matter into spirit.

Mannerism had its effect on the last sculpture of Michelangelo – the *Pietà Rondanini* (Fig. **9.40**), left unfinished and partly destroyed by its creator. The twisting lines of the two figures are far removed from the confi-

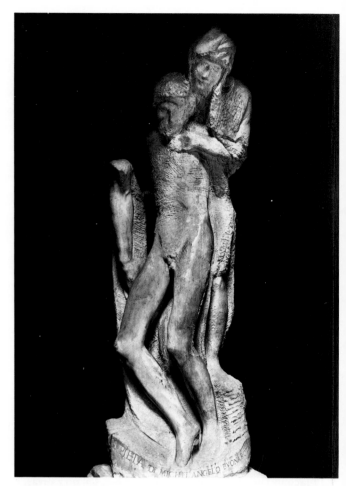

9.40 Michelangelo Buonarroti, *Pietà Rondanini*, c. 1554–64. Marble, height 5 ft 3³/₈ ins (1.61 m). Castello Sforzesco, Milan.

In his last sculpture (he labored on this *Pietà* just days before his death), Michelangelo absorbed some of mannerism's expressiveness and freedom of form. Compare his treatment of the human figure here to his vigorous *Moses* (Fig. 8.39) from forty years earlier.

dent contours of the same artist's *David* (see Fig. 8.24) or from the monumental compromises of St. Peter's (see Fig. 8.48). Michelangelo may have intended the sculpture for his own tomb. With its eloquent simplicity, the sculpture shows a deeply private sense of pain and grief, which may imply the artist's own soul-searching confrontation with death.

Chapter Summary

The Northern Renaissance. In sixteenth-century northern Europe, economic dynamism combined with humanism and religious ferment to stimulate a northern Renaissance. A commercial revolution and the discovery of the New World helped European monarchs consolidate their power. These rulers' courts – especially in Spain, France, and England – were centers of artistic patronage, and often attracted Italian painters and architects.

The Reformation. In 1517 the monk Martin Luther initiated a religious revolt, called the Reformation, that eventually split the Western Church into Protestant and Roman Catholic faiths. Luther's treatises disputed the authority of the pope and challenged religious practices that had no basis in Christian scripture. The Reformation appealed to its largely German followers with a message of simple piety and religious freedom and a critique of religious corruption. A second wave of Protestant reformation was initiated in Switzerland by the gifted thinker John Calvin, whose strict teachings stressed a "Protestant ethic" – moral uprightness, thrift, and the predestination of a righteous elect.

Painting in Northern Europe. Working in oil, northern Renaissance painters such as Jan van Eyck made stunning advances in pictorial realism and vivid detail. A northern sense of intense piety and emotionalism existed alongside the classicism of Albrecht Dürer, the only northern painter concerned with Italian humanism. Bruegel avoided religious subjects, and frankly depicted the humble and timeless life of European peasants.

Humanism in the North. Humanism's most important voice in the north was Erasmus, an evangelical humanist who exposed the pretensions and hypocrisy of humanity in his satire *In Praise of Folly*. As a scholar, Erasmus translated biblical texts and engaged Luther in debates on human nature and freedom. Erasmus' English friend Thomas More expressed his views of society's shortcomings in his *Utopia*, while, in his essays, the French skeptic Montaigne questioned intellectual pretensions and relied on his own experience for insight.

The Elizabethan Age. In England, Henry VIII's split with the Church aroused bitter religious divisions. When the wise queen Elizabeth I restored religious toleration, a new prosperity spawned the glittering Elizabethan age. Elizabethan theater produced England's greatest dramatist, Shakespeare, a man of the theater who succeeded by his verbal inventiveness and theatrical instincts. The hero of Shakespeare's *Hamlet* dramatized the psychological depths of humanist learning. Like the theater, Elizabethan music adapted Italian forms to English audiences and served the cult of Elizabeth. English composers excelled in the madrigal and other song forms.

The Late Renaissance in Italy. In late Renaissance Italy, the Counter-Reformation reacted conservatively against the excesses of Renaissance art and music. The composer Palestrina simplified and refined Renaissance polyphony. The Renaissance theater imitated classical dramatic forms and achieved significant advances in stage design.

The Venetian Renaissance and Mannerism. In Venice, the arts expressed the city's exuberant spirit and festive public life. Venetian composers developed a polychoral style to suit the city's great cathedral. The architect Palladio built grand residences and churches according to strict neoclassical rules. The versatile painter Titian used a mastery of color and Renaissance form to serve Venetian patrons, while mannerists throughout Italy sought a new expressiveness in stretching and distorting the principles of Renaissance art.

10 The Spirit of Baroque

Not since Emperor Hadrian built the Pantheon in Rome had a Western ruler expressed himself so perfectly in a building. The Palace of Versailles (Fig. 10.1) represented King Louis XIV's vision of the French nation under his reasonable and absolute control. The gilded palace, the gardens stretching beyond, the courtiers and servants in ordered ranks – all these were arranged according to the king's decree. They were all planets in orbit around the "Sun King."

*The palace at Versailles was a showpiece of the **spirit of baroque** – the love of extravagant and monumental beauty, the tension between simplicity and embellishment, the restless search for truth – that characterized the seventeenth century in Europe. In Spain, Italy, and France, kings and popes sponsored enormous projects and colonial expeditions to demonstrate their supreme power. In northern Europe, a more modest scale did not deter baroque creativity, and throughout Europe a new science was mastering the mysteries of the cosmos. This dynamic era – roughly 1600–1700 – was the time when modern science and modern government were born. It left an indelible mark on the Western world.*

THE BAROQUE IN SPAIN

Describe the transition from Renaissance to baroque in Spanish art.

The seventeenth century was an age defined by contradictions. Violent passions were balanced against a cool rationalism; extravagant excess contended with the restraint of neoclassicism; a search for cosmic order coexisted with a love of intricate embellishment. The turbulent seventeenth century created a rich diversity of art and ideas, manifest in all of Europe's major nations.

The art and music of the seventeenth century were characterized by a style called **baroque** [bar-OKE] – originally a disparaging term that meant "absurd or grotesque." The baroque style took different forms in Europe's nations and colonies – most significantly in Spain, Italy, France, and the Netherlands. In seventeenth-century Spain, the baroque style was shaped by two decisive forces, the Catholic Counter-Reformation and the rise of absolutist monarchy. The resurgent Catholic Church in Spain sponsored an art of mystical spirituality, while Spanish monarchs patronized major building projects and talented artists. Both the Counter-Reformation and the rise of absolutism had enormous consequences for the arts, not only in Spain but throughout Europe.

EL GRECO AND CATHOLIC MYSTICISM

By the early seventeenth century, the Counter-Reformation had spawned a wave of religious reform and piety in Spain and Italy. The counter-offensive against Protestantism led to such measures as the infamous Index, a list of books which devout Catholics were forbidden to read. However, the Counter-Reformation also saw genuine reforms in Catholic education and a revival of religious fervor.

The baroque master painter of religious feeling was El Greco (c. 1541–1614), who applied Renaissance technique to subjects of intense religiosity. Born Domenikos Theotocopoulos [THAY-o-to-KOH-po-luss] on the Greek island of Crete, the young El Greco (in Spanish, "The Greek") trained as a painter in Venice, where he absorbed the lessons of Titian and the Italian mannerists. Around 1570, he re-settled in Toledo, Spain's most religious city, and there he spent his career painting portraits and religious subjects for Toledo's churches.

10.1 Opposite **The Palace of Versailles, France, c. 1688.**
The symmetry and grandeur of the palace of Louis XIV symbolized the king's orderly rule over his nation. The monumental palace was the perfect setting for the spectacle and drama so beloved of baroque monarchs.

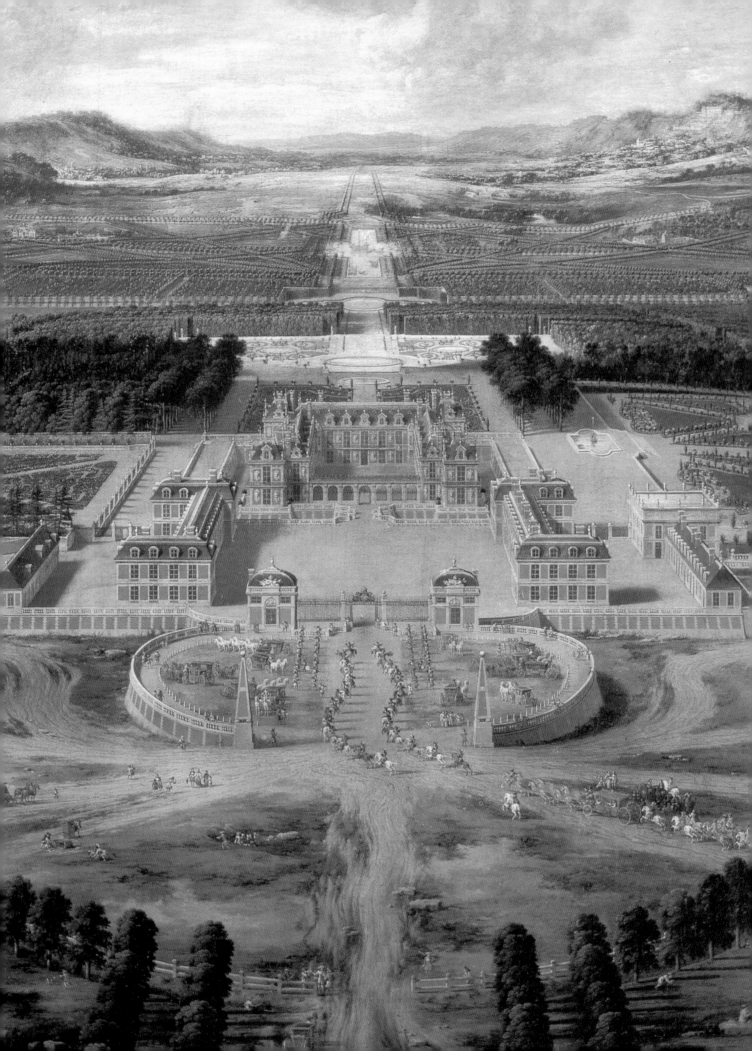

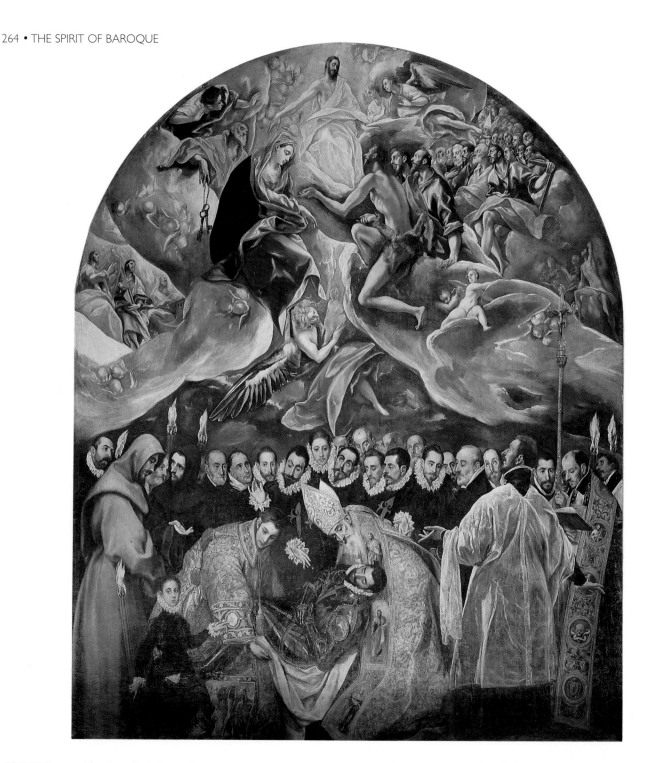

10.2 El Greco, *The Burial of Count Orgaz*, 1586. Oil on canvas, 16 ft x 11 ft 10 ins (4. 88 x 3.61 m). Santo Tomé, Toledo, Spain.
Trace the picture's horizontal and vertical axes. Note the contrary motion along the vertical axis (the count's soul flying up to heaven, his armored body falling into the crypt below) and the vividly realistic style of the human mourners versus the mannerist stylization of the host of heaven.

Typical of El Greco's church commissions is *The Burial of Count Orgaz* (Fig. **10.2**), painted above the count's tomb in a small church. The painting shows El Greco's command of color, inspired by his knowledge of Renais-sance Venetian art, and a philosophical depth reminiscent of Raphael. Yet, the picture is also suffused with the mystical aura and visual dynamism of the Catholic baroque. *The Burial of Count Orgaz* pays homage to a saintly knight at whose funeral St. Stephen and St. Augustine supposedly appeared. El Greco arranged the picture along a horizontal and a vertical axis. Horizontally, the mourners' heads form a division, the clarity of color in the faces and costumes below yielding to an acid contrast of blues, yellows, and greens in the heavenly host above. The austere figures of the Virgin Mary and John the Baptist implore Jesus to accept the count's soul. In this masterpiece, El Greco modulates styles the way a composer changes

THE BAROQUE AND ENLIGHTENMENT

	GENERAL EVENTS	ARCHITECTURE	VISUAL ARTS	MUSIC AND DANCE	LITERATURE AND PHILOSOPHY
1600					
THE BAROQUE	1618–48 Religious wars in Germany	1629 Bernini appointed architect of St. Peter's, Rome	1622–5 Rubens paints life of Marie de' Medici (**10.26**)	1607 Monteverdi, *Orfeo*	1632 Galileo, *Dialogues on Two Systems of the World*; condemned by Church 1633
				1600s Kabuki theater arises, Edo, Japan	
		1648 Taj Mahal, Agra, India (**10.5**)	1642 Rembrandt, *The Night Watch* (**10.35**)		
			1645–52 Bernini, *Ecstasy of St. Teresa* (**10.12**)		1639 Descartes, *Discourse on Method*
	1661 Louis XIV takes control of French government	1663 Bernini completes piazza of St. Peter's, Rome (**10.9**)		1653 Louis XIV dances as Sun King in *Ballet de la Nuit*	1664 Molière, *Tartuffe*
		1669–85 Le Vau and Mansart, garden façade, Versailles Palace, France (**10.22**)			
	1688 Glorious Revolution in England	1676–1710 Wren, St. Paul's, London (**10.39**)		1674 Lully's first opera performed at Versailles	1690 Locke, *Two Treatises on Government*
1700					
THE ENLIGHTEN-MENT	1715 Louis XIV dies		1717 Watteau, *Pilgrimage to Cythera* (**11.9**)		
				1721 Bach, *Brandenburg Concertos*	
					1740–42 Richardson, *Pamela*
				1747 Handel, *Messiah*	1762 Rousseau, *The Social Contract*
	1776–83 American war for independence	1770–84 Jefferson, Monticello, Virginia (**11.25**)	1784–5 David, *Oath of the Horatii* (**11.23**)	1786 Mozart, *Marriage of Figaro*	
1789	1789 French revolution begins		c. 1789 Vigée-Lebrun, *Self-portrait with Daughter* (**11.11**)	1788 Mozart, *Symphony No. 40*	

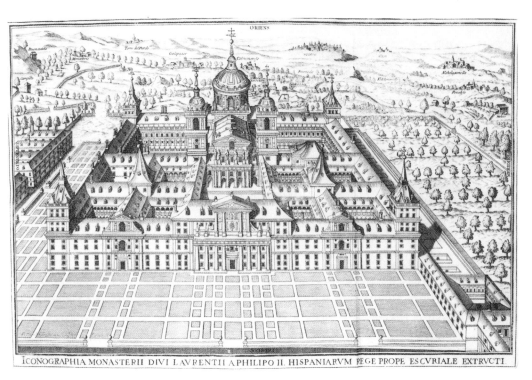

ICONOGRAPHIA MONASTERII DIVI LAVRENTII A PHILIPO II. HISPANIARVM REGE PROPE ESCVRIALE EXTRVCTI.

10.3 Juan Batista de Toledo and Juan de Herrera, Escorial Palace, near Madrid, Spain, 1553–84. Engraving. Louvre, Paris.
The domed central church served as the crypt for Philip II's father; the surrounding structure housed both the royal apartments and a monastery. The grid-like plan of the palace's inner sections had a gruesome symbolism: it represented the gridiron on which St. Lawrence was roasted to death. Compare this royal complex with Louis XIV's palace at Versailles (Fig. 10.1), which dates from a century later.

10.4 Cathedral of Mexico (1718–37), Mexico City.

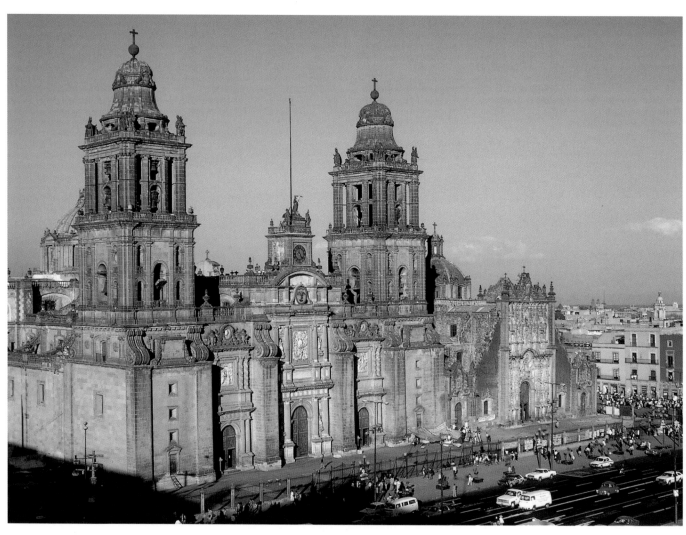

GLOBAL PERSPECTIVE

THE TAJ MAHAL

As European conquerors and missionaries colonized the Americas, Islam also extended its influence into India. From 1526 to 1761, a succession of Muslim rulers in India established the **Mughal Empire**, and under their reign India prospered from growing international trade. The first Mughal [MOO-gahl] conquerors originated in central Asia, descended from Mongols (hence the name Mughal or Mogul) but emphasizing their Turkish heritage. The Mughal rulers intermarried with Hindu nobility, and their civilization blended Muslim, Persian, and Indian cultures.

The most celebrated art work of the Mughal period was the tomb of Taj Mahal (Fig. **10.5**) at Agra in northern India. In general, Mughal rulers were more inclined to build monuments and tombs than Muslim mosques or shrines. The Taj Mahal [TAHZH muh-HAHL] followed a long-standing Turkish custom of commemorating a man's devotion to a woman – in this case, Mumtaz-i-Mahal, the favorite wife of Shah Jahan (ruled 1628–58).

In form, the Taj Mahal is a cube surmounted by a bulbous central dome, with archways on the four sides leading into the octagonal central space. The white marble building rests on a pink sandstone base and is approached by long reflecting pools on two sides. The building's setting is perhaps its most spectacular aspect, overlooking a river and set between a hospice and a mosque.

On the exterior and interior, the Taj Mahal is decorated with arabesques inlaid with semiprecious stones, Qur'anic script, and stone floral mosaics. The decoration is a blend of Islamic themes and the native Indian skill in stonecutting. Symbolically, the entire complex is both a profession of love and a vision of the Muslim paradise. A Mughal poet said the Taj Mahal was "wrapped in a veil of concord with the air."

10.5 Taj Mahal, Agra, India, 1632–48.
The tomb of a Mughal emperor's wife, the Taj Mahal floats on a pedestal of pink stone, above a garden and reflecting pools that suggest the pleasures of Islamic paradise. Compare the Taj Mahal's symmetry and balance to European neoclassical buildings like El Escorial in Spain (Fig. 10.3) or St. Paul's Cathedral in England.

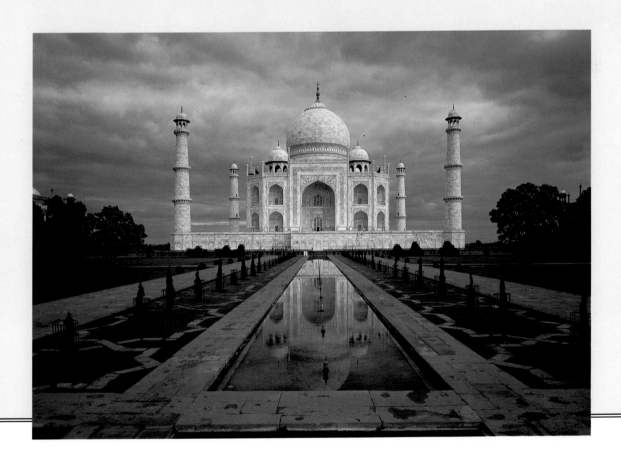

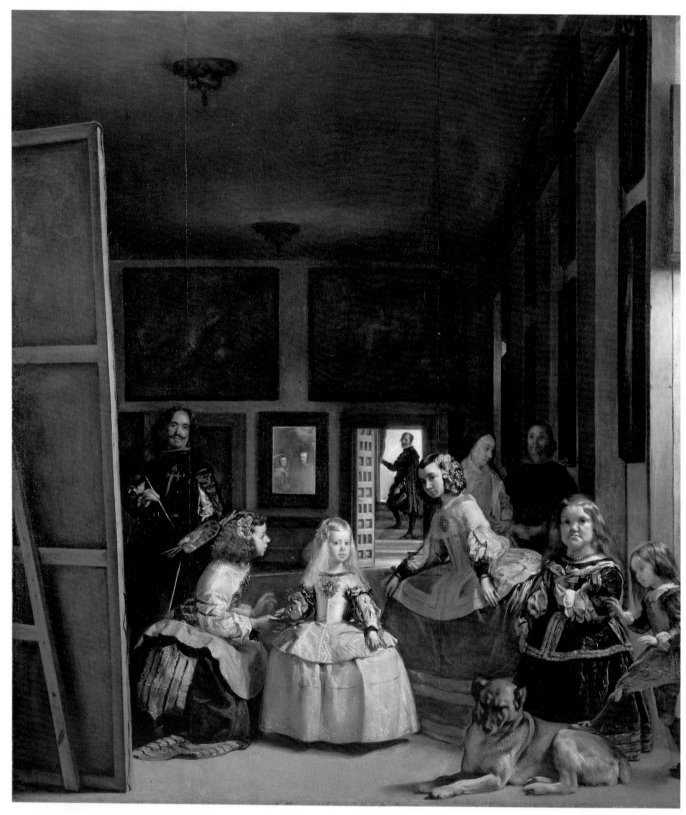

10.6 Diego Velázquez, *Las Meninas* (*The Maids of Honor*), 1656. Oil on canvas, 10 ft 5¹/₄ ins x 9 ft ³/₄ ins (3.18 x 2.76 m). Prado, Madrid.
By including his own portrait with those of his royal subjects, Velázquez assured himself a kind of artistic immortality. The red cross indicates his membership in the noble Order of Santiago, a sign of the status that Velázquez so avidly pursued.

musical keys. The painting's lower half states his debt to Titian, the Renaissance master; the upper half acknowledges his debt to mannerism. The dynamic whole announces his invention of a distinctively individual baroque style.

SPANISH BAROQUE ARCHITECTURE

It is curious that El Greco received few commissions from King Philip II of Spain (ruled 1556–98), since his style seemed well suited to the king's religious fervor. Instead, Philip imported Italian artists to decorate the stark palace that he had built at El Escorial, about 30 miles (48 km) outside the royal city of Madrid. Like El Greco's paintings, the Escorial Palace (Fig. **10.3**) was a bridge between Renaissance and baroque styles – inspired by the classicism of Renaissance Rome and decorated in the spirit of the baroque. The building complex functioned simultaneously as a palace for the king, a tomb for the king's father, and a monastery dedicated to St. Lawrence. The entire scheme of the Escorial borrowed from the rigorous classicism of Michelangelo's design for St. Peter's in Rome (see Fig. 8.46) – a debt evident in the dome of the central church. Three generations of Spanish royalty decorated the Escorial's galleries in baroque splendor, financed largely by gold and silver plundered from the Americas.

In Spain's American colonies, governors and missionaries erected baroque-style churches to assert the authority of Christian culture and promote the inhabitants' conversion. At the Inca capital of Cuzco, in modern Peru, the Jesuit church of La Compañia (begun 1651) was literally built on top of ancient Inca walls. La Compañia's distinctive facade contained stacked arches within a unifying trefoil (or cloverleaf) arch and a curving entablature. In Mexico City, the great Cathedral of Mexico (1718–37), Latin America's largest church (Fig. **10.4**), contained fantastically elaborate interior decoration. Its placement on the site of the Aztec Temple of the Sun, center of the Aztecs' sacred city of Tenochtitlán [tuh-NAHK-tit-LAHN], stated emphatically the triumph of Christian colonialism over native faiths. Baroque elements continued to predominate in Latin American building long after the style had faded in Europe.

VELÁZQUEZ

The Spanish court of the seventeenth century had a huge appetite for flattering portraits and ornate decoration. The only Spanish-born baroque artist to achieve distinction in royal service was Diego Velázquez [ve-LASS-kess] (1599–1660), court painter for Philip IV from 1623 to his death. As a painter, Velázquez achieved an unerring realism, communicated by bold color and brushwork. Despite his mastery, however, Velázquez was denied the social status that great painters such as Peter Paul Rubens (see page 285) enjoyed in other European nations.

The greatest work of Velázquez, *Las Meninas* (*The Maids of Honor;* Fig. **10.6**), presents itself as a genre picture, a scene of everyday life. The painting shows a casual moment in the artist's palace studio. Historians have identified the figures of the five-year-old Princess Margarita in her dazzling costume, her attendants, a pair of dwarfs, and the artist, standing before a canvas the size of *Las Meninas* itself. The most enigmatic figures are the king and queen, reflected in the mirror at the rear. The royal couple may be sitting for their portrait, in which case Velázquez paints them, not himself. Just as possibly, they may be visiting the painter and thus honoring him in his studio. Velázquez deepens these ambiguities with the figure of the courtier who has opened a door and gazes back at the scene.

The composition of *Las Meninas* is apparently accidental, yet it is more complex and ambiguous than a Renaissance painting such as Raphael's *School of Athens* (see Fig. 8.36). While lacking the intellectual unity of Renaissance painting, Velázquez explores the relations between illusion and reality, art and the court, and the artist and patron, with a subtlety that few painters have matched. His masterful illusion leaves the viewer wondering exactly who looks into whose eyes.

10.7 Don Quixote from Cervantes' *Don Quixote*, 1863 edition illustrated by Gustave Doré, Hachette, Paris.

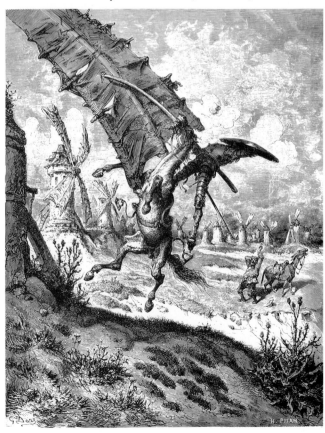

CERVANTES AND *DON QUIXOTE*

The tension between art and life visible in *Las Meninas* also inspired the greatest literary work of the seventeenth century, *Don Quixote*. The idealistic knight Don Quixote [DON kee-HOH-tay] de la Mancha constantly confuses the real world with his chivalric fantasy. Yet he draws others into his idealized world and ennobles them, much as Velázquez's palpable realism draws the viewer into his illusionary painter's studio.

The author of *Don Quixote* was Miguel de Cervantes (1547–1616), an impoverished veteran of foreign wars, slavery, and debtors' prison. When he began writing *Don Quixote*, at the age of fifty-seven, Cervantes [sair-VAHN-teez] was already author of dozens of undistinguished plays and romances. Desperate to overcome the poverty of his own prosaic world, Cervantes created one of the great utopian heroes of Western literature. His character Don Quixote deals with the world as it ideally should be, not as it really is.

The hero of Cervantes' tale begins as an impoverished Spanish noble who has spent too many hours in his library reading popular chivalric romances. Inspired to become a wandering knight, Quixote dresses himself in a ludicrous suit of armor and gains the services of a squire, Sancho Panza. Together, this unlikely pair sally forth on a series of adventures (Fig. **10.7**). Don Quixote, the gaunt and aristocratic knight, becomes so enamored of romantic fantasies that, in his eyes, a windmill is a giant and a rude tavern is a castle. Sancho Panza, the coarse peasant, is a realist who marvels at Quixote's delusions. The two extremes of idealism and realism illuminate one another, and highlight the limitations of each of these attitudes.

At this point they caught sight of thirty or forty windmills which were standing on the plain there, and no sooner had Don Quixote laid eyes upon them than he turned to his squire and said, "Fortune is guiding our affairs better than we could have wished; for you see there before you, friend Sancho Panza, some thirty or more lawless giants with whom I mean to do battle. I shall deprive them of their lives, and with the spoils from this encounter we shall begin to enrich ourselves; for this is righteous warfare, and it is a great service to God to remove so accursed a breed from the face of the earth."

"What giants?" said Sancho Panza.

"Those that you see there," replied his master, "those with the long arms some of which are as much as two leagues in length."

"But look, your Grace, those are not giants but windmills, and what appear to be arms are their wings which, when whirled in the breeze, cause the millstone to go."

"It is plain to be seen," said Don Quixote, "that you have had little experience in this matter of adventures.

If you are afraid, go off to one side and say your prayers while I am engaging them in fierce, unequal combat."[1]

CERVANTES
From *Don Quixote*, Part I

The novel, first published in 1605, was popular enough to inspire a plagiarized sequel by an anonymous author. Cervantes responded by writing his own Part II (published 1615), in which Quixote's adventures continue and the philosophical complexity of the novel increases. Quixote and Sancho are now famous for their exploits in Part I, and meet characters who seek to manipulate and deceive the heroes. In one telling episode, a friend of Quixote dresses himself as a "Knight of Mirrors," so that when they duel, Quixote is doing battle with his own reflected image. It is a duel that Velázquez might have liked to sketch. Quixote finally is unable to sustain his illusions, and his quest ends with a poignant scene. As Quixote, defeated and dying, relinquishes his chivalrous ambitions, it is Sancho Panza who urges him to revive his fantasies. To live in a disenchanted world is, as Sancho says, to die "in the hands of melancholy."

Throughout his tale, Cervantes explores the mismatch between appearance and reality, the boundary between truth and falsehood. In Counter-Reformation Europe, these were issues of life and death. In religion, the Inquisition – the Catholic tribunal that punished heresy – was executing heretics on the evidence of phantasms and enchantments such as Quixote's windmills. In science, thinkers such as Copernicus [koh-PURR-ni-kuss] and Galileo (see page 294) had to gauge (like Sancho Panza) the mind's inventions against the prosaic evidence of experience. In art, painters told the deepest truths through the skilled manipulation of appearance. Intending to write a popular bestseller, Cervantes wrote a philosophical masterpiece concerning, as one scholar puts it, "the chief intellectual problem of his age."

CRITICAL QUESTION

Would you agree with Sancho Panza's statement that we are sometimes better off because of our illusions? What beliefs of your own would you hold on to, even though they might be illusory?

10.8 Opposite **Gianlorenzo Bernini, altar canopy ("Baldacchino") of St. Peter's, Rome, 1624–33. Gilt bronze, height approx. 100 ft (30.5 m).**
Bernini's undulating columns and volutes provided a baroque counterpoint to the classical regularities of Michelangelo's dome and vaulting. Visible behind the canopy is the Throne of St. Peter, Bernini's last grand addition to the basilica.

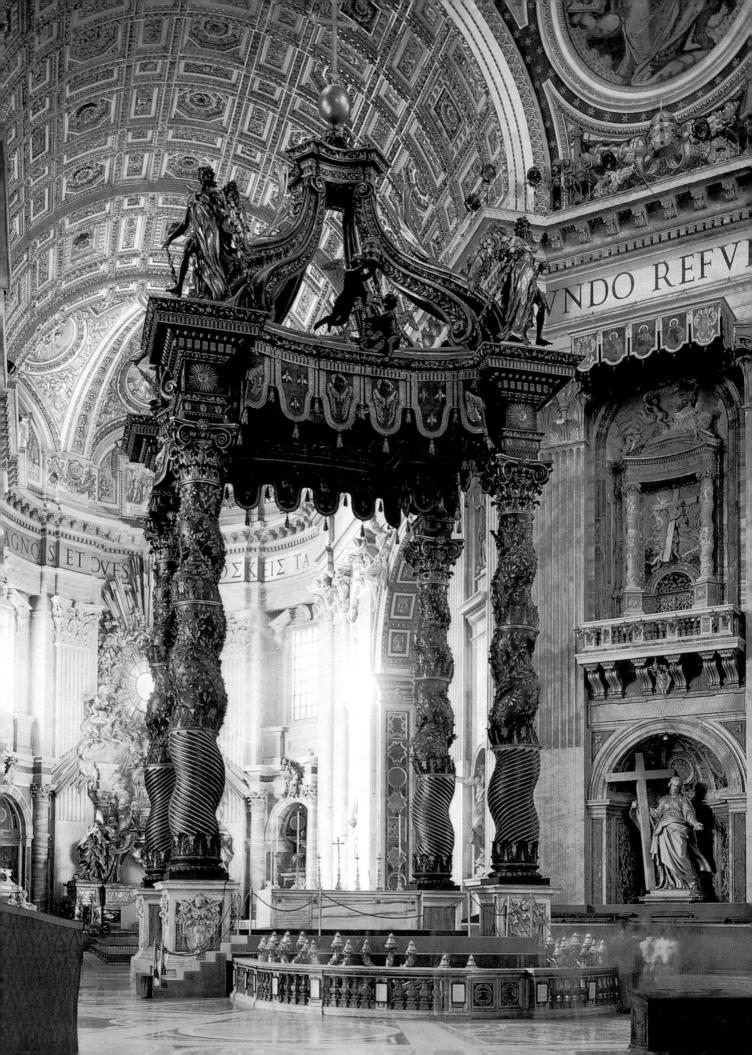

THE BAROQUE IN ITALY

Identify the important stylistic features of Italian baroque art and music.

Rome in the early seventeenth century was a city bursting with optimism and confidence. The Catholic Church had withstood the challenge of the Reformation and was celebrating its victory with a flurry of new building and artistic patronage, with the aim to exceed even the splendor of the Renaissance. The high-spirited Italian style

that developed encompassed the religious emotionalism and courtly splendor that had arisen in Spain. To these elements, the Italian baroque style added a love of ornamentation, a flair for the dramatic, and a dedication to works of monumental scale.

Artists in Rome were stimulated to excess by the Renaissance masterpieces that surrounded them. One was the painter Caravaggio [kair-a-VAH-jee-oh], who mastered the dramatic extremes of light and dark. Another, the prodigious Gianlorenzo Bernini, completely dominated the art scene of Counter-Reformation Rome. Bernini's artistic extravagance was matched by Italian opera, a secular art whose popularity soon filled new opera houses throughout Europe.

10.9 St. Peter's, Rome, aerial view. Nave and façade by Carlo Maderno, 1606–12; piazza, colonnades designed by Gianlorenzo Bernini, 1656–63. Height of façade 147 ft (44.81 m), width 374 ft (114 m).
Maderno's gigantic façade, with columns more than twice the height of the Parthenon's in Athens, completed the century-long project begun by the Renaissance pope Julius II.

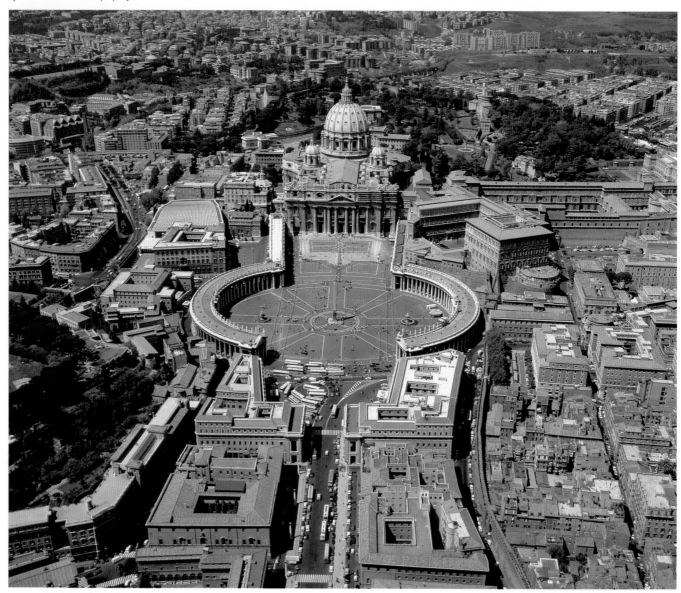

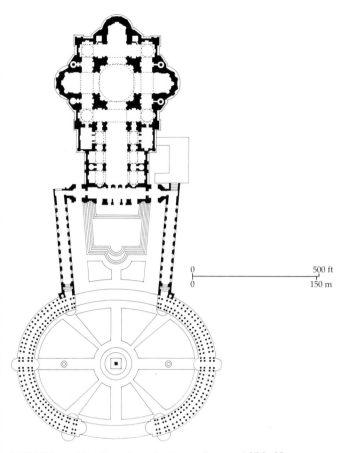

10.10 Plan of St. Peter's and piazza, Rome, 1656–63.

BERNINI AS ARCHITECT

When Maffeo Barberini became Pope Urban VIII in 1623, he said to the artist Bernini: "Your luck is great to see Cardinal Maffeo Barberini pope; but ours is much greater to have Cavalier Bernini alive in our pontificate." The pope was not being modest. He and his contemporaries recognized Bernini as the greatest living artist, a genius of the baroque.

Gianlorenzo Bernini (1598–1680) possessed an inexhaustible imagination and the energy to see his works through to completion. Propelled by the last great burst of Church-sponsored patronage, Bernini managed to exceed the Renaissance titans in the ambition and virtuosity of his art. His task was to complete and decorate St. Peter's basilica, the Renaissance project of Bramante, Michelangelo, and countless other architects. Bernini was instructed first to build an immense altar canopy of gilded bronze, to stand beneath Michelangelo's imposing dome. Abandoning his predecessors' classicism, Bernini supported the canopy or *baldacchino* (Fig. **10.8**) with twisted columns, ornately covered with laurel leaves (an emblem of his Barberini patron). As a triumph of sculpture and architecture, the *baldacchino* [bal-da-KEE-noh] mediates between the human worshiper and the superhuman scale of Michelangelo's basilica.

In 1656 Bernini took up the challenge to build a plaza in front of St. Peter's. The nave and façade of St. Peter's had been completed by Carlo Maderno in 1612, more than a century after the church was begun. Bernini's plaza had to begin at Maderno's wide façade and narrow to accommodate existing buildings. Then, it had to widen again, providing space for the many thousands of pilgrims and worshipers who gathered to receive the pope's blessing.

Bernini's solution was a triumph of ingenuity. The plaza began with a trapezoidal forecourt, then widened into two elliptical colonnades that opened like huge arms to enclose the faithful masses (Fig. **10.10**). The colonnades were composed of four rows of massive columns in the Tuscan order (much like the Doric). From a bird's-eye view (Fig. **10.9**), the plaza resembled a giant keyhole, symbol of the keys to God's kingdom given St. Peter by Christ. Bernini had completed St. Peter's with a triumphant baroque flourish, expanding its setting on a monumental scale and providing a dramatic entrance to the church of Bramante and Michelangelo.

10.11 Gianlorenzo Bernini, *David*, 1623–4. Marble, height 5 ft 6¹/₄ ins (1.68 m). Borghese Gallery, Rome.
The figure's tension and energy extend from the furrowed brow to the toes of the right foot, which clench the edge of the supporting plinth.

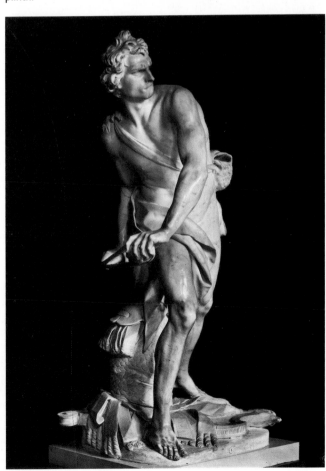

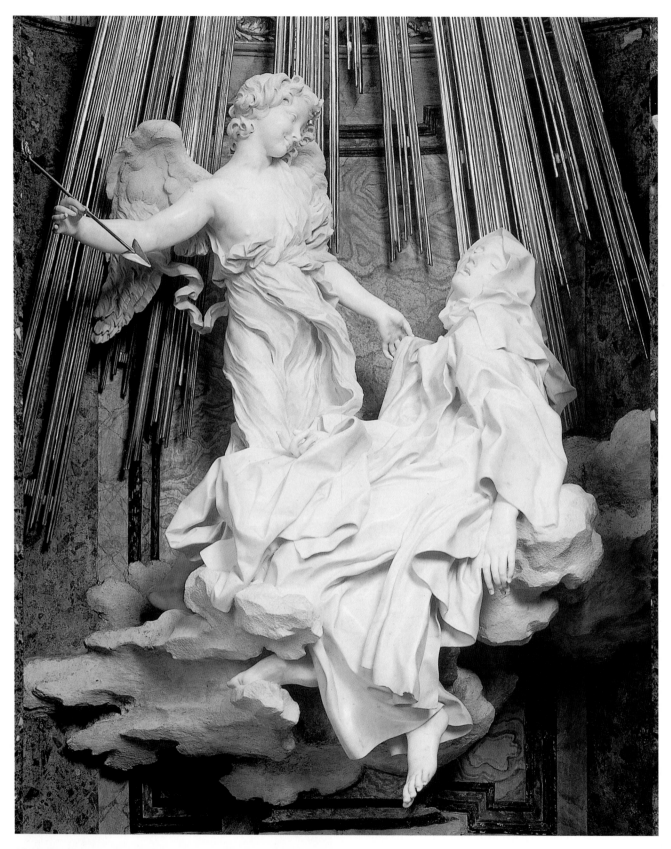

10.12 Gianlorenzo Bernini, *Ecstasy of St. Teresa*, 1645–52. Cornaro Chapel, Santa Maria della Vittoria, Rome. Marble and gilt bronze, life-size.
In a depiction of St. Teresa's ecstatic vision, the angel of God pierces Teresa's heart with the barb of divine love. The drama seems to be illuminated by the light of God; actually, the light comes from a hidden window above the sculpture.

BERNINI AS SCULPTOR

Like his designs for St. Peter's, Bernini's sculpture infused Renaissance technique with the dynamism and emotional force of the baroque style. His *David* (Fig. **10.11**), for example, provides a vivid contrast to Michelangelo's Renaissance *David* (see Fig. 8.24). As the giant Goliath approaches, Bernini's David prepares to cast his stone, creating the diagonal twisting so typical of baroque sculpture and painting. The determined grimace on David's face may be a self-portrait of Bernini's facial expression as he worked intensely at the stone. Although Bernini's *David* lacks the monumental presence of Michelangelo's hero, its emotional frankness is more dramatic and perhaps even more human.

10.13 Cornaro Chapel, Santa Maria della Vittoria, Rome. Observe Bernini's baroque fusion of the arts to create a theatrical setting for the *Ecstasy of St. Teresa*: a complex architectural niche for the main sculpture, backed by gilded rays of divine light; an elaborate ceiling painting, not visible in this photograph; and, most unusual, sculpted figures of the Cornaro family in balconies at either side, viewing Teresa's dream as if it were a staged drama.

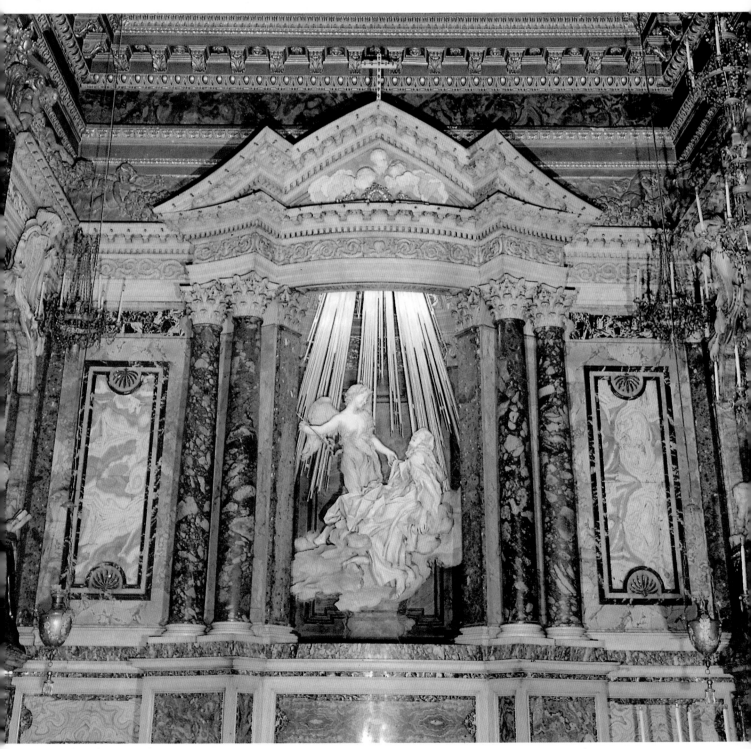

Among Bernini's many sculptural works, the Cornaro Chapel in Rome stands out as a masterpiece of illusionism and virtuoso technique – key elements of the baroque style. The chapel's sculptural centerpiece, the *Ecstasy of St. Teresa* (Fig. **10.12**), depicts the saint's ecstatic union with God. In sensuous language, Teresa described her vision of an angel:

In his hands I saw a great golden spear, and at the iron tip there appeared to be a point of fire. This he plunged into my heart several times so that it penetrated to my entrails. When he pulled it out, I felt that he took them with it, and left me utterly consumed by the great love of God. The pain was so severe that it made me utter several moans. The sweetness caused by this intense pain is so extreme that one cannot possibly wish it to cease, nor is one's soul then content with anything but God.[2]

In Bernini's depiction, the angel (which is also a cupid, symbol of erotic love) has withdrawn his spear. Teresa's lidded eyes and limp body show that she is overwhelmed by the "gentle wooing" of God, consumed in equal measure by sweetness and pain. The angel is draped in a swirling gown, while the sculptural group seems to float on a heavenly cloud.

The sculpture's illusionism is underlined by its theatrical setting in the Cornaro Chapel (Fig. **10.13**). The ceiling painting above shows the heavenly source of the divine light illuminating the statue. From theatrical boxes on either side, sculpted figures of the Cornaro family witness Teresa's vision and respond with different states of pious emotion. Bernini combines the visual arts of painting, architecture, and sculpture to present St. Teresa's ecstatic vision as if it were a piece of theater. This fusion of the arts is characteristic of the baroque.

CARAVAGGIO

The Italian painter Michelangelo Caravaggio (1573–1610) used dramatic contrasts of light and dark to depict realistic biblical scenes. Caravaggio's biblical characters looked so much like Italian peasants that his work was often

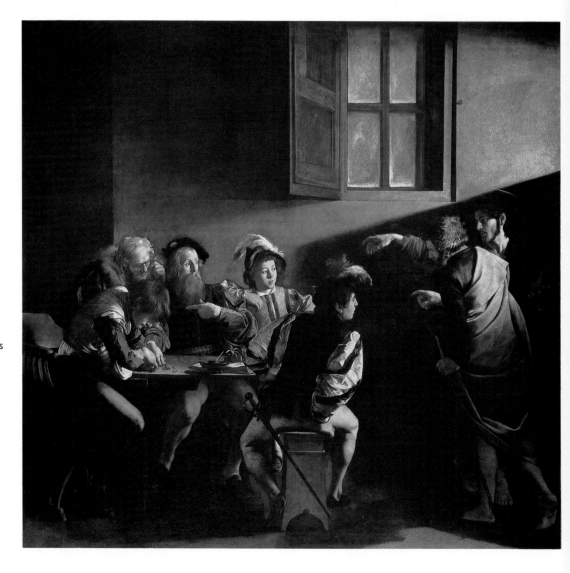

10.14 Caravaggio, *The Calling of St. Matthew*, c. 1547–8. **Contarelli Chapel, San Luigi dei Francesi, Rome. Oil on canvas, 11 ft 1 ins x 11 ft 5 ins (3.38 x 3.48 m).**
As Christ calls Matthew to discipleship, the tax collector (pointing to himself) responds with bewilderment and surprise. Christ's languid gesture is reinforced by the angled stream of light pouring into the room from right. Interpret the picture's symbolic contrasts: light vs. dark, rich garments vs. simple cloaks, dueler's sword vs. disciple's staff.

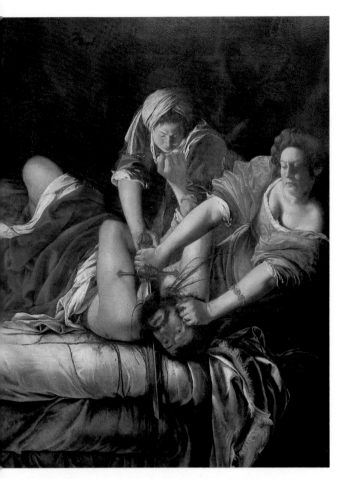

**10.15 Artemisia Gentileschi, *Judith Slaying Holofernes*,
c. 1620. Oil on canvas, 6 ft 6¹/₃ ins x 5 ft 4 ins (1.99 x
1.63 m). Uffizi, Florence.**
The Israelite heroine Judith slays the Assyrian general whose army
besieges her city. Trace the radiating lines that draw the eye to the
central action.

rejected by his patrons, who preferred idealized, conventional treatments to the graphic realism and contemporary settings of his paintings.

The *Calling of St. Matthew* (Fig. **10.14**) depicts a rude tavern much like those that Caravaggio frequented in his brief, turbulent life. On the left, Matthew is shown among a group of finely dressed Italian courtiers, who count the day's tax collections. Into this humble room steps Christ himself, accompanied by St. Peter. Christ calls Matthew to leave a dark world of sin and error (Matthew 9:9). The call is issued, not from Christ's shadowed face, but in the warm shaft of light that flows from an unseen window. The light, falling on Christ's pointing hand, singles out Matthew for a life of blessedness and discipleship. Caravaggio's message is much in the spirit of baroque religiosity: even a despised tax collector may be lifted from sin's darkness by the sudden light of God's grace.

Caravaggio's patrons had doubts about his effort to create a truly popular religious art. However, his dramatic use of *chiaroscuro*, or effects of light and shadow, quickly influenced artists in Italy and eventually throughout Europe. In Italy, one inventive follower was the artist Artemisia

Gentileschi [jen-ti-LESS-kee] (1593–1652), whose life and career show the challenges of being a female artist in Europe in the seventeenth century. As a pupil, Gentileschi was sexually abused by the painter employed by her artist father to train her. After a scandalous rape trial, Gentileschi resumed her career in Naples, taking Caravaggio's techniques to give dramatic effect to her paintings. One of Gentileschi's favorite themes was Judith and Holofernes, a Hebrew legend widely illustrated in Renaissance and baroque art. The Israelite heroine saved her besieged city by murdering Holofernes, commander of the attacking Assyrian army. In the version shown here (Fig. **10.15**), Gentileschi depicts the moment of violence itself. The brilliant foreground lighting pushes the action forward toward the viewer, increasing the sense of horror and violence.

THE BIRTH OF OPERA

By the middle of the seventeenth century, Italy was already losing the preeminence in the visual arts that it had held since the early Renaissance. In opera, however, Italy was to retain its position of superiority. **Opera** is musical theater in which all or most of the dialogue is sung, usually accompanied by an orchestra and staged with elaborate costumes and sets. It thus fuses the arts of music, theater, painting, and dance, making it one of Western civilization's most complete and extravagant artistic forms. Opera was born in the experiments of the Florentine Camerata (see page 205), grew to maturity in the baroque houses of Venice and Rome, and spread from Italy throughout Europe.

The first great operatic composer was Claudio Monteverdi (1567–1643), who was also a master of the madrigal and other musical forms. At the court of Mantua in 1607, Monteverdi [mohn-te-VAIR-dee] produced the first operatic masterpiece, *Orfeo* [or-FAY-o], based on the myth of Orpheus' journey to the underworld to rescue his beloved Euridice. Until this performance, opera had consisted of **recitatives** that told the story in a half-sung, half-spoken tone of limited emotional range. Monteverdi expanded the recitative musically to convey the intense feelings of his characters. In a famous solo, *Tu se' morta* (*You are dead*; Fig. **10.16**), Orpheus grieves his lover's death in a melodic line that draws him toward the underworld.

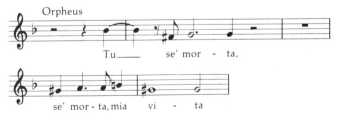

**10.16 Claudio Monteverdi, *Tu se' morta* (*You Are Dead*),
recitative from *Orfeo*, 1607.**

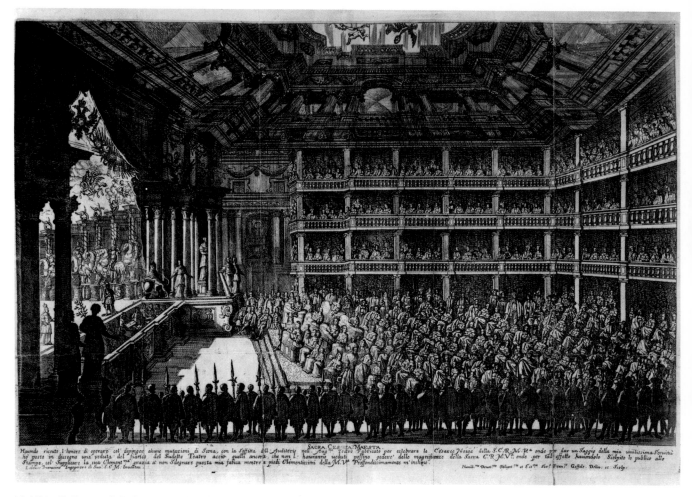

10.17 L. O. Burnacini, *Opera on the Cortina*, Vienna, 1665–6. Engraving. Historisches Museum der Stadt, Vienna.
Opera's commercial success in Italy led to the construction of lavish public opera houses throughout Europe. The rows of box seats permitted status-minded patrons to observe each other with as much interest as they viewed the performance.

You are dead, my life,
and I breathe?
You have left me,
Never, never more to return,
and I remain?[3]

Monteverdi applied the Renaissance technique of word-painting to reflect his characters' emotional state. More frequently than Palestrina, he used **chordal dissonances**, groups of tones that caused the listener to feel discomfort and to anticipate a resolution. This emotional expressiveness in Monteverdi's music corresponded to the interest in human emotion visible in Bernini's sculpture and Caravaggio's painting.

Throughout the seventeenth century, opera continued to develop as an art form. The expansion of recitative gave rise to the operatic **aria**, an independent song. The aria halted the story temporarily while the character revealed his or her feelings in song. The aria was often the occasion for crowd-pleasing virtuoso singing. Gradually, opera

evolved into two forms – **opera seria** and **opera buffa**. *Opera seria* was based on the lofty mythological themes favored by courtly aristocrats, while *opera buffa* was comic opera that had broader appeal to the urban middle class. Both forms were so popular that in 1637 the first public opera house opened in Venice. Similar theaters soon appeared in Rome, Naples, and throughout Europe (Fig. **10.17**), and Italian opera became an immensely popular international form.

Vivaldi and Italian Baroque Music It was in Venice that the best-known Italian baroque composer, Antonio Vivaldi (1678–1741), spent his entire career as musical director at a school for orphan girls and young women. The residents' musicianship must have been remarkably high to perform Vivaldi's difficult compositions.

Vivaldi was a master of the baroque **concerto** (or *concerto grosso* [kun-CHAIR-to GROH-so]), a musical form in which a small group of instruments plays in concert (or "conflict") with a larger orchestra. Vivaldi's most famous

KEY CONCEPT

ABSOLUTISM

The turbulence and emotion expressed in baroque art reflected deeper and more fatal divisions in seventeenth-century European society. Incessant war and civil disorder ravaged Germany, where the Thirty Years' War (1618–48) destroyed one-third of the population. England was split by a bitter civil war between Puritan parliamentarians and Catholic royalists. In 1649 English Puritan rebels beheaded King Charles I (1600–49), but only eleven years later agreed to a restoration of the English crown.

From this civil war and religious strife, the era's chief political problem emerged: how to maintain social order and the rule of law in the nations of Europe. One solution was to give absolute power to a monarch, who could then subdue the contending factions. This doctrine of **absolutism** dictated that a monarch exercise supreme political power and control every aspect of national life. An absolutist monarch was able to end quarrels among political factions and impose uniform national laws and economic policies. Although today it is a synonym for tyranny, in the seventeenth century absolutism was a progressive and modern political idea.

Absolutism's leading philosophical defender came from the royalist ranks of divided England. In 1651, while the Puritans ruled England, Thomas Hobbes (1588–1669) published *Leviathan* (1651), which defended the rule of a monarchy from a realist and secular perspective. Hobbes' treatise reflected his deep pessimism about humanity. Without a king to rule them, Hobbes believed people could expect a barren life that was "solitary, poor, nasty, brutish, and short." The all-powerful sovereign, or "Leviathan," imposed a brutal but benevolent order on the life of an unruly nation.

One need not share Hobbes' pessimism to see the advantages of the absolutist state. In France, the royal bureaucracy improved the efficiency of gov-

ernment, raised a standing army of half a million, and generously supported the arts. France's king symbolized the nation's unity and international prestige. According to the famous motto attributed to Louis XIV (Fig. **10.18**), *L'état, c'est moi* – "I am the state" – personal homage to the king was an act of patriotism. Indeed, many features of modern political life now associated with republican democracies first arose under the absolutism of the seventeenth century.

10.18 Hyacinthe Rigaud, *Louis XIV*, 1701. Oil on canvas, 9 ft 1¹/₂ ins x 6 ft 2⁵/₈ ins (2.78 x 1.9 m). Louvre, Paris.

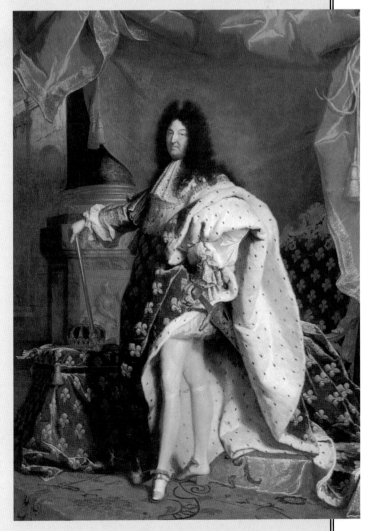

CRITICAL QUESTION
In times of war or crisis, leaders in modern governments often assume nearly absolute powers. What dangers are there in ceding extraordinary powers to government in times of war, imperiled national security, or social unrest?

work is *The Four Seasons* (1725), a suite of four concertos still widely performed today. The first concerto, *La Primavera* (*Spring*), is in three movements, with alternating tempos (fast-slow-fast). In the first movement of *Spring*, violins dramatize the arrival of spring: its birdsongs, murmuring streams, and sudden thunderstorms. These dramatic episodes are connected by a recurring melody (called a *ritornello*, or "something that returns"), which provides an explicit regularity to the composition. Within this somewhat rigid structure, Vivaldi achieved brilliant variations and embellishments. Music publishers disseminated Vivaldi's music to all corners of Europe, where it was studied by Johann Sebastian Bach and other masters of the later baroque.

THE BAROQUE IN FRANCE

Identify the neoclassical elements of architecture, theater, and music at Louis XIV's court.

10.19 Gianlorenzo Bernini, *Louis XIV*, 1665. Marble, height 33¹/₈ ins (84 cm). Palace of Versailles, France.
This idealized portrait of the Sun King suggests both the sun-god Apollo and the great Macedonian general Alexander the Great. Note how Bernini created a baroque sense of dynamic motion by dissolving the torso into a dramatic swirl of drapery.

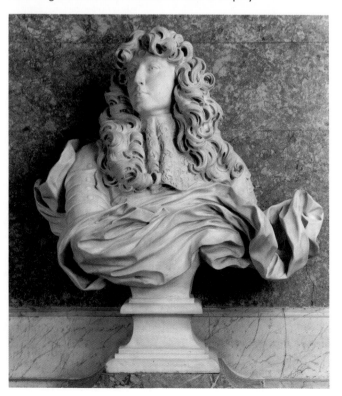

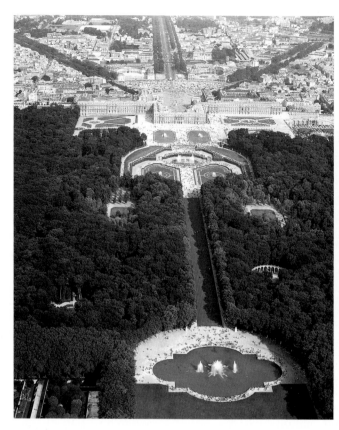

10.20 Louis Le Vau and Jules Hardouin-Mansart, an aerial view of the Palace of Versailles, France, 1669–85. Overall width of palace, 1935 ft (590 m).
The unified and rational design of the main palace and grounds expressed Louis XIV's desire for absolute control over the nation and nature. The majesty of Versailles inspired other European monarchs to build imitations and also influenced the plan of Washington, D.C., with its radiating axes and great mall.

The spectacle of power was never better understood, or more carefully manipulated, than during the reign of Louis XIV of France. In 1660 Louis took personal control of the French government with the words, "Now the theater changes." Planning to make France a grand stage for his majesty and power, within a year he began the construction of his palace at Versailles [vair-SIGH]. Louis XIV proved to be a master in the guises of absolutist power, assuming such roles as the "Sun-King" in a court ballet and commissioning a commanding portrait bust sculpted by Bernini (Fig. **10.19**).

An enthusiast of dance and theater, Louis XIV did not hesitate to enlist the arts in supporting his reign. He exerted absolutist control in cultural affairs via the **academies**, state-sponsored agencies that dictated standards of artistic training and taste. Under Louis XIV, academies governed all the major arts, including theater, dance, opera, and painting and sculpture. Although they brought order to the patronage of art in France, the academies also imposed conservative rules that stifled artistic innovation. These rules depended on the revival of classical Greek and Roman forms, creating a style termed **neoclassical**.

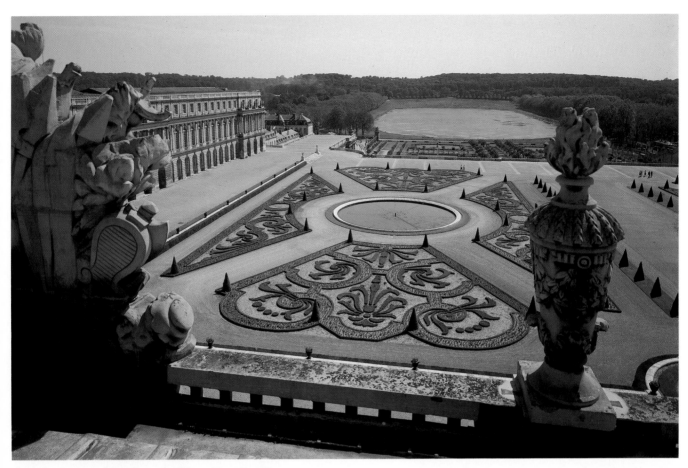

10.21 *Parterre du Midi*, **Palace of Versailles, France.**
Nature as viewed by absolutism: designed by reason and intended
for royal pleasure and spectacle.

THE PALACE OF VERSAILLES

The Palace of Versailles was balanced and restrained in its design, yet lavish in scale and decoration – a compromise between baroque excess and neoclassical rules, the ultimate synthesis of styles. Louis XIV's minister Colbert once advised him that "with the exception of brilliant military actions nothing speaks so eloquently of the grandeur and cleverness of princes as buildings." Taking this advice to heart, in 1661 Louis began enlarging his father's hunting château near the village of Versailles, about 20 miles (32 km) outside Paris. The château was located in a vast hunting reserve owned by the crown. The site offered the king's architects and planners the freedom they had lacked in remodeling the Louvre Palace in Paris. The original architect, Louis Le Vau [luh VOH], worked together with designers of the gardens (André le Nôtre) and interior decoration (Charles Lebrun). Later modifications, principally the long projecting wings, were made by Le Vau's successor, Jules Hardouin-Mansart [mahn-SAH(r)]. Together the designers created a unified and symmetrical design (Fig. **10.20**), an architectural universe with the king at the center.

The palace complex at Versailles expanded to accommodate Louis XIV's changing vision of the absolutist court. The palace was originally intended as a retreat from the bustle of the Paris court. Soon, however, Louis demanded that the influential French nobility come to live with him at Versailles, where he could control their influence – a move which impoverished the nobility by extravagant living. Eventually the palace accommodated a population estimated at fifty thousand, including government officials, courtiers, and a sizeable royal family. Aside from the main palace, the Versailles complex incorporated royal stables for twelve thousand horses and elaborate gardens covering several hundred acres (Fig. **10.21**). In later years, Louis had smaller palaces built on the grounds, in which he could escape the crush of courtiers. As a whole, Versailles projected absolutist power on a vast scale and according to a rationalized scheme that was to influence city planning for the next century.

The palace's garden façade (Fig. **10.22**) synthesized neoclassical and Italian baroque elements as designed by Jules Hardouin-Mansart. The neoclassical style was evident in the restraint of the three levels of the palace building: a plain ground arcade; the main level with its shallow

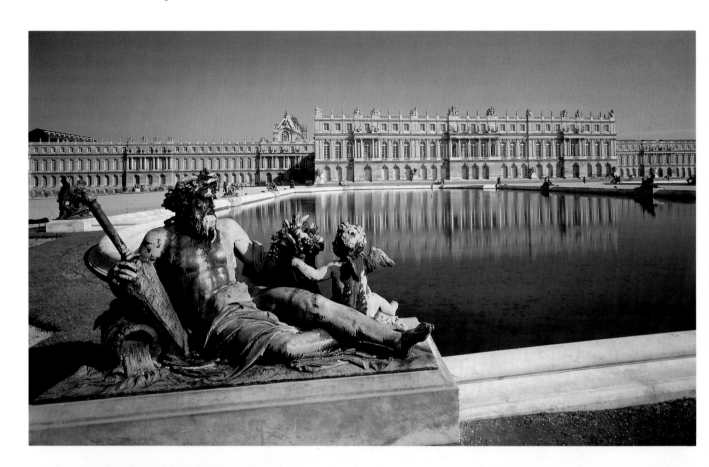

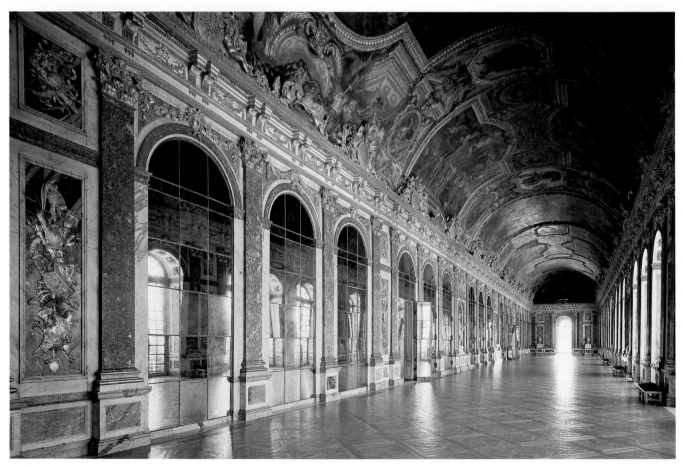

10.22 Opposite top Louis Le Vau and Jules Hardouin-Mansart, garden façade, Palace of Versailles, France, 1669–85.
Versailles' façade was mirrored in the pools and fountains that help create an atmosphere of grandeur and pomp.

10.23 Opposite below Jules Hardouin-Mansart and Charles Lebrun, Hall of Mirrors, Palace of Versailles, France, begun 1676. Length 240 ft (73.2 m), width 34 ft (10.36 m).
The spectacular hall was actually designed as a setting for Lebrun's rather undistinguished ceiling paintings. The arched mirrors create a sense of spaciousness that belies the room's modest width.

columned porticos; and the upper level topped by elaborate statues and balustrade. The simplicity and charm of Mansart's façade are dwarfed somewhat by the palace's wings, which stretch nearly 2000 feet (609 m) from end to end.

Mansart's greatest stroke of genius is visible inside the palace, in the famed Hall of Mirrors (Fig. **10.23**). Here, overlooking the garden, Mansart built a row of floor-length windows and on the facing wall placed matching windows of mirrored glass. With its grand length, the brilliant light and gilded decoration of the Hall of Mirrors embodies the lavish splendor of Louis XIV's court.

The Palace of Versailles was an achievement of the absolutist power of the monarch, Louis XIV, and of an evolving and distinctly French national style. Under Louis's patronage, the French arts finally threw off their dependence on Italian artists and models, enabling France to become an influential cultural center in its own right. For more than a century, France influenced the tastes of foreign rulers who aspired to the greatness and magnificence of the court at Versailles.

THE PERFORMING ARTS AT VERSAILLES

King Louis XIV generously patronized the theater and dance of his country, while enforcing stringent control. He granted dictatorial power over the performing arts to the academies, whose influence in the arts dates from 1636, when a royal minister asked a scholarly group called the *Académie Française* to judge a popular tragedy. The Academy quickly became official judge in matters of literary form and taste, imposing strict neoclassical rules on the theater. The Academy decreed that plays performed by Paris' emerging professional theater must be divided into five acts, obey the unities of time and place, and provide an uplifting moral.

Only an exceptional playwright could thrive under these restrictions. The age of Louis XIV could boast of two, the tragedian Jean Racine [rah-SEEN] and the comedian Molière [mohl-YAY(r)]. Jean Racine (1639–99), following the path of his older competitor Pierre Corneille [kor-NAY-(ee)], presented classical themes in a consciously artificial academic style. Racine's tragedies were strictly governed by the neoclassical unities, concentrating the plot in a single main action and locale. The characters spoke in an exalted rhymed verse, as dictated by the Academy. His themes were usually drawn from ancient Greek tragedy, though Racine's noble characters were often subject to ordinary human weakness and passion. Despite academic restrictions, Racine's tragedies presented a compelling drama of characters driven by their own desires and folly. He was often criticized for being too realistic. The neoclassical tragedies of Corneille and Racine have remained in the standard repertoire of French theater until this day.

Jean Baptiste Poquelin, known as Molière (1622–73), used his biting wit to attack the hypocrisy and vice of French society. Molière was a playwright, actor, and part-owner of his own theatrical company (Fig. **10.24**) and had early gained the favor of Louis XIV, who granted his company a theater inside the Louvre in Paris in 1658. Several of Molière's masterpieces were first performed at the court of Versailles. Among Molière's greatest comedies were *Tartuffe* (1664), the story of a religious hypocrite, and *Le Bourgeois Gentilhomme* (*The Would-be Gentleman*, 1671), which mocked France's boorish social climbers. Ironically, Molière was acting in his comedy-ballet *The Imaginary Invalid* (1673), the story of a hypochondriac, when he collapsed and died at Versailles. His plays were exceptional in their relentless wit and consistent moral attitude, and showed a careful observation of social manners of the time. Molière himself was a practical middle-class professional who always favored moderation and common sense over vanity and deceit.

Molière frequently collaborated in court entertainments with the composer and dance master Jean-Baptiste Lully [LOO-lee] (1632–87), the central figure in the devel-

10.24 Molière (Jean-Baptiste Poquelin) in the farcical role of Sganarelle from his own play *The Doctor in Spite of Himself*, a mocking depiction of medical quackery. Engraving. Bibliothèque Nationale, Paris.

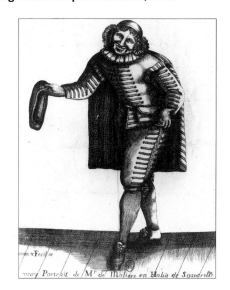

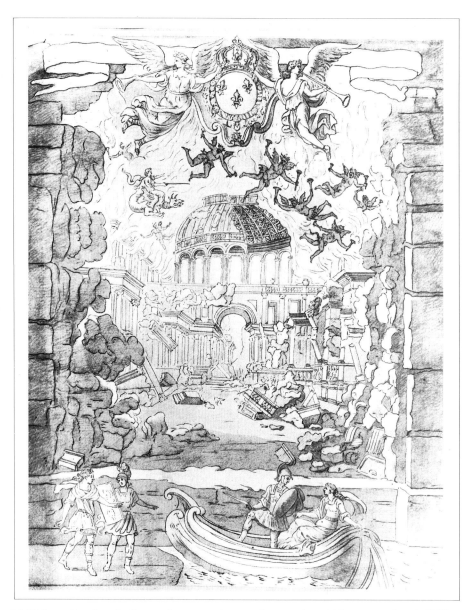

10.25 Jean-Baptiste Lully used spectacular staging to please his patron, Louis XIV. Here a palace collapses beneath a flight of devils during the opera _Armide_, first performed in 1686. Bibliothèque Nationale, Paris.

opment of classical ballet and French opera. Lully's royal sponsor, the young Louis XIV, appeared in his _Ballet de la Nuit_; by 1671, Lully had used his influence as royal dance master to become head of the Royal Academy of Music. From this position he ruled as virtual dictator over French music, opera, and dance.

In the baroque period, ballets were usually danced as interludes and entrées during the performance of a comedy or an opera. Ballet typically mimed or illustrated the drama's action. As an adjunct to the opera, Lully established a school of dance that developed what we know as the classical ballet – a regimented dance form based on five basic foot positions and a precisely defined vocabulary of movement. Under Lully's regime, the classical bal-

let evolved into a flexible and expressive art form. Among the dance school's advances were the first appearance of professional women dancers in ballet (1681) and the publication of a manual of choreography (1700) that standardized dance notation.

Lully also proved a versatile operatic composer: in fourteen years he wrote twenty operas that remained standards for more than a century. Like French architecture, French opera grew up under the shadow of the popular Italian version. The French aristocracy preferred their opera with Italian-style elaborate staging and elevated mythological themes (Fig. **10.25**). Lully developed a national style in opera that suited the French desire for pomp and spectacle.

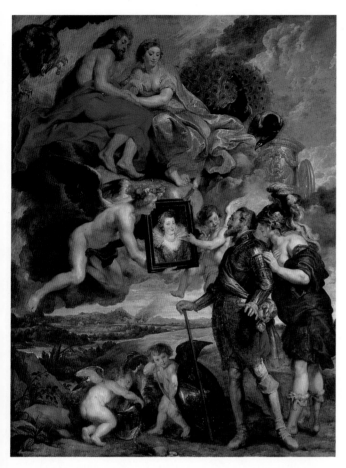

10.26 Peter Paul Rubens, *Henry IV Receiving the Portrait of Marie de' Medici*, 1622–5. Oil on canvas, 13 ft x 9 ft 8 ins (3.96 x 2.95 m). Louvre, Paris.
Note the centers of dramatic interest (Juno and Jupiter on the clouds, the portrait of Marie de' Medici itself, the goddess Minerva whispering in the king's ear, the cupids playing with the king's heavy armor). How does the sweeping line formed by these points highlight the painting's center of interest?

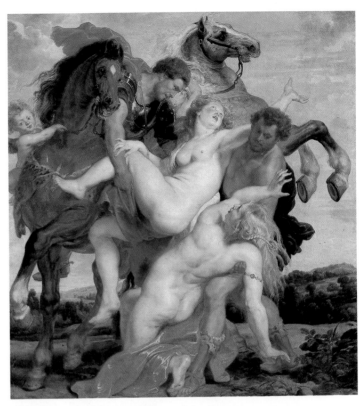

10.27 Peter Paul Rubens, *Rape of the Daughters of Leucippus*, c. 1618. Oil on canvas, 7 ft 3 ins x 6 ft 10 ins (2.21 x 2.08 m). Alte Pinakothek, Munich.
Amid the scene's furious motion, Rubens presents a striking contrast of textures in the translucent flesh of the nude women, Castor's swarthy skin and hard, shell-like armor, and the dappled horses. Trace the crisscrossing diagonal lines that draw the sisters' bodies together.

RUBENS AND POUSSIN: PAINTERS OF THE COURT

The seventeenth-century European nobility's favorite painter was a master of the baroque style, Peter Paul Rubens (1577–1640). His works decorated royal palaces from Spain to England, and the artist himself traveled frequently from his native Flanders (now Belgium) to the courts of Madrid, Paris, and London. Like Titian, the Renaissance master, Rubens earned a substantial fortune while serving his noble patrons.

Rubens' most famous commission illustrated his flair for dynamic composition and lavish color. In 1621, the artist was engaged to paint the life of Marie de' Medici, dowager queen of France. Ever the charming courtier, Rubens inflated the queen's life story into a monumental series of twenty-one canvases to hang in the new Parisian palace she was building. Rubens made it seem as if the

gods themselves had sponsored her career. In one scene, Marie's future husband, King Henry IV, is presented with her engagement portrait by the god Mercury (Fig. **10.26**). Minerva, the helmeted goddess of wisdom, counsels him to accept the match, while Juno and Jupiter look on approvingly from the heavens. Rubens completed the gigantic commission in just four years, employing assistants to paint background detail while he himself painted the figures.

Rubens excelled in the favorite themes of European aristocracy: hunting scenes, histories, classical and mythological subjects, and portraits. Such scenes permitted the aristocratic patron to identify with figures of military and romantic prowess. In Rubens' *Rape of the Daughters of Leucippus* (Fig. **10.27**), the two gods Castor and Pollux visit earth to take two mortal women as wives. The two sisters' energetic resistance to their violent kidnapping is emphasized in the twisted forms of their

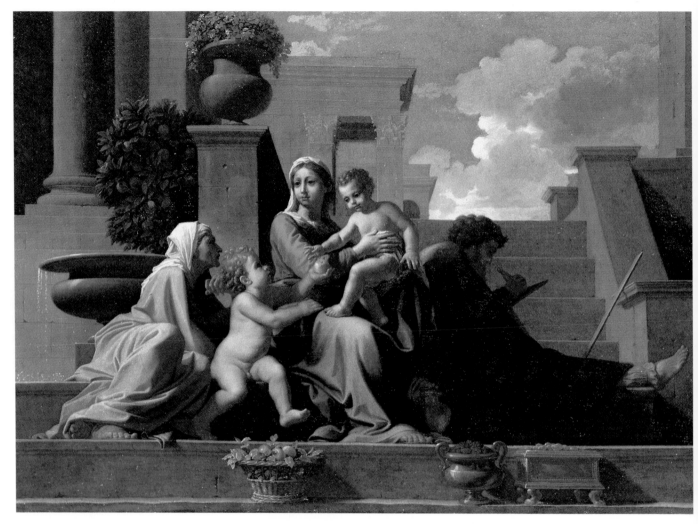

10.28 Nicolas Poussin, *The Holy Family on the Steps*, 1648. Oil on canvas, 28¹/₂ x 44 ins (72.4 x 111.7 cm). Cleveland Museum of Art, Leonard C. Hanna, Jr., Fund, 1981.18.
The painting's low horizon emphasizes the strong horizontal lines in the steps and temple roofs. Analyze the Christian symbolism of the three gifts and the oranges and apples. Note also the oddly positioned figure of Joseph at right, in shadow and studying a slate.

bodies. The furious motion of the picture leads upward, one sister being lifted awkwardly but inevitably toward heaven. The clash of textures, the diagonal lines, and the twisted forms, create a nearly unbearable drama of baroque violence and energy.

In contrast to the baroque dynamism of Rubens' paintings, the French painter Nicolas Poussin (1594–1665) was the essence of baroque neoclassicism, in both style and sensibility. While Rubens thrived among the intrigues of the court, Poussin [poo-SAN(h)] fled Versailles and spent most of his career quietly in Rome. Poussin's paintings gave a new expression to the tradition of classicism; his human figures were as cool and precisely defined as classical statues.

The clarity of Poussin's style is visible in all his later pictures, which include *The Holy Family on the Steps* (Fig. **10.28**). In this painting, Elizabeth and her infant son John the Baptist – figured on the left – visit the Holy Fam-

ily, who are framed by a rigorously neoclassical architectural setting. The light and shadow emphasize the pyramidal grouping of the figures. The repeated geometric shapes (rectangular pillars, ovoid vases, cylindrical columns) provide an explicit regularity of structure. Poussin's canvases so fully confirmed academic tastes that they soon became the model for all French painting. Ironically, the

CRITICAL QUESTION

Compare the violence of Gentileschi's *Judith Slaying Holofernes* with Peter Paul Rubens' depiction of the *Rape of the Daughters of Leucippus*. What do the two paintings say about the artists' attitude toward men, women, power, and sexuality?

academic style was advanced furthest by a painter who exiled himself from the absolutist court and its extravagant tastes.

MUSIC OF THE PROTESTANT BAROQUE

Define several musical forms, both sacred and secular, in which Bach excelled as a composer.

Germany in the seventeenth century was politically divided and suffered from the devastation of the Thirty Years' War (1618–48). Also, it had no absolutist monarchs to impose a national culture as had France and Spain. Artists had to find patronage at small German courts or in Germany's prosperous, mostly Protestant, cities. From such modest circumstances emerged the baroque composer Johann Sebastian Bach (1685–1750). Although hardly known in his lifetime outside a circle of friends, Bach is now acknowledged as one of the world's most prolific musical geniuses (Fig. **10.29**).

J. S. Bach

Bach excelled in the musical forms, both secular and sacred, that were regularly performed in Germany's courts and churches. His music typically exhibited two essential features of baroque concert music. One was elaborate **counter-**

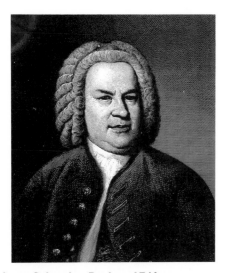

10.29 Johann Sebastian Bach, c. 1746.
Bach's younger contemporaries criticized his music for its old-fashioned baroque intricacy and virtuosity, although later generations highly praised these qualities.

point, that is, the combination of two or more melodies of equal importance. The term "counterpoint" is sometimes used as a synonym for polyphony, but traditionally is associated with the age of Bach. The second feature is the *basso continuo*, a prominent bass line that harmonically supports the polyphonic lines.

Both counterpoint and *basso continuo* are prominent features of the six *Brandenburg Concertos* (1721), which Bach composed for a friend of his noble patron. In the *Brandenburg Concerto No. 2*, a solo ensemble of flute, oboe, trumpet, and violin engage in a polyphonic conversation. A *continuo* provides a harmonic ground. Like his predecessor Antonio Vivaldi, Bach employs a recurring *ritornello* to punctuate the ensemble's melodic explorations.

In 1721 Bach was appointed music director and composer of the St. Thomas' choir school in Leipzig, a post of considerable civic and musical prestige. He composed music for the city's four major churches, served as organist for the church of St. Thomas, instructed the choirs, taught at the school, and undertook additional commissions for German nobles. Still, the composer found time to give music lessons to his children and hold musical concerts at home. Four of his sons became musicians, and two were famous composers in their own right.

For each week's religious service at St. Thomas' church, Bach provided a **cantata**, a choral work that provided the principal music of Lutheran worship. The text for the cantata was chosen for a particular Sunday or feast day, and celebrated the yearly cycle of the church calendar. Typically, the cantata contained recitative and aria-like forms, and served as a kind of sacred opera for the Lutherans. Bach frequently closed his cantatas with a familiar Lutheran hymn, which the congregation might join in singing. The tireless Bach composed about three hundred cantatas in all, enough for five complete cycles of the liturgical year.

The "Well-tempered Keyboard"

Bach's music illustrated the development of a new system of composition in baroque music. As early as 1600, European composers had devised a system of musical **keys** to replace the traditional modes used by ancient and medieval musicians. In a musical key, the seven intervals between the eight notes of an octave scale are arranged according to a specific formula of whole and half tones (Fig. **10.30**). Much like perspective in Renaissance painting, the major-minor key system provided composers with a carefully rationalized framework for their musical creations. Musical keys became so familiar to Western listeners that anything composed outside the system sounded "unnatural."

A musical key's principal pitch, called a **tonic**, serves as a tonal center to the entire composition. For example, a melody written in the key of C usually begins and ends on the tonic C. The baroque composers learned to trans-

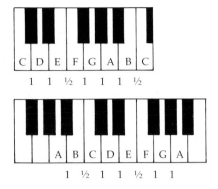

10.30 The major and minor scales.
The keyboards show the formulas of whole and half tones for the major and minor key systems. For the key of C major, the progression C-D-E-F-G-A-B-C can be played on a piano's white keys. Minor keys (A minor is shown here) are built on a different progression of whole and half tones. The key signatures of the major and minor keys show which sharps or flats are required to maintain the proper sequence of whole and half tones.

pose a melody from one key to another key without altering the tune. This technique of changing keys within a composition, called **modulation**, provided a new variety and range. Usually, a composer would modulate back to the beginning, or "home," key at the end of a musical work, providing a sense of closure and completion. The hierarchical sense of order and the possibility for seemingly infinite variation in this system appealed to the baroque sensibility.

Bach composed a set of musical exercises, entitled the *Well-Tempered Clavier* (1722), to prove that a clavier (any

stringed keyboard instrument) could be tuned to accommodate all twenty-four major and minor keys. ("Tempered" refers to the tuning, not a mood.) Bach's demonstrations took the form of preludes and fugues: the **prelude** (also called *toccata*) is a free form designed to show off the keyboard player's virtuoso ability. The **fugue** is a polyphonic musical form in which a theme is developed through elaborate counterpoint (Fig. **10.31**). The fugue begins with a theme (or "subject"), which is answered by another melodic line (the "counter-subject"). The voices continue to build, repeating the subject or counter-subjects and exploring contrapuntal variations. In fugues composed for the organ, the *basso continuo* is played on the foot pedals. Both these popular baroque forms displayed the virtuosity of composer and player and appealed to the baroque love of intricacy and embellishment.

Though Bach composed no operas, he was the author of a monumental masterpiece of musical storytelling, the *St. Matthew Passion* (1727). A "passion" recounted the last days of Christ's life, and its emotions ranged from the despair of the crucifixion of the triumphant joy of resurrection. The *St. Matthew Passion* was a gigantic work, calling for two orchestras, two choruses, organs, and solo voices. It was set to the text of the Gospel of St. Matthew (narrated by "the Evangelist," a tenor voice), with added recitatives and arias. Bach's music captures masterfully the story's emotional peaks and valleys. When Jesus announces he will be betrayed by one of his followers, the chorus (speaking as the apostles) answers with a ragged, panicked "Lord, is it I?" Realizing they all are sinners and all require salvation, they end in a melodic chorale, acknowledging to Christ "the scourges and shackles that You endured so that my soul might be delivered." From the virtuoso whims of the preludes to the dramatic sweep of Christ's passion, Bach proved his immense range as a composer.

THE DUTCH BAROQUE

Compare the style and subjects of Dutch baroque art with that of other regions of Europe.

In the baroque period, the Netherlands enjoyed an upsurge of national feeling and cultural vitality, especially in the art of painting. The Netherlands was a Protestant country, and did not permit art in its sober churches; nor did it embrace the lavish style of the absolutist court. Instead, the prosperous Dutch citizens decorated the walls of their town houses and public halls with paintings by their own Dutch artists. This demand for painting created a free mar-

10.31 Johann Sebastian Bach, *Prelude and Fugue in C Minor*, 1721 (above). Diagram of subject entries (below).

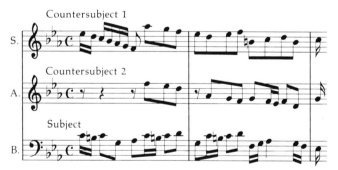

Soprano		S	C_1	S	C_1	S	C_2	S
Alto	S	C_1	C_2	C_2	S	C_1	C_1	
Bass			S	C_1	C_2	C_2	S	
Key	c	g	c	Eb	g	c	c	c

S subject C_1 countersubject 1 C_2 countersubject 2

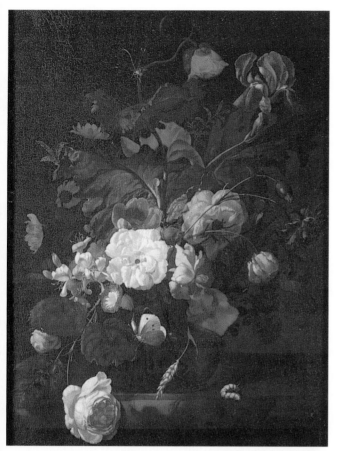

10.32 Rachel Ruysch, *Flowers in a Vase*, 1698. Oil on canvas, 23 x 17¹/₂ ins (58.5 x 44.5 cm). Städelsches Institut, Frankfurt.
The Dutch market in painting permitted women to enter the profession more easily than in France or Italy. Ruysch excelled in the popular genre of flower painting and was still painting at the age of eighty-three.

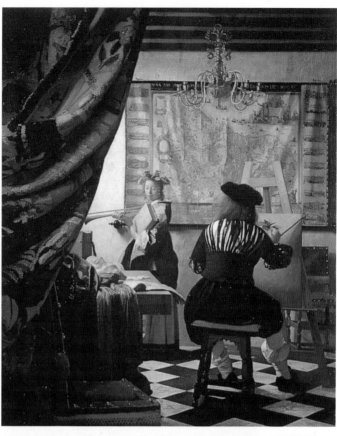

10.33 Johannes Vermeer, *The Allegory of Painting*, c. 1665–70. Oil on canvas, 4 ft ³/₁₈ ins x 3 ft 7¹/₄ ins (1.30 x 1.10 m). Kunsthistorisches Museum, Vienna.
The blurred points of light and enlarged foreground objects suggest that Vermeer composed his pictures with a camera obscura, a popular 17th-century optical device.

ket in art that bypassed the traditional channels of artistic patronage. Dutch painters often had to please anonymous buyers, who might purchase their works in a gallery or market stall. Artists responded with a style and themes suited to modest domestic interiors: landscapes and city-scapes, portraits, still lifes, and genre scenes (Fig. **10.32**). The most admired Dutch painters, Johannes Vermeer and Rembrandt van Rijn, were artists of very different temperaments.

VERMEER

The most remarkable painter of Dutch genre scenes was Johannes Vermeer (1632–75). Vermeer was virtually unknown in his day but is now regarded as a master of light and color. His paintings typically show a quiet interior scene illuminated by a cool, brilliant northern light.

There is often a subtle contrast between the naive intimacy of his subject and the objective tone created by light and composition (Fig. **10.34**).

Vermeer's feel for the Dutch interior is apparent even in his most philosophical work, *The Allegory of Painting* (Fig. **10.33**), an intricate fabric of allegorical and visual patterns. The painter's model is costumed as Clio, the muse of history. She holds a trumpet and a history book that will someday announce the fame of the anonymous painter in the foreground, who will also add to the fame of his city and nation, visible on the map against the back wall. The curtain drawn back on the left and the painter's fanciful costume enhance the painting's theatrical air. A cool light suffuses the entire scene. With this picture, Vermeer seemed to claim for himself and his modest art the respect accorded to tragedy and music, symbolized by the mask and sheet music on the table.

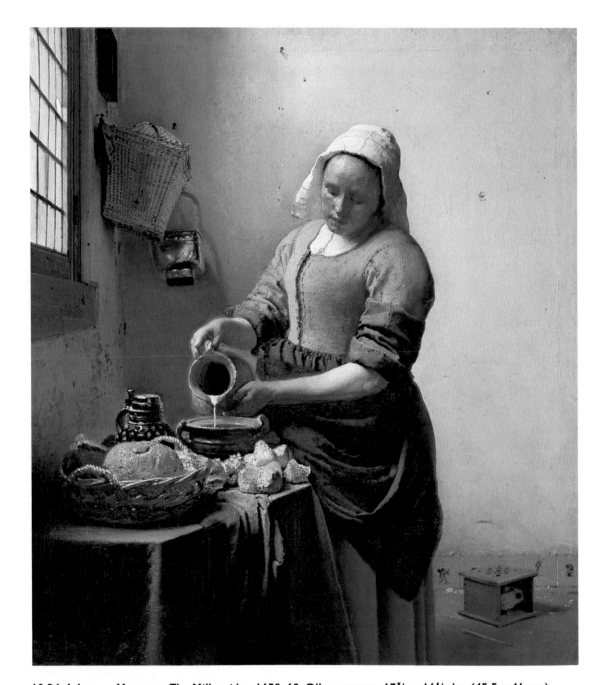

10.34 Johannes Vermeer, *The Milkmaid*, c. 1658–60. Oil on canvas, 17⁷/₈ x 16¹/₈ ins (45.5 x 41 cm). Rijksmuseum, Amsterdam.
Vermeer's genre scene lavishes loving attention on simple objects and modest, enduring truths: bread, milk, a maid's coarse dress (with its sleeves rolled). Note how the modulated light across the back wall serves to emphasize the maid's figure. What symbolic analogy might be made between the maid's white hat, the flowing milk, and the light pouring in from the window at left?

REMBRANDT

Rembrandt van Rijn [van RINE] (1606–69) spent most of his career in the Dutch capital of Amsterdam, where for a while he enjoyed prodigious success. He was an artist who mastered all the popular subjects of his age, taking from the Italian school of painting his religious and historical themes, and from the Dutch school his scenes of ordinary life and studies of human character. He transcended his peers in the visual and psychological richness of his achievement.

The height of Rembrandt's popularity is represented by the *Sortie of Captain Banning Cocq's Company of the Civic Guard* (Fig. **10.35**), an example of the group portraits often commissioned by Dutch civic groups. The picture was known as *The Night Watch* until a cleaning in the 1940s revealed a daytime scene. Rembrandt shows the guard on march from the city gate, led by the handsome captain and his dandified lieutenant in white. With muskets, spears, and swords, Rembrandt creates a complex rhythm of slashing diagonals. The theatrical lighting strikes the curious figure of the girl, who adds a whimsical air to the solemn occasion. The popular notion that the painting was rejected by the group who had commissioned it is unfounded. It was displayed proudly in the company's meeting hall, although one critic claimed that "Rembrandt paid too much attention to the grand design he had invented and too little to the portraits he was commissioned to make." Nevertheless, the painting's size and complexity may be compared to the masterpieces of El Greco and Velázquez (see Figs. 10.2 and 10.6).

Perhaps because of changing artistic fashion, Rembrandt suffered a loss of patronage in the 1640s. At the same time, his wife died and he floundered in self-imposed

10.35 Rembrandt van Rijn, *Sortie of Captain Banning Cocq's Company of the Civic Guard* (*The Night Watch*), 1642. Oil on canvas, 11 ft 9¹/₂ ins x 14 ft 4¹/₂ ins (3.59 x 4.38 m). Rijksmuseum, Amsterdam.
Note where Rembrandt has illuminated faces and figures arbitrarily, applying a theatrical (rather than naturalistic) principle of lighting.

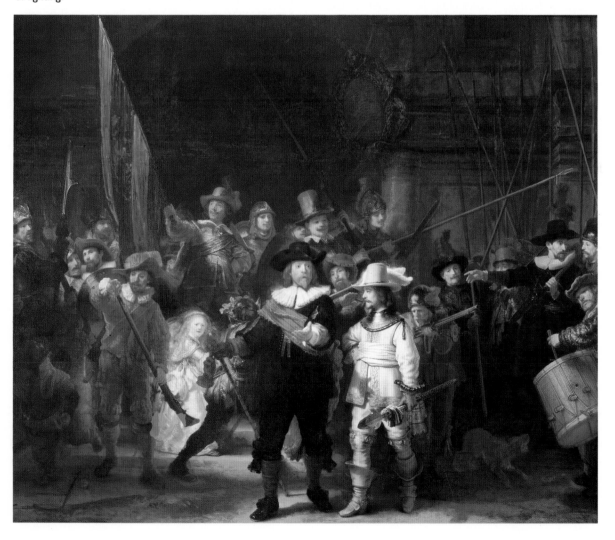

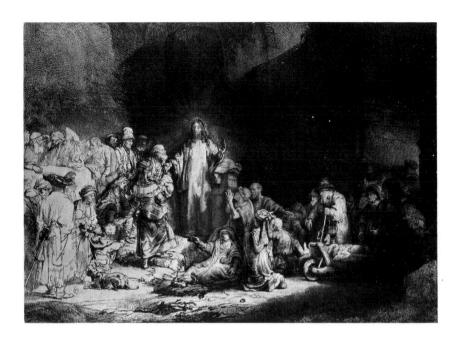

10.36 Rembrandt van Rijn, *Christ Healing the Sick (Hundred Guilder Print)*, c. 1649. Etching, 10⁷/₈ ins x 15³/₈ ins (28 x 39 cm). British Museum, London.
This etching is named for the high price it once fetched. Christ stands at the center, blessing the needy and healing the infirm, who crowd through an arch (right). Well-dressed elders at left argue Christ's violation of the religious law prohibiting work on the sabbath. What religious views might Rembrandt be expressing here?

personal and financial difficulties. During this period, Rembrandt created his most famous religious work, the etching of *Christ Healing the Sick* (Fig. **10.36**), also called the *Hundred Guilder Print*. In etching, lines are scratched on a wax-covered metal plate; the plate is treated with acid that "etches" the exposed metal; prints are then taken from the plate. The technique was well suited to Rembrandt's interest in light and dark. In *Christ Healing the Sick*, the poor and lame crowd into the picture from the right, while sanctimonious officials disapprovingly watch Jesus heal on the sabbath.

Rembrandt painted himself more than sixty times, more often than any other major artist in the Western tradition. Early in his career, Rembrandt often presented himself as a worldly sophisticate, dressed in fashionable attire. Later on, the self-portraits served to promote Rembrandt's international renown as painter, as when he portrayed himself as the Hellenistic painter Apelles (Fig. **10.37**). In his last decade, when age and troubles had punctured his vanity, Rembrandt painted himself dressed only in humble painter's clothes. The painter examined even his own failure with unflinching psychological insight.

10.37 Rembrandt van Rijn, *Self-Portrait*, c. 1665. Oil on canvas, 45 x 37¹/₂ ins (114 x 94 cm). The Iveagh Bequest, Kenwood House, London.
Rembrandt presents himself as the famed Hellenistic painter Apelles, who, like Rembrandt, was criticized for his unnatural use of light. Inclined to self-scrutiny, Rembrandt was not immune to self-promotion.

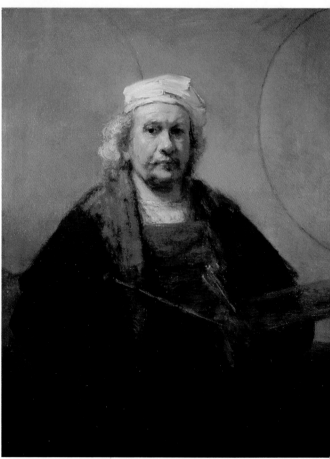

THE WRITE IDEA
Write character sketches of the artists you see in Vermeer's *The Allegory of Painting* (Fig. 10.33) and in Rembrandt's *Self-portrait* (Fig. 10.37). What differences do you see in the artists' attitudes toward themselves? What "face" does each present to the world?

KEY CONCEPT

THE SCIENTIFIC REVOLUTION

Thinkers in the seventeenth century faced profound new uncertainties. On the one hand, the Reformation and Counter-Reformation had weakened the Church's authority in intellectual matters; on the other, the sighting of unknown comets challenged the accepted truths of ancient science. Some thinkers withdrew into skepticism, such as the essayist Michel de Montaigne, who wrote that to know reality was like trying to clutch water. Others – including Galileo, Descartes, and Newton – were determined to build a new foundation for human knowledge. The discoveries made by seventeenth-century thinkers created the Scientific Revolution, a century of scientific progress that formed the basis for modern natural science (Fig. **10.38**).

The Scientific Revolution rested on two premises. First, scientists based their knowledge on experimental and observational data, a method called **empiricism**. The English philosopher Francis Bacon (1561–1626), a vigorous advocate of empiricism, wrote that science "must lead men to the particulars themselves, and their series and order." Galileo dramatically confirmed the new empirical approach when he, looking through his famous telescope, discovered four moons orbiting Jupiter. Traditional astronomy had said no moons could exist there.

The Scientific Revolution's second premise was to limit science to questions that could be quantified and expressed mathematically. The pioneer Galileo succeeded in expressing the motion of falling bodies as a simple, elegant mathematical formula: $v = 32t$; the speed (velocity = v) of a falling body equals thirty-two times the time (t) that it takes to fall. With such mathematical formulas, scientists showed that widely separate phenomena – such as a ball falling to earth and the orbit of the moon – obeyed the same laws.

The union of empirical observation and mathematical quantification formed the basis of the new science. Through the Middle Ages, science had been a branch of philosophy. After the Scientific Revolution, philosophers were left to speculate on matters that could not be expressed as a mathematical formula – ethics, aesthetics, metaphysics, and religion.

The Scientific Revolution did restore some certainty to human knowledge, but within a narrower field. Of course, the empirical and mathematical basis of modern science has not eradicated all opinion and ambiguity. The most intriguing areas of science are often those where the empirical record is incomplete (the fossil records of evolution) or the problems are difficult to quantify (the multiple variables involved in global climate). Today, Bacon's exhortation to "see to the particulars" is not always easy to follow.

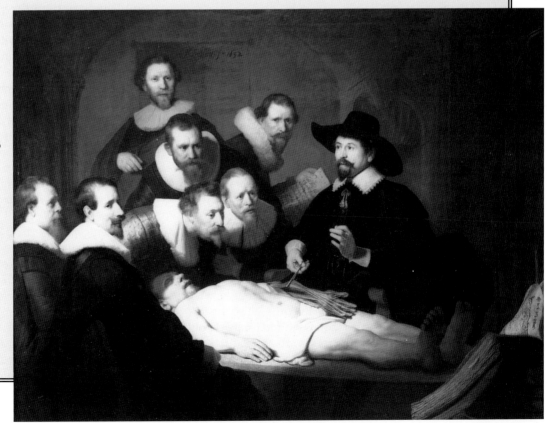

10.38 Rembrandt van Rijn, *The Anatomy Lesson of Dr Tulp,* **1632. Oil on canvas, 66⁵/₈ ins x 85¹/₄ ins (169.5 x 215.5 cm). Mauritshuis, The Hague.** The dissection of a cadaver was an important academic occasion, here depicted by Rembrandt with deference to the professor's vanity. The corpse's feet are most likely propped on a copy of *Vesalius' Anatomy,* the first modern work of human anatomy.

THE NEW SCIENCE

Identify examples of science's link to mathematics in the discoveries of the Scientific Revolution.

The body of scientific knowledge and methods of the Scientific Revolution emerged gradually over a century-and-a-half. Seventeenth-century scientists had to shed conventional opinions in small pieces, as if slowly shedding an old skin, and often mixed erroneous tradition with important discoveries. In the process, scientists found that they were altering Western conceptions of the universe and of humanity.

The Scientific Revolution began with the publication in 1543 of *De Revolutionibus Orbium Coelestium* (*On the Revolutions of Heavenly Bodies*) by Nicolaus Copernicus (1473–1543). The Polish astronomer proposed a **heliocentric** theory of the universe, that is, a sun standing stationary at the universe's center and the planets (including Earth) revolving around it. Copernicus' heliocentric scheme contradicted centuries of accepted science and challenged the Bible's authority in scientific matters.

Copernicus intended to simplify mathematical calculation of the planets' movements, which had become absurdly complex in the reigning astronomical system. In fact, Copernicus' tables of planetary motion were not much better, since he assumed (under the influence of Platonic ideas) that the planets orbited the sun in perfect circles. Despite his error, *De Revolutionibus* was the stimulus for further scientific challenges, and a potent symbol of the coming revolution in scientific thought.

TOOLS OF THE NEW SCIENCE

The successors of Copernicus created the tools of modern science and set in motion the technological progress of Western civilization. One tool was **scientific deduction**, the discovery of a truth through logical calculation. For example, the German astronomer Johannes Kepler (1571–1630) resolved the flaws in Copernicus' astronomical calculations by assuming that the planets moved in elliptical, not circular, orbits. The English physician William Harvey (1578–1657) clinched his theory of the blood's circulation by mathematical calculation, without being able to confirm his theory by observation.

Reasoning from observation, called **induction**, was essential to the discoveries of the Italian astronomer, physicist, and mathematician Galileo Galilei (1564–1642). Galileo constructed his own version of the newly invented telescope and touted it as a boon to Venetian merchants, who could better watch their ships arrive in port. Galileo's astronomical observations revealed moons around Jupiter, spots on the sun, and craters on the moon, all contradictions of conventional scientific wisdom. On the other hand, Galileo's discoveries in the physics of moving bodies were largely deductive. Galileo was able to treat the forces of motion as pure, mathematical abstractions.

Galileo's career also dramatized the conflict between the new scientific spirit and the authority of the Church. When the Catholic Church condemned Copernicus, Galileo published his *Dialogue on the Two Chief Systems of the World* (1632), which exposed the absurdities of traditional astronomy. The Church responded emphatically, threatening the scientist with trial and torture. Reluctantly, Galileo knelt in Rome and recanted his belief that "the sun is the center of the world and moves not, and that the earth is not the center of the world and moves".[4] In retirement and under house arrest, Galileo continued his studies and wrote his most important scientific work, *Discourses on Two New Sciences*. Prudently, he published the book in the Protestant Netherlands, where the long arm of the Counter-Reformation did not reach.

DESCARTES AND THE PHILOSOPHY OF SCIENCE

The troubles between Galileo and the Catholic Church caused the French mathematician René Descartes (1596–1650) to postpone publication of his own study of Copernicus. Descartes had already angered Church authorities with his provocative *Discourse on Method* (1639), a philosophical manifesto of the new science and a preface to his discoveries in mathematics and science. Descartes' *Discourse* is still regarded as a profound statement of scientific confidence and rigor.

In the *Discourse on Method*, Descartes describes the painful uncertainty and skepticism of his youth. In his rigorous education and broad experience, he had found nothing that he could believe with conviction – skepticism had poisoned everything but mathematics. Descartes wondered why all knowledge cannot resemble those "long chains of reasoning, quite simple and easy," that geometry used in its proofs. Determined to find certainty, Descartes practiced doubt. He rejected as completely false any thought which could be doubted for any reason. This rigorous doubt took him to the essential core of human thought.

> *But immediately afterwards I became aware that, while I decided thus to think that everything was false, it followed necessarily that I who thought thus must be something; and observing that this truth:* I think, therefore I am, *was so certain and so evident that all the most extravagant suppositions of the skeptics were not capable of shaking it, I judged that I could accept it without scruple as the first principle of the philosophy I was seeking.*[5]

Descartes had arrived at the first principle of his scientific method – *Cogito ergo sum* ("I think, therefore I am"). From this principle, he could deduce other perfectly clear and distinct ideas, including the existence of God and the certainty of his own mathematical propositions. With his methodical line of reasoning, Descartes had vanquished his own skepticism and expounded a philosophy of the new science.

Descartes' confidence in the rational mind was confirmed by the age's most important discovery, Newton's universal theory of gravitation. In his *Principia Mathematica* (*Mathematical Principles*, 1687), the Englishman Isaac Newton (1642–1727) synthesized the discoveries of Galileo and other scientists in a unified theory. Newton asserted that all bodies – large and small, earthly and heavenly, natural and mechanical – were subject to the same gravitational force. He showed how gravity's pull could be quantified precisely. At first, scientists rejected Newton's theory in favor of Descartes' deductively derived system. Only in the eighteenth century was Newton's theory of universal gravitation widely accepted among scientists.

THE ENGLISH COMPROMISE

Identify the diverse elements that were synthesized in the English baroque style.

The baroque was a robustly international style in the arts. However, Britain did not so readily absorb artistic styles and philosophical ideas from the rest of Europe: the English hesitated to accept artistic fashions that hinted at the absolutism of France and the Catholicism of Italy. Thus, continental styles were often compromised with native English traditions. The English also applied their skill for compromise to their own political conflicts, emerging from a bitter civil war in the mid-1600s with a political system carefully balanced between opposing forces.

The English were not great artistic innovators. Their greatest architect, Christopher Wren, was an amateur, and the English baroque's most acclaimed composer was, in fact, the German George Frideric Handel, who had settled in London. On the other hand, the English excelled in poetry and politics. Their baroque poets built on the achievement of Shakespeare, while seventeenth-century English philosophers – especially Thomas Hobbes and John Locke – examined the political issues that a century later exploded in the American and French revolutions.

ENGLISH BAROQUE POETRY

It was in poetry that seventeenth-century England found its most original geniuses. Some critics rank John Donne [dunn] (1572–1631) close to Shakespeare in the richness of his poetic achievement. Donne's intellectualized style and complexity of emotion place him in a group called the "metaphysical poets." A well-educated and widely traveled author, Donne was also a deeply religious man who applied his complex imagery to both sacred and secular themes. His famous poem *Death, Be Not Proud* is an affirmation of the triumph that salvation wins over death. Donne's love poetry is characterized by jarring associations and comparisons: in one poem, he compares the intertwined legs of lovers to the hands of a clock. The stanzas below are from one of his best-known love poems, *The Canonization*. Donne understood well the costs of love; in 1600 he sacrificed his career to marry the niece of his patron.

Call us what you will, we are made such by love;
Call her one, me another fly,
We're tapers too, and at our own cost die,
And we in us find the eagle and the dove.
The phoenix riddle hath more wit
By us; we too being one, are it.
So, to one neutral thing both sexes fit.
We die and rise the same, and prove
Mysterious by this love.

We can die by it, if not live by love,
And if unfit for tombs and hearse
Our legend be, it will be fit for verse;
And if no piece of chronicle we prove,
We'll build in sonnets pretty rooms;
As well a well-wrought urn becomes
The greatest ashes, as half-acre tombs,
And by these hymns, all shall approve
Us canonized for love . . .

JOHN DONNE
From *The Canonization*

John Milton (1608–74) wrote works of truly baroque scale. His masterpiece *Paradise Lost* (1667) is an epic poem that recounts the original drama of Christianity: the fall of Adam and Eve from the garden of Eden. The learned Milton was well aware of his classical precursors in the epic form, and interwove his Christian saga with allusions to classical mythology and literature. He portrays the loss of Eden as a tragedy that will be redeemed by the coming of Christ, as indicated in the poem's famous opening lines:

Of man's first disobedience, and the fruit
Of that forbidden tree whose mortal taste
Brought death into the world, and all our woe,
With loss of Eden, till one greater Man
Restore us, and regain the blissful seat,
Sing, Heavenly Muse . . .

JOHN MILTON
From *Paradise Lost*

Milton was also an outspoken critic of absolutist government. His most famous secular work is the *Areopagit-*

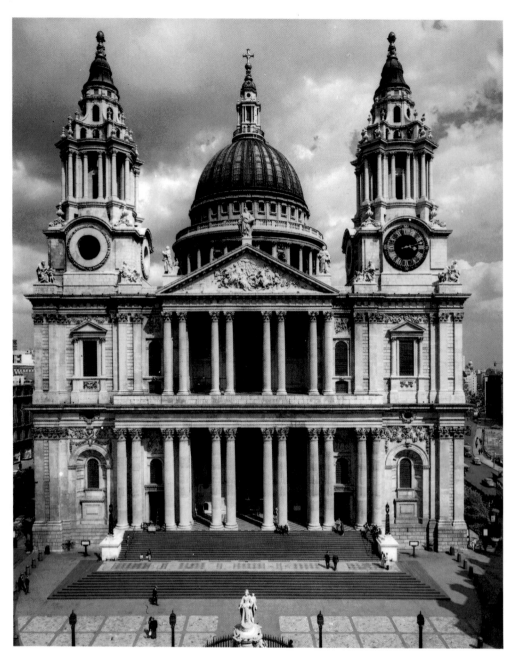

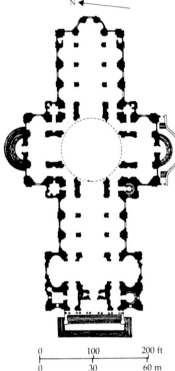

10.39 Christopher Wren, St. Paul's Cathedral, London, 1675–1710. Length 514 ft (156.7 m), width of façade 250 ft (76.2 m), height of dome 366 ft (111.6 m).

Wren's eccentric combination of Gothic, Renaissance, and baroque neoclassical elements responded to the contending forces of 17th-century English culture. It is the only major British building of the Renaissance and baroque built by a single architect.

10.40 Plan of St. Paul's Cathedral, London, 1675–1710.

N ◀

| 0 | 100 | 200 ft |
| 0 | 30 | 60 m |

ica (1644), which defended the right to publish without government censorship. Milton fervently asserted his belief that truth could prevail in "a free and open encounter" with error.

CHRISTOPHER WREN'S LONDON

The artistic compromises of late seventeenth-century England are perhaps best seen in St. Paul's Cathedral in London, designed by Christopher Wren (1632–1723). In St. Paul's, Wren achieved a synthesis of Gothic, Renaissance, and baroque styles and created London's most admired architectural landmark.

Until the 1660s, Wren was a professor of astronomy and founding member of London's Royal Society, a group of scientists and scholars. Wren's architectural hobby became his profession when he was appointed as the royal surveyor of works and asked to modernize English archi-

tecture. In 1665 he traveled to Paris, where he encountered continental baroque architecture through Bernini (who was there to redesign the Louvre) and Mansart, the architect of Versailles.

Wren's architectural task gained urgency when, in September 1666, a great fire destroyed three-quarters of London, including the original cathedral of St. Paul's. The disaster presented Wren with an unprecedented opportunity to leave his artistic signature on an entire city. He spent the remainder of his life rebuilding London's parish churches, gracing the city with their distinctive spires and neoclassical simplicity.

Wren's largest assignment was the construction of the new St. Paul's (built 1675–1710). His designs had to mediate between his patrons' traditional tastes and his own preference for the prestigious neoclassical style of Versailles. Wren's compromises are visible in St. Paul's façade and floor plan (Figs. 10.39, 10.40). The neoclassical double portico is flanked by towers that use the principles of both Gothic and baroque styles. The towers are most reminiscent of Bramante's Tempietto (see Fig. 8.45), by then a Renaissance standard. Above the portico rises the towering dome, indebted to Brunelleschi and Michelangelo, but somewhat obscured by the imposing façade. Wren's fusion of styles left unresolved tensions but evidently satisfied his patrons.

The interior of St. Paul's (Fig. **10.41**) is only barely related to the exterior. Wren, often more engineer than architect, placed little value on this connection. The architect aimed for the central unity of a Renaissance design, while his clerical patrons insisted on a traditional Gothic floor plan. The interior's most distinctive feature is the domed crossing. The dome rests on eight arches, four on the sides opening to the nave, choir, and transepts, and four on the corners closed off with apse-like niches. Originally the interior was austere in the Protestant fashion, but it is now decorated in mosaic.

HANDEL

The career of composer George Frideric Handel illustrates the international character of the baroque style and shows how art forms could be adapted to the tastes and

10.41 St. Paul's Cathedral, London, interior. Aquatint by Thomas Melton, 1798.
The domed crossing, with its alternating open and closed arches, was an up-to-date statement of neoclassicism. The Latin-cross plan was a concession to tradition.

WINDOW ON DAILY LIFE

THE FIRE OF LONDON

Diarist Samuel Pepys provides this eyewitness account of the devastating fire that consumed much of London in 1666.

So I down to the water-side, and there got a boat and through bridge, and there saw a lamentable fire. Poor Michell's house, as far as the Old Swan, already burned that way, and the fire running further, that in a very little time it got as far as the Steele-yard, while I was there. Everybody endeavouring to remove their goods, and fling into the river or bringing them into lighters [barges] that lay off; poor people staying in their houses as long as till the fire touched them and then running into boats, or clambering from one pair of stairs by the water-side to another. And among other things, the poor pigeons, I perceive, were loath to leave their houses, but hovered about the windows and balconies till they were, some of them burned, their wings, and fell down.[6]

The Diary of Samuel Pepys

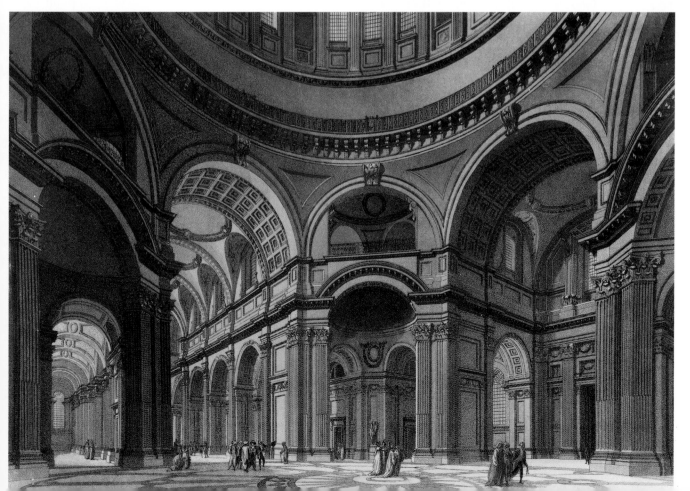

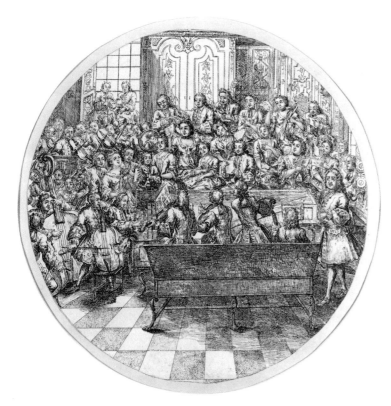

10.42 Handel directing a rehearsal.
Handel (far right) customarily used a choir of only about twelve singers and an orchestra of forty or so.

attitudes of audiences. Although German by birth, Handel (1685–1759) lived half his life in England and was honored as the nation's leading composer of the baroque period. As a youth, Handel studied and traveled in Italy, where he wrote popular Italian operas. In 1712, he took leave from his German patron to visit England and never returned. The patron eventually followed him to England to become King George I, causing some embarrassment to his wayward musical employee. In London, Handel was named musical director of the Royal Academy of Music (founded in 1720), which exploited the English fashion for Italian opera. Within a decade, however, the Academy failed and the debt-ridden Handel suffered a stroke and a mid-life career crisis.

Handel rescued his career by turning to a new musical form, the **oratorio**. The oratorio was a narrative choral work containing the musical elements of opera, but without action, scenery, or costumes. It offered its audience the narrative scope and musical grandeur of opera, without the expense of operatic staging. For Handel, working on a tight budget, this was a perfect compromise. In his remaining life, Handel composed and produced many oratorios, most written on biblical themes and performed in public concert halls (Fig. **10.42**).

Handel's most famous oratorio was the *Messiah*, first presented in Dublin, Ireland, in 1742 and still among the most widely performed baroque works. The *Messiah* recounts Jesus' birth, his death and resurrection, and the promised redemption of all humanity. The religious feeling and grandeur of the story were matched by Han-

del's music. The famous chorus "Hallelujah" (Hebrew for "Praise God") combines intricate counterpoint and imitation with simpler chordal passages of dignified majesty. The chorus builds to a jubilant finale, with a unison so magnificent that the English king stood up on first hearing it. Audiences ever since have traditionally stood at performances of this *Messiah* chorus. The commercial success of Handel's other oratorios was enhanced by the stirring Old Testament themes, which appealed subtly to the patriotism of his English audience.

THE POLITICS OF ENGLAND

The spirit of balance and compromise evident in the arts in baroque England was also evident in the practical solutions that the English found for their political conflicts in the seventeenth century. In 1642, a conflict between the king and the elected parliament erupted in bloody civil war, pitting royalists against the middle-class Puritans. In 1660, Puritan rule ended with the restoration of King Charles II, who was able to keep peace among England's religious and political factions. The peace was undone by his successor and brother, James II. By 1688 James had so enraged parliamentary forces that he fled London in fear of his life. Parliament immediately recruited a new king and queen, William and Mary of Orange, from the Protestant Netherlands (Mary was James II's daughter). The English called this political drama the "Glorious Revolution" of 1688 – glorious because the rebellion involved no bloodshed.

Two years later, John Locke (1632–1704) published a philosophical justification of the Glorious Revolution. Locke's *Two Treatises on Government* (1690) argued that governments resulted from the voluntary association of humans, acting in their rational self-interest. Thus, while asking the same questions as his predecessor Thomas Hobbes (see "Key Concept"; page 279), Locke reached very different conclusions. Where Hobbes claimed humans were naturally greedy and violent, Locke claimed they were reasonable and cooperative. Where Hobbes claimed only an absolute monarch – the "Leviathan" – could impose social order, Locke claimed absolute monarchy violated the purpose of civil society.

For Locke, free individuals had agreed to place the primary powers of government in the legislature, not the executive. This view is not surprising in a philosopher who sided with the English parliament against James II.

> *Wherever, therefore, any number of men so unite into one society, as to quit everyone his executive power of the law of nature, and to resign it to the public, there, and there only, is a political, or civil society. And this is done wherever any number of men, in the state of nature, enter into society to make one people, one body politic, under one supreme government, or else when anyone joins himself to, and incorporates with, any government already made. For hereby he authorizes the*

society, or, which is all one, the legislative thereof, to make laws for him, as the public good of the society shall require, to the execution whereof his own assistance (as to his own decrees) is due. And this puts men out of a state of nature into that of a commonwealth, by setting up a judge on earth with authority to determine all the controversies and redress the injuries that may happen to any member of the commonwealth . . .[7]

JOHN LOCKE
From *Two Treatises on Government* (1690)

Locke believed the power of government rested with the people, who lent this power to the legislature and gained the benefits of civil society. The idea of absolutism – that one person can rightly claim all power – violated Locke's balance between individual rights and social order. He concluded: "It is evident that absolute monarchy, which by some men is counted the only government in the world, is indeed inconsistent with civil society, and so can be no form of civil government at all."[8] Absolutism, expressed in Louis XIV's "I am the state," was a violation of natural order. In his last article, Locke considered the reasons that a people could overthrow one government and replace it with a better one. Locke was writing a license for political revolution. The compromise between reason and radicalism set the tone for the combative age of reason to come.

Chapter Summary

The Baroque in Spain. The seventeenth century in Europe saw the rise of the baroque, a varied and dynamic style in the arts. In Spain, the painter El Greco merged the religious feeling of the Counter-Reformation with mastery of Renaissance and mannerist technique. Spanish baroque architecture likewise borrowed from Renaissance classicism, but fused it with religious austerity (at El Escorial) and a militant colonialism (in New World churches). The painter Velázquez served the Spanish royal court with works of fascinating complexity, while the great novel of Cervantes, *Don Quixote*, also explored the tension between illusion and reality, art and life.

The Baroque in Italy. In Italy, the artist Bernini dominated the baroque era: his architectural and sculptural works embodied baroque extravagance and dynamism, often fusing several arts into a single, complex whole. In painting, Caravaggio's dramatic contrasts of light and dark and his graphic realism influenced generations of artists. Baroque Italy also was a center of musical innovation, nurturing the birth of opera and its first genius, Monteverdi, as well as the brilliantly embellished works of Vivaldi.

The Baroque in France. In seventeenth-century France, Louis XIV harnessed the baroque style to his absolutist designs. Louis's grand palace at Versailles served as a stage for projecting royal power, while combining baroque lavishness and neoclassical restraint. Louis patronized great masters of the performing arts, especially Molière in theater and Lully in ballet and opera. In painting, Rubens and Poussin represented the two trends of baroque pictorial style, exuberant virtuosity versus neoclassical order and balance.

Music of the Protestant Baroque. In northern Europe, baroque artists had to please both aristocratic and urban middle-class audiences. Johann Sebastian Bach proved a prolific innovator of baroque music, excelling in both secular and sacred forms (*concerto grosso*, cantata, fugue). His work demonstrated the flexibility of the new major-minor key system that was now widely employed in European music.

The Dutch Baroque. Without a royal court or wealthy nobility, the Dutch preferred the humble art of genre painting. The obscure master Johannes Vermeer rendered brilliantly lit interior scenes, while the more flamboyant Rembrandt painted group and individual portraits of great psychological insight and theatrical command of light and dark.

The New Science. The scientific discoveries of the Renaissance – especially Copernicus' proposal of a heliocentric universe – set off a scientific revolution in European civilization. Using scientific induction and deduction, scientists such as Galileo, Kepler, and Newton observed physical phenomena and calculated the movements of the heavens. Descartes' *Discourse on Method* offered a philosophical defense of scientific method and knowledge.

The English Compromise. Baroque England was a fertile ground for artistic innovation and political compromise. English baroque poets used richly embellished language to treat traditional themes of love and faith. Christopher Wren modernized English architecture with his combination of French neoclassicism and English traditionalism. The composer Handel pleased the English public with his operas and grand oratorios. In politics, Locke's theory of government justified England's sometimes precarious balance between individual freedom and the legitimacy of governments, setting the stage for a revolutionary age to come.

11 The Spirit of Enlightenment

It is a scene of frivolity and idle pleasure. A finely dressed young woman flings her slipper into the air, while casting a sly glance at her lover hidden in the shrubs (Fig. 11.1). The pair belong to the leisured and decadent nobility of eighteenth-century Europe, who wittily amused themselves with flirtation and conversation in elegant gardens, town houses, and country manors.

*Not everyone in Europe and America was so idly engaged. In middle-class parlors and coffee-houses, thinkers were fired by a **spirit of enlightenment** – the belief in the supremacy of reason over pleasure, and a conviction that humans could perfect society through the application of the intellect to human affairs. The thinkers of the Enlightenment published encyclopedias, pursued science, built neoclassical country homes, and eventually incited revolutions. In this age (c. 1700–1780), the sober advocates of reason and enlightenment endured an uneasy coexistence with an aristocratic society devoted to artful pleasure.*

THE ENLIGHTENMENT

Summarize the Enlightenment philosophes' program for reforming eighteenth-century society.

When Louis XIV died in 1715, the French nobility fled the crowded Palace of Versailles, where it had been captive for fifty years, and settled in new Parisian town houses decorated in the latest fashion. Noble ladies sponsored elegant gatherings where the French nobility mixed with middle-class wits and philosophers. Inevitably, new ideas began to percolate through these social conversations, ideas that challenged political and religious orthodoxy.

The preceding century had brought irreversible changes in European attitudes: exploration and colonization had widened Europe's horizon of experience; the Scientific Revolution had opened new vistas of intellectual inquiry; and the Glorious Revolution in England had improved national life. Suddenly, in eighteenth-century France, the authority of Church and king paled in the scrutinizing light of reason.

THE PHILOSOPHES

Paris became the cradle of the **Enlightenment**, a movement of intellectuals who popularized science and applied reason to human affairs. They educated and provoked with their writings, which included novels, plays, pamphlets, and, above all, the mammoth *Encyclopedia* (1751–72). These thinkers of Paris called themselves **philosophes**, a French term applied to eighteenth-century thinkers who advocated reason and opposed traditional ideas. The philosophes' intellectual godfathers were Isaac Newton (see page 293), discoverer of the universal laws of gravitation, and John Locke (see page 298), champion of individual rights. The philosophes were materialist and empiricist in their philosophical attitude: they believed that everything had a material cause and that all ideas came from experience. Above all, the philosophes sought the practical application of human reason to real human problems.

Inspired by the Scientific Revolution, the philosophes searched for universal laws in every sphere of human affairs. They believed politics and history must also be governed by an equivalent to the law of gravitation. They praised science for its promise of boundless material prosperity, and scorned superstition, including most of Chris-

11.1 Opposite **Jean-Honoré Fragonard, *The Swing*, c. 1768–9. Oil on canvas, 32 x 25½ ins (83 x 66 cm). Wallace Collection, London.**
Fragonard's scenes of seduction and dalliance appealed to the urbane and complacent French aristocracy under the reign of Louis XVI.

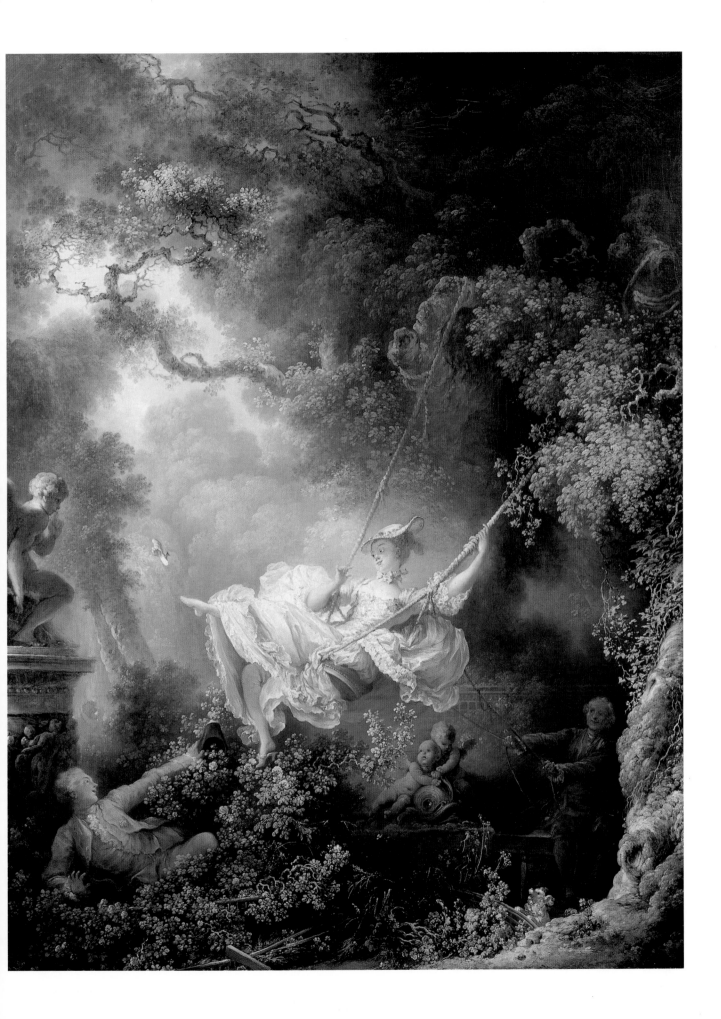

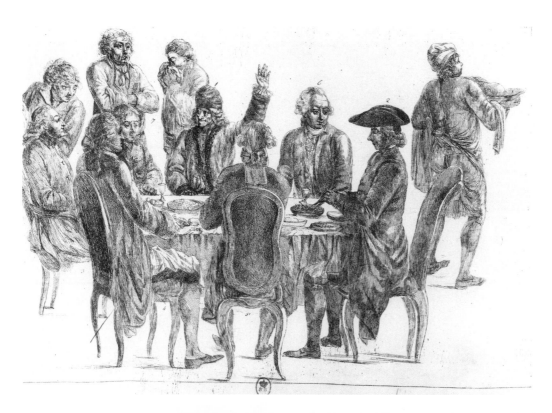

11.2 Jean Huber, *The Philosophers at Supper*, c. 1750. Engraving. Bibliothèque Nationale, Paris.

11.3 Below **Joseph Wright, *Experiment with an Air Pump*, 1768. Oil on canvas, 5 ft 11⁵/₈ ins x 7 ft 11³/₄ ins (1.82 x 2.43 m). National Gallery, London.** In this view of Enlightenment science, a lark suffocates as the air is pumped out of the glass bell, showing that air is necessary for life. The children exhibit a mixture of scientific curiosity and sentimental feeling.

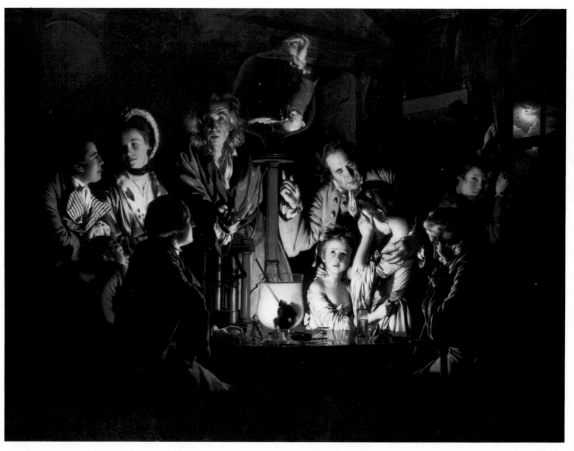

tian belief. They also believed that the chief barrier to human progress and happiness was not human nature, as Christianity taught, but social intolerance and injustice. The watchwords of the Enlightenment were freedom and reason. The German philosopher Immanuel Kant [kahnt] (1724–1804) defined "enlightenment" as the ability to reason for oneself, free of authority or received opinion. *"Sapere aude, "* he wrote – "Dare to know!" If humans would answer this challenge, they could dispel the darkness of tyranny and light the way to a perfect society.

The great project of the philosophes was the *Encyclopedia*, subtitled "A Classified Dictionary of the Sciences, Arts, and Crafts." The *Encyclopedia* was an ambitious attempt to compile systematically all human knowledge. The mammoth work appeared in twenty-eight volumes (including eleven volumes of illustrations) from 1751 to 1772. The editor, Denis Diderot [deed-uh-ROH], enlisted as authors the most progressive minds of his day: Rousseau, Montesquieu, Condorcet, Helvétius, and Voltaire, among others (Fig. **11.2**). With articles, both theoretical and practical, on topics from human language to surgery, the *Encyclopedia* was a fulfillment of the belief that reason should enhance humanity's material well-being. The Enlightenment's expansion of scientific knowledge, dramatized in Joseph Wright's painting *Experiment with an Air Pump* (Fig. **11.3**), confirmed the philosophes' belief that human knowledge was perfectible and that human progress was inevitable.

The philosophes' scientific attitude led them to doubt the articles of Christian faith; and most philosophes abandoned the Christian Church altogether. Many philosophes were **deists**, who believed that God created the universe to operate by rational laws. According to deism, God did not intervene in nature by miracles or reveal his will in a bible. Voltaire thought it impious even to pray, since prayer asked God to change his perfectly ordered world. As for morality, said the deists, "reason and conscience were perfectly adequate" to guide human conduct. The Scottish philosopher David Hume (1711–76), himself a figure of the Enlightenment, was shocked when he visited Paris and heard the philosophes' contempt for organized religion. Voltaire was perhaps the most vehement: "Every sensible man, every honorable man, must hold the Christian sect in horror." Church authorities in Switzerland, the Netherlands, France, and Italy burned Voltaire's *Philosophical Dictionary* (1764).

ROUSSEAU

The youngest of the French philosophes was Jean-Jacques Rousseau (1712–78), a radical and troubled man who was the most popular writer of the Enlightenment. The son of a Swiss watchmaker, Rousseau [roo-SOH] joined Parisian society in the 1740s, where his ideas stirred controversy even among the philosophes. Though Rousseau quarreled bitterly with other philosophes and frequently withdrew to live in rural solitude, he was probably the Enlightenment's most influential thinker. His sensitivity to nature

and praise for feeling over reason also made him the forerunner of the romantic movement (see page 337).

Rousseau's philosophy rested on the worth of the human individual and the value of human freedom and equality. Since all people are born free, he wrote, "their liberty is their own, and no person can dispose of it but they themselves." Not only are humans born free, he claimed, but they are also "naturally" good. The first sentence of his educational treatise *Emile, or Education* (1762) reads "God makes all things good; man meddles with them and they become evil." In other words, religion, government, even science and the arts, all corrupt innate human goodness – a notion which the philosophes vigorously attacked.

Rousseau recognized that children were not just small adults, but unique creatures requiring attention to their physical and moral development. In *Emile*, he describes the enlightened upbringing of a young boy. Emile is educated according to "the principles of nature," encouraged to explore the forests and to exercise his senses. Rousseau warned against rote learning and corporal punishment, urging instead a respect for the stages in child development.

If *Emile* describes the growth of an enlightened individual, then Rousseau's *Social Contract* analyzes the growth of an enlightened society. *The Social Contract* (1762) followed the tradition of Hobbes, Locke, and other theorists of the origins of civil government. Like these predecessors, Rousseau traced society's origins to a state of nature, in which individuals were absolutely free and equal (see "Key Concept"; page 304). The question for Rousseau was how to establish society, with all its safeguards, without sacrificing any of this natural freedom.

Rousseau sought a formula for reconciling the need for law with the individual's supreme right to freedom and autonomy. This formula he found in the concept of the "general will," a paradoxical and controversial notion of political authority. Rousseau's general will was not simply the sum of individual and private interests (what in today's language we would call public opinion). The general will was, instead, the collective desire of citizens guided by civic virtue and acting in the public interest. *The Social Contract* describes the transition to this state of civic and moral freedom as a passage from natural to civil liberty.

> *Man loses by the social contract his* natural *liberty, and an unlimited right to all which tempts him, and which he can obtain; in return he acquires* civil *liberty, and proprietorship of all he possesses. That we may not be deceived in the value of these compensations, we must distinguish natural liberty, which knows no bounds but the power of the individual, from civil liberty, which is limited by the general will; and between possession, which is only the effect of force or of the right of the first occupant, from property, which must be founded on a positive title. In addition we might add to the acquisitions of the civil state that of moral liberty, which alone renders*

THE WRITE IDEA

Write a diary entry of a philosophe who has traveled to your own historical time. What would the philosophe find most to criticize and to praise?

KEY CONCEPT

THE SOCIAL CONTRACT

For Christianity, human society had originated in the "fall" of Adam and Eve into sin. The philosophes likewise traced society's origins back to a decisive moment. Instead of a dramatic confrontation between God and humans, the Enlightenment saw this moment as a purely human decision, guided by human reason and self-interest.

According to the philosophes, civilization originated in the **social contract**, an agreement in which humans traded their natural freedom for the rule of law. The social contract was the basis for peaceful and orderly human relations. In the philosophes' view, every citizen was bound by the terms of the social contract and every government derived its powers from this original agreement among the people. Borrowing from the English philosopher John Locke (see page 298), the philosophes held that citizens retained "inalienable" rights that no government should ever violate. The American Declaration of Independence on July 4, 1776 (Fig. **11.4**) derived its rationale for revolution from Locke's political philosophy.

The Enlightenment's most famous version of the contract theory was Jean Jacques Rousseau's *The Social Contract* (1762), which began with the electrifying cry "Man is born free, and yet we see him everywhere in chains." Rousseau described humans living in a state of nature, that is, before the advent of law or government. He claimed that humans in the state of nature were "noble savages," creatures who were free, rational, and innately good. Rousseau acknowledged that humans could never return to a state of nature. In effect, the social contract was a philosophical fiction, not a historical or anthropological reality.

For eighteenth-century revolutionaries, the fiction was convenient. In all its versions, the social contract held that sovereignty – the ultimate authority for government – rested in the people. The people's sovereignty gave them the right to overthrow a government that violated their basic freedoms. Yet, in dissolving the bonds of government, humans risked a fall back into the anarchy that Hobbes envisioned as the state of nature.

CRITICAL QUESTION

Imagine that a group of young people was suddenly removed from society and reverted to a state of nature. Without the influence of social institutions, what kind of society do you think they would develop in the first months, in the first year, and in the first ten years?

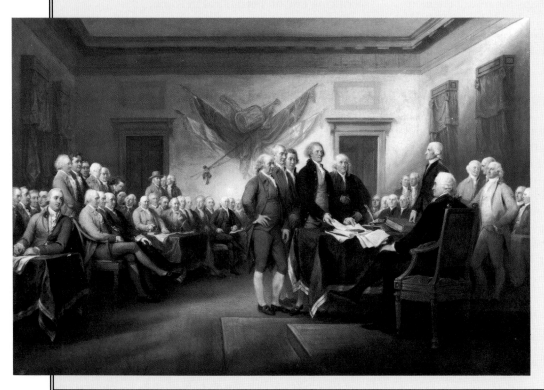

11.4 John Trumbull, *The Declaration of Independence, 4 July 1776*, 1787–1820. Oil on canvas, 21 1/8 ins x 31 1/8 ins (54 x 79 cm). Yale University Art Gallery, New Haven, Connecticut.
The calm exhibited here by the signatories of the American Declaration of Independence should not obscure their treasonous action. Author Thomas Jefferson (standing at the table in a dark cloak) justified the revolt with language from John Locke's version of the social contract, the second *Treatise on Civil Government*.

a man master of himself; for it is slavery to be under the impulse of mere appetite, and freedom to obey a law which we prescribe for ourselves.[1]

JEAN-JACQUES ROUSSEAU
From *The Social Contract* (1762)

Rousseau's concept of general will rested upon a paradox that brought him much criticism. Rousseau warned that when a citizen "refuses to obey the general will he shall be compelled to it by the whole body: this in fact only forces him to be free".[2] Some commentators see this as a rationale for the tyrannical excesses of the French Revolution, which were justified in the name of the "general will" and "public virtue."

Rousseau did not advocate a particular form of government, but he did plead for greater equality and freedom in all nations. Above all, he argued that flaws in society and its institutions, not flaws in human nature, were responsible for social injustice.

11.5 Clodion (Claude Michel), *Intoxication of Wine (Satyr and Bacchante)*, c. 1775. Terracotta, height 23¹/₄ ins (59 cm). The Metropolitan Museum of Art, New York, Bequest of Benjamin Altman, 1913.
This work of frank eroticism depicts worshipers of Dionysus who have given themselves over to sensual delight. The sculpture aptly expresses the playful mood of the rococo style.

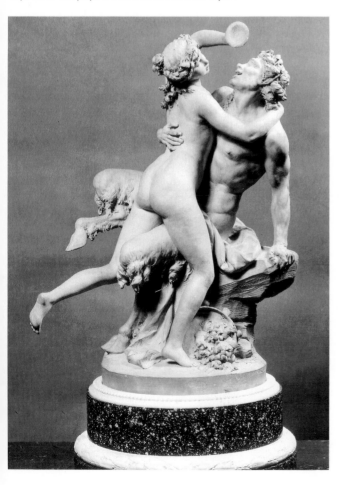

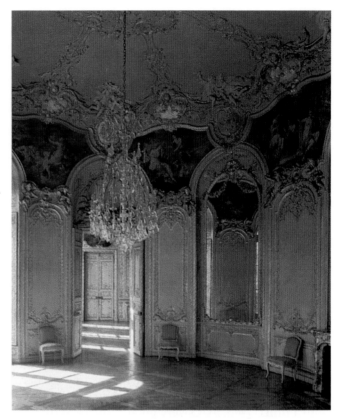

11.6 Gabriel Germain Boffrand, Salon de la Princesse, Hôtel de Soubise, Paris, c. 1740.
Note how the room is softened by its oval shape and the sculpted transition from wall to ceiling.

THE ROCOCO STYLE

Identify the qualities of eighteenth-century art that most appealed to art's patron classes.

The eighteenth century's dominant artistic style was called the **rococo** [ro-ko-KOH], a softer and more delicate style than the baroque. It was characterized by its intimate scale, soft colors and shapes, and playful, sensual themes, as in Clodion's *Satyr and Bacchante* (Fig. **11.5**). The name rococo probably derives from the French *rocaille*, the shell-like decoration used in fashionable gardens; the very sound of the word indicates something of the artistic style: gay, witty, and often frivolous.

The rococo style was most popular in France and Germany. In Paris, it was suited to the aristocratic town houses (or *hôtels*, as they were called), whose fanciful interior decoration (Fig. **11.6**) compensated for their modest exteriors. In these urbane and pleasant settings, the arts did not express profound ideas of political majesty or intense religious feeling. Instead, art could be witty and playful; succumb to melancholy or erotic fantasy; or distill the modest ideals of love, grace, and happiness. Rococo was art for pleasure and for decoration, and expressed perfectly the values and pastimes of the aristocracy.

THE WRITE IDEA

In your opinion, what ideas or teachings have been most abused by ignorant or zealous followers? To what extent would you hold a philosopher such as Rousseau responsible for the abuse of his ideas?

THE SALONS

The culture of the aristocracy centered around the Parisian salons. The salon was a regular social gathering that provided occasion for good food, music, and conversation – Paris' greatest art. It was customarily sponsored by a wealthy woman and held once or twice weekly in her *hôtel*. The most famous salons were those of Madame Geoffrin [ZHOFF-ran(h)] (Fig. **11.7**), whose husband had made a fortune manufacturing ice cream. Herself no intellectual, she entertained the leading figures of society, including the philosophes Rousseau, Diderot, and d'Alembert. Madame was known to cut short political discussions with a firm, "Well, that's very good!", thus avoiding the fate of one rival, whose guests so freely criticized the government that she was banned from the royal court.

The aim of the salon was to bring together "good company – a sort of association of the sexes" characterized by "the perfection of its charm, the urbanity of its usages, by an art of tact, indulgence, and worldly wisdom."[3] The salons provided an occasion for middle-class and aristocratic intellectuals to mix socially and exchange ideas. Through the salons, upper-class women became sponsors of music, art, and intellectual debate – indeed, Madame Geoffrin secretly helped to finance the philosophes' *Encyclopedia*. The *salonières'* social prominence and artistic patronage anticipated women's demands for greater rights and freedoms in the nineteenth century.

THE ART OF ROCOCO

The wistful mood of rococo painting was captured by Antoine Watteau (1684–1721), whose style set the tone for his eighteenth-century successors. Watteau [vah-TOH, wah-TOH] discarded the bold designs of the baroque style (Fig. **11.8**), preferring instead peaceful scenes with pastel colors and dreamy atmospheres. The painting which best expresses the rococo melancholy is *Pilgrimage to the Island of Cythera* (Fig. **11.9**). The painting shows a fashionable party of picnickers ready to leave Cythera [SITH-a-ra], the mythical island of the love-goddess Venus. The celebrants have decorated Venus' statue with flowers and now reluctantly leave their idyll. One lady turns for a last glance backward while her companion draws her toward the waiting boats, with their shell-shaped bows. The delicate colors give the painting a dream-like quality, tinged with sadness.

Watteau's picture created a new category of painting in the eighteenth century, the so-called *fête galante*, or "genteel celebration," of well-dressed and urbane revelers. The *fête galante* mirrored the fashionable and gay society of the eighteenth century, and provided the artists' patrons with an image of themselves worthy of exhibition in their homes and salons.

The more sensual and decorative side of rococo appears in the works of François Boucher (1703–70). Boucher [boo-SHAY] was the favored painter of Louis XV's mistress,

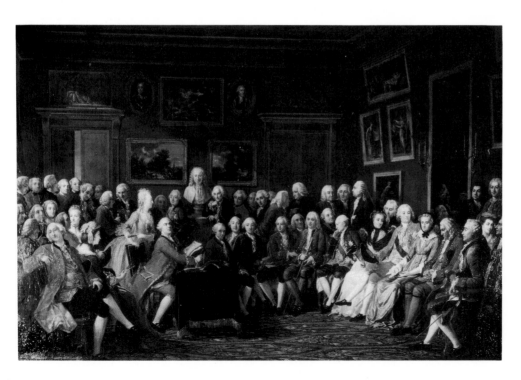

11.7 Madame Geoffrin's salon, Paris.
The imperious Madame Geoffrin oversees a musical performance at her Paris salon. Although prominent women sponsored most of the salons, note that most in attendance here are men.

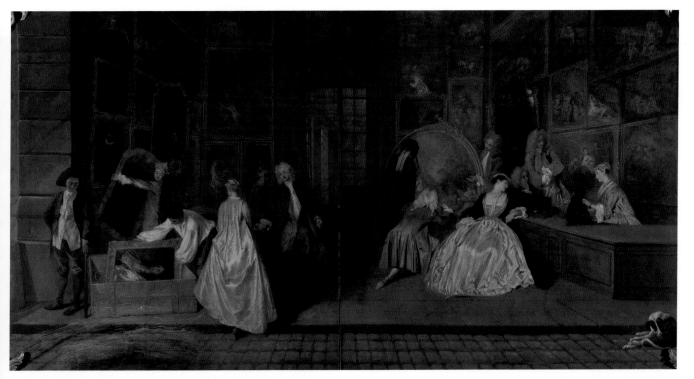

11.8 Antoine Watteau, *Gersaint's Signboard*, 1720–1. Oil on canvas, 5 ft 3⁷/₈ ins x 10 ft 1 ins (1.62 x 3.07 m). Staatliche Museen, Berlin.

Note how the composition is divided into two parts, dramatizing the change in painting fashion from baroque to rococo. While, at right, the gallery owner invites customers to examine a painting in the new style, at left a portrait of Louis XIV, emblem of the baroque past, is packed away into a crate.

11.9 Antoine Watteau, *Pilgrimage to the Island of Cythera*, 1717. Oil on canvas, 4 ft 2³/₄ ins x 6 ft 4³/₄ ins (1.29 x 1.94 m). Louvre, Paris.

Trace a line from the head of Venus' statue (right) along the party of picnickers to the boat at left. How does the shape of this line capture the mood of Watteau's rococo style? Observe also the rustic, golden colors and the aura of dreamy nostalgia.

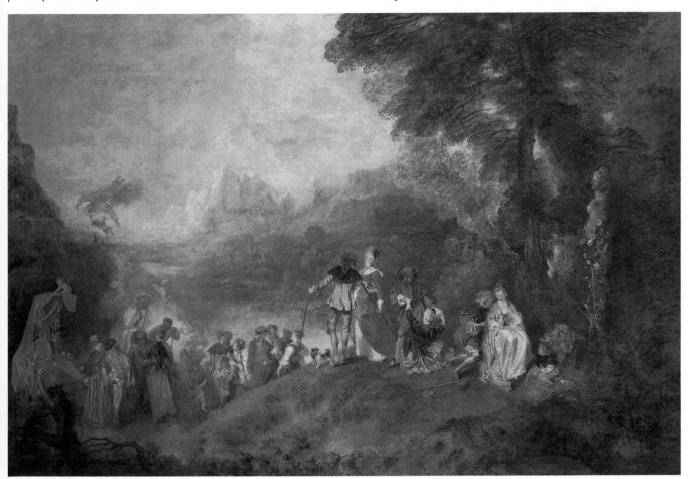

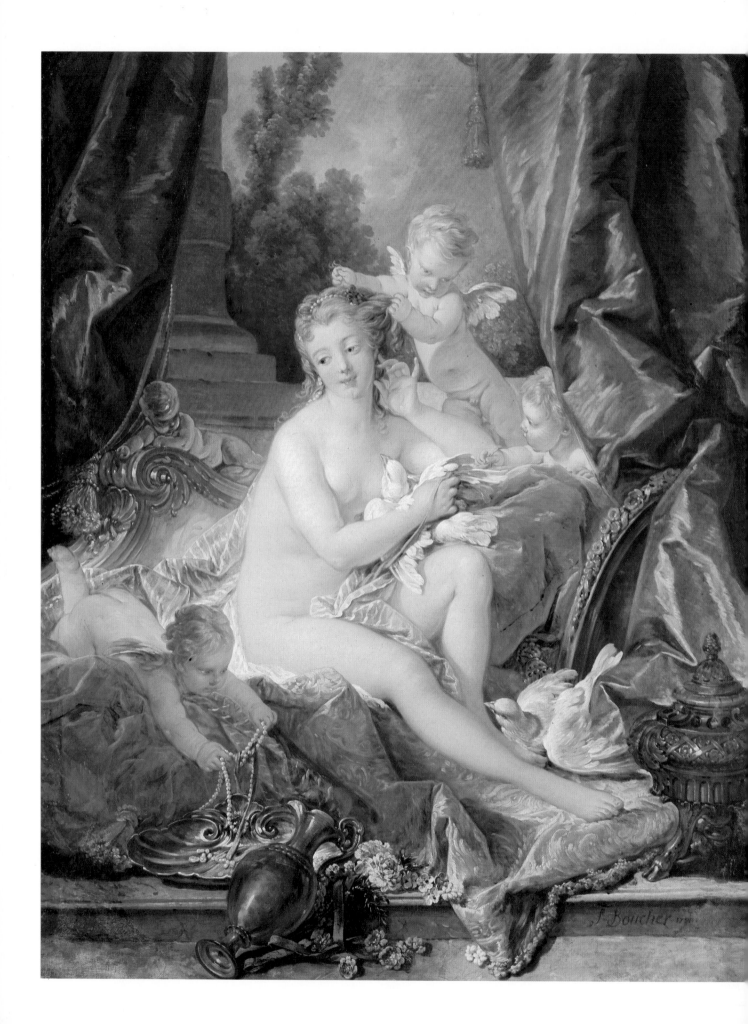

11.10 Opposite **François Boucher**, *The Toilet of Venus*, 1751. Oil on canvas, 42⁵/₈ x 33¹/₂ ins (108 x 85 cm). The Metropolitan Museum of Art, New York, Bequest of William K. Vanderbilt, 1920.
Analyze Boucher's scene as if it were a theatrical setting: how do the curtain, painted backdrop, props, and costume enhance the mood of dalliance and playfulness? What part do the minor characters (the cupids and doves) play in this erotic drama?

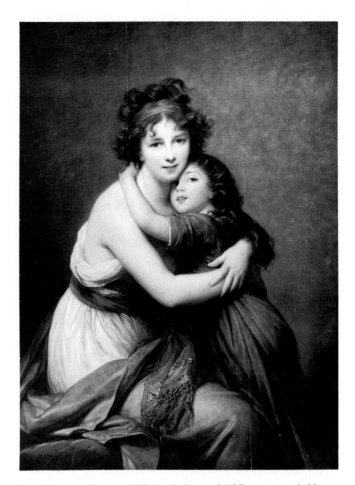

11.11 Marie-Elisabeth Vigée-Lebrun, *Self-Portrait with Her Daughter*, c. 1789. Oil on canvas, 51¹/₈ x 37 ins (130 x 94 cm). Louvre, Paris.
Vigée-Lebrun's self-portrait in neoclassical coiffure and costume helped fuel the Greek vogue of the late 1700s, while also appealing to the eighteenth-century cult of sentimentality (compare Fig. 11.17).

Madame de Pompadour, a patron of progressive writers and artists who decorated the Palace of Versailles in rococo fashion.

Boucher's *The Toilet of Venus* (Fig. **11.10**) was commissioned by Madame de Pompadour. While the picture is not her portrait, the beautiful royal mistress must have identified with the subject. The alluring goddess dreamily prepares herself for a visitor, as cupids coif her hair and toy with her jewels. Boucher achieved a luxurious surface with the gilded furnishings and glowing pinks and blues. Yet the picture has an aura of softness – in the doves, the flowers, the plump cupids – that half-conceals its erotic quality.

The frivolity and self-indulgence of the rococo style and its aristocratic patrons are clearly portrayed in *The Swing* (see Fig. 11.1) by Jean-Honoré Fragonard [frag-o-NAHR] (1732–1806), a genre scene of naughty gaiety. The central figure is the swinging young lady in her lavish gown. She looks coquettishly at the young gentleman positioned to gaze up her billowing skirts. The illicit pair is contrasted to the cleric, who stolidly swings his charge in the background. Fragonard's dreamy foliage provides the perfect setting for this dalliance. In contrast to the mythic power of Rubens' *Rape of the Daughters of Leucippus* (see Fig. 10.27), there is no pretense of a transcendent purpose in Fragonard's picture. It is a work of frank sensuality – charming but ultimately trivial.

The artist identified with the indulgent last days of the French monarchy is Marie-Elisabeth-Louise Vigée-Lebrun (1775–1842). Vigée-Lebrun [VEE-zhay luh-BRUH(n)] was portraitist and close friend of Marie Antoinette, queen of Louis XVI. She excelled in the delicate and flattering portraits preferred by the eighteenth-century nobility. Through the queen's influence, she was elected to the Royal Academy, which otherwise hindered the careers of women artists.

The sentimental self-portrait with her daughter (Fig. **11.11**) shows the sensitivity of Vigée-Lebrun's brush. The use of neoclassical coiffure and costume helped to fuel a Greek vogue in the late eighteenth century. A favorite of the court, Vigée-Lebrun made a dramatic escape from Paris during the French Revolution, fleeing the night that Marie Antoinette and the king were arrested. In exile from revolutionary France, Vigée-Lebrun charmed the nobility of Europe's capitals and earned a large fortune painting their portraits. She returned in 1802 to become a promi-

nent figure in Parisian society, sponsoring salons and writing charming memoirs.

The Rococo in Germany The rococo style of architecture was established in France, but found its most abandoned expression in eighteenth-century German palaces and churches. Indeed, with its grand scale and intense religiosity, German rococo art is sometimes considered a late variation of the baroque style.

In Catholic southern Germany and Austria, wealthy and powerful prince-bishops became ambitious sponsors of the new style. For the bishop of Würzburg, the architect Balthasar Neumann [NOY-mahn] (1687–1753) designed a grand palace, placing at its center a monumental staircase (Fig. **11.12**). The staircase's ceiling painting, showing angels carrying the bishop's portrait to dwell among the gods, is a masterwork of the Italian painter Giovanni Battista Tiepolo (1692–1770). Neumann's design of the pil-

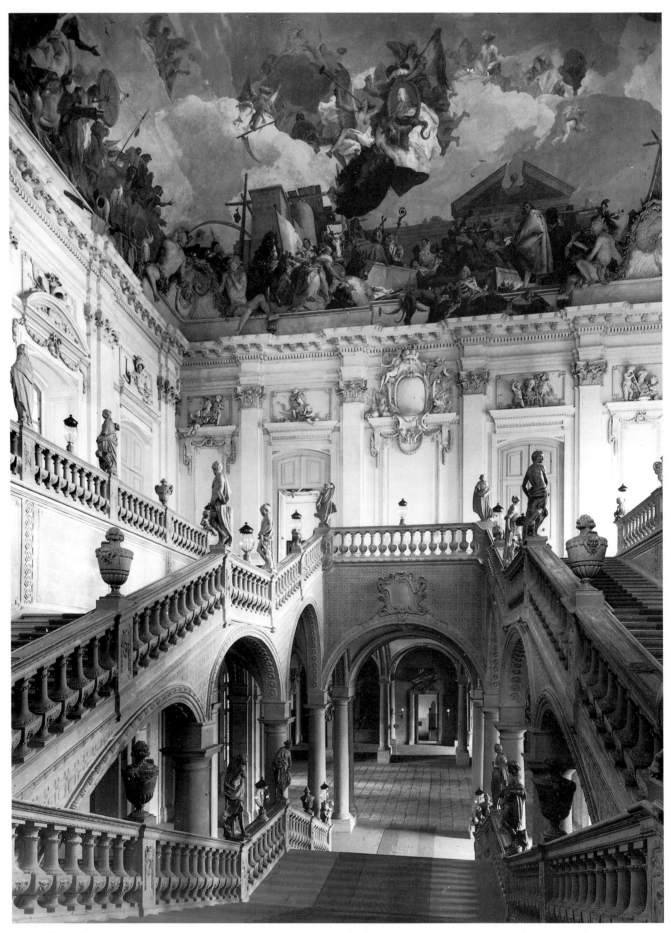

11.12 Above **Balthasar Neumann, staircase in the Residenz (Bishop's Palace), Würzburg, Germany, 1737–42.**
This vast staircase (one of the largest ever built) rises gradually from darkness to light. Tiepolo's vast ceiling painting (larger in area than Michelangelo's Sistine Chapel ceiling) extends the illusion with the temple pediment and scaffolding.

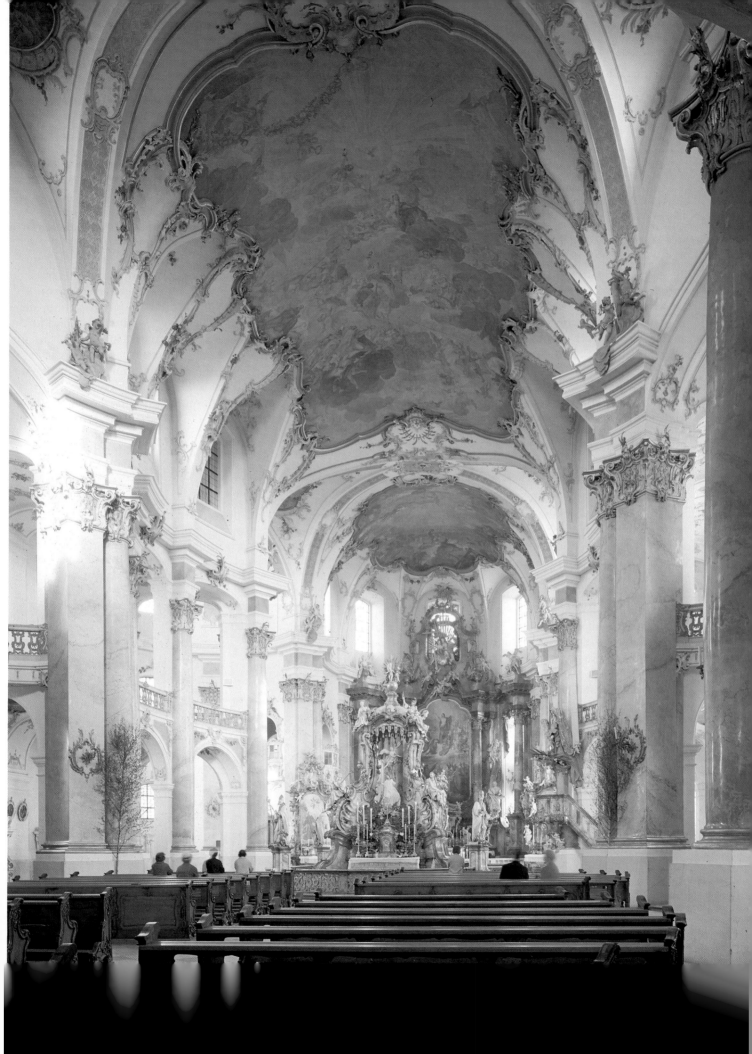

Previous page
11.13 Balthasar Neumann, interior of the Pilgrimage Church of the *Vierzehnheiligen*, near Bamberg, Germany, 1743–72.
Note the sculpted stucco and ceiling painting that soften the lines of the vaulting. The nave encloses worshipers in a large ellipse, a shape repeated in the island altar at center. Compare the character of this pilgrimage church to more traditional shrines such as Chartres Cathedral, France, or St. Peter's, Rome.

grimage Church of the *Vierzehnheiligen* [FEER-tsain-HIGH-lee-ghen] (the Fourteen Saints; Fig. **11.13**) in southern Germany is the purest expression of rococo architecture. The church's interior is a riot of rococo shapes and colors. The stucco decoration conceals the division between wall and ceiling, allowing the worshiper's eye to pass magically from the worldly to the spiritual realm. On first sight, the design seems to lack a unifying element. In fact, the church's floor plan consists of intersecting ovals that draw the pilgrim toward the elaborate altar. The *Vierzehnheiligen* offers the Christian pilgrim a pastel feast of the senses, a lavish celebration of piety.

EIGHTEENTH-CENTURY BALLET

The eighteenth century saw important developments in classical ballet, which had arisen under Lully's direction at the court of Versailles (see page 283). In 1713, the Paris Opera opened its own professional school of ballet. The Opera school produced a steady supply of well-trained dancers, including the famous Marie Anne de Cupis de Camargo, whom Voltaire called "the first woman to dance like a man" – meaning she danced with the technical virtuosity of male dancers. To demonstrate her technique, Camargo discarded the high-heeled dancing shoes of Louis XIV's era and shortened her skirts so audiences could see her feet.

These innovations in ballet training and costume were coupled with changes in the form and setting of the dance itself. In the baroque period, ballet had usually formed a pompous interlude in an opera or comedy, illustrating or adorning the larger dramatic work. During the eighteenth century, dancers created the *ballet d'action*, in which the ballet itself communicated dramatic action through dancers' movements. In *Letters on Dancing and Ballet* (1760), Jean Georges Noverre called for ballets to be "unified works of art" in their own right, with dance and music contributing to the narrative theme. Thus ballet emphasized less spectacular display and more emotional expression, changes made possible by new technique and greater freedom of costume.

MOZART AND OPERA

The painters and sculptors of rococo society were largely independent artists, but eighteenth-century musicians and composers were still servants of their patrons. Earlier in the century, Johann Sebastian Bach had been thrown into prison for asking his release from a patron. When the young Wolfgang Amadeus Mozart (1756–91) was rudely discharged by his patron in 1781, he migrated to the great musical capital of Vienna, where he barely supported himself as a freelance musician, tutor, and composer (Fig. **11.14**). Not until Beethoven, a generation later, did a European composer achieve an independent musical career, living only by the sale of his compositions.

Mozart [MOH-tsart] enjoyed the most storied musical career of the rococo era. He was famed as a child prodigy, and was performing for Europe's nobility at the age of six. By the time of his death, Mozart had composed more than six hundred works, including twenty operas and forty-one symphonies. His religious works include the famous *Requiem*, a Mass for the dead. Aside from these large works, he excelled in the shorter musical forms performed in the small palaces and town houses of rococo society.

In Vienna, Mozart sought the patronage of the enlightened Emperor Joseph II, who sponsored his entry into Viennese opera, a world of international prestige and cut-throat intrigue. Opera in Vienna had already felt the influ-

11.14 Joseph Lange, *Mozart at the Pianoforte*, 1789. Oil on canvas, 13¹/₂ x 11¹/₂ ins (35 x 30 cm). Mozart Museum, Salzburg.
The misery of Mozart's last years has been much exaggerated in the popular imagination, although he was unable to achieve the artistic independence that marked the later career of Ludwig van Beethoven.

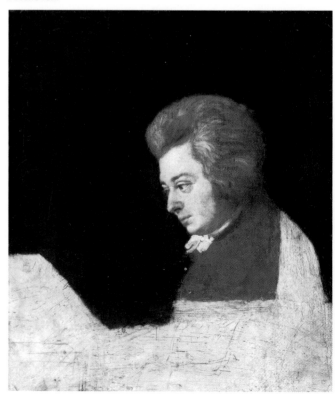

First Theme

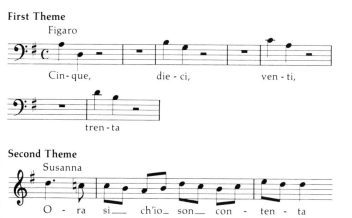

11.15 **Wolfgang Amadeus Mozart, opening measures of Figaro's and Susanna's entrances at the beginning of the opera, "Cinque . . . dieci," from** *Le Nozze di Figaro* **(***The Marriage of Figaro***), Act I, 1786.** Figaro's sturdy and naive manliness is expressed in the march-like melody of his part; Susanna provides a more lyrical counter-melody.

ence of reformers who wished to free German opera of ornamental singing and far-fetched plots. The reforms had the effect of widening opera's appeal to the mixed aristocratic and middle-class audiences of Vienna and Prague. In these great musical cities, Mozart enjoyed his greatest musical successes.

Mozart proved a genius at balancing music and drama in opera. He expressed in exquisite music his command of plot and interest in character psychology. One of his operatic masterpieces, *Le Nozze di Figaro* (*The Marriage of Figaro*, 1786), captures the rococo mood of gaiety and frivolity, while also presenting a musical drama of sophistication and wisdom. The *libretto*, or dramatic text, was written by Lorenzo da Ponte in Italian – still the language used in most eighteenth-century opera. *The Marriage of Figaro* recounts the impending marriage of Figaro and Susanna, servants in the house of Count Almaviva (Fig. **11.15**). Susanna fears that the philandering Count will force himself on her. She warns Figaro, who alternates between determination to foil the Count's intentions and suspicion of his fiancée. The complicated plot also involves a spurned suitor of Figaro's, and the Countess, who is embittered by the Count's infidelity.

The jealousies and angry threats never entirely obscure the humor and optimism underlying *The Marriage of Figaro*. The mistaken identities and disguises, distrust and suspicion, are all finally resolved in the opera's final scene, a virtuoso creation. Virtually all the characters are on-stage (visible or in hiding), singing in duets, trios, and ensemble. The climactic moment comes when the Count, totally outplayed, kneels and asks the Countess' pardon for his philandering, a moment of supreme musical reconciliation. The whole party celebrates this renewal of a candid and worldly love.

Mozart's later operas are also acknowledged as masterpieces of the operatic form. *Don Giovanni* [DON jee-oh-VAHN-ee] (1787) recounts the demise of the famous lover Don Juan, whose romantic exploits are enumerated in the famous "Catalogue" aria, sung by his sardonic servant Leporello. In the opera's finale, Don Giovanni refuses to repent of his sins and is cast into the flames of hell. In his last year, Mozart scored a popular success with *Die Zauberflöte* (*The Magic Flute*, 1791). Set in Egypt, the opera shows the influence of Mozart's membership of the secret Freemasons' society. The opera's magical atmosphere and light-hearted music delighted the Viennese public, while its Masonic symbolism celebrated the philosophical themes of harmony and enlightenment.

THE BOURGEOIS RESPONSE

Identify the artistic styles and themes that appealed to the middle-class public of the eighteenth century.

Mozart based the plot of *The Marriage of Figaro* on a stage play of the same name (written 1778) that had been censored in Vienna. The play criticized the arrogance of Europe's nobles and championed a morally upright servant. It contained a stirring indictment of aristocratic privilege: "Nobil-

11.16 **Jean-Baptiste-Siméon Chardin,** *Boy Spinning Top*, **1741. Oil on canvas, 26¹/₂ x 28³/₄ ins (67 x 73 cm). Louvre, Paris.** Chardin painted mostly still-life and genre scenes that possessed charm, simplicity, and a subtle moralizing tone. Here a boy has set aside his studies to play with a toy he has kept in the drawer – a mild pictorial sermon on the dangers of idleness.

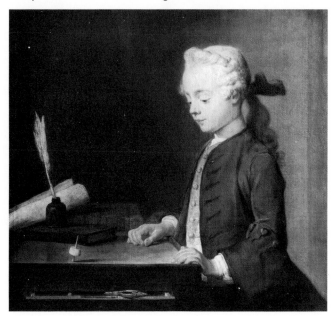

ity, wealth, a title, positions, and all of it makes you so proud! What have you done for all these blessings?" Figaro asks the Count. "You've had the trouble of being born, and nothing more."

In Paris, bourgeois audiences cheered Figaro's speech and the play's success was a sign of changing attitudes. As the middle classes gained influence, they demanded art that reflected their moral attitudes and artistic tastes. Instead of the frivolity of the rococo, bourgeois patrons desired sober virtue and a straightforward depiction of life. Yet, like the nobility, they wanted education for their children, entertainment for their leisure, and taste-fully decorated houses. In the eighteenth century, the arts of painting, literature, and theater provided the European middle class with works of sobriety and sentimentality, quite a different tone from that of the rococo style.

THE BOURGEOIS STYLE IN PAINTING

The bourgeois style in painting coexisted with the playful rococo style. The painter Jean-Baptiste-Siméon Chardin [shar-DAN(h)] (1699–1779), for example, countered the rococo style with a clarity of color and form. Chardin's paintings mostly depict ordinary scenes of the middle class, such as *Boy Spinning Top* (Fig. **11.16**). The subject and colors of his paintings are reminiscent of the seventeenth-century Dutch genre painting (see page 289) – adapted to the tastes of his French public. Chardin took great pleasure in the straightforward spatial order and palpable textures of his still lifes. His interior scenes present a world of domestic peace and contentment.

The most popular French painter of the mid-eighteenth century was Jean Baptiste Greuze (1725–1805). Technically, Greuze [gruhz] was a lesser painter than Chardin, but he was a greater phenomenon in his day. His genre pic-

11.17 Jean-Baptiste Greuze, *The Bride of the Village*, 1761. Oil on canvas, 46¹/₂ x 36 ins (118 x 91 cm). Louvre, Paris. Note the contrasting feelings among the principal females: the dreamy bride, the fretting mother, and (behind the father) the envious sister.

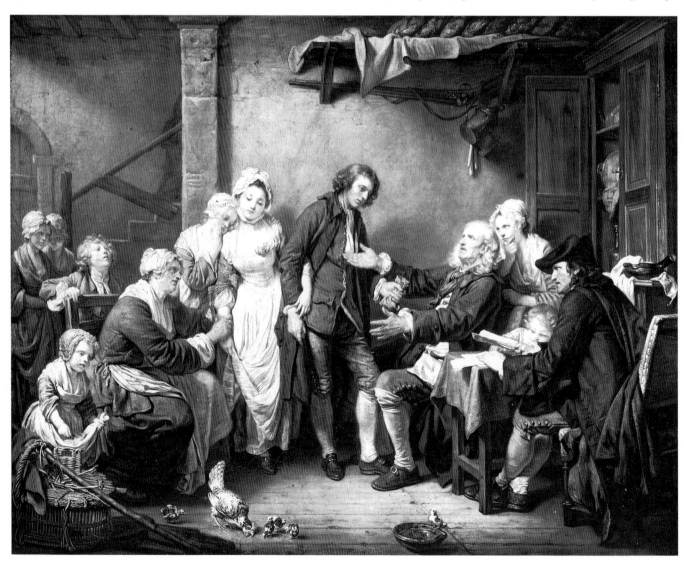

tures appealed directly to the cult of *sensibilité* ("feeling" or "compassion"), which swept over jaded Parisians at mid-century. Many of his pictures, such as *The Bride of the Village* (Fig. **11.17**), presented touching family scenes that might well be tableaux from the bourgeois sentimental drama. In this moralizing picture, the father hands over his daughter's dowry while delivering a sermon on the virtues of fidelity. The philosophe Diderot, who helped to popularize Greuze's paintings, said the spectator of such pictures "was seized by tender feeling." With his pictorial anecdotes, Greuze aroused a nostalgia for a simpler provincial life among Paris' sophisticates.

THE RISE OF THE NOVEL

A German philosopher once said of the novel that it was "the epic of the middle class," though, unlike the epics of ancient times, it did not retell tales from mythology or legend. Rather, the eighteenth-century **novel** was a long work of narrative fiction with realistic characters and settings – much as we know it today. Often taking the form of a journal or a series of letters (called an **epistolary novel**), the early novel provided ample latitude for its characters' introspection and moral self-examination.

The novel's popularity grew with the rising tide of literacy in eighteenth-century Europe. England was called "a nation of readers," with male literacy reaching perhaps sixty percent by 1750. The new reading public (which included a growing number of women) gathered in coffeehouses and cafés, sitting rooms and salons, to read and discuss newspapers and journals of criticism as well as novels (Fig. **11.18**). Eager for self-improvement, the middle class wanted books to uplift them, and novels gratified the bourgeois reader's expectations for an educational and moralizing literature.

The most important eighteenth-century English novelists were Daniel Defoe (1660–1731), Henry Fielding (1707–54), and Samuel Richardson (1689–1761). Richardson's epistolary novel *Pamela, or Virtue Rewarded* (1740–42) provided just the moral inspiration that bourgeois readers were seeking. The book's heroine, Pamela, is a simple country girl who must withstand the seductions of her wealthy employer. The psychological drama of her struggle is revealed through her letters, which form the bulk of the story. In a letter to her parents, Pamela sympathizes with young servant girls who have faced the assaults of their masters:

But, dear father and mother, what sort of creatures must the woman-kind be, do you think to give way to such wickedness? Why, this it is that makes every one to be thought of alike: and, a-lack-a-day! what a world we live in! for it is grown more a wonder that the men are resisted, than that the women comply. ... But I am sorry for these things; one don't know what arts and stratagems men may devise to gain their vile ends; and

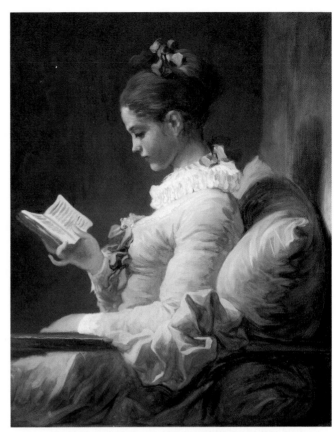

11.18 Jean-Honoré Fragonard, *A Young Girl Reading*, c. 1776. Oil on canvas, 32 x 25 1/2 ins (81 x 65 cm). National Gallery of Art, Washington, D.C., Gift of Mrs Mellon Bruce in memory of her father Andrew W. Mellon.
The 18th-century rise in literacy was fueled by the popularity of the novel, read in quiet solitude.

so I will think as well as I can of these poor undone creatures, and pity them. For you see, by my sad story, and narrow escapes, what hardships poor maidens go through whose lot it is to go out to service, especially to houses where there is not the fear of God, and good rule kept by the heads of the family.[4]

SAMUEL RICHARDSON
From *Pamela* (1740–42)

The most popular of these eighteenth-century sentimental novels was Rousseau's *Julie, ou la Nouvelle Héloïse* (*Julie, or the New Héloïse*, 1761), a best-seller that ran to 72 editions. Rousseau's novel was based on the famous medieval love story of Abelard and Heloïse (see page 160) and played on the racy themes of seduction and marriage between social classes. The virtue of Rousseau's heroine is suspect until she dies sacrificially in the last pages of the novel. All of Europe wept for Rousseau's *Julie*.

By the end of the century, the sentimental novel had evolved into a more subtle exploration of sensation and feeling. As perfected by Jane Austen (1775–1817), the

GLOBAL PERSPECTIVE

KABUKI THEATER

The rise of the European middle class as an artistic public finds an intriguing parallel in Japan during the Edo period (1616–1868). As Japan emerged from feudal wars, a new merchant class gained influence in Edo (Tokyo) and other commercial cities. These townspeople sought amusement in the entertainments of the *ukiyo*, the "floating world" of sensual pleasures – literally, districts containing restaurants, theaters, and brothels. In this atmosphere, a new form of theater arose called **kabuki** [kuh-BOO-kee], which combined stylized acting with song, dance, colorful costume, and spectacular staging. The invention of kabuki in 1603 is attributed to the young female dancer Izumo no Okuni. However, because of kabuki's early association with prostitution (both male and female), the authorities soon banned all but adult male actors from the stage.

By the eighteenth century, kabuki was so popular that commercial theaters were built to hold audiences of several thousand. At a time when European theater stressed simpler plots and staging, kabuki productions reveled in artifice. Elaborate theatrical devices – revolving stages, elevators, multiple curtains, intensely colored costumes, and elaborate scenery – made kabuki a visual spectacle. The kabuki stage's most distinctive feature was a ramp leading through the audience, called the *hanamichi*, or "flower path." The *hanamichi* [hahn-uh-MEE-chee] permitted theatrical entrances and exits by star actors, often with dramatic pauses and stylized poses. Kabuki staging borrowed from both the more traditional No drama, with its formalized gestures, and the exuberant Japanese puppet theater, called *bunraku*.

Some kabuki actors (all of whom were male) specialized in impersonating female characters, while others perfected a "rough" acting style suitable for gangster or soldier roles, or a "soft" style for playing merchants or lovers. The kabuki enhanced the actors' highly stylized gestures and poses with extravagantly colorful costumes and make-up. Typically, kabuki performances lasted for an entire day; a small orchestra provided a varied musical accompaniment to the action.

The stories of the kabuki theater included historical dramas, roughly equivalent to the history dramas of Shakespeare's theater, and domestic dramas with comic plots or tales of doomed lovers. In one typical plot, two lovers – a banished priest and a courtesan – both survive a mutual suicide attempt, but then continue their lives with each thinking the other has been lost. Often, as with European opera, the stories provided the occasion for spectacular effects and virtuoso performance.

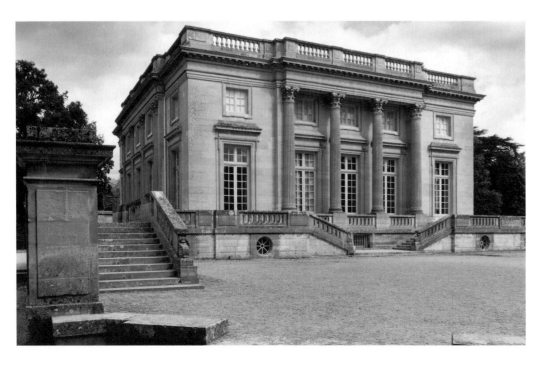

11.19 Ange-Jacques Gabriel, the Petit Trianon, Versailles, France, 1761–4. This small residence in the grounds of the Palace of Versailles expresses the elegance and decorum of the 18th-century neoclassical style. Compared to the main palace, the scale and decoration here are restrained and the residence's interior was ingeniously arranged for comfortable living.

so-called **novel of manners** was a carefully observed and gently satirical study of social life among the English gentry. In *Sense and Sensibility* (1811) and *Pride and Prejudice* (1813), Austen examined her heroines in the crucial moment of betrothal and marriage, as they sought a livable balance among affection, social standing, and personal integrity. Austen's finely wrought novels of manners gave the novel its first modern cast.

THE BOURGEOIS THEATER IN GERMANY

The bourgeois response in Germany was tinged with both sentimentality and nationalism. Through the early eighteenth century, Germany's dozens of small courts slavishly imitated the culture of absolutist France, with its artificial manners and neoclassical tastes. A rebellion against French influence was led by Gotthold Ephraim Lessing (1729–81), a critic and dramatist who single-handedly created a German national theater. Lessing was the founder of the *Aufklärung* [OWFF-klair-oonk], or "enlightenment," in Germany. To him, the term implied not only philosophical enlightenment but also a clarified national spirit in the German states. Lessing's critical works condemned neoclassical formalism, while his plays depicted characters of more direct and genuine feeling. A typical example of this bourgeois sentimental drama was his *Miss Sara Sampson*, the Greek tragedy of Medea refashioned with a bourgeois heroine.

Lessing's sentimental drama prepared the way for an impassioned group of young German authors called the *Sturm und Drang* [STOORM oont DRAHNK] (Storm and Stress) movement. Writers of the *Sturm und Drang* protested social injustice and praised rebellious genius. Dedicated to German nationalism, they hoped to free German culture from its insipid imitations of French neoclassicism. The movement's most important figure was Johann Wolfgang von Goethe (1749–1832). Goethe's [GUH(r)-tuh] sprawling play *Götz von Berlichingen* explicitly violated neoclassical norms and emulated Shakespeare's dramatic scope and diversity. Its hero, Götz [guhts], is a fiery medieval knight who joins a peasant revolt and thus proves a passionate commitment to justice and fairness. In Götz, Goethe gave to German theater its first great dramatic hero and a powerful expression of the *Sturm and Drang* movement.

CRITICAL QUESTION

In what areas can you see the impulse to "get back to basics" or "return to the past," as eighteenth-century neoclassicists wished to? In what areas might we benefit from reviving old values and ideas?

THE NEOCLASSICAL STYLE

Explain how neoclassicism could express both conservative and revolutionary values.

"There is but one way for the moderns to become great, and perhaps unequaled; I mean, by imitating the ancients." These were the words of the eighteenth century's greatest enthusiast of the "ancients," the German writer Johann Joachim Winckelmann (1717–68), in his *Thoughts on the Imitation of Greek Works in Painting and Sculpture*. Like so many enlightened thinkers, Winckelmann [VINK-el-mahn] praised the Greeks to condemn something in his own age, in particular the feeble softness and capricious excesses of the rococo. In the words of Winckelmann, ancient Sparta had produced heroes "fed on flesh," whereas the modern salons and academies produced heroes "fed on roses." Thus, Winckelmann's vision of antiquity served a modern purpose, which was to criticize the falseness of eighteenth-century art and society.

Winckelmann's teachings helped define the **neo-classical** style of the later eighteenth century, which explicitly imitated the art of ancient Greece and Rome. This era's neoclassicism was abstract, with little first-hand knowledge of antique art, and it was moral, imposing universal ethical principles on art. Neoclassicism was also versatile: under different circumstances, it was used to revive the grandeur of Versailles, to demonstrate the good taste of the rising middle class, and to educate and civilize an unsophisticated provincial nation.

NEOCLASSICAL ARCHITECTURE

Perhaps the purest example of the neoclassical taste and cultivation was the Petit Trianon [PUH-tee TREE-a-non(h)] (Fig. **11.19**), a residence built for Louis XVI on the grounds of Versailles Palace. The architect, Ange-Jacques Gabriel, avoided the main palace's pompous grandeur and instead aimed for perfect balance and austere simplicity. Except for the four subdued pilasters, the building is almost free of decoration. Nothing distracts from its geometric regularity.

In England, the bible of neoclassical building was Palladio's *Four Books of Architecture* – a collection of meticulous drawings of ancient Roman buildings by the famous Italian Renaissance architect (see page 259). The English gentry built imitations of Palladio's villas on their country estates, often combining neoclassical buildings with landscaped settings to achieve **picturesque** vistas. The English taste for the picturesque, with its balance between

KEY CONCEPT

NEOCLASSICISM

Western art had borrowed from the art of ancient Greece and Rome throughout history, but during the eighteenth century it swelled with a new enthusiasm for classical styles. This artistic fashion is called **neoclassicism**, meaning the conscious effort to revive the values of classical art and history. Compared with earlier classical revivals, eighteenth-century neoclassicism was particularly rigid and often austere. However, like other versions of classicism, it sought to recreate a world of timeless truth and beauty (Fig. **11.20**). It also had a great capacity for meaning different things to different people. To the royal court, it signaled a relief from the preciosity of the rococo style and a return to the grand style of Louis XIV. To the royal academies, it represented the authority of the past, a basis for teaching good taste and disciplined technique. To the newly educated middle classes, neoclassicism offered a high-minded moralism and a sure standard of taste and decorum.

It is no wonder, then, that an explosion of neoclassical paintings, buildings, and statues burst upon the later eighteenth century. The fashion was ignited by theorists such as Johann Winckelmann, who praised the "noble simplicity and quiet grandeur" of ancient Greece

11.20 Angelica Kauffmann, *Cornelia, Mother of the Gracchi*, 1785. Oil on canvas, 3 ft 4 ins x 4 ft 2 ins (1.02 x 1.27 m). Virginia Museum of Fine Arts, Richmond, Virginia, the Adolph D. and Wilkins C. Williams Fund.
Kauffmann was one of two female founding members of the British Royal Academy and excelled at history painting, the most prestigious category of 18th-century academic painting. This scene is taken from Roman history: when a visitor asked to see her family's jewels, Cornelia supposedly pointed to her two sons, who would become leaders of the Roman Republic.

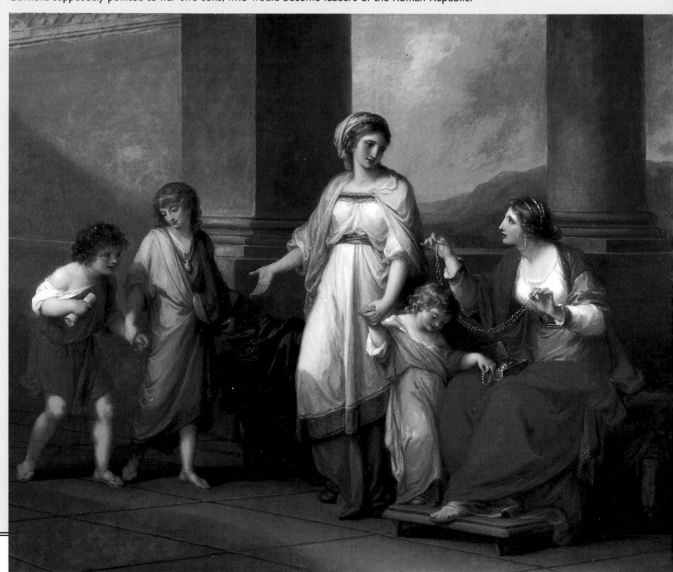

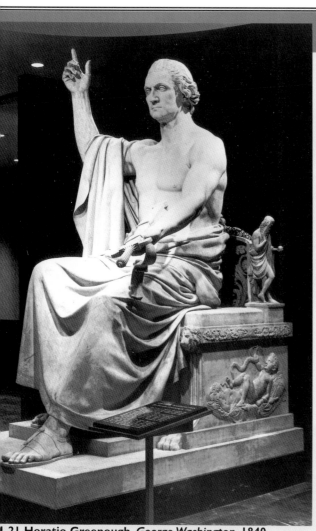

11.21 Horatio Greenough, *George Washington*, 1840.
Marble, height 11 ft 4 ins (3.46 m). National Museum of
American Art, Smithsonian Institution, Washington, D.C.
This statue idealizes the Virginia planter and first American
president as a heroic Greek god.

without ever having seen a Greek temple). Enlightened citizens lived in the style of antique heroes, modeling their lives and their clothes after the ancient Greeks
and Romans (Fig. 11.21).

This vision of antiquity was usually derived from earlier versions of neoclassicism rather than from antiquity itself. In fact, neoclassical theorists were somewhat
dismayed with excavations at the ancient cities of Herculaneum and Pompeii (begun in 1737). The bawdiness
of actual Roman wall paintings did not match neoclassicism's idealized image of antiquity. Whatever the illusions about antiquity, however, neoclassicism expressed
a desire for universal moral truths and enduring standards of reason and beauty. It responded to a common
impulse in Western civilization: the desire to return to
a simpler and more glorious past.

neoclassical order and the rustic irregularity of nature,
was evident in Henry Hoare's Park at Stourhead (Fig.
11.22).

The most ingenious of the neoclassical architects was
not English but American. Thomas Jefferson (1743–1826),
revolutionary philosopher and American president, was
also an accomplished builder. While ambassador to France
in the 1780s, he studied the neoclassical style and came to
believe it represented European cultivation and enlightenment. Jefferson adapted the neoclassical style in his
designs for buildings in America, such as his country estate
Monticello (Fig. **11.25**), built much in the spirit of Palladio's Italian villas. Monticello's hilltop site, overlooking
the mountains and farmland of central Virginia, can be
compared with Palladio's Villa Rotonda (see Fig. 9.33). In
some of Monticello's decorative details, Jefferson slavishly followed Palladio's architectural drawings. In other
cases, Jefferson showed his ingenuity as a designer. The
home's connecting outbuildings are hidden below ground
level, giving Monticello its elegant profile while serving
its function as a farmhouse. The famous dome and the
appearance of a single story (in fact there are three) were
elements borrowed from the fashionable *hôtels* that Jefferson had seen in Paris.

NEOCLASSICAL PAINTING

Many intellectual, artistic, and social figures of the eighteenth century were opposed to the frivolous mood and
pliable techniques of rococo art, especially in painting,
which was so ready to flatter or titillate. In 1765, the
philosophe Diderot claimed that the "degradation of taste,
of color, of composition, of character, of expression, of
drawing, is a consequence of the degradation of morals."
However, this moral condemnation of rococo art did
not translate immediately into great works of art. Instead,
it produced exhibitions full of undistinguished history
paintings. Not until Jacques-Louis David [da-VEED] was
the neoclassical style expressed in electrifying pictures.

Jacques-Louis David (1748–1825) astounded the art
public in 1784 with his stern tableau of Roman heroes, the
Oath of the Horatii (Fig. **11.23**). Visitors to the painter's
Rome studio placed flowers before the picture as if it were
an altar. King Louis XVI admired the work, and it was
purchased immediately by the French government. Today,
the picture is often seen as a premonition of the French
Revolution, which began four years later, in 1789. In
fact, the painting contains no criticism of French politics or society. It is a manifesto of neoclassicism, not of
revolution. In a scene from the history of Rome, three
brothers pledge to defend Rome's honor against the Curatius
family of a neighboring town. The Horatian women –
on the right – grieve because one is sister to the opposing
family and another is engaged to a Curatius. In David's
version, this gripping scene is purified of all ornament.
The statuesque quality of the male poses (borrowed from

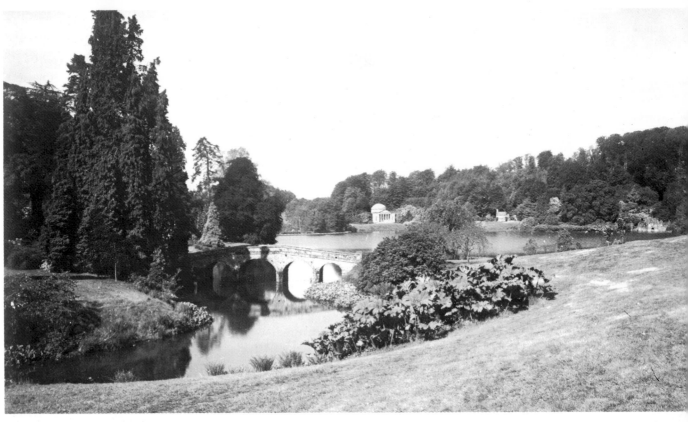

11.22 Above **Henry Hoare, the Park at Stourhead, 1743–4.**
In contrast to the formal gardens of Versailles, designers in England sought to reproduce the natural landscapes of the classical poets. Landscape designers strove for an effect called the "picturesque." Note in this view, the distant small-scale classical temple framed by the bridge, lake, and foliage.

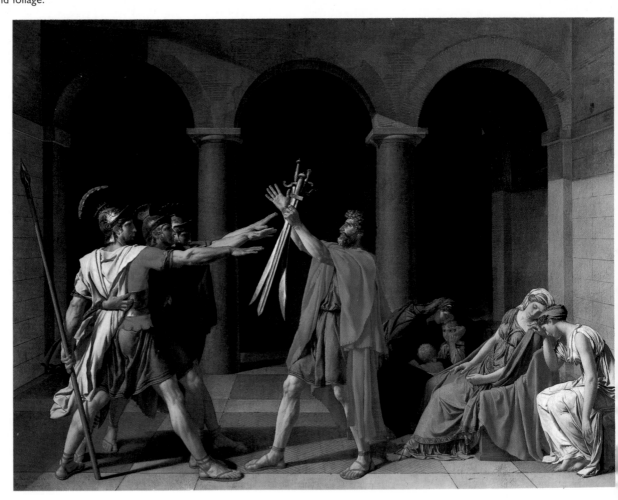

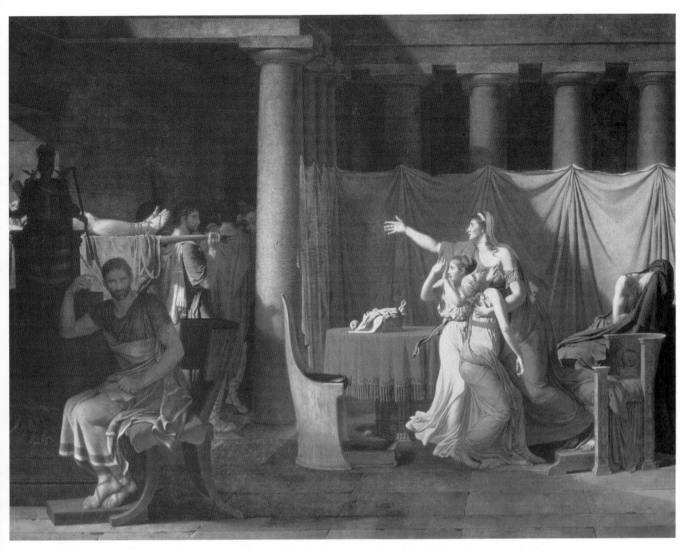

11.24 Jacques-Louis David, *Lictors Bearing to Brutus the Bodies of his Sons*, 1789. Oil on canvas, 10 ft 8 ins x 13 ft 10½ ins (3.25 x 4.23 m). Louvre, Paris.
With your finger, trace the planes defined by Brutus' feet (foreground), the mother's outstretched arm (middle ground), and the sewing basket on the table (background). How does the lighting define these planes and contribute to the painting's emotional drama?

11.23 Opposite below **Jacques-Louis David, *Oath of the Horatii*, 1784–5. Oil on canvas, 10 ft 10 ins x 14 ft (3.3 x 4.27 m). Louvre, Paris.**

Such scenes from Rome's history were a commonplace in neoclassical painting. David's statuesque figures and simplified design were the first to capture neoclassicism's moral passion in paint.

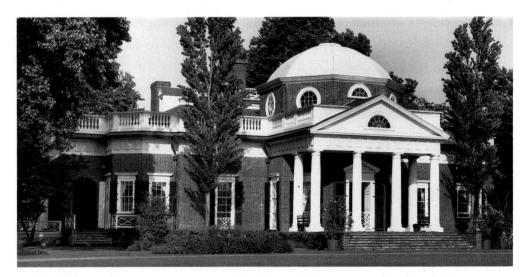

11.25 Thomas Jefferson, Monticello, near Charlottesville, Virginia, 1770–84; remodeled 1796–1806.
Compare the visual effect of Jefferson's neoclassical residence, with its use of native American materials (brick, wood), to the French palace Petit Trianon (Fig. 11.19). Note the use of round windows and the fan-shaped Palladian window in the triangular pediment.

Poussin) emphasizes the moral virtue of the men. By contrast, the languid lines of the women show their mournful emotion. The painting embodied the leading principles of neoclassical criticism: didactic purpose, purity of form, and deep passion restrained by good taste. In its simplicity and rigor, it was a declaration of neoclassicism's revolt against the whimsical style of the rococo.

David's neoclassical style is inevitably associated with his later political involvement in the French Revolution (see page 331), and scholars disagree about the political and artistic meaning of the last picture in his pre-revolutionary phase, *Lictors Bearing to Brutus the Bodies of his Sons* (Fig. **11.24**). Here again, the subject is drawn from early Roman history and the themes are self-sacrifice, honor, and commitment to principle. The consul Brutus has had to suppress a rebellion led by his own sons. Obeying his civic duty, Brutus has condemned his sons to die on the Senate floor. David shows us Brutus at home, sitting before a statue of the goddess Roma. Brutus' stoic calm contrasts with the distraught grief of the three women. Their gestures direct our eye to the doorway, where the sons' lifeless bodies are borne into the house.

Some art historians often attribute republican sentiment to this painting, seeing in it the sacrifices of revolutionary citizens. Others argue that David was chiefly interested in the painting's combination of strong feeling and bold visual style, not its political message.

THE CLASSICAL SYMPHONY

Eighteenth-century musicians could not reach back to classical sources in music, as neoclassical architects and painters could in their arts. Instead, composers in the late eighteenth and early nineteenth centuries – especially Haydn, Mozart, and Beethoven – adopted the neoclassical ideals of order, proportion, and harmony. Their works now constitute the "Classical" period (c. 1750–1820) in music because these composers are enduring "classics" who created a

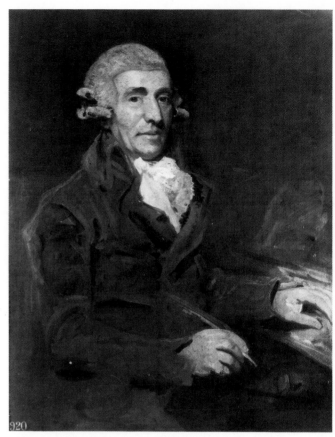

11.26 John Hoppner, *Portrait of Joseph Haydn*, 1791. The Royal Collection, London. © Her Majesty Queen Elizabeth II.
Prince Nikolaus I Esterházy engaged Joseph Haydn as court composer and conductor from 1762 until the year of his death in 1790. Musical life at court was extremely lively during Nikolaus I's reign.

standard for later music. The Classical period in music is thus doubly classical, in its rational and harmonious music style and its influence on later composers.

The first important Classical composers were Joseph Haydn and Wolfgang Mozart. Both composers were immensely prolific, composing music for court occasions, religious services, and public concerts that were the standard musical fare of the eighteenth century. The Austrian composer Haydn (1732–1809; Fig. **11.26**) spent nearly three decades as composer for the Esterházys, a family of Hungarian aristocrats. In service to his patrons, Haydn [HIGH-dn] composed with considerable range and originality within the limits of the Classical style. By the 1790s, he was recognized as Europe's leading composer, excelling in all the popular musical forms (see chart).

It was Haydn who developed the symphony in its Classical form. The **symphony** is an orchestral composition usually in four **movements** or sections. These movements are usually known by Italian terms which describe the tempo (speed) at which the music is played. The Classical symphony usually opens with a fast movement,

POPULAR CLASSICAL MUSICAL FORMS	
symphony	orchestral work, usually in four movements
concerto	work for single instrument and orchestra, usually in three movements with pattern of fast-slow-fast
sonata	work for solo piano or a piano with another instrument, usually in three or four movements
string quartet	work for violins, viola, and cello, usually in four movements

11.27 The sonata form.

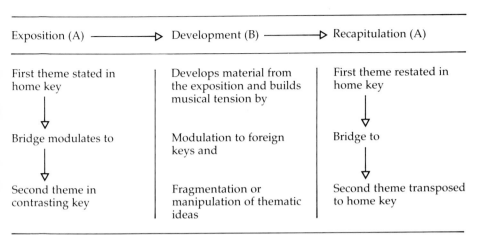

Exposition (A) ⟶ Development (B) ⟶ Recapitulation (A)

First theme stated in home key	Develops material from the exposition and builds musical tension by	First theme restated in home key
Bridge modulates to	Modulation to foreign keys and	Bridge to
Second theme in contrasting key	Fragmentation or manipulation of thematic ideas	Second theme transposed to home key

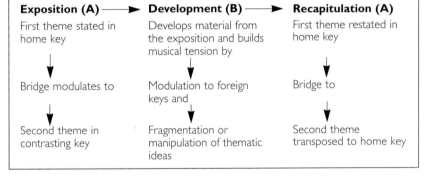

followed by a slow and lyrical movement, then a graceful dance in moderate tempo, and finally a fast and animated fourth movement. Haydn could achieve intricate musical effects in just the brief span of a minuet (a dance form), as in the Minuet and Trio from his Symphony No. 45 (1772). He was also a musical jokester: his "Surprise Symphony" and the "Joke Quartets" (1781) violate the predictable patterns of Classical form for comic effect.

Each symphonic movement was also written in a specific formal pattern. As developed by Haydn, the Classical symphony's first movement is most important, setting the musical tone for the entire work. This first movement was in the **sonata form** (Fig. **11.27**), which weaves two musical themes together in a three-part structure. In the sonata form, the two themes are first stated in the **exposition**, which presents the movement's basic musical ideas in a musical "argument." The first theme is stated in the home key, the second theme in a contrasting key. Then, in the **development**, the themes

undergo various musical changes. The melodies may be broken apart, turned backwards or upside down, or played in different musical keys. Finally, the tensions created in the development are resolved in the **recapitulation**, when both themes are restated in the home key. The movement may finish with a brief *coda*, or "tail." The sonata form offered classical composers an orderly, harmonious structure that could accommodate considerable musical variation. The form is so flexible that composers have continued to use it into the twentieth century, and most popular songs are written in a similar three-part structure (A-B-A).

The formal symmetry of the eighteenth-century Classical symphony is demonstrated in Mozart's precise symphonic compositions. In 1790, in the span of six weeks, Mozart composed three symphonies, including the Symphony No. 40 in G Minor. The symphony's first movement (Fig. **11.28**) begins with a **motif**, or melodic idea, of three rapid falling notes that create an insistent, almost neurotic energy. As was typical of the sonata form, the second theme (in a contrasting key) is more lyrical, even languid. The exposition is usually played twice. In Mozart's development, the first themes' three notes are sounded in different keys and build to a piercing climax. The tension is resolved in the recapitulation, as both themes return to the home key of G minor. The symphony demonstrates Mozart's ability to create effortless transitions between sections and to build a perfectly symmetrical structure for

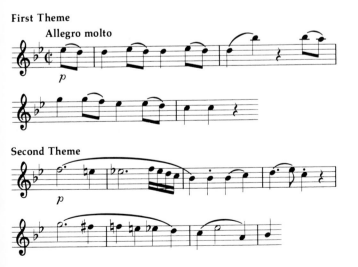

11.28 Wolfgang Amadeus Mozart, Symphony No. 40 in G minor. First movement, 1st and 2nd themes.

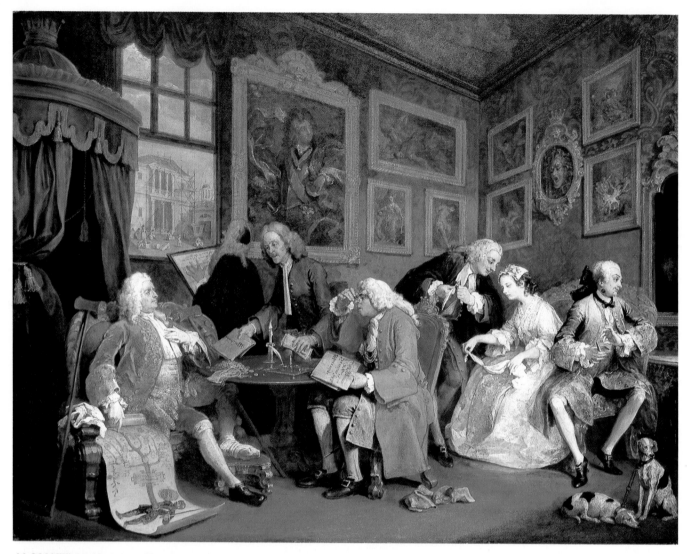

11.29 William Hogarth, *The Marriage Contract* from *Marriage à la Mode* (Scene I), 1744. Oil on canvas, 27 x 35 ins (69 x 90 cm). National Gallery, London.
Hogarth filled his painting with telling narrative detail: the botched neoclassical building, evidence of the aristocrat's faulty taste; the dogs chained together, symbolic of the couple's ill-fated union; and the syphilitic pox marks on the bridegroom's face, proof of his dissolute living.

his musical ideas. The work embodies the musical "enlightenment" of the Classical symphony, with its emphasis on clarity and balance.

THE AGE OF SATIRE

Identify the aspects of eighteenth-century society that were criticized by the age's great satirists.

The Enlightenment was as critical of human folly as it was convinced that social evils could be corrected. The age was characterized by **satire**, the literary or artistic attitude that aims to improve society by its humorous criticism. Imitating the satirical poets of ancient Rome (see page 94), Enlightenment satirists lightened their attacks on social ills with wit, mockery, and comic exaggeration. Often, they broadcast their satire in the pamphlets, engravings, and adventure tales that were staples of the reading public of the time. In every case, eighteenth-century satirists hoped that laughing at social evils would help to correct them.

SWIFT

Jonathan Swift (1667–1745), perhaps the greatest Enlightenment satirist, was a deeply pessimistic man who spent his literary talents on efforts for social reform. As an Anglican churchman, Swift led a highly public life that engaged him in the major political and social debates of his time. He was deeply sympathetic to the poverty and economic oppression in his native Ireland. In his famous pamphlet *A Modest Proposal* (1729), Swift made a bitterly ironic recommendation, that the children of the Irish poor be butchered, roasted, and served upon the Sunday dinner tables of their oppressive English landlords. Eating children, said Swift, would reduce surplus population and provide income for the children's impoverished parents. He even calculated the reasonable price a gentleman should pay for the "carcass of a good fat child."

I do therefore humbly offer it to public consideration, that of the hundred and twenty thousand children, already computed, twenty thousand may be reserved for breed, whereof only one fourth part to be males, which is more than we allow to sheep, black-cattle, or swine, and my reason is that these children are seldom the fruits of marriage, a circumstance not much regarded by our savages, therefore one male will be sufficient to serve four females. That the remaining hundred thousand may at a year old be offered in sale to the persons of quality and fortune, through the kingdom, always advising the mother to let them suck plentifully in the last month, so as to render them plump, and fat for a good table. A child will make two dishes at an entertainment for friends, and when the family dines alone, the fore or hind quarter will make a reasonable dish, and seasoned with a little pepper or salt will be very good boiled on the fourth day, especially in winter.[5]

JONATHAN SWIFT
From *A Modest Proposal* (1729)

Swift's satiric masterpiece was *Gulliver's Travels* (1726), a journal of the fantastic travels of Lemuel Gulliver. Its playful tone disguises a savage exposé of human folly and corruption. Swift recounts Gulliver's adventures in several lands, using each new encounter to mock human vices and political corruption. The bitterest episode describes Gulliver's encounter with the Houyhnhnms [HOO-ee-nimms], a race of horses "so orderly and rational, so acute and judicious" that they put humans to shame. The land of the Houyhnhnms is also inhabited by ignoble savages called Yahoos, who are disgusting and crude, prone to bickering, avarice, and gluttony. They possess, in other words, the worst features that Swift observed in his human companions. The Yahoos' leaders bear a striking resemblance to European monarchs and their fawning courtiers.

Swift's view of the world combined the Enlightenment's critical spirit with the traditional Christian belief in human sinfulness. He saw human beings as all the more responsible for their folly and cruelty, since humans could reason while the Yahoos could not. As the Houyhnhnm master observes, when a creature "pretending to reason" is able to commit the horrors of modern war, human rationality may be worse than the Yahoos' brutishness.

11.30 Thomas Gainsborough, *Mr. and Mrs. Andrews*, c. 1749. Oil on canvas, 27¹/₂ x 47 ins (69.8 x 119.4 cm). National Gallery, London.
Gainsborough's wedding portrait of this young couple is distinctly English: instead of a fanciful mythological background, he places the sitters before the grain fields and herds that they manage with such care and pride. How would you explain the painting's strongly asymmetrical composition and the contrast between portrait and landscape?

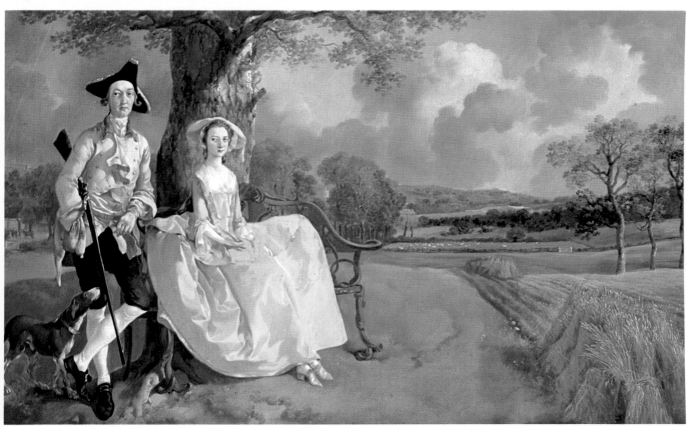

WINDOW ON DAILY LIFE

WOMEN GLADIATORS

English theater of the eighteenth century was still the scene of wild entertainments. A Frenchman who visited the theater at Lincoln's Inn Field in London gave this account of a gladiatorial combat between two women, which followed a performance of the opera *Orpheus in the Underworld*, with elaborate stage machinery:

The day I went to see the gladiators fight I witnessed an extraordinary combat, two women being the champions. As soon as they appeared on the stage they made the spectators a profound reverence [bow]; then they saluted each other and engaged in a lively and amusing conversation. They boasted that they had a great amount of courage, strength, and intrepidity. One of them regretted she was not born a man, else who would have made her

fortune by her powers; the other declared she beat her husband every morning to keep her hand in. Both these women were very scantily clothed, and wore little bodices and very short petticoats of white linen. … After a time the combat became very animated, and was conducted with force and vigor with the broad side of the weapons, for points there were none. The Irishwoman presently received a great cut across her forehead, and that put a stop to the first part of the combat. The Englishwoman's backers threw her shillings and half-crowns and applauded her. During this time the wounded woman's forehead was sewn up, this being done on the stage; a plaster was applied to it, and she drank a good big glass of spirits to revive her courage, and the fight began again… .[6]

CÉSAR DE SAUSSURE
From *A Foreign View of England* (1728)

Compared to the philosophes, Swift was less convinced that human decency and hard work could improve the world. In humans, he mused, reason is a quality "fitted to increase our natural vices."

SATIRE AND SOCIETY IN ART

Swift's mockery of eighteenth-century vice found its pictorial counterpart in the satirical paintings of William Hogarth (1697–1764). Hogarth is best known for several series of pictures telling stories of moral corruption. These pictorial narratives were engravings, which he sold by subscription to a middle-class public eager to laugh at the folly of their neighbors.

Hogarth's series *Marriage à la Mode* (1744) mocked the bourgeois social climbers and degenerate nobles who married off their children for their own advantage. In the first painting, *The Marriage Contract* (Fig. **11.29**), the dissolute Earl of Squander points to his family tree to prove the noble pedigree of his son, the prospective bridegroom. The mer-

chant, father of the bride, has laid the dowry on the table and scrutinizes the contract like a good businessman. Meanwhile, the bridal couple ignore both the negotiations and each other. The groom admires himself in the mirror and the bride is distracted by the flattery of the lawyer, Counselor Silvertongue. Later scenes in *Marriage à la Mode* recount the lawyer's seduction of the young countess, with disastrous results. Such moralizing, along with his command of narrative detail and satiric touch, made Hogarth's works highly successful among a new middle-class art public.

The English social classes that William Hogarth satirized sought more flattering portraits of themselves at the hands of Sir Joshua Reynolds (1723–92) and his student Thomas Gainsborough (1727–88). Reynolds pioneered a "grand style" of portraiture that showed his subjects sitting among antique statuary or portrayed as mythological figures. Pretentious portraits in this style adorn the nobleman's walls in Hogarth's *Marriage Contract*. Gainsborough's manner was more straightforward, as is evident in his portrait *Mr. and Mrs. Andrews* (Fig. **11.30**). The newly married couple sit somewhat stiffly in their country garden, with their fields and herds in the distance. The world of nature visible in this landscape is thoroughly domesticated, though less picturesque than the classical outbuildings of the Park at Stourhead (see Fig. 11.22). While Gainsborough clearly aimed to flatter his subjects, their air of self-satisfaction borders on smugness; in his candor, the painter may have exposed the vanity of this country aristocracy, with their Palladian houses, French silk gowns, and sculpture gardens.

CRITICAL QUESTION

Analyze Swift's ironic tone in the passage from *A Modest Proposal*. How does he manage to sound reasonable while making such a cruel and inhuman proposal?

VOLTAIRE

The Enlightenment's most famous satirical voice – indeed, the figure who came to symbolize enlightenment itself – was François Marie Arouet, known as Voltaire (1694–1778; Fig. 11.31). Voltaire [vol-TAIR] had a fertile literary intelligence and from his pen poured a stream of pamphlets, plays, tales, and poetry. His *Philosophical Letters* (1734), for example, helped to popularize English philosophy and science among French thinkers, while bitterly attacking France's political and religious establishment.

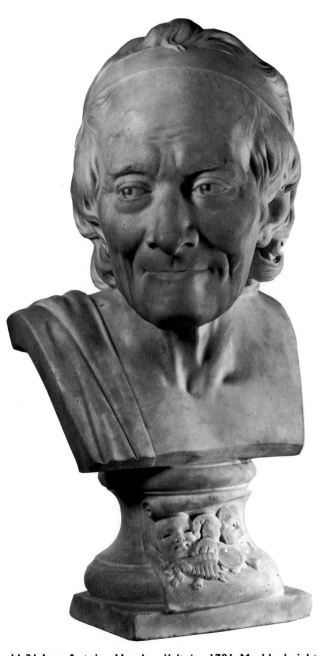

11.31 Jean Antoine Houdon, *Voltaire*, 1781. Marble, height 20 ins (51 cm). Victoria & Albert Museum, London.
Houdon's famous bust managed to capture the ironic tilt of the philosopher's head and the witty gleam of his eye.

A masterful conversationalist, Voltaire was a prized guest at Paris' court and salons. In later life, he moved to an estate in Ferney, Switzerland, just across the French border, where a stream of visitors paid homage to him. From the safety of Ferney, Voltaire attacked France's religious zealots with the battle-cry *"Écrasez l'infame"* ("Crush infamy") – by which he meant to oppose the evils of religious bigotry. He openly mocked his religious opponents, saying, "I have never made but one prayer to God, a very short one: 'O Lord, make my enemies ridiculous.' And God granted it."

***Voltaire's* Candide** The activism of Voltaire's later years dates from 1759, when he published his most famous and enduring work, the philosophical tale *Candide* [kan(h)-DEED]. This simple story of a naive young man's "enlightenment" lacks the fiery indignation of Voltaire's pamphlets, but truthfully exposes human vice and folly. With *Candide*, Voltaire addressed himself to the age's most perplexing philosophical problems: human suffering and evil, belief and doubt, and the possibility of reasoned action in an irrational world.

Voltaire's Candide (his name suggests his "candor" or innocence) subscribes to the philosophical "optimism" of Pangloss, his tutor. Pangloss' rationalist optimism is a parody of conventional Enlightenment belief. It resembles the ideas of the German philosopher Gottfried Wilhelm von Leibniz (1646–1716), who saw an absolute harmony between divine order and the material world. The rationalist Leibniz [LIPE-nits] was describing a world organized in an absolute hierarchical order, so that every part is perfectly balanced against all others. In a simplified version, Leibniz's ideas supported the optimism expressed in Alexander Pope's philosophical poem *An Essay on Man* (1734), which claimed that if humans could glimpse God's entire plan for the world, they would see that "Whatever is, is right."

This philosophical complacency infuriated Voltaire, who once wrote that "doubt is not a pleasant condition, but certainty is a ridiculous one." *Candide* is a relentless parody of rationalist optimism, since each new twist in the unlikely plot brings a new calamity. The tale is all the more horrifying because it portrays disasters and atrocities that could be documented in Voltaire's time. Candide and Pangloss witness the great Lisbon earthquake, an actual disaster in 1755, and suffer persecution by the Spanish Inquisition. Only in the New World land of Eldorado does Candide discover a society without bigotry, with no prisons or churches. However, he rashly abandons this land for the hope of being rich. When all the characters are reunited, they are still perplexed by the meaning of their suffering. They finally meet a Turkish merchant who rejects philosophical speculation altogether and works to make a comfortable life for his family: work, says the merchant, wards off the "three great evils: boredom, vice, and need." At the tale's conclusion Pangloss sums up the adventures and misfortunes from the entire tale, and Candide resolves to "work without theorizing."

The whole small fraternity entered into this praise-worthy plan and each started to make use of his talents. The little farm yielded well. . . . Pangloss sometimes said to Candide: "All events are linked up in this best of all possible worlds; for, if you had not been expelled from the noble castle, by hard kicks in your backside for love of Mademoiselle Cunegonde, if you had not been clapped into the Inquisition, if you had not wandered about America on foot, if you had not stuck your sword in the Baron, if you had not lost all your sheep from the land of Eldorado, you would not be eating candied lemons and pistachios here."
" 'Tis well said," replied Candide, "but we must cultivate our garden."[7]

VOLTAIRE
From *Candide* (1759)

Voltaire's solution to evil and bigotry is, as *Candide*'s ending suggests, a modest one. Candide finally does achieve a measure of enlightenment: to "cultivate our garden" means to reject speculative and merely philosophical solutions to the world's problems. It means to cultivate oneself, to work hard, and see that one's own life is comfortable and reasonable. Some have criticized Candide's solution as complacency of a different sort, claiming that it resembles the pursuit of middle-class self-interest. In another view, to "cultivate one's garden" means to act, with a sense of the limits of reason, to improve the world. Voltaire believed that humans had the resources, in their intelligence and industry, to make the world better – but not perfect. The revolutionary years that followed Voltaire's death would become a historical laboratory for testing his convictions.

Chapter Summary

The Enlightenment. The eighteenth century spawned an intellectual movement known as the Enlightenment, led by *philosophes* who aimed to reform society by applying reason and science. Parisian philosophes dedicated themselves to projects such as the *Encyclopedia* and defended freedom of thought, while criticizing orthodox religion. The philosophe Jean Jacques Rousseau propounded theories on child education and the origins of the state. His *Social Contract* traced the "general will" of society back to the agreement of free individuals that established civil society.

The Rococo Style. Art in the age of Enlightenment assumed the rococo style, a tamer and more light-hearted version of the baroque. Rococo wit and grace were displayed in the salons of Paris and other European capitals. The rococo style in painting was marked by nostalgia, frivolity, and an indulgence of the senses. In Germany especially, Neumann's rococo palaces and churches reached an extreme of ornate decoration and riotous color. In eighteenth-century dance, new attention was given to the skills of female dancers and to plot, through the rise of the *ballet d'action*. The composer Mozart excelled in many musical forms, especially in charming operas that appealed to the noble patrons and middle-class public of the later eighteenth century.

The Bourgeois Response. The middle classes preferred a less frivolous art that was nevertheless suffused with sentimental feeling. In painting, Chardin and Greuze painted simple genre scenes and moralizing dramas. In literature, the novel offered bourgeois readers a variety of uplifting moral tales and resourceful heroes and heroines. The German bourgeois theater, with heroes such as Goethe's Götz, helped to establish a German national culture.

The Neoclassical Style. The most versatile eighteenth-century style was neoclassicism, fueled by archeological discoveries and moralism. Neoclassical residences were built throughout Europe and America as symbols of good taste, universal truth, and elegance. In France, the painter David devised a stringent neoclassical style that seemed to criticize the indulgence and corruption of eighteenth-century society. The Classical symphony, as developed by Haydn and Mozart, demonstrated in music the same formal clarity and rigor as neoclassical painting.

The Age of Satire. The Enlightenment's critical spirit exerted itself in brilliant works of satire. The age's bitterest satirical works were penned by Swift, who exaggerated human vice and folly, while advocating social justice. The English painter Reynolds perfected the "grand style" of society portraiture, while Hogarth ridiculed the excesses and hypocrisy of the moneyed classes. The Enlightenment sage and activist Voltaire engaged in the period's central philosophical debates. His tale *Candide* recounts a young man's struggle to make sense of a world of violence and prejudice.

12 | Revolution and Romanticism

It is a vivid and dramatic scene, symbolic of its time: as the French revolutionary champion Jean-Paul Marat sits in his bathtub writing a pamphlet, a young noblewoman enters his quarters and stabs him fatally in the breast (Fig. 12.1). Marat becomes a martyr of the revolution, the woman an image of her nation's agony.

*As memorialized by the neoclassical painter Jacques-Louis David, the pale body of Marat is a symbol of the **spirit of revolution**: a dedication to the principles of equality, reason, and representative government. However, the overthrow of kings in America and France did not end injustice or establish a utopia of reason. As middle-class society took shape, a new sensibility arose, called **romanticism**, which glorified the individual and prized feeling over reason and intellect. This period of revolutionary change and romantic reaction (1775–1850) laid down the principles, and discovered the demons, of the first modern society.*

REVOLUTIONS AND RIGHTS

Identify the leading philosophical and political ideas of the American and French revolutions.

The political revolutions in America in 1776 and France in 1789 are turning points in the history of Western civilization. Today's leading political ideas, such as democracy, republicanism, and equality before the law, were first tested in those revolutionary upheavals. Many of today's political institutions – congresses, presidencies, consti-

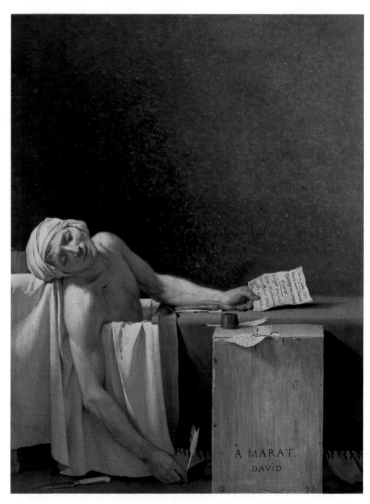

12.1 Jacques-Louis David, *The Death of Marat*, 1793. Oil on canvas, 5 ft 3³/₄ ins x 4 ft 2³/₈ ins (1.62 x 1.28 m). Musées Royaux des Beaux-Arts, Brussels.
The pathos of the revolutionary journalist's death is emphasized by the simplified design of rectangular shapes, contrasted with the drooping posture of Marat's head and shoulder.

tutions – resulted from those revolutionary conflicts. Yet scholars and politicians still debate whether the revolutions were righteous and the outcomes beneficial, and whether other nations can apply the lessons in other times. Since 1789, each generation has had to answer these questions for itself.

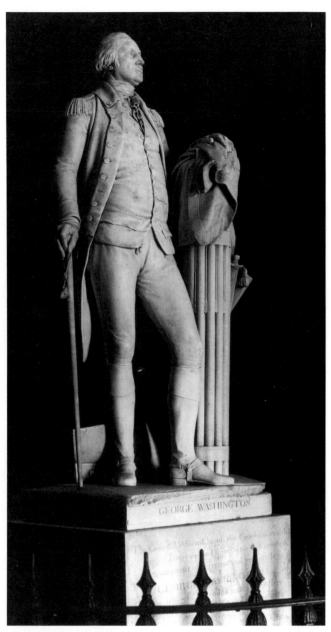

12.2 Jean-Antoine Houdon, *George Washington*, 1786–96. Marble, lifesize. State Capitol, Richmond, Virginia.
The famous French sculptor shows Washington as a dutiful republican, laying down his military authority to resume the guise of a gentleman farmer.

THE REVOLUTION IN AMERICA

The revolutionary wave began on the colonial fringes of Western civilization. Through the early eighteenth century, Britain's American colonies had grown prosperous from trade in fish, tobacco, and other New World commodities. By the mid-eighteenth century, the American colonists had begun to resent the burden of Britain's economic and political control. In summer 1776, a hand-ful of American colonists gathered to discuss boldly their grievances against the British king George III (ruled 1760–1820). In their minds, he had violated their basic rights as British citizens and threatened their prosperity with heavy taxation. Believing that the king's oppression left them no choice, they declared their independence of the British government and embarked on the danger-ous course of revolution.

The American revolutionaries readily cited historical precedents for their rebellion: they alluded to the Romans' revolt against the Etruscan kings and compared their leader George Washington (Fig. **12.2**) to the ancient Roman Cincinnatus, who left his plow to defend the Roman Republic. The Americans also used the principles of Enlightenment political philosophy to defend their war of colonial rebellion. Thomas Jefferson's Declaration of Independence was drawn almost verbatim from John Locke's *Treatise on Civil Government* (1690) and in turn set a precedent for Simón Bolívar and the other liberators of Spanish America in the early nineteenth century.

The Declaration of Independence, written principally by Thomas Jefferson, applied the doctrines of equality, civil rights, and popular sovereignty that had been developed by the Parisian philosophes. Drawing from Locke, Jefferson claimed:

> ... *that whenever any Form of Government becomes destructive of these ends, it is the Right of the People to alter or to abolish it, and to institute new Government, laying its foundation on such principles and organizing its powers in such form, as to them shall seem most likely to effect their Safety and Happiness.*[1]

The Declaration was followed in 1787 by the Americans' equally radical constitution. The United States Constitution established, for the first time among Western nations, a republican government with an elected executive and a guarantee of individual rights.

The new constitution was defended in a remarkable series of political essays known as the *Federalist* papers. Published anonymously in newspapers during 1787–8, the *Federalist* papers analyzed the new government's balance between state authority and the rights of the individual. Applying the theories of Enlightenment philosophes, the *Federalist* authors rationalized the constitution's complex system of checks and balances among the branches of government. The tenth essay, written by future U.S. president James Madison (1751–1836), explained how republican government might support a genuinely pluralistic society and mediate among contending factions.

For all their brilliance, the *Federalist* papers did not address one central question of the American republic: slavery. Despite declarations on the equality of all men, the new constitution allowed the continuation of slavery as an economic necessity. Since early colonial days, slaves had been imported from Africa to work on plantations in the southern American colonies and the Caribbean islands. The new United States, founded on liberal principles, continued to sanction slavery until the practice was ended by the American Civil War (1861–5).

THE REVOLUTION IN FRANCE

The American revolutionary doctrine was not easily contained. Frenchmen who fought with the American colonists returned to their homeland fired with radical ideas. Their fervor helped to ignite a revolutionary inferno that consumed France in Europe's widest and most divisive upheaval since the Reformation.

The revolutionary drama began in earnest in early 1789, as King Louis XVI (ruled 1774–93) and France's ruling factions jockeyed for power. Representatives of the educated and wealthy middle classes pressed their political demands for a constitutional monarchy. At a crucial moment, middle-class delegates and aristocratic sympathizers gathered in a royal tennis court at Versailles. There, on June 20, 1789, they swore the "Oath of the Tennis Court," vowing to remain in Paris until France had a constitution. David immortalized the scene in a famous sketch, in which delegates struck the noble pose of his painting of the Horatii brothers, while the French people applauded from the windows.

Two events followed the Oath of the Tennis Court that epitomized the revolution's fusion of ideas and violence. On July 14, 1789, a Parisian crowd assaulted the royal prison, the Bastille – a symbol of royal authority and the medieval past. When the warden surrendered, the crowd executed him and triumphantly paraded his head on the end of a pike to the city hall. The Bastille's fall foreshadowed the crucial role of the Paris crowd in the revolutionary decade that followed.

Then, on August 27 the same year, revolutionary delegates issued the Declaration of the Rights of Man and the Citizen, listing the principles of a new French government. The Declaration was clearly derived from Enlightenment political doctrines, especially Rousseau's belief in equality and popular sovereignty. It promised a society of merit, where success depended on talents and not on inherited rank. It proclaimed the legal equality of all citizens and their right to basic freedoms. Like the United States Constitution, the Declaration also enshrined property as an inviolable right. The delegates, many of them wealthy bourgeois and nobles, did not care to sacrifice their fortunes to equality. Still, more than any other single document, the Declaration of the Rights of Man embodied the ideas of Enlightenment political philosophy. Its principles of liberty, equality, and brotherhood would be quoted by every contending faction in France's revolutionary struggle.

Between 1789 and 1795, France was seized by political intrigue and revolutionary turmoil. In 1793, King Louis XVI and his hated queen, Marie Antoinette, were beheaded by the new "scientific" instrument of execution, the guillotine. Economic crisis and the threat of invasion led to the so-called "Reign of Terror" (May 1793–July 1794), a period in which a small group of revolutionary leaders sent thousands of French citizens to the guillotine. Meanwhile, a huge and patriotic French army managed some victories against the Revolution's foreign opponents, most notably in Italy, where it was commanded by a charismatic young general named Napoleon Bonaparte.

THE NAPOLEONIC ERA

By 1799 France was exhausted from a decade of revolution and war. The French had lived through a number of constitutions, and disillusioned revolutionaries found their republic of virtue inhabited by citizens full of greed and prejudice. Having beheaded a king, the French were now ready to entrust their hard-won liberties to the military hero Napoleon Bonaparte (1769–1821). For fifteen years, Napoleon inspired the French with dreams of imperial glory and spread republican ideas throughout Europe.

To many French people, Napoleon personified the principles of revolution, even as he imposed dictatorial control over the nation. As a young military officer, Napoleon had risen through the ranks by his own genius for leadership. His success in leading the French revolutionary

THE WRITE IDEA
If you were writing a contemporary "Declaration of Human Rights" for today, how would you revise or expand the revolutionary documents of 1776 and 1789? Explain how your "Declaration" reflects the leading ideas of today.

REVOLUTIONARY MILESTONES

1776	American colonists declare their independence from the British crown
1788	Constitution ratified in the United States
1789	Paris mob storms royal prison at Bastille; French parliament declares "Rights of Man and the Citizen"
1799	Napoleon seizes control of French revolutionary government
1793–1802	Toussaint-l'Ouverture leads rebellion against slavery and colonial rule in Haiti
1817–1825	Simón Bolívar leads independence struggles in South America

THE NINETEENTH CENTURY

	GENERAL EVENTS	ARCHITECTURE	VISUAL ARTS	MUSIC	LITERATURE AND PHILOSOPHY
1789	1789–99 French Revolution; Reign of Terror 1793–4		1793 David, *Death of Marat* (**12.1**)		1794 Blake, *London*
ROMANTICISM	1799–1814 Napoleon rules France		1808 Canova, *Pauline Bonaparte as Venus* (**12.7**)	1804 Beethoven, Symphony No. 3 (*Eroica*)	1808, 1832 Goethe, *Faust*, Parts I and II
		1815–21 Nash, Royal Pavilion, Brighton, England (**12.22**)	1814–15 Goya, *Executions of the Third of May, 1808* (**12.14**)	1814–15 Schubert, *Lieder* (songs) settings of Goethe's poetry	
					1818 Mary Shelley, *Frankenstein*
	1830 "July Revolution" in Paris			1830 Berlioz, *Symphonie fantastique*	
	1830–70 Industrialization of Europe and the United States	1840–65 Barry and Pugin, Houses of Parliament, London (**12.21**)		1838 Schumann, *Kinderszenen*	
	1848 Revolutionary uprisings throughout Europe		1844 Turner, *Rain, Steam, and Speed* (**12.18**)		
1848					1848 Marx, *Communist Manifesto*
		1851 Paxton, Crystal Palace, London (**13.7**)	1850s Hokusai and Hiroshige, Japanese color print-makers (**13.25**)		
	1859 Darwin publishes *Origin of Species*	1854–75 Labrouste, National Library, Paris (**13.8**)		1869 Wagner, *Das Rheingold*; entire *Ring des Nibelungen* cycle performed 1876 at Bayreuth, Germany	1869 Flaubert, *A Sentimental Education*
REALISM			1874 First impressionist exhibition		
					1880 Dostoyevsky, *The Brothers Karamazov*
		1887–9 Eiffel Tower, Paris (**13.10**)			
			1892–7 Rodin, *Balzac* (**13.20**)	1894 Debussy, *Prélude à "L'après-midi d'un faune"*	
1900					

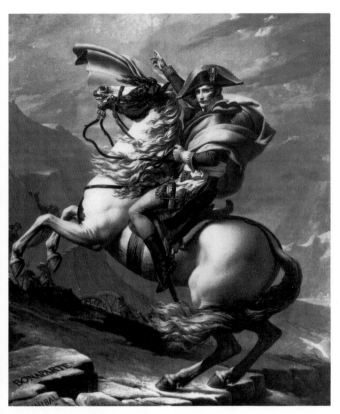

12.3 Jacques-Louis David, *Napoleon Crossing the Alps*, 1800. Oil on canvas, 8 ft x 7 ft 7 ins (2.44 x 2.31 m). Musée de Versailles.
David's stirring portrait of Napoleon depicts him following the path of ancient generals such as Hannibal and Charlemagne (whose names are carved in the rocks). Like many revolutionaries, David approved of Napoleon's rule, believing that he could restore order to a weary France.

army in Italy made him a national hero and positioned him to take power in November 1799. Napoleon satisfied his middle-class supporters by revising France's legal system and modernizing its government, thus erasing the vestiges of absolute monarchy and aristocratic privilege. However, Napoleon's ambitions extended far beyond a more efficient government. He dreamed of a French empire and a Napoleonic dynasty.

Crowning himself emperor in 1804, Napoleon embarked on a military campaign that devoured virtually the whole European continent (Figure **12.3**). He proclaimed the revolutionary values of liberty and republicanism in conquered nations, while in France he created a dictatorial government and quietly suppressed the rights of French citizens. Military defeats finally forced his abdication in 1814 and then, after a brief return, exile to the remote island of St. Helena in 1815.

Napoleon and the Arts Napoleon was a skillful propagandist for his own reign, disguising his power and cleverly manipulating the symbolism of the Revolution.

Where the revolutionaries had seen themselves as heroes of the Roman Republic, Napoleon now presented himself as a Roman emperor and set out to make Paris an imperial capital on the scale of ancient Rome.

Like the Roman emperors, Napoleon advertised his power by patronizing the arts and starting an ambitious building program. The royal palace of the Louvre became a museum to hold the artistic plunder brought from Italy and Egypt. He erected arches of triumph on public squares (Fig. **12.4**) and a triumphal column (modeled after the Column of Trajan in Rome) cast from the metal cannons of defeated armies. Facing the Place de la Concorde (where the guillotine had stood), he commissioned a great neoclassical temple dedicated to the soldiers of his army. Known as La Madeleine (Fig. **12.5**), the temple stood atop a 23-feet (7m) high podium and was surrounded by a gigantic Corinthian colonnade.

Only two artists of distinction served Napoleon: the painter Jacques-Louis David and the Italian sculptor Antonio Canova. David's devotion to the emperor earned him the title of "First Painter," and the control of the

12.4 Jean-François Chalgrin, Arc de Triomphe de l'Étoile, Paris, 1806–37.
Napoleon's great arch surpassed in scale any comparable triumphal work of ancient Rome (compare the Arch of Trajan, Fig 4.5). The monument's sculptures, including François Rude's stirring rendition of *Departure of the Volunteers, 1792 (La Marseillaise)*, were not finished until the 1830s, years after Napoleon's fall.

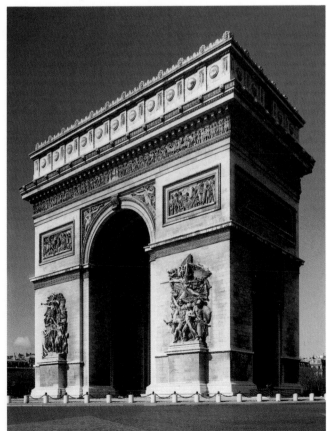

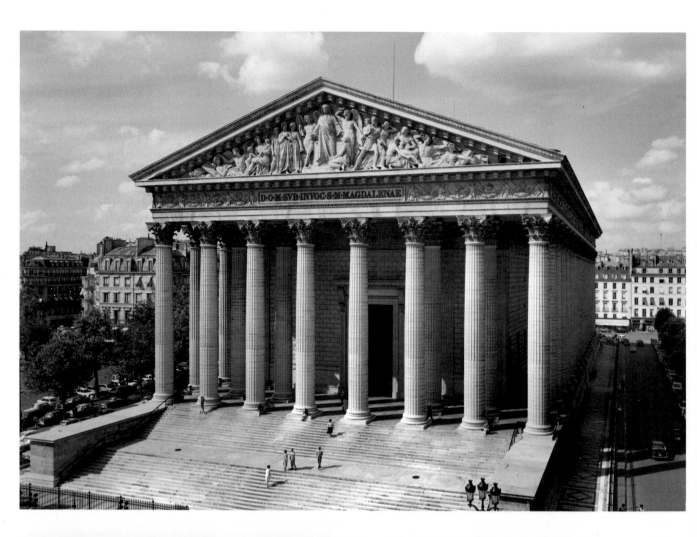

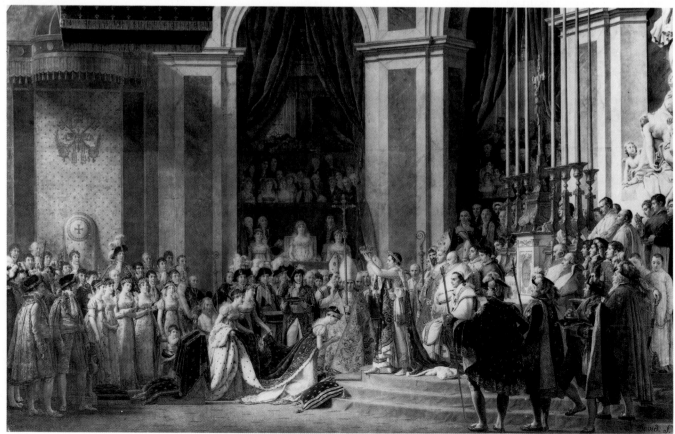

12.5 Opposite top **Pierre-Alexandre Vignon, La Madeleine, Paris, 1762–1829. Length 350 ft (106.7 m), width 147 ft (44.8 m), height of base 23 ft (7 m).**
Compare this Napoleonic monument to the ancient Roman Temple of Portunus (Fig. 4.12). Note differences and similarities in construction, scale, and decoration. How did such artistic connections to imperial Rome serve the propagandistic purposes of Napoleon's own imperial regime?

12.6 Opposite below **Jacques-Louis David, Le Sacre (The Coronation of Napoleon), 1805–7. Oil on canvas, 20 ft x 30 ft 6¹/₂ ins (6.1 x 9.31 m). Louvre, Paris.**
At Napoleon's direction, David took liberties with the truth in this giant portrait. Although Napoleon's republican mother refused to attend, David nevertheless shows her sitting in the balcony.

government's artistic patronage. David's most famous commission in this period was the portrait of Napoleon's coronation, *Le Sacre* (Fig. **12.6**), painted in an opulent style very different from the rugged simplicity of the *Oath of the Horatii* (see Fig. 11.23). Napoleon personally instructed David to show him crowning Josephine, his empress wife, rather than placing the crown on his own head. To celebrate France's reconciliation with the Catholic Church, the pope attended the ceremony and was shown raising his

hand in benediction. The event was a mixture of Christian rite and imperial paganism, much as Napoleon's own rule was a mixture of republicanism and tyranny.

Napoleon also imported to Paris the most famous sculptor of his day, the Italian Antonio Canova (1757–1822). Canova was commissioned to portray members of the Bonaparte family, whom Napoleon had placed on the thrones of conquered Europe. Canova's portraits for Napoleon's family were frigidly neoclassical. His sculpture of Napoleon's sister Pauline Bonaparte, shows her as Venus (Fig. **12.7**), reclining on a divan that might almost have been excavated from Pompeii.

Colonial Revolutionaries The revolutionary turmoil in Europe had repercussions in the American colonies of France and Spain. In 1793, on the Caribbean island of Hispaniola (present-day Haiti and the Dominican Republic), the freed slave François Dominique Toussaint-l'Ouverture [TOO-san(h) LOO-vuh-tyoor] (*c.* 1743–1803) assumed command of a slave revolt. By 1801, Toussaint's skilled and ruthless leadership secured the abolition of slavery in the island's French and Spanish colonies. Though professing republican ideals, Toussaint imposed a constitution on Hispaniola that gave him nearly absolute power. In 1802, he surrendered to a French military force

12.7 **Antonio Canova, *Pauline Bonaparte as Venus*, 1808. Marble, lifesize. Galleria Borghese, Rome.**
Canova shows Pauline holding the apple of Venus, the prize of beauty granted to the goddess by Paris' famous judgment. What is the effect of the figure's awkward posture, which presents her head in profile but turns her nude torso entirely to the front?

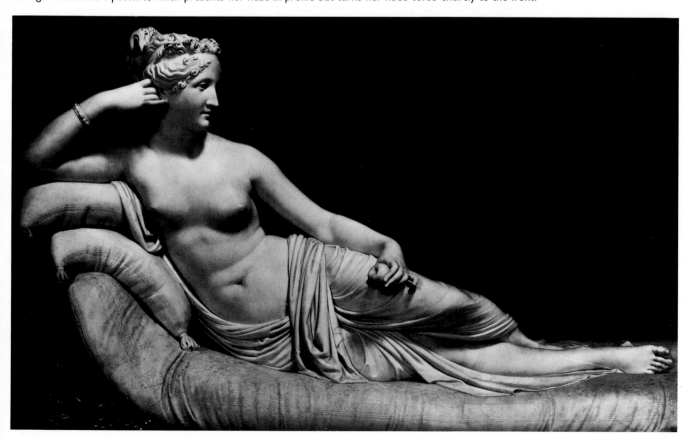

KEY CONCEPT

ROMANTIC GENIUS

At the heart of the romantic attitude was the concept of genius, the extraordinary powers of imagination and creativity possessed by exceptional individuals and expressed in their works. The romantic concept of genius rejected strict rules of composition and

12.8 Carl Friedrich Auguste von Kloeber, *Ludwig van Beethoven*, c. 1818. Pencil drawing. Beethovenhaus, Bonn.
Beethoven's fiery musical works and his private life tortured by deafness qualified him as a romantic genius. As the French painter Delacroix wrote in his journal, "obstacles and difficulties which repel mediocre men are a necessity and nourishment to genius."

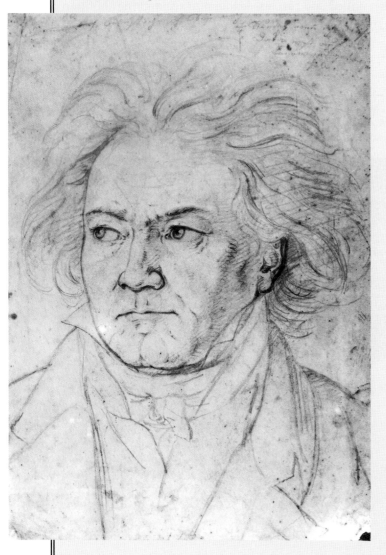

aesthetic judgment. True genius created its own rules, as the French writer Victor Hugo (1802–85) wrote in his *Preface to Cromwell* (1827): "Genius, which divines rather than learns, devises for each work the general rules from the general plan of things, the special rules from the separate ensemble of the subject treated."[2] A genius required no mechanical rules for manufacturing a work of art. The romantics believed a work of genius grew by its own organic laws of truth and beauty.

The romantic concept of genius resulted partly from a historical trend in the arts. Since the Renaissance, European artists had struggled to achieve a status equal to their patrons. Indeed, artists such as Velázquez and Mozart had chafed at their role as artistic servants. In the romantic age, however, artists finally stood on the same social plane as their middle-class public. In fact, beginning with the romantic era, creative artists often felt superior to the mediocrities around them, and could claim to be an exceptional elite.

The romantics used several metaphors to describe genius. The pre-romantic poet Edward Young (1683–1765) compared poetic composition to a vegetable process. The truly original work of art "rises spontaneously from the vital root of genius; it grows, it is not made,"[3] wrote Young in his *Conjectures on Original Composition* (1755). The painter Eugène Delacroix described genius as a "sacred fire," like "the fire of a volcano which must absolutely burst into the open, because its nature absolutely compels it to shine, to illuminate, to astonish the world."[4]

The romantic concept of genius survives today. So much art and thought in twentieth-century culture defies traditional rules and common sense that it is convenient to attribute it to "genius." From the physicist Albert Einstein to the artist Pablo Picasso, the twentieth century has often applied the label of genius to its most powerful and perplexing creators (Fig. **12.8**). In our age, it is often a label for those whom we admire but do not understand.

CRITICAL QUESTION
What type of person do you think best deserves the label of "genius"? What are the implications of this label in today's setting? Should we continue to use the concept of genius?

dispatched by Napoleon, demanding only a French promise not to re-impose slavery. Toussaint died a year later in a French prison.

In South America, it was the Creoles – native-born colonials of European descent – who instigated the struggle for independence from Spain. Their charismatic leader was Simón Bolívar (1783–1830), nicknamed *El Libertador* (The Liberator) for his role in liberating much of South America from Spanish rule. Inspired by Napoleon's example, Bolívar envisioned a united Spanish America, governed by constitutional republics and a president elected for life. From 1817 to 1822, he undertook a long campaign that eventually freed the Spanish colony of Gran Colombia (present-day Colombia, Venezuela, and Ecuador). By 1825 Bolívar had also defeated Spanish forces in Peru, and had been named president of a Latin American federation. But Bolívar's grand vision succumbed to his own authoritarian tendencies and the forces of regional independence. Civil war flared and the federation disintegrated, leaving South American nations independent but insecurely republican, and still governed by the Creole elite.

THE ROMANTIC HERO

Identify the essential characteristics shared by the romantic heroes, both historical and fictional, discussed here.

Napoleon can be seen as the first great romantic hero. In his sweeping ambition, his powerful individualism, and his haughty distance from the ordinary, Napoleon was a figure larger than life. Even in exile on St. Helena, he was seen as the political genius brooding in isolation from an unappreciative world of mediocrity. The hero Napoleon appealed to a nineteenth-century sensibility called **romanticism**. The romantics preferred feeling and imagination to the sober dictates of intellect and reason. They were attracted to the picturesque in nature and in the past, and above all, they prized the powers of creative genius, discounting the value of mechanical laws or neoclassical restraint. The romantic attitude arose gradually between 1775 and 1850, appearing first in England and Germany, then in post-revolutionary France and North America.

The romantic sensibility was a reaction against the widening industrialism of Western society and its dull materialism. It often involved an escape into nature or a fascination with the grotesque and macabre. The romantic age was dominated by a few artists who towered over others in their restless genius and passionate vision. In their lives and their works, such romantic individuals as Byron, Goethe, and Beethoven were measured on a heroic scale of grand achievement and tragic suffering. They were the Napoleons of the romantic sensibility.

BEETHOVEN

In his life, the German composer Ludwig van Beethoven (1770–1827) seemed cast by fate to assume the role of the suffering romantic genius. Beethoven [BAY-toh-ven] endured the pains that were the "nourishment" of romantic genius – as the nineteenth-century romantic painter Delacroix once said. Beethoven was abused by an alcoholic father and appointed his brothers' guardian before the age of eighteen. By the age of twenty-five, the composer's hearing began to fail. In 1802, Beethoven wrote a desperate "testament" to his brothers, confessing his ailment and its emotional effects. It reveals a man tortured by his social isolation and convinced that others misunderstood him – the epitome of the romantic hero. Thinking of suicide, Beethoven confessed that "art alone restrained my hand." He wrote:

> But, think for 6 years now I have been hopelessly afflicted, made worse by senseless physicians, from year to year deceived with hopes of improvement, finally compelled to face the prospect of a lasting malady (whose cure will take years or, perhaps be impossible). Though born with a fiery, active temperament, ever susceptible to the diversions of society, I was soon compelled to withdraw myself, to live life alone…. Ah, how could I possibly admit an infirmity in the one sense which ought to be more perfect in me than in others, a sense which I once possessed in the highest perfection, a perfection such as few in my profession enjoy or ever have enjoyed.[5]

Beethoven made his name as a pianist, performing in the courts and concert halls of Vienna. Passionately committed to the republican ideals of the French Revolution, he was often disdainful of his aristocratic audiences – a position he could afford to take, since, unlike Mozart, Beethoven supported himself largely through the publication of his compositions. The profound crisis caused by deafness did not hamper Beethoven's work as a

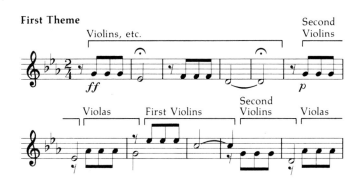

12.9 Ludwig van Beethoven, score of opening bars of Symphony No. 5 in C Minor, 1808, first movement. The relentless rhythm of the opening four-note motif is audible throughout the symphony's four movements.

composer: he recovered from his depression to compose works of unprecedented scope and feeling. Beethoven enlarged the symphonic orchestra, adding the piccolo and trombone, and he exchanged the elegant dance movement of Haydn's and Mozart's symphonies for a rougher, more vigorous *scherzo* [SKAIR-tso] (Italian, "joke"). Beethoven's Symphony No. 3, called the *Eroica*, was a watershed between the Classical style in music (see page 322) and the more ambitious and adventurous romantic style.

Beethoven's expansion of the Classical sonata form is audible in his Symphony No. 5 in C Minor, with its compelling theme and volcano of sound. This symphony has been interpreted as the composer's confrontation with fate, a struggle depicted in the shifting modulations between minor keys. The composer himself supposedly described the symphony's opening four tones as "Fate knocking at the door." Their menacing rhythm – three short beats and one long – dominates the symphony's long first movement (Fig. **12.9**). Beethoven enlarges the Classical mold through the recurring four-note **motif** (a term for a short musical idea). The motif moves through repeated moments of harmonic tension and ends the movement with a dynamic *coda*, or closing. Even here Beethoven has still not exhausted his motif, which recurs throughout the symphony, unifying its complex structure and further expanding the Classical symphonic form. At the end of the third movement, Beethoven added yet another innovation. Instead of the customary pause, the music continues directly into the last movement. Symphony No. 5 achieves a heroic grandeur that matches the legend of its composer.

Musical Virtuosos

The romantic era in music was marked by the unprecedented fame acquired by musical **virtuosos** – performers of spectacular ability whose flair appealed to the wider audiences of the nineteenth century. In his day, perhaps the most famous of these virtuosos was the Italian violinist Niccolò Paganini (1782–1840), who toured Europe displaying his dazzling technical ability. Paganini [pah-gah-NEE-nee] employed a showman's tricks, but also inspired several composers to more daring compositions for violin.

On the piano, the era's greatest virtuoso was the Polish musician Frédéric Chopin (1809–49). Chopin's [SHOH-pan(h)] delicate appearance and rhapsodic compositions defined a romantic musical type very different from the burly Beethoven. Chopin's compositions used smaller musical forms, including Polish dances such as the mazurka and polonaise. He was famous also for his love affair with the flamboyant George Sand (the male pseudonym of the female novelist Aurore Dudevant). Sand nursed Chopin as he slowly died of tuberculosis, and later described their relationship in a novel. Romantic genius was often associated with ecstatic states that bordered on madness. Composer Robert Schumann (1810–56) even-

tually succumbed to mental illness (probably manic depression), but managed to compose the most lyrical of romantic songs and symphonies. He composed several song cycles and other music of literary inspiration. His *Kinderszenen* (*Scenes from Childhood*, 1838) creates the mood of play and daydream that Schumann remembered from his own childhood. After his mental collapse and death, Schumann's wife, Clara (1819–96), continued to perform his music and support their family with her own professional career. Despite her considerable achievement as pianist and composer, Clara felt acutely the constraint of living in her husband's shadow. "I once thought that I possessed creative talent, but now I have given up this idea. A woman must not desire to compose. Not one has been able to do it, so why should I?" she once asked.

Goethe and Faust

One literary hero above all symbolized the romantic desire to burst all human constraint and to taste of every possible experience. That striving hero was Faust [fowsst], the creation of German writer Johann Wolfgang von Goethe (1749–1832), himself a towering figure of the romantic age. Byron called Goethe "the undisputed sovereign of European literature," a kind of Napoleonic poet. During the early 1770s, Goethe had been a leader of the pre-romantic *Sturm und Drang* movement (see page 317), though for a period afterwards he rejected his youthful emotionalism and the label of "romantic," saying "Romanticism is sickness, classicism is health." Only later in his career did Goethe regain a sympathy for his youthful works and return to themes that were unmistakably romantic. Among these late writings was the completion of Goethe's romantic masterpiece, the two-part drama *Faust* (1808, 1832).

Goethe's drama was based on the same medieval legend that had provided the basis for Christopher Marlowe's *Doctor Faustus* in the sixteenth century (see page 248). In Goethe's version, Faust is a striving hero who discards his stale academic life and indulges his unquenched desire for all human experience. Faust bargains with the devil – disguised as the wily Mephistopheles [meh-fiss-TOFF-e-less] – for the power to feel all "that is allotted to humankind," to "embrace all human selves." If his striving spirit is ever once satisfied, Faust vows, then Mephistopheles may have his soul. Having signed this pact in his own blood, Faust voices the romantic desire for an experience without limit.

> *In the depths of sensuality*
> *Let us now quench our glowing passions!*
> *And at once make ready every wonder*
> *Of unpenetrated sorcery!*
> *Let us cast ourselves into the torrent of time,*
> *Into the whirl of eventfulness,*
> *Where disappointment and success,*
> *Pleasure and pain may chop and change*

his love has evaporated. As Mephistopheles pulls him away, Faust hears a voice from heaven intone that Gretchen is redeemed. Faust himself, however, is left unsatisfied.

In the second part of *Faust*, the hero's quest for the whole range of human experience extends to science, politics, and history. The action ranges across great stretches of space and time. Although the work is a drama, no stage could accommodate its fantastic plot, which includes a journey to the realm of myth. Faust finds that he cannot balance his visionary designs with a sympathy for human limitations. However, he does not regret his endless quest for satisfaction and achievement.

The scope of Faust's ambitions reflect those of Goethe himself. The poet had supervised building projects, engaged in diplomatic missions, and directed cultural affairs for his patron, the Duke of Weimar [VYE-mar]. The poet's romantic vision, however, far exceeded the narrow limits of the provincial court at Weimar, where he spent much of his career, and like Faust, Goethe felt that his achievements never quite matched his designs, leaving him with a residue of longing and desire. The heroism of *Faust* expresses the sense of infinite horizons that was a part of the romantic sensibility.

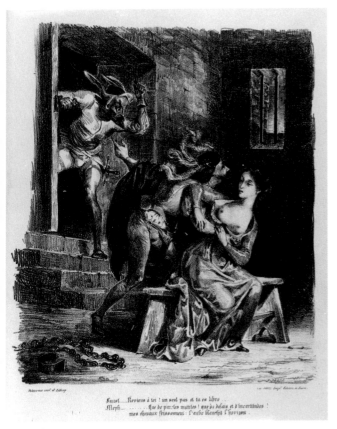

12.10 Eugène Delacroix, *Faust Visits Marguerite in Prison*, illustration from the French edition of Goethe's *Faust*, 1828.
Goethe's romantic tragedy inspired many artistic and musical imaginations.

As chop and change they will and can,
It is restless action makes the man.[6]

J. W. VON GOETHE
From *Faust*, Part 1 (1808)

I have only galloped through the world
And clutched each lust and longing by the hair;
What did not please me, I let go,
What flowed away, I let it flow.
I have only felt, only fulfilled desire,
And once again desired and thus with power
Have stormed my way through life; first great and strong,
Now moving sagely, prudently along.[7]

J. W. VON GOETHE
From *Faust*, Part 2 (1832)

As Mephistopheles promises "No limit is fixed for you," Faust embarks on a romantic quest for all that love, power, and science can bring him. In Part 1, he explores the world of personal feelings through his love affair with the innocent girl Gretchen. In his attempts to seduce Gretchen, Faust destroys her. She eventually is imprisoned for drowning the child of her union with Faust. When Faust tries to rescue her, Gretchen refuses, recognizing that

12.11 Thomas Phillips, *Lord Byron in Albanian Costume*, 1814. Oil on canvas, 29¹/₂ x 24¹/₂ ins (75 x 62 cm). Courtesy of the National Portrait Gallery, London.
The romantic hero as noble savage: Byron dressed in native Albanian costume, on his first trip to aid the Greek rebellion against the Turks.

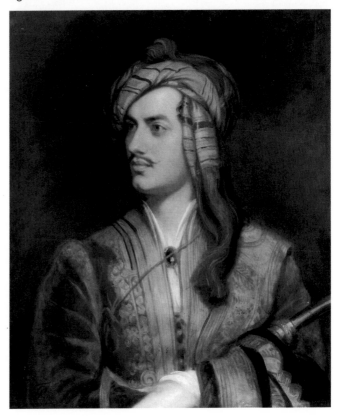

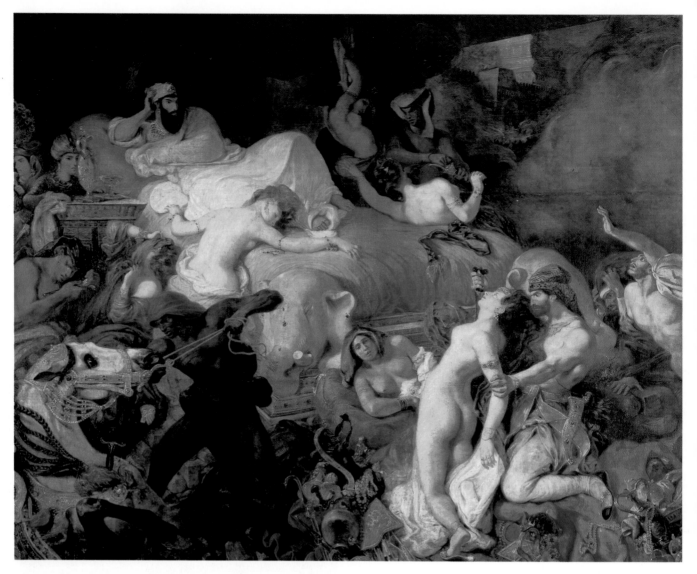

12.12 Eugène Delacroix, *The Death of Sardanapalus*, 1826. Oil on canvas, 12 ft 11¹/₂ ins x 16 ft 3 ins (3.95 x 4.95 m). Louvre, Paris.
An Oriental monarch presides over the destruction of his wives and possessions, in preparation for his own suicide. What emotional effect does the painter create by placing Sardanapalus at the back of the scene? How does the use of color and line here add to the atmosphere of erotic violence?

Faust in Music Goethe's drama exercised a great stimulus on the romantic imagination. The painter Eugène Delacroix illustrated a French translation of the first part of *Faust* with appropriately demonic lithographs (Fig. **12.10**). In music, the Viennese composer Franz Schubert (1797–1828) composed several songs (in German, *Lied*, pl. *Lieder* [leet, LEE-der]) from the poetry in *Faust*, capturing a poignant tenderness of feeling from the romantic heroism of Goethe's drama. Among the most famous of Schubert's *Lieder* (composed at age seventeen) was *Gretchen at the Spinning Wheel*, depicting a scene from the earliest version of Faust. The song's accompaniment creates the musical image of the spinning wheel, while in the song's text Gretchen alternates between passion and despair. The song begins and ends with the same words: "My heart is heavy, my peace is gone." In 1859, the French composer Charles Gounod (1818–93) based a successful opera on

Faust. Gounod's [goo-NOH] stirring finale is set in Gretchen's prison cell, where Mephistopheles insistently calls Faust to leave, Faust implores his lover to escape, and Gretchen prays for forgiveness for murdering her child.

DELACROIX AND THE BYRONIC HERO

French romantic artists of the 1820s were not much interested in the scientific ambition and German conscience of Goethe's Faust. The French were more attracted to the defiant sensuality figured in the life and works of Lord Byron, the English poet. Byron (1788–1824) lived a life of sexual freedom, political idealism, and exotic travel (Fig. **12.11**). His unfinished poetic masterpiece was *Don Juan* (begun 1819), in which he portrays himself as the legendary lover. Byron's works and life defined what came to be known as the Byronic hero, the rebellious genius whose intellectual and moral freedom isolated him from an unsympathetic world. The Byronic hero appealed to young French artists repelled by the conventional morality and avid commercialism of middle-class society.

The French artist most inspired by the Byronic hero was the painter Eugène Delacroix (1798–1863). Delacroix [dell-ah-KWAH] cut a dashing and aristocratic figure in the Parisian salons. He was one of a generation of young romantics that included the composer Hector Berlioz, the novelist Alexandre Dumas, and the spokesman of French romanticism, dramatist Victor Hugo (author of *Les Misérables*). As a painter, Delacroix mounted his own rebellion against the official academic style of French painting, which emphasized line and skillful drawing. Delacroix instead preferred riotous color, turbulent compositions, and exotic themes. He painted an enormous range of sub-

jects – many drawn from literary works (including Byron's) – which reflect an artistic rebellion against the society in which he lived.

The Death of Sardanapalus (Fig. **12.12**), for example, expresses an orgy of egoism, violence, and sexuality that scandalized Parisian art circles. The theme is taken from a play by Byron. According to legend, the Assyrian monarch Sardanapalus [sar-da-NAP-a-luss] destroyed himself and all his possessions when threatened by a rebellion. In Delacroix's version, slaves deliver the fatal blow to a concubine (on the right) and to the king's struggling horse (on the left). Meanwhile, Sardanapalus lies propped on his pillow in sadistic detachment, his own cup of poison at hand. Delacroix unifies the tumultuous scene by means of bold colors – the reds, greens, and golds are visible in every detail. Both Delacroix's subject and

12.13 Eugène Delacroix, *Liberty Leading the People*, 1830. Oil on canvas, 8 ft 6 ins x 10 ft 8 ins (2.59 x 3.25 m). Louvre, Paris.
Delacroix's visual hymn to patriotic revolution is unified by his use of the French tricolor flag. The red, white, and blue are echoed in the uniform of the guardsman who gazes up at Liberty and in smoke rising above the cathedral of Notre Dame at right.

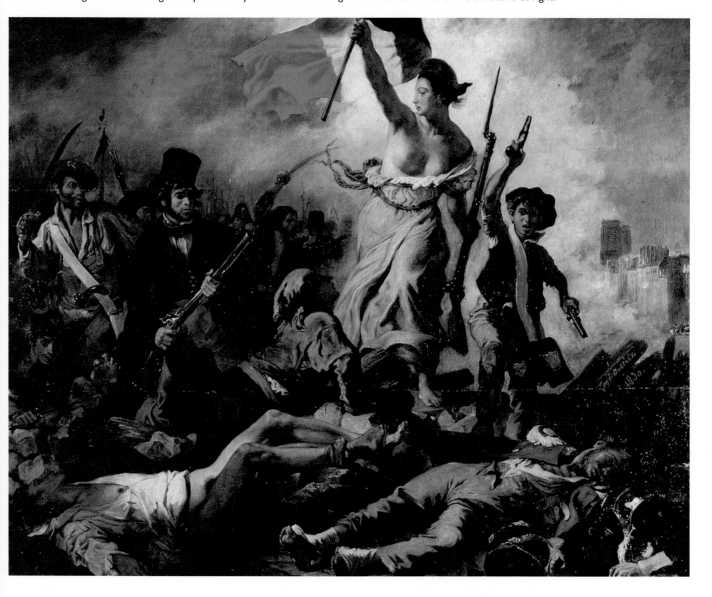

technique were condemned by academic critics, who rightly saw the picture as an assault on academic painting and moral principle.

Delacroix was among the many French romantics inspired by the July 1830 revolution in France. Recalling the revolutionary spirit of 1789, Paris' citizens barricaded their streets in July 1830, and again overthrew their king – the Bourbon monarchy that had ruled France for fifteen years. The Bourbon king abdicated and was replaced by the "Citizen-King," Louis-Philippe, whose monarchy endured until insurrection again convulsed France in 1848.

During the July insurrection, some romantic novelists and artists took their places on the barricades, while Delacroix observed the events from a balcony. He said months later, "If I did not fight for our country, at least I will paint for her." His depiction of the July revolution, *Liberty Leading the People, 1830* (Fig. **12.13**), embodies the event's romantic spirit, with a combination of the grotesque and the ideal. Delacroix's picture centers on the allegorical figure of Liberty, de-sexualized enough to be heroic. Liberty strides triumphantly across a barricade littered with the naked bodies of fallen rebels. On the left, a grimy worker fights beside a dandified student in top hat, symbolizing the unity of working and middle classes. The painting's dominant element is the red, white, and blue of French revolutionary patriotism. Caught in France's moment of political romanticism, Delacroix momentarily forgot his Byronic irony and detachment, and joined in the revolutionary enthusiasm of his fellow French citizens.

ELEMENTS OF ROMANTICISM

Link the different elements of romanticism to the historical and social circumstances of the romantic age.

The heroic individualism evident in *Faust* and in the life and works of Lord Byron is just one element of the romantic movement. Other common elements recur in the arts and movements of the romantic period (c. 1800–1850). Romantics in several nations raised a protest against political and social injustice. Some romantics were attracted to nature or indulged in a nostalgia for the medieval past, while others exhibited a fascination with the evil and exotic. Thus, romanticism was a mosaic of artistic and philosophical concerns, not a unified movement or style. What the romantics shared was a sensibility that responded to their social and historical circumstances.

ROMANTIC SOCIAL PROTEST

The early romantics thrilled at the revolutionary declarations of equality and freedom issued in 1776 and 1789.

On the other hand, the romantics were witness to the misery and bondage of large-scale industrial society, especially in the towns of England. In factory towns, workers starved in the midst of industrial plenty; women turned to prostitution to feed their families; children labored frantically in factories and mines. Fierce images of urban oppression appeared in the early poetry of the Englishman William Blake (1757–1827). Blake was a visionary mystic who created his own elaborate personal mythology, saying he "must create a system or be enslaved by another man's." He was a sympathetic observer of those enslaved by the industrial city and passionately condemned the evils of urban existence with dense, powerful images.

In Blake's poem *London*, the miserable faces of London's poor are portrayed. The poem rails against the "mind-forg'd manacles" of law, religion, and marriage – social institutions which Blake believed had the effect of creating their opposites: poverty, violence, and prostitution. One of Blake's "Proverbs of Hell" reads: "Prisons are built with stones of Law, Brothels with bricks of Religion." Industrialism had degraded human labor, symbolized by the chimney-sweep (hazardous labor reserved for young boys) and the prostitute (the only sure employment for poor urban women). Blake's protest was romantic in the emotional idealism of its last image, the wedding carriage seen as hearse. What ought to bear a couple full of love and optimism, instead carries the harlot's child, blighted by venereal disease.

> I wander thro' each charter'd[a] street,
> Near where the charter'd Thames does flow.
> And mark in every face I meet
> Marks of weakness, marks of woe.
>
> In every cry of every Man,
> In every Infants cry of fear,
> In every voice: in every ban,[b]
> The mind-forg'd manacles I hear
>
> How the Chimney-sweepers cry
> Every blackning Church appalls,
> And the hapless Soldiers sigh,
> Runs in blood down Palace walls
>
> But most thro midnight streets I hear
> How the youthful Harlots curse
> Blasts the new-born Infants tear,
> And blights with plagues the Marriage hearse.[8]

WILLIAM BLAKE
London (1794)

---

a. charter'd, Blake suggests that the streets and the river have been licensed to private commerce.

b. ban, a curse or public denunciation.

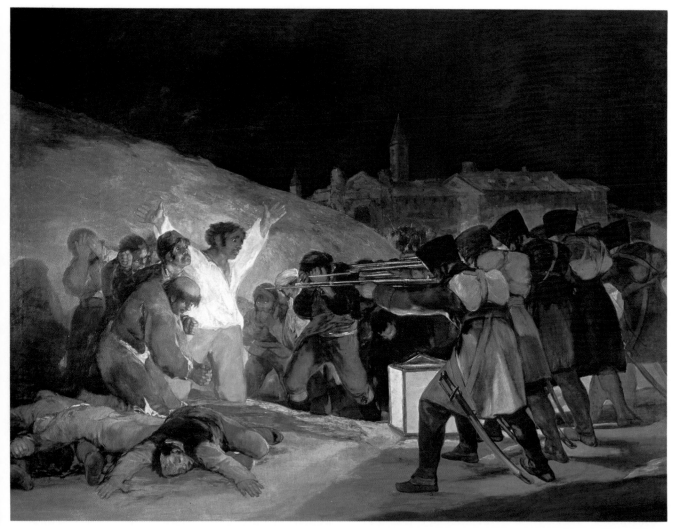

12.14 Francisco Goya, *Executions of the Third of May, 1808*, 1814–15. Oil on canvas, 8 ft 8³/₄ ins x 13 ft 3³/₄ ins (2.66 x 3.45 m). Prado, Madrid.

Goya finds no redemption in this gruesome slaughter, either in the symbolism of light, the teachings of the Church (symbolized by the falling monk), or in the revolutionary ideals of freedom and equality, embodied ironically in the faceless shapes of the French soldiers.

Romantic Feminism A more genteel romantic protest was heard in the writings of Mary Wollstonecraft (1759–97), author of the first feminist manifesto. Wollstonecraft lived a life of intellectual and personal freedom. She became the lover of the radical social theorist William Godwin (1756–1836), and died soon after the birth of their daughter Mary (author of *Frankenstein*). In applying the French Revolution's principles to women, Wollstonecraft answered conservatives such as Edmund Burke (1729–97), the British politician and theorist, and the revolution's philosophical godfather, Jean Jacques Rousseau. Rousseau had patronized women in his writings on education, calling for the protection of wives and mothers from society's harsh demands. Wollstonecraft countered this idea, claiming that sheltering women from society stifled their creative energies and deprived society of their contribution.

In her manifesto *A Vindication of the Rights of Women* (1792), Wollstonecraft boldly compared middle-class women to soldiers. Both received a narrow training and suf-

fered from their assigned roles. Her startling comparison – soldiering was supposedly the most masculine of occupations – supported her advocacy of women's education. It also responded to Rousseau's claim that women were inferior because they could not perform military duty. Wollstonecraft's appeal for recognition by men was to be echoed by later generations of feminists:

> *Would men but generously snap our chains, and be content with rational fellowship instead of slavish obedience, they would find us more observant daughters, more affectionate sisters, more faithful wives, more reasonable mothers – in a word, better citizens. We should then love them with true affection, because we should learn to respect ourselves …*[9]

However, the revolutions that sought the liberty and education of men merely added to legal and social restrictions on women. In France, Napoleon's revision of the legal code denied women the right to hold property within marriage, and most Western nations denied women the right to vote. Mary Wollstonecraft's protest for the rights of women was largely forgotten until the revival of the woman's suffrage movement in the 1840s.

Goya and Spain The greatest artist of romantic protest was the Spanish painter Francisco Goya (1746–1828), whose paintings and drawings depicted the senseless brutality of war and oppression. Goya was court painter in Madrid when Napoleon's army invaded Spain in 1808 to overthrow the weakened Spanish monarchy. Spanish citizens rose in sporadic but violent resistance to the French army, fighting the first *guerrilla*, or "little war." The uprising generated mutual reprisals of extreme brutality, which Goya sketched in a horrifying series called *The Disasters of War*. Goya's protest is best captured in the painting *Executions of the Third of May, 1808* (Fig. **12.14**). The picture portrays the execution of Spanish insurgents in Madrid by a French firing squad. The scene is presented with such a raw truthfulness that the picture has been called "the explosion of modern painting." Goya shows us two groups of men, the Spanish citizens being led to slaughter and the faceless French soldiers coldly mowing them down. The soldiers' stance provides an unconscious echo of the noble Romans in David's *Oath of the Horatii* (see Fig. 11.23). Goya shows us a sacrifice without ideals, a martyrdom without redemption. In his white shirt, the Christ-like central figure draws the viewer's eye to his dead compatriots. The scene is lighted by a stable lantern, normally a symbol of enlightenment and grace that here merely serves to illuminate the soldiers' grisly work. The moral realism in Goya's painting is a testimony of the demonic forces of war, loosed on a world without reason or optimism.

THE ROMANTICS AND NATURE

As Western societies became more urbanized, nature assumed a new significance for the romantic sensibility. Since ancient Greece, nature had symbolized the divine cosmos, of which human society was a part. For the romantics, however, nature became the negation of society, a world of beauty unspoiled by human endeavor. Among the English romantics, nature also represented a child-like existence that was lost to adults, except through moments of poetic transcendence. In their imagination, English romantic poets momentarily felt communion with the natural world and, through nature, with themselves.

The poetry of English romanticism often portrayed the poet's imaginative union with nature, such as John Keats (1795–1821) contemplating a nightingale's song, or Percy Bysshe Shelley (1792–1822) listening to the west wind. The English poet William Wordsworth (1770–1850) was the leading nature poet of the romantic age. Wordsworth's poetry recorded moments of transcendental insight gained during his contemplation of nature.

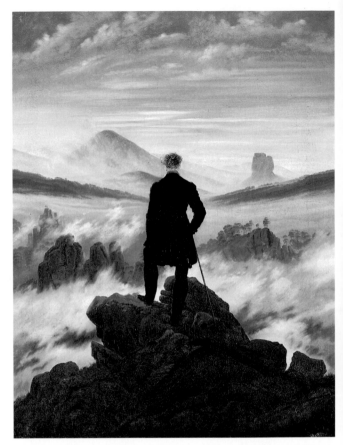

12.15 Caspar David Friedrich, *The Wanderer Above the Mists*, c. 1817–18. Oil on canvas, 29¹/₂ x 37¹/₄ ins (75 x 95 cm). Kunsthalle, Hamburg.
The German romantic painter Caspar David Friedrich depicts a wanderer struck by the sublime power of nature. In Friedrich's view, much like Wordsworth's, all of nature contained the presence of God. "The Divine is everywhere," he said, "even in a grain of sand."

Where Goethe's *Faust* had sought "infinitude" in human ambition, Wordsworth found infinity in the sublime experience of nature. Nature served as the catalyst to the poet's own spiritual development or renewal, reflecting and confirming his own powers of imagination (Fig. **12.15**). This correspondence between nature and the artist's inner soul was a commonplace of romanticism. In this passage from *The Prelude, or Growth of a Poet's Mind* (1799–1805), Wordsworth's poetic powers are stimulated by his nighttime excursion to Mt. Snowdon in Wales:

> *There I beheld the emblem of a mind*
> *That feeds upon infinity, that broods*
> *Over the dark abyss, intent to hear*
> *Its voices issuing forth to silent light*
> *In one continuous stream; a mind sustained*
> *By recognitions of transcendent power ...*[10]

Often, the romantic's contemplation of nature caused a profound sense of melancholy. The purity of nature reminded the romantics of their lost innocence and alienation from the natural world. In the poem *The World is Too Much With Us*, Wordsworth bemoans the distractions of a "too busy world" and envies the ancient Greeks' naive vision of nature. The knowledge that his wish is impossible makes his melancholy all the more acute.

> *The world is too much with us; late and soon,*
> *Getting and spending, we lay waste our powers:*
> *Little we see in Nature that is ours;*
> *We have given our hearts away, a sordid boon!*
> *The Sea that bares her bosom to the moon;*
> *The winds that will be howling at all hours,*
> *And are up-gathered now like sleeping flowers;*
> *For this, for everything, we are out of tune;*
> *It moves us not. – Great God! I'd rather be*
> *A Pagan suckled in a creed outworn;*
> *So might I, standing on this pleasant lea,*
> *Have glimpses that would make me less forlorn;*
> *Have sight of Proteus*[a] *rising from the sea;*
> *Or hear old Triton*[a] *blow his wreathèd horn.*[11]

WILLIAM WORDSWORTH
The World is Too Much With Us (1807)

a. Proteus and Triton, Greek gods of the sea.

THE WRITE IDEA

Write a commentary on Wordsworth's assertion that "getting and spending we lay waste our powers," from the poem *The World is Too Much With Us*. Which human abilities are "wasted" in the acquisition of material wealth? Which are developed?

The romantic return to nature reached a final expression in the writings of the Americans Ralph Waldo Emerson (1803–82) and Henry David Thoreau (1817–62). Emerson's musings on nature had a kinship with the mysticism of Hindu philosophy. He claimed that all humanity was part of the divine "Over-soul," and that individuals possessed within themselves the capacity to know all things. Thoreau's love of nature was more matter-of-fact, as expressed in the famous book *Walden, or Life in the Woods* (1854). By living for a year close to nature, Thoreau hoped he could learn the essentials of human existence and escape the "lives of quiet desperation" led by most inhabitants of the modern world.

12.16 John Constable, *The Hay Wain*, 1821. Oil on canvas, 4 ft 2¹/₂ ins x 6 ft 1 ins (1.28 x 1.85 m). National Gallery, London.
A master colorist, Constable created his brilliant foliage from overlaid dabs of green. The green is balanced by its complementary color (red) in the horses' harness and the scarf of a fisherman barely visible above the row boat at right.

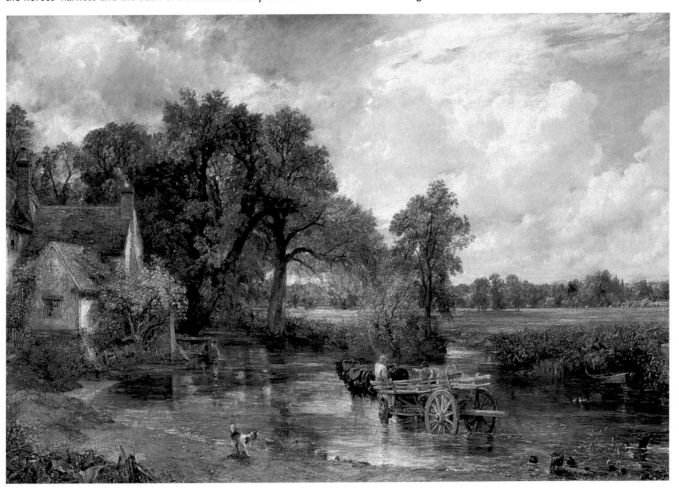

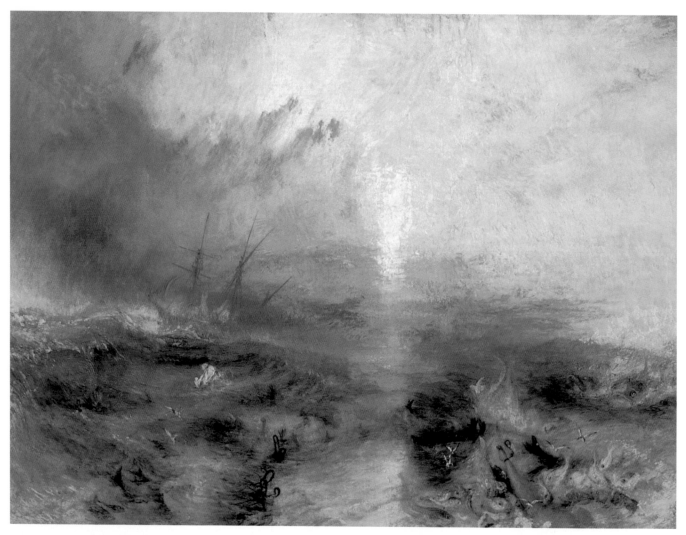

12.17 Joseph Mallord William Turner, *The Slave Ship* (*Slavers throwing Overboard the Dead and Dying – Typhoon Coming On*), 1842. Oil on canvas, 35³/₈ x 48¹/₄ ins (91 x 123 cm). Courtesy, Museum of Fine Arts, Boston, Henry Lillie Pierce Fund.
In this phantasmagoria of natural and human violence, fishes devour the body of a cast-off slave (lower right), while the doomed ship sails into a blood-red storm. Compare Turner's perspective on humans' relation to nature to John Constable's (see Fig. 12.16).

ROMANTIC LANDSCAPES

If Wordsworth was romanticism's greatest nature poet, his compatriot John Constable (1776–1837) was its great-

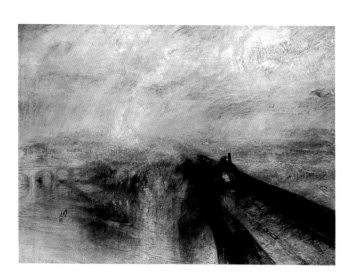

est nature painter. Constable's favorite subjects were rustic landscapes in which, in Wordsworth's words, "the passions of man are incorporated with the beautiful and permanent forms of nature." Constable's nature scenes may have been commonplace, but his technique as a painter was not. He applied color aggressively to the canvas, laying down daubs and dashes of pure color that created a shimmering vitality in his pictures. The picturesque calm in *The Hay Wain* (Fig. **12.16**), for example, renders the changing light and brilliant hues of the English countryside, visible in the red of the oxen's yoke and the dappled sunlight on the distant pasture. His intense use of color influenced Delacroix to adopt his bold method of coloring, and was

12.18 Joseph Mallord William Turner, *Rain, Steam, and Speed: The Great Western Railway*, 1844. Oil on canvas, 35¹/₂ x 47⁵/₈ ins (90 x 121 cm). National Gallery, London.
Compare the picturesque stone arches of the bridge at left and the sooty railroad trestle. The picture at full size also contrasts the party of picnickers on the river's shore with the train's passengers, who fly by in open cars.

KEY CONCEPT

THE NOBLE SAVAGE

The romantic idealization of nature was not limited to mountain peaks and bucolic countryside. The romantics also idealized people, especially peasants, blacks, and other groups, who were seen as "noble savages" (Fig. **12.19**) – primitives who lived close to nature and were presumed to be more reasonable or morally upright than civilized Europeans. The notion of a morally pure savage stemmed – like so many romantic ideas – from Jean Jacques Rousseau, who claimed that humans were most free and happy in a time before they were civilized. Sophisticated Europeans such as Wordsworth and Byron tried to rediscover this uncorrupted human nobility in peasants and primitives.

In literature, the noble savage appeared in romantic narratives, especially stories dealing with exploration and the frontier. In Herman Melville's *Moby Dick*, the young sailor Ishmael is terrified by his first encounter with the tattooed savage Queequeg. Later the narrator admits: "Through all his unearthly tattooings, I thought I saw the traces of a simple honest heart; and in his large, deep eyes, fiery black and bold, there seemed tokens of a spirit that would dare a thousand devils."[12]

Romantic authors used the idea of the noble savage to create the opposite of their own over-civilized and morally corrupt selves. Modern anthropology is still inspired by the noble savage. The twentieth-century anthropologist Margaret Mead praised the sexual freedom of primitive peoples in *Coming of Age in Samoa* (1928), and French anthropologist Claude Lévi-Strauss admiringly entitled one study of tribal peoples *La Pensée Sauvage*, meaning both "the wild flower" and "the primitive mind." An apparently simpler, truer mode of living is still attractive to Westerners who see themselves as overly sophisticated and exploitative. The irony of this view is that, since the romantic age, candidates for noble savagery have been steadily disappearing, their cultures disrupted by colonization and commerce.

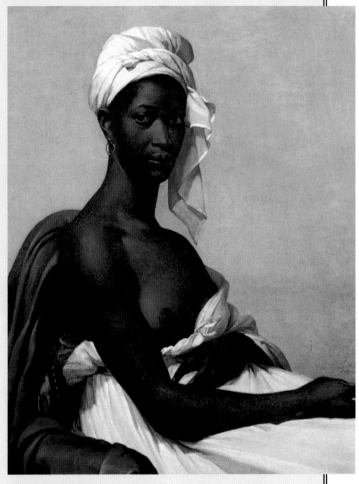

12.19 Marie Guillemine Benoist, *Portrait of a Black Woman*, 1800. Oil on canvas, 32 x 25 ¹/₂ ins (81 x 65 cm). Louvre, Paris.
The exotic beauty of an African woman is idealized in this portrait by a student of Jacques-Louis David's. The romantic idealization of the noble savage often coincided with harsh colonial policies.

later imitated by French impressionist painters (see page 375).

Constable depicted nature as a picturesque idyll. The paintings of Joseph Mallord William Turner (1775–1851), however, show nature as a violent and mysterious force, overwhelming the puny inventions of humanity. Even more obsessively than Constable, Turner experimented with color – especially blues and yellows – frequently transforming and fusing his colors to convey the effects of fog, steam, or smoke. Sometimes, it seems, color was the mystic veil through which Turner revealed humanity and nature.

In *The Slave Ship (Slavers Throwing Overboard the Dead and Dying – Typhoon Coming On)* (Fig. **12.17**) a turbulent sea swallows up the bodies of diseased slaves. The slaves had been cast overboard because the slavers' insurance

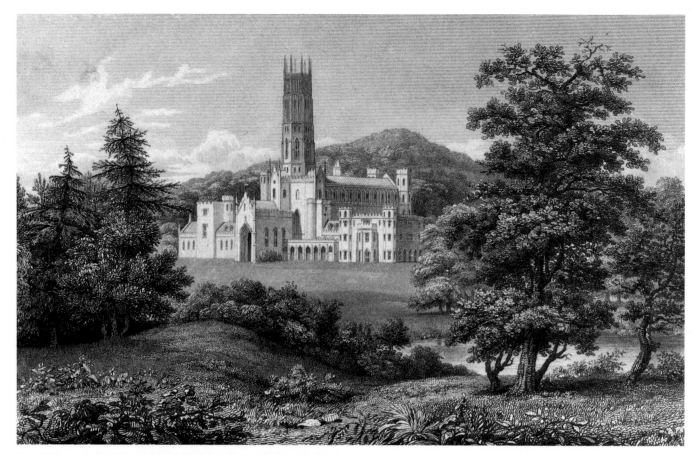

12.20 View of Fonthill Abbey, Wiltshire, England, from John Butter, *Delineations of Fonthill and its Abbey*, 1823. Frontispiece.
The mock Gothic tower collapsed in 1825, leaving a "Gothic" ruin that symbolized to romantics both organic growth and organic decay. What examples can you cite from today of a similar nostalgia for or recreation of medieval civilization?

would pay only on cargo lost at sea. Britain's slave trade had been abolished for twenty years, so Turner perhaps chose the subject for its potential to produce an apocalyptic atmosphere. In his later career, Turner privately experimented with techniques of increasing abstraction. His late masterpiece *Rain, Steam, and Speed: The Great Western Railway* (Fig. **12.18**), painted in 1844, was a landmark in modern painting. A party of picnickers and a cowherd with his beasts are details suggested rather than shown, so that no human drama distracts from the spectacular atmosphere of color and light. Turner's merger of human device and natural landscape was a technical tour-de-force that had few equivalents in romantic painting.

Romantic landscape painting in North America thrived under the influence of Thomas Cole (1801–48), founder of the Hudson River school. Cole was famed for his painstaking scenes of the Hudson River Valley in New York. Other painters of the Hudson River school specialized in grand views of the Rocky Mountains. Nineteenth-century American landscape painters shared an awe at the sweep of their continent's unspoiled natural beauty.

THE RETURN TO THE PAST

Each age finds in the past a reflection of its own values, and the romantics were no exception. The romantics viewed history from a different perspective than their predeces-

sors. The French Revolution had caused such a cataclysmic break in history, that the period that followed felt more distant from any past age. Romantic historians were more likely to recognize that each age had its own unique sensibility. Romantic works sought to recreate the past in historical detail, evidence that some romantics preferred reconstructing the past to observing the present.

The romantic period saw a Gothic revival that included the imitation of Gothic architecture and the use of Gothic settings in literary works. Heinrich Heine [HIGH-nuh] (1797–1856), the German poet, defined romanticism as "the re-awakening of the life and thought of the Middle Ages." The medieval Gothic cathedral became a feast of romantic symbolism: the ancient, the mystic, the picturesque, and the organic. In Germany, romantics engineered the completion of Cologne's Gothic cathedral in 1834, a project that fused romantic medieval nostalgia with German cultural nationalism. It did not matter to German romantics that the Gothic style had originally been known as the "new French style."

One striking example of the Gothic revival in England was William Beckford's estate at Fonthill Abbey (begun 1796; Fig. **12.20**), which grew into an elaborate Gothic fantasy. Gothic ruins were thought especially picturesque, so Beckford employed the architect John Wyatt to construct a ruined convent at his summer home. However, a fake Gothic convent was not enough for Beckford's romantic

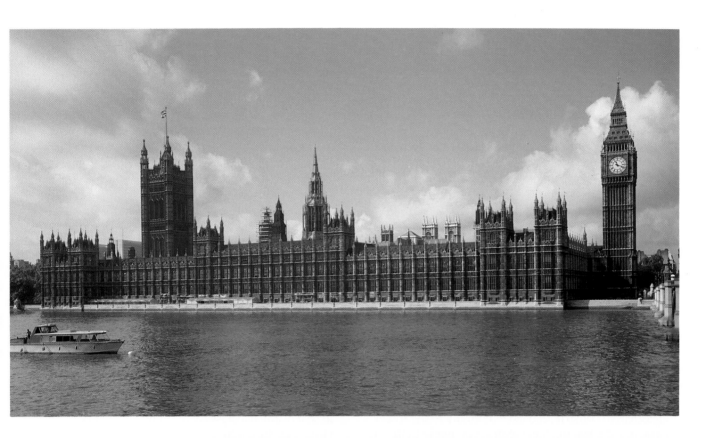

12.21 Above **Sir Charles Barry and A. W. Pugin, Houses of Parliament, London, 1840–65. Length 940 ft (286.5 m).** The massive Houses of Parliament in England were the Romantic era's greatest public building in the Gothic style. What elements of regularity and order can you observe in the buildings? What elements fail to conform to the regular patterns?

12.22 Right **John Nash, Royal Pavilion, Brighton, England, 1815–21.** Nash's Royal Pavilion resembles Fonthill Abbey in its arbitrary and fanciful combination of exotic styles. Both structures contradict the geometric regularity of neoclassical architecture.

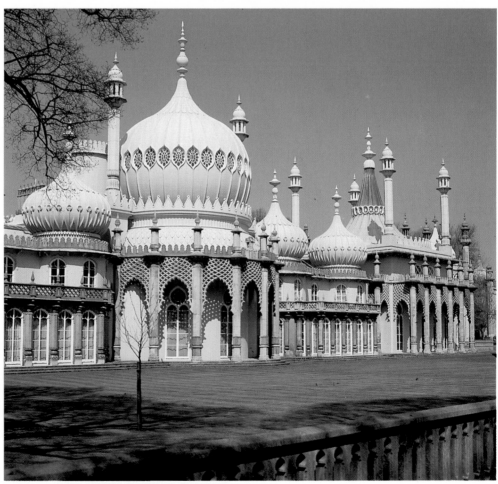

WINDOW ON DAILY LIFE

NATIVE STORYTELLERS

The native peoples contacted or uprooted by European colonialism often struggled to maintain the integrity of their cultural traditions. Here, an American Indian woman born in Arizona in 1837 describes an Apache custom for etching stories in the memories of young people.

In the old days when a person got ready to be told a story, from the time the storyteller started no one there ever stopped to eat or sleep. They kept telling the story straight through till it was finished. Then when the story was through, the medicine man would tell all about the different medicines. There would be a basket of corn seeds there, and for each line that was spoken, that person who was listening would count out one corn seed. This way there would be sometimes two hundred corn seeds. Then that person would have to eat them all. If he could eat them, then he would remember all the words he had been told. If you fell asleep during this time, then the story was broken and was no good. That is the way we used to do.[13]

GRENVILLE GOODWIN
From *Western Apache Raiding and Warfare*

tastes. He rapidly added a Gothic tower and a jumble of other additions, creating a stone concoction that bore no resemblance to any genuinely Gothic building. Haste and carelessness in construction led eventually to the tower's collapse in 1825, leaving the building's owner with the picturesque Gothic ruin that Beckford had originally intended.

A more lasting example of the Gothic style is the Houses of Parliament in London (Fig. **12.21**), rebuilt after a dis-astrous fire in 1834. The gigantic new building was more Gothic in its decoration than in its construction – the imposing façade facing the Thames is as regular and geometric as that of any neoclassical building. Augustus Welby Pugin (1812–52), the Gothic decoration's designer, called his work "Tudor details on a classic body." Still, the famous irregular towers and the building's intricate exterior carving make it an impressive presence in London architecture.

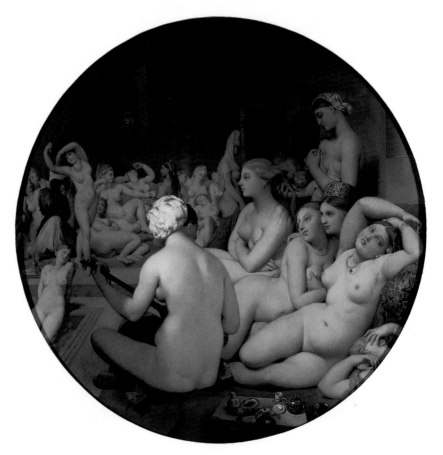

12.23 Jean Auguste Dominique Ingres, *The Turkish Bath,* **c. 1852–63. Oil on canvas, diameter 3 ft 6¹/₂ ins (1.08 m). Louvre, Paris.**
Ingres' combination of neoclassical refinement and romantic exoticism prompted one critic to call him a "Chinese loosed on the streets of Athens." How does the painter explicitly appeal to each of the five senses? How would you assess the painting's implied assumptions about women, men, sensuality, and Eastern cultures?

ROMANTIC EXOTICISM

With the end of the Napoleonic wars in 1815, the societies of Europe and North America settled into a comfortable routine of middle-class life. The appropriate symbol of this complacency was France's bourgeois king, Louis-Philippe (ruled 1830–48), who dressed in a businessman's frock coat and gambled his fortune on the stock market. Ironically, as European societies succumbed to conservatism, they were drawn to art of the exotic and grotesque. Middle-class readers and patrons wished to be transported outside the narrow limits of middle-class experience. Artists reacting against Enlightenment rationalism were also eager to explore the domains of evil and exoticism.

The European colonization of Africa and Asia brought the romantic sensibility into contact with exotic Oriental cultures. In England, when the Prince of Wales redesigned his residence at Brighton, architect John Nash (1752–1835) created a fantastic confection of Arabic, Chinese, and Indian styles. Nash's Royal Pavilion at Brighton (Fig. **12.22**) used Oriental and Moorish elements in a willful disregard for authenticity and carried the exotic themes over into the building's interior decoration. Nash's creation was typical of exotic designs, removed from their culture of origin and merged into an artificial but delightful combination.

Not to be outdone by English exoticism, French romantics followed in the wake of French colonial expeditions to northern Africa. In 1832, the painter Delacroix embarked on an unlikely (and dangerous) mission to Morocco. Fascinated by the rich colors of Arab dress, he sketched a Moorish harem and succeeded in getting an invitation to a Muslim wedding. Even Delacroix's rival, the academic painter Jean Auguste Dominique Ingres (1780–1867) was not immune to the seductions of exoticism. His *Turkish Bath* (Fig. **12.23**) offers a key-hole view of a Turkish harem as he imagined it, an erotic feast of the senses. While appealing to the voyeuristic pleasure of his male public,

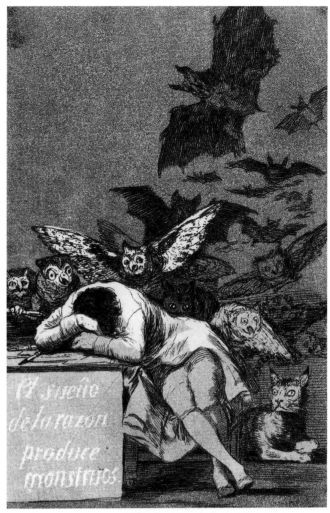

12.24 Francisco Goya, *The Sleep of Reason Brings Forth Monsters*, from *Los Caprichos*, 1796–8. Etching, 8¹/₂ x 6 ins (21.6 x 15.2 cm). British Museum, London.
This etching was the frontispiece to a book of drawings that demonstrated Goya's early interest in the grotesque; late in his career, disillusioned by repression in his country, he painted even fiercer demons and monsters.

12.25 Francisco Goya, *Witches' Sabbath*, c. 1819–23. Oil on canvas, 4 ft 7¹/₈ ins x 14 ft ¹/₂ ins (1.4 x 4.38 m). Prado, Madrid.
Darkened by the pessimism of his old age, Goya's scene depicts the devil, in the form of a goat, addressing a gathering of witches and warlocks. The picture can be seen as a commentary on the moral transformation of individuals when they join a mob or crowd.

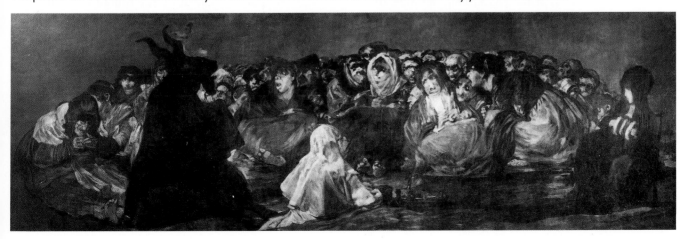

Ingres [ang(r)] maintained the cool restraint of his academic style. The form of the lute-player in the left foreground might be a classical statue.

ROMANTIC DEMONS

Illustrate the romantic fascination with the demonic and grotesque by examples from several arts.

Where Enlightenment rationalists expected evil to be defeated by moral diligence, the romantics found it to be as mysterious and irrepressible as the human imagination itself. In some romantic works, evil took the recognizable form of demons and witches; in others, grotesque and bizarre creatures hinted at the twisted feelings inside apparently ordinary people.

The Spanish artist Francisco Goya (see page 344) provided the most succinct image of the romantic fascination with evil. In *The Sleep of Reason Brings Forth Monsters* (Fig. **12.24**), from a series of etchings on Spanish superstitions, he drew a man asleep at a work-table, with his brushes beside him. As he sleeps, the demons of his imagination liberate themselves and rise with triumphant energy above him. The enigmatic caption reads, "The sleep of reason produces monsters." It suggests that behind wakeful reason, the destructive fiends of the human imagination are lurking. With such insights, the romantics anticipated the discoveries of modern psychology.

BERLIOZ'S *FANTASTIC SYMPHONY*

One of the most bizarre romantic tales of evil was told in Hector Berlioz' *Symphonie fantastique* (*Fantastic Symphony*, 1830). Berlioz [BAIR-lee-ohz] (1803–69) was an innovator of romantic **program music**, music that explicitly tells a story or describes a place. Berlioz' program for the *Fantastic Symphony*, printed as a pamphlet to be distributed at performances, was based on his own obsessive love for an Irish actress who had rejected him:

> *A young musician of morbid sensibility and ardent imagination in a paroxysm of lovesick despair has poisoned himself with opium. The drug, too weak to kill, plunges him into a heavy sleep accompanied by strange visions. His sensations, feelings, and memories are translated in his sick brain into musical images and ideas. The beloved one herself becomes for him a melody, a recurrent theme that haunts him everywhere.*[14]

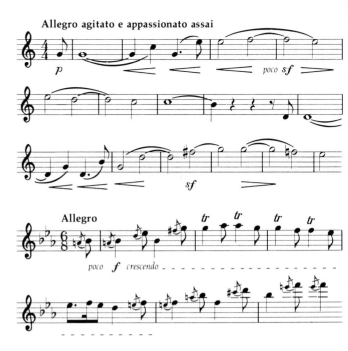

12.26 Hector Berlioz, *idée fixe* **from the first and fifth movements of** *Symphonie fantastique.*
In its first version (introduced by solo flute and violins), the *idée fixe* represents the musician's lover in a noble and idealized guise. The second version, from "Dream of the Witches' Sabbath," is vulgar and grotesque, played by a high-pitched clarinet.

The fifth and last movement of the *Symphonie fantastique* is a phantasmagoria of the demonic and macabre. In his dream, the musician has been executed for murdering his sweetheart. He sees himself "at a witches' sabbath surrounded by a host of fearsome specters who have gathered for his funeral" (Fig. **12.25**). His beloved joins the celebration through the recurring *idée fixe* [ee-DAY FEEKS], the musical theme that symbolizes her throughout the symphony (Fig. **12.26**). In earlier movements the *idée fixe* had been "noble and reserved." In the fifth movement's demonic atmosphere, it becomes "trivial and grotesque," a vulgar tune played by a mocking clarinet. The *idée fixe* is interwoven with other melodies: a ponderous version of the *Dies irae* (Latin, "day of wrath") from a medieval Mass for the dead, and a rapid "witches' dance." Berlioz' symphony not only captured the romantic spirit of the macabre, it also exudes a romantic sense of excess and vitality, with its extremes of loud and soft and its programmatic form.

THE ROMANTIC NOVEL

The literary fascination with evil and the demonic was evident in the **Gothic novel**, a genre characterized by horror, supernatural occurrences, and often a medieval setting. The most spectacular Gothic atmospheres were created in the stories of American author Edgar Allan Poe (1809–49). Such tales as *The Pit and the Pendulum* and *The Fall of the House of Usher* demonstrate Poe's mastery of Gothic horror and his insight into human fear and remorse. Another

American novelist, Nathaniel Hawthorne (1804–64), used supernatural effects to explore the torments of sin and guilt in *The Scarlet Letter* (1850).

In Europe, the sisters Charlotte and Emily Brontë both used the wild landscapes of their remote English homeland to frame stories of tortured and willful souls. In Charlotte's *Jane Eyre* and Emily's *Wuthering Heights* (both published 1847), the central figures are impelled by their passion and loneliness to confront social obligation and moral choice. Similar themes animate Victor Hugo's novel *The Hunchback of Notre Dame* (1831), with its grotesque hero and Gothic setting.

Mary Shelley's **Frankenstein**   The best-known Gothic novel today is Mary Shelley's *Frankenstein, or the Modern Prometheus* (1818), which synthesized Gothic atmosphere with the romantic themes of genius and the noble savage. The life of Mary Wollstonecraft Shelley (1797–1851; Fig. **12.27**) might well have been a romantic drama, with its acts of passionate abandon and lonely struggle. The daughter of free-thinking radicals, the precocious Mary eloped with the young romantic poet Percy Bysshe Shelley, who was estranged from his wife and child. The Shelleys became companions of Lord Byron in his dissolute European exile. Their idyll ended when Percy Shelley drowned in Italy. Mary Shelley returned to England with the couple's son and became a professional writer, earn-

12.27 Mary Wollstonecraft Shelley, shown in a miniature by Reginald Easton. Bodleian Library, Oxford.

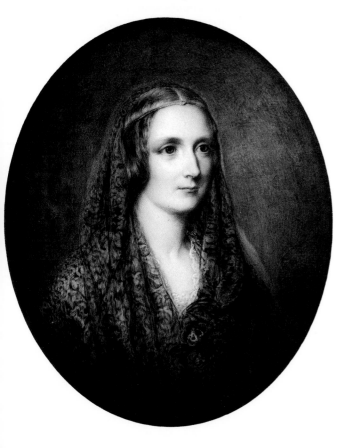

ing a living and educating her son, while also editing and publishing her husband's poetic works.

Mary Shelley traced the genesis of her *Frankenstein* to a night in Switzerland, when she and her literary companions had challenged each other to a ghost-story competition. She had dreamed that night about a "hideous phantasm of a man stretched out" who, "on the working of some powerful engine, shows signs of life, and stirs with an uneasy, half vital motion." In Shelley's novel, this "phantasm" – the grotesque creature – owes its existence to Victor Frankenstein, a romantic version of the Greek hero Prometheus, who stole fire from the gods. Believing that he has discovered the secret to life, Victor chortles that "a new species would bless me as its creator and source; many happy and excellent natures would owe their being to me." But when his hideous creation springs to life, Victor is horrified and abandons the monster, who embarks on his own odyssey of loneliness and despair. The creature finally appeals to Frankenstein to fashion a mate for him, an "Eve" to share his miserable state:

> *"What I ask of you is reasonable and moderate; I demand a creature of another sex, but as hideous as myself: the gratification is small, but it is all that I can receive, and it shall content me. It is true, we shall be monsters, cut off from all the world; but on that account we shall be more attached to one another. Our lives will not be happy, but they will be harmless, and free from the misery I now feel. Oh! my creator, make me happy; let me feel gratitude towards you for one benefit! Let me see that I excite the sympathy of some existing thing; do not deny me my request!"*[15]
>
> MARY SHELLEY
> From *Frankenstein* (1818)

Victor refuses the appeal, and the two figures – creator and creature – are finally locked in a tortuous pursuit, determined to destroy each other.

More than other Gothic novels, Mary Shelley's story engaged the romantic themes of genius, alienation, and the evils of society. In Frankenstein, she created a hero who suffers a conflict between his God-like ambitions and his moral blindness. In the creature, she imagined the noble savage, who learns hatred and cruelty from humans whose civilization has failed to make them kind. With all its interwoven themes, Shelley's Gothic tale is one of the richest documents of romanticism.

THE WRITE IDEA

Recall a horror novel or film that struck your imagination. How would you explain modern civilization's continued fascination with evil, the demonic, and the grotesque?

Chapter Summary

Revolutions and Rights. The revolutionaries of 1776 in America and 1789 in France justified themselves with the principles of Enlightenment philosophy. In America, the Declaration of Independence put into bold action the principle of popular sovereignty, while the *Federalist* writers defended the new American constitution with enlightened rationalism. In France, the revolutionary drama included the Declaration of Rights of Man and the Citizen (1789) as well as European war and the Reign of Terror.

During the Napoleonic era (1799–1815), the military hero Napoleon presented himself as the champion of revolutionary principles while seizing absolute power. Taking ancient Rome as a model for his imperial capital Paris, Napoleon employed the arts to project his imperial ambitions, though only two artists – David and Canova – served him with genuine distinction. In the Americas, the leaders Toussaint-l'Ouverture in Haiti and Simón Bolívar in South America overthrew colonial rule and established constitutional governments.

The Romantic Hero. In the wake of Napoleon's defeat (1815), a new sensibility suffused European society – romanticism, which preferred feeling over reason and individual genius over mechanical laws. In the romantic period (1800–1850), heroic geniuses were prized for their extraordinary powers and achievements.

In music, the titanic and tortured genius Ludwig van Beethoven composed expansive symphonies that bridged the Classical and romantic styles. Musical virtuosos such as Paganini and Chopin were international stars whose abilities appealed to wide musical audiences.

In literature, the great German poet Goethe re-cast the Faust legend as a romantic striving to taste all human experience; Goethe's *Faust* inspired artists and composers. The life of poet Lord Byron defined the romantic hero, advocate of moral and intellectual freedom, which powerfully influenced the French painter Delacroix.

Elements of Romanticism. The elements of romantic art and literature arose in response to different social and historical circumstances. Romantic-era poets such as William Blake protested the social injustices of early industrial society, while Mary Wollstonecraft demanded equal rights for women. In Spain, the painter Goya bitterly and passionately depicted the cruelties of war.

In England and America, romantic authors such as Wordsworth and Emerson saw nature as a mirror of the human imagination. They often imputed special nobility to people – peasants, American Indians, or Pacific tribes – who seemed unspoiled by civilization. The painters Constable and Turner used new effects of color and light to render the natural landscape's elusive beauty.

Still other romantics sought escape in the past, fostering a taste for picturesque medieval architecture. As industrial life became more routine, the lure of exotic lands spurred the imaginations of architects such as Nash and painters such as Delacroix and Ingres.

Romantic Demons. The romantics were fascinated by evil, the demonic, and the grotesque. Berlioz's *Fantastic Symphony* told the bizarre tale of an artist's obsessive love, ending with a fantastic dream of a witches' sabbath. The Gothic novel evoked horrific effects with its medieval setting and characters tortured by remorse. While the master of Gothic effects was the American Poe, the most accomplished Gothic novel was Mary Shelley's *Frankenstein,* the tale of a gifted scientist whose grotesque creation, the monster, pursues and tortures him. *Frankenstein* is a summation of romantic motifs: the genius, the noble savage, the protest against injustice, and the fascination with evil.

13 The Industrial Age: The Spirit of Materialism

*Finely dressed shoppers stroll down a rainy boulevard in 1870s Paris (Fig. **13.1**), the "capital of the nineteenth century." Fashionable apartments rise like modern pyramids behind them. Within a decade, the great Eiffel Tower, a masterpiece of engineering and design, will be erected nearby. Like other capitals of modernity – Berlin, New York, Chicago – this glistening Paris is a triumph of **materialism**: the belief that science, technology, and industry can know all truth, solve all problems, and create human happiness.*

*But we must ask about these urbane citizens of the industrial age, striding purposefully into a modern future: Do they feel a bit of nostalgia for the old Paris? Are they alienated from the others – the workers, the poor, the powerless – who share their sidewalk? What, ultimately, are the spiritual costs of their materialism and prosperity? These are the questions that came to perplex the great **age of industry** (1850–1910), when modernity prevailed in Western civilization and brought astounding material progress.*

13.1 Gustave Caillebotte, *Paris Street: Rainy Weather*, 1877. Oil on canvas, 6 ft 11¹/₂ ins x 9 ft ³/₄ ins (2.12 x 2.76 m). Art Institute of Chicago (Charles H. and Mary F. S. Worcester Collection, 1964.336). This scene of Paris' modern boulevards shows the painter's fascination with oblique angles and uneven proportions. Compared to the Romantics' view of humans in nature, what does this picture say about humans in the urban landscape? What elements of the picture make it feel "modern?"

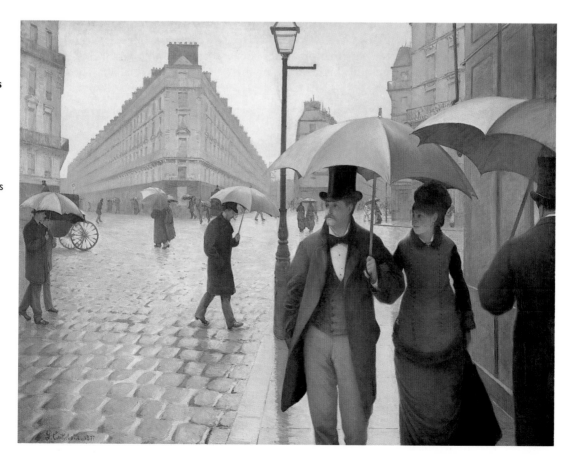

REALISM

Define realism as it was practiced in nineteenth-century art and literature.

In the mid-nineteenth century, Western societies were entering a new age of material production, a triumph of machines and commodities. Much of Europe and North America was in the midst of a great economic boom, fueled by discoveries in applied science and industrial technology. New railroads, the symbol of material progress, criss-crossed England, transporting manufactured goods of high quality from the factories of the new industrial towns. Optimists claimed that science would soon answer all questions and material prosperity satisfy all wants.

Material prosperity did not bring greater political freedom. In Europe, political repression doused the romantics' hopes for a society of democracy and individual freedom (Fig. **13.2**). In 1848, Paris' citizens again overthrew the French king and briefly established another republic. Inspired by the French example, patriots in Poland, Germany, and Italy mounted their own revolutions, hoping to establish liberal republics. But their hopes crumbled as one after another, the republics fell to repression.

Artists and writers reacted to Western industrial society with sober detachment and practicality, an attitude called **realism**. Realism in the arts aimed to give a truthful and objective representation of the social world, without illusion or imaginative alteration. Although committed to social reform, the realists were determined to depict society as it really was. Where the romantics considered the artist an inspired genius, the realists saw the artist as a scientific observer of detail. The American journalist and novelist William Dean Howells (1837–1920) said that realism was "nothing more or less than the truthful treatment of material."

Despite its straightforward claims, the realist attitude led to different results in painting, the novel, and philosophy. Realism in the visual arts scandalized the official art world, which expected painters to depict idealized allegories and historical subjects. Instead, realist painters portrayed ordinary subjects from daily life. Novelists and philosophers mocked the utopian illusions of romanticism and the promises of middle-class society. In all, the realists raised a powerful and sometimes passionate indictment of industrialism's harshness and hypocrisy. In many cases, realism in art was a reaction against the optimistic prophecies of material progress.

REALISM IN PAINTING

The most militant realist painter was the French artist Gustave Courbet (1819–77), whose scenes of ordinary provincial life outraged the Parisian art public. Courbet [koor-BAY] declared boldly that painting "can only consist of the presentation of real and existing things." In his own work, he found artistic truth in the ordinary lives and routine events of industrial society, presenting his subjects without nobility or sophistication.

When Courbet's *Burial at Ornans* [or-NAHN(h)] (Fig. **13.4**) was shown in 1851 at the official Salon – the annual exhibition of work by professional artists – the Paris connoisseurs were scandalized. They attacked the picture of funeral-goers from Courbet's native town as the incarnation of socialism. They considered the picture to be care-

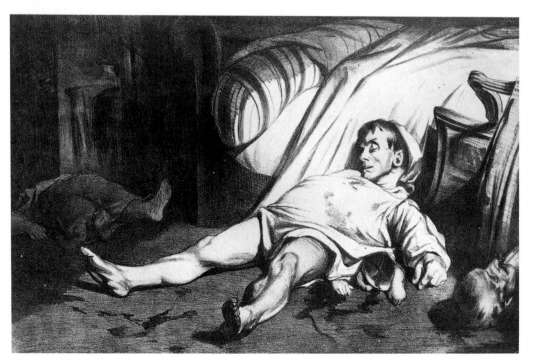

13.2 Honoré Daumier, *Rue Transnonain, April 15, 1834.* 1834. Lithograph, 11¹/₂ x 17¹/₂ ins (29 x 44.5 cm). This is the aftermath of an atrocity by government soldiers against a poor Parisian family, as depicted by the caricaturist and illustrator Honoré Daumier. Daumier's sketches and lithographs achieved an immediacy and evocative power that would later characterize journalistic photography.

13.3 Thomas Eakins, *The Gross Clinic,* **1875. Oil on canvas, 96 x 78 ins (2.44 x 1.98 m). The Jefferson Medical College, Philadelphia, Courtesy Thomas Jefferson University.**
The light falls across the doctor's forehead to the patient's exposed thigh, where attendants with bloody hands hold open an incision. Compare the emotional responses of Dr. Gross, the note-taking scribe, and the female relative of the patient (left, middle ground).

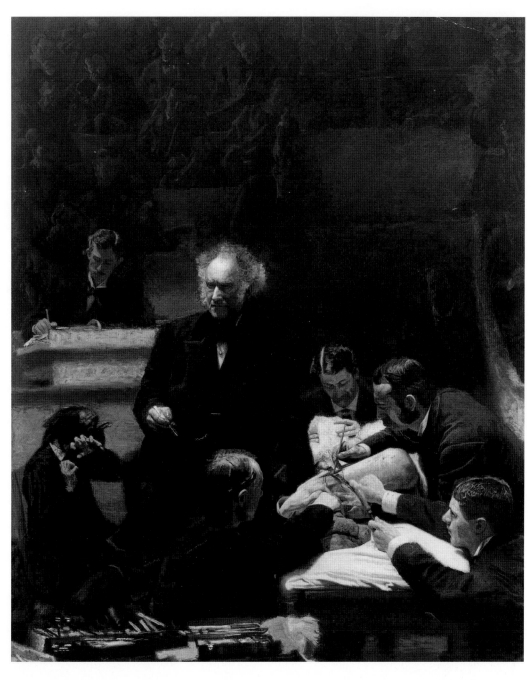

lessly composed, and complained that the subject lacked any hint of heroism or exalted truth. Courbet had, in fact, portrayed the mourners crowded around the open grave with no regard for social hierarchy – the priest, pall-bearers, and attendants are depicted with utter honesty, including a beadle (in red) flushed with drink. Realism, Courbet would say, was "democracy in art." The *Burial at Ornans* was a triumph of the ordinary citizen, reason enough for it to be reviled as socialism in paint.

Critics found a more palatable brand of realism in the works of Rosa Bonheur (1822–99), the most famous female painter of her day. Bonheur's [BOHN-err] father belonged to a socialist group that believed firmly in women's equality, and Rosa lived by his teachings. She wore men's clothes (which required a police permit), smoked cigarettes, and never married, living instead with female companions. Her painting was as bold as her life. *The Horse Fair* (Fig. **13.5**), painted between 1853 and 1855, depicts a sweeping parade of horses with the same wild energy that Delacroix

---

THE WRITE IDEA

Write a "realistic" and "objective" description of the event depicted in Courbet's *Burial at Ornans.* To what degree must you rely on the artist's perceptions? How might your description be different if you were looking at a photograph of the funeral, or if you had witnessed the event firsthand?

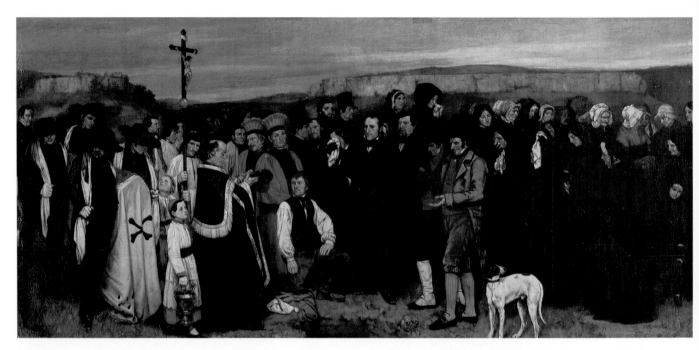

13.4 Gustave Courbet, *Burial at Ornans*, 1849. Oil on canvas, 10 ft 3⁵/₈ ins x 21 ft 9³/₄ ins (3.14 x 6.65 m). Louvre, Paris.
The painting's monumental size contradicts the drab ordinariness of its subject. With this portrait of villagers from his provincial home, what might the realist Courbet be saying about the grand history paintings and heroic subjects that were typical of official painting?

had found in exotic beasts. Bonheur studied her animal subjects with visits to slaughter houses and livestock markets. The result, though, was more rustic and less threatening than Courbet's crude scenes of provincial life.

In the United States, the painters Winslow Homer (1836–1910) and Thomas Eakins (1844–1916) combined realist technique with American matter-of-factness. After working as a magazine illustrator during the American

Civil War, Homer visited Paris, where he saw the works of Courbet and Edouard Manet (see page 375). Homer's favorite subjects were scenes of children at play or of high drama at sea. Eakins [AY-kunz] studied in Paris with an academic history painter and composed his outdoor subjects – rowers, sailors, and swimmers – with precise attention to perspective and balance. In *The Gross Clinic* (Fig. 13.3), he portrayed a famous Philadelphia doctor demon-

13.5 Rosa Bonheur, *The Horse Fair*, 1853–5. Oil on canvas, 8 ft ¹/₄ ins x 16 ft 7¹/₂ ins (2.44 x 5.07 m). The Metropolitan Museum of Art, New York, Gift of Cornelius Vanderbilt, 1887.
Analyze the complex movements of Bonheur's majestic parade. What relation does she pose between the brute animal power of the horses and their human keepers?

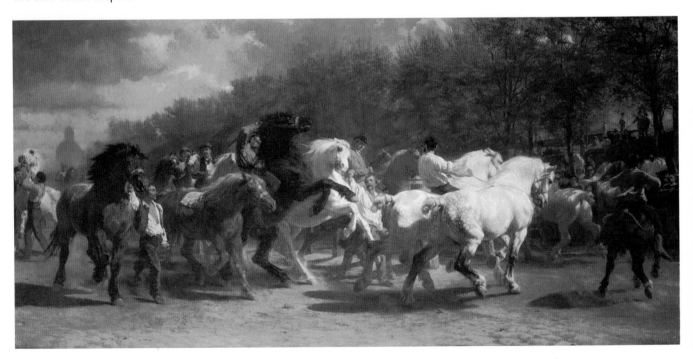

strating a daring surgical procedure. The physician holds open the bloody incision in the patient's thigh, while impassively lecturing his medical student audience. Eakins' choice of subject and theatrical use of light were influenced by Rembrandt's famous *Anatomy Lesson of Dr. Tulp* (see Fig. 10.38). But the graphic realism of his presentation repelled art connoisseurs. Like both Courbet and Manet, Eakins suffered the rejection of the artistic public for his uncompromising realism.

THE REALIST NOVEL

While the romantic sensibility was most intensely expressed through lyric poetry, the description of industrial society was best accomplished in the social novel, which became the dominant literary form of the later nineteenth century.

Of the many novelists who flourished in this age, the English novelist Charles Dickens (1812–70) was perhaps the most outspoken in his protests against the injustices of industrialism. His novels portrayed the social evils of nineteenth-century England, particularly its cruelty to children. Dickens knew this cruelty from experience – his father was often in debtors' prison and he himself was working in a factory by the age of twelve. Young Dickens educated himself, becoming a lawyer's assistant and later a parliamentary reporter. By the age of twenty-four, he was a literary success and was soon serializing his novels in his own weekly publications. He later fictionalized his rise from poverty to literary prominence in the novel *David Copperfield* (1849–50). His other novels also drew from his experience as a child and young adult – for example, *Bleak House* (1852), a bitter portrait of the English legal system.

Dickens' ability to draw memorable characters and to fill his novels with unlikely coincidences and sentimentality made his books immensely popular. They too were a product of industrialism, appearing in installments beside advertisements for new products. The novels often appealed directly for industrial and social reform. Dickens' anger from his early life of poverty never cooled. His works pointedly compared the miseries of industrial society with the complacent life of the wealthy.

The French novelist Gustave Flaubert (1821–80) was in many ways the opposite of Dickens. Where Dickens suffered an impoverished London childhood, Flaubert [floh-BAIR] grew up in a comfortably middle-class French provincial family. Where Dickens wrote quickly, sometimes only days ahead of publication, Flaubert spent hours searching for *le mot juste*, the most appropriate word. Flaubert was recognized as a master stylist in fiction and associated with the "art for art's sake" movement of the later nineteenth century (see page 371).

Flaubert's best-known work was *Madame Bovary* (1865), the story of a naive provincial woman overwhelmed by the sophistication of the modern world. Emma Bovary's idealized view of life and sentimentality lead her to adultery, debt, and finally suicide. The novel's plot scandalized the French public and Flaubert stood trial for obscenity after its publication.

Flaubert's most complex novel, *L'Education sentimentale* (*The Sentimental Education*, 1869), was his cynical reflection on French political events in the revolutionary period of the 1840s. The novel deals with themes of illusion and disillusionment, romantic hope and cynical realism, lofty principle and mean-spirited hypocrisy. The novel's hero, the young provincial Frédéric Moreau, is a fool in both love and politics. Throughout the novel he is so absorbed in his own sentimental conceits that he fritters away opportunities for success, while history swirls around him.

From Flaubert's acerbic perspective, the decisive political events of 1848 involve the same combination of folly and cynicism as Frédéric's personal life. In February 1848, an uprising of Parisian workers, poor people, and middle-class radicals overthrew the Citizen-King, Louis-Philippe, and established a republic. However, Flaubert saw the new government and its quarreling supporters as self-serving and corrupt. He bitterly portrays the brutal slaughter of June 1848, when the French National Guard turned against the republic's supporters – newspapers, political clubs, demonstrators – and brutally suppressed a new popular uprising. To Flaubert, all sides of the struggle had achieved equality – an equality of human savagery.

13.6 Käthe Kollwitz, *Uprising*, 1899. Klipstein 44. Courtesy, Galerie St. Etienne, New York.
Socialism tapped the anger of 19th-century workers and peasants, who often futilely revolted against their miserable living and working conditions. The Berlin artist Käthe Kollwitz depicts in this painting an uprising of weavers led by an angry angel of revolution.

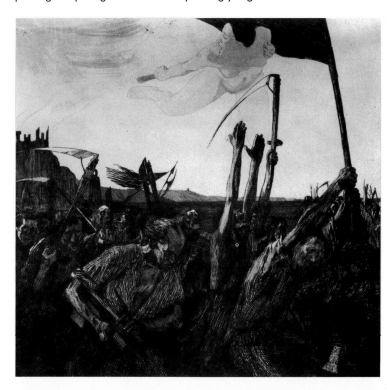

KEY CONCEPT

SOCIALISM

The suffering of factory workers and the extremes of industrial wealth and poverty created vigorous demands for social reform. Some of industrialism's critics favored **socialism**, a system in which the wealth of a society is collectively owned and distributed equally among its members. The idea of socialism can be traced to Plato's *Republic*, the Greek philosopher's vision of the ideal state (see page 63). A Christian version of socialism thrived in medieval monasteries and in fictions such as Thomas More's *Utopia* (see page 245), which criticized early capitalism's selfishness and ac-quisitiveness.

Nineteenth-century socialists proposed schemes to relieve the hardship of industrial labor and re-organize industrial society. The Scottish factory-owner Robert Owen instituted progressive reforms in his own mills and founded an experimental socialist com-munity at New Harmony, Indiana. The French reformer Charles Fourier proposed that industrial society be organized into efficient units of 1600 persons, called phalanxes. Members of a phalanx were to live and work in the same building and share equally in the products of their labor. Scoffing at such utopian schemes, Karl Marx argued that socialism would arise as a nec-essary stage of historical development, not from a phil-anthropic or philosophical fancy. Marx's proletarian state would abolish the private ownership of factories and fields, thus eliminating the basis for social classes. Compared with the utopian socialists, though, Marx was vague in describing life under future socialism. He imagined a society in which the enforced divisions of labor gave way to free productivity:

> *In communist society, where nobody has an exclusive area of activity and each can train himself in any branch he wishes, society regulates the general production, making it possible for me to do one thing today and another tomorrow, to hunt in the morning, fish in the afternoon, breed cattle in the evening, criticize after dinner, just as I like …*[1]

By the late nineteenth century, socialism was the leading revolutionary doctrine of its day, appealing to industrialism's poor and disenfranchised (Fig. **13.6**). Socialists also called for more practical reforms, many of which would eventually be widely adopted: the right to vote for all citizens, including women; an eight-hour work day with a minimum wage; free medical care; and the right to organize unions.

Most of the National Guardsmen[a] were pitiless. Those who had not fought in the streets hoped to distinguish themselves now. In a panic, they were taking their revenge at once against the newspapers, the clubs, the demonstrations, the doctrines, against everything that had infuriated them during the last three months; and, despite their victory, equality (as if to rebuke its defenders and taunt its enemies) emerged triumphant – an equality of brutish beasts, a common level of bloodstained savagery. For the fanaticism of the rich was as great as the frenzy of the poor, the aristocracy was as prey to the same madness as the rabble, and the cotton nightcap proved as hideous as the revolutionary bonnet. The mind of the nation was unbalanced, as it is after great natural upheavals. Certain intelligent men stayed fools for life because of it.[2]

GUSTAVE FLAUBERT
From *The Sentimental Education* (1869)

---

a. National Guardsmen, citizen soldiers who had supported popular uprisings in July 1830 and February 1848.

CRITICAL QUESTION

What radical ideas appeal to the poor and oppressed peoples of today's world? From what political, religious, or ethnic traditions are these radical ideas drawn?

KARL MARX AND COMMUNISM

Like Flaubert, the philosopher Karl Marx (1818–83) looked with scorn on the romantic illusions of his fellow radicals. Marx intended to base his revolutionary theory on a sober analysis of history and economics, though his hopes for revolution remained unfulfilled. Eventually, Marx led an international laborers' movement and became the nine-teenth century's dominant socialist thinker. In the twen-tieth century, his writings guided revolutionaries in every part of the world.

Marx's revolutionary statement was the *Communist Manifesto*, by coincidence published in February 1848, the month of the Paris workers' insurrection. In its famous opening lines, the *Manifesto* summoned factory laborers to rise and overthrow their bourgeois masters: "Workers of the world, unite! You have nothing to lose but your chains." The *Manifesto* declared that Europe stood at the threshold of a great historical upheaval. The impending conflict between the owners of industry and the mass of industrial workers, wrote Marx, would inaugurate the last and highest stage of human progress.

Marx's concept of history expressed his philosophical **materialism**, the belief that matter is the basis of all reality. In Marx's version of materialism, human thought and values were determined by one's material conditions of life. By Marx's own account his theory mirrored the practical attitude of nineteenth-century industrialists, who also placed supreme value on material things. Industrial capitalism had installed money and profit as the basis of all human relations, thus making labor something to be bought and sold. He wrote in the *Communist Manifesto*:

> *In proportion as the bourgeoisie, i.e., capital, is developed, in the same proportion is the proletariat,[a] the modern working class, developed – a class of laborers, who live only so long as they find work, and who find work only so long as their labor increases capital. These laborers, who must sell themselves piecemeal, are a commodity, like every other article of commerce, and are consequently exposed to all the vicissitudes of competition, to all the fluctuations of the market.[3]*

a. proletariat, the urban class of factory workers.

Nevertheless, Marx recognized that capitalism had unleashed the creative powers of human productivity and represented the highest stage of historical development.

While Marx's revolutionary hopes were not realized, the efforts of reformers and trade unions did soften some of industrialism's abuses: for example, child labor was outlawed and the English workhouses abolished. The ongoing development of industrial capitalism continued also to produce critics of its excesses and injustices.

THE SPIRIT OF PROGRESS

Explain how industrial-age cities and buildings reflected the era's optimism.

The later nineteenth century was an age of stunning material progress in Western civilization. In 1876, the first transatlantic telegraph cable connected Europe with North America, enabling swift telecommunication. Programs of sanitation and vaccination began to eradicate epidemic diseases such as smallpox and typhus. By the end of the century, water-powered electrical plants were providing electricity for Thomas Edison's newly invented light bulbs. Voices of the new age produced compelling scientific and poetic statements of progress. The materialist future took shape in urban reconstruction and innovative buildings that put a new face on the modern city.

VOICES OF A NEW AGE

Perhaps the age's most compelling example of progress was not an invention but an idea: the theory of evolution. The biologist Charles Darwin (1809–82) argued that nature itself obeyed the laws of progress in his *Origin of Species* (1859). Darwin described how the genetic adaptability of species determined their survival in nature. According to Darwin, competition between species – a process of "natural selection," as he called it – provided for extinction or gradual evolution. Thus all species, including human beings, had evolved from lower forms, having proved their adaptability in the "struggle for life." Religious objections nearly buried Darwin's theory under a storm of controversy. However, some social thinkers seized on Darwinism as an explanation for Western industrial nations' world dominance, applying Darwin's naturalist principle of the "survival of the fittest."

The American poet Walt Whitman (1819–92) saw the unity of all being in a different light. Whitman affirmed the vibrant and vulgar diversity of modern life. In his book of poems *Leaves of Grass*, first published in 1855, he confidently proclaimed his "song of myself." Where earlier romantics had contemplated nature in solitude and found a mystic oneness, Whitman roamed the raucous streets of New York City, celebrating not only his own sense of being alive but also the teeming life of the modern city. He greeted the city's residents and affirmed their vitality. He was the most enthusiastic poet of modernity and American-style democracy.

> *I celebrate myself,*
> *And what I assume you shall assume,*
> *For every atom belonging to me as good as belongs to*
> * you…*
> *Walt Whitman, a kosmos, of Manhattan the son,*
> *Turbulent, fleshy, sensual, eating, drinking and breeding,*
> *No sentimentalist, no stander above men and*
> * women or apart from them,*
> *No more modest than immodest.[4]*
>
> WALT WHITMAN
From *Leaves of Grass* (1855)

MONUMENTS OF PROGRESS

The mid-nineteenth century in Europe saw an unprecedented diversity of architectural styles: Neoclassicism contended with Gothic and Renaissance revivals as the proper

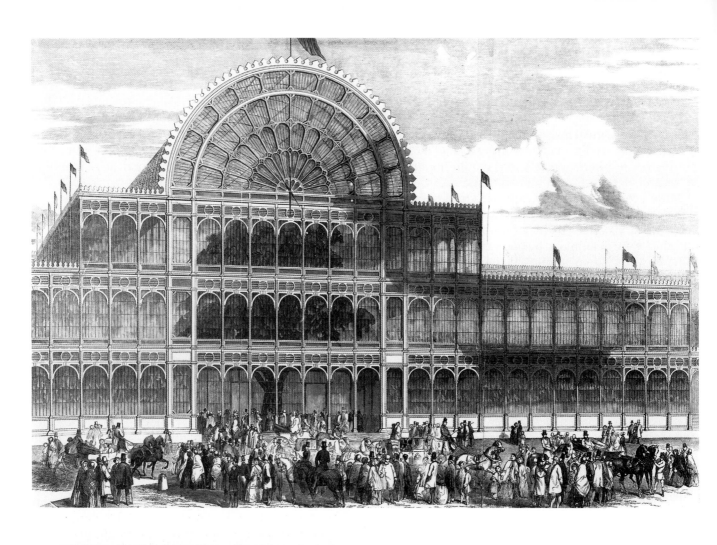

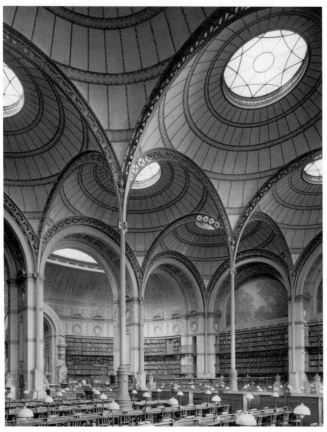

13.7 Above **Joseph Paxton, Crystal Palace, London, 1851. Cast iron and glass, length 1851 ft (564.2 m).**
The prefabricated parts of cast and wrought iron were so precisely manufactured that the entire building was assembled in a few months, then later disassembled and rebuilt on a different site.

13.8 Left **Henri Labrouste, reading room of the Bibliothèque Nationale, Paris, 1854–75.**
The use of slender iron arches and glass skylights lends Labrouste's interiors a graceful airiness that compares favorably to ancient Roman baths or Gothic-style churches. Note the recurring geometric pattern of circles, arcs, and rectangles.

style for new urban buildings. The only genuinely new style in architecture was based on a new material, the combination of iron and glass in building. Not since the ancient Romans introduced concrete had a building material so revolutionized construction. During the nineteenth century, iron-and-glass construction was mostly used to enclose large, open spaces, such as railroad stations or the shopping arcades of Paris.

The nineteenth century's romance with iron-and-glass construction culminated in the Crystal Palace (Fig. **13.7**), the gigantic hall built for the 1851 Great Exhibition in London. The building was designed by Joseph Paxton (1801–65), a former gardener, whose plan resembled a monumental greenhouse. The building's materials were manufac-

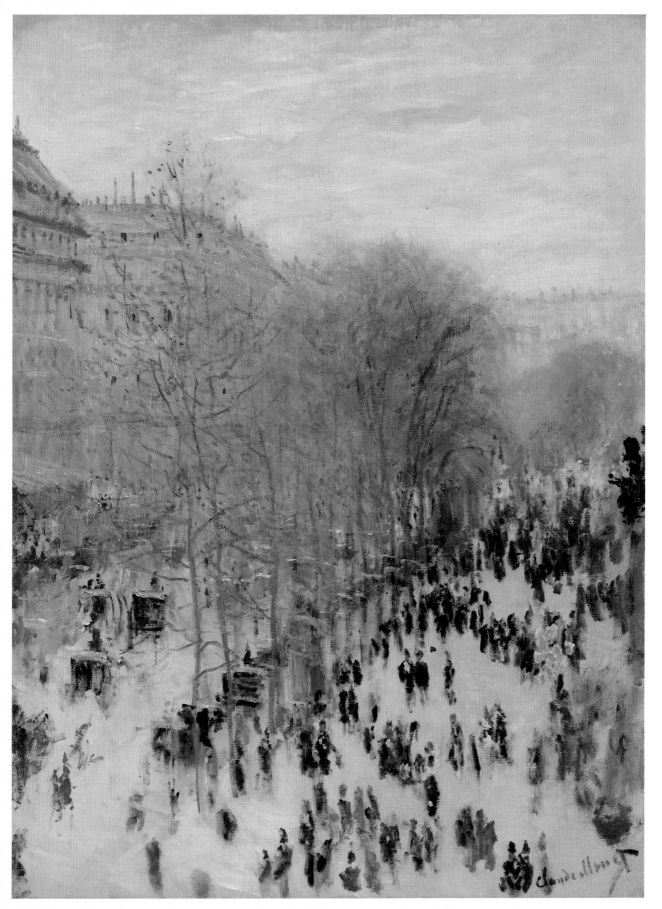

13.9 Claude Monet, *Boulevard des Capucines, Paris*, 1873. Oil on canvas, 31³/₄ x 23¹/₂ ins (81 x 58 cm). The Nelson-Atkins Museum of Art, Kansas City, Missouri, purchase: the Kenneth A. and Helen F. Spencer Foundation Acquisition Fund F72–35.
This impressionist view of a modern Parisian boulevard captures the bustle and excitement of 19th-century urban life. The painting's lack of explicit composition or a unified center of interest shows the influence of photography. In fact, Monet painted this scene from the balcony of the pioneering photographer Nadar.

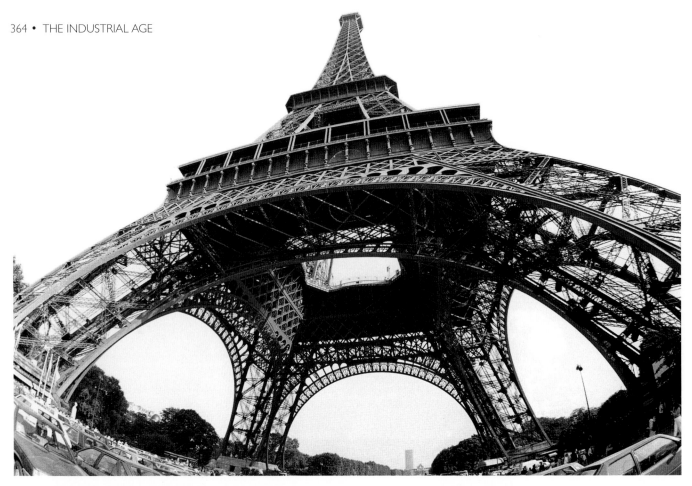

13.10 Gustave Eiffel, Eiffel Tower, Paris, 1887–9. Cast and wrought iron, height 984 ft (299.9 m).
Except for the decorative arches connecting the legs, the Tower is the pure expression of engineering in metal. It echoes the technical virtuosity of such engineering achievements as the Brooklyn Bridge, New York, begun in 1868.

tured off-site, pre-fabricated to be easily assembled and disassembled. The entire building, nearly 2000 feet (*c.* 610 m) long and covering 26 acres (10.5 hectares), was constructed in less than ten months. From the outside Paxton's building was a glistening palace on the scale of Versailles. Inside, it achieved a transparency that Gothic architects could not have dreamed of. The Crystal Palace embodied the spirit of progress and Britain's pride in her industrial know-how.

The aesthetic possibilities of iron construction were mastered by Henri Labrouste (1801–75) in his Bibliothèque Nationale (National Library) in Paris (1854–75). Labrouste showed iron's flexibility in handling different spaces. The library stacks rise to five levels on iron girders, while the reading room has the flavor of a Romanesque monastery (Fig. **13.8**). Its terracotta vaulting and glass-covered oculi are outlined by iron and supported on graceful iron columns. Despite Labrouste's elegant handling of his materials, however, the decorative use of iron had fallen out of fashion by the time his project was complete.

By the end of the century, iron was being used primarily in bridges and other industrial buildings. The age's most ambitious iron structure was the Eiffel Tower (Fig. **13.10**), the controversial landmark of Paris' 1889 World Exhibition. Like Paxton's Crystal Palace, the cast-iron tower

designed by Eiffel (1832–1923) was a feat of engineering more than of architecture. It soared to a height of 984 feet (*c.* 300 m), an obelisk in pure metal that far surpassed Napoleon's imperial monuments. For more than forty years, the Tower was the tallest structure in the world.

THE MODERN CITY

The audacious optimism of the age of materialism expressed itself above all in the modern city. Nineteenth-century architects and city planners were sometimes called to build entire cities from scratch, such as the United States capital, Washington, D.C., and St. Petersburg in Russia, each built on a vacant site. The designs of these new cities were heavily influenced by Louis XIV's Palace of Versailles, with its rationalized plan and imposing neoclassical buildings.

To build a fine modern city in a vacant swamp was one thing. It was quite another to transform an ancient city, with its cramped streets and dingy quarters, into a plan of grand boulevards and spacious parks. This greater challenge – to modernize the city of Paris – was taken up by Baron Georges-Eugène Haussmann (1809–91), inventor of the modern city. Haussmann [(h)OHSS-mahn] was appointed by Emperor Napoleon III (Bonaparte's nephew), who wanted an opulent imperial capital and an efficient

13.11 Louis H. Sullivan, Guaranty Building, Buffalo, New York, 1894–5.
Note how the first two stories create a monumental base, from which the upper stories rise like a fluted column, capped by an emphatic cornice.

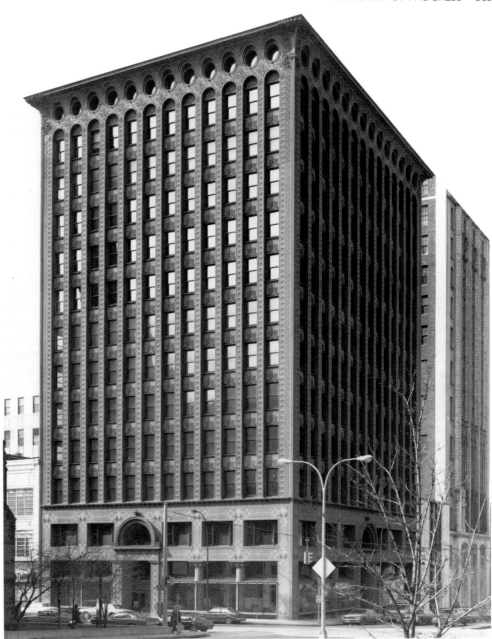

center of modern commerce and industry. The emperor also wanted a seat of government secure from Paris' habitual political uprisings.

To build the straight new boulevards, Haussmann plowed through traditional neighborhoods, demolishing some twelve thousand buildings, including many homes of the poor and working classes. He lined his boulevards with uniform, fashionable apartment buildings and punctuated his streets with broad plazas, where Parisians could stroll and play (Fig. **13.9**). In all, Paris gained some 95 miles (150 km) of new streets and a feeling of spaciousness and regularity. Not surprisingly, Haussmann's Paris was best suited to the city's affluent middle class, who gained fashionable housing, parks for their leisure, and a chance to profit in Haussmann's complicated financial schemes.

Perhaps the most enduring element of the modern city rose out of the North American heartland in the 1880s. Chicago architect Louis Sullivan (1856–1924) responded to the needs of commercial patrons by designing the modern skyscraper – a building of several stories made practical by the invention of the mechanical elevator. Buildings such as Sullivan's Guaranty Building in Buffalo (Fig. **13.11**) were constructed of an interior cage of welded steel beams. This **steel-cage** frame was covered with a windowed, stone façade that expressed the underlying rectangular frame. To soften the sometimes harsh rigidity of this design, Sullivan often added floral decoration in cast iron, borrowing from the highly decorative style called Art Nouveau (see page 372). Sullivan's buildings were "commercial palaces," grand settings for the pursuit of material wealth.

MUSIC AND MODERNITY

Explain Wagner's concept of the "total work of art" as it was realized in his operas.

The centerpiece of Baron Haussmann's modern Paris was the opulent Opéra (completed in 1875). In this luxurious building, fashionable Parisians could enjoy the age's most spectacular musical art. Given opera's popularity at the time, it is not surprising that the industrial age should spawn two geniuses of the art. Giuseppe Verdi [VAIR-dee] was the idol of Italy's opera-loving public, hailed like today's popular-music and sports stars. Richard Wagner [VAHG-ner] envisioned himself as musical high priest of the German nation and his operas as a mythic ritual. Verdi brought to a climax Italy's centuries-long operatic tradition. Wagner blazed a musical path into the twentieth century.

VERDI'S OPERAS

Giuseppe Verdi (1813–1901) rose from humble beginnings to become the national hero of Italian opera. Born to a family of small landowners, he learned music helping play the town organ. His career reached a climax in 1851–3, with the success of three operatic masterpieces: *Rigoletto*, *Il Trovatore*, and *La Traviata*. All three had stories touched by tragedy, and featured dramatically telling songs of luscious beauty. At the height of his fame, Verdi retired to the life of a gentleman farmer, but the world still sought him out. Egypt's ruler commissioned an opera to mark the opening of the Suez Canal, one of the age's great engineering feats. The result, *Aïda* [eye-EE-duh] (1871), was staged in Egypt with a cast of three hundred, a production so bombastic that even Verdi was disgusted.

Though his operas excelled in lyric beauty and dramatic effect, Verdi had not been a great technical innovator. Late in his career, however, he was spurred by two challenges: the musical ideas of his contemporary Richard Wagner, and the chance to set Shakespeare to music. In his last operas, Verdi proved able to match Shake-

13.12 Bayreuth Festspielhaus, Bavaria, Germany, 1876.
Wagner's entire *Der Ring des Nibelungen* (*The Ring of the Nibelung*) was first performed in 1876 at this special festival playhouse in southern Germany. Designed to Wagner's specifications, the playhouse allowed audiences to stroll through the grounds and refresh themselves between acts of sometimes five-hour performances.

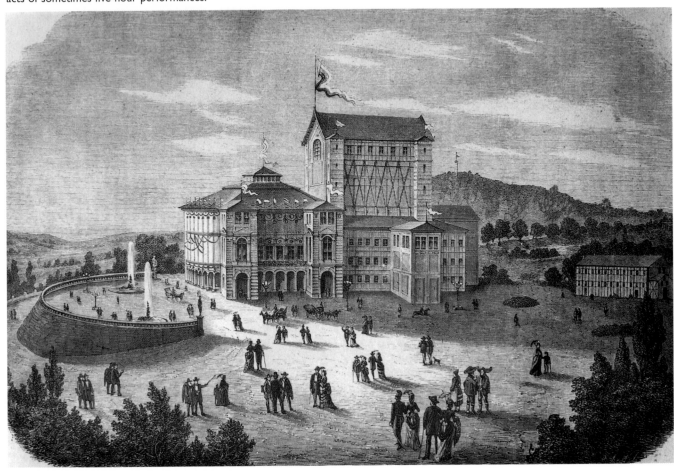

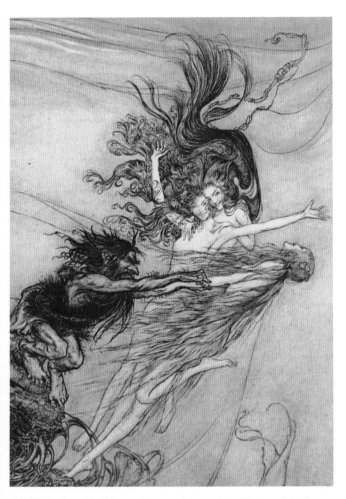

13.13 Arthur Rackham, illustration to _Das Rheingold (The Rhine Gold)_, 1910.
Wagner enjoyed a great vogue among Symbolist poets and artists at the turn of the century. Here the illustrator Arthur Rackham imagines the heated grasping of Alberich (the Nibelung of the cycle's title) at the elusive Rhine maidens; the dwarf's frustration leads him to renounce love altogether and seize the Rhine Gold.

speare's breadth of action and depth of character. In _Otello_ (1887), he dramatized the tragedy of the Moorish general Othello, who is incited to murder his bride by the evil Iago. In _Falstaff_ (1893), Verdi captured the comic vigor of Shakespeare's lusty braggart from _Henry IV_.

Musically, Verdi's Shakespearean operas followed Wagner's lead, advancing beyond the standard opera form of aria alternating with recitative. Verdi experimented with "accompanied recitative," which instead of stopping for a song kept the plot moving forward. The orchestral accompaniment mirrored the characters' moods and emphasized the action, much as today's film sound-tracks. Verdi's scenes of intense emotion were such a rousing success that when _Otello_ premiered at the famous opera house La Scala in Milan, the aging composer had to answer twenty curtain calls. Afterwards, admirers pulled his carriage through the streets in triumph.

Musical scholars still debate whether Verdi was influenced by Wagner's more systematic innovations. Verdi himself refused to be cast as Wagner's rival. He attributed their differences to the differing musical sensibilities of Germany and Italy. He once said to a German conductor: "Everyone ought to keep the characteristics inherent in their nation. Well for you, who are still sons of Bach! And we? We too, sons of Palestrina."

WAGNER'S MUSICAL REVOLUTION

Compared with the humble Verdi, Richard Wagner (1813–83) was a flamboyant artistic egoist whose life had enough passion and betrayal, triumph and failure, to be an opera itself. He blamed his initial musical failures on opera's commercialism and finally convinced a mad Bavarian king to finance his operas at the lavish Festspielhaus (Festival House) at Bayreuth (Fig. **13.12**). Throughout his career, he engaged in titanic love affairs with the wives of patrons and musical colleagues. Late in life, the composer used to receive his fanatical disciples at Bayreuth [BEYE-roit] while dressed in velvet cap and satin gown.

Wagner's musical ideas exceeded even the extravagance of his life. Wagner envisioned opera as the synthesis of all the arts – myth, music, poetry, drama, and pictorial design. He called this concept the _Gesamtkunstwerk_ [ghe-SAHMT-koonst-vairk] (the "total work of art") and compared it to the classical tragedy in ancient Greece. To achieve this all-embracing experience, Wagner believed that he had to control everything about his operas: the text, music, design, and production.

Opera as a _Gesamtkunstwerk_ required stories different from the conventional opera that Wagner despised. The composer turned to Germanic myth and legend, explaining that myth "is true for all time; and its content, no matter how terse or compact, is inexhaustible for every age."[5] Even Wagner's own erotic passions took mythic form. A love affair with a merchant's wife prompted him to write _Tristan and Isolde_ (1859), based on a medieval tale. The hero and heroine unknowingly drink a love potion that unites them in a doomed passion. At the opera's end, Isolde holds her dead lover while singing the famous _Liebestod_ [LEE-buss-toht] (_Love-Death_), in which she succumbs to her yearning for transcendental oneness with Tristan.

**Wagner's Musical Innovations** Wagner's _Tristan and Isolde_ demonstrates the basic elements of Wagner's musical revolution:

- the primary importance of the orchestra over singing
- the _Leitmotif_ as unifying element
- chromatic, or "colored," harmonies.

In Wagner's theory, the orchestra should be the master of the dramatic action, not a mere accompaniment to the singing. The orchestra was able to reflect every feeling and action through his use of the *Leitmotif* ("leading motive"). A *Leitmotif* [LITE-moh-teef] was a distinct melody or melodic fragment associated with a character, object, or idea; when any element appeared in the drama, its *Leitmotif* appeared in the orchestral music. Wagner intertwined his motives in complex developments, so that the motives evolve with the opera's action. In Isolde's *Liebestod*, for example, two motives ("yearning" and "love-death") are unified in a third ("transcendental bliss"), the last chords representing the lovers' blissful union in death.

Wagner's third musical innovation is more technical. Since Bach's era, Western composers had employed the major-minor key system, with its seven-tone scale (*do-re-mi* etc.). Traditional composers occasionally "colored" their music with the five dissonant half-steps in this scale (when playing in the key of C major on the piano, these will be the black keys). In his music, Wagner increasingly used all of these twelve tones, which make up the **chromatic scale** (from *chroma*, meaning "coloring"). Wagner's use of chromaticism gave his music its restless emotionalism and dissolved the boundaries of tonality.

Wagner's musical innovations culminated in his gigantic four-opera masterpiece titled *Der Ring des Nibelungen* (*The Ring of the Nibelung*, 1876). The *Ring* tells how the Nordic gods are corrupted and ultimately destroyed by their own desires, a story that takes some sixteen hours in performance. The mythic scenarios of the *Ring* struck some as far-fetched and tedious. The French composer Claude Debussy exclaimed, "My God! how unbearable these people in skins and helmets become by the fourth night."

Wagner's *Ring* contains some of the operatic tradition's most famous moments. At the opening of *Das Rheingold* (*The Rhine Gold*), the dwarf Alberich chases the elusive river maidens and then barters for the gold that will doom the gods (Fig. **13.13**). In *Siegfried*, the hero tastes the blood of the slain dragon and hears the song of nature. The loping music of the "Ride of the Valkyries" from *Die Walküre* (*The Valkyrie*) has become associated with doom. In the finale of *Götterdämmerung* [guh(r)-ter-DEMM-er-oonk] (*Twilight of the Gods*), the heroine Brünnhilde rides onto her own funeral pyre, while the palace Valhalla collapses in flames. But no list of highlights can do justice to the musical complexity of Wagner's masterpiece or its impact on his own and future generations.

LATE ROMANTIC MUSIC

Where Wagner's music was relentlessly innovative, his principal rival, the late romantic composer Johannes Brahms (1833–97), looked back to the Classical era. Of the titanic Beethoven, Brahms once wrote, "You will never know how the likes of us feel when we hear the tramp of a giant like him behind us." Despite his reservations, Brahms' four

KEY CONCEPT

MODERNITY

Baron Haussmann's urban renewal was guided by the spirit of **modernity**, the process by which the new, up-to-date, and the contemporary replace the outmoded and traditional. In the nineteenth century, modernity swept away the antiquated remnants of traditional existence, what Marx called "the dead weight of the years," and in its place installed the standardized products and routines of modern life. The cities of Paris, Berlin, New York, and Chicago were dynamic metaphors of modernity, with their vibrant industry and busy avenues. Economic modernity usually involved replacing human or animal labor with machines, or inefficient machines with more efficient ones. For example, horse-drawn street cars were replaced by electric cars, and antiquated iron foundries by new open-hearth furnaces. The advance of modernity in the late nineteenth century accomplished a "second industrial revolution," in which first-generation machinery was replaced with more efficient improvements. Even today, "modernizing" an industrial plant or office usually means installing new machinery and uprooting workers from old places or habits.

The critics of modernity ranged from the sentimental to the visionary. To some, modernity was an assault on the human spirit. The French poet Charles Baudelaire reflected on Haussmann's changes to Paris, saying that "old neighborhoods turn to allegory, and memories weigh more than stone." The Russian novelist Fyodor Dostoyevsky (see page 386) was perhaps the most impassioned critic of modernity. He symbolized all of modernity's promises in the "tower of Babel," an emblem of human vanity and self-destruction. In Dostoyevsky's view, modernity would lead ultimately to a cannibalistic mass society (Fig. **13.14**).

The conflict between modernity and tradition is not yet resolved. Today, voices still defend traditional family life or education from modernity's negative effects. Nations hold fiercely to their religious or cultural traditions, while accommodating themselves to a constantly modernizing world. Faced with modernity's ceaseless changes, people still wonder about the human heart.

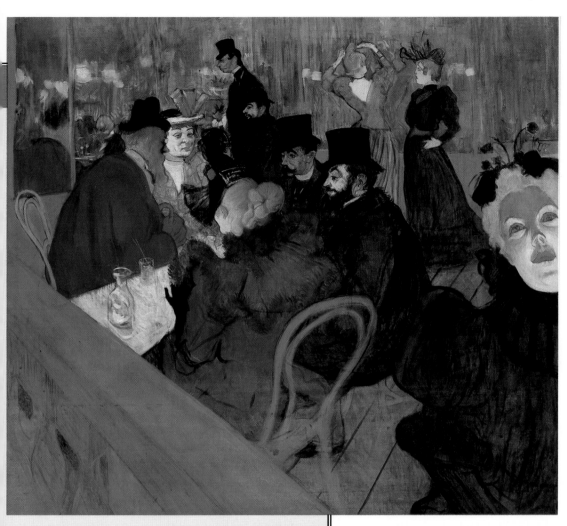

13.14 Henri de Toulouse-Lautrec, *At the Moulin Rouge,*
1892–5. Oil on canvas, 4 ft¹/₂ ins x 4 ft 7³/₈ ins (1.23 x
1.41 m). The Art Institute of Chicago, Helen Birch
Bartlett Memorial Collection, 1928.610.
The garish faces and heated atmosphere in this cabaret scene
imply a spiritual alienation peculiar to modern city life. How
does the framing of the singer at right and the table at lower
left contribute to the claustrophobia of the scene and its
central group?

CRITICAL QUESTION

In what cases does the victory of modernity over
tradition represent genuine progress? In your discussion, consider such areas as medicine, industry,
computers, and urban development. How does one
judge modernity's benefits against the value of
traditional ways of life?

symphonies come closer than any others to matching
the scope and sophisticated design of Beethoven. Brahms
rejected romantic-style program music and all his symphonies (composed between 1876 and 1885) possess the
weighty structure and inspired variations that he admired
in his Classical predecessors. Brahms represents the last
great composer of "absolute" music in the tradition of
Mozart and Beethoven.

Another development of late romantic music was the
rise of musical nationalism, especially among composers

LATER NINETEENTH-CENTURY MUSIC

Giuseppe Verdi	Italian	*La Traviata* (1853); *Aïda* (1871); *Otello* (1887); *Falstaff* (1893)
Richard Wagner	German	*Tristan and Isolde* (1865); *Ring of the Nibelung* (1876); *Parsifal* (1882)
Johannes Brahms	German	Symphony #4 (1885)
Claude Debussy	French	*Prélude à "L'après-midi d'un faune"* (1894)

WINDOW ON DAILY LIFE

A MUSICAL CAREER

Lillian Nordica (1857–1914) was an American-born soprano who succeeded as an opera singer in Europe, performing notable Wagnerian roles at Bayreuth. On her first trip to Europe, her mother describes the hardships that industrial-age women encountered in pursuing a professional career.

It is no child's play to learn an opera. If you think so, listen to five or six hours of digging at Aïda every day, besides two hours [of] French verbs. . . . Lilly has done an immense amount of work in the last four months, taking into account the seventy concerts. Since the twelfth of August she has had forty lessons with Belari in Italian repertory, and the same number or more from Delsarte in dramatic action, besides her French lesson every day.

I take care of everything connected with her dress and wait upon her by inches, because I know that she is doing all she can consistently. She sings most charmingly, and could, if at home, no doubt have all [the engagements] that she could do. But the question now is, study!!! . . .

Lilly commences at nine o'clock every morning a preparatory lesson in acting; at ten a pianist from Belari comes to the house to assist her in learning the notes and Italian of operas; at half past eleven she practices until twelve, then breakfasts; then French for two hours; at three music study; at four acting with Delsarte. So her whole time is occupied. She generally lies on the sofa while studying or reciting French and in that way gets rested. . . .

The truth of the matter is, Lilly can be great, *but she must have time to study without injury to her health, just the same as others have done.*[6]

(1878)

---

from eastern Europe. The *1812 Overture* by the Russian Peter Tchaikovsky [tcheye-KOFF-skee] (1840–93) and *The Moldau* by the Czech Bedrich Smetana [SMET-tun-uh] (1824–84) celebrated the valor of the two composers' peoples and the beauty of their homelands. The musical nationalists typically incorporated native folk music and programmatic musical descriptions into their compositions.

THE LAST ROMANTICS

Explain why the symbolists and like-minded artists rejected the artistic tastes of middle-class society.

Wagner's explorations of inner experience found a deep sympathy among artists in the late nineteenth century. On first glance, these artists appear to be latter-day romantics because of their praise for artistic genius and fascination with evil and the exotic. They also rejected crass materialism and the superficial entertainments preferred by the middle classes. Yet, in withdrawing from modern industrial society, these last romantics anticipated the artis-

tic techniques that defined the artistic modernism of the twentieth century. These included:

- in poetry, the dense and enigmatic works of the symbolists
- in the visual arts, the decorative plant motifs of *Art Nouveau*
- in music, the dreamy compositions of Debussy
- in sculpture, the rugged figures of Rodin.

In their reaction against Western industrial society, the late romantics foreshadowed the coming modern revolution.

SYMBOLISM AND ART FOR ART'S SAKE

The French symbolist poets were a literary group known for their dream-like and deeply symbolic poetic works. The symbolists created a poetic language of rich ambiguities that expressed their intuitive insights and fascination with language. At the same time, they emphatically rejected the moral hypocrisy and greedy materialism of modern civilization. The later symbolists withdrew into a world of mysticism and decadence, mocking the banality of middle-class existence.

The symbolists' acknowledged inspiration was the poet Charles Baudelaire [boh-de-LAIR] (1821–67), whose poetry explored the sensational connections between the sordid and the sublime. Baudelaire's collection *Les Fleurs du Mal* (*The Flowers of Evil*, 1857) was so frankly erotic that Baudelaire was prosecuted on morals charges after its publication. Many Baudelaire poems were morbid in their self-analysis and grotesque imagery. In the prologue to *Les Fleurs du Mal*, entitled "To the Reader," Baudelaire draws the reader into the poet's satanic world of violence and oblivion.

Like a poor profligate who sucks and bites
the withered breast of some well-seasoned trull,
we snatch in passing at clandestine joys
and squeeze the oldest orange harder yet.

Wriggling in our brains like a million worms,
a demon demos holds its revels there,
and when we breathe, the Lethe[a] in our lungs
trickles sighing on its secret course.

If rape and arson, poison and the knife
have not yet stitched their ludicrous designs
on to the banal buckram[b] of our fates,
it is because our souls lack enterprise!

But here among the scorpions and the hounds,
the jackals, apes and vultures, snakes and wolves,
monsters that howl and growl and squeal and crawl,
in all the squalid zoo of vices, one

is even uglier and fouler than the rest,
although the least flamboyant of the lot;
this beast would gladly undermine the earth
and swallow all creation in a yawn;

I speak of Boredom which with ready tears
dreams of hangings as it puffs its pipe.
Reader, you know this squeamish monster well,
– hypocrite reader, – my alias, – my twin![7]

CHARLES BAUDELAIRE
From *Les Fleurs du Mal* (1857)

a. Lethe, the mythic river of forgetfulness; Baudelaire may refer to opium smoking.

b. buckram, a stiff cloth used to line clothing.

Baudelaire became an icon for the symbolist group but where he had praised the busy boulevards and fashions of modern Paris, the symbolists flatly rejected the values of industrial mass society. They saw themselves as an artistic elite, aloof from the petty lives of the middle class. The leading poet of the symbolists, Stephane Mallarmé [MALL-ar-may] (1842–98), said, "Let the masses read works on morality, but for heaven's sake do not give them our poetry to spoil." The symbolists' philosophy also included the principle of *l'art pour l'art* or "art for art's sake," – a slogan coined by the English writer Walter Pater in 1868 – which placed art in a parallel universe to the real world,

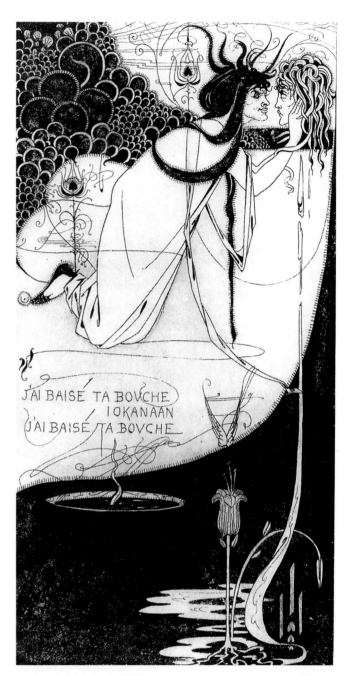

13.15 Aubrey Beardsley, *Salomé,* **1892. Pen drawing, 10⁷/₈ x 5³/₄ ins (27.6 x 14.6 cm).**
In an advertisement for Oscar Wilde's play *Salomé*, Beardsley revels in the erotic evil of the princess who demanded the head of John the Baptist (called in the play Jokanaan) and here addresses it, "I have kissed your lips, Jokanaan."

CRITICAL QUESTION

Do you agree with the symbolists that great art is, by its nature, *un-popular?* Using examples from your experience, discuss the fate of literature, art, and music in a mass society.

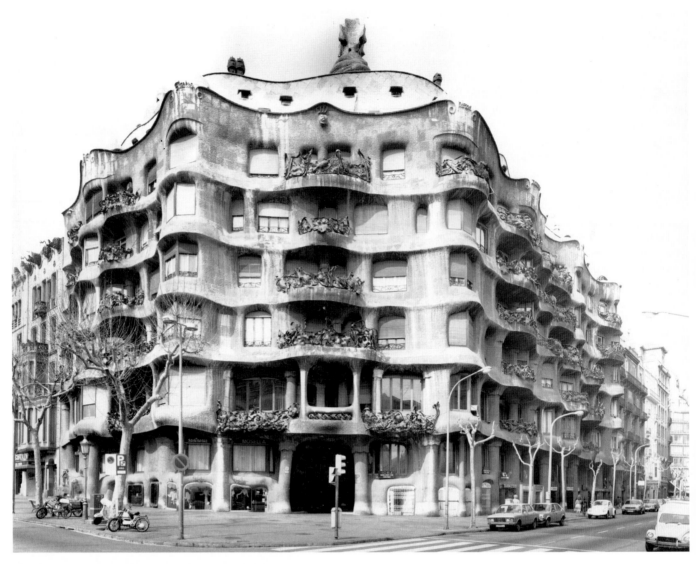

13.16 Antonio Gaudí, Casa Milá, Barcelona, 1905–7.

governed by its own special rules and methods. The symbolist poets polished their works like jewels of language, full of secret symbols and cryptic phrases. Though the doctrine of *l'art pour l'art* was rooted in romantic ideas of artistic genius, it was later sustained by twentieth-century artists who escaped from mass society into a separate universe of art.

Art Nouveau Symbolism's reaction against industrialism was shared by **Art Nouveau** [arr noo-VOH], a style of decorative art and architecture that used floral motifs and stressed the organic unity of artistic materials and form. Art Nouveau's love for sinuous, vegetal forms can be seen in the illustrations of Aubrey Beardsley (Fig. **13.15**), which often achieved a sinister combination of eroticism and evil. A favorite Art Nouveau medium was colored glass: the workshops of American Louis Tiffany, for example, produced popular glassware, lamps, and furniture in floral design.

In architecture, Art Nouveau was largely a decorative style applied to the surface of otherwise conventional buildings. The style's originator, Belgian Victor Horta (1861–1947), typically employed Art Nouveau motifs in wrought iron details, wall decoration, and floor tiles. The one architect who integrated Art Nouveau principles into a building's form was the Catalan Antonio Gaudí y Cornet (1852–1926). Built over a modern steel frame, the walls of Gaudí's [gow-DEE] Casa Milá apartment building in Barcelona (Fig. **13.16**) undulate like the gently rocking ocean waves. The wrought-iron balcony railings writhe like seaweed or sea creatures. Gaudí's buildings were the most ambitious example of Art Nouveau's attempt to unify the work of art in one organic piece. Whatever it was called – in Spain *Modernismo*, in Germany *Jugendstil*, in Vienna the *Sezession* – Art Nouveau reached back to romantic organicism while pushing forward to modernity.

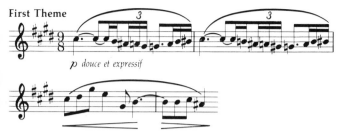

13.17 Claude Debussy, opening theme of *Prélude à "l'après-midi d'un faune"* (*Prelude to the Afternoon of a Faun*), 1894.

DEBUSSY'S MUSICAL IMPRESSIONS

The musician closest to the symbolist group was French composer Claude Debussy (1862–1918), whose works explored new harmonic relationships and exotic tone colors. Debussy [deh-BYOO-see] was affected by two musi-

cal influences: Wagner's operas, heard on a visit to Wagner's Bayreuth playhouse, and the gamelan [GAMM-uh-lan] orchestras of Java (part of today's Indonesia), which toured Paris in the 1880s. The Javanese **gamelan orchestra** consisted of various gongs, chime-bars, and a solo string instrument called the *rebab*, producing a rich blend of tone colors and playing in harmonic modes rather than Western keys. Drawing on these musical influences, Debussy's compositions evoke dream-like moods and suggestive impressions, much like the symbolists' poetic images. Even Debussy's titles – *Clouds, Waves at Play, Reflections on the Water* – suggested poetic reverie.

Debussy's most famous work was inspired by a Mallarmé poem about a satyr and wood nymphs. The *Prélude à "L'après-midi d'un faune"* (*Prelude to "The Afternoon of a Satyr"*, 1894) was the musical equivalent of an idle erotic daydream. The opening flute sounds a musical theme that dreamily dissolves into another musical idea (Fig. **13.17**). The vagueness derives in part from Debussy's use of a

13.18 Auguste Rodin, *The Gates of Hell*, begun 1880. Bronze (cast from plaster model), height 20 ft 8 ins (6.3 m), width 13 ft 1 ins (3.99 m). Philadelphia Museum of Art, Gift of Jules E. Mastbaum.

Rodin's masterpiece contained in its last (though not necessarily finished) version some 186 figures, including the famous *Thinker*, the pensive genius who broods over the tortured products of his imagination. Compare the roiling figures of Rodin's *Gates* to the Renaissance clarity of Ghiberti's *Gates of Paradise* in Florence (Fig 8.10).

13.19 Auguste Rodin, *The Three Shades*, 1880. Bronze, height 3 ft 2 ins x 3 ft x 1 ft 9¼ ins (96.6 x 92 x 54.1 cm). Musée Rodin, Paris, S1191.
As he did with many figures from *The Gates of Hell*, Rodin detached this group from the top of the door's lintel and enlarged it into a life-size sculpture.

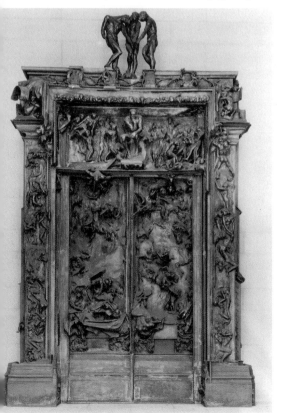

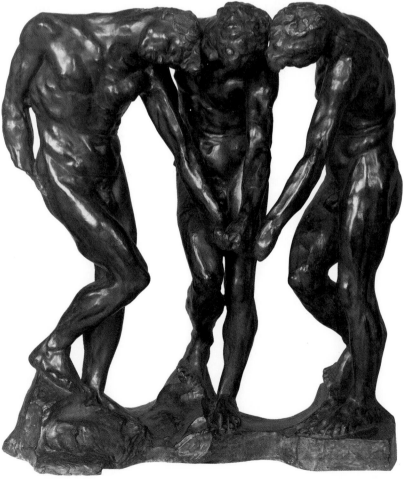

whole-tone scale, the six whole tones of a normal scale without the half-steps. The whole-tone scale sounds unstable to anyone more accustomed to conventional Western major and minor scales, and creates a musical fuzziness akin to the impressionist style of painting.

While discarding conventional harmony, Debussy also rejected the formal structures of the baroque and Classical traditions. In contrast to the forward-moving structures of Brahms, Debussy's compositions were comparatively static, full of languid moods and harmonic nuances. This was music wafting into the twentieth century like a nymph's song.

RODIN

Where Debussy rejected the rational structure of German music, the French sculptor Auguste Rodin (1840–1917) broke with the heroic style of commemorative public sculpture represented by Auguste Bartholdi's *Statue of Liberty*, a gift of the French government to the United States in honor of the American centennial. By exploring a new mode of figural sculpture, Rodin [roh-DAN(h)] established himself as the precursor of modern sculpture but also

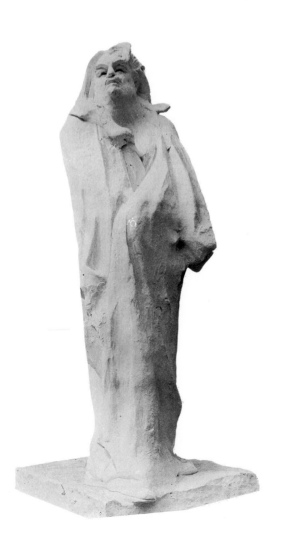

exposed himself to ridicule and scorn. An uncomprehending public hooted at his rough figures, much as earlier generations had scoffed at the innovations of Delacroix and Turner.

In 1877, Rodin was engaged to sculpt a decorative portal for a Paris museum. He modeled the portal loosely after Ghiberti's *Gates of Paradise* in Florence (see Fig. 8.10). However, Rodin conceived his portal as *The Gates of Hell* (Fig. **13.18**), intending to depict the tortured souls of Dante's *Inferno* (see page 184). *The Gates of Hell* soon took on a life of its own, as Rodin worked intensely for eight years, furiously adding and subtracting figures, and generating sculptural ideas that he later turned into separate life-size figures. When *The Gates of Hell* (in plaster model) was exhibited in 1900, the two massive panels seethed with dozens of tortured figures. Above the door lurks the now-familiar form of *The Thinker*, originally conceived as the poet Dante brooding over his creation. Below him are figures seared by the hot pangs of unfulfilled desires and above are the so-called *Three Shades* (Fig. **13.19**). The whole work is an essay on the vanity of human hope and the tortures of guilt. In the end, Rodin's figures seemed drawn more from a symbolist hell than from Dante's.

Rodin's most controversial work was a statue of the French novelist Honoré de Balzac [ball-ZAHK], who had died thirty years before the commission. The sculpture became an object lesson in modern art's testy relations with its tradition-bound public. To grasp his subject, Rodin had a suit made by Balzac's old tailor, found some lost photographs, and finally made seven life-size studies in his studio. Atop the striding figure, a massive lion-like head suggested the immense appetites and prolific energy of the great novelist.

Rodin's *Honoré de Balzac* (Fig. **13.20**) appalled the public, and was rejected by the literary society that had commissioned it. Critics condemned it as an insult to France and compared it (with some accuracy) to a heathen god – an effect that Rodin was striving for. Despite the criticisms, Rodin insisted that the statue was a "pivot" of his aesthetic. He wrote, "I had forged a link between the great, lost traditions of the past and my own time which each day will strengthen." In other words, the connection of *Balzac* to the great bronzes of ancient Greece was perceptible to the artist's inner sense, though not immediately visible to the viewing public. With Rodin, as with other late romantics, art was becoming an increasingly private and subjective affair, not to be shared with society at large.

13.20 Auguste Rodin, *Honoré de Balzac*, 1892–7. Plaster, height 9 ft 10 ins (3 m). Musée Rodin, Paris, S163.
Even to the sophisticated members of the literary society that commissioned it, Rodin's portrait of the novelist Balzac was too bold. This statue, like most of Rodin's works, was modeled in plaster and afterwards cast in bronze.

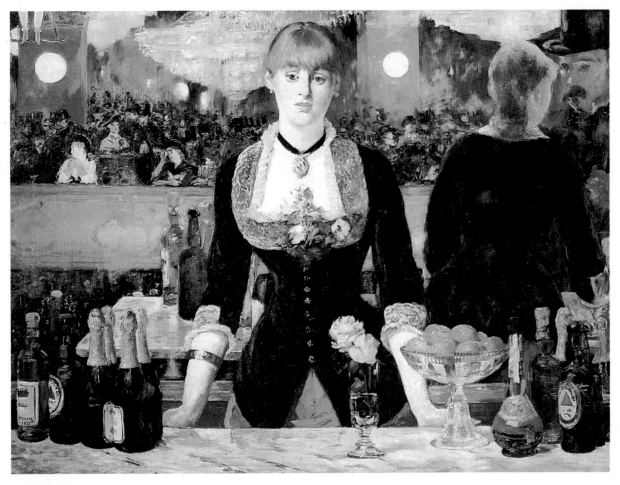

13.21 Edouard Manet, *The Bar at the Folies-Bergère*, 1881–2. Oil on canvas, 37¹/₂ x 51 ins (95 x 130 cm). Courtauld Institute Galleries, London.
A barmaid stands before a great mirror reflecting the customer who addresses her and a balcony full of gaily dressed theatergoers enjoying a circus performance. Analyze the relation between the background image (influenced by impressionist technique) and the solid shapes of the barmaid, bottles, and fruit.

IMPRESSIONISM AND BEYOND

Summarize the principal characteristics of the impressionist and post-impressionist styles in painting.

In the 1860s, painting was still largely governed by history paintings in a neoclassical style. However, a few artists were determined to paint modern life as they saw it. Their subjects were the dynamic streets and anonymous citizens of modern Paris. Adopting the pose of the detached observer, these artists painted their impressions of the moment: the glistening steam of a locomotive, the oblique angle of a dancer's leg, the bold outline of a champagne bottle on a marble bar.

These first painters of modernity were called the **impressionists**, and in the 1870s they defined new techniques of light, color, and visual form. Unlike the symbolist poets,

the impressionists delighted in the life of the café and boulevard. They captured on their canvases the pulsing energies and sudden changes of the modern city. Manet's painting *The Bar at the Folies-Bergère* (Fig. **13.21**), for example, shows the riotous gaiety of a café scene, contrasting with the emotional detachment of the barmaid, who has succumbed to dreamy boredom. The impressionists' innovations and modern subjects laid the foundation of modernist painting.

MANET: PRELUDE TO IMPRESSIONISM

The impressionist style grew directly from the roots of realism. A generation earlier, Courbet had scandalized the art world by simply "painting what he saw." In the 1860s, a controversial painter stepped from Courbet's shadow and boldly presented his views of modern life. Edouard Manet (1832–83) was more interested in vivid contrasts of light and color than in sympathetic portrayals of ordinary subjects. Manet demonstrated his daring modernity in *Le*

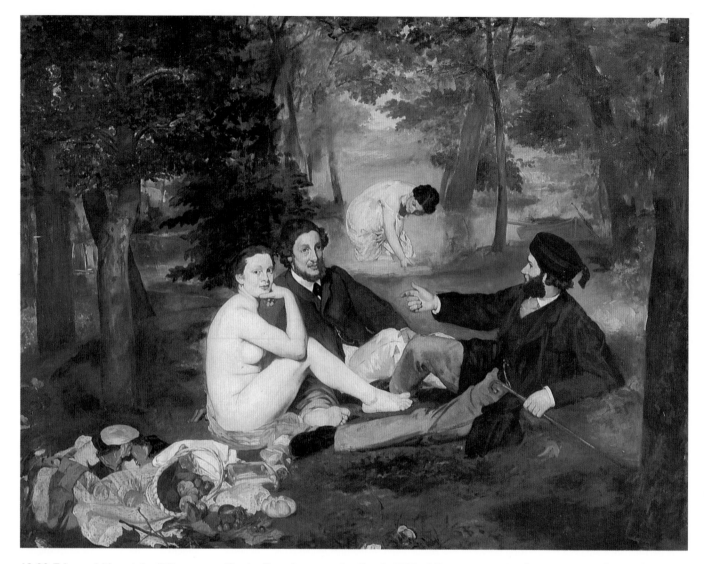

13.22 Edouard Manet, Le Déjeuner sur l'herbe (Luncheon on the Grass), 1863. Oil on canvas, 7 ft ³/₄ ins x 8 ft 10³/₄ ins (2.15 x 2.71 m). Musée d'Orsay, Paris.
Manet's painting was as outrageous in its subject (the frank nudity of the woman next to her clothed companions), as in its style (the flat, unmodeled form of the woman against the dark coats). What is the effect of the nude's bold gaze at the viewer and the woman at rear wading in the Seine?

Déjeuner sur l'Herbe (*Luncheon on the Grass*; Fig. **13.22**). The *Déjeuner* [DAY-zhuh-nay] roused greater official outrage in 1863 than Courbet's *Burial at Ornans* had done fifteen years earlier. The picture shows a party of Parisian picknickers – a nude woman sitting between her dandified male companions. The Paris critics were shocked by the vivid juxtaposition of nude female and clothed men in a contemporary setting. Even more, they protested Manet's style of painting the nude form, which was not modeled according to the academic tradition. Instead, Manet painted the woman in a flat, chalky white, contrasting pale flesh with dark eyes that gazed boldly at the viewer.

Manet painted the *Déjeuner* with a sly self-consciousness of art history, knowing that his subject resembled a well-known Renaissance picture hanging in the Louvre. While the public accepted nudity in the traditional masterpiece,

they rejected Manet's modernized version because he violated painterly tradition.

MONET AND THE IMPRESSIONISTS

In the early 1870s, Manet encouraged a group of younger artists led by the painter Claude Monet (1840–1926). Finding their work rejected by the official Salon, this group mounted their own exhibition in 1874. Labelled impressionists by a derisive critic, who took the name from Monet's painting of a harbor called *Impression: Sunrise* (Fig. **13.23**), this group formed a loose circle and exhibited their works together for about a decade. They included Monet, Pierre Auguste Renoir, Edgar Degas, Camille Pissarro, and the American expatriate Mary Cassatt. Together the impressionists shocked the traditional art world with their

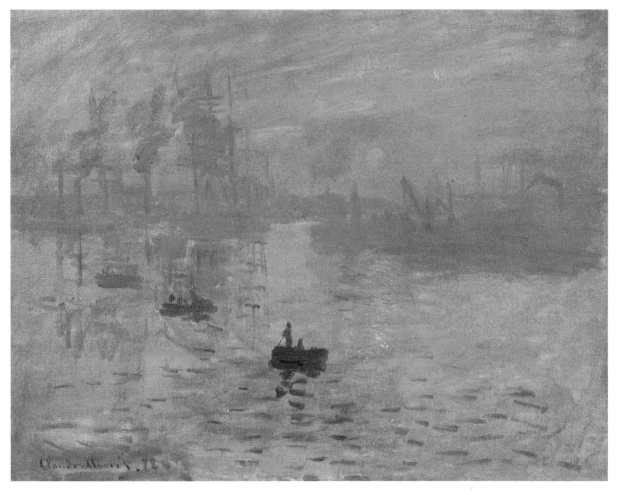

13.23 Claude Monet, *Impression: Sunrise*, 1872. Oil on canvas, 19¹/₂ x 24¹/₂ ins (49.5 x 62 cm). Formerly Musée Marmottan, Paris.
Note the use of broad, sketchy brushstrokes to suggest the ghostly ships at rear and the Japanese-like diagonal of the foreground boats.

13.24 Claude Monet, *St. Lazare Station*, 1877. Oil on canvas, 29¹/₂ x 41 ins (75.5 x 104 cm). Musée d'Orsay, Paris.
Compare the transforming effect of the sunlit steam on this modern city scene to J. M. W. Turner's country landscape in *Rain, Steam, and Speed* (Fig. 12.18).

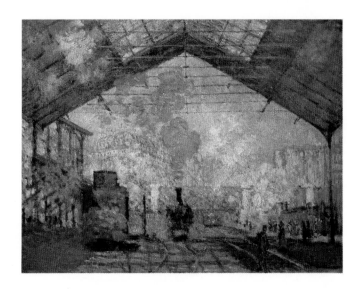

GLOBAL PERSPECTIVE

THE JAPANESE COLOR PRINT

The Paris of the impressionists was awash in a great wave of Japanese art, especially the inexpensive color prints called *ukiyo-e* [OO-kee-yoh-AY] – "scenes of the floating world." The "floating world" referred to the pleasure districts of Japan's commercial cities in the Edo period (1616–1868; see page 316). The principal visual art of this milieu was the multi-color (or **poly-chrome**) wood-block print, usually depicting scenes of everyday life. The early *ukiyo-e* printmakers excelled in portraits of gracious courtesans and actors from the kabuki theater. The master Kitagawa Utamaro (*c.* 1753–1806) portrayed geisha entertainers with a wistful delicacy that has been compared to the French rococo painter Antoine Watteau. *Ukiyo-e* prints were immensely popular in Japan and also inexpensive, selling usually in series or bound in books.

The polychrome print enjoyed a late flowering in the nineteenth-century works of Katsushika Hokusai [HOHKS-eye] and Ando Hiroshige [hee-ruh-SHEE-gay]. In 1822, Hokusai produced his famous *Thirty-six Views of Mount Fuji*, portraying Japan's famous mountain in various aspects – transformed by rain, set against blossoming trees or a tossing sea (Fig. **13.25**). Hokusai's younger rival, Hiroshige, created a competing series entitled *Fifty-three Stations of the Tokaido*, which depicted life on the busy road from Edo to Kyoto.

The Japanese aesthetic expressed in these prints exercised an immense influence on the impressionist and post-impressionist Europeans. In the prints of Hokusai and Hiroshige, especially, we find the techniques that helped revolutionize European painting: dramatic settings, the tension between foreground and background, high and low points-of-view, and decorative fields of solid color.

13.25 Katsushika Hokusai, *The Great Wave off Kanazawa*, from the *36 Views of Mount Fuji*, 1823–9. Polychrome woodblock print, 10 x 14 ins (25.5 x 37.5 cm). Victoria & Albert Museum, London.
In this famous print, Hokusai contrasts the heaving waves against the quiet stability of Mt. Fuji in the background. What statement does this image make about the place of humans in the natural world?

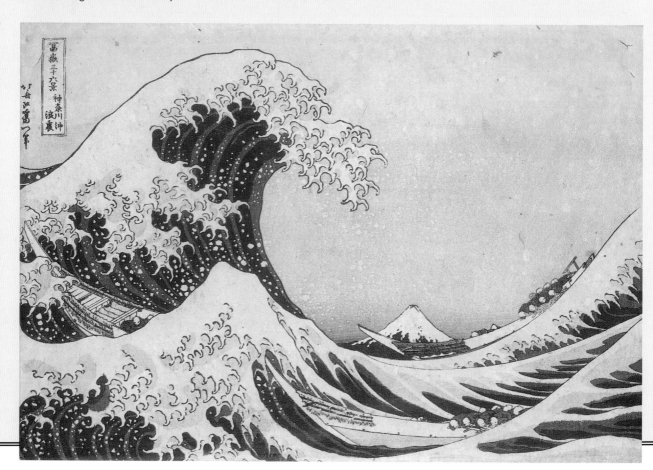

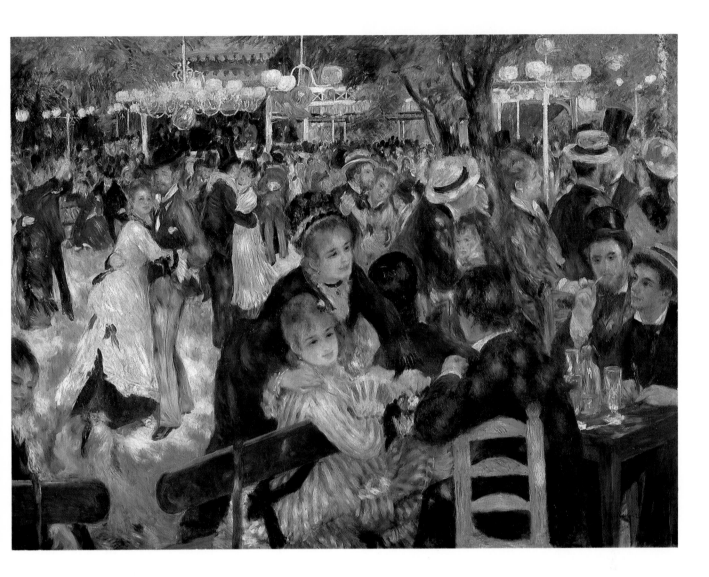

13.26 Pierre-Auguste Renoir, *Le Moulin de la Galette*, 1876. Oil on canvas, 4 ft 3¹/₂ ins x 5 ft 9 ins (1.31 x 1.75 m). Musée d'Orsay, Paris.
In this painting of ordinary city-dwellers at their leisure, Renoir used the full range of impressionist colors, dominated by the yellow of the straw hats and the chairback on the right.

daring use of light and color, their spontaneity of technique, their almost scientific detachment, and their innovations in design.

The "pure" impressionist style of Monet and Renoir sought to capture the fleeting effects of light and color with rapid, sketchy brush strokes. Monet [moh-NAY] disregarded the pompous subjects of academic painting. Taking his canvases outside into the "open air," he sought to capture the shifting light of the suburban landscape and the ceaseless motion of the boulevard. Monet applied colors directly to the canvas without mixing them on his palette. The canvas was painted with small strokes of bright color, so that when one looked closely, the painting consisted of daubs of color. At a longer range the colors formed an image – Rouen Cathedral, grain stacks near Monet's home in Giverny, or water lilies. The results were pictures of vibrant, shimmering color that carried no evident psychological or intellectual values. Monet's moral and emotional flatness puzzled critics as much as his crude, unfinished style. Here was an artist who wished, like a photographer, only to capture the moment of vision.

Yet he endeavored, like the artist, to make the moment last forever.

Monet applied his method to painting the St. Lazare railroad station in Paris. The railroad was a symbol of material progress, while urban rail stations were temples of modernity. Yet Monet seemed chiefly interested in the changes of light and color beneath St. Lazare's glass roof. The station's image became for him like a Wagnerian musical motif, transforming itself in different moods and times of day. In Fig. **13.24**, the locomotive is nearly obscured by steam, the anonymous figures linger on the platform, and a modern apartment building rises in the background.

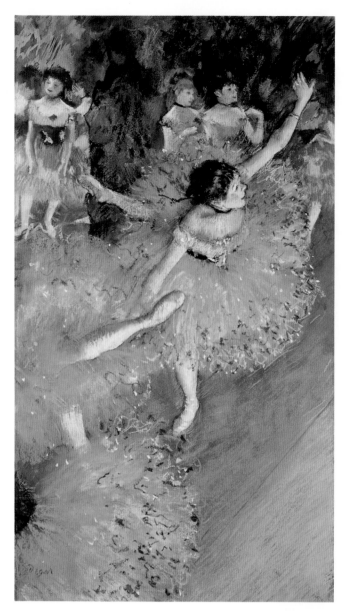

The impressionist paintings of Pierre Auguste Renoir (1841–1919) were more lyrical than Monet's, less bound to the empirical facts of perception. Renoir [ren-WAH(r)] captured the informal mood of city life in his café scene *Le Moulin de la Galette* (Fig. **13.26**). In the open-air dance hall, young working women enjoy their day off, dancing rather gracelessly with male companions. Sunlight falls in a dappled pattern across the foreground group. Typical of impressionist composition, Renoir has created an accidental pattern of yellow straw hats and a variation in the prints of the women's cheap dresses. The whole scene can be taken as a modern and unpretentious version of the rococo *fête galante* (see Fig. 11.9).

The works of Edgar Degas (1834–1917), socially the most conservative of the impressionists, have an undertone of alienation and spiritual exhaustion. In style and subject, Degas [duh-GAH] was close to the realists. But the arbitrary framing of his subjects made his paintings as disconcerting as Monet's sketchiness. Typically he created off-center compositions, such as *The Dancer in Green* (Fig. **13.27**), whose figures seem to be anonymous robots of the ballet. Degas plots the foreground figures along a sharp diagonal, outlined by the central dancer's arms. The perspective nearly tilts the dancer into our laps, and two other figures appear only as torsos and legs. This painting uses devices that were characteristic of Japanese prints – an off-center composition, with objects placed along a receding diagonal or cut off by the picture's edge. Such techniques gave Degas' colorful scenes a disorientating tension.

Degas was close friends with the American expatriate painter Mary Cassatt (1844–1926), who joined the impressionists and exhibited in their 1879 group exhibition. Like

13.27 Above **Edgar Degas, *The Dancer in Green*, c. 1879. Pastel. Thyssen-Bornemisza Collection, Lugano.**
The figures in Degas' paintings of commonplace subjects are off-center and the whole composition unbalanced in a vaguely disturbing way. Thus Degas communicated something of the nervous disorientation of modern life.

13.28 Right **Mary Cassatt, *The Boating Party*, 1893–4. Oil on canvas, 35¹/₂ x 46¹/₄ ins (90 x 117 cm). National Gallery of Art, Washington, D.C., Chester Dale Collection.**
This is one of many Cassatt paintings focussed on the intimacy between a mother and child. Note how the rower's arm and oar form a flattened pyramid with its apex at the child.

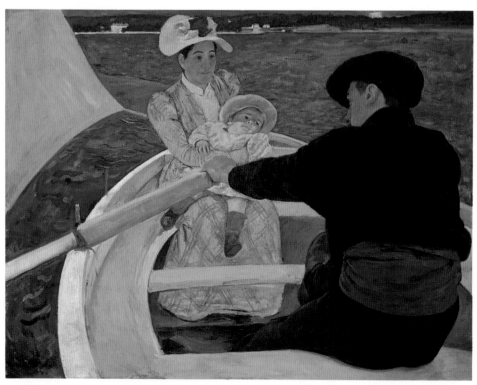

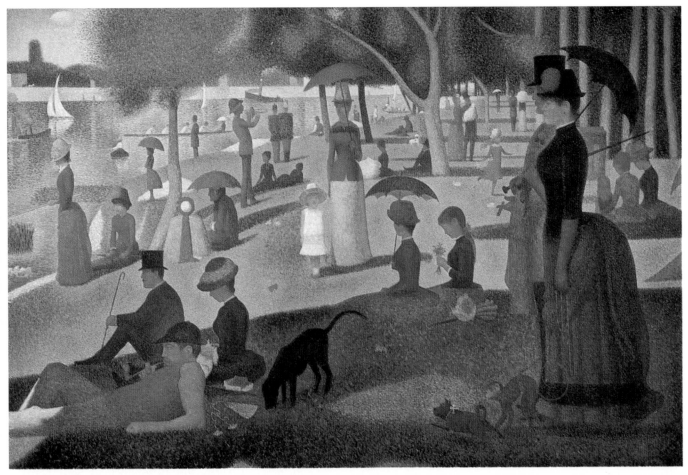

13.29 Georges Seurat, *Sunday Afternoon on the Island of La Grande Jatte*, 1884–6. Oil on canvas, 6 ft 9¹/₂ ins x 10 ft ³/₄ ins (2.07 x 3.05 m). Art Institute of Chicago, Helen Birch Bartlett Memorial Collection, 1926.224.
Consider the several shapes that Seurat repeats throughout this scene. Does this formal rhythm create a mood of unity and tranquillity among these city-dwellers enjoying their leisure? Or is the mood better described as the anonymity and self-absorption of life in the modern city?

most of the group, Cassatt was influenced by the popularity in Paris of Japanese art. She was especially attracted to the large areas of unbroken color and the flattened perspective of Japanese prints. In *The Boating Party* (Fig. **13.28**), the mother and child in the bow of the boat are framed against a brilliant field of blue water. The boat and sail, together with the rower's dark form, provide contrasts that are interesting in themselves. By the time of this painting (1893–4), Cassatt was pursuing a path toward greater abstraction. Color and form were gaining an intrinsic value, quite apart from the subject depicted.

POST-IMPRESSIONISM: SEURAT AND CÉZANNE

In the 1880s and '90s, several important artists intensified the impressionists' break with tradition. These artists are now termed **post-impressionists** because their works extended impressionist techniques in different directions. The most important post-impressionists are Georges Seu-

rat, Paul Cézanne, Paul Gauguin, and Vincent van Gogh. Each represented a step, in form or style, away from impressionism toward modernist painting.

Of the post-impressionists, Georges Seurat [surr-AHH] (1859–91) was the closest in technique to Monet's pure impressionism, depicting scenes of urban life and applying unmixed colors directly to the canvas. However, Seurat reacted against the improvisation and informality of the impressionist style. Where Monet had dashed his brush across the canvas, Seurat applied paint in tiny, meticulous dots, a method he called **pointillism**. With his pointillist technique, Seurat claimed he could scientifically control the mood of a painting. This careful calculation resulted in pictures that were cousins to impressionism but more formal and distant in their effect.

Seurat's most famous picture, *Sunday Afternoon on the Island of La Grande Jatte* (Fig. **13.29**), illustrates the complex formality of the pointillist style. The subject, a typical scene of Parisian modernity, shows Sunday afternoon strollers on an island park. Had an impressionist painted this scene, we might have expected the casual manner of Renoir's *Le*

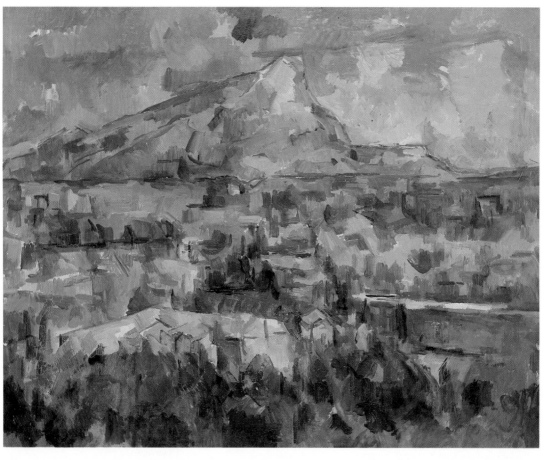

13.30 Paul Cézanne, *Mont Sainte-Victoire from Les Lauves,* **1902–4. Oil on canvas, 27¹/₂ x 35¹/₄ ins (70 x 89.5 cm). Philadelphia Museum of Art, George W. Elkins Collection.**
Cézanne's paintings of nature are as fresh and immediate as those of the impressionists; yet he also sought the solid, enduring structures beneath the surface of nature. The painter said of the neoclassical painter Nicolas Poussin: "I want to do Poussin over again, after nature."

13.31 Below Paul Cézanne, *Apples and Oranges,* **1895–1900. Oil on canvas, 29 x 36³/₄ ins (74 x 93 cm). Musée d'Orsay, Paris.**
Compare Cézanne's carefully defined shapes and complex composition to the orderliness of Chardin's commonplace scenes (Fig. 11.16).

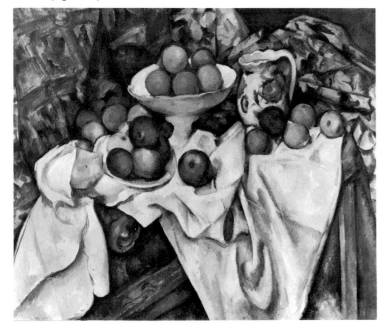

Moulin de la Galette (see Fig. 13.26). Instead, Seurat creates a subtle pattern of parallel lines and interlocking shapes. The pattern is created in the repeated shapes of the umbrellas, the ladies' bustles and bodices, and the gentlemen's hats and canes. Each figure is treated with scientific dispassion and precision, flattened and contained by Seurat's formulas. What might be a scene of gaiety instead communicates something of the psychic alienation and social divisions of modern city life.

Under the same influences, many have said Paul Cézanne (1839–1906) made a great new beginning – the beginning of modernist art. Cézanne [say-ZAHN] wanted to "make of impressionism something solid and durable like the art of the museums." That is, he wanted to find in impressionist subjects the enduring forms of nature that were the basis of traditional art. Like his impressionist contemporaries, Cézanne painted directly from nature in brilliant colors, especially greens, blues, and yellows. But in his landscapes, he sought more than transient effects of light and color. Cézanne studied the permanent structure of natural forms, once advising a young painter to "treat nature through the cylinder, the sphere, the cone."

Cézanne's style as a painter matured when he abandoned Paris in the 1880s and returned to his native southern France. There he frequently painted outdoors in the warm Mediterranean light, striving to capture nature's immediacy while also exploring its essence. Dozens of times he painted Mont Sainte-Victoire, a low peak near his home town (Fig. **13.30**). In Cézanne's paintings, the mountain is an enduringly solid arrangement of masses and planes, a monumental puzzle of nature's forms. While Monet could not paint fast enough to be true to his subject, Cézanne let the fruit rot on the plate while he studied his still-life models (Fig. **13.31**).

The impact of Cézanne's vision on other painters has been compared to Giotto's re-invention of painting in the fourteenth century (see page 188). Giotto's innovations in visual realism set the stage for the Renaissance masters and a five-hundred-year phase of art that followed. In the view of some critics, Cézanne brought that long phase of painting to an end. His works prepared for a new painting of abstraction and formal purity.

TOWARD EXPRESSIONISM: GAUGUIN AND VAN GOGH

Two other painters, Paul Gauguin and Vincent van Gogh, used impressionist techniques to achieve a more intense visual expressiveness. There were parallels in their careers as well as their styles. Gauguin abandoned his career as a bank clerk and family man to pursue the impoverished life of the bohemian artist; van Gogh took up painting after proving too unstable to hold any other job. When the two lived together briefly in the provincial town of Arles in southern France, their quarreling resulted in van Gogh's famous mutilation of his own ear. In life, their feelings were never far from the surface; in painting, they achieved emotional power through bold design and intense color.

Paul Gauguin (1848–1903; Fig. **13.32**) sought to express the elemental forces of human feeling, to enter through his painting "the mysterious center of thought." Gauguin [go-GAN(h)] was drawn to the primitive beliefs and customs of the French provincial countryside of Brittany, in north-west France, where he found a "wildness and primitiveness" among the peasants and in the landscape. In 1891, he withdrew even further from conventional society, going to live in the South Pacific islands and taking a Polynesian wife. In Polynesia, Gauguin satisfied his love of exoticism and his desire to find the primitive core of human imagination.

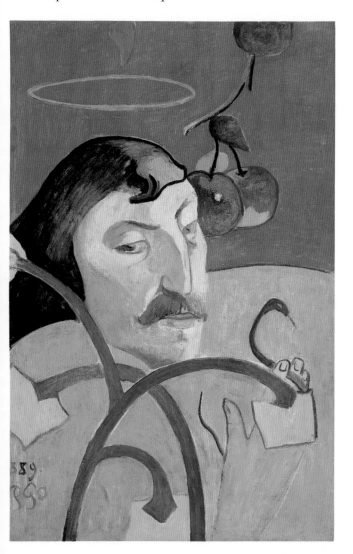

13.32 Paul Gauguin, *Self-Portrait with Halo*, 1889. Oil on wood, 31³/₈ x 20³/₈ ins (79.6 x 51.7 cm). National Gallery of Art, Washington, D.C., Chester Dale Collection, 1962. Amid the hardship of his artist's career, Gauguin saw himself as a misunderstood genius. In a letter to a fellow artist, he wrote: "What does it matter to me if I'm setting myself apart from the rest, for the masses I'll be an enigma, for a few I'll be a poet, and sooner or later quality finds its true place."

Gauguin resembled the romantics in his search for the exotic and picturesque, but his style as a painter was something the romantics could hardly have imagined. He used unnatural colors, heavily drawn boundaries, and flattened shapes to achieve a consciously symbolic visual style. In *The Vision after the Sermon* (*Jacob Wrestling with the Angel*) (Fig. **13.33**), superstitious Breton peasant women imagine Jacob's struggle with the angel of God (Genesis 32). The picture's sense of unreality derives from the bright field of red and the cow wandering across the boundary, formed by the trunk of a tree, between the women and their vision. As with his later pictures of Tahitian subjects, Gauguin simplified and stylized shapes and chose colors according to the dictates of his artistic imagination. With these techniques, Gauguin created an aura of mysticism and a highly decorative visual style.

The Dutchman Vincent van Gogh (1853–90) was also drawn to the countryside and peasant life. Instead of Gauguin's rather self-conscious primitivism, however, van Gogh [van GOH] was motivated by a religious sympathy for the peasants' harsh existence. In his realist early pictures, he painted dark and crudely powerful images of the rural poor. When he came to Paris in 1886, however, his painting career took a remarkable and fateful turn. The Dutchman was struck by the intoxicating energy of the modern city and the bright hues of impressionist paintings. Color became such an extension of feeling that, as he said of one painting, he could "express the terrible passions of humanity by means of red and green."

In his *Starry Night* (Fig. **13.34**) van Gogh expresses the terrible forces of the cosmos by means of blue and yellow. The painting's swirling lines generate a palpable, almost

13.33 Paul Gauguin, *The Vision after the Sermon (Jacob Wrestling with the Angel)*, 1888. Oil on canvas, 28³/₄ x 36³/₄ ins (73 x 92 cm). National Galleries of Scotland, Edinburgh.
Gauguin employs powerful visual elements to communicate the vision of these Breton women: the white caps of their folk dress are set off against the field of mystical red color. How does the diagonal line of the tree trunk serve to define the picture's two main sections?

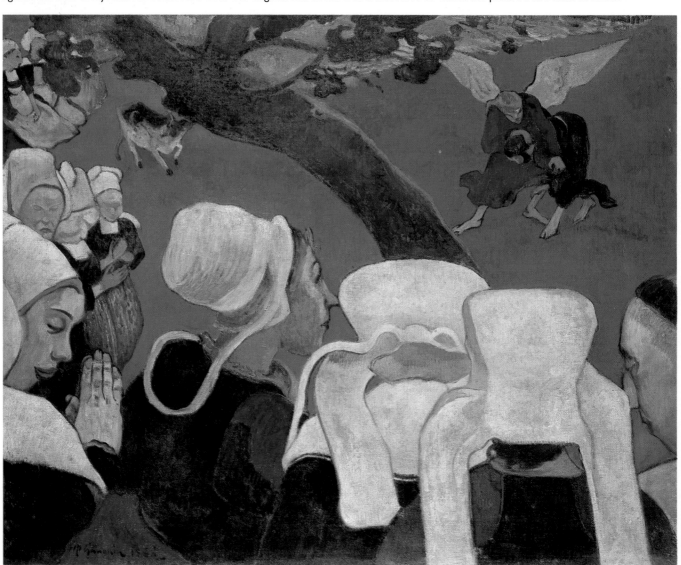

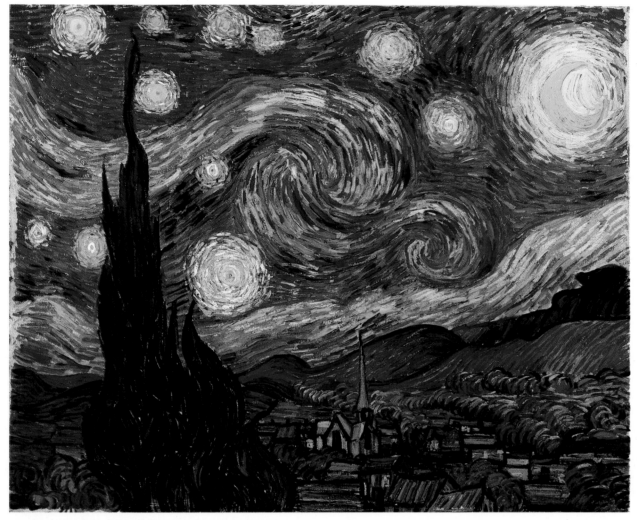

13.34 Vincent van Gogh, *Starry Night,* **1889. Oil on canvas, 29 x 36¹/₄ ins (74 x 92 cm). Collection, The Museum of Modern Art, New York, acquired through the Lillie P. Bliss Bequest.**
With your finger, trace the swirling lines of the sky across the scene, then down to the tranquil village below, and over to the cypress trees at left. What might this composition say symbolically about the relation of humans to the cosmos?

violent energy. The pulsating life of the skies, released in vivid yellows, overwhelms the quiet innocence of the village and countryside below. Although the work may seem a spontaneous expression of emotion, van Gogh's sketches show the painter's careful plan for the picture's formal elements. He applied the paint thickly, often with a palette knife, creating a bold design that was influenced by his love of Japanese art.

Inevitably, we associate van Gogh's paintings with his unhappy life. Yet, some of his most brilliant, joyous canvases were painted in his last year, before depression finally led him to suicide. In a letter to his art-dealer brother, the dying van Gogh despaired whether the modern world could recognize what he and the post-impressionists had defined as modern art.

THE DARK SIDE OF PROGRESS

Summarize the criticisms made by Ibsen and Dostoyevsky of Western industrial society.

The astounding material progress of the industrial age exacted an awful toll of suffering in mines and factories. While Western nations prospered through global trade and technological inventions, these same forces brought colonial oppression to Asia and Africa. Western civilization's dedication to wealth, science, and progress had unleashed immense powers of change. But some feared that progress had been purchased with spiritual impoverishment.

In the last decades of the nineteenth century, a handful of thinkers explored the darker side of the materialist spirit. The dramatists Chekhov and Ibsen explored beyond the formal limits of realism, into the realms of psychology and symbolism. The novelist Dostoyevsky [doss-stoy-EFF-skee] unraveled the conflicts between belief and doubt, while the philosopher Nietzsche [NEETS-shuh] embraced the egoism of the industrial age, preaching that an elite race of supermen would rule mass society.

THE REALIST THEATER

By 1870, theaters throughout Europe were recovering from a decline suffered during the romantic era. This recovery was based in part on the success of plays in the realist mode. Realist plays were usually written in prose, with plots contrived according to strict rules of plausibility. Such "well-made plays," as they were called, absorbed the audience in a compellingly logical plot. Stage directions and sets were carefully defined, and the use of curtains and electric lighting further enhanced the stage's realism.

In the late nineteenth century, playwrights began to employ realist techniques to delve into human psychology. In Russia, Anton Chekhov (1860–1904) emphasized the complexity of human character in realistic settings. His greatest plays, *The Three Sisters* (1901) and *The Cherry Orchard* (1904), deal with the Russian land-owning class in crisis. Chekhov's characters are caught between Russia's slow modernization and their bonds with their aristocratic heritage. Typically, in confronting the changes in Russian society, they prove unable to face the reality that impinges on their idealistic dreams.

Ibsen's **A Doll's House** The Norwegian Henrik Ibsen (1826–1906) also examined the inner conflicts of middle-class society. The topics of his plays were often controversial – venereal disease, marriage, the role of women – but Ibsen was also widely praised for exploring subjects of social and philosophical interest. Among his masterpieces were *The Wild Duck* (1884) and *Hedda Gabler* (1890). Ibsen's psychological insight into character shifted theater away from merely ingenious plots. His use of powerful and ambiguous symbols such as the wild duck explored a symbolic depth in theater that reached beyond realist conventions. His psychological realism probed beneath the appearances of middle-class society. There, he found spiritual emptiness and hypocrisy.

Ibsen's most shocking play was *A Doll's House* (1879), in which the heroine, Nora, has committed forgery to pay for her husband's medical treatment. Nora's husband, Helmer, condemns her deceit, even though the money has saved his life. Nora realizes that she is expected to act like a doll, adorning her husband's household and bearing his children, but taking no decisive actions on her own. In the play's final scene, Nora declares to her patronizing husband her intention to leave him and seek her freedom:

When you'd recovered from your fright – and you never thought of me, only of yourself – when you had nothing more to fear – you behaved as though none of this had happened. I was your little lark again, your little doll – whom you would have to guard more carefully than ever, because she was so weak and frail. At that moment it suddenly dawned on me that I had been living here for eight years with a stranger and that I'd borne him three children. I can't bear to think about it! I could tear myself to pieces![8]

HENRIK IBSEN
From *A Doll's House* (1894)

The final scene ends as Nora closes the door of her past life with a decisive reverberation. It was said that the sound of that door echoed across the theaters of Europe.

THE NOVEL AND MODERN PHILOSOPHY

Like the realist theater, the late nineteenth-century novel was increasingly concerned with the inner life of psychologically complex characters. Two examples are the American novelists Henry James (1843–1916) and Edith Wharton (1862–1937), who shifted their stories' focus from external action toward their characters' perceptions and feelings. These writers aimed to reveal subtle shifts in consciousness and ironically complex social situations. James' exquisitely crafted novels were associated with the *l'art pour l'art* movement of the late nineteenth century.

The psychological novels of the Russian Fyodor Dostoyevsky (1821–81) voiced a profoundly philosophical criticism of modern progress. In his early career, Dostoyevsky championed humanitarian values and utopian socialist schemes, steeped himself in Western philosophy and literature, and voiced his disgust at Russia's backwardness and its repressive czarist regime. He was nearly executed for political activity and then sent to Siberian exile for eight years. In Siberian prisons, he experienced the moral anarchy and class hatred that would be such a force in his later novels.

Dostoyevsky's prison experience convinced him that only Christian love and the simple faith of the Russian peasantry could redeem Western society, which had been seized by materialism and spiritual alienation. Dostoyevsky's mature works reflect a profound ambivalence between his religious conviction and the rationalist skepticism of modern civilization. He believed that God was necessary, yet could not answer the skeptics' doubts that God even existed. In a letter he wrote, "If someone proved to me that Christ is outside the truth and that *in reality* the truth were outside of Christ, then I should prefer to remain with Christ rather than with the truth."[9] Dostoyevsky's ambivalence infects his literary works; each character's beliefs are "tried in the crucible of doubt," as Dostoyevsky called it.

Dostoyevsky's Grand Inquisitor Dostoyevsky's great novels – including *Crime and Punishment* (1866) and *The Idiot* (1869) – deal with a spiritual crisis in which the characters' moral kindness and generosity inexplicably turn into cruelty and murder. The most complex of his works is *The Brothers Karamazov* (1880), which concerns four brothers, one of whom is accused of murdering their father. Dostoyevsky weaves his characters into a vast, richly detailed narrative. Despite its realistic tone, *The Brothers Karamazov* achieves an atmosphere of mystery and evil, and explores the moral and psychological alienation of humans in an age of material progress. The characters' faith in redemption is balanced against their moral freedom to commit the most hideous crimes.

At the heart of *The Brothers Karamazov* is the story of the Grand Inquisitor, a "poem" that Ivan recounts to Alyosha. It tells of a fictional second coming, when Christ appears in Spain during the Great Inquisition. Christ is challenged by the Grand Inquisitor, who explains how a priestly elite has "corrected" Christ's message of moral freedom. The elite offer the masses material wealth and mystic rituals, he says, rather than the anguished doubt of freedom. The Inquisitor ominously predicts that society will be misled by the promises of materialism and modernity, and in the end will submit to a powerful and charismatic elite that offers them security and certainty.

Oh, ages are yet to come of the confusion of free thought, of their science and cannibalism. For having begun to build their tower of Babel[a] without us, they will end, of course, with cannibalism. But then the beast will crawl to us and lick our feet and spatter them with tears of blood. And we shall sit upon the beast and raise the cup, and on it will be written, "Mystery." But then, and only then, the reign of peace and happiness will come for men....Oh, we shall persuade them that they will only become free when they renounce their freedom to us and submit to us. And shall we be right or shall we be lying? They will be convinced that we are right, for they will remember the horrors of slavery and confusion to which Thy freedom[b] brought them.[10]

FYODOR DOSTOYEVSKY
From *The Brothers Karamazov* (1880)

---

a For Dostoyevsky, a symbol of materialism and human vanity; see Genesis 11.

b The "free verdict of the human heart" that Christ offered to his followers.

In defending his Christian belief, Dostoyevsky anticipated the most modern of conditions: mass society governed by an elite who offer them material comforts and the illusion of freedom.

Nietzsche and the Superman The specter of submissive masses and authoritarian elite took a different shape in the works of the German philosopher Friedrich Nietzsche (1844–1900). Nietzsche rejected both Christianity and democracy, which were based on what he called a "slave morality" of self-denial. He believed that every conception of God prevented humans from affirming their true power and creativity. "God is dead," a Nietzschean character declared, and so modern society had to re-create its values without regard to Judeo-Christian definitions of "good" and "evil."

The humans able to free themselves from moral constraints were called *Übermenschen* [YOO-ber-mentsh-en] ("over-men" or supermen) in Nietzsche's works. The superman was an artist of the self, able to create a personal life and system of values in total freedom. Of such figures, Nietzsche wrote, "They have awoken again and again the sense of comparison, of contradiction, of joy in the new, daring, untried, they have compelled men to set opinion against opinion, model against model." Nietzsche imagined the poet Goethe as such a superman and also himself, portrayed as his philosophical alter-ego in *Thus Spoke Zarathustra* (1892).

Nietzsche's ideas anticipated the psychological theories of Sigmund Freud and the post-modern idea that no absolute truth or morality exists. Nietzsche's attacks on conventional religion and morality were a prelude to the assaults on tradition that characterized the twentieth century.

THE WRITE IDEA

In your opinion, is human progress best achieved through greater human freedom or less? What would be the likely consequences, both constructive and destructive, of expanding or restricting humans' freedom to make moral decisions?

Chapter Summary

Realism. In the spirit of mid-nineteenth-century materialism, the realist style sought to depict the world without illusion or fantasy. Realist painters such as Courbet and Bonheur portrayed ordinary life with sober detachment. In the hands of Dickens and Flaubert, the realist novel mercilessly exposed the injustice and hypocrisy of middle-class society and the sometimes desperate lives of ordinary citizens. The radical philosopher Karl Marx declared that the inevitable progress of history would overthrow industrial society and establish a socialism without a class structure.

The Spirit of Progress. In the industrial age, many saw technology and science as agents of progress. Architects applied the new techniques of pre-fabrication and iron construction in such wonders as the Crystal Palace and the Eiffel Tower. Grand modern cities were built from scratch, such as Washington, D.C., or rebuilt in a grand manner, like Baron Haussmann's Paris. The architect Sullivan built the first steel-cage skyscrapers in American cities. This sense of incessant change and loss of traditions defined the spirit of modernity.

Music and Modernity. The industrial age's taste for musical spectacle fostered a golden age in opera. In Italy, Verdi enjoyed a long career that culminated in a series of operas based on Shakespearean plays. In Germany, Wagner's revolutionary operas presented Nordic myths as morality tales of modern life. Musically, Wagner revised and modernized the operatic tradition, unifying opera with his *Leitmotifs* and expanding the harmonic possibilities of Western music.

The Last Romantics. A number of late romantic poets and artists concentrated on symbol, mood, and the artist's inner sensibility. Inspired by Baudelaire, the symbolist poets pursued the principle of *l'art pour l'art* ("art for art's sake") in their poetry of dense meaning. The same idea could be found in the decorative style of Art Nouveau, embodied in the buildings of the Spaniard Gaudí. The composer Debussy devised a "musical impressionism" of dreamlike moods and musical colors. The sculptor Rodin mystified the artistic public with his impassioned renderings of the human figure.

Impressionism and Beyond. In painting, impressionism sought to depict the modern city and capture the transient effects of light and color. Manet inspired the impressionists with his boldly anti-traditional versions of traditional subjects. The pure impressionism of Monet and Renoir sketched open-air scenes in vibrant color, while Degas and Cassatt were more interested in the human figure and pictorial design. Following impressionism, the post-impressionists Seurat and Cézanne sought greater formal order through abstraction; Gauguin and van Gogh aimed for a more intense expressiveness and decorative effect.

The Dark Side of Progress. Using the devices of realism, the dramatists Chekhov and Ibsen explored the complexity of human character and the alienation of middle-class society. Ibsen explicitly addressed such issues as women's rights and modern marriage. Dostoyevsky's panoramic novels explored the dark side of social progress, depicting the conflicts among materialism, modernity, and moral freedom. The philosopher Nietzsche rejected traditional morality and boldly declared the freedom of self-defining "supermen."

14 The Spirit of Modernism

In 1913, a new mode of thought and expression seemed to explode across the Western world. In Paris, an innovative ballet called The Rite of Spring – pulsing with primitive rhythms and unconventional dancing – incited an audience riot at the premier. In New York, an exhibition of strange new art scandalized the American public. Visitors to the Armory Show were especially outraged by Nude Descending a Staircase (Fig. 14.1), which one critic called "an explosion in a shingle factory." The year 1913 saw the public debut of the **spirit of modernism** – the aggressive style of 1900-50 that demolished cultural traditions and conventions and defined a bewildering future for the twentieth century.

A TURBULENT CENTURY

Identify the historical events and forces that shaped the rise of modern mass society.

The early twentieth century was shaken by a series of catastrophes whose tremors reached the entire globe. In 1914 the complacent European powers blundered into a war that soon involved virtually the whole world and eventually killed nine million people. Before the war ended, a revolution in Russia instituted the first communist state. In the war's aftermath, workers' revolts and race riots threatened stability in other Western countries.

To many, Western civilization's core values and enduring traditions were disintegrating under the force of these events. The Irish poet William Butler Yeats [yates] (1865–1939) registered the century's disorientation in vivid

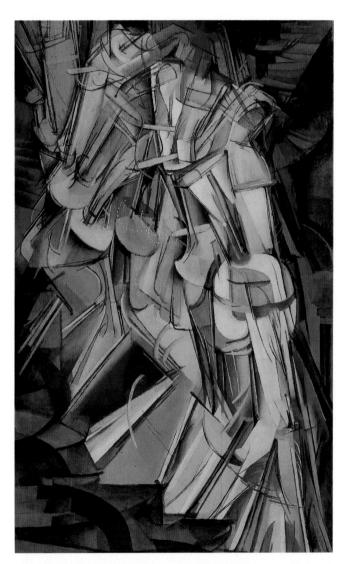

14.1 Marcel Duchamp, *Nude Descending a Staircase No. 2*, 1912. 58 x 35 ins (147.3 x 89 cm). Philadelphia Museum of Art, Louise and Walter Arensberg Collection.
Duchamp's abstract painting was the most notorious work in the 1913 Armory Show, which stunned the American public with art by Picasso, Matisse, and other early modernist masters.

poetic images. A falcon soars beyond his master's call. A bloody tide of war and revolution washes over the grace and civility of culture:

> *Turning and turning in the widening gyre*[a]
> *The falcon cannot hear the falconer;*
> *Things fall apart; the center cannot hold;*
> *Mere anarchy is loosed upon the world,*
> *The blood-dimmed tide is loosed, and everywhere*
> *The ceremony of innocence is drowned;*
> *The best lack all conviction, while the worst*
> *Are full of passionate intensity.*[1]
>
> WILLIAM BUTLER YEATS
From *The Second Coming* (1920)

---

a. gyre, gyration; here, circling flight.

Yeats' poem ends in a mood of foreboding with the question, "And what rough beast, its hour come round at last,/Slouches towards Bethlehem to be born?" Yeats' anxious query might have been echoed by many who surveyed the cultural landscape of the early twentieth century. In the period 1910–40, world war and revolution stimulated the rise of powerful new forces. Communism, fascism, and Western-style democracy all sought to shape mass society through the arts of mass appeal.

THE GREAT WAR

In 1914, with the nations of Europe locked in conflicting alliances, a political assassination in central Europe set off a war of unprecedented carnage and futility. World War I, also called the "Great War," was the first industrialized world conflict, a triumph of industrial invention and productivity. It demonstrated how effectively Western societies could mobilize vast armies, supply them with efficient weapons, and annihilate human lives in pointless conflict. Barbed wire and rapid-fire machine guns made troop entrenchments virtually impregnable. Poison gas was used to early effect by German and British troops, and the tank and the airplane made their first appearance.

The Great War's technologies of destruction produced a three-year stalemate on the battlefield. Dug into their defensive trenches, troops suffered constant and fearsome artillery bombardment. Under this deadly fire, the novelist Erich Remarque wrote, "the world as they had taught it to us broke into pieces." Offensive assaults on trench lines were as lethal as they were ineffective. At the Battle of the Somme in 1916, both sides lost together more than a million dead or wounded, though barely 100 square miles (259 ha) changed hands. In all, World War I caused more than nine million deaths.

The Russian Revolution The deprivations of war produced an event in Russia as momentous as the Great War itself. In October 1917, the radical Bolsheviks – the Russian Social Democratic Party – overthrew a temporary government and established the first socialist state in Europe. The Bolshevik Revolution was led by V. I. Lenin (1870–1924), who determinedly applied Marxian socialism to backward Russia. Lenin theorized that a highly trained party elite could compensate for Russia's lack of a class-conscious proletariat.

In fact, Lenin centralized power in the hands of party leaders, who used the czarist secret police to suppress dissent. Lenin's successor, Joseph Stalin (1879–1953), undertook a massive industrialization, increasing the Soviet Union's steel production five-fold in a single decade. Along with this progress came widespread suffering, including mass starvation, caused by Stalin's forced collectivization of farming. As many as twenty million Soviet citizens died, many in a brutal system of prison camps.

14.2 Vladimir Tatlin, model for *Monument to the Third International*, 1919–20. Wood, iron, and glass. Contemporary photograph.
Tatlin's projected structure was 1300 feet (396.2 m) tall, and was to be built of iron and glass. It would have had three levels, each rotating slowly at different speeds – truly a revolutionary design for a revolutionary age.

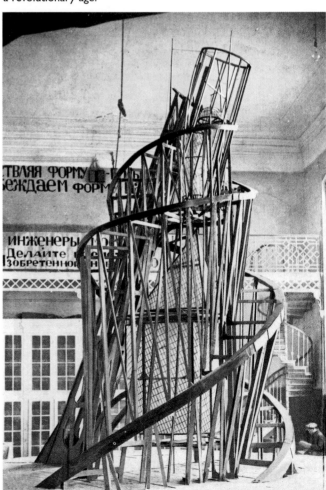

THE TWENTIETH CENTURY

	GENERAL EVENTS	VISUAL ARTS	MUSIC AND DANCE	ARCHITECTURE	LITERATURE
1900					1900 Freud, *Interpretation of Dreams*
MODERNISM		1907 Picasso, *Les Demoiselles d'Avignon* (**14.4**)			
		1912 Matisse, *Blue Window* (**14.14**)	1912 Schoenberg, *Pierrot Lunaire*		
	1914–18 World War I		1913 Ballets Russes, *Rite of Spring*		1922 Joyce, *Ulysses;* Eliot, *The Waste Land*
	1929 Stock market crash, beginning of Great Depression	c. 1928 Brancusi, *Bird in Space* (**14.11**)	1925 Louis Armstrong, jazz soloist, records with "Hot Five"	1925 Gropius, Bauhaus studio, Dessau, Germany (**14.26**)	1929 Woolf, *A Room of One's Own* 1944 Sartre, *No Exit*
	1933 Hitler takes power in Germany			1936–7 Wright, "Falling Water," Pennsylvania (**14.33**)	
1945	1939–45 World War II; Holocaust of Nazi death camps; first atomic weapons	1940–50 Rise of New York avant-garde			
				1950–54 Le Corbusier, Notre-Dame-du-Haut, Ronchamp, France (**15.14**)	1952 Ellison, *Invisible Man*
			1956 Stockhausen, *Gesang der Jünglinge*	1959 J. Utzon begins Sydney Opera House; completed 1972 (**15.16**)	
THE POST-WAR AGE	1963 Civil rights movement; march on Washington, D.C.	1965 Calder, *Spring Blossoms* (**15.8**)			1967 García Marquéz, *One Hundred Days of Solitude*
	1970 Feminist movement gains influence		1971 A. Ailey and J. Jamison, *Cry* (**15.27**)		
		1979 Chicago, *Dinner Party* (**15.28**)	1976 Glass, *Einstein on the Beach* 1983 Anderson, *United States*	1980–83 Graves, Public Services Building, Portland, Oregon	
1990	1989 Fall of Berlin Wall; end of Cold War		1990 Corigliano, *AIDS Symphony*	1990 Isozaki, Team Disney Building, Florida (**15.30**)	1993 Kushner, *Angels in America*

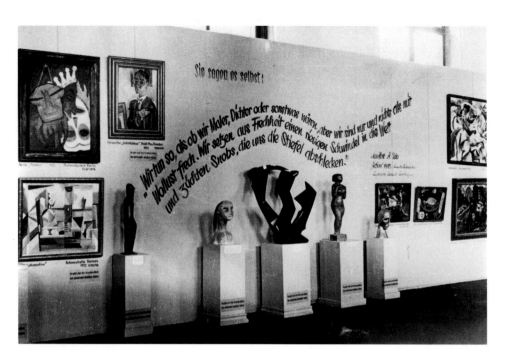

14.3 Nazi exhibition of "Degenerate Art," Munich, 1937. Stadtarchiv, Munich.
The Nazis scorned modernist art as "degenerate" and "Jewish," censoring modernism in favor of idealized images of blond-haired, blue-eyed Germans. Although the Nazis intended to ridicule modernism with this 1937 exhibition, it drew huge crowds and was closed hastily.

The first years of Soviet communism stimulated a lively artistic avant-garde. Soviet artists put themselves at the service of the workers' state, and produced works of abstract design that won praise from modernist groups in western Europe (Fig. **14.2**). Soviet actors and dramatists organized **agit-prop** (for "agitation-propaganda") troupes who carried the revolutionary message to Russian villages. Agit-prop theater rejected the subtleties of realism, aiming for a bold impact on its largely uneducated audiences. Soviet artistic experiments were gradually suppressed by Stalin, whose henchmen finally declared "socialist realism" as the only true revolutionary style. Modernist art was suppressed and artists either fled to the West or disappeared into prison camps.

FASCISM AND THE RISE OF MASS SOCIETY

Western political leaders feared that Lenin's revolution would be an incentive to the workers in Western Europe and the United States. Instead, anti-communist revolutions in Italy and Germany spawned the new ideology of fascism, which proved just as devastating and fatal. Fascism (from *fasces*, an ancient Roman symbol of authority) prized nation and race above all individual rights, and typically used government power to regiment social life and suppress opposition. The fascist movement was originated in 1919 in Italy by Benito Mussolini (1883–1945) and copied effectively in Germany by Adolf Hitler (1889–1945) and his National Socialist (Nazi) party. The term "fascist" is still applied to authoritarian groups who use paramilitary dress and practice racial violence.

In Germany, the fascists proved to be masters in appealing to the masses of unemployed. The skillful orator Hitler pounded away at Nazi themes of German pride, anti-

communism, and anti-Semitism (the hatred of Jews). When the Nazis took power in 1933, they applied their anti-Semitic doctrines, forcing Jews from official positions and stripping them of German citizenship. The Nazis were masters of political rhetoric and symbolism, using the mass media of radio and film for political purposes. Hitler's radio addresses hypnotized audiences with their emotional appeal and simplified slogans. Nazi party rallies, like the one depicted in Leni Riefenstahl's film *Triumph of the Will* (see page 414), massed thousands of supporters in festivals adorned with flags, banners, and uniforms. The Nazis condemned modernist art as "cultural Bolshevism" and stigmatized intellectual dissenters as "Jewish" (Fig. **14.3**). In German town squares, Nazis burned the literary works of well-known intellectuals and most prominent artists quickly left Germany after 1933.

While fascism never flourished in the United States, Americans responded enthusiastically to the new mass media. The new art of commercial film-making established itself in Hollywood, California, churning out movies with standardized story-lines and star actors. President Franklin Roosevelt (1882–1945) gave "fireside chats" on radio to reassure an American people beleaguered by the Great Depression, following the Wall Street crash of 1929. To justify his economic programs, dubbed the "New Deal," Roosevelt's administration sent legions of writers and artists into rural areas. Their mission was to document poverty and suffering by using **documentary arts** (reportage, photography, and film), that recorded social conditions directly and objectively. Documentary photographs by Margaret Bourke-White, Walker Evans, and Dorothea Lange graphically illustrated the hardships of the rural poor. Concerned for artists' survival during the Depression, Roosevelt's New Deal agencies also provided direct support to more

CRITICAL QUESTION
What kinds of political ideas are best communicated through the images and messages of television, radio, and mass advertising? Why were such ideas so important during the 1920s and '30s?

traditional arts. The success of American artists after World War II (1939–45) was rooted in Depression-era government patronage.

The influence of communism, fascism, and the New Deal produced a new kind of art, often intensely political and shaped for mass appeal. These arts of mass appeal effectively employed the media to achieve the political assent of the masses. Even in the United States, where parliamentary democracy remained intact, Roosevelt's New Deal exploited radio to achieve a broader approval than traditional politics allowed. In this role, the arts were not a medium for individual creativity and expression, but the vehicle for propagating messages to mass audiences.

MODERNISM IN ART

Discuss the ways in which modernists discarded or transformed long-standing traditions in the visual arts.

The arts of the early twentieth century sought to find a new place in the emerging mass societies. Yeats had described the disintegration of Western society as the widening spiral of a falcon's flight. A better metaphor might have been the title of British painter Wyndham Lewis' modernist journal – *Blast!* Artists in this age were blasting away at artistic and social conventions, exploding a tradition in the visual arts that had remained intact for five hundred years.

The diverse artistic innovations of the period 1900–50 are grouped loosely under the label of **modernism**. Like romanticism, modernism was more an attitude than a coherent philosophy or style. Nearly all modernists negated some part of the realist tradition in art, whether it was rejecting perspective, abandoning the human form in sculpture, or treating plumbing as art. With the rejection of tradition came a shared interest in new artistic forms and materials. Rather than telling a story or depicting a scene, modernist art was often "about" color or fear or harmony. Above all, it created an art of ideas, feelings, and form that was not bound to the exterior world of visible reality.

The modernists often banded together to defend themselves against detractors and to educate the public about

WINDOW ON DAILY LIFE

WAR, FASHION, AND FEMINISM

Shortly after the Great War ended, women in Britain and in the United States gained the right to vote. Their cause was aided by the dislocations of war, which forced changes in women's fashion. Here Ray Strachey, a British feminist, associates the new freedom in dress with women's growing social independence and opportunity.

For a long time fashion fought valiantly against any further development of physical freedom for women. . . . The war, however, brought deliverance. Under the necessities of the time fashion gave way, and short-skirted uniforms, and even breeches, became familiar sights. Women, when they had once really tasted the joys of this deliverance, refused to be put back into the old costumes. The trade tried, indeed, when the war was over, to reinstate the old ideas; but they did not "take." Skirts grew shorter and shorter, clothes grew more and more simple and convenient, and hair, that "crowning glory of a woman," was cut short. With one bound the young women of 1919 burst out from the hampering conventions, and with their cigarettes, their motor-cars, their latch-keys, and their athletics they astonished and scandalized their elders.[2]

RAY STRACHEY
From *"The Cause": A Short History of the Women's Movement in Great Britain*, 1928

their artistic aims. These groups formed different branches or movements – such as cubism, expressionism, and surrealism – in modernist art. According to conventional understanding, modernism in painting and sculpture begins with Picasso and cubism, and develops along one branch of modernism toward formal abstraction. Along another branch, modernism developed toward more direct expression. Other modernist groups, such as the dadaists and the surrealists, directly attacked traditional definitions of arts. For all their differences, modernist artists were responding to similar forces: to a historical time of war and revolution, to an exhausted artistic tradition, and to each other's radical new vision of artistic truth.

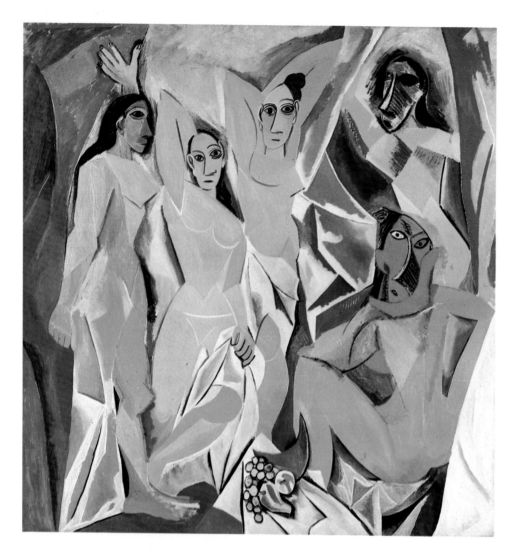

PICASSO'S REVOLUTION IN ART

The Spaniard Pablo Picasso (1881–1973) was to become the twentieth century's most versatile and influential artist. The young Picasso had mastered traditional techniques of drawing and form, as was evident in his first original works, the paintings of his "blue period" and "rose period." By 1907, already a success in the Paris art world, Picasso was determined to discard the Renaissance artistic tradition and formulate a new set of artistic rules.

The first great manifesto of modernist painting was Picasso's *Les Demoiselles d'Avignon* [lay demm-WAW-zell dah-veen-YOHN(h)] (Fig. **14.4**), which depicts a group of nude prostitutes parading themselves before their customers. Instead of the traditional alluring female nude, these women are grotesque mannikins, who project an aggressive threat to the viewer. In the figure at left, Picasso decomposed the female form into transparent slabs of color. The central pair gazes frankly out at the viewer from faces that resemble archaic Spanish sculpture. Most disturbing of all, the masked figures at right project an unmasked hostility toward their male customers. The figures pose against a blue curtain that folds around their forms and flattens the picture into a two-dimensional space.

Scholars identify two creative influences on Picasso in the years 1906 and 1907. At a retrospective Cézanne exhibition, Picasso saw a Cézanne sketch entitled *The Bathers* that clearly influenced his treatment of the nude form. In the same period, Picasso visited a museum of non-Western art in Paris. There he saw African and Polynesian masks that stylized the human face in ways reflected in Picasso's grotesque prostitutes. Despite the painter's later denials, *Les Demoiselles* unmistakably shows the influence of **primitivism** (see page 396).

A third factor in shaping *Les Demoiselles* was Picasso's own experimentation with the elements of visual expression. By disassembling the human form, Picasso was violating a centuries-long artistic tradition, formed from the lessons of Renaissance painters. Moreover, though the rules of perspective had loosened with the post-impressionists, none of their pictures was so boldly flat as *Les Demoiselles*. With his innovations in space and the human figure, Picasso attacked the Renaissance pictorial tradition more aggressively than any painter before him.

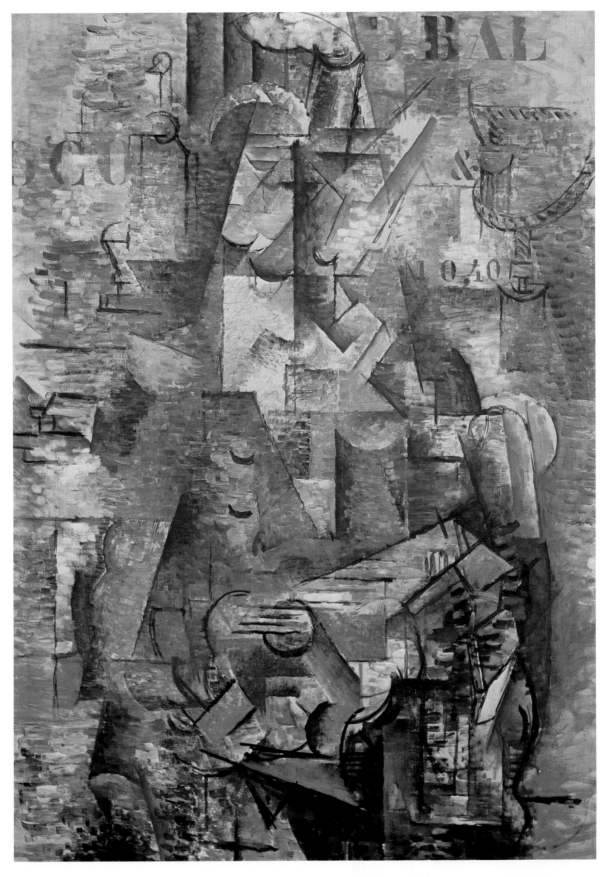

14.5 Georges Braque, *The Portuguese*, 1911. Oil on canvas, 46¹/₄ x 32¹/₄ ins (117.5 x 82 cm). Kunstmuseum, Basel.
Braque's portrait of a bar-room singer with guitar is punctuated by the cryptic lettering "Bal" ("dance") and "10.40" (evidently a drink tab). Can you recognize an underlying pyramidal form?

KEY CONCEPT

PRIMITIVISM

No study of Picasso's paintings fails to mention the evidence in his work of **primitivism**, the influence of arts from supposedly "primitive" tribal cultures in Africa, Oceania, and the Americas. Picasso and other modernists collected tribal art the way the impressionists collected Japanese prints. The modernists had little interest in the anthropological study of primitive art or its place in tribal culture. They were more concerned with the formal inventiveness of tribal artists who were unschooled in realist techniques. Some modernists also hoped to tap the savage vigor (real or imagined) they felt in tribal art, thus shocking their own exhausted civilization into new life.

The works of tribal artisans exhibited formal qualities that paralleled the innovations of modernist artists. Tribal artists did not show things as they were seen by the eye, a rule that had governed Western art since the Renaissance. Tribal masks and sculpture were governed by abstract or symbolic representation: Picasso owned an African mask that depicted the eyes as protruding cylinders and the mouth as a block. In tribal styles, some modernists found confirmation of their search for an art of concept rather than empirical perception. Others sought in primitivism an art of intense

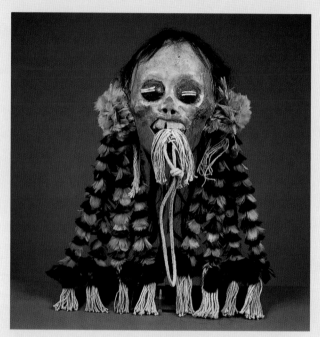

14.7 Trophy head, Mundurucú, Brazil. Human head, cotton, and feathers. Head 6¼ ins (16 cm) high. Museum für Völkerkunde, Berlin.

14.6 Emil Nolde, *Still Life of Masks I*, 1911. Oil on canvas, 28³/₄ x 30¹/₂ ins (73 x 77.5 cm). The Nelson-Atkins Museum of Art, Kansas, Missouri, gift of the Friends of Art.
Nolde combined popular carnival masks (center) with versions of Oceanic and South American tribal masks that he had seen.

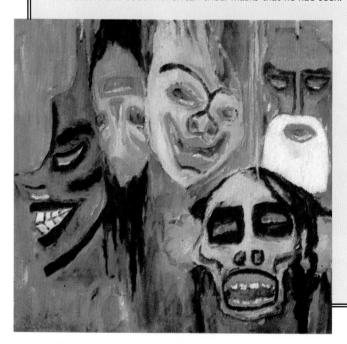

feeling, as in the German expressionist Emil Nolde's *Still Life of Masks I* (Fig. **14.6**). Nolde combines popular carnival masks with versions of Oceanic and South American tribal masks (Fig. **14.7**) that he had seen in European collections.

In one sense, modernists were responding to tribal artists' use of a universal visual language. Removed from its cultural and religious context, tribal art struck the modernists as remarkably free and inventive in its use of shape, line, and proportion. In another sense, the modernists were refurbishing the myth of the noble savage (see page 347). Some presumed that tribal art delved closer to the core of human experience, beneath the falsifying veneer of Western civilization. But where the romantics saw in the noble savage a model of reason and nobility, the modernists saw in the primitive a violent expressiveness that violated the polite boundaries of Western art. Inevitably, the modernists judged primitive art purely in terms of their own culture and artistic interests, welcoming its affirmation of their own artistic inventions. Their borrowings cannot be taken as a measure of tribal art's meaning or value.

CRITICAL QUESTION

What parts of your speech, dress, manner, or interests are drawn from "different" or "foreign" culture? Are your borrowings conscious or unconscious?

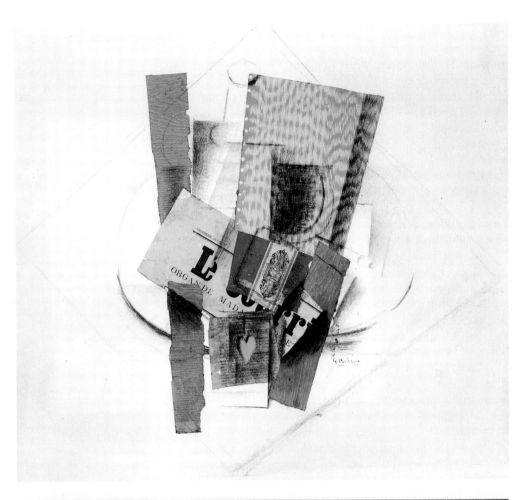

14.8 Georges Braque, *Le Courrier*, 1913. Pasted paper and charcoal, 20 x 22¹/₂ ins (51 x 57 cm). Philadelphia Museum of Art, A. E. Gallatin Collection.
By gluing paper, string, and other objects to the canvas – the technique of collage – Braque hoped to make "the reality in the painting" compete with "the reality in nature."

14.9 Pablo Picasso, *The Three Musicians*, 1921. Oil on canvas, 6 ft 7 ins x 7 ft 3³/₄ ins (2.06 x 2.23 m). Collection, The Museum of Modern Art, New York, Mrs. Simon Guggenheim Fund.
Two figures from the *commedia dell'arte*, a pierrot and harlequin, join a somber monk in a carnival concert. Note the comically irregular shapes, such as the harlequin's gaping jaw and the dislocated dog.

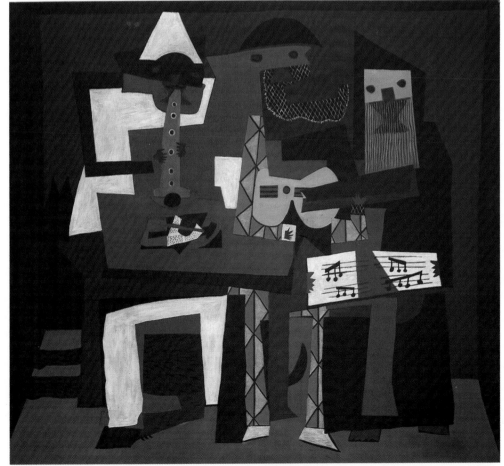

CUBISM

By painting *Les Demoiselles d'Avignon*, Picasso began to define the modernist style called **cubism**, a style that analyzed natural forms into planes, angles, and geometric shapes. The co-inventor of cubism with Picasso was Frenchman Georges Braque [brawk] (1882–1963), a less brilliant artist but a determined innovator. Between 1907 and 1914, the two worked so closely – "roped together like two mountain climbers," said Braque – that some of their paintings are virtually indistinguishable. During these years, Picasso and Braque methodically decomposed the pictorial tradition, defining a technique of formal abstraction that established an entire branch of modernism.

At first, cubism analyzed the object as a visual idea, producing not a picture of the object but a picture of the idea. In Braque's *The Portuguese* (Fig. **14.5**), the sitter's features dissolve into flattened shapes, distinguishable as a fez-like hat, shoulder epaulets, and guitar. Neither the tantalizing lettering nor the image itself can be fully reconstructed. In this so-called analytical phase of cubism, Picasso and Braque largely restricted their colors to browns and grays. They wanted no color to distract from the abstracted lines and intersecting planes of their portraits, still lifes, and landscapes. Picasso later said that he adopted cubism to escape painting in two dimensions. By abandoning perspective – the Renaissance trick of showing three dimensions in two – analytical cubism had achieved a fourth dimension, the object as seen in time or motion. In *The Portuguese*, Braque presents the figure as if in multiple exposure, captured not by the eye but by the intellect.

By 1912 the cubists entered a second phase, called synthetic cubism, in which they glued objects – newspaper, string, even sawdust – directly to the painting surface. This technique was called **collage** (from the French *coller*, "to glue"), and it restored (literally) a third dimension to cubist pictures. Instead of dissolving objects into planes and angles, as in analytic cubism, the cubists now constructed their paintings from scraps of paper and other "real" objects. In *Le Courrier* (Fig. **14.8**) Braque overlaid his drawing of a cafe table with pasted scraps representing a newspaper, playing card, and cigarette pack. The collage technique also extended cubism's original purpose, which was to supersede the pictorial tradition. The pasted paper shapes define the picture as a construction, not an illusionary window through which the viewer sees the object.

Picasso's collaboration with Braque ended abruptly with the outbreak of war in 1914, although cubist techniques enjoyed a vigorous afterlife in his later works. In 1920 he painted two versions of *The Three Musicians*. In the version here (Fig. **14.9**), the raucous shapes and colors are more vivacious than in the cubist paintings. Three figures are dressed for Mardi Gras in the costumes of (from left) a pierrot, a harlequin, and a monk. The painting appears to be a collage of disparate pieces that nevertheless merge into an amusing whole.

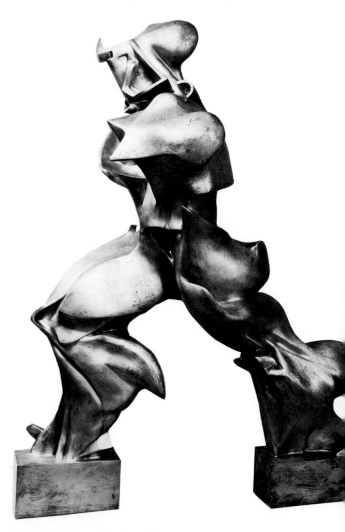

14.10 Umberto Boccioni, *Unique Forms of Continuity in Space*, 1913. Bronze (cast 1931), 43⁷/₈ x 34⁷/₈ x 15³/₄ ins (112.2 x 88.5 x 40 cm). Collection, The Museum of Modern Art, New York, acquired through the Lillie P. Bliss Bequest. Boccioni's sculpture captures in three dimensions the dynamism of analytical cubism, but in more fluid and organic shapes.

TOWARD FORMAL ABSTRACTION

Some cubist painters stepped back from the brink of pure abstraction and returned to representational painting. Other artists followed the cubist path to its logical end, and created works of pure line, shape, and color. The result was called **non-objective** (also non-figurative) art, which depicts no object at all. The trend toward a non-objective sculpture was visible already in the works of the Italian **futurists**. The futurists were an aggressively modernist group who toured the capitals of Europe in the pre-war years. Their scandalous performances and outrageous calls for a "machine art" gained them notoriety. World War I brought an early end to their ambitions, including their uncritical view of new technology as the salvation of the world. One memorable futurist work is the fluid sculpture entitled *Unique Forms of Continuity in Space* (1913; Fig.

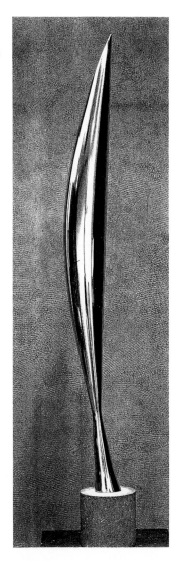

14.11 Constantin Brancusi, *Bird in Space*, c. 1928. Bronze (unique cast), height 4 ft 6 ins (1.37 m). Collection, The Museum of Modern Art, New York, given anonymously.
Denying that his works were abstract, Brancusi said, "I pursue the inner, hidden reality, the very essence of objects in their own intrinsic fundamental nature." To increase the viewer's sense of motion and freedom, Brancusi sometimes placed his works on a rotating base.

drian's flat, rectangular grids of red, yellow, and blue lines. Mondrian believed that line and color were the "pure" materials of painting, rectangles were "pure" forms, and both should be liberated from "the particulars of appearance." Once painting was freed from the representational Mondrian believed it could represent pure harmony and order. *Broadway Boogie Woogie* (Fig. **14.12**) shows Mondrian's characteristic grid of horizontal and vertical lines, broken with blue dashes. The picture communicates visually the musical rhythm of the "boogie woogie" – music with a rocking bass line and an improvisational melody above it. Mondrian's vertical and horizontal bars suggest the underlying rhythm and the irregular blue dashes the free improvisation.

14.12 Piet Mondrian, *Broadway Boogie Woogie*, 1942–3. Oil on canvas, 50 x 50 ins (127 x 127 cm). Collection, The Museum of Modern Art, New York, given anonymously.
Mondrian linked his abstract painting style to hopes for a future of social harmony and universal order. His vision of New York City imagines a calm but vibrant order, animated by the irrepressible rhythms of a boogie-woogie piano tune.

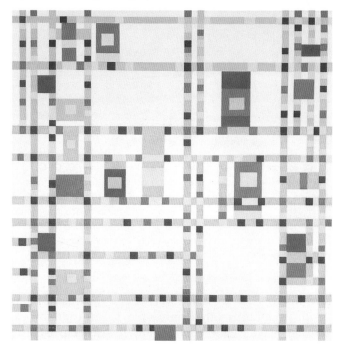

14.10) by Umberto Boccioni [boh-chee-OH-nee] (1882–1916). Although clearly a striding human form, the figure's surface also resembles a windswept sea. The twisting undulations of bronze define the figure's volume, while also enclosing space.

As sculpture became less figurative, sculptors emphasized the textures and expressive potentials of the material itself. In Constantin Brancusi's *Bird in Space* (Fig. **14.11**), the highly polished bronze surface and the streamlined shape suggest the ease of a bird soaring through space. Brancusi [bran-KOO-zee] (1876–1957) usually began with an organic shape, such as the bird or egg, and sought to define the formal or abstract idea in that shape. With *Bird in Space*, Brancusi sought "the essence of flight," as he called it, aiming at pure concept and not a visual representation. For this reason, his sculptures depended on titles to explain their elemental meanings.

The modernist trend toward formal abstraction reached its zenith in the paintings and writings of Dutch artist Piet Mondrian [pee-ETT MOHN-dree-ahn] (1872–1944). One wonders what could be more non-objective than Mon-

Mondrian had an almost Platonic faith in the power of formal abstraction to bring harmony and order to the modern world. Although he was disappointed in his social and moral goals, Mondrian's vigorous defense of abstract art would powerfully influence future art trends.

DADA AND ANTI-ART

The redefinition of art was undertaken by a modernist group called dada, which devoted itself to an attack on

a bicycle wheel attached to a kitchen stool, was also the first mobile sculpture. Duchamp once submitted a standard porcelain urinal, entitled *Fountain*, to a New York art exhibition. Such iconoclasm reached its height (or low point, depending on one's perspective) with Duchamp's "rectified" version (Fig. **14.13**) of Leonardo's famous *Mona Lisa*. Duchamp penciled in a graffito beard and a caption that, when pronounced in French, makes an obscene suggestion about *Mona Lisa*. Most likely Duchamp was also alluding to Leonardo's homosexuality, then a taboo subject. More significantly, Duchamp mocked the work's status as an icon of traditional art.

Despite its self-indulgence, dadaism successfully broadened the definition of art, and prepared the way for such later innovations as happenings, performance art, and pop art – all stimulating elements of the contemporary scene.

14.14 Henri Matisse, *The Blue Window*, Issy-les-Moulineaux, 1912. Oil on canvas, 51¹/₂ x 35⁵/₈ ins (130.8 x 90.5 cm). Collection, The Museum of Modern Art, New York, Abby Aldrich Rockefeller Fund.
Matisse flattened the picture's space so that the table, vases and lamp, and bulbous blue trees outside all seem to occupy the same plane. This child-like indifference to perspective enhances the picture's quiet, reassuring mood.

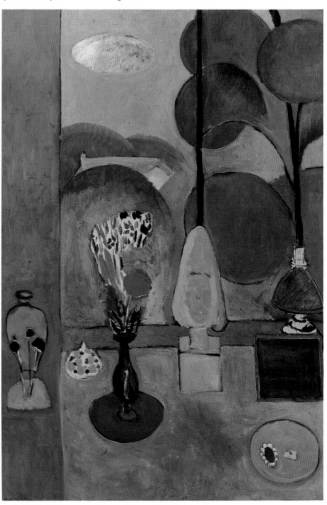

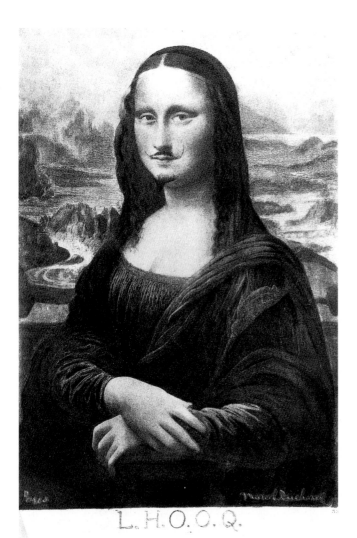

14.13 Marcel Duchamp, *La Boîte en Valide (L. H. O. O. Q.)*, 1919. Rectified readymade, pencil on reproduction, 7³/₄ x 4⁷/₈ ins (19.7 x 12.2 cm). Collection of Mrs Mary Sisler.
Duchamp's "rectified" version of Leonardo's masterpiece, the *Mona Lisa*, mocked the work's status as an icon of traditional art. Dada frequently made such outrageous assaults on conventional definitions of art.

art, philosophy, and Western values. The nonsensical name "dada" symbolized the group's playful attitude toward conventional meaning. Founded in 1916 in Zurich, dadaism established outposts in Paris, New York, and later Berlin. The dadaists frequently engaged in scandalous so-called "manifestations," raucously improvised performances of poetry and art that sometimes turned into riots. With their rejection of reason and order as sources of meaning in art, the dadaists represented the opposite of Mondrian's philosophical abstraction.

The most inventive associate of this group was Marcel Duchamp (1887–1968), who playfully redefined art by stressing idea over fabrication. With his **ready-mades**, Duchamp [doo-SHAN(h)] presented manufactured or "found" objects as unique works of art. One ready-made,

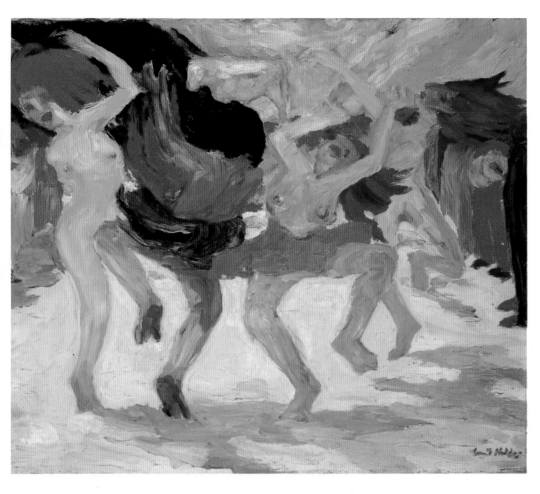

Describe the mood created by Nolde's reds, yellows, and purples. Why might the artist choose this scene from the story of the Israelites in the Sinai desert?

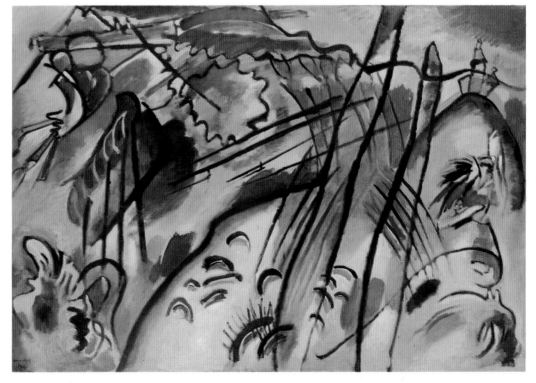

Kandinsky wrote color was like the keys of the piano that the artist touched "to cause vibrations in the soul." Here the swirling lines and colors seem to coalesce into a landscape of the soul.

EXPRESSIONISM

Alongside the trend toward formal abstraction, other modernists moved toward an art of more intense expression. The expressionist branch of modernism also began in Paris, in the works of French painter Henri Matisse (1869–1954). Matisse was a pioneer in the use of color to represent both form and feeling. Somewhat older than Picasso, Matisse rivalled the brilliant Spaniard in his influence on the course of modernist art.

Matisse expressed himself in the decorative arrangement of a picture's elements, including boldly unnatural colors that created their own pictorial structure. "Expression to my way of thinking," he wrote in 1908, "does not consist of the passion mirrored upon a human face or betrayed by a violent gesture. The whole arrangement of my picture is expressive. The place occupied by figures or objects, the empty space around them, the proportions, everything plays a part."[3] Compared to the other modernists, Matisse harbored no revolutionary ambitions. In his *Notes of a Painter*, he said his dream was "an art of balance, of purity and serenity devoid of troubling or depressing subject-matter."[4] *The Blue Window* (Fig. **14.14**) illustrates precisely Matisse's desire to make of art "something like a good armchair in which to rest from physical fatigue."[5]

Matisse was associated with a group labeled the **fauvists** [FOH-vists] (from the French *fauve*, or "wild beast"), named by a critic who said a statue at their 1905 exhibition was like "Donatello among the wild beasts." Actually, the pictorial subjects of fauvist works were quite gentle; the critic was responding to their bold use of color. Matisse followed the example of Cézanne and Gauguin in making color the primary component of the picture. Everything else – including the subject – was subordinated to the logic of color.

German Expressionism The German expressionists achieved an art of morbid, volcanic energy, more dynamic and psychologically intense than Matisse's gentle shapes and liquid colors. Two groups of German expressionism formed in the wake of the fauves: *Die Brücke* ("The Bridge"), formed in Dresden in 1905, and *Der Blaue Reiter* ("The Blue Rider"), organized in Munich in 1911. *Die Brücke*'s [BRY-OOK-uh] leading painter was Emil Nolde (1867–1956), whose pictures showed a preoccupation with religion. In *Dance around the Golden Calf* (Fig. **14.15**), Nolde [NOLL-duh] depicted the pagan abandon of the Israelites worshiping an idol. From the Judeo-Christian tradition, so concerned with sin and divine law, Nolde chose a scene of orgiastic pleasure. Painted in torrid colors, the forms and features of the dancers dissolve in Dionysian intoxication.

Der Blaue Reiter [BLOW-uh RYE-ter] (named for its almanac published in 1919) included the Russian artist Wassily Kandinsky (1866–1944). Like Mondrian's abstraction of line and form, Kandinsky's work pushed artistic expression to the very limits of non-objectivity. His most innovative pictures consisted of swirling colors and freely drawn lines and shapes, with no discernible subject. To stress their non-objectivity, Kandinsky numbered these paintings, titling many of them *Improvisation*. Kandinsky's style clearly had an improvisational spirit since the line and color flowed directly from Kandinsky's feelings (Fig. **14.16**). Kandinsky wanted to achieve an immediate effect on the viewer, and believed the effect of color was most powerful if not mediated through a pictorial subject.

Another member of *Der Blaue Reiter* was Paul Klee (1879–1940), a painter whose career intersected with every major style in the modernist idiom: cubism, expressionism, and the Bauhaus style of modern design. Klee [klay] tapped the primitivism of the child, recapturing by intellectual effort the freshness and simplicity of a child's consciousness. Klee's paintings are nearly all small and childlike in their scale and imagery. For example, in *All Around the Fish* (Fig. **14.18**), the central image is surrounded by vases containing fancifully symbolic flowers. The pictorial techniques of modernism – abstraction, the autonomy of shape and color, the preeminence of feeling and intellect over pictorial subject – are all subordinated to Klee's own private and mystical vision.

THE FREUDIAN REVOLUTION

Summarize Freud's view of the role of sexuality in human thought.

In 1900, seven years before Picasso painted *Les Demoiselles d'Avignon*, the psychologist Sigmund Freud (1856–1939) published his study *The Interpretation of Dreams*. In this work, Freud [froyd] outlined a theory of the human mind that would revolutionize psychology, much as Matisse and Picasso transformed modern art.

According to Freud, the mind was not the center of reason and self-mastery, but a battleground between unconscious desires and the oppressive demands of society. The family was not a sanctuary of innocent love, but a cauldron of incestuous attachments and murderous wishes. Freud applied his scientific analysis to subjects that were normally taboo – masturbation, incest, perversion. His writings gave us a new vocabulary for understanding human thought, including now-familiar terms such as "unconscious," "ego," and "Oedipus complex." Every domain of the humanities, from surrealist art to philosophy and religion, has been affected by Freud's theories.

FREUD AND HUMAN SEXUALITY

Freud was the inventor of **psychoanalysis**, a method of treating mental illness by analyzing unconscious desires. One psychoanalytic method required the patient to talk freely about his or her thoughts and feelings. This "free association" of ideas revealed the unconscious thoughts behind the mental symptom and exposed the patient's thoughts to interpretation. Through analysis, the patient eventually could acknowledge the sexual wish or fear that caused the symptom. All human activity was motivated by a powerful psychic energy that Freud called **libido** (Latin for "wish" or "desire"). Most people had successfully

MODERNIST "-ISMS"

Style	Main Figures	Features
fauvism	Matisse	intense colors, tendency toward abstraction
cubism	Picasso, Braque	multiple perspectives, collage
futurism	Boccioni	praise of technology
dada	Duchamp	anti-art, ready-mades
expressionism	Nolde, Klee	religious symbolism, dream images

repressed their libido along the paths of marriage, work, parenthood, and other ordinary human activities. The person who suffered from mental illness or sexual perversion, however, had unsuccessfully repressed the libido. Freud drew no clear line between the normal and abnormal psyche. The actor who stepped before an audience every night was gratifying the same libido as the sexual exhibitionist.

The most controversial aspect of Freud's theory was his view of child sexuality. Western civilization had long thought children were free of sexual motives. However, Freud asserted that children were driven by libido from the beginning of their psychic lives. The child was reluctant to give up the erotic attachment to his or her parents and, according to Freud, mentally re-enacted the Greek legend of Oedipus (see page 61). In the "Oedipus complex," the child unconsciously wished to murder his or her parental rival and preserve a sexual attachment to the parent of the opposite sex. According to Freud, the experience of the Oedipus complex influences our future relations with our parents, our choice of a mate, even our choice of an occupation.

In later years, Freud generalized his psychological theories to the domains of mythology, religion, and politics. In *Civilization and its Discontents* (1925), for example, he argued that civilization was built on an inevitable conflict between humans' true desires and the requirements of work and achievement. In other works on religion and mass psychology, Freud daringly tested his theories on the major social and psychic phenomena of his day, usually with controversial results.

SURREALISM

Freud's interest in dreams corresponded to a trend already established in the visual arts, especially in the dream-like images of Giorgio de Chirico (1888–1978). De Chirico [day KEE-ree-koh] was an Italian who arrived in Paris at the height of cubism. Working without any knowledge of Freud, he captured something of the eerie, compelling

logic of the unconscious mind. Painted in 1914, *The Mystery and Melancholy of a Street* (Fig. **14.17**) shows a girl playing on a street that narrows between two arcaded walls. Like a dream, the images possess a startling clarity – the brightly illuminated arcade, for example – but are combined in obscure and ominous associations.

The first artists consciously to adopt Freud's theory of the unconscious mind were the **surrealists**, a group of writers and painters initially based in Paris who sought to release unconscious images and words in their art. The result was an art "beyond" reality (in French, *surréalisme*), or, as the surrealists claimed, a transmutation of dream and reality. The surrealists' leader, French writer André Breton [breh-TOHN(h)] (1896–1966), issued a manifesto in 1924 in which he defined surrealism as "pure psychic automatism" – that is the straightforward "dictation" of unconscious thoughts into writing or art, without any rational control. Automatism in writing produced a poetry of dream-like associations and arbitrary word play. The surrealists compared automatism with the free association of thoughts and feelings in Freudian psychoanalysis. Inspired by Freud, they called aggressively for liberation from sexual taboos.

The most accomplished painter of the Paris surreal-

14.17 Giorgio de Chirico, *The Mystery and Melancholy of a Street*, 1914. Oil on canvas, 33¹/₂ x 27¹/₄ ins (85 x 69 cm). Resor Collection, New Canaan, Connecticut.
Interpret the looming shadow between the arcaded walls. What is the shadow's relation to the profile of the girl?

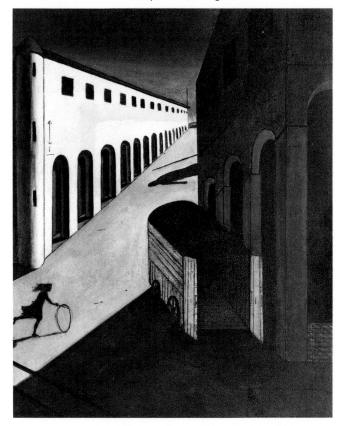

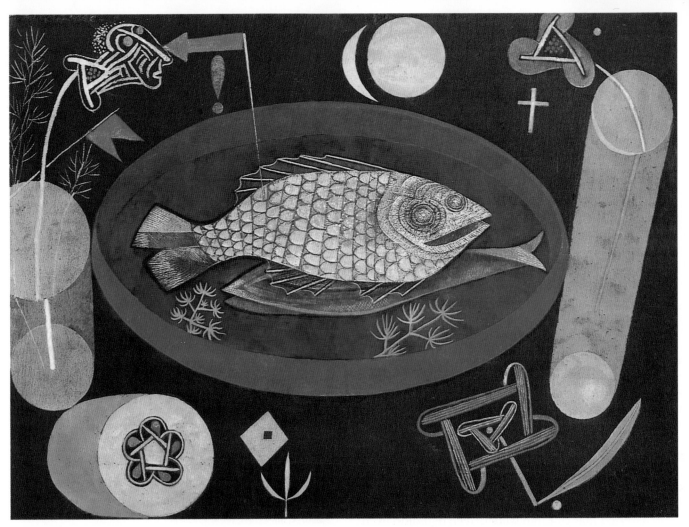

14.18 Paul Klee, *All Around the Fish,* **1926. Oil on canvas, 18³/₄ x 25³/₈ ins (46.67 x 63.82 cm). Collection, The Museum of Modern Art, New York, Abby Aldrich Rockefeller Fund, 1939.**
Speculate on the symbolism of the flowers, fish, cross, and other elements of this mystical scene.

KEY CONCEPT

THE UNCONSCIOUS

A century before the modernists, the romantics had praised the mysterious source of creativity in the unconscious mind. The philosopher Friedrich Nietzsche (see page 387) had mocked the puny efforts of reason to control the irrational powers of dream and imagination. Not until Sigmund Freud, however, did the concept of an unconscious mind enter the philosophical calculation of Western civilization. In Freud's theory, the unconscious was composed of powerful memories suppressed from consciousness, but still affecting thinking and behavior. The unconscious was like an underground river, hidden but powerful, that might erupt in an eerie dream or a caustic slip of the tongue.

Freud saw the unconscious as a psychic repository, a mental attic stuffed full of old memories. Stored there were the psyche's most powerful and frightening thoughts – thoughts of death, violence, and sex-

ual desire. To protect against its own dangerous ideas, the conscious mind censored these thoughts, repressing them into the unconscious. However, Freud found that this repression was never entirely successful. Unconscious thoughts reappeared as dreams or neurotic symptoms, disturbing normal thought with their insistent desires and fears. In Freud's mental system, the conscious mind had to work constantly to control unconscious thoughts and transform their energy into socially acceptable activity.

Freud found evidence of the unconscious mind in virtually every aspect of human thinking. The apparently accidental forgetting of a friend's name revealed an unconscious desire that she die. The artistic works of Sophocles and Leonardo, men long dead, left a record of their unconscious fantasies. Above all, the dream – that ordinary but puzzling mental work performed by every human every night – revealed the work-

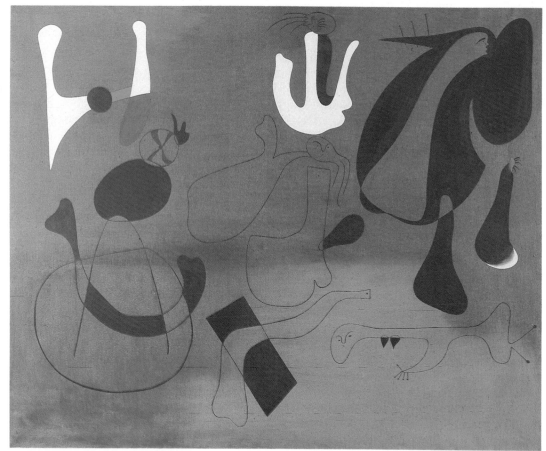

14.19 Joan Miró, *Composition*, 1933. Oil on canvas, 4 ft 3³/₈ ins x 5 ft 3³/₄ ins (1.3 x 1.63 m). Wadsworth Atheneum, Hartford, Connecticut, Ella Gallup Sumner and Mary Catlin Sumner Collection.
Miró admitted that, even with a dream-like canvas such as this, only the first stage of painting was "free, unconscious." The second stage required control and discipline.

The door

The wind

The bird

The valise

magritte

ings of the unconscious. The dream was, as Freud said, the "royal road" to the unconscious (Fig. **14.20**).

The existence of an unconscious mind put a question mark beside the entire history of Western thought. Since Plato and Aristotle, Western philosophy had enshrined reason as the core of human thinking. In his theory of the human psyche, however, Freud claimed that unconscious thoughts were more powerful and in a sense truer than conscious thinking. Logic and rationality were a necessary, but inadequate defense mechanism against repressed desires and fears. After Freud, reason would never be the same again.

14.20 René Magritte, *The Key of Dreams*, 1932. Oil on canvas, 16³/₈ x 11 ins (41.5 x 28 cm). Collection Jasper Johns, New York.
The illogical "logic" of the unconscious was captured by the surrealist Magritte, who arbitrarily associated pictures with unrelated captions.

ists was Joan Miró (1893–1983), a Spaniard whose method foreshadowed the abstractions of post-World War II art. Of his painting, Miró [mee-ROH] said, "I begin painting and as I paint, the picture begins to assert itself, or suggest itself under my brush. The form becomes a sign for a woman or a bird as I work."[6] Miró used "biomorphic" shapes that suggested organic creatures without defining them. In his *Composition* (Fig. **14.19**), for example, the shapes suggest human figures drifting in space, appearing to be governed not by the artist's design but by the playful logic of dream.

The method of another surrealist, Salvador Dalí (1904–89), was more mannered and self-conscious. Dalí [dah-LEE] called his paintings "hand-painted dream photographs," and works such as *The Persistence of Memory* (Fig. **14.22**) combined minute detail with bizarre images and vividly painted landscapes. Of the limp watches in *The Persistence of Memory*, Dalí said they "are nothing more than the soft, extravagant, solitary, paranoiac-critical Camembert cheese of space and time."[7] Dalí also contributed, with director Luis Buñuel [boon-(y)-WELL] (1900–83), to the surrealist film *Un Chien Andalou* (*An Andalusian Dog*, 1928), which contained a famous scene of a razor slicing open an eyeball. Dalí's eccentric flamboyance made him the most famous surrealist, though the sober Miró was to have a greater influence on artists of later generations.

MODERNISM IN LITERATURE

Identify the literary techniques that enabled modernist authors to depict the inner reality of human thought and experience.

Twentieth-century literature explored new forms with the same intensity as the other arts and with the same disorienting effects on the public. Storytellers could not make their works entirely non-objective, as Mondrian and Kandinsky did in painting. They could, however, experiment with poetic language and narrative form. Modernist poets often discarded poetic meter and rhyme, writing in *vers libre* [VAIR leeb(r)] ("free" or non-metrical verse). Novelists concentrated more on the inner lives of their characters, registering subtle gradations of consciousness. As a result, the action in many modernist novels was less coherent than in conventional works, with fewer causal connections.

Such innovations marked the modernist style in writing as distinct from literature of the modern era. The modernist style was distinguished by its writers' desire to alter or expand traditional literary forms and discover new topics for the literary imagination. The works of Virginia Woolf, James Joyce, T. S. Eliot, and Franz Kafka projected the anxieties and desires of modern experience into powerful new forms of literary expression.

THE MODERNIST STYLE

Modernist writers boldly experimented with new styles; in prose, the novel sought to free itself from the conventions of realist narrative. Novelists accomplished this by concentrating on their characters' inner thoughts, recording unconscious associations. Such inwardness characterized the novels of Virginia Woolf (1882–1941). Woolf developed the technique of interior monologue (also called "stream of consciousness"), which reproduces the flow of a character's inner thoughts. Interior monologue gave to fiction the same kind of subjective complexity and relativism that we find in cubist painting. In Woolf's *Mrs. Dalloway* (1925), for example, the events of a single day are described through the interior thoughts of several characters. Woolf's *A Room of One's Own* (1929) was the first modern work of feminist criticism, addressing the question of why there had been no female Shakespeare. Woolf determined that a woman who wanted to write required an independent income and "a room of one's own."

The most influential modernist novelist was the Irishman James Joyce (1882–1941). His novel *Ulysses* (1922) is the story of a day in the life of Dubliner Leopold Bloom. This long novel recounts Bloom's adventures selling newspaper advertisements and arguing with friends, comparing them (often ironically) to the exploits of the epic hero Ulysses. As the title suggests, *Ulysses* is the modern version of Homer's great epic, the *Odyssey*. The language is packed with the dense allusions and symbolic associations of the symbolist poets (see page 370). Joyce's stylistic techniques make *Ulysses* difficult to read, but give the novel a rich texture of meaning that more conventional novels lack. Because of the novel's sensuous language, *Ulysses* was banned for obscenity in the United States until 1934.

In poetry, the path to modernism had been blazed by the symbolists. Poets such as Paul Valéry, Rainer Maria Rilke, and Pablo Neruda extended the symbolists' use of intensely imagistic and allusive language, and wrote in *vers libre*. In 1922 Anglo-American poet T. S. Eliot (1888–1965) published *The Waste Land*, probably the most influential modernist poem in English. Eliot's poem evoked disturbing images of spiritual desolation, contrasting modern despair with ancient symbols of fertility and regeneration. To achieve unity, *The Waste Land* relied on literary allusion and recurring mythic symbols, drawn from anthropology, religion, and the musical works of Richard Wagner. By his use of symbolism, Eliot contradicted the romantic idea that a poem expresses the author's inner state of mind or emotion. Instead, Eliot's poem adopts a pose of ironic detachment, speaking through images that are chosen – sometimes quite arbitrarily – from diverse sources.

THE MODERN HEROES

The new forms in literature were coupled with a new type of hero. While the traditional realist novel was still pri-

THE WRITE IDEA

Describe a literary or film hero that represents, to your mind, the antithesis of the modernist ironic hero. What do these opposing kinds of heroes tell you about the world you live in? Which is truer, in your experience?

marily focused on the exploits or moral development of a central character, modernist literature was more likely to present an ironic hero, a character who frustrates or disappoints the reader's expectations for decisive action and moral growth. The modernist hero is over-self-conscious, unable to bring himself or herself to action, immobilized by anxieties. One Eliot character asks with neurotic insecurity, "Shall I part my hair behind? Do I dare to eat a peach?"

The stories and novels of Czech author Franz Kafka (1883–1924) had a more sinister cast than Eliot's ironic wit. Kafka imagined his central characters caught in absurd and terrifying circumstances, yet recounted their experiences with detached matter-of-factness. His novels created an insane, nightmarish world which we now describe with the adjective "Kafka-esque." In Kafka's story *Die Verwandlung* (*The Metamorphosis*), for example, the character Gregor Samsa awakes one morning to find himself transformed into a giant insect:

> *As Gregor Samsa awoke one morning from uneasy dreams he found himself transformed in his bed into a gigantic insect. He was lying on his hard, as it were armor-plated, back and when he lifted his head a little he could see his dome-like brown belly divided into stiff arched segments on top of which the bed quilt could hardly keep in position and was about to slide off completely. His numerous legs, which were pitifully thin compared to the rest of his bulk, waved helplessly before his eyes.*
>
> *. . . What about sleeping a little longer and forgetting all this nonsense, he thought, but it could not be done, for he was accustomed to sleep on his right side and in his present condition he could not turn himself over. However violently he forced himself towards his right side he always rolled on to his back again.*[8]

FRANZ KAFKA
From *The Metamorphosis* (1924)

Gregor's family gradually abandons him to his degraded condition and he dies in loneliness and desperation. Such modern themes of impotence, alienation, and despair recur in some of Kafka's more traditional modernist contemporaries, including Ernest Hemingway (1899–1961) and Thomas Mann (1875–1955).

MODERNIST MUSIC AND ARCHITECTURE

Explain why modernist music often outraged or alienated popular audiences.

Modernist currents in music led in two different directions. In one of these, exemplifed by Stravinsky's ballets, music achieved its own version of modernist primitivism, while the other path led toward esoteric innovation. Modernist architects strived for a rationalism and functionality that would make architecture the most accessible of the modernist arts.

STRAVINSKY AND BALLET

The scandalous Paris debut of *Le Sacre du Printemps* (*The Rite of Spring*) in 1913 announced a new agenda for the performing arts. Where traditional works had intended to entertain and delight their audiences, modernist perfor-

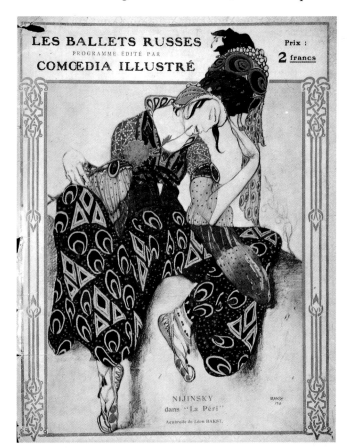

14.21 Vaslav Nijinsky, portrayed by costume designer Leon Bakst.
Russian dancer and choreographer Nijinsky intentionally violated the rules of classical ballet with his angular movements.

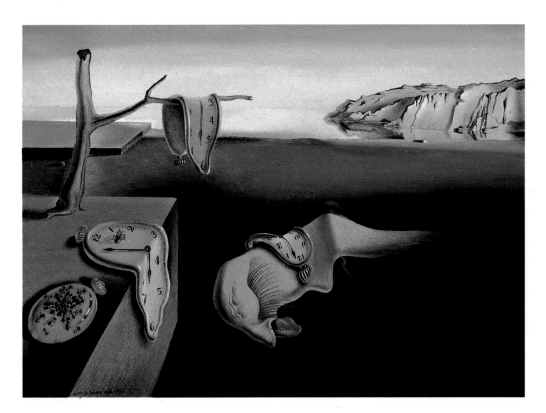

14.22 Salvador Dalí, *The Persistence of Memory*, 1931. Oil on canvas, 9¹/₂ x 13 ins (24 x 33 cm). Collection, The Museum of Modern Art, New York, given anonymously.
What elements of this Dalí scene most directly evoke the logic and imagery of dreams? How might the symbols here be interpreted?

mances seemed determined to provoke and perplex, even when rejected by an artistic public that was comfortable with traditional arts.

The Rite of Spring involved the collaboration of several geniuses of modernism. Sergei Diaghilev (1872–1929) was artistic director of the Ballets Russes, an innovative Russian dance troupe. Diaghilev's [DYAW-ghe-lev] daring productions made him the single most important figure in the rise of modernist ballet. His principal dancer was Vaslav Nijinsky (1888–1950; Fig. **14.21**), a brilliantly inventive dancer and choreographer who had outraged Parisian audiences with his erotic ballet for Debussy's *Prélude à "L'après-midi d'un faune."* Composer Igor Stravinsky (1882–1971) achieved his first recognition with his ballets for Diaghilev. His score for *The Rite of Spring* – with its pounding rhythms and dissonant melodies – was a work of primitivism as provocative as Picasso's *Les Demoiselles d'Avignon*.

Stravinsky's music attacked the truisms of traditional music, the use of a consistent meter and key. Instead of using a single meter, Stravinsky employed numerous meters

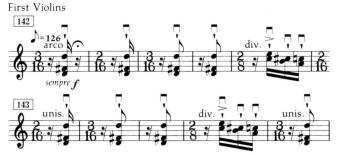

14.23 Igor Stravinsky, section of first movement from *Le Sacre du Printemps* (*The Rite of Spring*), 1913.

within a section, often changing the number of beats from one measure to the next (Fig. **14.23**). The use of different time signatures simultaneously or in rapid succession is called **polyrhythm**, and it gave Stravinsky's music a jagged, "primitive" pulse. The *Rite of Spring* also exploited **polytonality**, the use of two or more musical keys at the same time. Polytonality expanded the harmonic possibilities of music and allowed for broader dissonances – the tension created by unexpected chords. The dissonances in *Rite of Spring* are pronounced and prolonged, accounting for its disturbing effect on the audience at its premier.

Stravinsky later moved from the primitivism of his compositions for the Ballets Russes to music structured somewhat in the Classical style of Haydn or Mozart. The composer was partly motivated by his opposition to the cult of Wagner, with its subordination of music to feeling, story, and myth. Stravinsky's later compositions, though Classical in form, continued to rely on modernist techniques of dissonance and innovative rhythms. Much of Stravinsky's influence in modern music can be attributed to this eclectic attitude – a borrowing from many sources, both modern and traditional.

SCHOENBERG AND ATONAL MUSIC

While Stravinsky's music was rooted in Russian folk traditions, the musical ideas of Arnold Schoenberg (1874–1951) were formed by the intense aestheticism and expressionist fervor of early twentieth-century Vienna. Schoenberg [SHUH(r)N-bairk] rejected the Classical tradition of orchestral music as completely as Kandinsky broke with objective painting. His innovations in tonality had wide influence on modern music.

A Viennese contemporary of Freud and associate of expressionist painters, Schoenberg packed his early music with chromatic scales (scales using the half-tones of a musical key). By his use of chromaticism and dissonance, Schoenberg dissolved the boundaries of the major-minor key system and created the first **atonal** music – that is, music not composed in a musical key. His atonal compositions were called musical "expressionism" because of their intense emotionality.

The move toward atonality is illustrated in *Pierrot Lunaire* [PEE-(uh)-roh loo-NAIR] (*Pierrot of the Moon*, 1912), a series of twenty-one songs written for a female vocalist and five musicians. The poetic texts, which relate the neurotic jokes and bizarre stories of someone on the verge of mental breakdown, heave with the symbolism of expressionist poetry. According to Schoenberg's direction, the poems were to be half-sung, half-spoken, in a haunting method of delivery called *Sprechstimme* [SPREKH-stimm-uh] (German for "speaking voice"). In the music for *Pierrot*, there is no tonal center, no "home" tone where the music begins and ends. Instead, the melodic line is broken into small fragments that are not bound together by a major or minor scale.

The most popular work of atonal music was the opera *Wozzeck* (1925), composed by Schoenberg's student Alban Berg (1885–1935) and considered a masterpiece of musical expressionism. Based on a fatalistic nineteenth-century play, *Wozzeck* [VOH-tsek] depicts opera's most compelling modernist hero. The soldier Wozzeck is humiliated by his captain and betrayed by his lover, Marie. Overwhelmed by a dehumanizing world, Wozzeck goes mad: he stabs Marie to death and drowns himself. The opera's atmosphere of paranoia and despair relies upon Berg's intricate musical score and frequent use of *Sprechstimme*. Its atonal harmonies are contained within tightly defined traditional forms, such as the sonata and fugue. In the opera's final scene, Berg uses children's songs to give the tragic story a final, aching twist.

Musically, Berg's opera already contains elements of Schoenberg's most radical innovation: the elimina-

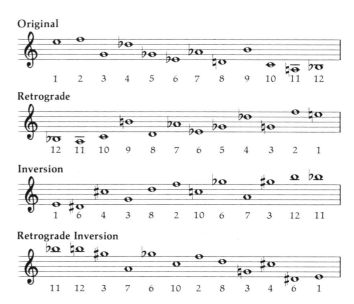

14.24 Tone-row for a Schoenberg piano concerto.
The original tone-row is also shown retrograde (backwards), inverted, and retrograde-inverted.

tion of all tonality, in favor of his own compositional system. In the 1920s, Schoenberg achieved this with the **tone-row** – the twelve tones of the chromatic scale arranged in a fixed sequence, or "series." Schoenberg's method dictated that every tone in the tone-row had to be played before any tone could be repeated. The discipline of the tone-row guaranteed that no tone could be heard more than any other. Hence, there was no tonic note toward which the music gravitated.

Schoenberg's system of composition was called **serialism** or the **twelve-tone method**, and it was also practiced by another of Schoenberg's students, Anton Webern [VAY-bern] (1883–1945). In serial composition, the tone-row of a particular composition was fixed, although it could be developed in a variety of ways. The tone-row might be played backwards or upside-down, tones might be played simultaneously as a chord, or the rhythm varied (Fig. **14.24**). The tone-row gave the composition a unity

14.25 Le Corbusier, Villa Savoye, Poissy, France, 1929–30.
The ribbon window became a common feature in modernist building. Le Corbusier called his houses "machines for living in."

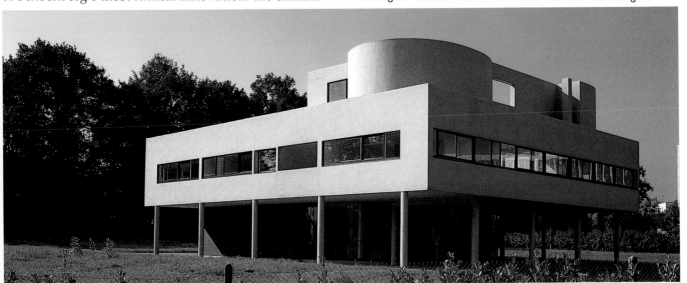

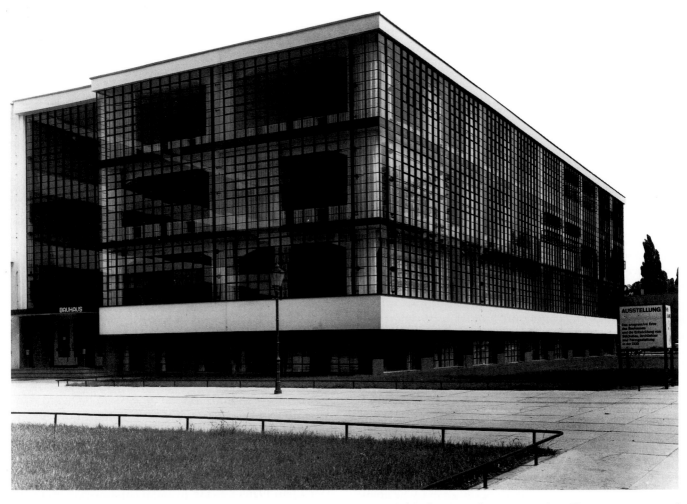

14.26 Walter Gropius, Workshop Wing, Bauhaus, Dessau, Germany, 1925–6.
The sheer simplicity of Gropius' glass and steel design recalls the purified painting of Mondrian (Fig. 14.12). Gropius became an influential teacher in America and a founder of the so-called International Style in architecture.

and coherence traditionally achieved by use of a musical key or a pattern of exposition and development. However, there were no melodic themes or motifs, as in traditional musical composition, to orient the audience. As with non-objective art, serial composition discarded an exhausted tradition and led music in a bold new direction.

MODERNIST BUILDING

Modernist architects discarded the decorative styles of the nineteenth century and sought to merge architecture with industry. The result was a simple, logical, functional building style, as much industrial as artistic. Twentieth-century architects had the advantage of working with new architectural forms and materials. To begin with, there was steel, from which strong building frames or cages could be constructed (see page 365). Steel was the heart of ferroconcrete, or steel-reinforced concrete, which is still the principal

material in large-scale construction. Ferroconcrete made possible a technique called **cantilevering**, in which a block or floor is supported at one end and hangs free at the other.

The architects of modernism sought forms that were suited to the industrial and social needs of the early twentieth century. In Germany and the Netherlands especially, architects responded to the need to serve large urban populations. The young German architect Walter Gropius (1883–1969) determined that modernist principles should be united with industrial design. He invited such leading modernist artists as Kandinsky and Klee to teach at his art school in Germany called the Bauhaus ("Building House"). When the Bauhaus [BOW-howss] moved from Weimar to Dessau in 1926, Gropius constructed the new campus according to his philosophy of clean, functional, modern design. The Bauhaus studio is a conglomeration of cubes, built of steel, ferroconcrete, and glass (Fig. **14.26**). Gropius' most important contribution was the so-called "curtain wall," the exterior wall of glass that also displays the building's interior design. The Bauhaus architects designed modernist furniture and household utensils to match the functional style of Bauhaus interiors.

The most visionary of the modernist architects was the Frenchman Charles Edouard Jeanneret, known as Le Corbusier (1887–1965). Trained by the same teacher as Gropius,

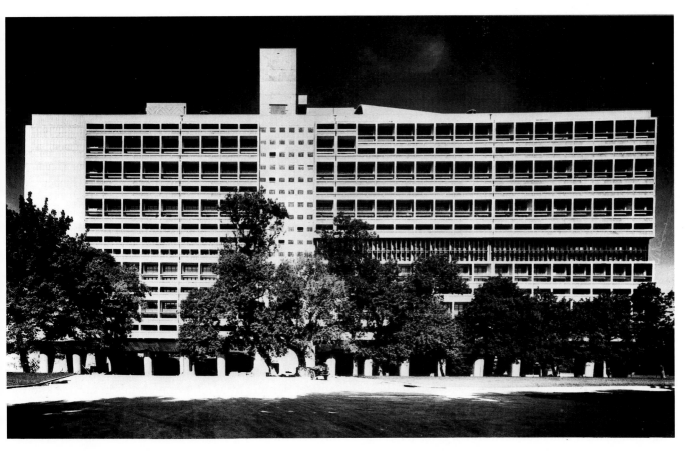

14.27 Le Corbusier, *L'Unité d'Habitation*, Marseilles, France, 1947–52. Length 550 ft (167.64 m), width 79 ft (24.08 m), height 184 ft (56.08 m).
Le Corbusier's high-rise apartment towers were the inspiration for much post-war public housing.

Le Corbusier [luh kor-BOO-zee-AY] shared the German's aim of a socially useful architecture. He envisioned "radiant cities" based on his designs of glass skyscraper apartments and super-highways. Le Corbusier's actual buildings in the 1920s and 1930s were more modest than his visionary designs. The Villa Savoye (Fig. **14.25**) in Poissy, France, embodied his principles of geometric regularity and utility. The cubical box, 60 feet square (18.3 m²), is supported on pylons. The exterior is rigorously simple with a ribbon window stretching along the whole wall, a design which became a common feature in modernist building. The building's design is more forgiving on the interior, with its pastel colors and roof garden. The American architect Frank Lloyd Wright disparaged such designs as "boxes on stilts," but Le Corbusier maintained his principles in later, more ambitious buildings.

Larger commissions for architects in the 1920s and 1930s were blocked by the Depression and then by war. In the 1940s, Le Corbusier was able finally to build an apartment building that realized his ideal of city living. The building in Marseilles, France, called *L'Unité d'Habitation* (Fig. **14.27**), is, in effect, a vertical street. Each apartment is on two levels and is equipped with a two-story garden; half-way up the building is a full-scale shopping and service area; and on the roof, Le Corbusier placed a garden decorated with curving concrete sculpture, providing space for the building's occupants to stroll and play. In effect, the street had been moved to the roof.

The *Unité d'Habitation* [OO-nee-tay dab-i-TA-si-ohn] embodied the urban ideal that Le Corbusier had envisioned since the early 1920s. His simple, cubical designs became the basis of the International Style in architecture, the modernist style practiced widely in Europe and North America in the period after World War II.

ART AND POLITICS

Compare the different political beliefs that were communicated in the works of modernist artists.

Just as in the Reformation and the French Revolution, so too in the 1920s and '30s artists and writers were drawn into the political conflicts of their time. Sharp lines were drawn over such issues as communism, fascism, labor unions, and the poor. Modernists spoke with eloquence from many points on the political spectrum, commenting on events and agitating for change through the media of drama, painting, film, and photography.

BRECHT'S EPIC THEATER

Devastated by inflation and unemployment, Germany in the late 1920s was splintered into political factions, with increasing polarization between left-wing parties and the

Nazis. An atmosphere of decadence and political cynicism pervaded German cities, where party shock troops battled in the streets and cabaret singers mocked the corruption of wealth.

German artists responded with an ironic soberness exemplified in the works of poet and dramatist Bertolt Brecht (1898–1956). Brecht was early influenced by the extravagant staging and didactic tone of expressionist theater in Germany. By the late 1920s, he had devised a theory of acting and dramatic presentation that he called epic theater. Epic theater dictated that the action should be interrupted by song, narrative commentary, and other techniques intended to break the spell of realism over the stage. In the epic theater, audiences would act as experts able to judge the action, like spectators at a boxing match. By 1928 Brecht had combined his theory of epic theater with Marxist doctrine, and his most important plays taught lessons about human relations under capitalism. At the time Brecht was first studying Marxism, he and the composer Kurt Weill [vile] (1900–50) had a gigantic theatrical hit with *Die Dreigroschenoper* (*The Threepenny Opera*, 1928), a ballad opera based on John Gay's *Beggar's Opera* (1728). Brecht and Weill's bitter satire compared the decadent bourgeoisie to the criminal underworld of gangsters, beggars, and prostitutes. The two worlds – upper class and underclass – were shown as morally equivalent. Weill's music was full of bitter melancholy and modernist dissonance. The opera's tone contrasted sharply with the Wagnerian pomp so popular with the rising Nazis.

In 1933, Brecht went into exile, not long before Nazi censors ordered his works to be burned. His later plays expressed his Marxist ideas, and were more didactic, usually centering on a character torn between virtue and expedience. In *Mutter Courage and ihre Kinder* (*Mother Courage and her Children*, 1939), for example, Mother Courage makes her living from the war that eventually devours all her children. Brecht intended such plays to have an "alienation effect" on the audience, challenging them to consider social and political contradictions. After World War II, Brecht returned to socialist East Germany and directed many of the plays he had written in exile. His work as playwright and director widely influenced theater in the later twentieth century.

PICASSO'S *GUERNICA*

The great political issue of the late 1930s was the Spanish Civil War (1936–9), in which liberals and communists battled against the rising forces of conservatives and fascists. Spain's progressive republican government was aided by Soviet Russia and attracted sympathetic volunteer fighters from left-wing parties in Europe and the United States; the fascist regimes of Hitler and Mussolini aided the Spanish rebels, who eventually succeeded in overthrowing the republic. One infamous event in the Civil War inspired the artist Pablo Picasso to create a modernist masterpiece. In 1937 German bombers attacked the Basque city of Guernica [GAIR-nee-ka] in the first massive aerial bombardment of a civilian target. The city, which had no military value, was gutted, its citizens obliterated.

In outrage at the barbarous attack, Picasso painted *Guernica* (Fig. **14.28**), a modernist allegory of suffering and

14.28 Pablo Picasso, *Guernica,* **1937. Oil on canvas, 11 ft 5¹/₂ ins x 25 ft 5³/₄ ins (3.49 x 7.77 m). Museo Nacional Centro de Arte Reina Sofía, Madrid.**
Picasso's masterpiece protested the Germans' massive bombing of a Spanish Basque city in 1937. The horse, he said, represented the people, the bull "not fascism, but brutality and darkness."

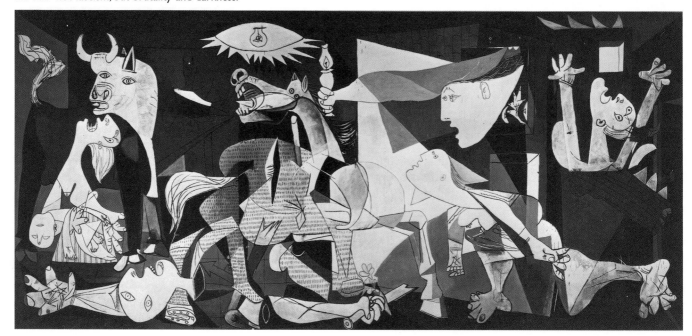

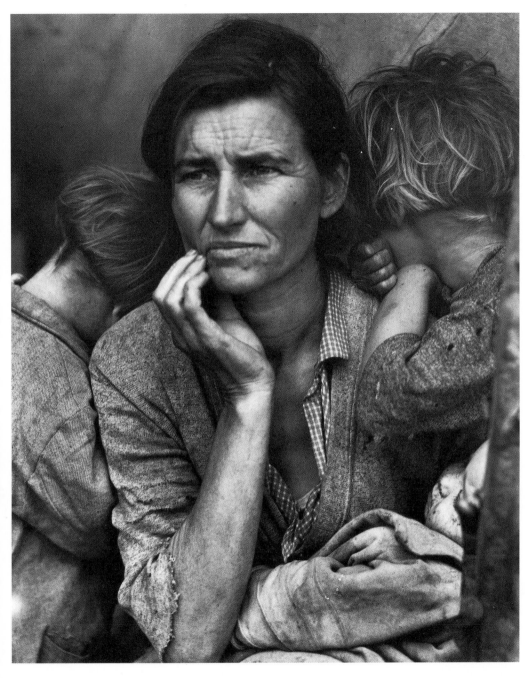

14.29 Dorothea Lange,
Migrant Mother, Nipomo,
***California,* 1936. Gelatin**
silver print. Library of
Congress, Washington, D.C.
What details of pose and
gesture in this affecting scene
communicate the subjects'
anguish?

brutality. The central figure is a horse, pierced by a spear and fragmented into planes. Its anguished cry is shared by human figures engulfed in flames of the burning city. A mother shrieks in agony over the body of her child. Hulking behind her is the bull, a figure of "darkness and brutality," according to Picasso. The scene is illuminated by an eerie eye, with a light bulb as its pupil. Although Picasso clearly drew from his own private symbolism, the picture nevertheless achieves a powerful propagandistic effect.

THE POLITICAL ART OF THE CAMERA

The young arts of photography and film-making were pressed into political service during the tumultuous decades

of 1920 to 1940. In the United States, the effects of the Great Depression stimulated an outburst of photographic realism. To document rural poverty and help justify government aid programs, the United States government sent photographers into rural areas, where they collected more than two hundred and fifty thousand documentary photographs. **Documentary** is the name given to a straightforward photographic record of social reality. One famous photo-document of the Depression was Dorothea Lange's image of a mother and her children in a California migrant workers' camp (Fig. **14.29**). Lange and other documentary photographers wished to arouse the sympathy of the viewer, while endeavoring to keep a balance as they truthfully recorded the visual facts.

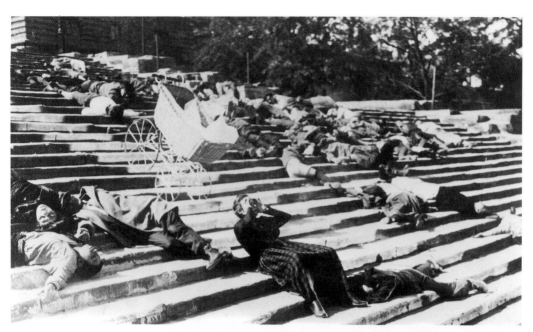

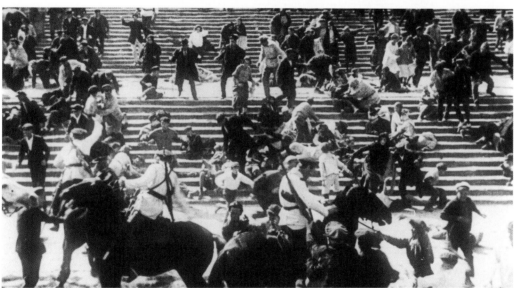

14.30 Sergei Eisenstein, shots from the "Odessa Steps" sequence from the film *Battleship Potemkin*, 1925.
Eisenstein's editing technique, called montage, rapidly switched from one shot to another, building an emotional response in the viewer.

By the 1920s, the cinema was a well-established commercial enterprise, already out-pacing the theater in the size of its public. Film-making was quickly adapted to political purposes in the Soviet Union, where a generation of pioneering filmmakers emerged from the Bolshevik Revolution of 1917. In 1925, Sergei Eisenstein (1898–1948) made the classic film *Battleship Potemkin*, an international success, and one of the most influential films in the history of cinema, symbolizing to many Westerners the cultural progress of revolutionary Russia.

Battleship Potemkin recounts a 1905 mutiny on a czarist warship, an uprising that foreshadowed the Bolshevik Revolution. To tell the story, Eisenstein [EYE-zen-STINE] used an editing technique called **montage**, the rapid juxtaposition of different images to create an idea or emotion in the viewer. *Potemkin's* most famous montage sequence is the "Odessa Steps," when czarist soldiers slaughter the townspeople who are cheering the mutineers. At its climax the Odessa steps sequence cuts back and forth between the fleeing townspeople and the czarist soldiers marching relentlessly forward. Interspersed among these shots is an image of a baby carriage careering down the steps (Fig. **14.30**) – an image symbolizing the vulnerability and innocence of the people.

A different kind of politics inspired the films of German filmmaker Leni Riefenstahl (b. 1902), whose documentary films *The Triumph of the Will* (1934) and *Olympia* (1936) glorified the regime of Adolf Hitler. Riefenstahl [REEF-en-stahl] was invited to make a documentary of a Nazi party rally at Nuremberg, with finance from the Nazi government. The resultant film *The Triumph of the Will* contained visually stunning shots of massed troops and Nazi flags, as well as endearingly human scenes of Nazi youths. Although presenting itself as documen-

THE WRITE IDEA

Choose a contemporary work of film, video, or photography that you would classify as propaganda. Analyze the political message of the work, paying special attention to its use of the visual medium.

tary, *Triumph of the Will* effectively communicated both Hitler's hypnotic power as an orator and his ordinariness and vulnerability. Riefenstahl's film was a masterful work of political propaganda, an artistic work in the service of political ideology.

IN THE AMERICAN GRAIN

Identify the most significant American innovators of the modernist era.

The modernist period – about 1910–1940 – saw an artistic flowering in a North America no longer culturally dominated by Europe. Some Americans were drawn to London and Paris, and became American modernists on European soil. Others stayed home to create a modernism in the American grain.

REGIONALISM AND RENAISSANCE

The expatriate Americans who made notable contributions to modernism included: T. S. Eliot (see page 406) and another hugely influential poet, Ezra Pound (1885–1972); Gertrude Stein (1874–1946), an author and center of a famous literary circle in Paris; and Ernest Hemingway, a novelist who depicted the lives of American expatriates like himself. New York City was a modernist center in its own right: there, a gifted group of Americans gathered around the photographer Alfred Stieglitz (1864–1946) and defined a modernist style with an American flavor. The best-known representative of this style is painter Georgia O'Keeffe (1887–1986), whose works transmuted organic shapes – flowers, skeletons, landscapes – into abstract forms.

In Harlem, uptown from Stieglitz's New York avant-garde gallery, a dynamic group of poets and artists created the **Harlem Renaissance**, a flowering of African-American letters in the 1920s. Among its most important figures were poets Countee Cullen (1903–46) and Langston Hughes (1902–67). Hughes powerfully expressed the frustrated desires of black Americans in such poems as *Harlem*, with its potent questions: "What happens to a dream deferred?

Does it dry up like a raisin in the sun? . . . *Or does it explode?*" The Harlem Renaissance also included the young folklorist Zora Neale Hurston, author of *Their Eyes Were Watching God* (1937), a novelistic rendering of a young black woman's search for love.

Outside New York, American artists drew their literary or artistic innovations from the speech and landscape of the American locales – the kind of distinctively American scenes captured by painter Edward Hopper (Fig. **14.31**). Among these American "regionalists," known by their association with various American regions, were the novelist Willa Cather (1876–1947), whose novels were set in Nebraska, and William Faulkner (1867–1962), who created an imaginary Mississippi county filled with intriguing characters. Faulkner's most important novels, such as *Absalom, Absalom!* (1936), achieved a richness of language and complexity of form that ranked him with Joyce, Kafka, and other masters of the modernist style in fiction.

THE AMERICAN SCENE

The invention of **modern dance** – the expressive and often spontaneous dance form based on a rejection of ballet's classical rules – is often credited to the free-spirited American Isadora Duncan (1878–1927). Duncan earned her first dancing job after she exclaimed, "I have discovered the art which has been lost for two thousand years." Thinking she was re-creating the ancient art of Greek dance, Duncan was actually challenging the regimented world of classical ballet with her freely interpretive movements. She was famous for her "free dances," in a flowing white costume, moving lyrically on her scandalously bare feet to the strains of Beethoven or Wagner. She was an early and outspoken feminist and proponent of free love, and her hatred of convention was visible in her inimitable dance style. She died in a manner fitting a legend. Saying to her friends, "I go to my glory," she climbed into an open car. The long scarf she was wearing caught in the wheel spokes and as the car started, her neck was snapped.

Less flamboyant but no less legendary experimenters followed Duncan's example. Martha Graham (1894–1991) fashioned a system of teaching modern dance that made it as rigorous as ballet. Graham taught dance as a means of directly expressing inner states of mind. Her dancers learned to feel opposing forces in their bodies – forces that would draw their bodies down to the floor and then back upright again. Graham's methods were proved in dance works that usually centered on her own performance. She first worked only with female dancers, and she often worked with women's themes. Her works included *Primitive Mysteries* (1931) and *Appalachian Spring* (1944; Fig. **14.32**), a portrayal of a heroic pioneer woman. The music to *Appalachian Spring* was composed by Aaron Copland (1900–90), whose works frequently quoted from American ballads and folk songs.

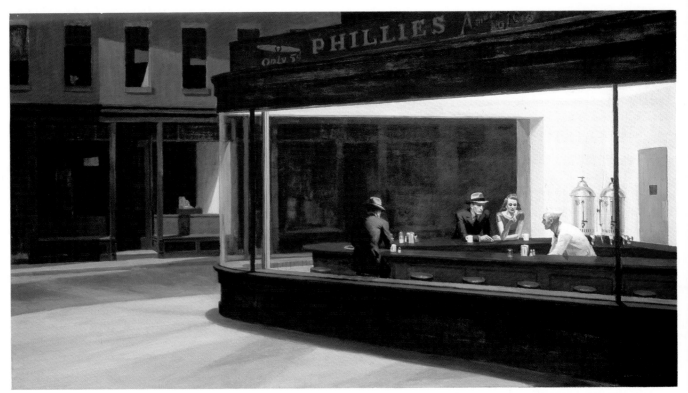

14.31 Edward Hopper, *Nighthawks*, 1942. Oil on canvas, 33 x 60 ins (84 x 152 cm). Art Institute of Chicago, Friends of American Art Collection 1942.51.
Hopper presented his cityscapes as lonely pastorals of American urban life.

14.32 Martha Graham's *Appalachian Spring*, 1944, with music by the American composer Aaron Copland and sets by the Japanese-American sculptor Isamu Noguchi.
Copland's music for the last scene of *Appalachian Spring* builds on variations of the familiar tune "Simple Gifts," a melody from the Shaker faith.

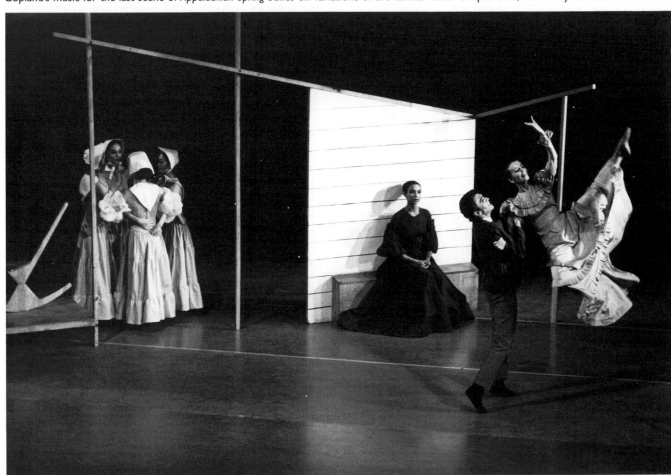

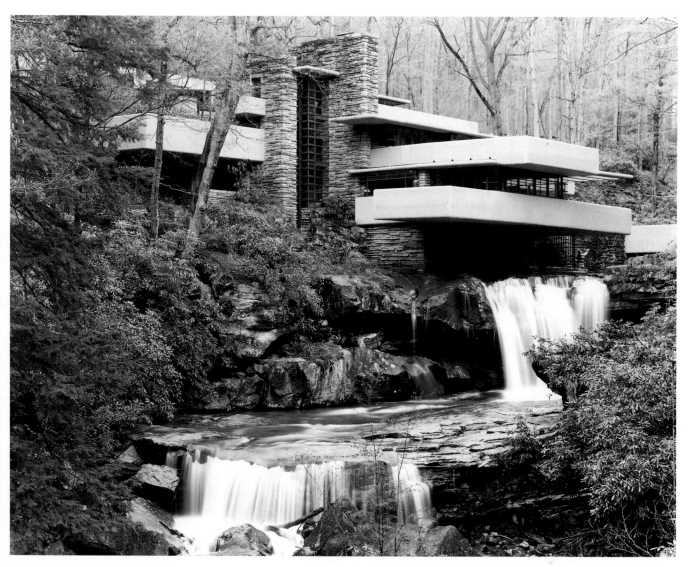

14.33 Frank Lloyd Wright, "Falling Water" (Kaufmann House), Bear Run, Pennsylvania, 1936–7.
Wright's organic use of setting and materials contrasts sharply with the self-contained modernist designs of Le Corbusier (Fig. 14.25).

The American scene also fostered a budding genius in symphonic music. Composer Charles Ives (1874–1954) captured the aural flavor of American popular life – the Fourth of July, marching bands, and camp meetings – in his *Three Pieces in New England* (1903–11). One of the work's movements, called "Putnam's Camp," records the sounds of an Independence Day festival, punctuated by a dream sequence full of musical energy. Ives' musical techniques had none of the abstract rigor of Schoenberg's methods, but did explore broad dissonances.

Frank Lloyd Wright The same special affinity for the American place and people was apparent in the architecture of Frank Lloyd Wright (1869–1959). Influenced by his boyhood summers on a Wisconsin farm, Wright believed that a building should reflect its natural surroundings and mediate between its occupants and their natural environment. Though he designed many types of buildings, Wright's organic sense of form is best expressed in his houses.

Wright's organic theory of architecture is demonstrated in "Falling Water" (Fig. **14.33**), a vacation house on Bear Run in Pennsylvania. The house is built literally around a waterfall: from its central core, concrete terraces were cantilevered out over the stream, creating a daring, airy effect. Inside, the treatment was just as fluid. Space flowed around a central fireplace, with glass walls looking out over the wooded site. Inside and out, surfaces were faced with native stone. Although technically daring, "Falling Water" had a solidity and serenity that derived from its harmony with the natural setting.

THE AGE OF JAZZ

The most distinctly American art form was jazz, a music of popular melodies played with improvisational invention and a characteristic "swing" rhythm. By 1920, jazz music could be heard in the clubs and dance halls of every city with a large African-American population, and by the 1930s it had become popular throughout America and Europe. Mainstream composers adapted jazz melodies and rhythms to concert music, particularly George Gershwin (1893–1937) in his *Rhapsody in Blue* (1924) and his opera *Porgy and Bess* (1935).

Jazz originated as an ensemble music, usually played in collective improvisation, that blended diverse African and European musical elements. **Improvisation** is the technique of composing the musical work while it is being performed. Typically, a jazz soloist improvises variations on a familiar melody, inventing new rhythmic or melodic ideas at the moment of performance.

The first great genius of the jazz solo was trumpeter Louis Armstrong (1900–71; Fig. **14.34**), probably the best-known figure in the history of jazz. Armstrong migrated from New Orleans to Chicago, where he eventually led his own jazz groups, the "Hot Five" and the "Hot Seven." With his cornet or trumpet, Armstrong was able to mimic jazz singers by bending notes up or down, creating a mournful effect. In songs such as *Hotter than That* (1927), composed by his wife, the pianist Lil Hardin, Armstrong altered the tempo for dramatic effect and "played around the tune," exploring melodic variations in improvisational style. Armstrong also invented **scat singing**, vocals of nonsense syllables that imitate a jazz instrumental solo.

The jazz ensemble was revived with the large dance bands of the 1930s and 1940s. These so-called "swing" bands expanded jazz's appeal as dance music, especially to white audiences. To meet the enormous demand for jazz compositions, several important jazz composers became prominent, among them Duke Ellington (1899–1974). As one of his players said, "Duke played the piano but his real instrument was the band." Although he composed longer works, Ellington's most famous pieces, such as *Concert for Cootie* (*Take the A-Train*) and *Satin Doll*, were short enough to be recorded on 78-rpm records.

The 1940s saw a revival of improvisational purism in jazz in a style called "be-bop." Be-bop's more jagged, adventurous style was perfected by saxophonist Charlie "Bird" Parker (1920–55). On such be-bop classics as *Little Benny* (1947) and *Bloomdido* (1950), Parker's searching improvisations maintained only the chords of the original tune. As a relentlessly innovative improviser, Parker's influence in jazz is rivaled only by Louis Armstrong's.

The exploratory solos of be-bop jazz indicated the direction that jazz would take in the post-war era. The insistent experimentation of musicians such as Parker, John Coltrane, Miles Davis, and their successors later restricted jazz to small and musically knowledgeable audiences. Still, it gave rise to the immensely popular forms of rock-and-roll and rhythm-and-blues, the basis of most contemporary pop music.

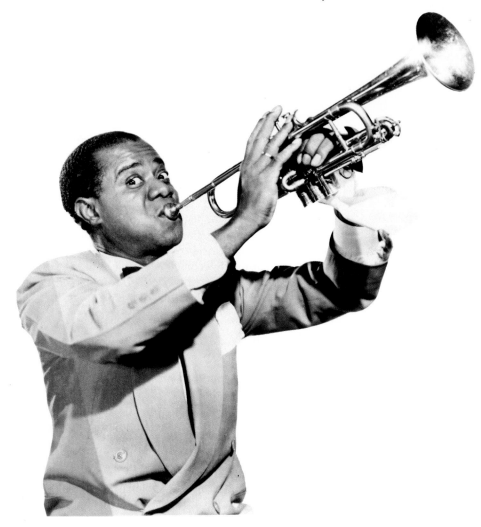

14.34 Louis Armstrong – respectfully known as "Pops" by fellow jazz musicians, or less respectfully as "Satchmo" (satchel-mouth) – virtually invented the improvisational solo in jazz.

Chapter Summary

A Turbulent Century. The Great War of 1914–18 set off a series of shocks and upheavals within Western civilization. In Russia, Lenin engineered the Bolshevik revolution, establishing the first self-proclaimed socialist state. In Germany, fascism employed authoritarian rule and anti-Semitic doctrines to gain control of government. Hitler's Nazis and Roosevelt's New Deal used mass media and new documentary art forms to appeal to disaffected masses.

Modernism in Art. Artistic modernism discarded artistic tradition and embraced the "primitive" style of African and Pacific art. Picasso's primitivist masterpiece *Les Demoiselles d'Avignon* ignited the cubist style, blazing a path toward greater abstraction in art. The trend intensified in the nonobjective works of Kandinsky, Brancusi, and Mondrian. Duchamp and the dadaists attacked the very idea of art, mocking conventional definitions of art. German expressionists, inspired by the example of Matisse, pursued an art of unbridled expressiveness.

The Freudian Revolution. Like artistic traditions, Western intellectual traditions were shaken in the twentieth century. Freud's theory of the mind located the origins of human thought in the unconscious, while psychoanalysis sought the key to psychological development in childhood sexuality. The surrealists applied Freud's theory in their works of "psychic automatism" and bizarre symbolism, embodied in Miró's biomorphic shapes and Dalí's dream images.

Modernism in Literature. Modernist writers revealed their characters' inner psychic life through stream-of-consciousness narrative, while poets employed dense allusion and fragmented form. Ironic modern heroes such as Kafka's Gregor Samsa suffered deep alienation from a perplexing and nightmarish social world.

Modernist Music and Architecture. Working with Diaghilev's daring dance company the Ballets Russes, the modernist composer Stravinsky developed new complexities of rhythm and harmony that disturbed tradition-minded audiences. Schoenberg's atonal method discarded the major-minor key system and eventually replaced it with the twelve-tone or serial method. Berg's atonal opera *Wozzeck* was notable for its atmosphere of paranoia and despair. By contrast, modernist architects devised a logical, functional building style typified by Bauhaus architect Gropius' glass and steel cubes. Le Corbusier's Villa Savoye employed ferroconcrete to achieve a look of modern clarity and sophistication.

Art and Politics. Art in the modernist era served as a vehicle for political protest and propaganda. Brecht's epic theater sought to stimulate a critical attitude in audiences through his "alienation effect." Picasso's *Guernica* protested against the brutality of modern war, using the whole language of modernism. American photographers documented the poverty of the Great Depression, while the film-makers Eisenstein in the Soviet Union and Riefenstahl in Nazi Germany employed new cinematic techniques in their compelling works of propaganda.

In the American Grain. The modernist period brought a new confidence to American artists and authors. One important center was New York, where the Harlem Renaissance nurtured a brief but intense flowering of African-American literature and art. American regionalists captured the distinctive character of American locales. In dance, Isadora Duncan and Martha Graham helped invent the expressive and spontaneous form of modern dance, while the composer Ives typified a budding American genius in music. Architect Frank Lloyd Wright organically linked his eclectic buildings to people and place. North America produced a genuinely new art form in jazz, pioneered by the improvisational genius of jazz musicians such as Armstrong, Ellington, and Parker.

15 The Contemporary Spirit

One might say the spirit of contemporary civilization was "wrapped up" by an event in the mid-1990s. For two weeks, the artists Christo and Jeanne-Claude cloaked Germany's past and future parliament building with silver fabric (Fig. *15.1*). The building in Berlin was a potent historical symbol, recalling the horrors of war and Germany's long division between democracy and communism. The crowds that gathered to view the Christos' project were animated by the **contemporary spirit**:

exhilarated by global unity, alive with the possibility of new technologies, but a little perplexed by what it all meant and how quickly it changed.

15.1 Christo and Jeanne-Claude, *Wrapped Reichstag*, Berlin, 1971–95.
Crowds gather around the Christos' work of art entitled *Wrapped Reichstag*. The past and future Parliament building is located near the site of the Berlin Wall and the Brandenburg Gate. All are symbols of Germany's troubled political past.

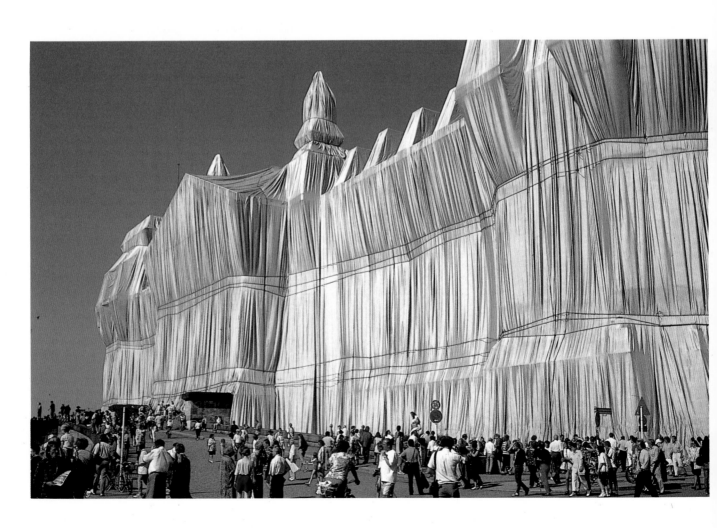

HOLOCAUSTS

Describe the responses of artists and writers to the horrors of World War II and the rise of consumer society.

World War I had thrown into doubt the question of human progress. In the trenches, the certainties of enlightenment and universal order were shattered under the first artillery barrage. World War II (1939–45) raised questions of a different sort. The war demonstrated that Western civilization had made considerable progress, if only in its powers of destruction. Motorized weapons, the aerial bombardment of cities, and the atomic bomb indicated great strides in technological violence. The question was whether technological progress would now lead humanity toward total self-destruction.

The aftermath of World War II revealed new horrors and new hopes for the course of Western civilization. The Allied soldiers who conquered Germany and Eastern Europe discovered death camps full of emaciated survivors. In such camps as Auschwitz in Poland, the Nazis had systematically slaughtered millions of Jews, Slavs, gypsies, and other groups, a calamity now called the **Holocaust**. The long-standing Western tradition of anti-Jewish prejudice had culminated in the Nazis' "final solution," a program to eradicate European Jewry and other supposed inferior races. Revelations of the death camps shocked Westerners and seemed to question the core of Western values. One German philosopher said, "After Auschwitz there can be no more poetry."

A holocaust of another sort was unleashed by the United States' invention and use of atomic weaponry. The incineration of Hiroshima and Nagasaki in Japan in 1945 by atomic bombs ushered in a new era of human destructiveness. From its beginnings, the technology of atomic weapons assumed a life of its own, sustained by scientists' pursuit of pioneering research and politicians' hope for the ultimate weapon. The rivalry between the United States and the Soviet Union, known as the Cold War, threatened a nuclear war that would destroy the entire planet. Meanwhile, Europe's overseas colonial territories struggled for their independence. In some cases, efforts of national liberation were advanced with friendship and peace, in others (for example, Algeria and Vietnam) they were bitterly and bloodily contested.

Despite the philosphers' warnings, artists were able to respond to an age of mass destruction and global anxiety. Romanian-born novelist Elie Wiesel [VEE-zell] (b. 1928) wrote a moving account of his experience as a survivor of the Jewish Holocaust in *Night* (1958). In his *Threnody for the Victims of Hiroshima* (1960), Polish composer Krzysztof Penderecki [penn-der-ETT-skee] (b. 1933) captured the anguish of Hiroshima's residents in piercing violins and the thump of musicians pounding the bodies of their instruments.

POST-WAR AMERICA

In the United States, a post-war mood of self-confidence, expansion, and consumerism prevailed. North American artists responded with misgivings to the widening consumer culture around them. As in the nineteenth century, materialism was associated with spiritual alienation and emptiness. The poet Allen Ginsberg (1926–97) belonged to a 1950s group of writers called the Beats, American writers who explored themes of rootlessness and the endless quest for meaning. In one poem, Ginsberg describes an encounter with the ghost of Walt Whitman, the nineteenth-century American poet, in a California supermarket. Ginsberg's consumer images seem to ask whether well-stocked supermarket aisles mask a spiritual desolation in the midst of material prosperity.

> *I saw you, Walt Whitman, childless, lonely old*
> *grubber, poking among the meats in the refrigerator*
> *and eyeing the grocery boys.*
> *I heard you asking questions of each: Who killed the*
> *pork chops? What price bananas? Are you my*
> *Angel?*
> *I wandered in and out of the brilliant stacks of cans*
> *following you, and followed in my imagination by*
> *the store detective.*
> *We strode down the open corridors together in our*
> *solitary fancy tasting artichokes, possessing every*
> *frozen delicacy, and never passing the cashier.*
>
> *Where are we going, Walt Whitman? The doors close*
> *in an hour. Which way does your beard point*
> *tonight?*
> *(I touch your book and dream of our odyssey in the*
> *supermarket and feel absurd.)*
> *Will we walk all night through solitary streets? The*
> *trees add shade to shade, lights out in the houses,*
> *we'll both be lonely.*
> *Will we stroll dreaming of the lost America of love*
> *past blue automobiles in driveways, home to our*
> *silent cottage?*
> *Ah, dear father, graybeard, lonely old courage-teacher,*
> *what America did you have when Charon[a] quit*
> *poling his ferry and you got out on a smoking bank*
> *and stood watching the boat disappear on the black*
> *waters of Lethe?*[1]

ALLEN GINSBERG
From *Howl* (1955)

---

a. Charon, mythological figure who rows the souls of the dead across the river Lethe to the underworld.

While the Beats' quest took them "on the road" (the title of a Beat novel), a group of self-searching American women authors turned inward. Called the "confessional poets," these writers recorded intensely intimate accounts of their personal lives. Their spiritual self-searching was compounded with their protest against the subordinate roles often forced on them as women. The confessional poet Anne Sexton (1928–74) employed graphic images of female sexuality and menstruation, topics seldom explored by male poets. Another confessional, Sylvia Plath (1932–63), was author of the autobiographical novel *The Bell Jar* (1963), which described her fascination with suicide. Both Plath and Sexton eventually took their own lives, succumbing to their own private holocaust of despair.

EXPLORING THE ABSURD

Describe the situation of the existential hero, as depicted in absurdist theater and fiction.

Amid the horror and spiritual desolation left by World War II, a new philosophy explored the possibilities for human freedom and meaningful action in the nuclear age. The philosophy of **existentialism** [eks-iss-STEN-shull-ism] (see "Key Concept") sought engagement in a world that was essentially "absurd," empty of fundamental or ultimate meaning. The existential hero typically faced a circumstance that negated all human effort, like the doctor who combats the bubonic epidemic in Camus's novel *The Plague* (1947). In the face of a meaningless universe, Camus's

KEY CONCEPT

EXISTENTIALISM

In the post-war world, the fresh memories of holocaust were overlaid by Cold War confrontations and a mass society of avid consumption. Some philosophers responded to this situation by rebelling against all systems, asserting the need for authentic, individual action in an indifferent world. This attitude was called **existentialism**, a philosophy determined to live without the illusions of a universal order or an essential human nature. Jean-Paul Sartre (see page 423), a prominent French existential philosopher, said human "existence precedes essence." That is, humans must live their lives without absolute values or divine laws. For the existentialist, there were no assurances of human happiness or worth. There was an absolute freedom – for better or worse – to define what humanity was.

The existentialist hero typically was caught in a Kafkaesque world, faced with a choice between conformity and an anguished but genuine freedom. The French writer Albert Camus (1913–60) described this predicament in his reinterpretation of the ancient myth of Sisyphus. Sisyphus was condemned by the gods to push a stone perpetually up a hillside. To Camus [kam-YOO], Sisyphus' labor was a metaphor for the absurdity of all human action. The hero recognizes that his efforts will never lead anywhere, never attain fruition or transcendence. Yet, in Camus' version, Sisyphus resumes his perpetual labor with a smile, thus affirming his absurd condition.

Although easily exaggerated and caricatured, existentialism was rooted in a long-standing philosophical issue. Christian philosophers had long assumed that God controlled the universe and gave purpose to human life. Enlightenment philosophers had assumed that reason guided human history; existential philosophers stripped away such presumptions. Sartre believed humans were "condemned to freedom." No divine order had prevented the Nazis' horrible crimes against humanity. On the other hand, no innate human nature prevented humans from acting kindly and responsibly toward each other.

In the works of Sartre and Camus, existentialism was ultimately an affirmative philosophy. In their view, humans could live decently and "in good faith," but only if they understood how precarious and uncertain their values were. To live life fully and responsibly required a recognition of the universe's final absurdity.

THE WRITE IDEA

Recall an experience in your life that taught you about the essential nature of human existence. How does your insight compare with the assertions of existentialist philosophy?

existential hero can only savor brief moments of joy or achievement.

Both the novel and the theater proved to be suitable media for existentialist reflection. In the post-war years, a "theater of the absurd" dramatized the futility of human language and action. In the novel, existentialist heroes struggled to assert an individual will against a bureaucratic but irrational system.

THE EXISTENTIALIST IN ACTION

Jean-Paul Sartre (1905–80) was an existentialist man of action. With Camus, Sartre [SART(r)] was a leader of the French Resistance during World War II, writing and producing his first play in Nazi-occupied Paris. After the war, he associated himself with the French communists and the movement to free France's colonies, declining the Nobel Prize for Literature in 1964 for political reasons. When Parisian students and workers revolted in May 1968, they acclaimed Sartre as an intellectual father of the student movement. Sartre followed his own prescription for *l'homme engagé*, the human individual engaged in the struggles of his own time.

Sartre expressed his complex and often contradictory philosophical positions in literary works. His best-known play was *Huis clos* (*No Exit*, 1944), in which three characters serve as each other's tormentors in hell. In a revealing scene, a woman guilty of over-riding vanity finds that there are no mirrors in her part of hell. She must rely on a companion to apply her lipstick, and finally despairs that her perceptions of herself must be transmitted through others. The characters' pessimistic conclusion is the play's famous motto: "*L'enfer, c'est les autres*" – "Hell is other people."

Sartre's literary works reinforced his teaching that every human must ultimately take responsibility for his or her own actions. For this reason, Sartre found the existence of God to be incompatible with human freedom. Like Dostoyevsky and Nietzsche before him, Sartre argued that, even if God existed, then humans were still left utterly free. He wrote:

> Dostoyevsky said, "If God didn't exist, everything would be possible." That is the very starting point of existentialism. Indeed, everything is permissible if God does not exist, and as a result man is forlorn, because neither within him nor without does he find anything to cling to. He can't start making excuses for himself.[2]

Sartre was closely associated with the existentialist woman of action Simone de Beauvoir (1908–86). De Beauvoir [BOH-vwah(r)] was author of *The Second Sex* (1947), a founding text of modern feminism that criticized "the feminine" as a philosophical category. When women were treated as essentially different from men, she argued, they were robbed of their existential freedom. Their value as persons was defined by and against men's. De Beauvoir wrote frequently about the obstacles to free and equal male-female relationships, including her lifelong relationship with Sartre. As an activist, she closely linked the personal and the political. Her study of existentialism and action, *The Ethics of Ambiguity* (1949), examined the difficulty of making ethical choices in a world without universal rules or values.

THE THEATER OF THE ABSURD

The "theater of the absurd" rejected realistic devices or explicit political messages. Instead, absurdists used dream, burlesque comedy, and nonsensical language as dramatic metaphors for the emptiness of the human condition. The dramatist who most vividly dramatized a world without God was Samuel Beckett (1906–89), whose comically pathetic characters inhabit a waste land of empty hopes and futile action. Beckett was an Irishman who lived for many years in Paris. He often translated his own plays into French, or even wrote original works in that language. His plays stripped drama to its bare essentials – pairs of characters yoked to each other by dependency, speaking words that barely communicate, acting in the grotesquely exaggerated gestures of slapstick comedy. More emphatically than Sartre, Beckett demonstrated that hell was – or at least, could be – other people.

As Beckett's theater frequently illustrated, hell was also being without other people. Loneliness and alienation are afflictions that dwarf all other human suffering. In Beckett's "tragicomedy" *Waiting for Godot* (1952), the tramps Vladimir and Estragon spend their days waiting for a command from "Godot" [go-DOH] that will give their lives purpose. These characters spend their days in pointless triviality – no work, no love, no sense of time. They encounter only the sado-masochistic pair of Pozzo and Lucky. It is the blind Pozzo who renders the play's bitterest commentary on human life, describing it as the brief flash of light between womb and grave: "They give birth astride of a grave, the light gleams an instant, then it's night once more."[3] In the play's poignant final scene, Vladimir and Estragon consider hanging themselves from the nearby tree. That solution is rejected because neither of them wants the other to be left alone. Better to confront the futility of their wait for Godot together, than for one to be condemned to loneliness.

The theater of the absurd of the 1950s anticipated a more politicized theater of the next decade. One example is *The Persecution and Assassination of Jean-Paul Marat as Performed by the Inmates of the Asylum of Charenton under the Direction of the Marquis de Sade* (1964), written by the German Peter Weiss [vice] (b. 1915) and usually known under the shortened title *Marat/Sade*. The play within a play mixes political commentary, history, and ritualized violence, and centers on a debate between the revolutionary orator Marat and the sexual eccentric Sade.

THE EXISTENTIAL HERO

In the fiction of the 1950s, a kind of existential hero emerged who was searching for individual identity in the face of an oppressive or insanely bureaucratic system. The archetype of this existential hero appears in Ralph Ellison's stunning novel *Invisible Man* (1952). Ellison (1914–94) relates a young black man's encounters with a white-dominated world, including racist civic leaders in his home town, a hypocritical college president, and a political party that wants only to exploit his talents.

Invisible Man is an existentialist *Bildungsroman* (novel of education), a form established in the eighteenth century. The main character (whose name we never learn) struggles to find his own identity, while the absurd world perceives him through stereotyped masks. His invisibility, the narrator says, is not simply a consequence of the color of his skin. It is a condition of the eyes through which others see him. As the narrator says in the novel's prologue, when others "approach me they see only my surroundings, themselves, or figments of their imagination – indeed, everything and anything except me."[4]

In Joseph Heller's novel *Catch-22* (1961), World War II is a symbol of the absurdity of human existence. Heller (b. 1923) portrays the futile efforts of the bomber captain Yossarian to escape from his maniacal commander. The commander keeps raising the quota of bombing missions necessary to be sent on leave. Yossarian hopes to save himself by claiming insanity, but is trapped by the impossible situation of a "Catch-22," which gives the book its title: a pilot "would be crazy if he wanted to fly more missions and sane if he didn't, but if he was sane, he had to fly them. If he flew them he was crazy and didn't have to; but if he didn't, he was sane and had to."[5]

Like Beckett and Ellison, Heller exploited irony and wit to expose the insanities of Yossarian's world. Underneath the comedy, however, is an unrelenting horror at the senselessness of human suffering.

15.2 Below **Jackson Pollock,** *Number 1*, **1948. Oil on canvas, 5 ft 8 ins x 8 ft 8 ins (1.73 x 2.65 m). Collection, The Museum of Modern Art, New York.**
Though he discarded all subject or symbol, some critics saw existential despair in Pollock's abstract canvases. Others interpreted his "drip" method as a pure, "existential" encounter between artist and materials.

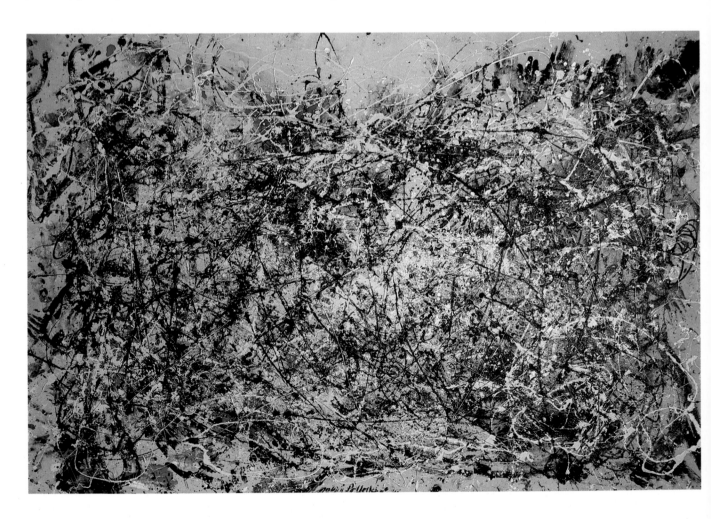

ART IN THE POST-WAR ERA

Identify the modernist trends and techniques that were extended or developed by the post-war avant-garde.

For a long while, Western artists had migrated to Paris to join the newest movements or study the latest style. After 1945, the French capital lost its preeminence in the visual arts to the American upstart New York City. In the post-war era, New York was to be the heart of the artistic avant-garde (see page 427) – the newest wave of artistic experiment.

One reason for New York's prominence was the war itself. Major European artists such as Piet Mondrian and Walter Gropius had fled Nazi Europe to the United States, where they were an enormous stimulus to American artists.

15.3 Mark Rothko, The Rothko Chapel, Rice University, Houston, 1961–5. Oil on canvas. Chapel designed by Philip Johnson.

Meanwhile, the European art world was suppressed by the war's aftermath and dominated by aging masters of modernism like Matisse, Picasso, and Braque (see page 398). The innovative spirit that was temporarily suppressed in Europe, erupted in New York. Radical new styles were often encouraged as a symbol of the West's artistic freedom, and compared to the repression of Soviet-style communism.

With few exceptions, the most important post-war trends in the visual arts emanated from New York. These trends included the tightly knit but diverse group called the "New York school"; the mixture of art and popular culture called "pop art"; and the sculptural innovations of Henry Moore, David Smith, and others.

THE NEW YORK SCHOOL

Out of the heady atmosphere of post-war America arose a confident group of artists now called the New York school, whose artistic styles pushed aggressively toward abstraction. Taking their cue from European modernists, the New York school developed a style called **abstract expressionism**.

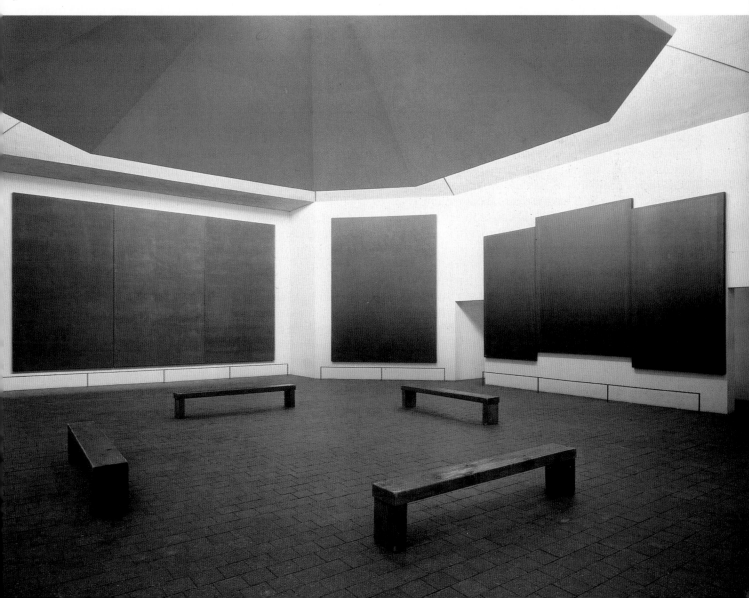

While each painter had an individual style, most abstract expressionists shared a non-objective style that also had the emotional directness of the expressionists. Hence the combination of "abstract," in the manner of Mondrian and Kandinsky, and "expressionist," in the manner of Matisse and Nolde.

The best-known abstract expressionist was Jackson Pollock (1912–56), an intense artist whose radical methods symbolized the New York avant-garde. Pollock had been trained as a realist, but in the 1940s his work grew increasingly abstract. Finally, he discarded the brush altogether and took to dripping and splattering paint on the canvas, often mixing paint with sand or crushed glass (Fig. **15.2**). Pollock described his painting method in these words:

> *My painting does not come from the easel. I hardly ever stretch my canvas before painting. I prefer to tack the unstretched canvas to the hard wall or the floor. I need the resistance of a hard surface. On the floor I am more at ease. I feel nearer, more a part of the painting, since this way I can walk around it, work from the four sides and literally be in the painting. This is akin to the method of the Indian sand painters of the West.*
>
> *I continue to get further away from the usual painter's tools such as easel, palette, brushes, etc. I prefer sticks, trowels, knives, and dripping fluid paint or a heavy impasto with sand, broken glass, and other foreign matter added.*[6]

In the language of existential philosophy, Pollock's paintings were a transcript of his existential encounter with his materials. His method was self-consciously unconscious, akin to the psychic automatism of the surrealists. Such a spontaneous method was also called "action painting." He said, "I have no fears about making changes, destroying the image, etc., because the painting has a life of its own. I try to let it come through. It is only when I lose contact with the painting that the result is a mess."[7]

A host of other New York painters practiced similar principles of abstraction, but with substantially different results. Willem de Kooning (1904-97), Arshile Gorky (1905–48), Barnett Newman (1905–70), and Robert Motherwell (1915–93) were among the most prominent New York painters. The works of Mark Rothko (1903–70) are interesting in part because of the religious overtones in his luminous rectangles of color. Rothko left the edges of his rectangular shapes vaguely defined, so that the fields of color gently merged. Hence critics gave the name "color-field painting" to his work. Rothko himself wished his paintings to destroy the "finite associations" of ordinary life and refer to a "transcendent realm" of human experience. His majestic canvases often evoked in viewers a mood of spiritual contemplation, which was Rothko's aim in the eleven canvases he painted for the Houston Chapel at Rice University in Texas (Fig. **15.3**).

POP, MINIMALISM, AND THE AVANT-GARDE

The New York avant-garde that followed abstract expressionism was **pop** (for "popular") art, a style far removed from the drip paintings of Jackson Pollock. Pop art borrowed from the mass-produced commercial art of magazines, television, and movies. By crossing over the division between elite and mass culture, pop art brought a refreshing irreverence and accessibility to the avant-garde.

The most flamboyant pop artist was Andy Warhol (1928–87), whose works of mass-culture images show little visible attempt at artistic creativity. Warhol worked with the most banal and familiar images he could find, like a Campbell's soup can (Fig. **15.5**) or a Coca-Cola bottle. His silk-screened images of Elvis Presley and stacks of Brillo boxes directly challenged the aesthetics of abstraction. By repeating these consumer icons, however, Warhol invested them with an aesthetic value that the same objects lacked sitting on a supermarket shelf. In other words, any image could be art, just as any person (including himself) could be a celebrity. Warhol became famous for his pronouncement, "everyone will be famous for fifteen minutes." In fact, Warhol himself became a media image as familiar as any of his works.

The pop artist Robert Rauschenberg [ROW-shun-berg] (b. 1925) studied at Black Mountain College in North Carolina, where he came into contact with other avant-garde innovators. Rauschenberg's pop works followed in the tradition of dada artists, who often created art from discarded objects. In the late 1950s, Rauschenberg devised his "combine paintings," mixed-media compositions of photographs, silk-screens, and "found" objects. His *Monogram* (Fig. **15.6**) rehabilitated the refuse of mass society and charged it with new meaning. At the work's center is a stuffed goat wearing a used tire as its girdle. Rauschenberg has been one of the most resourceful figures in the American avant-garde. His later works have been autobiographical and documentary, including the ongoing *Quarter-Mile Piece*, a collage of objects and images from the artist's career.

In avant-garde sculpture, an abstractionist trend led to an extreme objectivity, removing virtually all evidence of the artist's hand. This trend toward stripping sculpture of all content or decoration was called **minimalism**. Minimalists often limited themselves to simple and unadulterated materials and form, such as plain

---

CRITICAL QUESTION

If society had followed the lead of the post-1945 avant-garde, in what direction would it have developed? Besides artists, what other group or part of contemporary society might be considered an avant-garde?

KEY CONCEPT

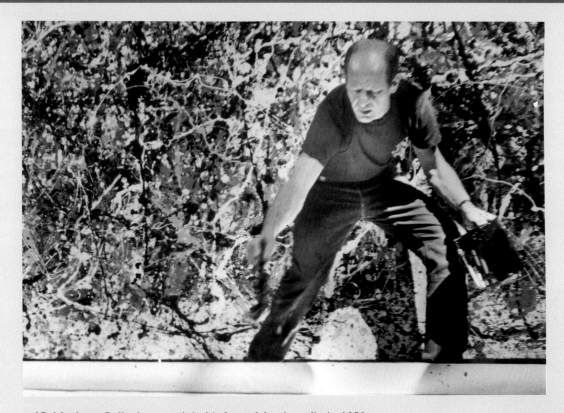

15.4 Jackson Pollock at work in his Long Island studio in 1950.
Pollock's radical painting methods and cryptic abstract canvases were an emblem of the post-1945 avant-garde.

THE AVANT-GARDE

In the 1950s, the New York school represented the latest incarnation of the **avant-garde**, the label applied to artists and writers who define the newest wave of artistic experiment. Although the modernists did not consciously use the term, their rejection of traditional forms in art, music, and literature was an important phase of the avant-garde. Inevitably, however, modernism itself became the artistic tradition which the New York school claimed to be "in advance of."

As often happens in cultural history, the New York school of painters relied on critics to explain their significance as the new avant-garde. The New York art critic Clement Greenberg argued that Jackson Pollock (Fig. **15.4**) and the abstract expressionists represented the next logical development of modernism because their work was *new*. Innovation, along with artistic technique and vision, became an essential criterion for judging the arts. The novelty of abstract expressionism was so radical, however, that Greenberg feared

it would estrange wealthy collectors and patrons. He pleaded for New York's elite to buy avant-garde works, so that genuine art would not lose its "umbilical cord of gold."

Greenberg's writings revealed the continuing paradox of the idea of the avant-garde. To forge ahead, avant-garde artists could not be too bound to social or artistic conventions. Yet if their work was to be understood (and purchased), it had to communicate intelligibly to a significant audience. Greenberg's essays on abstract expressionism were intended to educate potential patrons about the value of avant-garde innovations.

Today, much publicly funded art seen in university and public galleries suffers from the same paradox. How do avant-garde artists achieve innovation and freedom of artistic expression, and still find understanding among the public that supports their work? On the other hand, what fresh insights are lost to a public that does not support an artistic avant-garde, the very artists who challenge conventional assumptions about art's definition or meaning?

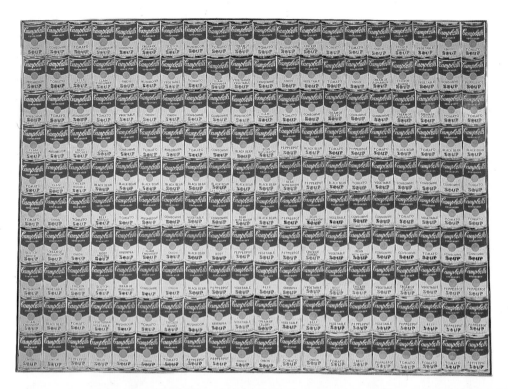

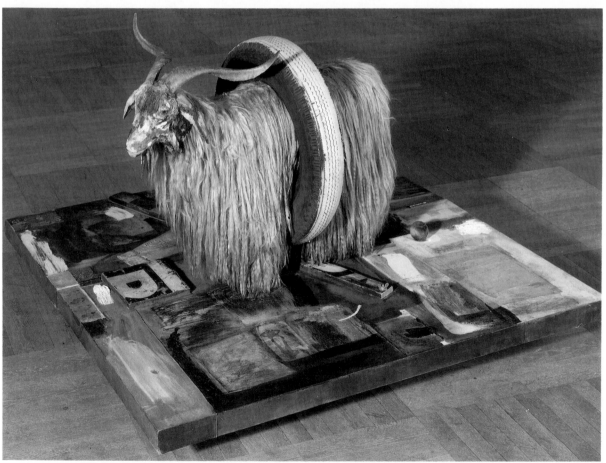

lacquered planks or precisely machined aluminum boxes. Minimalism may be seen as a reaction against the expressive excesses of the avant-garde and the clutter of consumer culture.

The sculpture of Donald Judd (b.1928) is often called minimalist because Judd purged his work of any reference to objects or ideas. In sculpture, he wanted to do away with the "illusionism" of painting; he believed that "actual space is intrinsically more powerful and specific than paint on a flat surface." Judd's metal boxes and other minimalist

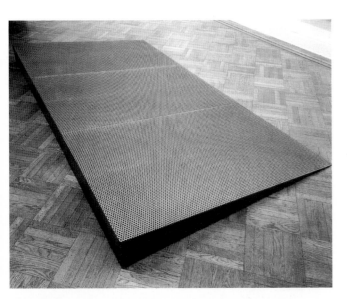

**15.7 Donald Judd, *Untitled (Perforated Steel Ramp)*, 1965.
Perforated steel, 119¹/₄ x 8¹/₄ x 65³/₄ ins (303 x 21 x 167
cm). Collection Giuseppe Panza di Biumo-Varese.**
The minimalist Donald Judd created radically understated sculptural
works, like this metal ramp.

works (Fig. **15.7**) were the antithesis of Jackson Pollock's
abstract expressionism. Their polished surfaces reflected
only their gallery surroundings. The artist was even removed
from the works' fabrication, since Judd drew up exact specifications for his works and then had an industrial shop
produce the object itself.

A different direction in the post-war avant-garde
stressed art as idea and process, rather than finished work.
This notion was extended by **happenings**, intentionally
provocative and quasi-artistic events executed by artists.
One happening involved an artist drinking paint, pouring paint over his head, and then diving through the
canvas. Happenings had the effect of engaging all the spectator's senses, even when their meaning was to say the
least, unclear. Happenings were descended from the dada
manifestations and were usually limited in their appeal to
the avant-garde community.

Happenings had a positive effect on other kinds of
performance art, especially dance. Merce Cunningham
(1919–91), a graduate of Martha Graham's modern dance
school, incorporated the avant-garde spirit of happenings
into his dance works. Although Cunningham's dance
choreography was classically abstract and technically
demanding, he built spontaneity into his performances
– sometimes choosing the sequence of movements in a
dance by flipping a coin. Several of his works were performed with sets designed by Rauschenberg and other
artists of his time, and he believed that music, dance,
and setting should be independent of one another,
creating visual dissonances that arrested the audience's
attention (Fig. **15.9**).

SCULPTURE IN THE POST-WAR ERA

At mid-century the sculptural arts fell under the influence
of Englishman Henry Moore (1898–1986), whose smoothly
carved organic forms added a new element to the vocabulary of modernism. Moore, a younger contemporary of
the modernists, acknowledged that Constantin Brancusi
(see page 399) had succeeded in purifying sculpture. After
experimenting with non-objective sculpture, however,
Moore began to work in the massive human forms that he
saw in Aztec and other native American sculpture.

Moore crafted his works to look as if they had been
shaped by the timeless forces of nature. He said, "I have
always paid great attention to natural forms, such as bones,
shells, and pebbles."[8] His sculptures frequently contained
hollowed-out voids, creating an interaction between the
void and the sculptural mass of wood or bronze. Moore's
works were less severe than earlier modernism and contrasted sharply to the hard-edged works of minimalism.
Often suggesting the solidity of the earth and the human
body, Moore's carvings took on a "human, or occasionally
animal character and personality." The *Recumbent Figure*
(Fig. **15.10**) suggests the primal archetypes of woman or
mother and child.

Like Moore, the American sculptor Alexander Calder
(1898–1976) was a contemporary of Miró and Mondrian.
Calder's characteristic works were assemblages of cut-out
shapes suspended in air, dubbed by Duchamp as **mobiles**.
The different shapes of Calder's mobiles seemed to be borrowed from Miró's surrealist paintings (see Fig. 14.19). By
suspending them on wire, however, Calder introduced an
element of chance into the parts' movement and interaction (Fig. **15.8**). Other Calder mobiles were motorized
so that the motion was constant and predictable. From the
1940s, Calder became interested in monumental works

**15.8 Alexander Calder, *Spring Blossoms*, 1965. Painted
metal and heavy wire, height 4 ft 4 ins (1.32 m). Museum of
Art, The Pennsylvania State University.**
Calder often suspended his mobiles from the ceiling, where a breath
of air might set them in motion. The lyrical whimsy of his mobiles
provided an important connection between the modernists and
post-war sculpture.

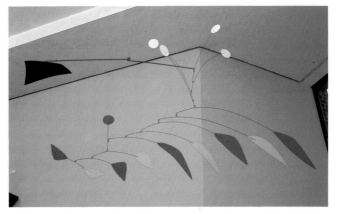

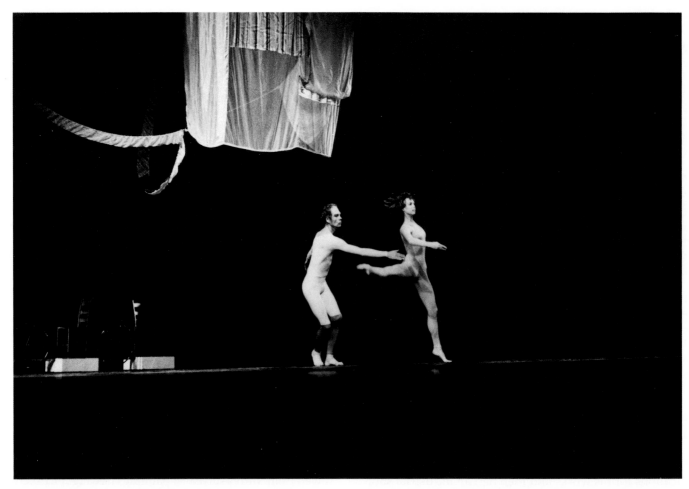

15.9 Above **Merce Cunningham in *Travelogue*, 1977. Set designed by the pop artist Robert Rauschenberg.**
Merce Cunningham's dance works achieved something of the spontaneity of artistic happenings.

that interacted with the surrounding environmental space. He called these "stabiles," large stationary works made from cut-out metal plate, which often stood on plazas.

Constructed metal sculpture was the preferred medium of David Smith (1906–65), the most important North American sculptor in the post-war era. Smith had no academic training as a sculptor or first-hand contact with the modernists. Having learned to weld in an automobile plant, he created large metal constructions whose abstract shapes were inspired by the Soviet constructivists and their effort to unite art with industrial design and technology. He produced works that clearly represented the machine age; metal, he said, "possesses little art history." His machinist skills enabled Smith to explore the aesthetic qualities of steel: sometimes the surface was polished to a high sheen and other times it was scraped away to create texture. His *Cubi* series (Fig. **15.11**) illustrates the dynamic, un-"stabile" quality of his assemblages.

Louise Nevelson (1900–88) used the refuse of industrial society to compose her sculptures of discarded boxes,

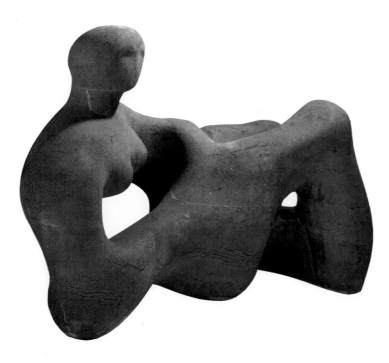

15.10 Henry Moore, *Recumbent Figure*, 1938. Green Horton stone, length 4 ft 7 ins (1.40 m). Tate Gallery, London.
Moore's smoothly carved figures suggest primal archetypes of woman or mother and child, akin to the pre-Columbian sculpture that he admired.

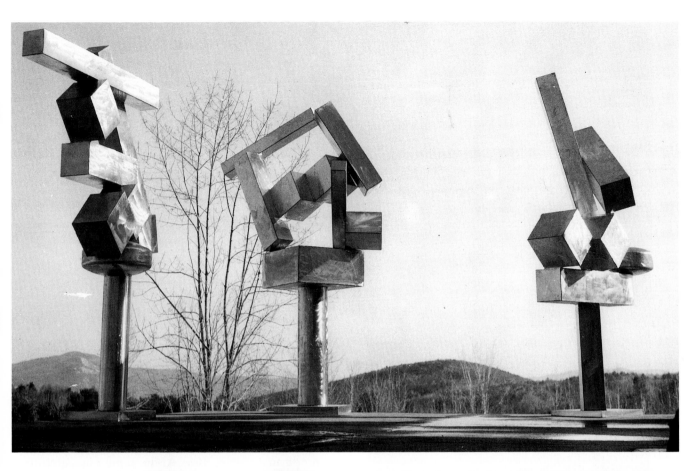

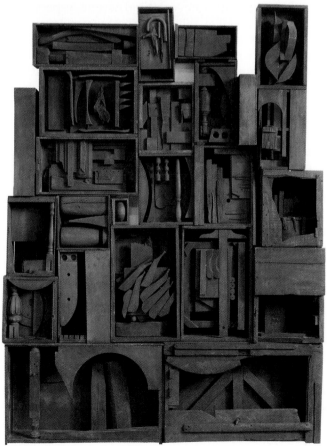

15.11 Above **David Smith, *Cubi XVIII, Cubi XVII, Cubi XIX*, 1964, 1963, 1964. Heights 9 ft–9 ft 8 ins (2.74–2.95 m). Tate Gallery, London.**
Consider Smith's play with balance and mass in these monumental standing constructions. How is their visual impact enhanced by the natural setting shown here?

15.12 Left **Louise Nevelson, *Black Wall*, 1959. Wood, 112 x 85¹/₄ x 25¹/₂ ins (264.2 x 216.5 x 44.8 cm). Tate Gallery, London.**
Catalogue some of the interesting shapes that Nevelson collects in this wall assemblage. Compare her use of "found" objects (wood scraps) to Rauschenberg's in *Monogram* (Fig. 15.6).

furniture, and other off-casts. Sculpture built up from such disparate, often "found" materials, is called **assemblage**, a method pioneered by cubism and Duchamp. Nevelson composed her assemblages from found wood objects – chair slats, spindles, and benches. These odd components, enclosed within crate-like boxes and built into an imposing wall of shapes and textures, were often unified by the single color of the paint. The paint reminded the viewer to see these as artistic shapes, as well as the rehabilitated refuse of modern urban society (Fig. **15.12**). In a sense, Nevelson's wood assemblages were the opposite of Warhol's pop art, an art of authentic objects instead of an art of image.

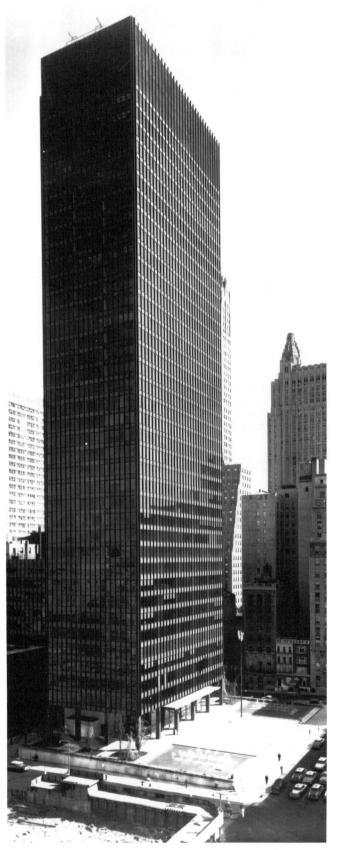

15.13 Ludwig Mies van der Rohe and Philip Johnson, Seagram Building, New York, 1954–8. Height 512 ft (156.2 m). Mies' glass-and-steel box was the logical outcome of the International Style, invented by modernist pioneers Walter Gropius and Le Corbusier. Similar skyscrapers dominated the skylines of North American cities in the 1960s and 1970s.

THE WRITE IDEA
Compare the works featured here of sculptors Henry Moore, Louise Nevelson, and David Smith. Which of these works best represents the way you see the contemporary world? Do the works' materials and the way they are shaped seem appropriate to contemporary experience?

THE TRIALS OF MODERN ARCHITECTURE

Summarize the artistic goals of post-war architecture, as evident in the works of the International Style.

The Great Depression and World War II suspended most large-scale building projects in the United States and Europe through the 1940s. As architecture was revived in the post-war period, the monolithic glass towers of the International Style became the dominant language of urban building. The centers of North American cities became forests of glass skyscrapers in the austere, geometric style of modernist architecture. At the same time, architects experimented with more sculptural designs, especially in smaller-scale building. While these post-war styles realized the architects' artistic aims, they also often suffered from a tension between architectural form and intended function. In the post-war era, modern architecture's artistic vision was put to the test of social usefulness and durability.

TRIUMPH OF THE INTERNATIONAL STYLE

The German architect Ludwig Mies van der Rohe [MEES van-der-ROH] (1886–1969) was already a leading architect of the pre-war International Style when he emigrated to the United States. When Mies settled in Chicago in 1938, he adopted the city's skyscraper tradition and built a number of high-rise apartment buildings along Chicago's lake shore. Mies' style of glass-and-steel towers was to dominate not just Chicago, but the skylines of nearly every major North American city.

The archetypal Miesian skyscraper is the Seagram Building (Fig. **15.13**) in New York, co-designed with Philip Johnson. Mies was recruited for the project by the daughter of the president of the Seagram distilling company, who liked Mies' use of steel beams as both a decorative and a structural element. She compared it to the Greek architectural orders. Mies' design was a simple box shape on a giant scale, with an exterior of bronze I-beams and a gray-tinted glass skin. The thirty-eight-story building stood on two-story metal stilts. It was set back 100 feet (30.5 m) from the street (to meet a New York building code), creating a dramatically spacious plaza. The Seagram Building offered North American corporations a style of unadorned purity on a grand scale.

In its post-war variations, the International Style became the architectural synonym of wealth and prestige, much like neoclassical architecture in previous centuries. Miesian glass towers sprang up in the Americas, Asia, and even Europe, as glistening symbols of the contemporary spirit.

The International Style became truly internationalized in the post-war building boom, though not always with happy results. Miesian skyscrapers created inhospitable urban centers in booming cities such as Houston, Texas, and Brasilia, the new capital of Brazil. When used in mass housing, modern skyscrapers frequently deteriorated and became unlivable Babels of crime, violence, and human alienation. Le Corbusier's confident vision of a "radiant city" of glass towers turned into bitter failure.

BUILDING AS SCULPTURE

The triumph of Mies' angular purity did not prevent other architects from seeking new directions. Even the pioneer of International Style, Le Corbusier, increasingly abandoned his box-like "machines for living" to explore the potential of building as sculpture. But like the glass-box skyscraper, the innovative use of plastic shapes and sculp-

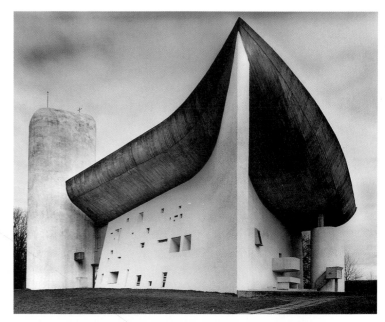

15.14 Le Corbusier, Notre-Dame-du-Haut ("Our Lady of the Heights"), pilgrimage church of Ronchamp, France, 1950–4.
Compare the swooping lines of this church exterior to the rectilinear logic of the architect's Villa Savoye (Fig. 14.25).

15.15 Frank Lloyd Wright, Solomon R. Guggenheim Museum, New York, 1957–9. Largest diameter 128 ft (39 m), height 92 ft (28 m). Guggenheim Museum, New York.
Completed after Wright's death, the Guggenheim realized his ambition to create a purely sculptural building.

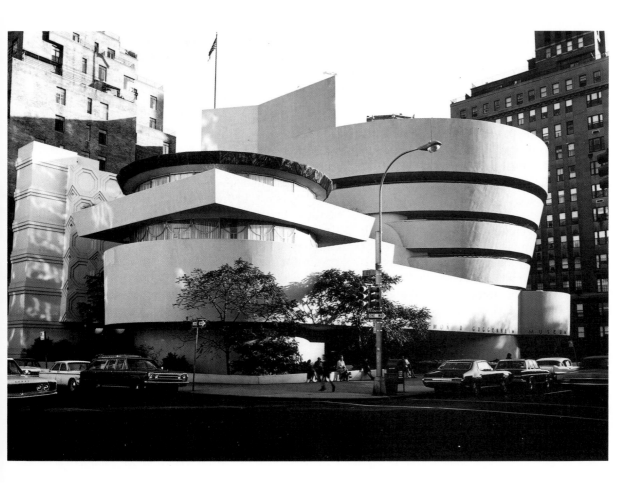

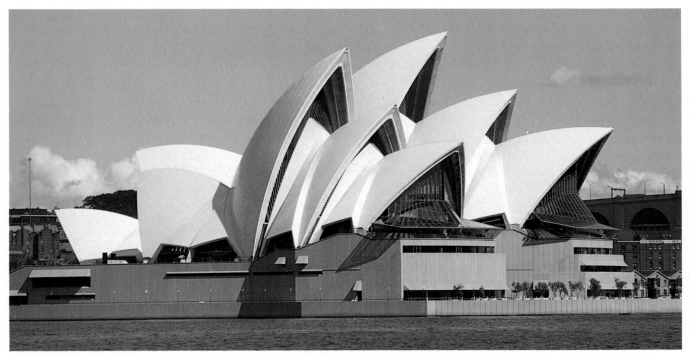

15.16 Jörn Utzon, Opera House, Sydney, Australia, 1959–72. Height of tallest shell 200 ft (61 m).
Utzon's daring visual design presented considerable technical difficulties in construction. "Instead of making a square form," he wrote, "I have made a sculpture."

tural forms did not always achieve a happy union with practicality and function.

A dramatic example of building as sculpture was Le Corbusier's Ronchamp [rohn(h)-SHAHN(h)] Chapel (Fig. **15.14**), a small pilgrimage church in a village in eastern France. The church's trademark is the swooping roof, whose curves rise to form what resembles the prow of a ship. The shape was also compared to a nun's hat or a crab shell (Le Corbusier's own organic metaphor). The building's sculptural plasticity carries over to the interior, where the massive sloping walls are pierced by irregular funnel-like windows. Gone was Le Corbusier's interest in a smooth, mechanical "skin" for his buildings. Instead, the roof showed his use of rough (in French, *brut* or "raw") concrete, an unfinished surface that showed the marks of the wooden forms.

In his Solomon R. Guggenheim Museum (Fig. **15.15**), his last great building commission, Frank Lloyd Wright achieved a plasticity that few modern buildings surpassed. As Wright said, "Here for the first time architecture appears plastic, one floor flowing into another (more like sculpture) instead of . . . stratified layers cutting and butting into each other."[9] The building's interior was a helix of spiral ramps, widening as they rose, enclosing a central, glass-domed atrium. The same spiral was expressed on the exterior in a shape resembling an inverted beehive.

The Guggenheim Museum was, indeed, a beautiful work of sculptural architecture. However, built to house a famous collection of modern art, the Guggenheim's curving walls and narrow exhibition space were ill-suited to its primary function. Some hinted that the Guggenheim

was Wright's last joke on artistic modernism, which he always disliked. The joke was on New York, too. One can hardly imagine a building less married to its surroundings than the Guggenheim Museum, which perches on New York's Fifth Avenue like a giant concrete snail among the city's tall apartment blocks.

The height of sculptural vision in post-war architecture was attained by Jörn Utzon (b. 1918), who designed the Sydney Opera House in Australia (Fig. **15.16**). Utzon's [OOT-tsohn] prize-winning design for the cultural center envisioned gleaming, sail-like shells lifting from a rectangular base. The shells would serve as both ceiling and wall, with the open faces encased in a curtain of glass. Built on a spit of land jutting into Sydney harbor, the arching shells would present a splendid view to all four sides. However, the problems in constructing Utzon's design proved to be enormous. Utzon had to invent the technology to build the ferroconcrete shells (ten in all), which were all curved to the same radius. The construction delays and cost overruns were so frustrating that Utzon resigned from the project in 1966, to be replaced by a team of architects. This group had to redesign the building's interior and the original estimated cost of seven million dollars rose eventually to one hundred million dollars.

Utzon compared the soaring lines of his opera house to a Gothic cathedral. The comparison applies not only to the Opera House's stunning visual beauty, but also to the length and difficulty of construction. This most difficult trial of modern architecture illustrates the uneasy relation between the modern architectural imagination and practicality.

POST-1945 MUSIC

Describe the two major trends in avant-garde music after 1945.

Music in the 1950s and 1960s saw an avant-garde scene move farther from popular audiences, while popular music itself was revitalized by a rebellious new form called rock-and-roll. The use of electronic instruments and computers satisfied the desire of some composers for total musical control. Spontaneity, chance, and a rocking good time were still the goals of others.

THE AVANT-GARDE IN MUSIC

One trend in post-war music extended the experiments of serial composer Arnold Schoenberg toward a music of ever more precise calculation. The French composer Pierre Boulez [boo-LEZZ] (b. 1925) devised a method called **total serialism**, in which he calculated every aspect of a composition – pitch, duration of notes, dynamics – according to numerical formulas. In his two-piano composition *Structures I* (1952), the prescribed patterns interact to create a shifting, sometimes elusive texture of sound. Boulez was probably the single most influential composer in post-war concert-hall music.

The trend toward total control intensified still further with the advent of electronic music. Electronic devices – synthesizers, electronic instruments, and computers – allowed composers to manipulate rhythm, tone, harmony, and dynamics with complete precision. The composer no longer had to rely on the interpretation or execution of a performer. Milton Babbitt (b. 1916) was among the first to use a music synthesizer, carefully controlling tone color and tempo. Babbitt acknowledged the difficulty of his works for audiences in an essay entitled, only half-jokingly, "Who Cares if You Listen?".

The best-known composer of electronic music was the German Karlheinz Stockhausen [SHTOK-how-zen] (b. 1928), whose *Gesang der Jünglinge* (*Song of Youths*, 1956) consisted of a biblical text sung and chanted against an electronic accompaniment. The singer's voice was altered electronically so that it ranged between the extremes of pure noise (unorganized sound) and pure musical tones. The composer explained, "Whenever speech momentarily emerges from the sound-symbols in the music, it is to praise God."[10] In 1977, Stockhausen began work on a mammoth cycle of operas entitled *Licht* (*Light*), to be completed in the year 2000.

John Cage and the Music of Chance
A quite different avant-garde trend was defined by John Cage (1912–92), a witty creator of highly unconventional music. Cage joined the New York avant-garde scene in the 1940s, after studying in Europe with Schoenberg. In New York, he became interested in Oriental philosophy, especially the Zen Buddhist principle of non-intention, or "mindlessness." Under the influence of Zen, Cage composed works that reduced the role of choice or decision in composition. In 1951, he wrote a piece for piano by flipping a coin to decide the sequence of tones – hence the term **aleatory music** [AY-lee-uh-tor-ee] (from the Latin *alea*, or dice).

The signature composition of aleatory music was Cage's *Imaginary Landscape No. 4* (1951), which called for twelve radios, each tuned to a different frequency. Another famous Cage work reached to the very boundary of music itself – silence. His *4′33″* (1952) instructed the performer to sit with his or her instrument for the specified time, playing nothing. The "music" consisted of the audience's reaction and other chance sounds in the auditorium. Cage collaborated closely with dance choreographer Merce Cunningham (see page 429), who also employed chance operations in his dance.

THE POP REBELLION

Despite the avant-garde's esoteric experiments, the concert hall did not lose all its popular appeal. Conductor and composer Leonard Bernstein (1918–1990) introduced classical music to wide audiences through children's concerts and television programs. Bernstein's works for musical theater, including *Candide* (1956) and *West Side Story* (1957), were both updated versions of literary classics.

Bernstein's finger-snapping melodies were no match, however, for the hip-rolling rebellion of **rock-and-roll** music – a pop style featuring electric guitars and a strong rhythmic drive. The charismatic Elvis Presley and other early rock stars skillfully re-interpreted traditionally African-American blues styles for their white audiences and infused this tradition with youthful energy.

Elvis and other North American rock-and-rollers transmitted their music via tours and recordings to Britain, where it was taken up by bands in working-class cities. The resultant "British wave" of rock-and-roll was led by the Beatles, a clean-cut group from Liverpool whose love songs charmed the Anglo-American public. The Beatles' revolutionary album *Sergeant Pepper's Lonely Hearts Club Band* (1967) was a landmark in popular music. It was the first rock-and-roll record to present itself as a coherent musical whole, rather than a collection of popular tunes.

Meanwhile in the United States, the civil rights movement and racial integration provided new avenues for African-American musicians. The signature style of this new era was rhythm-and-blues (also called "soul"), a music with a strong rhythmic ground and blues inflections. Talented rhythm-and-blues singers such as Wilson Pickett, James Brown, and Diana Ross became pop stars on a great scale.

POST-MODERN STYLES

Illustrate the stylistic tendencies of post-modern art with examples from several media or forms.

One social critic called the later twentieth century a "post-industrial society," dominated by the exchange of information rather than material production. This new age was characterized by rapid social change, shifting boundaries, and a loss of certainty. In response, a new sensibility emerged called **post-modernism**, which could be summarized as:

- scepticism toward any representation of reality that claimed to be universal or objective
- a focus on the "construction of reality" through language and symbol
- an emphasis on the local and particular rather than the universal
- in the arts, a tendency toward parody, pastiche, and an eclectic mixture of styles.

Post-modernism had learned to stop seeking redemption or expecting life to make sense. As one commentator said, post-modern humanity had "stopped waiting for Godot":

To the existentialists, the discovery of a world without meaning was the point of departure; today a loss of unitary meaning is merely accepted; that is just the way the world is.[11]

Post-modern artists had to find their place between two overwhelming cultural forces. On the one side were modernism and its heroic inventors – Picasso, Joyce, and Schoenberg. On the other side was the mass culture of television, film, and advertising, with its capacity to absorb avant-garde techniques. Toward their modernist predecessors, contemporary artists adopted an attitude of ironic or playful quotation. In an installation at the Guggenheim Museum, for example, Jenny Holzer (b. 1950) used the museum's spiraling white interior as a billboard for her provocative slogans (Fig. **15.17**). By choosing her artistic medium from the realm of advertising, however, Holzer sought to compete with the blaring commercial messages of mass culture.

For this reason, noted one critic, the challenge for post-modern artists is "to choose and combine traditions selectively, to *eclect* (as the verb of eclecticism would have it) those aspects from the past and present which appear most relevant for the job at hand."[12] Post-modern works were often stylistic hybrids. A post-modern novel such as Umberto Eco's *The Name of the Rose* (1980) could be detective fiction, Gothic novel, and learned treatise, all in one. Post-modern buildings quoted decorative motifs from Renaissance and neoclassical architecture. Meanwhile, post-modern phi-

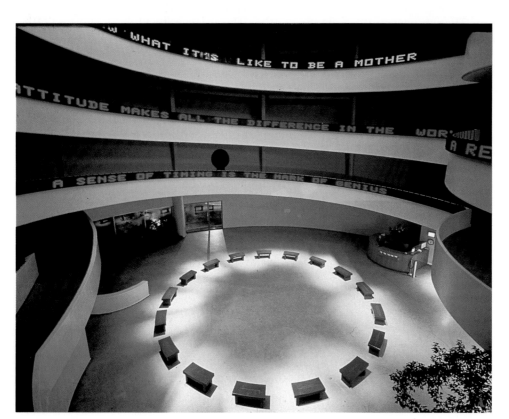

15.17 Jenny Holzer, *Installation "Jenny Holzer"*, **Solomon R. Guggenheim Museum, New York. Extended helical tricolor L. E. D. signboard and 17 Indian red granite benches.**
Holzer's banal "mock clichés" flash along the spiraling ramps of Frank Lloyd Wright's Guggenheim Museum. Post-modern art often consciously quoted from classical modernism as well as the slogans and images of mass culture.

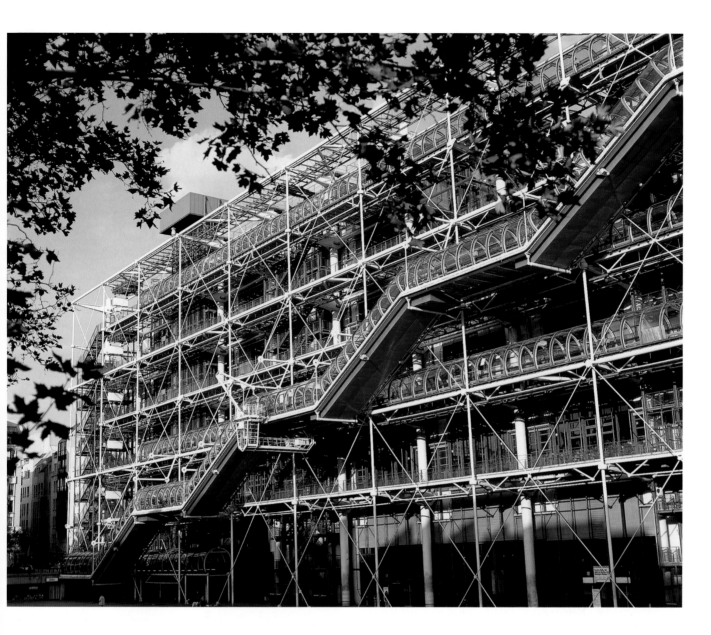

15.18 Renzo Piano and Richard Rogers, Georges Pompidou National Center for Arts and Culture (the "Beaubourg"), Paris, 1977.
The high-tech exterior of exposed struts and pipes explicitly violates the modernist ideal of a smooth exterior shell.

losophy questioned whether the author or artist really existed. It claimed that, in the post-modern era, the human "subject" – the autonomous, individual, rational self – was disappearing. Its place was being taken by the "protean" self, a constantly changing and evolving self, made of the interwoven voices and images of post-industrial culture.

Under such circumstances, buildings still managed to get built, novels written, plays produced, and music performed. Contemporary architecture brought a spirit of levity to the austere face of modernity; minimalism in music found a welcoming audience among pop fans; and the "exhausted" literary form of the novel nevertheless produced new masters of the narrative art. Postmodernism's announcement of the "end" of culture may have been premature.

POST-MODERN ARCHITECTURE

Post-modern architecture arose from a reaction against modernism's negation of the architectural past. Modernists such as Mies van der Rohe insisted on buildings in which nothing distracted from the clarity of form. Contemporary architects responded with an open-minded eclecticism, a willingness to borrow and compromise. Robert Venturi (b. 1925), a pioneer of this new eclecticism, wrote in 1966: "Architects can no longer afford to be intimidated by the puritanically moral language of orthodox Modern architecture. …I am for messy vitality over obvious unity."[13]

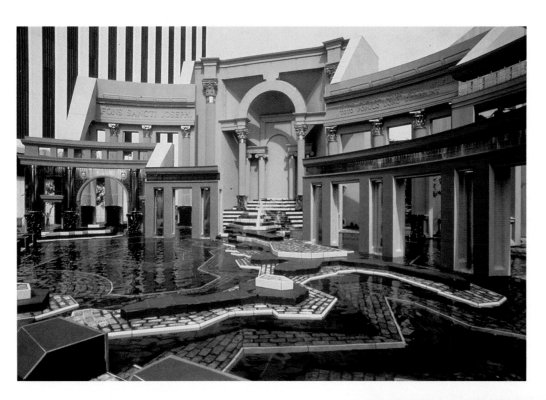

15.19 Left **Charles Moore, Piazza d'Italia, New Orleans, 1978–9.**
Note the concoction of neoclassical elements (Corinthian columns, arches) employed in mocking ways (doorways that lead nowhere, capitals of steel, columns of water).

15.20 Below **Michael Graves, Public Services Building ("the Portland"), Portland, Oregon, 1980–3.**
What decorative elements (note the "eyebrow" ledges, the wreaths on the side) does Graves employ to create the effect of his building as an image?

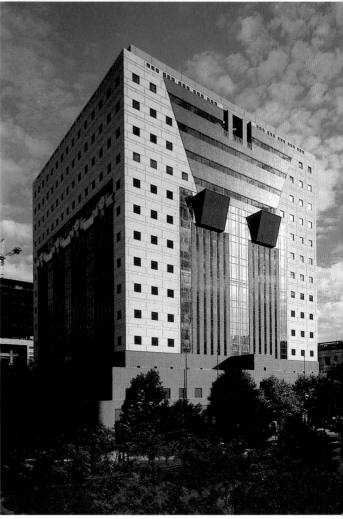

With Venturi as their leader, contemporary architects escaped from the doctrinaire purity of modernist predecessors.

One flamboyant response to modernist purism was the high-tech architecture of the Georges Pompidou National Center for Arts and Culture (1977) in Paris (Fig. **15.18**). Like so much French public architecture, this museum was a political monument (dedicated to a former French president) and a statement of French nationalism. With this brash museum dedicated to contemporary art, music, and culture, Paris hoped to regain some of the prominence lost to New York in the 1950s.

Designed by Renzo Piano (b. 1937) and Richard Rogers (b. 1933), the Pompidou Center, known as the "Beaubourg," was a high-tech fantasy. The building's mechanical guts – heating and cooling ducts, plumbing, service elevators – are its skin, brightly colored for visual emphasis. By placing these normally hidden elements on the outside of the building, the architects intended to expand the interior space available for art exhibitions. Although Parisians initially opposed this brazenly non-traditional building, the museum's plaza soon became a lively stage for Parisian street life. As a tourist attraction, the Beaubourg [BOH-boorg] surpassed both the high-brow Louvre Museum and the Eiffel Tower.

One danger in post-modernism was that its eclectic spirit would end in mere pastiche, a hodgepodge of earlier styles. This warning might be raised about the buoyant post-modern historicism of Charles Moore (b. 1925). Charles Moore's Piazza d'Italia (Fig. **15.19**) in New Orleans is a fountain complex that pays homage to the heritage of New Orleans' Italian-Americans, and was intended as a

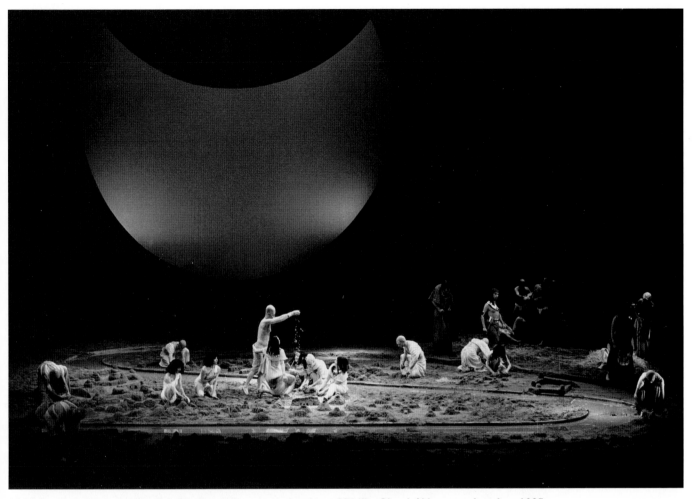

15.21 A scene from the English National Opera production of Philip Glass' *Akhenaten*, **London, 1985.**

site for Italian-American ethnic festivals and community activities. The Piazza is a feast of historical styles, illuminated by neon lights and bright paint. The pseudo-façades incorporate witty post-modern substitutions, such as "columns" of sheets of water and columns and capitals made of stainless steel. Steps rise to the highest façade, where the arch and entablature are outlined in neon.

In the 1980s, post-modern architecture proved itself in constructing the large, urban office towers that had been the staple of modernism. The first significant public building in post-modern style is Michael Graves' Portland Public Services Building (Fig. **15.20**) in Oregon, known as "the Portland." The building's decorative façade distinguishes it immediately from the uniformity of modernism. Two piers rise on either side of a seven-story barred window, ending in "eyebrow" ledges. Graves (b. 1934) mounted the squat tower on a base of darker granite, a technique adapted from the Art Deco of the 1920s. The whole façade has an Egyptian flavor, and its symbolism is punctuated by the statue of "Portlandia" in front. Graves' Portland blazed the path for similarly inventive post-modern towers in other North American cities.

MINIMALISM IN MUSIC

Compared with the bare abstractions of minimalist painting and sculpture, minimalism achieved considerable popular success in music. Music critics applied the term minimalist to a small group of avant-garde composers, chiefly Terry Riley, La Monte Young, Steve Reich, and Philip Glass. In the 1960s, the minimalists broke away from their training in the twentieth-century tradition of atonality. They stripped music down to a few bare musical fragments that were repeated with slow and subtle variations. For example, Terry Riley's *In C* (1964) consists of fifty-nine musical fragments in the key of C, to be played by the ensemble in any order they choose.

The best-known minimalist composer is Philip Glass (b. 1937), who developed minimalist technique in more ambitious works involving dance and theater. His early music consists of interwoven melodic patterns, described by one unappreciative critic as "sonic torture." However, Glass achieved a remarkable popular success with his opera entitled *Einstein on the Beach* (1976), which sold out performances in the traditionalist Metropolitan Opera in New York. As staged by Robert Wilson, Glass' opera

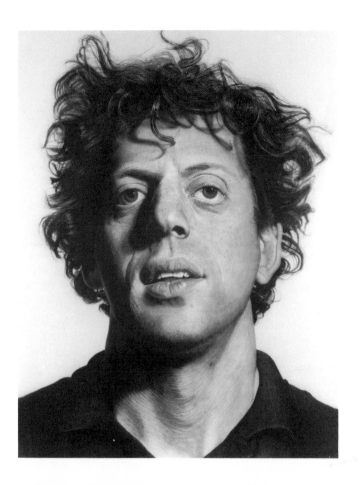

consisted of oversized dramatic tableaux suggesting physicist Albert Einstein's scientific theories. Glass followed *Einstein* with two more accessible minimalist operas, particularly *Akhenaten* (1984), which in mesmerizing chanted music retold the story of Egypt's "heretic pharaoh" (Fig. **15.21**).

Part of Glass' enthusiastic audience consisted of fans crossing over from rock music, drawn by Glass' use of amplified instruments. The success of *Einstein on the Beach* paved the way for others, most significantly John Adams' *Nixon in China* (1987) and *The Death of Klinghoffer* (1991), both topical and well-received operas staged by theatrical designer Peter Sellars. This revival of opera as a popular form ranked as one of the most surprising developments of the post-modern era.

15.22 Left **Chuck Close, *Phil*, 1969. Synthetic polymer on canvas, 9 x 7 ft (2.74 x 2.13 m). Whitney Museum of American Art, New York, Purchase with funds from Mrs. Robert M. Benjamin, 69.62.**
Close meticulously reproduced photographic images in paint, resulting in giant portraits far beyond the scale of the photographs he copied. Here the subject is minimalist composer Philip Glass.

15.23 Below **Robert Smithson, *Spiral Jetty*, 1970. Black basalt, limestone rocks, and earth. Length 1500 ft (457.2 m). Great Salt Lake, Utah.**
Smithson's earth art not only tended to minimalize the artist but also the spectator. Because the site was virtually inaccessible, the work could be viewed only through photographs.

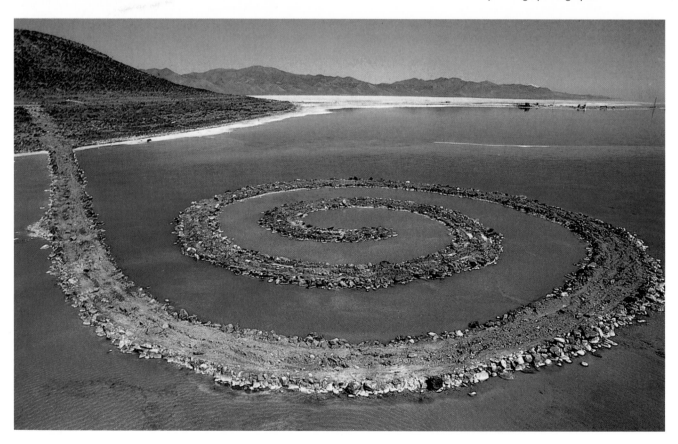

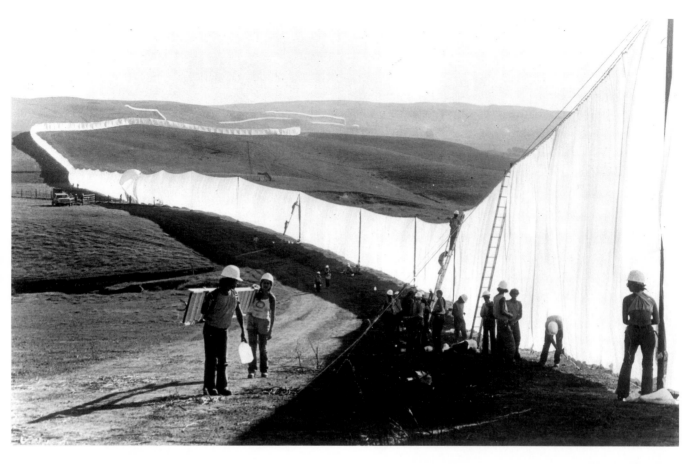

THE CONTEMPORARY VISUAL ARTS

Painting and sculpture in the post-modern era explored several directions, with no one style or influence predominating. The variety of trends includes the wholesale revival of earlier styles, including neo-expressionism and neo-romanticism, and the frequent "quoting" of historical styles in an artistic pastiche.

One contemporary revival grew directly out of pop art. **Superrealism** in painting faithfully reproduced in paint the qualities of the photographic image. Chuck Close (b. 1930) was quite explicit in his aim to transfer photographic information to paint, often painting oversize portraits directly from photographs (Fig. **15.22**). Sculptor Duane Hanson (1925–96) sculpted mannequin-like figures faultlessly crafted of polymers to resemble breathing humans. Placed in airports or banks, Hanson's figures were often mistaken for real people.

Another trend in art was to move outside the studio and find a new relation to nature and the social world. An outgrowth of minimalist sculpture, called **earth art** (or **land art**), merged sculpture with the environment. Earth art was constructed of materials virtually identical to the surrounding natural site, often primeval landscapes in the desert or prairie. The best-known work of earth art was Robert Smithson's *Spiral Jetty* (1970; Fig. **15.23**), a spiral form built from black basalt, limestone rocks, and earth in the Great Salt Lake of Utah. For Smithson (1938–73), the

15.24 Christo and Jeanne-Claude, *Running Fence*, Sonoma and Marin Counties, California, 1972–6. Woven nylon fabric, steel cables, and steel poles, height 18 ft (5.49 m), length 24¹/₂ miles (39.2 km).
Erected for two weeks in 1976, *Running Fence* meandered across miles of California countryside, ending at the Pacific Ocean.

work evoked a geological time that superseded the brief history of artistic fashion. In 1977, James Turrell (b.1943) undertook the re-shaping of Roden Crater in the wilderness of Arizona. Turrell constructed tunnels beneath the crater that aligned with the cardinal directions in the manner of ancient temples. Said Turrell, "the separation that occurs in a gallery between spectator and artwork is impossible when the 'work' surrounds you and extends for a hundred miles in all directions."[14]

Like the earth artists, the artists Christo and Jeanne-Claude (both b. 1935) conceived works that burst the bounds of the studio and gallery. The Christos' projects transform their rural or urban settings and usually require a lengthy process of gaining permits and erecting the work with a legion of workers. Their *Running Fence* (Fig. **15.24**) was a white nylon curtain hung on steel cable suspended on poles across 24½ miles (39 km) of California landscape. The Christos' recent projects include *The Umbrellas, Japan–USA* (1984–91) and the *Wrapped Reichstag* in Berlin (see Fig. 15.1).

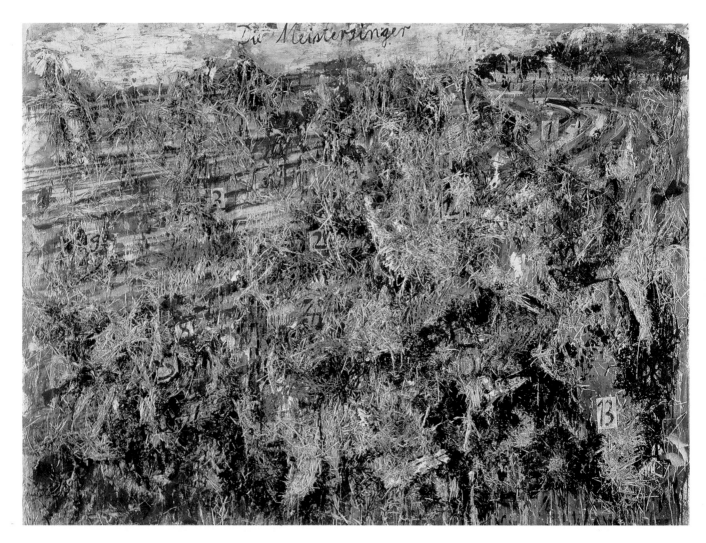

15.25 Anselm Kiefer, *Die Meistersinger*, 1982. Oil and straw on canvas, 9 ft 3 ins x 12 ft 6 ins (2.8 x 3.8 m). The Saatchi Collection, London.
Some of the grotesque power of Kiefer's works is explained by their large scale and their enigmatic materials.

In Germany the meditative painter Anselm Kiefer [KEE-fer] (b. 1945) was part of a wave often labeled neo-romanticism. Kiefer's brooding canvases showed his fascination with evil and grotesque themes, and his preoccupation with Germany's heroic past. Kiefer describes himself as "bringing to light things that are over, that are forgotten," and *Die Meistersinger* (Fig. **15.25**) illustrates the rather ominous overtones of his work. The canvas suggests a ringed pyramid encrusted with straw and paint. The title, borrowed from a Wagnerian opera, evokes Germany's long-repressed Nazi past.

THE NEW FICTION

When the novelist John Barth (b. 1930) suggested in the 1960s that literature was "exhausted," he meant that the novel and the short story had been used up by literary modernists such as Joyce and Kafka. Using these exhausted fictional forms, works such as Barth's *The Sot-Weed Factor* (1967) and Thomas Pynchon's *Gravity's Rainbow* (1973) exhibited a dizzying self-consciousness of language and form, with convoluted plots and shifts among different fictional forms.

These post-modern works were often called **meta-fiction** because they seemed to be stories about stories and fictions about fictions. The acknowledged master of contemporary meta-fiction was the Argentinean writer Jorge Luis Borges (1899–1986), whose metaphysical style influenced a generation of post-modern writers. Borges' [BOR-hayss] short fiction and essays (he never wrote a novel) are largely concerned with the sphere of intellectual games and fantasy. Borges admitted quite readily that his stories did not describe social reality, as narrative fiction had done for three centuries. Instead, he created intricate but artificial literary worlds that were more interesting and more intelligible than the real.

Borges' dominant metaphor for this artificial world is the labyrinth, a self-contained maze that defines its own rules and signposts. In one well-known story, *Tlön, Uqbar,*

Orbis Tertius, Borges tells of a forty-volume encyclopedia describing life on the imaginary planet of Tlön. The encyclopedia has been written by a secret society who "came together to invent a country" and instead described an entire fictional planet. The encyclopedia of Tlön resembles a labyrinth (and life, for that matter) in its apparently infinite complexity.

> *One of the schools in Tlön has reached the point of denying time. It reasons that the present is undefined, that the future has no other reality than as present hope, that the past is no more than present memory.*[a] *Another school declares that the* whole of time *has already happened and that our life is a vague memory or dim reflection, doubtless false and fragmented, of an irrevocable process. Another school has it that the history of the universe, which contains the history of our lives and the most tenuous details of them, is the handwriting produced by a minor god in order to communicate with a demon. Another maintains that the universe is comparable to those code systems in which not all the symbols have meaning, and in which only that which happens every 300th night is true. Another believes that, while we are asleep here, we are awake somewhere else, and that thus every man is two men.*[15]

JORGE LUIS BORGES
From *Tlön, Uqbar, Orbis Tertius* (1956)

---

a Bertrand Russell (*The Analysis of Mind*, 1921, page 159) conjectures that our planet was created a few moments ago, and provided with a humanity which "remembers" an illusory past. [Borges' note]

Borges' narrator compares the benevolent fantasy of Tlön's inventors to the ideological fictions of modern politics. "Why not fall under the spell of Tlön and submit to the minute and vast evidence of an ordered planet?" the narrator asks. "Tlön may be a labyrinth, but it is a labyrinth plotted by men, a labyrinth destined to be deciphered by men."[16]

Magic Realism In Latin America, Borges was precursor to an adventurous new style called **magic realism**, for its blend of realistic narrative and elements of fantasy and myth. The Colombian novelist Gabriel García Márquez (b. 1928) received international acclaim for his *One Hundred Days of Solitude* (1967). The novel recounts the lives of seven generations of a family in the fictional village of Macondo. García Márquez [gar-SEE-a MAR-kez] merged surreal circumstances with realistic observations of social class and politics. At one point, for example, the villagers all lose their memory and need to erects signs to remind them of the names of things. One sign reads simply, "God exists." In a typical post-modern gesture, the narrative's last pages incorporate characters from other Latin American novels, acknowledging their influence by giving their charac-

ters a new fictional life. García Márquez' splendid mix of fantasy and realism inaugurated a new wave of Latin American fiction. In its wake came novels from Carlos Fuentes, Julio Cortázar, and the Peruvian Mario Vargas Llosa.

REVISING THE CANON

Summarize the arguments for broadening the literary and artistic canons of Western civilization.

The 1960s and 1970s saw a rising consciousness among groups long denied a strong voice in Western politics and culture. In the United States, a determined movement arose to overthrow racial segregation and gain basic civil rights for American blacks. By 1970, an international women's movement arose to demand equal rights for women. In Africa, Latin America, and other former European colonies, writers and artists established new national traditions.

In literature and the visual arts especially, these movements challenged the ascendancy of a history and heritage created largely by European and American men. They demanded a revision of the **canon**, the body of artistic and philosophical works recognized as the best and most important. To its proponents, broadening the canon was necessary to reflect a more diverse, egalitarian, and global culture. Their efforts brought recognition to a new generation of artists and fresh controversy to debates over artistic and historical value.

African and American Voices

As African nations gained their independence from colonial powers, Africans stepped onto the world's literary stage. In 1959 Nigerian Chinua Achebe [ah-CHAY-bay] (b. 1930) published his landmark novel *Things Fall Apart*, an anguished tale of the clash between traditional Africans and missionary intruders. Another Nigerian, Wole Soyinka [shah-YENG-kah] (b. 1934), often criticized Africa's political authoritarianism in his poems, plays, and essays, applying the existentialist ideal of the "engaged" writer.

In the United States, the African-American artist Romare Bearden [ROH-muh-ree BEER-dun] (1912–88) rose to prominence in the 1960s, when he turned from an abstract style to techniques of collage and **photomontage**. A contemporary of the New York school, Bearden was never entirely comfortable with subjective abstraction or hard-edged minimalism. Partly through his activism in the civil rights movement, Bearden's works increasingly celebrated African-American ritual, myth, and community. Rejecting the extreme individualism of avant-garde art, he drew explicitly from African-American community life.

Bearden composed his works from fragments of photographs, cloth, and other ordinary objects. He compared the process of composition to mosaic, in which the artist carefully chooses and arranges small pieces of glass. His works are more clearly representational than those of many contemporary artists, with recurring visual motifs such as

15.26 Romare Bearden, *Baptism*, 1964. Collage, 22 x 18 ins (56 x 46 cm). Estate of Romare Bearden, Courtesy of ACA Galleries, New York.
Bearden himself noted the "prevalence of ritual" in his collage works – rituals of work, play, and religious faith. Here, with cut-out figures against a painted landscape, he invokes the ecstatic immersion of baptism.

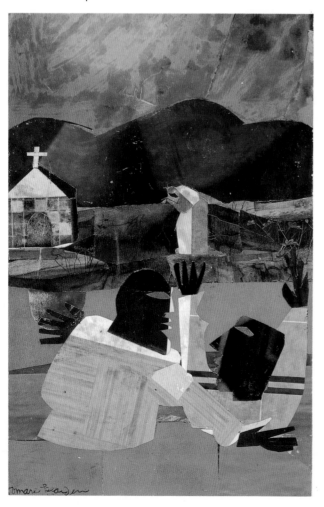

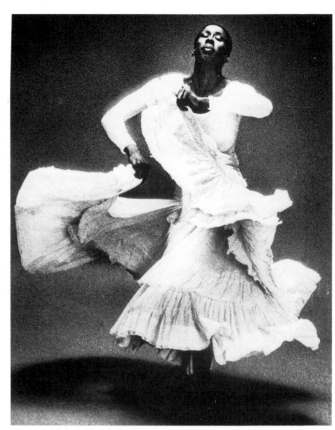

15.27 Judith Jamison in her acclaimed performance of *Cry*, 1971, a work symbolizing the nobility of spirit in "black women everywhere." Courtesy American Dance Theater, New York.
In 1991 Jamison became director of the American Dance Theater following the death of its founder, Alvin Ailey.

trains, baptism (Fig. **15.26**), and African-American "conjure women" with magical powers.

Often through bitter struggle, opportunities grew for American blacks in other media. In 1958, Alvin Ailey (1931–91) formed the American Dance Theatre, creating dance works based on the rhythms of blues and jazz. He created for dancer Judith Jamison the demanding solo piece *Cry* (1971), which was set to jazz and soul music and dedicated to "all black women everywhere – especially our mothers." Jamison, dressed in a flowing white dress, gave a landmark performance of modern dance (Fig. **15.27**).

African-American authors gained broad readership and critical esteem as the canon widened to include them. The poet Gwendolyn Brooks (b. 1917) recorded racial wounds in soft-spoken poems with an uncommon candor and sensitivity. Novelist Toni Morrison (b. 1931) gained wide acknowledgment for her novel *Beloved* (1988) and in 1994 won the Nobel Prize for Literature. On the stage, playwright August Wilson (b. 1945) enjoyed a string of successes with such plays as *Fences* (1987) and *The Piano Lesson* (1990). Wilson's plays dealt principally with African-American characters and experience of society. In *Fences*, for example, the main character, Troy Maxson, bitterly recalls the baseball career denied him by racial segregation. The spiritual costs of a life of responsibility lead him to alienate his son and wife, building "fences" between himself and his loved ones.

WOMEN'S VOICES

The feminist movement of the 1970s brought to prominence a host of women writers and artists. The new feminists were buttressed by a long-standing but largely subterranean tradition of women's voices, from Mary Wollstonecraft (see page 343) to Simone de Beauvoir (see page 423). High on the feminist agenda was the recovery of a lost tradition of women's history and art.

One example of this determined effort was *The Dinner Party* (1979), a work of installation art by feminist avant-garde artist Judy Chicago (b. 1939). **Installation art** is artistic work created for a particular site (that is, museum or gallery) and then usually dismantled. In *The Dinner Party* (Fig. **15.28**), Chicago set up a three-sided dinner table with place settings for thirty-nine women figures, both historical and mythological. Chicago wanted to acknowledge the domestic decorative arts of china-painting and embroidery, long practiced by American women. However, the suggestive design aroused such controversy that the show was closed soon after its opening. Women's groups responded by raising enough funds to send the exhibition on a successful North American tour.

The 1970s and '80s saw an unprecedented flowering of women writers, including among many others, the British writers Margaret Drabble and Doris Lessing, the French writers Marguerite Duras and Monique Wittig, the Canadian writer Margaret Atwood, and in the United States, writers Maxine Hong Kingston and Joyce Carol Oates. These women writers found considerable life in the "exhausted" literary forms of the novel, short story, and lyric poem.

15.28 Judy Chicago, *The Dinner Party*, 1979. Multimedia installation, china painting on porcelain with needlework, 48 x 48 x 48 ft (14.6 x 14.6 x 14.6 m). Copyright © Judy Chicago 1979.
Chicago's thirty-nine painted plates commemorated goddesses, queens, poets, and other women figures of historical note. Each setting contains a hand-painted plate decorated with an abstract design of butterflies or vulva-like flowers.

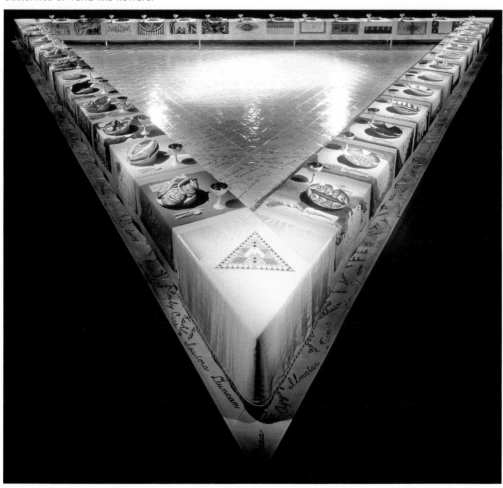

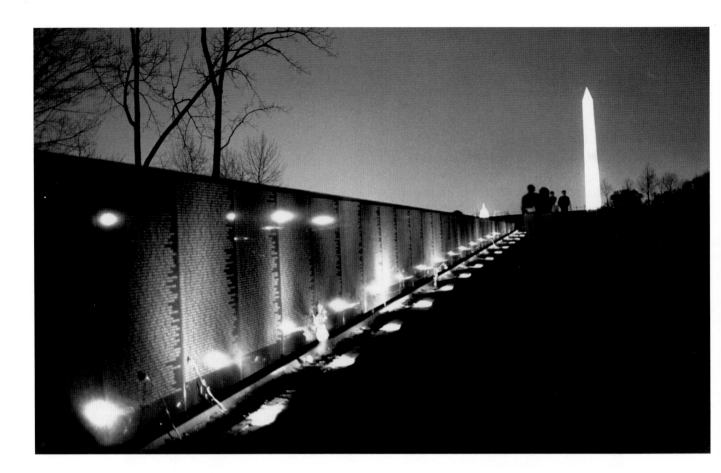

15.29 Maya Lin, Vietnam War Memorial, 1981–4. The Mall, Washington, D.C. Black polished granite, two wings, each 246 ft (75 m) long.
Consisting of little more than a V-shaped granite wall engraved with names of the dead, Lin's minimalist memorial became a shrine at which mourners leave flowers, war medals, and other mementoes.

The poet Denise Levertov [LEFF-er-toff] (1923–97) maintained an outspoken commitment to poetry as a literary enterprise rather than a vehicle for ideas. Yet she was also actively involved in protests against the Vietnam War and nuclear proliferation. Her poem *In Mind* aptly expresses an ambivalence that many women of her era felt.

There's in my mind a woman
of innocence, unadorned but
fair-featured, and smelling of
apples or grass. She wears
a utopian smock or shift, her hair
is light brown and smooth, and she
is kind and very clean without
ostentation –
but she has
no imagination.
And there's a
turbulent moon-ridden girl
or old woman, or both,
dressed in opals and rags, feathers
and torn taffeta,
who knows strange songs –
but she is not kind.[17]

DENISE LEVERTOV
In Mind (1964)

The Vietnam War was commemorated in a powerful but controversial war memorial designed by Maya Lin (Fig. **15.29**). Lin's simple design of two monolithic black walls inscribed with the names of American soldiers killed in the war inspired protests from veterans' groups. Opponents successfully demanded that a more realistic and heroic sculpture of three soldiers be placed nearby. But Lin's simple wall proved itself as the more powerful remembrance, becoming a shrine that helped to heal the divisions of a troubled era.

THE WRITE IDEA

In Levertov's poem *In Mind*, compare the clothing of the two kinds of women she describes. How does their garb symbolize the two types of women? Consider how you are also drawn to be two such contrasting types of people.

THEMES FOR A NEW AGE

Speculate on one cultural development that you expect to see in the twenty-first century.

The last decades of the twentieth century were marked by several significant developments. One was the devastation of a new plague, while another was the promise of a new global culture.

AIDS AND THE ARTS

By the 1990s, the spread of AIDS, a usually fatal virus infection, had killed millions world-wide and had struck arts communities especially hard. As with the medieval Black Death, the condition stimulated creative responses, including the NAMES project: a gigantic quilt of panels, each created by family and loved ones to memorialize an AIDS victim. Each NAMES panel was the size of a grave and decorated with materials ranging from chintz to black leather, all symbolizing the remnants of lost life. When first exhibited on the Capitol Mall in Washington, D.C., the AIDS quilt covered the area of two football fields. By the mid-1990s, the project comprised more than twenty-five thousand panels, and could only be exhibited in sections.

A more traditional memorial was the so-called "AIDS Symphony," the Symphony No. 1 by John Corigliano [kor(g)-lee-AHH-noh] (b. 1938). In this haunting work, composed in memory of colleagues lost to AIDS, one friend "appears" in the sound of a single piano, playing a favorite melody offstage. The symphony's second movement is a *tarantella*, a frantic Italian dance that recalls the madness often associated with the final stages of AIDS. Corigliano acknowledged that he was inspired by the AIDS quilt, and compared the symphony to "a quilt-like interweaving" of melodic motifs.

The AIDS epidemic was also a central theme in the exhilarating theater piece *Angels in America* by Tony Kushner (b. 1956). Subtitled *A Gay Fantasia on National Themes*, Kushner's 1993 drama mixed historical with fictional characters, incorporating the themes of homosexuality, AIDS, and politics in the conservative era of the 1980s. In keeping with the play's somber subject, the author asserted, "If we are to be visited by angels we will have to drag them out of the skies, and the efforts we expend to draw the heavens to an earthly place may well leave us too exhausted to appreciate the fruits of our labors."[18]

TOWARD A WORLD CULTURE

The 1980s and '90s saw a widening world culture that was no longer limited by national or regional boundaries. With the break-up of the former Soviet Union, the symbol of Europe's long-standing division, the Berlin Wall, was joyously demolished in 1989. In Africa, the last bastion of white supremacy, South Africa, achieved a peaceful transition to black majority rule.

In this atmosphere, artists and writers circulated more easily across traditional boundaries, too. The Japanese architect Arata Isozaki [ee-so-ZAH-kee] was commissioned to build corporate offices at a Disney theme park (Fig. **15.30**), while artist Robert Rauschenberg undertook a series of works based on exchanges with Asian cultures. A new idiom of "world music" developed from such influences as the Indian musical master Ravi Shankar (Fig. **15.31**) and pop musicians Paul Simon's and David Byrne's samplings of African music.

The dissolution of traditional boundaries was not without its tensions and fractiousness. On the pop music scene, the mood was often despair and aggression, as evident in the names of such styles as "punk" and "grunge." Out of the urban black culture arose "hip-hop" and the music

WINDOW ON DAILY LIFE

LIVING AND DYING WITH AIDS

Here is novelist and poet Paul Monette's account of the early days of the AIDS crisis, soon after his gay companion had been diagnosed with AIDS symptoms:

Has anything ever been quite like this? Bad enough to be stricken in the middle of life, but then to fear your best and dearest will suffer exactly the same. Cancer and the heart don't sicken a man two ways like that. And it turns out all the certainties of health insurance and the job that waits are just a social contract, flimsy as the disappearing ink it's written in. Has anything else so tested the medical system and blown all its weakest links? I have oceans of unresolved rage at those who ran from us, but I also see that plague and panic are inseparable. And nothing compares. That is something very important to understand about those on the moon of AIDS. Anything offered in comparison is a mockery to us. If hunger compares, or Hamburger Hill or the carnal dying of Calcutta, that is for us to say.[19]

PAUL MONETTE
Borrowed Time: An AIDS Memoir (1988)

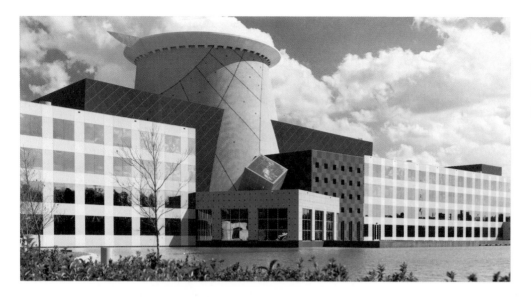

15.30 Arata Isozaki, Team Disney Building, Lake Buena Vista, Florida, 1990.
Note the variety of intersecting shapes in the building's center. The central turret is hollow and functions as a gigantic sundial.

of **rap**, chanted lyrics accompanied by vocalized or synthesized percussion. Rap lyrics were often explicitly violent and sexist, and were sometimes censored by governments and record companies. Rap's aggressiveness was countered by traditional musicians such as Wynton Marsalis, a classically trained trumpet player who undertook a vigorous reclamation of the jazz heritage.

The dissolving boundaries of a worldwide culture were accelerated by computerized creativity and communication. Performer Laurie Anderson (b. 1950) created multi-media extravaganzas, such as the six-hour, two-night mixed-media performance entitled *United States* (1983). Through computers, the media of photography and film

became totally manipulable. An apparently inexhaustible fund of information became available on the appropriately named World Wide Web, the network linking computers across the world. Video communication too was exploited by artists such as the Korean Nam June Paik (b. 1932) with his *TV Buddha* (Fig. **15.32**). It seemed that Jorge Luis Borges' vision of an endless labyrinth of virtual realities had been realized.

One characteristic of Western civilization had become part of the world culture: the relentless innovation and pace of change. But questions were raised about the viability of traditional cultures in the new world of "cyber" culture. Would people still need to visit museums if the

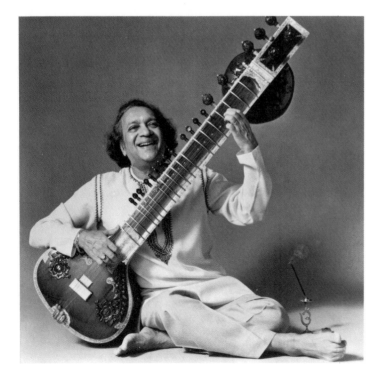

15.31 Ravi Shankar playing the sitar.
Shankar instructed a variety of contemporary musicians, from the Beatles to minimalist La Monte Young.

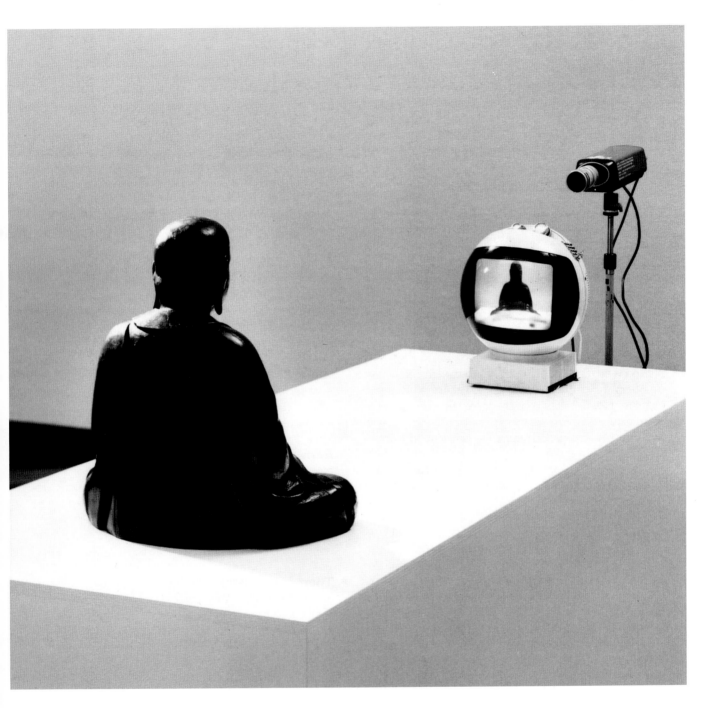

world of art was easily accessible through the computer network? Would a new audience be found for live performances of Mozart if his music was perfectly preserved on digital recording? Would the accessibility of culture mean an inevitable loss of authenticity? Would human creativity be absorbed into a virtual world of ephemeral sounds and images?

These and many other questions await answers in the new century.

15.32 Nam June Paik, *TV Buddha*, 1974. Video installation with statue. Stedelijk Museum, Amsterdam.
This installation parodies the contemplative pose of a traditional Buddha by placing the statue before a video screen. What ironic juxtapositions do you find in this work?

Chapter Summary

Holocausts. The holocausts of World War II – the war itself, as well as the Nazi death camps and the first use of atomic weapons – created an atmosphere of alienation and anxiety among Western artists and thinkers. In the United States, the beat writers and the confessional poets responded to the rise of Western consumer society with misgiving and soul-searching.

Exploring the Absurd. The existentialists stressed the absurdity and utter moral freedom of human life. Yet Sartre, de Beauvoir, and Camus all engaged in political activism against injustice. Beckett's absurdist theater portrayed characters condemned to loneliness, living in a world without redemption. Novels such as *Invisible Man* and *Catch-22* dramatized the plight of the existential hero in an indifferent universe.

Art in the Post-War Era. The artistic avant-garde was revived in the aggressively abstract works of the New York school, ranging from Pollock's "drip paintings" to Rothko's majestic fields of color. "Pop" art borrowed icons from the mass culture – Warhol's soup cans and music stars – while minimalist sculpture and happenings continued to challenge conventional definitions of art. In post-war sculpture, modernist abstractionists such as Calder and Smith gave way to the constructions and assemblages of a generation seeking authenticity.

Trials of Modern Architecture. The International Style of urban architecture reached a triumphant height in the monolithic glass-and-steel skyscrapers of Mies van der Rohe. On a smaller scale, buildings such as Wright's Guggenheim Museum and Utzon's Sydney Opera House treated building as sculpture, achieving striking organic forms that were beautiful, if not always practical and durable.

Post-1945 Music. Avant-garde music composers such as Babbitt and Stockhausen turned to synthesizers and electronic instruments to achieve total control over the musical performance. Cage employed Zen Buddhist ideas in a music of chance that stretched the definitions of music to the limit. While traditional classical music and musical theater demonstrated continuing popular appeal, the charismatic stars of rock-and-roll led a youthful pop rebellion that crossed racial and national boundaries.

Post-Modern Styles. The rapid changes of the late twentieth century produced a sensibility called the "post-modern," sceptical of universal truths and eclectic in its approach to art and ideas. Post-modern architecture abandoned modernist purity in favor of a colorful flamboyance and historicism. Minimalist composers such as Glass won a broader audience for the musical avant-garde. In the arts, superrealists reduced art to direct copies of photographs, while earth art and conceptual art escaped the bounds of the studio and the gallery with art on a superhuman scale. The self-conscious "meta"-fictions of post-modern writers, modeled on Borges' labyrinthine stories, culminated in the "magic realism" of Latin American novelists.

Revising the Canon. The civil-rights and feminist movements brought a call to broaden the canon of artistic and philosophical master works. Post-colonial nations produced important new literary voices. With unprecedented opportunities, African-American artists excelled in painting, dance, and drama. Women novelists and poets flourished without post-modern conceits.

Themes for a New Age. The end of the twentieth century brought a sobering epidemic of AIDS and profound artistic responses to this new plague. The increasingly global culture of images and information promised a new integration of ideas and experience, but at the risk of losing authentic traditions.

NOTES

Chapter 2

1   Herodotus, *History of the Persian War*, Book II.78, trans. George Rawlinson. See Charles A. Robinson, Jr., ed., *Selections from Greek and Roman Historians*. New York: Holt, Rinehart & Winston, 1957, pp. 12–13.

2   *The Great Hymn to Aten*, quoted in N. Grimal, *A History of Ancient Egypt*, trans. Ian Shaw. Oxford: Blackwell, 1992, pp. 228–9.

Chapter 3

1   *The Iliad of Homer*, trans. Richard Lattimore. Chicago: U. of Chicago Pr., 1951, pp. 488–9.

2   Willis Barnstone, *Sappho and the Greek Lyric Poets* (rev. ed. of *Greek Lyric Poetry*). New York: Schocken, 1988. Copyright © 1962, 1967, 1988 by Willis Barnstone. Reprinted by permission of Schocken Books, published by Pantheon Books, a division of Random House, Inc.

3   Thucydides, *History of the Peloponnesian War*, Book II.52, trans. Richard Crawley. See Thucydides, *The Peloponnesian War*, ed. John H. Finley. New York: Modern Library, 1951, p. 113.

4   Thucydides, *History of the Peloponnesian War*, trans. Benjamin Jowett. In Charles A. Robinson, Jr., ed., *Selections from Greek and Roman Historians*. New York: Holt, Rinehart & Winston, 1957, p.80.

5   Sophocles, *Antigone*, trans. Robert Fagles. In *The Three Theban Plays*. Harmondsworth: Penguin, 1982, pp. 76–7. Translation copyright © 1982 by Robert Fagles. Used by permission of Viking Penguin, a division of Penguin Books USA Inc.

6   *The Great Learning*, in W. T. de Bary and others, *Sources of Chinese Tradition*, Vol. 1. New York: Columbia U. Pr., 1960, p. 115.

Chapter 4

1   Virgil, *Aeneid*, trans. W. F. Jackson Knight. Harmondsworth: Penguin Classics, 1956, p. 173. Reproduced by permission of Penguin Books Ltd. Copyright © G. R. Wilson Knight, 1956.

2   Renate Bridenthal and Claudia Koonz, eds., *Becoming Visible: Women in European History*, 1st ed. Boston: Houghton Mifflin, 1977, p. 75. Copyright © 1977 by Houghton Mifflin Company. Used with permission.

3   From *The Poems of Catullus* by Catullus, trans. James Michie. Copyright © 1969 James Michie. Reprinted by permission of Random House, Inc.

4   Virgil, *Aeneid*, p. 27.

5   Virgil, *Aeneid*, p. 116.

6   Juvenal, *Satires*, trans. Rolfe Humphries. Indianapolis: Indiana U.Pr., 1958. © 1958 Indiana U. Pr.

7   Lucretius, *On the Nature of the Universe*, trans. R. E. Latham. Harmondsworth: Penguin Classics, 1951, p. 124. Reproduced by permission of Penguin Books Ltd. Copyright © R. E. Latham 1951.

8   Lucretius, *On the Nature of the Universe*, pp. 24–5.

9   Marcus Aurelius, *The Meditations*, trans. G. M. A. Grube. Indianapolis: Liberal Arts Pr., 1963, Book VII.9, pp. 62–3.

10   Marcus Aurelius, *The Meditations*, Book II.5, p. 13.

Chapter 5

1   Genesis 1:26–28. Scripture quotations are from the Revised Standard Version of the Bible, copyright 1946, 1952, 1971 by the Division of Christian Education of the National Council of the Churches of Christ in the USA.

2   Genesis 3:1–5.

3   Job 38:1–11.

4   Matthew 5:27–29, 38–42.

5   Josephus, *The Jewish Wars*, trans. William Whiston; see *The Works of Flavius Josephus*. Philadelphia: International Pr. [1904], p. 818.

6   St. Augustine, *The Confessions*, trans. E. B. Pusey. In *Great Books of the Western World*, Vol. 18. Chicago: Encyclopedia Britannica, 1952, pp. 10–11.

7   John Julius Norwich, *Byzantium: The Early Centuries*. New York: Knopf, 1989, p. 203.

8   The Koran (Qur'an), trans. N. J. Dawood. Harmondsworth: Penguin Classics, 1956, 6th rev. ed. 1990. Copyright © N. J. Dawood 1956, 1959, 1966, 1968, 1974, 1990.

Chapter 6

1   Russell Chamberlin, *The Emperor: Charlemagne*. New York: Franklin Watts, 1986, pp. 144–5.

2   Charlemagne, quoted in Pierre Riché, *Daily Life in the World of Charlemagne*, trans. Jo Ann McNamara. Philadelphia: U. of Pennsylvania Pr., 1983, pp. 133–4.

3   Ramon Llull, *Book of the Order of Chivalry*, quoted in Maurice Keen, *Chivalry*. New Haven: Yale U. Pr., 1984.

4   From *The Song of Roland* by Frederick Goldin, translator. Copyright © 1978 W. W. Norton & Company, Inc. Reprinted by permission of W. W. Norton & Company, Inc.

5   The Rule of St. Benedict, quoted in David Knowles, *Christian Monasticism*. New York: McGraw-Hill, 1969, pp. 34–5.

6   Katharina Wilson, *Medieval Women Writers*. Athens, Georgia: U. of Georgia Pr., 1984, p. 38.

7   Wilson, *Medieval Women Writers*, p. 38.

8   Bernard of Clairvaux, "Apologia" to William, Abbot of St.-Thierry. In Elizabeth G. Holt, ed., *A Documentary History of Art*, Vol. 1. *The Middle Ages and Renaissance*. New York: Doubleday, 1957, p. 20.

9   Hildegard of Bingen, *De Sancta Maria*, from *Hildegard of Bingen's Book of Divine Works*, ed. Matthew Fox. Santa Fe, New Mexico: Bear & Co., 1987. Reprinted with permission. © 1987 Bear & Co.

Chapter 7

1   François Villon, "For His Mother to Our Lady," in *French Lyrics in English Verse*, trans. William Frederic Giese. Madison, Wisconsin: U. of Wisconsin Pr., 1946.

2   Gerda Panofsky-Soergel, ed. *Abbot Suger on the Abbey Church of St.-Denis and its Art Treasures*, 2nd ed. Princeton: Princeton U. Pr., 1979, p. 49.

3   Panofsky-Soergel, *Abbot Suger*, p. 51.

4   Andreas Cappellanus, *The Art of Courtly Love*. New York: Columbia U. Pr., 1990.

5   Bernart de Ventadorn, from "Singing is Not Worth a Thing," trans. Harvey Birenbaum, in Flores, ed., *Medieval Age*. New York: Dell, 1963, p. 181.

6   Beatriz de Dia, "A chantar m'er de so qu'ieu non volria" (Of things I'd rather keep in silence), from Magda Bogin, *The Women Troubadours*, p. 87. New York: Norton, 1980. Reprinted by permission.

7   Henry Knighton, from C. Olson and M. Crow, eds., *Chaucer's World*. New York: Columbia U. Pr., copyright © 1948, pp. 353–4. Reprinted with permission of the publisher.

8   Dante Alighieri, *The Divine Comedy*. Vol. 1: Inferno, Canto V, trans. Mark Musa. Indianapolis: Indiana U. Pr., 1971. © 1971 Indiana U. Pr.

9   Geoffrey Chaucer, *The Canterbury Tales*, trans. Neville Coghill. London: Penguin, 1977, p.279.

10   Petrarch, Sonnet CCXCII, "Gli occhi di ch'io parlai sí caldamente," *Sonnets*, trans. Edwin Morgan.

Chapter 8

1   Pico della Mirandola, *Oration on the Dignity of Man*, trans. Elizabeth Forbes. In Robert Warnock and George K. Anderson, eds., *The World in Literature*. Chicago: Scott, Foresman, 1959, p. 546.

2   Lorenzo de' Medici, "A Carnival Song," trans. J. A. Symonds. In James Bruce Ross and Mary Martin McLaughlin, eds., *The Portable Renaissance Reader*. New York: Viking, 1953, pp. 432–4.

3   Benvenuto Cellini, *The Autobiography of Benvenuto Cellini*, Book VIII,

trans. J. A. Symonds. Immortal Classics edn, p. 62.

4 Niccolò Machiavelli, *The Prince*, trans. and ed. Thomas G. Bergin. Wheeling, Illinois: Crofts Classics Series, © 1947 Harlan Davidson Inc., pp. 25–26, 48, 50–52, 70–71, 75. Used by permission.

5 Baldassare Castiglione, *The Book of the Courtier*, trans. George Bull. Harmondsworth: Penguin, 1967, p. 221.

6 *Leonardo on Painting*, Martin Kemp, ed. and trans. New Haven, Connecticut: Yale U. Pr., 1989, p. 48.

Chapter 9

1 Diane de Poitiers, in Katherine M. Wilson, ed., *Women Writers of the Renaissance and Reformation*. Athens: U. of Georgia Pr., 1987, p. 166.

2 Albrecht Dürer, from a letter. In Wolfgang Stechow, *Northern Renaissance Art 1400–1600: Sources and Documents*. Englewood Cliffs, New Jersey: Prentice-Hall, 1966, p. 91.

3 Albrecht Dürer, from a draft of his study of proportion. In Elizabeth G. Holt, ed., *A Documentary History of Art, Vol. 1. The Middle Ages and Renaissance*. New York: Doubleday, 1957, p. 311.

4 Erasmus, *Handbook of the Militant Christian*. In John P. Dolan, *The Essential Erasmus*. New York: New American Library, 1964, p. 39. Copyright © 1964 by John P. Dolan. Used by permission of New American Library, a division of Penguin Books USA Inc.

5 Erasmus, *In Praise of Folly*, trans. Betty Radice. Harmondsworth: Penguin Classics, 1971, pp. 150, 179, 161–2. Reproduced by permission of Penguin Books Ltd. Translation copyright © Betty Radice, 1971.

6 William Shakespeare, *Hamlet*, Act II, sc. ii, 319 ff.

7 Shakespeare, *Hamlet*, Act III, sc. i, 160–71; p. 66.

8 Quoted in Gustave Reese, *Music in the Renaissance*, rev. ed. New York: Norton, 1959, p. 449.

Chapter 10

1 Miguel Cervantes, *Don Quixote*. In *The Portable Cervantes*, trans. Samuel Putnam. New York: Viking, 1951, pp. 110–11. Translation copyright © 1949, 1950, 1951 by Viking Penguin, Inc. Used by permission of Viking Penguin, a division of Penguin Books USA Inc.

2 *Life of St. Teresa*, trans. J. M. Cohen. Harmondsworth: Penguin, 1957, p. 210.

3 Claudio Monteverdi, *L'Orfeo*. London: J. & W. Chester, 1923, pp. 51–2.

4 Galileo quoted in Giorgio de Santillana, *The Crime of Galileo*. Chicago: U. of Chicago Pr., 1955, p. 312.

5 René Descartes, *Discourse on Method and the Meditations*. Harmondsworth: Penguin, 1968, pp. 53–4.

6 *Samuel Pepys's Diary*, ed. Richard Le Gallienne. New York: Modern Library, n.d., pp. 199–200.

7 John Locke, *Essay on Civil Government*. In Edwin A. Burtt, ed., *The English Philosophers from Bacon to Locke*. New York: Modern Library, 1939, p. 438.

8 Locke, *Essay on Civil Government*, p. 438.

Chapter 11

1 Jean-Jacques Rousseau, *The Social Contract*, trans. Charles Frankel. New York: Hafner, 1947, p. 19.

2 Rousseau, *The Social Contract*, p. 18.

3 Edmond and Jules de Goncourt, *The Woman of the Eighteenth Century*, trans. Jacques de Clercq and Ralph Roeder. New York: Minton, Balch, 1927, p. 44.

4 Samuel Richardson, *Pamela*. London: Dent, 1962, p. 57.

5 Jonathan Swift, *A Modest Proposal*. See Swift, *Satires and Personal Writings*, ed. W. A. Eddy. London: Oxford U. Pr., 1973, pp. 23–4.

6 César de Saussure, "A Foreign View of England." In *Eyewitness to History*, ed. John Carey. Cambridge, MA: Harvard U. Pr., 1987, p. 215.

7 Voltaire, *Candide, or Optimism*. Wheeling, Illinois: Harlan Davidson, 1946, pp. 114–15.

Chapter 12

1 *The Declaration of Independence*. New York: Oxford U. Pr., 1947, pp. 3–7.

2 Victor Hugo, "Preface to *Cromwell*," trans. George Burnham Ives. In

Morse Peckham, ed., *Romanticism: The Culture of the Nineteenth Century*. New York: George Braziller, 1965, p. 161.

3 Quoted in M. H. Abrams, *The Mirror and the Lamp: Romantic Theory and the Critical Tradition*. London: Oxford U. Pr., 1953, p. 199.

4 Quoted in Lorenz Eitner, *Neoclassicism and Romanticism, 1750–1850*. Englewood Cliffs, New Jersey: Prentice-Hall, 1970, p. 101.

5 Ludwig van Beethoven, "Heiligenstadt Testament," in *Thayer's Life of Beethoven*, rev. ed., Vol. 1, Elliot Forbes, ed. Princeton: Princeton U. Pr., 1967, pp. 304–6.

6 *Goethe's Faust*, Parts I and II, trans. Louis MacNeice. Copyright © 1951, 1954 by Frederick Louis MacNeice; renewed by Hedli MacNeice. Reprinted by permission of Faber & Faber Ltd, p. 61.

7. *Goethe's Faust*, p. 282.

8. William Blake, "London," from *Songs of Experience*. In Northrop Frye, ed., *Selected Poetry and Prose of William Blake*. New York: Modern Library, 1953, p. 46.

9 Mary Wollstonecraft, *A Vindication of the Rights of Women*. New York: Norton, 1988, pp. 149, 150.

10 William Wordsworth, *The Prelude*, Book XIV, 70–75. In Mark van Doren, ed., *Selected Poetry*. New York: Random House, 1950, p. 384.

11 William Wordsworth, "The World is Too Much With Us." In *Selected Poetry*, p. 536.

12 Herman Melville, *Moby Dick*. New York: Norton, 1967, p. 52.

13 Grenville Goodwin, *Western Apache Raiding and Warfare*, ed. K. Basso. Tucson: U. of Arizona Pr., 1971, p. 29.

14 Berlioz's program for *Symphonie fantastique*, quoted in Joseph Machlis, *The Enjoyment of Music*, 4th ed. New York: Norton, 1977, p. 106.

15 Mary Shelley, *Frankenstein*. Harmondsworth: Penguin, 1985, pp. 190–1.

Chapter 13

1 Karl Marx, *The German Ideology*. In Loyd D. Easton and Kurt H. Guddat, eds., *Writings of the Young Marx on Philosophy and Society*. Garden City, New York: Doubleday Anchor, 1967, pp. 424–5.

2 Gustave Flaubert, *The Sentimental Education*, trans. Perdita Burlingame. New York: Signet, 1972, p. 330. Translation copyright © 1972 Perdita Burlingame. Used by permission of New American Library, a division of Penguin Books USA Inc.

3 Karl Marx, *The Communist Manifesto*, trans. Samuel Moore. Harmondsworth: Penguin, 1985, p. 87.

4 Walt Whitman, *Leaves of Grass*. In *Complete Poetry and Collected Prose*. New York: Library of America, pp. 188, 210.

5 Richard Wagner, quoted in Bryan Magee, *Aspects of Wagner*, rev. ed. Oxford: Oxford U. Pr., 1988, p. 5.

6 Lillian Nordica, *Lillian Nordica's Hints to Singers*. New York: Dutton, 1923, pp. 13–14.

7 Charles Baudelaire, "To the Reader," *Les Fleurs du Mal*, trans. Richard Howard. Boston: Godine, 1982, pp. 5–6. Translation © 1983 Richard Howard. Reprinted by permission of David R. Godine Publishers.

8 Henrik Ibsen, *A Doll's House*, trans. Eva LaGallienne. In *Six Plays by Henrik Ibsen*. New York: Random House, 1957.

9 Dostoyevsky quoted in Peter Conradi, *Fyodor Dostoyevsky*. New York: St. Martin's Pr., 1988, p. 17.

10 Fyodor Dostoevski (Dostoyevsky), from *The Brothers Karamazov*, trans. Constance Garnett, edited with a foreword by Manuel Komroff, © 1960 by Manuel Komroff. Reprinted by permission. Indianapolis: Bobbs-Merrill, 1948, pp. 37–8.

Chapter 14

1 W. B. Yeats, "The Second Coming," in *The Poems of W. B. Yeats: A New Edition*, ed. Richard J. Finneran. New York: © 1924 Macmillan Publishing Co, renewed 1952 by Bertha Georgie Yeats. Reprinted with permission of Simon & Schuster, Inc.

2 Ray Strachey, *"The Cause": A Short History of the Women's Movement in Great Britain*. Port Washington, New York: Kennikat Pr., 1969, p. 389.

3. Henri Matisse quoted in Nikos Stangos, *Concepts of Modern Art*. London: Thames and Hudson, 1981, pp. 23-4.

4 Henri Matisse quoted in John Canaday, *Mainstreams of Modern Art*.

New York: Simon & Schuster, 1959, p. 407.

5 Henri Matisse quoted in Robert Goldwater, ed., *Artists on Art*, 3rd ed. New York: Pantheon, 1958, p. 98.

6 Joan Miró quoted in Herschel Chipp, *Theories of Modern Art*. Berkeley, California: U. of California Pr., 1968, p. 435.

7 Salvador Dalí, quoted in Robert Descharnes, *Salvador Dalí*. New York: Abrams, 1976, p.30.

8 Franz Kafka, *The Metamorphosis*, from *Short Stories of Franz Kafka*. New York: Random House. Copyright © 1952 Random House Inc, pp. 19, 20.

Chapter 15

1 Allen Ginsberg, "A Supermarket in California," from *Collected Poems 1947–1980*. Copyright © 1955 Allan Ginsberg, copyright renewed. San Francisco: City Lights, 1959, pp. 29–30. Reprinted by permission of HarperCollins Publishers Inc.

2 Jean-Paul Sartre, "Existentialism," trans. Bernard Frechtman. In *Existentialism and Human Emotions*. New York: Philosophical Library, 1957, p. 22.

3 Samuel Beckett, *Waiting for Godot*. New York: Grove, 1966, p. 57.

4 Ralph Ellison, *Invisible Man*. New York: Modern Library, 1952, p. 3.

5 Joseph Heller, *Catch-22*. New York: Dell, 1961, p. 47.

6 Jackson Pollock quoted in Herschel Chipp, *Theories of Modern Art*. Berkeley, California: U. of California Pr., 1968, pp. 547–8.

7 Pollock quoted in Chipp, *Theories of Modern Art*, pp. 547–8.

8 Henry Moore quoted in Chipp, *Theories of Modern Art*, p. 595.

9 Frank Lloyd Wright quoted in Spiro Kostof, *A History of Architecture*.

New York: Oxford U. Pr., 1985, p. 742.

10 Karlheinz Stockhausen quoted in H. H. Stuckenschmidt, *Twentieth Century Music*. New York: McGraw-Hill, 1969, p. 187.

11 Steiner Kvale, "Themes of Postmodernity," in *The Truth about the Truth*, Walter Truett Anderson, ed. New York: Tarcher/Puttnam, 1995, p.25.

12 Kvale, p.27.

13 Robert Venturi, *Complexity and Contradiction in Architecture*, 2nd ed. New York: The Museum of Modern Art, 1977, p. 16.

14 James Turrell, quoted in Suzi Gablik, *Has Modernism Failed?* New York: Thames and Hudson, 1984, p.83.

15 Jorge Luis Borges, "Tlön, Uqbar, Orbis Tertius," from *Ficciones*, trans. Alastair Reid, © 1962 by Grove Pr., renewed copyright © 1990 Grove Weidenfeld. Used with permission of Grove/Atlantic Monthly Pr. In Emir Rodriguez Monegal and Alastair Reid, eds., *Borges: A Reader*. New York: E. P. Dutton, 1981, pp. 116–17.

16 Borges, pp. 121–22.

17 Denise Levertov, "In Mind," from *Poems 1960–1967*. Copyright © 1966 by Denise Levertov. Reprinted by permission of New Directions Publishing Corp.

18 Tony Kushner, "Angels in America, A Gay Fantasia on National Themes," quoted in Rob Baker, *The Art of AIDS*. New York: Continuum, 1994, p. 221.

19 Excerpt from Paul Monette, *Borrowed Time: An AIDS Memoir*. New York: Harcourt Brace. Copyright © 1988 Paul Monette, reprinted by permission of Harcourt Brace & Company.

GLOSSARY

absolutism The political philosophy that a monarch should exercise absolute political power and control all aspects of national life.

abstract expressionism The term commonly applied to a group of painters active in New York City in the 1940s and 1950s; their works are characterized by the highly abstract use of color, line, and shape.

academy The Academy was originally the school established by Plato in Athens; generally, the term refers to an officially established school or group that dictates (usually conservative) rules and standards of taste.

additive sculpture *Sculpture* which is fashioned by building up a shape (as with plaster or clay), constructing a shape from raw materials (such as metal), or assembling a shape from various materials.

aleatory music Music in which significant choices in the composition or performance are left to chance or whim (from Latin *alea*, "dice").

allegory A literary or artistic device in which characters, objects, or actions represent abstract ideas or meanings; in Dante's *Divine Comedy*, for example, the poet's journey stands allegorically for every human's journey through life.

ambulatory The walkway around the *choir* of a Christian church, giving access to the *apse* and *chapels*.

analytical cubism See *cubism*.

antiphonal Music in which two or more groups sing or play in alternation (hence "antiphonal singing").

apse Originally the semicircular niche at the ends of a Roman *basilica*; in Christian architecture, the niche-like eastern end of a church, usually housing the altar.

arabesque An intricate surface decoration, often consisting of repeating linear designs and, in Islamic art, containing no figures.

arch The architectural form in which a curved construction spans the distance between two columns or walls (Fig. 4.14).

Archaic A period of ancient Greek art (c. 700–480 B.C.), typified in sculpture by the stylized *kouros* and *koré* figures.

architrave In classical architecture, the horizontal beam that forms the lowest part of the *entablature*.

archivolt The molding that frames an arched doorway.

aria A song usually found in operas, oratorios, and cantatas, commonly sung as a solo and often the occasion for virtuoso singing (Italian, "air").

Ars Nova In music, a style of *polyphony* (current c. 1320–1400) characterized by greater refinement and expressiveness (Latin, "new art").

Art Nouveau In art, a style of decoration and architecture (current c. 1890-1910) characterized by floral and plant motifs (French, "new art").

assemblage A process in which a work of art is built up, or "assembled," from miscellaneous three-dimensional materials.

atmospheric perspective (also **aerial perspective**) The *perspective* technique that creates the illusion of depth by blurring the outlines and altering the color tones of distant objects.

atonal Music that is not composed in a *key*.

atrium The inner courtyard of a Roman house; also, the forecourt of an Early Christian church.

aulos A pipe instrument used in ancient Greece, usually played in pairs, one held in each hand.

avant-garde The group of artists or writers who are considered at the time to be the most "advanced" in their methods or subject matter.

ballet A dramatic art combining dance, pantomime, and music, usually to tell a story or evoke a mood; also, a musical composition to accompany ballet.

baptistery The part of a church where baptism is performed; in Early Christian and medieval churches, often a separate building constructed on a circular plan.

baroque A style of European art and music in the period c. 1600–1750, characterized by theatricality, elaborately decorative design, and monumental scale.

barrel vault (also **tunnel vault**) A *vault* composed of an extended, continuous arch (Fig. 4.14).

basilica In ancient Roman architecture, a colonnaded hall used for law courts or other public functions; form later adapted to Christian churches (Fig. 5.13).

bass The lowest range of the male voice; also, any bass instrument.

blank verse Poetic meter consisting of iambic pentameter, or five iambs (˘ ¯) in a line.

Bronze Age Period of human culture in Europe and Asia characterized by use of bronze tools and weapons (from c. 4000–3000 B.C. to c. 1000 B.C.).

buttress In architecture, a supporting arm or post, usually to brace a wall, arch, or *vault* (Fig. 7.7).

cadence In music, a conclusion or resting place.

caliph Ruler of the Muslim community.

canon In architecture or sculpture, a set of rules for proportion; generally, any officially prescribed set of books.

cantata A form of musical composition for voice and orchestra, consisting of several movements or sections, often including opera-like *arias* and *recitative*; as developed by Bach in the baroque period, the most important musical component of Lutheran worship.

capital The upper part of a column; see *orders*.

casting A sculptural process in which a liquid material (wax, plaster, clay, or metal) is poured into a mold; when the liquid has hardened, the mold is removed, leaving a replica of the original shape.

catharsis According to Aristotle, the cleansing of the emotions experienced by the audience of an ancient Greek *tragedy* (Greek, "purgation").

cella The inner room of a Greek temple, usually containing a cult image of a deity.

chant See *plainchant*.

chapel A small space in a church or other building usually containing an altar.

chiaroscuro In painting, the use of shades of light and dark to suggest volume; also, strong contrasts of light and dark for dramatic effect (Italian, "light-dark").

chivalry The rules and customs governing knightly conduct in the Middle Ages, requiring loyalty to the lord, fairness in combat, and courtesy toward women (from French *chevalier*, "horseman", "knight").

choir The part of a church where the service is sung, usually east of the nave (Fig. 6.30).

chord Any combination of two or more notes sounded together.

choreographer The artist who devises and directs the movements of dancers.

chorus In ancient Greek theater, a group of singers and dancers who commented on the action; in music, a group of singers who perform together, usually singing in parts; also, the section of a musical work designated for choral singing.

classical Pertaining to the civilization of ancient Greece and Rome; also (usually *Classical*), the period in European music, c. 1750–1820, as defined by the works of Haydn, Mozart, and Beethoven.

clef The sign placed at the beginning of a *staff* to indicate the pitch of one line, and hence establishing the range of notes for all the lines and spaces (French, "key").

clerestory The row of windows along the top of the *nave* walls of a basilica or church.

cloister The enclosed courtyard of a Christian monastery, often surrounded by covered, arcaded walkways.

collage The technique of pasting materials – paper, string, cloth, etc. – to a canvas or board, often combined with painting (from French *coller*, "to paste").

colonnade A row of columns.

column An upright post, usually a support but sometimes built independently as a monument (Fig. 4.10); in the classical *orders* (Fig. 3.13), consists of *shaft*, *capital*, and base.

comedy A literary or dramatic form involving wit, humor, and ridicule, usually intended to provoke laughter.

composition The formal arrangement of parts within a work of art; also, a work of music.

concerto A musical composition for an ensemble of voices and instruments; in the baroque *concerto grosso*, a small group of instruments plays in contrast with a larger orchestra; in the Classical concertos of Mozart and Beethoven, a solo instrument plays with an orchestra.

contrapposto A pose of the human figure in which the upper torso is twisted slightly, so that the shoulders and hips form an oblique angle (Italian, "opposite"; Fig. 8.24).

Corinthian order A classical *order* of architecture, with finely carved leaf capitals, popular in Hellenistic Greece and imperial Rome.

cornice In classical architecture, the horizontal ledge overhanging the *entablature*; hence, any horizontal projection along the top of a wall.

counterpoint As a synonym for *polyphony*, the musical technique of combining two different melodic lines played simultaneously; also applies to systematized methods in Renaissance and baroque music for combining contrapuntal voices (from Latin *contrapunctum*, "against note").

cross vault (also **groin vault**) *Vault* formed by the intersection of two *tunnel vaults* (Fig. 4.14).

cubism The abstract style of art developed by Picasso and Braque in the period 1907–14; its early phase, *analytic cubism*, decomposed objects into abstract planes and shapes; its later phase, *synthetic cubism*, combined *collage* with abstract painting.

dada The movement of European artists characterized by provocation and mockery of traditional art; active c. 1916–22 in Zürich, Paris, and Berlin.

deism Religious belief in the existence of a God who has created the universe and left it to operate according to rational laws; prominent among *Enlightenment* intellectuals.

dissonance A combination of notes that violates the prevailing harmonic system, producing discord and a feeling of tension in the listener.

dome A hemispherical *vault*, composed of an arch rotated 180 degrees.

Doric A classical *order* of architecture characterized by austere simplicity (Fig. 3.13).

dynamics The aspect of music that determines the variations of loudness or softness of the sound.

empiricism Philosophical belief that all knowledge is derived from experience and the senses; denies the existence of innate ideas independent of experience; compare *rationalism*.

engraving Process of printmaking by incising a metal plate, which is then inked and used to print an image; also, the print itself.

Enlightenment The term given to the eighteenth-century intellectual movement that sought to apply reason and science to human affairs; also the period (c. 1715–1800) of the movement's greatest prominence.

entablature In classical architecture, the horizontal section above the columns, consisting of *architrave*, *frieze*, and *cornice* (Fig. 3.13).

entasis The slight outward swelling in the *shaft* of a classical *column*.

epic A long narrative poem recounting the adventures of a heroic central figure, who is usually aided by supernatural forces.

Epicureanism The philosophical belief that the universe is composed of atoms and void, and that the highest good lies in moderate pleasure.

epistles Letters, especially the letters of Paul and the apostles in the Christian New Testament.

epistolary novel A novel that recounts its story through letters written by one or several of the characters.

essay In literature, a brief work of analytic, interpretive, or critical prose, often dealing with its subject from a personal point of view.

etching The process of *engraving* in which the metal plate is incised, or eaten away, by acid.

ethics The branch of philosophy concerned with human conduct.

ethos In ancient Greece, the belief that music could shape human character (Greek, "character").

Eucharist In Christian belief, the ritual celebration of the Last Supper or Lord's Supper, consisting of bread and wine that symbolize the body and blood of Christ (Greek, "thanksgiving").

Evangelist One of the four authors of the Christian Gospels (Matthew, Mark, Luke, and John).

existentialism Philosophical belief that asserted the absurdity of human existence and stressed the necessity for human struggle and individual responsibility; popularized by Sartre and Camus during the period 1940–60.

exposition See *sonata form*.

expressionism An artistic or literary style that seeks to express the author's emotions or inner vision; as a movement, applies to writers and artists active, especially in German-speaking Europe, in the period c. 1910–30.

façade The front of a building.

farce A *comedy* of exaggerated expressions and ludicrous situations.

fauvism A style of painting emphasizing free use of color, practiced by a group of French artists, led by Matisse, in the years 1905–7.

feudalism the system of landholding and political alliance prevalent in medieval Europe, in which oaths of allegiance and military service are exchanged for possession of land.

fluting In architecture, vertical grooves carved into the *shaft* of a *column*.

flying buttress The external support of a Gothic church, formed by an arched arm that braces the *nave* wall and transfers its *thrust* to a vertical *buttress* (Fig. 7.7).

form The overall design or structure of a literary, musical, or artistic work.

fresco A technique of wall or ceiling painting in which paint is applied to wet plaster (Italian, "fresh").

frieze Any horizontal band of sculptural decoration; in classical architecture, the sculpted band above the *architrave* and beneath the *cornice*.

fugue A form of musical composition in which a *theme* is developed usually by *counterpoint*.

futurism The movement of artists and intellectuals who rejected tradition and exalted the speed and machines of modern life; active in Italy and Russia c. 1909–28.

gallery In architecture, the passageway above the church *aisles*.

genre In painting, the depiction of scenes from ordinary life; generally, a type or category of art or literature (portraiture as a *genre* of painting, the novel as a *genre* of literature).

Gesamtkunstwerk (German, "total work of art") The term coined by Wagner to describe his vision of opera as the perfect union of music, theater, dance, and the visual arts.

Golden Age A period of exceptional cultural achievement; in ancient Greece, refers to Athens in 480–404 B.C.

Gospels The first four books of the Christian New Testament (Matthew, Mark, Luke, and John), devoted to accounts of, and commentaries on, the life of Jesus (Greek, "good news").

Gothic In art history, a style associated with the later European Middle Ages (c. 1200–1450); in literature, a genre employing horror, supernatural effects, and medieval settings.

Greek cross A cross with arms of equal length.

Gregorian chant A form of *plainchant* attributed to Pope Gregory I (590–604) but probably unified as a body of sacred vocal music during the reign of Charlemagne, c. 800.

Guidonian hand A method of musical notation, attributed to Guido of Arezzo (active early eleventh century), in which different parts of the hand represented different tones.

hamartia Aristotle's term for the tragic error that brings a hero's downfall.

Harlem Renaissance Movement of African-American authors and artists in Harlem (New York City) during the 1920s.

harmony The combination of notes to produce *chords* and the successive use of chords in a progression that pleases the ear.

high-relief See *relief*.

hippodrome In ancient Greece and Rome, an oval stadium for horse races.

homophonic The term for the type of *polyphony* in which a principal melodic line is accompanied by subordinate lines in chordal *harmony*, as distinct from *counterpoint*, in which the melodic lines move independently (Greek, "like-voiced").

hubris Greek for arrogant or excessive pride.

humanism The philosophical belief in the nobility of human character and achievement; in the Renaissance, a scholar who studied ancient Greek and Latin authors.

hydraulis An ancient type of organ that used water to control the wind pressure in the organ's pipes.

hymn A religious song of praise and adoration.

icon In the Byzantine Church, paintings on panel representing holy persons (Greek, "image").

iconoclasm A movement in the Byzantine Christian Church (730–843) to destroy *icons* and other visual images (Greek, "image smashing").

iconography Any system of symbols and their meanings.

idealism The philosophical belief that a permanent and unchanging world exists apart from the world known through sense experience.

idée fixe The term coined by Berlioz for a melody that recurs, with variations, in different movements of a work.

imitation In music, the immediate or overlapping repetition of a melodic phrase by different voices, often at a different pitch.

impasto In painting, thick applications of oil paint.

imperialism The domination by a single nation or city-state over the life of other areas.

impressionism The movement and style of painting developed by Monet and others, chiefly in the period 1870–90, characterized by the effort to capture the transient effects of light and color in outdoor scenes.

improvization Spontaneously creating or adding to a musical work as it is being performed; especially prominent in baroque music and *jazz*.

installation art A work of art erected or arranged (usually temporarily) in a particular site or exhibition space.

interval The distance between two musical pitches; designated by counting up or down on the seven-tone scale from the starting point (C up to G is an interval of a "fifth").

Ionic A classical *order* of architecture with slender columns and elegant scrolled *capitals* (Fig. 3.13).

jamb The vertical member that frames a doorway.

jazz A type of popular music characterized by *improvization* on popular melodies and a swinging rhythm; originated by African-American musicians in the early 1900s.

jongleur A medieval wandering minstrel.

key The tendency of a musical work to gravitate toward a tonal center (the "key" note, or *tonic*); also, in keyboard instruments, the lever that causes sound to be made.

keystone The central stone in an arch or vault.

Koran See *Qur'an*.

kouros A nude male statue of the *archaic* period in ancient Greece, characterized by a frontal stance and stylized anatomical features; the female version (**koré**) was always clothed.

Latin cross A cross with a longer vertical arm that bisects the shorter crossing arm.

Leitmotif In opera, a well-defined theme that symbolizes a character, object, or idea, often recurring with variations to reflect developments in the dramatic action (German, "leading motif").

libretto The written text of an opera (Italian, "small book").

linear perspective The *perspective* technique that creates the illusion of depth by making parallel lines converge in the far distance.

lintel The horizontal beam that spans the opening between posts or columns.

liturgy The formalized and official rites used in public worship.

lyric A *genre* of poetry, originally designating poetry recited with musical accompaniment; generally, any brief poem, often expressing direct emotion and suggestive of song (Greek *lura*, "lyre," a stringed instrument).

madrigal A type of song popular in Renaissance Italy and England; the Italian madrigal (popular 1350–1560) was a two- or three-voice song of several verses with repeating music; the English madrigal (popular in Elizabethan England) was a secular song in five or six voices often set to love poetry.

major In music, a seven-tone scale or *key* which contains half-step *intervals* between the third and fourth and seventh and eighth steps in the scale (Fig. 10.30).

mannerism In painting and sculpture, a style prominent in Italy between the Renaissance and baroque periods, characterized by elongated figures and deliberate distortions of color, *perspective*, and scale.

masonry In architecture, stone or brick-work.

mass In religion, the *liturgy* of the *Eucharist* in the Catholic Church, composed of the Ordinary (text always the same) and the Proper (texts vary according to liturgical season); in music, a musical composition to accompany the mass.

materialism The philosophical belief that matter is the basis of all reality and that all things, including ideas and emotions, can be explained by reference to physical conditions.

medium (pl. **media**) In general, the physical or technical means by which a work of art is realized (in painting, for example, oil paint vs. *fresco*).

megalith A large stone block, often arranged or aligned in stone-age structures.

melisma In *Gregorian chant*, a chain of several notes sung on a single syllable.

melody A series of musical tones arranged in succession, in a *rhythmic* pattern, to form a recognizable unit.

meter In poetry, any regular scheme of stressed and unstressed syllables; in music, a regular pulse of beats, grouped in larger units called measures (or bars), usually containing two (duple meter) or three (triple meter) beats per measure; see *time signature*.

metopes Square slabs, often decorated with sculpture, that alternate with *triglyphs* in the *frieze* of a Doric temple.

minimalism In the arts, a highly conceptual style of the 1960s that sought to eliminate art's expressive or symbolic qualities; in music, a style of composition using repetition and static harmony, prominent in the U.S. in the 1970s.

minor In music, a seven-tone scale or *key* which, in its natural version, contains half-step *intervals* between the second and third and fifth and sixth steps in the scale (Fig. 10.30).

miracle play A medieval drama depicting the life and martyrdom of a saint (see *mystery play*).

mobile A type of sculpture in which different parts move freely or are moved by a motor.

mode Any group of notes that form a musical *scale* and serve as the basis for a musical composition.

modernism The styles and movements in the arts, literature, and music associated with the rise of the modern world, especially in the period 1910–45.

modulation In music, the change from one *key* to another.

monophonic The term for music consisting of a single melodic line, such as *plainchant* (Latin, "one-voiced"); compare *polyphony*.

monotheism Religious belief in a single, usually all-powerful deity.

montage In film, the rapid editing of brief film segments so as to create a powerful effect on the viewer; see also *photomontage*.

morality play A medieval drama that illustrates a Christian moral teaching, usually through *allegory*.

mosaic A pictorial *medium* consisting of colored pieces of glass, stone, and tile cemented to a wall, floor, or ceiling.

mosque A Muslim religious building for communal prayer.

motet A *polyphonic* musical form used widely in the period c. 1250–1750; in medieval and Renaissance versions, the upper voices often sang different texts (French *mot*, "word").

motif (also **motive**) A brief, often fragmentary musical idea, usually elaborated or developed in a larger composition.

movement In music, a section of a larger composition, such as a symphony.

mural A painting on a wall.

mystery play A medieval religious drama that depicts Biblical stories.

myth Ancient story or belief usually explaining, in metaphoric or symbolic terms, cosmic origins or sacred truths.

narthex The porch or vestibule of a church.

naturalism In the visual arts, any style that seeks fidelity to nature.

nave The rectangular space of a church where worshipers congregate (Latin, "ship").

Near East Region of the ancient world from present-day Turkey to Iran and Arabia.

neoclassicism The revival of the styles and tastes of ancient Greece and Rome, especially as pursued in France and England in the seventeenth and eighteenth centuries.

Neoplatonism A late classical philosophy derived from Plato that asserts three levels of reality leading to the One or the Good; widely adapted by Christian philosophers in the medieval and Renaissance eras.

notation Any system for writing music.

octave The *interval* between one note and the next note of the same pitch, for example, from middle C to the next C higher or lower; on the seven-tone scale, the interval of an "eighth."

opera A musical drama in which all or some of the dramatic text is sung to orchestral accompaniment.

oratorio An extended musical composition for voice and orchestra, usually with a sacred text; contains the musical elements of opera but without costume or theatrical staging.

orchestra In ancient Greek theater, the circular space where the chorus danced and sang its part; in music, an instrumental group that includes stringed instruments, organized to perform musical works (Greek, "dancing place").

order In architecture, a style of decorating a classical temple, distinguished by the treatment of *column* and *entablature* (Fig. 3.13).

organum Generally, the forms of medieval *polyphony* based on *plainchant*; usually with a slow-moving lower voice and one or more higher, more rapid voices.

overture An orchestral composition that introduces an opera, oratorio, or ballet.

pantomime (also **mime**) A dramatic form in which actors use gestures without words.

parable A simple story that teaches a lesson or illustrates a moral principle.

Passion The events of Jesus' last hours, from the Last Supper to his death; also, an oratorio recounting these events.

pediment The triangular area formed by the gabled roof and *cornice* of a classical temple.

pendentives Concave, triangular devices that support a dome (Fig. 5.17).

performance art Type of art consisting of performances by visual or musical artists, rather than actors or dancers, often provocative in nature.

perspective In the visual arts, techniques for creating the illusion of three-dimensional depth on a flat surface.

philosophes Eighteenth-century French intellectuals who professed *Enlightenment* beliefs.

photomontage A *collage* of photographic images.

pier A masonry support, usually square or rectangular, for a roof or vault.

pietà A painting or sculpture depicting the Virgin Mary grieving over the dead Christ.

pilgrimage A journey to a shrine or holy place.

pitch The quality of a sound that fixes it, high or low, on a scale.

plainchant (also **plainsong**) The *monophonic*, unaccompanied vocal music arising in early Christianity and performed with the Christian *liturgies* (see *Gregorian chant*).

polyphonic The term for music in which two or more independent melodic lines sound simultaneously; compare *monophonic* and *homophonic* (Greek, "many-voiced").

polytheism Religious belief in many gods.

pop art A style of art based on "popular" or mass cultural forms such as advertising, commodity packaging, popular music, and film; prominent in the U.S. during the 1960s.

post-and-lintel An architectural form based on columns supporting horizontal beams, as in a Greek temple.

post-impressionism A style in painting (about 1880–1900) that developed from *impressionism*.

prelude In music, a *movement* that introduced a larger instrumental work; often performed unattached as an independent work.

proscenium In ancient Greek theater, the area in front of the *skene* building where the principal actors performed their parts (Greek, "before the skene").

psalter Book containing the Psalms of the Bible.

quadrivium In medieval learning, the higher division of the seven liberal arts, consisting of arithmetic, geometry, astronomy, and music.

Qur'an The Muslim sacred scriptures, as recorded by the prophet Muhammad.

rationalism The philosophical belief that emphasizes the power of human reason over emotion or divine revelation; also, in contrast to *empiricism*, the belief that some ideas are innate to the human mind.

realism An artistic and literary style of the mid-nineteenth century that sought truthfulness to life, instead of traditional idealized representations; used generally, a synonym for *naturalism*.

recitative In opera and similar forms, a style of singing that follows the natural rhythms of the voice, as distinguished from song-like *arias* and ensembles.

Reconquest (also *Reconquista*) Campaign by medieval Spanish Christians to regain Muslim-held territories in Spain.

relics Objects (often bones or possessions) venerated because of their association with a holy person.

relief Sculpture attached to, and projecting from, a backing wall or panel; *low-relief* sculpture projects slightly, while *high-relief* sculpture projects farther.

reliquary A container for a sacred remain, such as a saint's bones.

Renaissance The literary and artistic period, c. 1400–1600, characterized by artistic innovation, new confidence in human abilities, and interest in classical civilization.

responsorial singing A form of *plainchant* in which a soloist sings and a chorus responds.

rhythm In music, a regular pulse or beat; in the visual arts, the repetition of some element (line, shape, etc.).

ribbed vault A *vault* supported by thin ribs of stone (Fig. 7.5).

rococo An eighteenth-century artistic style, especially in France, characterized by soft colors, decorative designs, and frivolous mood (French *rocaille*, "shell-work").

Romanesque The medieval artistic style of c. 900–1200, in architecture characterized by the use of rounded arches, *tunnel vaults*, and other features of Roman architecture (hence the name "Romanesque").

romanticism An artistic movement or sensibility prominent c. 1775–1850, characterized by heroic individualism, a nostalgia for nature or the past, and the prevalence of feeling over reason.

satire Any work that criticizes wickedness and folly through wit and humor, usually with the intent to correct and improve.

scale In music, a sequence of tones in ascending or descending order of *pitch*; in general, the relative size or proportion of an object of art.

scholasticism The method in medieval theology and philosophy characterized by a synthesis of Christian doctrine and the works of Aristotle.

sculpture Any type of art in which a three-dimensional object is fashioned either by removing material (*subtractive* sculpture) or by building up a shape from one or several materials (*additive* sculpture).

serial composition (also **twelve-tone method**) The method of musical composition, devised by Schoenberg c. 1920, based on the varied combination of a series, or "row," of twelve tones.

skene In ancient Greek theater, the building that housed costumes and props and served as a backdrop for the performance.

socialism The philosophical and political belief that society should be based on collective ownership and control of the production of goods.

sonata form A three-part musical form, employed in the Classical *symphony*, consisting of musical themes elaborated through an exposition, development, and recapitulation (Fig. 11.27).

sonnet A form of *lyric* poem composed of fourteen lines in one of several traditional rhyme schemes.

sophists A group of teachers in fifth-century Athens who taught persuasion in argument and questioned the independence of knowledge from the knower (Greek *sophos*, "wisdom").

squinches A system of columns or beams placed diagonally so as to support a dome.

staff In music, the set of horizontal lines and intervening spaces on which music is written.

stoicism The philosophical belief, prominent in classical Rome, that reason governs the universe and that individuals should accept events beyond their immediate control.

subtractive sculpture *Sculpture* fashioned by carving or chipping away material (such as wood or marble) from an unshaped block.

superrealism In the visual arts, a style of extreme realism, prominent in the U.S. in the 1970s.

Symbolism A literary and artistic movement, c. 1885–1910, characterized by a reaction against *realism* and the use of evocative but often private symbols.

symphony An extended form of musical composition for *orchestra*, usually with three or four *movements*.

synthetic cubism See *cubism*.

tempera A paint made of pigment, water, and egg yolk.

tempo The "time" of a musical composition, determining the speed of its performance; traditionally designated by Italian terms (for example, *allegro*, "quick").

tenor In medieval *organum*, the lower voice consisting of long, sustained notes (Latin, *tenere*, "to hold"); also, the highest range of the male voice in regular use.

theme The self-contained melody on which all or part of a composition may be based.

thrust The force that causes a roof to push supporting walls outward.

tonality In music, the series of relationships among *pitches* as based on one central note (the *tonic*); in particular, the system of *keys* governing Western music from the seventeenth to the twentieth centuries.

tone (also **note**) A musical sound of particular *pitch*.

tone row In *serial composition*, the series of twelve tones which forms the basis of the composition.

tonic The main note in a musical *key*.

tracery Decoratively shaped openings in a Gothic church window.

tragedy In ancient Greece, a form of poetic drama involving song and dance, usually relating the fall of a hero through some tragic error; in general, a serious drama involving a character's courageous struggle against destiny or defeat (Greek *tragoidia*, "goat song").

transept The crossing arm of a cross-shaped church.

triforium Arcaded wall passage facing onto the *nave* of a church.

triptych A painting on three panels.

trivium In medieval learning, the lower division of the seven liberal arts, consisting of grammar, rhetoric, and dialectic.

troubadours Poet-musicians of southern France, prominent c. 1100–1350.

tympanum In medieval architecture, the area enclosed by the *lintel* and framing arch of a doorway.

utilitarianism The attitude or philosophical belief that utility, or usefulness, should be the standard for judging an object or action.

utopia An ideal society (Greek for "no-place").

vanishing point In *linear perspective*, the point at which parallel lines seem to converge.

vault A masonry ceiling or roof constructed on the principle of the *arch*.

vernacular The spoken language of a region or country, as opposed to a literary or cultured language; for example, Luther translated the Bible into vernacular German from medieval Latin.

virtuoso In music, a performer of exceptional brilliance or skill.

voice In musical composition, one of the several melodic strands or parts of a polyphonic work; for example, the *tenor* voice or a *fugue* in three voices.

whole tone scale Musical *scale* consisting only of whole-tone *intervals*, without the half-tone steps in a traditional musical *key*.

woodcut The process of printmaking by incising a plank of wood, which is then inked and used to print an image; also, the print itself.

word painting The musical depiction of the meaning of a word or phrase in the text; for example, a quickened rhythm on the word "joyous."

ziggurat Mesopotamian stepped pyramid.

BIBLIOGRAPHY

Chapter 1

BROWN, J. R. *The Oxford Illustrated History of Theatre*. Oxford: Oxford U. Pr., 1996.

CASS, J. *Dancing Through History*. Englewood Cliffs, NJ: Prentice Hall, 1993.

CUMMING, R. *Annotated Art: The World's Greatest Paintings Explored and Explained*. London: Dorling Kindersley, 1995.

JANSON, H. W. *History of Art*, 5th ed. New York: Abrams, 1995.

Chapter 2

ALDRED, C. *Egyptian Art*. London: Thames and Hudson, 1980.

BAHN, P. *Images of the Ice Age*. New York: Facts on File, 1988.

CHAUVET, J., and others. *The Dawn of Art: The Chauvet Cave*. New York: Abrams, 1996.

FRANKFORT, H. *The Art and Architecture of the Ancient Orient*, 4th ed. Pelican History of Art. New Haven: Yale U. Pr., 1970.

GRIMAL, N. *A History of Ancient Egypt*, trans. Ian Shaw. Oxford: Blackwell, 1992.

SAGGS, H. W. F. *Civilization before Greece and Rome*. New Haven: Yale U. Pr., 1989.

Chapter 3

BOARDMAN, J. *The Oxford History of Classical Art*. New York: Oxford U. Pr., 1993.

BOARDMAN, J. *The Parthenon and Its Sculptures*. Austin: U. of Texas Pr., 1985.

CANTARELLA, E. *Pandora's Daughters*. Baltimore, MD: Johns Hopkins U. Pr., 1987.

COMOTTI, G. *Music in Greek and Roman Culture*, trans. R. Munson. Baltimore, MD: Johns Hopkins U. Pr., 1989.

FORD, A. *Homer: The Poetry of the Past*. Ithaca, New York: Cornell U. Pr., 1992.

GREEN, P. *Alexander to Actium: The Historical Evolution of the Hellenistic Age*. Berkeley: U. of California Pr., 1990.

HOWATSON, M. C., ed. *Oxford Companion to Classical Literature*, 2nd ed. Oxford: Oxford U. Pr., 1989.

POLLITT, J. J. *Art and Experience in Classical Greece*. Cambridge, England: Cambridge U. Pr., 1972.

Chapter 4

BOARDMAN, J., J. Griffin, and O. Murray, eds. *The Oxford History of the Classical World*. Oxford: Oxford U. Pr., 1986.

FREEMAN, C. *The World of the Romans*. New York: Oxford U. Pr., 1993.

GRANT, M. *The Art and Life of Pompeii and Herculaneum*. New York: Newsweek, 1979.

KLEINER, D. *Roman Sculpture*. New Haven: Yale U. Pr., 1992.

WALKER, S. *Roman Art*. Cambridge, MA: Harvard U. Pr., 1991.

WARD-PERKINS, J. B. *Roman Imperial Architecture*. Pelican History of Art. Harmondsworth: Penguin, 1981.

Chapter 5

ALTER, R. *The World of Biblical Literature*. New York: Basic Books, 1992.

ARMSTRONG, K. *A History of God*. New York: Knopf, 1993.

BREND, B. *Islamic Art*. Cambridge, MA: Harvard U. Pr., 1991.

CROSSAN, J. D. *The Essential Jesus: Original Sayings and Earliest Images*. San Francisco: Harper, 1994.

FRIEDMAN, R. *Who Wrote the Bible?* New York: Summit, 1987.

FRYMER-KENSKY, T. *In the Wake of the Goddesses: Women, Culture, and the Biblical Transformation of Pagan Myth*. New York: Free Press, 1992.

KRAUTHEIMER, R. *Early Christian and Byzantine Architecture*. Pelican History of Art. London: Penguin, 1975.

McMANNERS, J., ed. *The Oxford Illustrated History of Christianity*. Oxford: Oxford U. Pr., 1990.

SELTZER, R. *Jewish People, Jewish Thought: The Jewish Experience in History*. New York: Macmillan, 1980.

Chapter 6

BECKWITH, J. *Early Medieval Art*. London: Thames and Hudson, 1969.

BERNSTEIN, D. *The Mystery of the Bayeux Tapestry*. Chicago: U. of Chicago Pr., 1986.

CONANT, K. *Carolingian and Romanesque Architecture 800-1200*. London: Penguin, 1979.

HARKSEN, S. *Women in the Middle Ages*. New York: Universe, 1975.

HUBERT, J., and others. *The Carolingian Renaissance*. New York: Braziller, 1970.

LAWRENCE, C. H. *Medieval Monasticism*, 2nd ed. London: Longman, 1989.

MARENBOM, J. *Early Medieval Philosophy (480-1150)*. London: Routledge, 1983.

Chapter 7

FAVIER, J. *The World of Chartres*. New York: Abrams, 1990.

HOPPIN, R. *Medieval Music*. New York: Norton, 1978.

HYMAN, A., and J. Walsh, eds. *Philosophy in the Middle Ages: The Christian, Islamic, and Jewish Traditions*, 2nd. ed. Indianapolis: Hackett, 1983.

KNOWLES, D. *The Evolution of Medieval Thought*. Baltimore: Helicon, 1962.

LOYN, H. R. *The Middle Ages: A Concise Encyclopedia*. London: Thames and Hudson, 1989.

WARNER, M. *Alone of All Her Sex*. New York: Knopf, 1976.

Chapter 8

BRAMLY, S. *Leonardo: Discovering the Life of Leonardo da Vinci*. New York: HarperCollins, 1991.

DE GRAZIA, S. *Machiavelli in Hell*. Princeton: Princeton U. Pr., 1989.

FENLON, I. *The Renaissance*. Man & Music. Englewood Cliffs, NJ: Prentice Hall, 1989.

HARTT, F. *History of the Italian Renaissance Art*, 3rd ed. New York: Abrams, 1987.

HAY, D. *Italy in the Age of the Renaissance*. New York: Longman, 1989.

Chapter 9

ARNOLD, D. *Giovanni Gabrieli and the Music of the Venetian High Renaissance*. New York: Oxford U. Pr., 1979.

McGRATH, A. *Reformation Thought: An Introduction*. London: Blackwell, 1988.

NAUERT, C. *The Age of Renaissance and Reformation*. Lanham, MD: U. Pr. of America, 1981.

ROSAND, D. *Painting in Cinquecento Venice: Titian, Veronese, Tintoretto*. New Haven: Yale U. Pr., 1982.

ROWSE, A. L. *Elizabethan Renaissance: The Cultural Achievement*. New York: Scribner, 1972.

SNYDER, J. *Northern Renaissance Art*. New York: Abrams, 1985.

Chapter 10

BAZIN, G. *The Baroque: Principles, Styles, Themes*. New York: Norton, 1978.

BROWN, J. *The Golden Age of Painting in Spain*. New Haven: Yale U. Pr., 1991.

DOWNES, K. *The Architecture of Wren*. New York: Universe, 1982.

MAINSTONE, M. *The Seventeenth Century*. Cambridge, England: Cambridge U. Pr., 1981.

MONTCLOS, J.-M. *Versailles*. New York: Abbeville, 1991.

SCHWARTZ, G. *Rembrandt: His Life, His Paintings*, 2nd ed. London: Penguin, 1991.

Chapter 11

BROOKNER, A. *Jacques-Louis David*. New York: Thames and Hudson, 1980.

DOWNS, P. *Classical Music: The Era of Haydn, Mozart, and Beethoven*. New York: Norton, 1992.

GAY, P. *The Enlightenment: An Interpretation*, 2 vols. New York: Knopf, 1966, 1969.

HONOUR, H. *Neo-classicism*. Harmondsworth: Penguin, 1977.

JONES, S. *The Eighteenth Century*. Cambridge, England: Cambridge U. Pr., 1985.

YOLTON, J., and others. *The Blackwell Companion to the Enlightenment.* Cambridge, MA: Blackwell, 1992.

Chapter 12

BENNETT, B., and C. ROBINSON, eds. *The Mary Shelley Reader.* New York: Oxford U. Pr., 1990.

BOIME, A. *Art in an Age of Revolution 1750-1800.* Chicago: U. of Chicago Pr., 1987.

HOBSBAWM, E. J. *The Age of Revolution. Europe 1789-1848.* London: Weidenfeld and Nicolson, 1962.

ROSEN, C. *The Romantic Generation.* Cambridge, MA: Harvard U. Pr., 1995.

ROSENBLUM, R., and H. W. JANSON. *19th Century Art.* New York: Abrams, 1984.

SCHAMA, S. *Citizens: A Chronicle of the French Revolution.* New York: Knopf, 1989.

WOOD, G. *The Radicalism of the American Revolution.* New York: Knopf, 1992.

Chapter 13

BERMAN, M. *All That Is Solid Melts Into Air: The Experience of Modernity.* New York: Simon and Schuster, 1982.

CONRADI, P. *Fyodor Dostoyevsky.* New York: St. Martin's Press, 1988.

DONINGTON, R. *Opera and its Symbols: The Unity of Words, Music, and Staging.* New Haven: Yale U. Pr., 1990.

HERBERT, R. *Impressionism: Art, Leisure, and Parisian Society.* New Haven: Yale U. Pr., 1988.

HOBSBAWM, E. J. *The Age of Empire, 1875-1914.* London: Weidenfeld and Nicolson, 1987.

WHITTALL, A. *Romantic Music: A Concise History from Schubert to Sibelius.* London: Thames and Hudson, 1987.

Chapter 14

ARNASON, H. H. *A History of Modern Art,* 3rd. ed. New York: Abrams, 1986.

CANTOR, N., *Twentieth-Century Culture: Modernism to Deconstructionism.* New York: Peter Lang, 1988.

COLLIER, J. *The Making of Jazz.* New York: Delta, 1978.

GRIFFITHS, P. *Modern Music: A Concise History.* New York: Thames and Hudson, 1985.

NEU, J., ed. *The Cambridge Companion to Freud.* Cambridge, England: Cambridge U. Pr., 1991.

OPPLER, E., ed. *Picasso's Guernica.* New York: Norton, 1988.

VARNEDOE, K. *A Fine Disregard: What Makes Modern Art Modern.* New York: Abrams, 1990.

Chapter 15

BRINDLE, R. *The New Music: The Avant-garde since 1945,* 2nd ed. New York: Oxford U. Pr., 1987.

CHADWICK, W. *Women, Art, and Society.* London: Thames and Hudson, 1990.

DOCHERTY, T., ed. *Postmodernism: A Reader.* New York: Columbia U. Pr., 1993.

JENCKS, C. *What is Postmodernism?,* 3rd ed. New York: St. Martin's Press, 1989.

KAUFMANN, W., ed. *Existentialism from Dostoevsky to Sartre,* rev. ed. New York: New American Library, 1975.

STILES, K., and P. Selz, eds. *Theories and Documents of Contemporary Art: A Sourcebook of Artists' Writings.* Berkeley: U. of California Pr., 1996.

INDEX

Aachen, Germany: Palace Chapel of Charlemagne 123, 138–9, 149, **6.8, 6.9**
Abd-ar-Rahman 145
Abelard, Peter 159, 160, 178, 181, **6.36**
Abraham 101, 105, 131
absolutism 262, 279
abstract expressionism 425–6
absurd, theater of the 423
academies 49; French 280, 280, 283, 284
Achebe, Chinua: *Things Fall Apart* 443
Adam and Eve (Dürer) **5.11**
Adams, John 440
Adoration of the Magi (Botticelli) 196, **8.4**
Aeneid (Virgil) 72, 93, 95, **4.3**
Aeschylus 60; *Oresteia* 60
African art 210, **8.26**
Afro-American art and literature 443–5, 447–8
"Agamemnon, Mask of" 40, **2.18**
Agesander *et al.*: *Laocoön* 59, **3.27**
AIDS 447
Ailey, *Cry* 444, **15.27**
Akhenaten 33, 35; "Hymn to Aten" 35
Akhenaten (Glass) 440, **15.21**
Alberti, Leon Battista 206, **8.19**
Alcuin of York 135, 139
aleatory music 435
Alexander the Great 32, 48, 58, 63, 66; *Alexander at the Battle of Issus* 66, **3.33**
Alexandria 67, 85, 86, 112
Alhambra, Granada 146, **6.17**
All Around the Fish (Klee) 402, **14.18**
Allegory of Painting, The (Vermeer) 18, 289, **10.33**

al-Mansur 146
Amarna 35
"*Ambassadors, The*" (Holbein) **9.2**
Ambrosian chant 124
American Revolution 329, 330–1
Americans, Native 350
Amiens, France: Cathedral 165
Anatomy Lesson of Dr. Tulp, The (Rembrandt) 359, **10.38**
Anderson, Laurie 448
Andokides: vase **3.3**
Anselm, St. 159–60, 181
Anthemius of Tralles and Isidorus of Miletus: Hagia Sophia 116–17, **5.15, 5.17, 5.18**
antiquarianism 86
Aphrodite of Cnidos (Praxiteles) 58, **3.25**
Apollo (Etruscan statue) 71, **4.2**
Apollodorus of Damascus: Basilica Ulpia 77, **4.9**; Trajan's Column 77–8, **4.10, 4.11**
Appalachian Spring (Copland) 415, **14.32**
Apples and Oranges (Cézanne) 383, **13.31**
Aquinas, Thomas 181
Ara Pacis Augustae 75–6, **4.3, 4.7**
arch construction 79, 81, 166, **4.14, 7.4**
Archaic period (Greece) 45–7
archetypes 31
architecture 20–1
archivolts 154, 172
Arena Chapel, Padua: Giotto frescoes 189, **7.26**
Aristophanes 61; *Clouds* 61; *Lysistrata* 49, 61

Aristotle 49, 63–4, 66, 104, 131, 160, 178, 180, 181; *Nicomachean Ethics* 64, **7.21**; *Poetics* 61, 64
Armstrong, Louis 418; **14.34**
Arnolfini Marriage (van Eyck) 237–8, **9.12, 9.13**
Ars nova 183
ars perfecta 217
Art Nouveau 365, 370, 372
Arthurian legends 183
Aryans 36
Ashoka, Emperor 97
Aspasia 49–50
Aspendos: Roman theater 90, **4.28**
assemblages 431
Assyrians 32
At the Moulin Rouge (Toulouse-Lautrec) **13.14**
Athenodorus *see* Agesander
Athens 48–50, 62, 67; *see also* Parthenon
Augustine of Hippo 112, 113, 125, 233; *City of God* 112, 114, 135; *Confessions* 112, 178
Augustus, Emperor 72, 73, 83; *Augustus of Primaporta* (marble) 73, 75, **4.6**
Aurelius, Marcus 72, 95, 96; equestrian statue 98; *Meditations* 98
Austen, Jane 315, 317
automatism 403
Autun Cathedral, France: *Last Judgment* (Gislebertus) 133, 153, **6.1, 6.26**
avant-garde 427
Averroës 180–1
Avicenna 180

Babbitt, Milton 435
Babylon/Babylonians 32
Bacchus and Ariadne (Titian) 259–60, **9.37**
Bach, J.S. 280, 287–8, 312, **10.29, 10.31**
Bacon, Francis 293
Baghdad 129, 131, 145
Bakst, Leon: *Nijinsky* **14.21**
ballet 23, 284, 312, 407–8, **1.10**
Ballets Russes 408
Balzac (Rodin) 374, **13.20**
Baptism (Bearden) 444, **15.26**
Bar at the Folies-Bergère, The (Manet) 375, **13.21**
Barcelona: Casa Milá (Gaudí) 372, **13.16**
baroque style 262, 265; Dutch 288–92; in England 295–8; French 280–3, 285–6; Italian 272–7
Barry, Sir Charles: Houses of Parliament 350, **12.21**
Barth, John 442
Basilica of Constantine, Rome 81, **4.15, 4.16**
basilicas, Christian 114–15, **5.12, 5.13**
baths, Roman 81–2
Battleship Potemkin (Eisenstein) 414, **14.30**
Baudelaire, Charles 368, 370; *Les Fleurs du Mal* 371
Bauhaus 410, **14.26**
Bayeux Tapestry 140, 143, 145, **6.14**
Bayreuth Festspielhaus 367, **13.12**
Bearden, Romare 444; *Baptism* 444, **15.26**
Beardsley, Aubrey: *Salomé* 372, **13.15**
Beatles, the 435
Beatriz de Dia 182

Beats, the 421–2
Beauvais, France: Cathedral 165
Beauvoir, Simone de 423
Becket, Thomas à 164, **7.3**
Beckett, Samuel 423; *Waiting for Godot* 423
Beckford, William: Fonthill Abbey 348, 350, **12.20**
Beethoven, Ludwig van 337–8, **12.8**; Symphony No. 5 338, **12.9**
Bellini, Gentile: *Procession in St. Mark's Square* **9.32**
Benedict of Nursia, St. 146, **6.15**
Benevento, Italy: Arch of Trajan 75, **4.5**
Benin bronzes 210
Benoist, Marie Guillermine: *Portrait of a Black Woman* 347, **12.19**
Beowulf 43
Berg, Alban: *Wozzeck* 409
Berlioz, Hector 341; *Symphonie fantastique* 352, **12.26**
Bernard of Clairvaux, St. 154, 156
Bernart de Ventadorn 182
Bernini, Gianlorenzo 272, 273, 296; "Baldacchino" 273, **10.8**; *David* 20, 275, **10.11**; *Ecstasy of St. Teresa* 276, 10.12, **10.13**; *Louis XIV* **10.19**; St. Peter's piazza 273, **10.9, 10.10**
Bernstein, Leonard 435
Bible 31, 32, 102–5, 106–7, 109, 112
Bird in Space (Brancusi) 399, **14.11**
Birth of Spring (Botticelli) 204, **8.17**
Black Death 186, 187
Black Wall (Nevelson) 431, **15.12**
Blake, William 342; *London* 342
Blaue Reiter, Die 402
Blue Window, The (Matisse) 402, **14.14**
Boating Party, The (Cassatt) 381, **13.28**
Boccaccio, Giovanni: *Decameron* 187
Boccioni, Umberto: *Unique Forms of Continuity in Space* 398–9, **14.10**
Boethius 124; *De institutione musica* 124, **5.29**
Boffrand, Gabriel: Hôtel de Soubise 305, **11.6**
Boîte en Valide, La (Duchamp) 400, **4.13**
Bolívar, Simón 330, 337
Bonaparte, Pauline: *Pauline Bonaparte as Venus* (Canova) 335, **12.7**
Bonheur, Rosa 357; *Horse Fair* 357–8, **13.5**
Borges, Jorge Luis 442, 448; *Tlön, Uqbar, Orbis Tertius* 442–3
Borobudur, Java: temple 174
Botticelli, Sandro 197, 210; *Adoration of the Magi* 196, **8.4**; *La Primavera (Birth of Spring)* 204, **8.17**
Boucher, François 306, 309; *The Toilet of Venus* 309, **11.10**
Boulevard des Capucines, Paris (Monet) **13.9**
Boulez, Pierre 435
Bourke-White, Margaret 392
Boy Spinning Top (Chardin) 314, **11.16**
Brahms, Johannes 22, 368–9, 374
Bramante, Donato 219; St. Peter's, Rome 224, **8.46**; Tempietto 224, 297, **8.45**
Brancusi, Constantin: *Bird in Space* 399, **14.11**
Braque, Georges 398, 425; *Le Courrier* 398, **14.8**; *The Portuguese* 398, **14.5**
Brecht, Bertolt 412
Breton, André 403
Bride of the Village (Greuze) 315, **11.17**
Brighton, England: Pavilion (Nash) 351, **12.22**
Broadway Boogie Woogie (Mondrian) 399, **14.12**
Brontë sisters 353
Brooks, Gwendolyn 444

Brücke, Die 402
Bruegel, Pieter, the Elder 229, 241; *The Hunters' Return* 241–2, **9.17**; *The Parable of the Blind* 242, **9.18**; *Tower of Babel* **9.21**
Brunelleschi, Filippo 48; Florence Cathedral (dome) 198, 201, 224, **8.8, 8.13, 8.18**; Pazzi Chapel, S. Croce 201–2, **8.14, 8.15**
Buddha 96–7, 174
Buddhism 37, 96–7, 167, 174, 435
Buffalo, New York: Guaranty Building (Sullivan) 365, **13.11**
Bull-leaping fresco (Knossos) 39, **2.16**
Buñuel, Luis: *Un Chien Andalou* 406
Burgmair, Hans: *Maximilian with His Musicians* **8.32**
Burial at Ornans (Courbet) 356–7, **13.4**
Burial of the Count of Orgaz (Greco) 264, 269, **10.2**
Burke, Edmund 343
Byrd, William 250–1
Byrne, David 447
Byron, Lord 337, 338, 340, 353, **12.11**; *Don Juan* 340–1
Byzantine empire 114, 115–23, 125, 127, 140

cadences 175, 257
Caesar, Julius 70, 72, 83
Cage, John 435
Caillebotte, Gustave: *Paris Street: Rainy Weather* 355, **13.1**
Calder, Alexander 429–30; *Spring Blossoms* 429, **15.8**
Callicrates *see* Ictinus
Calling of St. Matthew, The (Caravaggio) 277, **10.14**
Calvin, John 233, **9.7**
Calvinism 233, 234, 235, 248
Camargo, Marie Anne de Cupis de 312
Campbell's Soup Cans (Warhol) 426, **15.5**
Camus, Albert 422; *The Plague* 422–3
Candide (Voltaire) 327–8
Canonization, The (Donne) 295
Canova, Antonio 333, 335; *Pauline Bonaparte as Venus* 335, **12.7**
cantatas 23, 287
Canterbury Tales (Chaucer) 93, 183, 187
cantus firmus 176, 183
capitalism 361
Cappellanus, Andreas: *The Art of Courtly Love* 182
Caravaggio, Michelangelo 272, 276–7; *The Calling of St. Matthew* 277, **10.14**; *David with the Head of Goliath* **1.4**
Carolingian renaissance 135–9
Cartesianism *see* Descartes, René
caryatids 54, **3.20**
Cassatt, Mary 376, 380–1; *The Boating Party* 381, **13.28**
Castiglione, Baldassare **8.31**; *The Book of the Courtier* 214–15, 250
Catch-22 (Heller) 424
Cather, Willa 415
Catullus 92–3
cave paintings 27–8, **2.2**
cella 52; cella frieze 53, **3.16, 3.19**
Cellini, Benvenuto 197
Cervantes, Miguel de: *Don Quixote* 270
Cézanne, Paul 381, 382–3, 394, 402; *Apples and Oranges* 383, **13.31**; *Mont Sainte-Victoire from Les Lauves* 383, **13.30**
Chalgrin, Jean-François: Arc de Triomphe 333, **12.4**
Chambord, Château de 231, **9.4**
Chardin, Jean-Baptiste-Siméon 314; *Boy Spinning Top* 314, **11.16**

Charlemagne 124, 127, 135, 137, 141, 149; Aachen chapel 123, 138–9, **6.8, 6.9**
Charles V, Emperor 212, 251
Chartres Cathedral, France 165, 168–9, 176, **7.8–7.10**; sculpture 171–3, **7.13–7.15**; stained glass 162, 170–1, **7.1, 7.11, 7.12**
Chaucer, Geoffrey 187, **7.6**; *Canterbury Tales* 93, 183, 187
Chekhov, Anton 386
chiaroscuro 204, 215, 277
Chicago, Judy: *Dinner Party* 445, **15.28**
Chien Andalou (Buñuel and Dalí) 406
China 37–8, 64
chivalry 142
Chopin, Frédéric 338
choreography 23, 284
Chrétien de Troyes 183
Christ as the Good Shepherd 120, **5.20**
Christ Healing the Sick (Rembrandt) 292, **10.36**
Christ Pantocrator (mosaic) 125, **5.30**
Christians, early 97, 100, 106–11; music 91, 123–4; philosophy 112–14
Christine de Pisan 187; *The Book of the City of Ladies* 187–8
Christo and Jeanne-Claude 441; *Running Fence* 441, **15.24**; *Wrapped Reichstag* 420, **15.1**
Cicero 96; bust 89, **4.26**
Cimabue: *Madonna Enthroned* 188, **7.25**
city-states, Italian 192, 194
Clodion (Claude Michel): *Satyr and Bacchante* 305, **11.5**
Close, Chuck 441; *Phil* **15.22**
Clouet, Jean [?]: *Francis I* **9.3**
Cluny Abbey, France 149, 150–1, 153, 156, 160, **6.21, 6.22**
Cole, Thomas 348
collage 398, 444
Cologne Cathedral 348
Colosseum, Rome 82, **4.17**
Coltrane, John 418
comedy, Greek 61
commedia dell'arte 254, **9.31**
communism, Soviet 390, 392
Communist Manifesto (Marx) 114, 360–1
Composition (Miró) 406, **14.19**
concrete: Roman 81; steel-reinforced 410
Confucius 64
Constable, John 346; *Hay Wain* 346–7, **12.16**
Constantine, Emperor 97, 98, 109, 110, 114, 115; Head **5.10**
Constantinople 110, 114, 115, 188, 200; *see also* Istanbul
contrapposto 58
Copernicus, Nicolaus 294
Copland, Aaron: *Appalachian Spring* 415, **14.32**
Córdoba, Spain 131, 146; Great Mosque 129, 131, **5.36, 5.37**
Corigliano, John: "AIDS Symphony" 447
Corinthian order 52, **3.13**
Corneille, Pierre 283
Cornelia (Kauffmann) 318, **11.20**
Counter-Reformation 251, 262, 270, 272, 293
Courbet, Gustave 356, 358, 375; *Burial at Ornans* 356–7, **13.4**
Courrier, Le (Braque) 398, **14.8**
Courtier, Book of the (Castiglione) 214–15, 250
courtly love, medieval 181–2
Cranach, Lucas, the Elder: *Luther* **9.1**
Cranach, Lucas, the Younger: *Luther and the Wittenberg Reformers* **9.5**
Crete: Minoan civilization 39
Crucifixion (Grünewald) 238–9, **9.14**
Crusades/Crusaders 140, 163–4, 167, 188,

7.5; map **7.2**
Cry (Ailey) 444, **15.27**
Crystal Palace, London (Paxton) 362, 364, **13.7**
Cubi series (Smith) 430, **15.11**
cubism 393, 398
Cullen, Countee 415
Cunningham, Merce 429, 435, **15.9**

dada/dadaists 393, 399–400
Dalí, Salvador 406; *Un Chien Andalou* (with Buñuel) 406; *The Persistence of Memory* 406, **14.22**
dance 23–4, 141; modern 23, 415, 429
Dance Around the Golden Calf (Nolde) 402, **14.15**
Dancer in Green, The (Degas) 380, **13.27**
Dancers at the Court of Elizabeth I **9.26**
Dante Alighieri 160; *Divine Comedy* 183–4, 186, **7.23**
Daphne, Greece: Church of the Dormition (mosaic) 125, **5.30**
Darwin, Charles 181, 361
Daumier, Honoré: *Rue Transnonain* 356, **13.2**
David (Bernini) 20, 275, **10.11**
David (Donatello) 20, 205, **8.22**
David (Michelangelo) 208–9, 220, **8.24**
David, Jacques-Louis 319, 333; *The Death of Marat* 329, **12.1**; *Lictors Bearing to Brutus the Bodies of his Sons* 322, **11.24**; *Napoleon Crossing the Alps* **12.3**; *Oath of the Horatii* 319, 322, 335, 344, **11.23**; *Le Sacre* 335, **12.6**
David, King 101
David with the Head of Goliath (Caravaggio) **1.4**
Davis, Miles 418
Death of Marat, The (David) 329, **12.1**
Death of Sardanapalus, The (Delacroix) 341–2, **12.12**
Debussy, Claude 370, 373; *Prélude à "l'après-midi d'un faune"* 373–4, 408, **13.17**
Decameron (Boccaccio) 187
de Chirico, Giorgio 403; *The Mystery and Melancholy of a Street* 403, **14.17**
Declaration of Independence 330, **11.4**
Defoe, Daniel 315
Degas, Edgar 376, 380; *The Dancer in Green* 380, **13.27**
Déjeuner sur l'herbe, Le (Luncheon on the Grass) (Manet) 375–6, **13.22**
de Kooning, Willem 426
Delacroix, Eugène 336, 341, 342, 351; *The Death of Sardanapalus* 341–2, **12.12**; *Faust Visits Marguerite in Prison* 340, **12.10**; *Liberty Leading the People* 342, **12.13**
Delian League 49
Demoiselles d'Avignon, Les (Picasso) 394, 398, **14.4**
Depression, Great 392–3, 413
Descartes, René 293, 294–5
Diaghilev, Sergei 408
Diane de Poitiers 231
Diaspora, Jewish 102
Dickens, Charles 359
Diderot, Denis 303, 306, 315, 319
Dinner Party, The (Chicago) 445, **15.28**
Diocletian, Emperor 72, 98, 125
Dionysian dances 59, 61, 65
Dionysian Mysteries 87, **4.24**
Dipylon vase 46, **3.5**
Discobolus (Discus Thrower) (Myron) 57–8, 59, **3.24**
Disney Building, Florida (Isozaki) 447, **15.30**
Divine Comedy (Dante) 183–4, 186, **7.23**
documentary arts 392, 413–14

Doll's House, A (Ibsen) 386
dome construction 81, 117, **4.14**, **5.16**
Domenico di Michelino: *Dante and his Poem* **7.23**
Don Quixote (Cervantes) 270
Donatello 205; *David* 20, 205, **8.22**; *Judith* 209
Donne, John 295; *The Canonization* 295
Doric order 50, 54, **3.13**
Doryphorus (Polyclitus) 48, **3.9**
Dostoyevsky, 368, 386–7; *The Brothers Karamazov* 387
"drip paintings" 426
Duchamp, Marcel 20, 400; *La Boîte en Valide* 400, **14.13**; *Nude Descending a Staircase No. 2* 389, **14.1**
Dufay, Guillaume 205
Duncan, Isadora 415
Dura Europos 109–10
Dürer, Albrecht 229, 239, 240–1; *Adam and Eve* **5.11**; *Erasmus ...* **9.19**; *Knight, Death, and the Devil* 240, **9.16**; *St. Jerome ...* **9.20**; *Self-portrait ...* 240, **9.15**
Dying Gaul (marble) 58–9, **3.26**

Eakins, Thomas 358; *The Gross Clinic* 358–9, **13.3**
earth art 441
Eco, Umberto: *The Name of the Rose* 436
Ecstasy of St. Teresa (Bernini) 276, **10.12**, **10.13**
education 135, 159, 160, 164, 178, 179–80
Egypt, ancient 32–5, 66, 67, 86
Eiffel Tower, Paris 364, **13.10**
Einstein on the Beach (Glass) 439–40
Eisenstein, Sergei: *Battleship Potemkin* 414, **14.30**
Eleanor of Aquitaine 182, 183
Eliade, Mircea 31
Eliot, T. S. 406, 407, 415; *Waste Land* 406
Elizabeth I 244, 247, 250, **9.26**
Elizabeth of Schöngau 156
Elizabethan drama 247–8; *see also* Shakespeare, William
Ellington, Duke 418
Ellison, Ralph: *Invisible Man* 424
Emerson, Ralph Waldo 345
Emile (Rousseau) 303
empiricism 293
Encyclopedia 300, 303, 306
Enlightenment, the 265, 300, 302, 304, 327
entablature 50
Enuma elish (creation myth) 30
epic theater 411–12
epics 32, 43–4, 141, 142, 143; *see also Aeneid*; *Divine Comedy*
Epicurus 67, 95; epicureanism 95
Epidaurus, Greece: theater 59, **3.28**
Erasmus, Desiderius 95, 240, 242–3, 244, **9.19**; *In Praise of Folly* 243
Erechtheum, Athens 54, **3.20**
Escorial Palace 269, **10.3**
Este, Isabella d' 205, 214–15
ethics 65
Etruscans 71; *Apollo* 71, **4.2**
Euclid 67
Euphronios: *Death of Sarpedon* 46, **3.4**
Euripides 61; *Medea* 61
Evans, Walker 392
Everyman 178
Executions of the Third of May, 1808 (Goya) 344, **12.14**
existentialism 55, 422–4, 426, 436
Experiment with an Air Pump (J. Wright) 303, **11.3**
expressionism 393, 401–2
Eyck, Jan van 236; *Ghent Altarpiece* 236, **1.2**, **9.10**, **9.11**; *Marriage of Giovanni Arnolfini...* 237–8, **9.12**, **9.13**

"Falling Water" (F. L. Wright) 417, **14.33**
fascism 392, 393
Faulkner, William 415
Faust (Goethe) 338–9, 344
Faust Visits Marguerite in Prison (Delacroix) 340, **12.10**
fauvists 402
Federalist papers 330
feminists 31, 342–3, 393, 406, 423, 445
fêtes galantes 306
feudalism 133, 140–3, 160, 164, 181
Ficino, Marsilio 196, 205
Fielding, Henry 315
Flaubert, Gustave 359; *The Sentimental Education* 359–60
Fleurs du Mal, Les (Baudelaire) 371
Florence, Italy 192, 194, 197, 200, 205, 208–9, 212, **8.1**; Baptistery doors 200–1, 205, 207, 260, **8.9–8.12**; Brancacci Chapel frescoes, S. Maria del Carmine 204, **8.16**; Camerata 253, 255; Cathedral 198, 202, 224, **7.23**, **8.8**, **8.13**, **8.18**; Laurentian Library 196, **8.6**; Pazzi Chapel, S. Croce 201–2, **8.14**, **8.15**
Flowers in a Vase (Ruysch) 289, **10.32**
Fonthill Abbey, Wiltshire, England 348, 350, **12.20**
Formation (Frankenthaler) **1.3**
Fouquet, Jean: miniature **7.20**
Fourier, Charles 360
Fragonard, Jean-Honoré: *The Swing* 309, **11.1**; *A Young Girl Reading* **11.18**
Francis, St., of Assisi 144, **6.16**
Francis I, King of France 229, 231, **9.3**
Frankenstein (M. Shelley) 353
Frankenthaler, Helen: *Formation* **1.3**
Franks, the 135
French Revolution 329, 331, 348
frescoes 189, 204; *see also* Sistine Chapel frescoes
Freud, Sigmund 86, 402–3, 404–5
Friedrich, Caspar David: *The Wanderer Above the Mists* 344, **12.15**
friezes 52, 53, 67, **3.16**, **3.18**, **3.19**, **3.34**
frottole 205
fugues 288, **10.31**
futurists, Italian 398–9

Gabriel, Ange-Jacques: Petit Trianon, Versailles 317, **11.19**
Gabrieli, Giovanni 255
Gainsborough, Thomas 326; *Mr. and Mrs. Andrews* 326, **11.30**
Galileo Galilei 293, 294
gamelan orchestra 373
García Márquez, Gabriel: *One Hundred Days of Solitude* 443
Gates of Hell, The (Rodin) 374, **13.18**
Gates of Paradise (Ghiberti) 200–1, 205, 207, 260, **8.9–8.12**
Gaudí, Antonio: Casa Milá, Barcelona 372, **13.16**
Gauguin, Paul 381, 383–4, 402; *Self-Portrait with Halo* **13.32**; *The Vision after the Sermon* 384, **13.33**
genius 336
genre painting 241, 314–15
Gentileschi, Artemisia 277; *Judith Slaying Holofernes* 277, **10.15**
Geoffrin, Madame: *salon* 306, **11.7**
Gersaint's Signboard (Watteau) 306, **11.8**
Gershwin, George 417
Gesamtkunstwerk 60, 367
Ghent Altarpiece (van Eyck) 236, **1.2**, **9.10**, **9.11**
Ghiberti, Lorenzo: *Gates of Paradise* 200–1, 205, 207, 260, **8.9–8.12**
Gilgamesh, Epic of 32, 43

Ginsberg, Allen 421; *Howl* 421
Giorgione 259; *Tempest* 259, **9.36**
Giotto di Bondone 187; *Madonna Enthroned* 188–9, **7.24**; *Pietà (Lamentation)* 189, **7.26**; [?] *St. Francis Renouncing His Father* **6.16**
Gislebertus: *Last Judgment* tympanum 133, 153, **6.1**, **6.26**
Giza, Egypt: pyramids 33, **2.9**
Glass, Philip 439; *Akhenaten* 440, **15.21**; *Einstein on the Beach* 439–40
Globe Theater, London 247–8, **9.23**
"Glorious Revolution" (1688) 298
Goethe, Johann von 317, 337; *Faust* 338–9, 344; *Götz von Berlichingen* 317
Gogh, Vincent van 381, 383, 384, 384; *Starry Night* 384–5, **13.34**
Goodwin, Grenville 350
Gorky, Arshile 426
Gospel Books, Carolingian 137, **6.2–6.4**
Gospels, the 106–7, 109
Gothic novel 352–3
Gothic style 162; cathedrals 160, 165–6, 168–71; sculpture 171–3
Gothic revival architecture 349–50
Goths, the 115
Gounod, Charles: *Faust* 340
Goya, Francisco 344; *Executions of the Third of May, 1808* 344, **12.14**; *The Sleep of Reason ...* 352, **12.24**; *Witches' Sabbath* 352, **12.25**
Graham, Martha 415, 429; *Appalachian Spring* 415, **14.32**
Granada, Spain: the Alhambra 146, **6.17**
Graves, Michael: Portland Public Services Building 439, **15.20**
Great Schism (1378–1417) 164
Great Wave off Kanazawa, The (Hokusai) 378, **13.25**
Greco, El 262; *Burial of the Count of Orgaz* 264, 269, **10.2**
Greenberg, Clement 427
Greenough, Horatio: *Washington* **11.21**
Gregorian chant 124, 154
Gregory I, Pope 124, **5.28**
Greuze, Jean-Baptiste 314–15; *The Bride of the Village* 315, **11.17**
Gropius, Walter 410, 425; Bauhaus **14.26**
Gross Clinic, The (Eakins) 358–9, **13.3**
Grünewald, Matthias: *Crucifixion* (from *Isenheim Altarpiece*) 238–9, **9.14**
Guernica (Picasso) 412–13, **14.28**
Guggenheim Museum, New York (F. L. Wright) 21, 434, 436, **15.15**
Guido of Arezzo 155; staff 155–6, **6.31**
Gulliver's Travels (Swift) 325–6

Hadrian, Emperor 72, 82–3; Villa **4.22**
Hagia Sophia, Istanbul 116–17, **5.15**, **5.17**, **5.18**
Hammurabi, King 32; Code 32
Handel, George Frideric 295, 297–8, **10.42**; *Messiah* 298
Hanson, Duane 441
happenings 429
Harappa 36; male torsos 36, **2.12**, **2.13**
Hardouin-Mansart, Jules 296; Versailles 281, 283, **10.20–10.23**
Harlem Renaissance 415
Harvey, William 294
Hatshepsut, Queen 35
Haussmann, Baron G. E. 364–5, 366, 368
Hawthorne, Nathaniel 353
Hay Wain, The (Constable) 346–7, **12.16**
Haydn, Joseph 322–3, **11.26**
Hegeso, stele from **3.10**
Heine, Heinrich 348
Hellenistic civilization 66–7; sculpture 58–9; theater 61, 90

Heller, Joseph: *Catch-22* 424
Hemingway, Ernest 407, 415
Henry II, King of England 164, 182, 183
Henry IV, King of England 164
Henry IV Receiving the Portrait of Marie de' Medici (Rubens) 285, **10.26**
Henry VIII, of England 229, 231, 244
Hermes and the Infant Dionysus (Praxiteles) 55, 58, **3.21**
Herodotus: *The Persian Wars* 35
Hildegard of Bingen 156, **6.33**
Hilliard, Nicholas: *Ermine Portrait of Queen Elizabeth I* **9.22**; *Youth Leaning Against a Tree* 249, **9.25**
Hinduism 37
Hiroshige, Ando 378
Hitler, Adolf 75, 392, 412, 414–15
Hoare, Henry: Stourhead Park 319, **11.22**
Hobbes, Thomas 295; *Leviathan* 279, 298
Hogarth, William 326; *Marriage Contract* 326, **11.29**
Hokusai, Katsushika 378; *The Great Wave off Kanazawa* **13.25**
Holbein, Hans, the Younger 231; "The Ambassadors" **9.2**
Holocaust, the 421
Holy Family on the Steps (Poussin) 286, **10.28**
Holzer, Jenny: *Installation...* 436, **15.17**
Homer, Winslow 358
Homeric poems 42, 43–4, 86, 93
Hopper, Edward: *Nighthawks* 415, **14.31**
Hoppner, John: *Joseph Haydn* **11.26**
Horace 94
Horse Fair, The (Bonheur) 357–8, **13.5**
Horta, Victor 372
Houdon, Jean-Antoine: *Voltaire* **11.31**; *Washington* **12.2**
Houses of Parliament, London 350, **12.21**
Houston Chapel (Rothko) 426, **15.3**
Howells, William Dean 356
Howl (Ginsberg) 421
Hrotsvit 149
Huber, Jean: *Philosophers at Supper* **11.2**
hubris 61
Hudson River School 348
Hughes, Langston 415
Hugo, Victor 336, 341, 353
humanism 55, 187, 193, 196, 233, 239, 242–4
Hume, David 303
Hundred Guilder Print (Rembrandt) 292, **10.36**
Hunters' Return (Bruegel) 241–2, **9.17**
Hurston, Zora Neale 415
Hypatia 112

Ibn Hazm 146
Ibn-Rushd 180–1
Ibn-Sina 180
Ibsen, Henrik 386; *A Doll's House* 386
iconoclasm 125, 127, **5.31**
icons 110
Ictinus, Callicrates: Parthenon 50, 52, **3.12**
idealism 62
idée fixe 352, **12.26**
Ife bronze head 210, **8.26**
Iliad (Homer) 43–4, 93
imitation, musical 217–18, **8.35**
imperialism 72, 74–5
Impression: Sunrise (Monet) 376, **13.23**
impressionism 375–6, 379–81
Improvisations (Kandinsky) 402, **14.16**
In Mind (Levertov) 446
In Praise of Folly (Erasmus) 243
Indus Valley civilization 36
Ingres, Jean-Auguste-Dominique: *Turkish Bath* 351–2, **12.23**
Installation... (Holzer) 436, **15.17**

installation art 445
International Style (architecture) 432–3
Intoxication of Wine (Clodion) 305, **11.5**
Invisible Man (Ellison) 424
Ionic order 52, 54, **3.13**
Isaac, Heinrich 205
Isenheim Altarpiece (Grünewald) 238–9, **9.14**
Isidorus of Miletus *see* Anthemius
Islam/Islamic culture (Muslims) 127–32, 145–6, 163–4, 167, 180–1
Isozaki, Arata: Team Disney Building 447, **15.30**
Israelites 101–5
Istanbul 110; *see* Hagia Sophia
Ives, Charles 417

James, Henry 386
Jamison, Judith 444, **15.27**
Japan: kabuki theater 316; prints 378, 380
jazz 417–18, **1.9**
Jefferson, Thomas 319; Declaration of Independence 330; Monticello 319, **11.25**
Jerome, St. 112, 244; *St. Jerome in His Study* (Dürer) **9.20**
Jerusalem 107, 163–4; Dome of the Rock 131, **5.38**; temples 101, 102, **5.2**, **5.3**
Jesus of Nazareth 106–7
Jews: Sephardic 146; *see* Israelites
Job, Book of 105
Johnson, Philip (with Mies): Seagram Building, New York 432–3, **15.13**
Josephus: *Jewish Wars* 107
Josquin des Préz 205, 217–18, **8.34**, **8.35**
Joyce, James 406; *Ulysses* 406
Judd, Donald 428–9; *Untitled (Perforated Steel Ramp)* **15.7**
Judith Slaying Holofernes (Gentileschi) 277, **10.15**
Jugendstil 372
Julius II, Pope 217, 218, 219, 223–4, 243; tomb (Michelangelo) 219–20, **8.38**
Jung, C. G. 31
Justinian, Emperor 115–16, 117; *Justinian and His Courtiers* 100, 123, **5.1**, **5.26**
Juvenal: *Satires* 94–5

kabuki theater 316
Kafka, Franz 406, 407; *Metamorphosis* 407
Kandinsky, Wassily 402, 406, 410; *Improvisations* 402, **14.16**
Kant, Immanuel 302
Kauffmann, Angelica: *Cornelia* 318, **11.20**
Kaufmann House (F. L. Wright) 417, **14.33**
Keats, John 344
Kepler, Johannes 294
Key to Dreams, The (Magritte) 405, **14.20**
keys, musical 287–8
Kiefer, Anselm 442; *Die Meistersinger* 442, **15.25**
Klee, Paul 402, 410; *All Around the Fish* 402, **14.18**
Knight, Death, and the Devil (Dürer) 240, **9.16**
Knighton, Henry 186
Knossos, Crete: Bull-leaping fresco 39, **2.16**; *Snake Goddess* 39, **2.17**
Koran *see* Qur'an
koré 47, **3.8**
kouroi 47, 54, 56, **3.6**, **3.7**, **3.22**
Kouros (Noguchi) **1.6**
Kritios Boy (marble *kouros*) 56, **3.22**
Kushner, Tony: *Angels in America* 447

Labrouste, Henri: Bibliothèque Nationale 364, **13.8**
Lamentation (Giotto) 189, **7.26**
land art 441

Lange, Dorothea 392; *Migrant Mother...* 413, **14.29**
Laocoön (Agesander *et al.*) 59, **3.27**
Lascaux, France: cave paintings 27–8, **2.2**
Last Supper (Leonardo) 207, 214, 260, **8.20**, **8.21**
Last Supper (Roman mosaic) **5.7**
Last Supper (Tintoretto) 260, **9.39**
Leaves of Grass (Whitman) 361
Lebrun, Charles: Versailles 281, **10.23**
Le Corbusier 410–11, 433; Notre-Dame-du-Haut, Ronchamp 434, **15.14**; *Unité d'Habitation* 411, **14.27**; Villa Savoye 411, **14.25**
Leibniz, Gottfried Wilhelm von 327
Lenin, V. I. 390
Leo X, Pope 205, 217, 232, 243
Leonardo da Vinci 197, 200, 212, 215, 219, 224, 229, 400; *Last Supper* 207, 214, 260, **8.20**, **8.21**; *Madonna of the Rocks* 214–15, **8.29**; *Mona Lisa* 215, 400, **8.30**; *Notebooks* 212, 214, **8.28**; *Proportions of the Human Figure* 193, **8.3**; *Treatise on Painting* 214, 215
Léonin 175
Lessing, Gotthold Ephraim 317
Le Vau, Louis: Versailles 281, **10.20**, **10.22**
Levertov, Denise 446; *In Mind* 446
Leviathan (Hobbes) 279, 298
Lévi-Strauss, Claude 347
Liberty Leading the People (Delacroix) 342, **12.13**
Lictors Bearing to Brutus the Bodies of his Sons (David) 322, **11.24**
Lin, Maya: Vietnam War Memorial 446, **15.29**
Lindau Gospels 137, **6.4**
literature 25; *see* epics; novels; poetry; satire
Llull, Ramon: *Book of ... Chivalry* 142
Locke, John 295, 300, 304; *Two Treatises on Government* 298–9
London: Crystal Palace 362, 364, **13.7**; Fire (1666) 297; Globe Theater 247–8, **9.23**; Houses of Parliament 350, **12.21**; St. Paul's 296–7, **10.39**, **10.40**
London (Blake) 342
lost-wax casting 210
Louis XI, of France 164, **7.5**
Louis XIV, of France 262, 279, 280, 281, 283, 284, 299, 300, **10.18**, **10.19**
Louis XVI, of France 319, 331
Lucretius 95
Lully, Jean-Baptiste 283–4, **10.25**
Luther, Martin 193, 217, 227, 229, 231, 232–3, 240–1, 244, 251, **9.1**, **9.5**; "Ein' feste Burg..." 233, **9.6**
lyres 65; soundbox (from Ur) 29–30, **2.5**

Machaut, Guillaume de 183
Machiavelli, Niccolò 211, **8.27**; *The Prince* 211–12
Madonna Enthroned (Cimabue) 188, **7.25**
Madonna Enthroned (Giotto) 188–9, **7.24**
Madonna of the Rocks (Leonardo) 214–15, **8.29**
Madonna with the Long Neck (Parmigianino) 260, **9.38**
madrigals 251
magic realism 443
Magritte, Henri: *The Key to Dreams* 405, **14.20**
Mahabharata 36–7
Maids of Honor (Velázquez) 269, **10.6**
Maimonides, Moses 181
Malinowski, Bronislav 31
Mallarmé, Stéphane 371
Manet, Edouard 358, 359; *The Bar at the Folies-Bergère* 375, **13.21**; *Le Déjeuner*

sur l'herbe 375–6, **13.22**
Manicheism 112
Mann, Thomas 407
Mannerism 260
manuscript illumination 135, 137, **6.2–6.5**
Manutius, Aldus 193
Marat/Sade (Weiss) 423
Marie de France 183
Marlowe, Christopher 248; *Doctor Faustus* 248, 338
Marriage at Cana (Veronese) 259, **9.35**
Marriage Contract (Hogarth) 326, **11.29**
Marriage of Arnolfini... (van Eyck) 237–8, **9.12**, **9.13**
Marriage of Figaro (Mozart) 313–14, **11.15**
Marseilles, France: *Unité d'Habitation* (Le Corbusier) 411, **14.27**
Marx, Karl 114, 245, 360–1, 368
Masaccio 204; *The Tribute Money* 204, 206, **8.16**
Massys, Quentin: *Moneychanger and His Wife* **9.8**
materialism 62, 355, 356, 361
mathematics 62, 67, 131, 293
Matisse, Henri 401–2, 425; *The Blue Window* 402, **14.14**
Maximilian with His Musicians (Burgmair) **8.32**
Maya civilization 147, **6.18**
Mead, Margaret 347
Medea (Euripides) 61
Medici, Cosimo de' 194, 196
Medici, Lorenzo de' 196–7, 202, 205, **8.7**
Medici family 192, 196, 212
megalithic structures 28, **2.3**
Meistersinger, Die (Kiefer) 442, **15.25**
melismatic chant 154
Melville, Herman: *Moby Dick* 347
Menander 61, 67
Meninas, Las (Velázquez) 269, **10.6**
meta-fiction 442
metopes 53
Mexico 126–7, 147, 269
Mexico City: Cathedral 269, **10.4**
Michelangelo 197, 200, 208, 210, 219, **8.37**; *David* 208–9, 220, **8.24**; *Moses* 220, **8.39**; Laurentian Library 196, **8.6**; *Pietà* 18, 208, **8.23**; *Pietà Rondanini* 260, **9.40**; St. Peter's 223, 225, **8.46–8.48**; Sistine Chapel frescoes 210, 217, 220, 223, **8.40–8.44**; tomb of Julius II 219–20, **8.38**
Mies van der Rohe, Ludwig 432, 437; (with Johnson) Seagram Building 432–3, **15.13**
Migrant Mother... (Lange) 413, **14.29**
Milkmaid, The (Vermeer) 289, **10.34**
Milton, John 295–6
minimalism 426, 428–9; in music 439–40
Minnesänger 182
Minoan civilization 39
miracle plays 178, **7.20**
Miró, Joan 403, 406; *Composition* 406, **14.19**
Mnesicles: Erechtheum, Athens 54, **3.20**
mobiles 20, 429
modernism 389, 393
modernity, concept of 368
modes, Greek 66, **3.32**
Modest Proposal, A (Swift) 324–5
Mohenjo-Daro 36
Molière 89, 283, **10.24**
Mona Lisa (Leonardo) 215, **8.30**
monasteries and monasticism 135, 137, 144, 146, 148–9, 155, 156, 160
Mondrian, Piet 399, 406, 425; *Broadway Boogie Woogie* 399, **14.12**
Monet, Claude 376, 379, 380; *Boulevard des Capucines, Paris* **13.9**; *Impression,*

Sunrise 376, **13.23**; *St. Lazare Station* 379, **13.24**
Monette, Paul 447
Monk, Thelonius **1.9**
monody 205
Monogram (Rauschenberg) 426, **15.5**
monotheism 104
Mont Sainte-Victoire from Les Lauves (Cézanne) 383, **13.30**
montage 414
Montaigne, Michel de 244, 293
Monteverdi, Claudio 277, 278; *Orfeo* 277–8, **10.16**
Monticello, Charlottesville, Virginia (Jefferson) 319, **11.25**
Moore, Charles: Piazza d'Italia, New Orleans 438–9, **15.19**
Moore, Henry 425, 429; *Recumbent Figure* 429, **15.10**
morality plays 178
More, Thomas 243; *Utopia* 245, 360
Morley, Thomas 251; *The Triumphes of Oriana* 251, **9.27**
Morrison, Toni 444
mosaics 87–8, 119, 120–1, 123, **3.33**, **4.25**, **4.29**, **5.1**, **5.7**, **5.20–5.22**, **5.25–5.27**
Moses 101, 104
Moses (Michelangelo) 220, **8.39**
mosques 129, 131, **5.36**, **5.37**
motets 183, 217, **8.35**
Motherwell, Robert 426
Moulin de la Galette, Le (Renoir) 380, **13.26**
Mozart, W. A. 22, 23, 312–13, 322, 336, **11.14**; *Don Giovanni* 313; *Magic Flute* 313; *Marriage of Figaro* 313–14, **11.15**; Symphony No. 40 323–4, **11.28**
Mr. and Mrs. Andrews (Gainsborough) 326, **11.30**
Mughal Empire 267
Muhammad, Prophet 127, 128–9, **5.34**
mumming 141
music and musical instruments 21–3; ancient Greek 45, 65–6; ancient Roman 91; baroque 278, 280; "Classical" 322–4; early Christian 91, 123; and Counter-Reformation 251–3; Elizabethan 250–1; medieval 154–6, 174–5, 183; 19th–c. 368–70; Renaissance 204–5, 217–18; romantic 338, 340, 352; Sumerian 29–30; 20th–c. 408–10, 417–18, 435, 439–40; *see also* opera
Muslims *see* Islam
Mycenaean civilization 39, 40, 41
Mycerinus and Khamerernebty **2.10**
Myron: *Discobolus* 57–8, 59, **3.24**
Mystery and Melancholy of a Street, The (de Chirico) 403, **14.17**
mystery plays 178, **7.19**
myths 30, 31

NAMES project 447
Napoleon 75, 331, 333, 335, 337; *Napoleon Crossing the Alps* (David) **12.3**
Nash, John: Brighton Pavilion 351, **12.22**
naturalism 46, 47, 56, 58
Nazism 392, 411–12, 414–15, 421, 422, 425
Nebuchadnezzar II 32
Nefertari, Queen 35; tomb 35, **2.11**
neoclassicism 280, 317, 318–19; in architecture 317, 319, 361; in painting 319–22
Neoplatonism 112
Neruda, Pablo 406
Neumann, Balthasar: Residenz staircase 309, **11.12**; *Vierzehnheiligen* Church 312, **11.13**
Nevelson, Louise 430–1; *Black Wall* 431,

15.12

New Deal, American 392–3

New Orleans: Piazza d'Italia (C. Moore) 438–9, **15.19**

New York 425–6; Guggenheim Museum 21, 434, 436, **15.15**; Seagram Building 432–3, **15.13**; Trans World Flight Center 21, **1.7**

Newman, Barnett 426

Newton, Isaac 293, 295, 300

Nietzsche, Friedrich 386, 387, 404

Night Watch, The (Rembrandt) 291, **10.35**

Nighthawks (Hopper) 415, **14.31**

Nijinsky, Vaslav 408, **14.21**

Nîmes, France: Pont du Gard 79, 81, **4.13**

No Exit (Sartre) 423

Noguchi, Isamu: *Kouros* **1.6**; set **14.32**

Nolde, Emil: *Dance Around the Golden Calf* 402, **14.15**; *Still Life with Masks I* 396, **14.6**

non-objective art 398

Nordica, Lillian 370

Notebooks (Leonardo) 212, 214, **8.28**

Notre-Dame-du-Haut, Ronchamp (Le Corbusier) 434, **15.14**

novels 25, 245, 270, 315–16, 352–3, 359–60, 386–7, 406–7, 422, 442–3, 444, 445

Noverre, Jean Georges 312

Nude Descending a Staircase No. 2 (Duchamp) 389, **14.1**

Number 1 (Pollock) 426, **15.2**

Oath of the Horatii (David) 319, 322, 335, 344, **11.23**

Octavian *see* Augustus, Emperor

Odyssey (Homer) 43, 93

Oedipus (Seneca) 90

Oedipus the King (Sophocles) 61, 253, 255

O'Keeffe, Georgia 415

Olivier, Laurence **1.1**

opera 25, 277–8, 284, 312–13, 366–8, 409, 440

Oration on the Dignity of Man (Pico della Mirandola) 193

oratorios 298

orchestras 22, 60, 373, **1.8**

orders, Greek 50, 52, **3.13**

Oresteia (Aeschylus) 60

Orfeo (Monteverdi) 277–8, **10.16**

organum 174–5, 176, **7.16–7.18**

original sin 113

Orwell, George: *1984* 114, 245

Ottonian dynasty 146, 149–50

Ovid 93: *Metamorphoses* 93

Owen, Robert 360

Padua, Italy: Arena Chapel frescoes (Giotto) 189, **7.26**

Paganini, Niccolò 338

Paik, Nam June: *TV Buddha* 448, **15.32**

Palestrina, Giovanni da 251, 252–3, 255; *Missa Brevis*, "*Kyrie*" **9.28**

Palladio, Andrea 254, 257; *Four Books of Architecture* 259, 317; (with Scamozzi) Teatro Olimpico, Vicenza 254, **9.29**; Villa Rotonda 259, 319, **9.33, 9.34**

Pamela (Richardson) 315

Pannini, Giovanni: *Interior of the Pantheon* **4.20**

Pantheon, Rome 81, 82–3, 116–17, **4.18–4.20**

pantomimes 90

Parable of the Blind (Bruegel) 242, **9.18**

Paradise Lost (Milton) 295

Paris, France 364–5, 368; Arc de Triomphe 333, **12.4**; Bibliothèque Nationale 364, **13.8**; Eiffel Tower 364,

13.10; Hôtel de Soubise 305, **11.6**; La Madeleine 333, **12.5**; Notre Dame School 175–6; Pompidou Center 438, **15.18**; St. Denis 165–6; salons 306, 309, **11.7**; University 179

Paris Street: Rainy Weather (Caillebotte) 355, **13.1**

Parker, Charlie "Bird" 418

Parmigianino: *Madonna with the Long Neck* 260, **9.38**

Parthenon 42, 50, 52, 56–7, **3.1, 3.11, 3.12, 3.14, 3.15**; sculptures 18, 52–4, 76, **1.5, 2.8, 3.16–3.19**

Pater, Walter 371

Paul, St. 107, 109, 232

Paxton, Joseph: Crystal Palace 362, 364, **13.7**

Pazzi Chapel, Florence (Brunelleschi) 201–2, **8.14, 8.15**

pediments 52, 53, **3.16, 3.17**

Peloponnesian Wars 49

Penderecki, Krzysztof: *Threnody for the Victims of Hiroshima* 421

Pepys, Samuel 297

Pergamon, Turkey 86; Altar of Zeus 67, **3.34**

Pericles 49, 50, **3.1**

Pérotin 175–6

Persepolis, Iran 32, **2.8**

Persistence of Memory, The (Dalí) 406, **14.22**

perspective 201; atmospheric 204; linear 204, 206–7, **8.19**

Petrarch (Francesco Petrarca) 187

Phidias 52, 57

Phil (Close) 441, **15.22**

philosophers: Greek 61–4; medieval 159–60, 178, 180–1, 187–8; Muslim 180–1; 19th-c. 387; Roman 95–6, 98; and Scientific Revolution 293–5

Philosophers at Supper, The (Huber) **11.2**

philosophes 300, 302–3, 304

photomontage 444

Piano, Renzo, and Rogers, Richard: Pompidou Center 438, **15.18**

Picasso, Pablo 393, 394, 396, 398, 425; *Les Demoiselles d'Avignon* 394, 398, **14.4**; *Guernica* 412–13, **14.28**; *The Three Musicians* 398, **14.9**

Pico della Mirandola, Giovanni 239; *Oration on Dignity of Man* 193, 197

Pierrot Lunaire (Schoenberg) 409

Pietà (Giotto) 189, **7.26**

Pietà (Michelangelo) 18, 208, **8.23**

Pietà Rondanini (Michelangelo) 260, **9.40**

pilgrimage 167; churches 151, 153, 167

Pilgrimage to the Island of Cythera (Watteau) 306, **11.9**

Pissarro, Camille 376

plainchant *see* Gregorian chant

Plath, Sylvia 422

Plato 49, 62, 63, 64, 65, 66, 112, 180, 193, 196; *Apology* 62–3; *Crito* 62; *Phaedo* 63; *Republic* 63, 211, 245, 360, **3.30**

Plautus 90, 215, 248

Poe, Edgar Allan 352

poetry 25; baroque 295–6; lyric 45; 19th-c. 361; Roman 92–3; romantic 342, 344–5; symbolist 370–2; 20th-c. 389–90, 421, 446; *see also* epics

pointillism 381–2

Poissy, France: Villa Savoye (Le Corbusier) 411, **14.25**

Pollock, Jackson 426, **15.4**; *Number 1* 426, **15.2**

Polyclitus: *Doryphorus* 48, **3.9**

Polydorus of Rhodes *see* Agesander

polyphony 174

polytheism 33

Pompadour, Madame de 309

Pompeii, Italy 66, 83, 85, 87, 319, **3.33, 4.23, 4.24**

Pompidou Center, Paris (Piano and Rogers) 438, **15.18**

Pont du Gard, Nîmes 79, 81, **4.13**

pop art 425, 426, 431

Pope, Alexander: *An Essay on Man* 327

Portland Public Services Building, Oregon (Graves) 439, **15.20**

portrait sculpture, Roman 88–9

Portuguese, The (Braque) 398, **14.5**

post-and-lintel 50, 79

post-impressionism 381–3

post-modernism 436–9

Pound, Ezra 415

Poussin, Nicolas 48, 286–7, 322; *The Holy Family on the Steps* 286, **10.28**

Praxiteles: *Aphrodite of Cnidos* 58, **3.25**; *Hermes and the Infant Dionysus* 55, 58, **3.21**

Prelude, The (Wordsworth) 344

Prélude à "l'après-midi d'un faune" (Debussy) 373–4, 408, **13.17**

preludes 288, **10.31**

Primavera, La (Botticelli) 204, **8.17**

primitivism 394, 396

Prince, The (Machiavelli) 211–12

program music 352

Prophet, the *see* Muhammad, Prophet

prophets, Hebrew 105

Propylaea, Athens 54

Protagoras 55, 62

Protestant ethic 234

Protestantism 231–5, 244, 247, 251

psychoanalysis 402–3; *see also* Freud

Pugin, A. W. N.: Houses of Parliament 350, **12.21**

Punic Wars 71

Puritans 234, 279, 298

Pynchon, Thomas: *Gravity's Rainbow* 442

pyramids, Egyptian 33, **2.9**

Pythagoras 48, 62, 65–6

Qur'an 129, **5.35**

Racine, Jean 283

Rackham, Arthur: *Rheingold* **13.13**

Rain, Steam, and Speed (Turner) 348, **12.18**

Ramayana 36–7

Ramesses II 35

rap 448

Rape of the Daughters of Leucippus (Rubens) 285–6, 309, **10.27**

Raphael (Rafaello Sanzio) 218, 225; *Castiglione* **8.31**; *School of Athens* 201, 218–19, **8.36, 8.37**

rationalism 48

Rauschenberg, Robert 426, 447; *Monogram* 426, **15.5**; sets 429, **15.9**

Ravenna, Italy 115, 119; Sant'Apollinare in Classe 119–20, **5.19**; Sant' Apollinare Nuovo 107, 121, **5.7, 5.21, 5.22**; S. Vitale 100, 123, **5.1, 5.23–5.27**

Razi 131

ready-mades 400

realism: humanist 211–12; 19th-c. 332, 356–60, 386

recitatives 277

Recumbent Figure (Moore) 429, **15.10**

reflection, modes of 175

Reformation, the 231–5, 243–4; in England 244, 247

Reich, Steve 439

reliquaries 137–8, **6.6**

Remarque, Erich 390

Rembrandt van Rijn 289, 291–2; *The Anatomy Lesson of Dr. Tulp* 359, **10.38**; *Christ Healing the Sick* 292, **10.36**; *Self-*

Portrait 292, **10.37**; *Sortie of Captain Banning Cocq's Company...* 291, **10.35**

Renaissance: Italian 191, 192, 195; Northern 227–31, 235–8; Late 251–60

Renoir, Pierre Auguste 376, 379, 380; *Le Moulin de la Galette* 380, **13.26**

Republic, The (Plato) 63, 211, 245, 360, **3.30**

Reynolds, Sir Joshua 326

Riace Warrior (bronze) 57, **3.23**

Richardson, Samuel: *Pamela* 315

Riefenstahl, Leni: *Triumph of the Will* 392, 414–15

Rigaud, Hyacinthe: *Louis XIV* **10.18**

Riley, Terry 439

Rilke, Rainer Maria 406

Rite of Spring, The (Stravinsky) 407–8, **14.23**

rock-and-roll 435

Rodin, Auguste 370, 374; *Balzac* 374, **13.20**; *The Gates of Hell* 374, **13.18**; *The Three Shades* 374, **13.19**

Rogers, Richard *see* Piano, Renzo

Roland, Song of 141, 142, 143, **6.12**

Roman de la Rose 183

Romanesque style: architecture 150–3, 166, 170; sculpture 153–4

romanticism 329, 332, 336, 337, 342; literature 338–9, 340, 342–5, 347; music 338, 340; painting 340–2, 344, 346–8

Rome 69, 71–3, 98, 115, 216–217, 251, 272; *Ara Pacis Augustae*, 75–6, **4.3, 4.7**; Arch of Titus **5.4**; Basilica of Constantine 81, **4.15, 4.16**; Basilica Ulpia 77, **4.9**; baths 81–2; catacombs 110, **5.8**; Colosseum 82, **4.17**; equestrian statue of Aurelius **4.31**; forums 73, 76–7, **4.8**; Pantheon 81, 82–3, 116–17, **4.18–4.20**; St. Peter's 114–15, **5.12** (old), 223–5, 273, **8.46–8.48**, **10.8–10.10**; Sarcophagus of Junius Bassus 110, **5.9**; scale model **4.1**; Sistine Chapel 210, 217, 220, 223, **8.40–8.44**; Tempietto 224, 297, **8.45**; Temple of Portunus (Fortuna Virilis) **4.12**; Theater of Marcellus 90, **4.27**; Trajan's Column 77–8, **4.10**

Ronchamp, France: Notre-Dame-du-Haut (Le Corbusier) 434, **15.14**

Roosevelt, Franklin D. 392–3

Rothko, Mark 426; Chapel 426, **15.3**

Rousseau, Jean-Jacques 303, 306, 343, 347; *Emile* 303; *Julie* 315; *Social Contract* 303, 304, 305

Rubens, Peter Paul 269, 285; *Henry IV Receiving the Portrait of Marie de' Medici* 285, **10.26**; *Rape of the Daughters of Leucippus* 285–6, 309, **10.27**

Rue Transnonain (Daumier) 356, **13.2**

Running Fence (Christo and Jeanne-Claude) 441, **15.24**

Russian Revolution 390

Ruysch, Rachel: *Flowers in a Vase* 289, **10.32**

Saarinen, Eero: Trans World Flight Center 21, **1.7**

Sacre, Le (David) 335, **12.6**

Sacre du Printemps, Le (Stravinsky) 407–8, **14.23**

St. Domingo de Silos, Spain **6.20**

St. Gall, Switzerland 148–9, 154, 156, 157, **6.19**

St. Lazare Station (Monet) 379, **13.24**

St. Paul's Cathedral, London 296–7, **10.39–10.41**

Salomé (Beardsley) 372, **13.15**

salons, Parisian 306, 309, **11.7**

Santiago de Compostela, Spain 167

Sappho 65, 92; lyric poetry 45
Sarcophagus of Junius Bassus 110, **5.9**
Sartre, Jean-Paul 422, 423
satire 94–5, 243, 324–8, 412
Satyr and Bacchante (Clodion) 305, **11.5**
Saussure, César de 326
Savonarola, Girolamo 209–10, **8.25**
Scamozzi, Vincenzo *see* Palladio, Andrea
scat singing 418
Schliemann, Heinrich 40
Schoenberg, Arnold 21, 408–9, 417, 435
scholasticism 146, 178
School of Athens (Raphael) 201, 218–19, **8.36, 8.37**
Schubert, Franz 340
Schumann, Clara 338
Schumann, Robert 338
Scientific Revolution 293, 294
Second Coming, The (Yeats) 390
Self-Portrait (Rembrandt) 292, **10.37**
Self-Portrait in a Fur-collared Robe (Dürer) 240, **9.15**
Self-Portrait with Halo (Gauguin) 383, **13.32**
Self-Portrait with Her Daughter (Vigeé-Lebrun) 309, **11.11**
Sellars, Peter 440
Seneca 90, 248; *Oedipus* 90
Sens, France: Cathedral 165
Sentimental Education, The (Flaubert) 359–60
serialism 409; tonal 435
Serlio, Sebastiano: stage setting **9.30**
Seurat, Georges 381; *Sunday Afternoon on the Island of La Grande Jatte* 381–2, **13.29**
Sexton, Anne 422
Sezession, Vienna 372
sfumato technique 215
Shakespeare, William 25, 89, 229, 248, 249, 295, **9.24**; *Comedy of Errors* 90; *Hamlet* 16, 158, 249, **1.1**; *A Midsummer Night's Dream* 93
Shang dynasty 37–8; bronzes 37, **2.14**
Shankar, Ravi 447, **15.31**
Shaprut, Hisdai ibn 146
Shelley, Mary 343, 353, **12.27**; *Frankenstein* 353
Shelley, Percy Bysshe 344, 353
Sistine Chapel *see* Michelangelo
Skinner, B. F.: *Walden II* 245
skyscrapers 365, 411, 432
Slave Ship, The (Turner) 347–8, **12.17**
Sleep of Reason ... (Goya) 352, **12.24**
Smetana, Bedrich: *The Moldau* 370
Smith, David 425, 430; *Cubi* **15.11**
Smithson, Robert: *Spiral Jetty* 441, **15.23**
Snake Goddess (Minoan) 39, **2.17**
Social Contract (Rousseau) 303, 304, 305
socialism 360
Socrates 62, 96
solmization 155
Solomon, King 101
sonata form 323, **11.27**
sonatas 322
Song of Roland 141, 142, 143, **6.12**
sonnets 187
sophists 62, 178
Sophocles 60–1; *Antigone* 55; *Oedipus the King* 61, 253, 255
Sortie of Captain Banning Cocq's Company ... (Rembrandt) 291, **10.35**
Sosus: *Unswept Floor* 87–8, **4.25**
Soyinka, Wole 443
Spear-bearer (Polyclitus) 48, **3.9**
Spiral Jetty (Smithson) 441, **15.23**
Spring Blossoms (Calder) 429, **15.8**
staffs, musical 155–6, **6.31, 6.32**
stained glass 170–1, **7.1, 7.11, 7.12**

Stalin, Joseph 390
Starry Night (van Gogh) 384–5, **13.34**
Stein, Gertrude 415
Stieglitz, Alfred 415
Still Life with Masks I (Nolde) 396, **14.6**
Stockhausen, Karlheinz 435
stoicism/stoics 95–6, 98
Stonehenge, England 28, **2.3**
Stourhead Park, England (Hoare) 319, **11.22**
Strachey, Ray 393
Stravinsky, Igor: *The Rite of Spring* 407–8, **14.23**
stupas 174
Sturm und Drang 317, 338
Suger, Abbot 165–6
Sullivan, Louis 365; Guaranty Building, Buffalo 365, **13.11**
Sumerians 29–30
Sunday Afternoon on the Island of La Grande Jatte (Seurat) 381–2, **13.29**
superrealism 441
surrealism 393, 403, 406
Swift, Jonathan 324; *Gulliver's Travels* 325–6; *A Modest Proposal* 324–5
Swing, The (Fragonard) 309, **11.1**
Sydney Opera House (Utzon) 434, **15.16**
symbolists, French 370–2
Symphonie fantastique (Berlioz) 352, **12.26**
symphonies 22, 322–4, 338, 352, **1.8**

Taj Mahal, Agra, India 267, **10.5**
Tatlin, Vladimir: model for *Monument to the Third International* 392, **14.2**
Tchaikovsky, Peter: *1812 Overture* 370
Tempest (Giorgione) 259, **9.36**
Teotihuacán, Mexico 126–7, **5.32**
Terence 90, 149, 215, 248
theater 24–5; of the absurd 423; and early Christians 125; *commedia dell'arte* 154; Elizabethan 247–9; French 283–4; German 317, 411–12; Greek 49, 59–61; Japanese *kabuki* 316; medieval 156–9, 176–9; 19th-c. realist 386; Renaissance 253–4; Roman 89–90, 125
Theodora, Empress 116, 125; *Theodora and Retinue* (mosaic) 123, **5.27**
Thoreau, Henry David 345
Three Musicians, The (Picasso) 398, **14.9**
Three Shades, The (Rodin) 374, **13.19**
Threepenny Opera (Brecht) 412
Thucydides: *Peloponnesian War* 49
Tiepolo, Giovanni Battista: Residenz ceiling 309, **11.12**
Tiffany, Louis 372
Tintoretto, Jacopo: *Last Supper* 260, **9.39**
Titian (Tiziano Vecelli) 254, 259, 262; *Bacchus and Ariadne* 259–60, **9.37**
Tivoli, Italy: Hadrian's Villa **4.22**
Tlön, Uqbar, Orbis Tertius (Borges) 442–3
Toilet of Venus (Boucher) 309, **11.10**
Toledo, Spain 146, 180, 262
Torah 101, 105
Toulouse, France: St. Sernin 151, 153, **6.23–6.25**
Toulouse-Lautrec, Henri de: *At the Moulin Rouge* **13.14**
Toussaint-l'Ouverture, François 335, 337
Tower of Babel (Bruegel) **9.21**
towns, medieval 164–5
tragedy, Greek 59–61
Trajan, Emperor 75, 77; Trajan's Arch, Benevento 75, **4.5**; Trajan's Column, Rome 77–8, **4.10, 4.11**; Trajan's Forum 73, 77, **4.9**
Trent, Council of 251
Tribute Money (Masaccio) 204, 206, **8.16**
triglyphs 53

Tristan and Isolde (Wagner) 367–8
Triumph of the Will (Riefenstahl) 392, 414–15
Triumphes of Oriana (Morley) 251, **9.27**
trobairitz 182–3
tropes 155
troubadours/*trouvères* 182, 183
Trumbull, John: *The Declaration of Independence* **11.4**
trumeaux 154
Turkish Bath (Ingres) 351–2, **12.23**
Turner, J. M. W. 347; *Rain, Steam, and Speed...* 348, **12.18**; *The Slave Ship* 347–8, **12.17**
Turrell, James 441
Tutankhamen, King 35; mask 27, **2.1**
TV Buddha (Paik) 448, **15.32**
twelve-tone method (music) 409
tympana 153–4, 171–2, **6.26, 6.27, 7.13**

ukiyo-e prints 378
Ulysses (Joyce) 406
unconscious, the 404–5
Unique Forms of Continuity in Space (Boccioni) 398–9, **14.10**
Unité d'Habitation, Marseilles (Le Corbusier) 411, **14.27**
universities 164, 179–80, **7.21**
Unswept Floor (Sosus) 87–8, **4.25**
Untitled (Judd) 428–9, **15.7**
Upanishads 36
Ur, Iraq: lyre soundbox 29–30, **2.5**; ziggurat 30, **2.6**
Utamaro, Kitagawa 378
Utopia (More) 245, 360
Utrecht Psalter 137, 143, 145, **6.5**
Utzon, Jörn: Sydney Opera House 434, **15.16**

Valenciennes Mystery Play 178, **7.19**
Valéry, Paul 406
van Gogh *see* Gogh, Vincent van
Vasari, Giorgio: *Lives of the Painters* 217
vases, Greek 45–6, 59, **3.2–3.5, 3.29**
vaults: barrel 81, **4.14**; cross 81, **4.14**; ribbed 166, **7.4, 7.7**
Vedas, the 36
Velázquez, Diego 269, 336; *Las Meninas (Maids of Honor)* 269, **10.6**
Venice 21, 164, 254, 257, 259, **9.32**; music 255, 257; painting 259–60
Venturi, Robert 437–8
Verdi, Giuseppe 366–7
Vermeer, Johannes (Jan) 289; *The Allegory of Painting* 18, 289, **10.33**; *The Milkmaid* 289, **10.34**
Veronese, Paolo: *Marriage at Cana* 259, **9.35**
Verrocchio, Andrea del 197; *Lorenzo de' Medici* **8.7**
Versailles, France: Palace 262, 281, 283, 300, **10.1, 10.20–10.23**; Petit Trianon 317, **11.19**
Vézelay, France: La Madeleine 153–4, **6.27, 6.28**
Vicenza, Italy: Teatro Olimpico 254, **9.29**; Villa Rotonda 259, 319, **9.33, 9.34**
video installations 448, **15.32**
Vierzehnheiligen Church, Germany (Neumann) 312, **11.13**
Vietnam War Memorial (Lin) 446, **15.29**
Vigée-Lebrun, Marie-Elisabeth 309; *Self-Portrait with Her Daughter* 309, **11.11**
Vignon, Pierre-Alexandre: La Madeleine 333, **12.5**
Vikings 139, 143, 147
Villa Rotonda, Vicenza (Palladio) 259, 319, **9.33, 9.34**
Villa Savoye, Poissy (Le Corbusier) 411,

14.25
Vindication of the Rights of Women, A (Wollstonecraft) 343–4
Virgil 72; *Aeneid* 72, 93, 95, **4.30**
virtuosos, musical 338
Vision after the Sermon, The (Gauguin) 384, **13.33**
"*Vitruvian Man*" (Leonardo) 193, **8.3**
Vivaldi, Antonio 278, 287; *The Four Seasons* 280
Voltaire 303, 312, 327, **11.31**; *Candide* 327–8

Wagner, Richard 60, 366, 367–8, 370, 373, 406, 408, 412; *Das Rheingold* 368, **13.13**
Waiting for Godot (Beckett) 423
Wanderer Above the Mists, The (Friedrich) 344, **12.15**
Warhol, Andy 426, 431; *Campbell's Soup Cans* 426, **15.5**
Washington, George 330, **11.21, 12.2**
Waste Land, The (Eliot) 406
Watteau, Antoine 306, 378; *Gersaint's Signboard* **11.8**; *Pilgrimage to the Island of Cythera* 306, **11.9**
Weber, Max 234
Webern, Anton 409
Weill, Kurt 412
Weiss, Peter: *Marat/Sade* 423
Wexler, Peter: scene design **1.11**
Wharton, Edith 386
Whitman, Walt 361, 421; *Leaves of Grass* 361
Wiesel, Elie 421
Willendorf, Woman from 31, **2.7**
William the Conqueror 143, 145
Wilson, August 444; *Fences* 444–5
Wilson, Robert: *Akhenaten* 440, **15.21**
Winckelmann, Johann Joachim 317, 318
Witches' Sabbath (Goya) 352, **12.25**
Wollstonecraft, Mary 343; *A Vindication of the Rights of Women* 343–4
women: in ancient Greece 49–50; in ancient Rome 83, 85, 87, 109; as "gladiators" 326; medieval 149, 156, 182–3; Renaissance 214–15; *see also* feminism
Woolf, Virginia 406
word-painting (music) 205
Wordsworth, William 344, 346; *The Prelude* 344; *The World is Too Much With Us* 344–5
World War I 390, 421
World War II 421, 422, 423
Wozzeck (Berg) 409
Wrapped Reichstag (Christo and Jeanne-Claude) 420, **15.1**
Wren, Sir Christopher: St. Paul's Cathedral 296–7, **10.39–10.41**
Wright, Frank Lloyd 411, 417; "Falling Water" 417, **14.33**; Guggenheim Museum 21, 434, **15.15**
Wright, Joseph: *Experiment with an Air Pump* 303, **11.3**
Würzburg, Germany: Residenz 309, **11.12**

Yaxchilán, Mexico 147, **6.18**
Yeats, William Butler 389; *The Second Coming* 390
Young, Edward 336
Young, La Monte 439
Young Girl Reading, A (Fragonard) **11.18**
Youth Leaning Against a Tree (Hilliard) 249, **9.25**

Zeno 67, 96
ziggurats 30, 32, **2.6**